THE
NEW BOOK
OF
KNOWLEDGE

The
New Book
of
Knowledge

Scholastic Library Publishing, Inc.
Danbury, Connecticut

VOLUME 5

E

ISBN 0-7172-0540-1 (set)

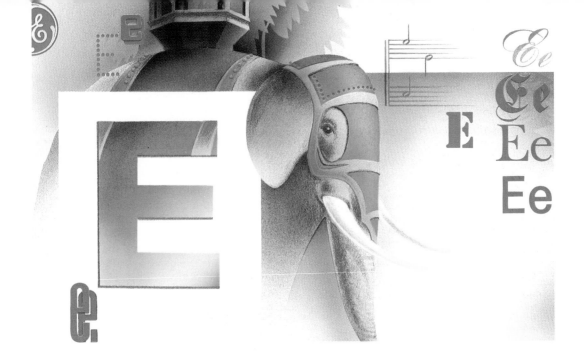

E, the fifth letter in the English alphabet, was also the fifth letter in the Phoenician, Hebrew, and Greek alphabets. The Phoenicians and Hebrews called it *he,* pronounced "hay." The Greeks called it *epsilon.*

Most language scholars believe that the Phoenician letters were simple pictures of objects. The Phoenician letter *he,* however, is still a puzzle to them. Some think that it may have represented a comb for carding wool. Others say it was just a name for a sound. The *he* looked like this: ∃

In the Phoenician alphabet the *he* had the sound of a consonant, which the Phoenicians pronounced like an H. When the Greeks adapted the Phoenician alphabet, they changed the name of the letter to *epsilon* and gave it the vowel sound of E, as in *sled.* The Romans in turn borrowed the letter E, but its sounds varied greatly. It is the Roman E that is used in English today.

In English too the letter is pronounced many different ways, and some of these ways have changed over the years. Short E, as in *sled,* has remained more or less the same, but long E now represents the sound heard in the word *be.* The main sounds of the letter in English are contained in the words *here, there, be, acme, sled,* and *pest.* The E is used more than any other letter in the alphabet.

In many words the E is silent. A silent E at the end of a word in which there is another vowel often shows that the first vowel is long. For example, we say *haste* instead of *hast, dine* instead of *din.* E also "softens" the letters C and G when it is placed after them, as in the words *place* and *cabbage.*

In music E is the third note in the scale of C major, and in chemistry Er stands for the element erbium.

In a series E stands for the fifth member. An E on a report card usually means excellent.

Reviewed by MARIO PEI
Author, *The Story of Language*

See also ALPHABET.

See also ALPHABET.

SOME WAYS TO REPRESENT E:

Ee *Ee*

The **manuscript** or printed forms of the letter (left) are highly readable. The **cursive** letters (right) are formed from slanted flowing strokes joining one letter to the next.

The **Manual Alphabet** (left) enables a deaf person to communicate by forming letters with the fingers of one hand. **Braille** (right) is a system by which a blind person can use fingertips to "read" raised dots that stand for letters.

The **International Code of Signals** is a special group of flags used to send and receive messages at sea. Each letter is represented by a different flag.

International Morse Code is used to send messages by radio signals. Each letter is expressed as a combination of dots (•) and dashes (––).

The scream of the eagle is usually meant for another eagle. It can be a warning or a greeting.

EAGLES

Eagles are big, powerful birds. Some are more than 3 feet (about 1 meter) long from head to tail. Their wingspread may be more than 7 feet (about 2 meters). An eagle's beak is large and hooked. Its toes end in talons, which are strong claws. Its eyes are many times keener than those of a person.

The eagle is a bird of prey—that is, a hunter. It catches and eats small animals and fish. The eagle swoops down, picks up the prey in its talons, and flies off. An eagle, which weighs 8 to 12 pounds (3.5 to 5.5 kilograms), may be able to carry off an animal weighing almost as much as itself. With its beak, it tears the food to pieces. Eagles hunt only in the daytime.

Eagles of North America belong to the same family as the hawks. Their closest relatives are other broad-winged hunting birds, called buzzard hawks. Female eagles are usually bigger than the males.

▶THE BALD EAGLE

The bald eagle is found only in North America. Most live in Alaska. In spite of its name, the bald eagle is not really bald. The adult bald eagle has white feathers covering its head. (This bird was named at a time when "bald" meant "white" or "streaked with white.") The bald eagle's tail is white, too. Its body and wings are dark brown. The upper portions of its legs are covered with feathers. Its eyes, beak, and feet are yellow.

The bald eagle is fond of fish and likes to live near water. Sometimes the eagle steals its catch from the osprey, another large fishing bird. The bald eagle also eats small animals, such as rabbits or birds. It is closely related to the sea eagles of Greenland, Europe, Asia, and Africa.

The bald eagle is the national emblem of the United States.

▶THE GOLDEN EAGLE

The golden eagle breeds in the mountainous or hilly regions of North America and other parts of the world. It is somewhat golden only on the back of its neck. The rest of the bird is brown. The golden eagle's legs are covered with feathers all the way to its feet.

▶LIFE OF THE EAGLES

An eagle keeps the same mate for life. Eagles build their nests at the tops of very tall trees or on rocky ledges. The nest, called an **aerie**, is built of sticks. The largest aerie on record is about 9½ feet (3 meters) wide and 20 feet (6 meters) deep. Many eagles use the same nests year after year.

The female eagle usually lays two eggs. When the eaglets hatch, both parents feed them and later teach them to fly. The eaglets are covered with dark feathers. They are 3 or 4 years old before their feathers look like their parents'. At age 4 or 5, they start to raise their own young. An eagle may live 30 years.

In the 1960's, despite a law protecting them, bald eagles were in danger of extinction because of hunting, habitat loss, and harmful pesticides in the environment. Wildlife officials made great efforts to save these majestic birds. And by the late 1990's, the bald eagle had made a comeback and was no longer considered endangered.

Reviewed by SHIRLEY MILLER
National Audubon Society

Thomas Eakins painted many scenes in and around his native Philadelphia. His painting *Max Schmitt in a Single Scull* (1871) portrays a champion rower on the city's Schuylkill River. The painting is typical of the artist's realistic style.

EAKINS, THOMAS C. (1844–1916)

The American artist Thomas Eakins is considered by modern critics to be a master of 19th-century realism. However, fame for the Philadelphia artist came late. In his own day, when most popular art was entertaining and often sentimental, the public rejected his truthful portrayals of the people and scenes around him.

Almost all of Eakins' life was spent in Philadelphia, where he was born on July 25, 1844. He studied drawing at the Pennsylvania Academy of Fine Arts and anatomy at Jefferson Medical College. In 1870, after four years of study in Europe, Eakins returned to Philadelphia. He became a teacher at the Pennsylvania Academy in 1876 and was made its director in 1882.

Eakins painted scenes of everyday life in and around Philadelphia. Yet hidden in these "ordinary" scenes are the techniques of a masterful painter. A good example is an early work, *Max Schmitt in a Single Scull* (1871), which is reproduced on this page. Eakins' expert rendering of the reflections in the water gives his objects solidity and helps establish a tranquil mood. In the foreground, the rowing champion Max Schmitt approaches the viewer. To suggest the enormous strength of Schmitt's body, Eakins repeats the arch of the railroad bridge in the bend of Schmitt's back and shoulder. The second rower (Eakins himself) leads the eye back into the painting. From there, nine more boats can be found. Each has its own function in the tightly balanced design of the painting.

The painting's history is typical of Eakins' life. Unpopular when it was painted, it lay in Schmitt's attic for 60 years. When it was rediscovered in the 1930's, it was immediately recognized as a masterpiece.

Later in his career, Eakins painted many revealing portraits. He liked to show his subjects at their work, relating their occupations to their character. One of his most powerful works, *The Gross Clinic* (1875), shows the famous surgeon Samuel D. Gross performing an operation. Its uncompromising realism shocked the public.

Eakins' interest in realistically portraying the human body led him to pioneering work in photography, which he used to capture the body in action. But Eakins' passion for scientific accuracy was not widely understood. His insistence that female as well as male students at the academy draw the male nude from life caused a scandal and led to his resignation in 1886.

Eakins continued to paint, mainly portraits, for the rest of his life. He won some honors and awards in his later years but never achieved worldly success. He died in Philadelphia on June 25, 1916.

ERNEST GOLDSTEIN
Author, *Let's Get Lost in a Painting*

EAR

The ear is much more complicated than it might first appear. Each of your two ears is actually a double sense organ. First, as an organ of **hearing**, the ear receives sound waves and changes them into signals that the brain can translate into the sensation of sound. An ear is also an organ of **balance**. It tells you whether your head is upright or tilted and helps you keep your balance, whether you are standing, walking, or riding a bicycle.

▶PARTS OF THE EAR

The "ear" you see on the side of a person's head is actually only a part of the **outer ear**, which leads into a hollow chamber called the **middle ear**. Deeper inside is the **inner ear**, the parts of which work in hearing and balance.

The visible part of the outer ear is called the **pinna** or auricle. It has an inner framework of rubbery cartilage (like the gristle on the end of a chicken bone). The curves and folds of the pinna help direct sound into the **ear canal**, which is about an inch (2.5 centimeters) long. Bristly hairs and waxy secretions help keep out dust particles and small insects. At the end of the channel is the **eardrum**, a tightly stretched membrane of very thin skin.

The middle ear is a small, air-filled cavity behind the eardrum. A series of three tiny bones links the eardrum with another membrane called the **oval window**, which is the entrance to the inner ear. The bones of the middle ear are named for their shapes: **hammer**, **anvil**, and **stirrup**. A narrow tube called the **Eustachian tube** runs from the middle ear to the back of the throat. The Eustachian tube helps keep the air pressure inside the ear equal to the air pressure outside. Normally this tube is closed except for a brief time during yawning or swallowing. When you ride in a fast elevator or descending airplane, there may be a rapid change in air pressure. If the air pressure in the middle ear cannot change as quickly as the outside air pressure, your ears may "pop" as the Eustachian tubes open to allow air into or out of the middle ear.

The inner ear is sometimes called the **labyrinth**, for its mazelike channels and passageways. The oval window opens into the **vestibule**, a sort of "front hallway" containing the baglike **saccule** and **utricle** (parts of the balance system). The vestibule leads into the **cochlea**, which is coiled like a snail shell, and three **semicircular canals**. The cochlea is the sound-processing part of the ear; the semicircular canals are parts of the balance system. The inner-ear cavity is filled with a watery fluid. A second membrane-covered opening, the **round window**, acts like a kind of safety valve. When a wave of pressure flows through the fluid in the inner ear, the membrane covering the round window can bulge out or in, allowing for the vibrations of the membrane of the oval window.

The cochlea coils for about two and a half turns. Inside, it is divided by two membranes into three channels that run the length of the spiral. The **basilar membrane** forms the floor of the middle channel. The **organ of Corti**, resting on the basilar membrane, contains about 15,000 hair cells that are sensitive to vibrations. Thousands of nerve fibers from the hair cells form a bundle of fibers called the **cochlear nerve**.

▶HOW DO WE HEAR?

Sound is a form of energy that travels in waves of compression, carried by molecules that bump into each other. (For more information, see the article SOUND AND ULTRASONICS in Volume S.) Sound travels from a vibrating object to your ear by means of a sound carrier, or medium. The medium may be a gas (such as air), a liquid, or a solid. Sounds may be high or low, loud or soft. The **pitch** of a sound (whether it is high or low) depends on its **frequency**, or the number of sound waves that pass by (cycles) each second. The **loudness** of a sound depends on how many molecules are involved in carrying it along.

What happens when a sound reaches your ear? Sound waves that have been traveling through the air are funneled into the ear canal and bump against the eardrum, making it vibrate. The vibrations of the eardrum set the three tiny ear bones jiggling in the middle ear. These jiggling bones amplify (strengthen) the sound waves and make the oval window vibrate, too. Pressure waves are set up in the inner-ear fluid and race up and down the coils of the cochlea. These waves push against the basilar membrane. The hair cells of the organ of Corti are bounced about and bend back and forth. Their movement is picked up by tiny nerve fibers attached to the hair cells.

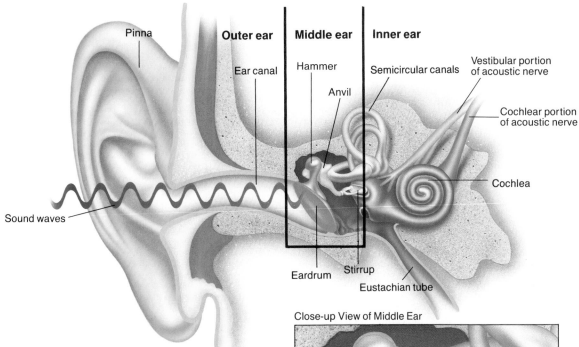

Pinna

Outer ear   **Middle ear**   **Inner ear**

Ear canal

Hammer

Anvil

Semicircular canals

Vestibular portion of acoustic nerve

Cochlear portion of acoustic nerve

Cochlea

Sound waves

Eardrum   Stirrup

Eustachian tube

Close-up View of Middle Ear

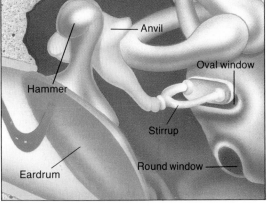

Anvil

Oval window

Hammer

Stirrup

Eardrum

Round window

The cochlear nerve carries messages from the ear to various parts of the brain. In a special hearing center in the cerebral cortex (the outer part of the brain), the messages are sorted out. The pitch of the sound is determined according to which hair cells were excited. The strength of the nerve message indicates the loudness of the sound. (Loud sounds move many hair cells and make the nerve cells fire faster.) The brain sorts out all the information from the ears, and at last we hear.

▶**KEEPING YOUR BALANCE**

With every step you take, you are performing an amazing juggling act. Muscles in almost every part of your body have to be carefully co-ordinated to keep you moving smoothly without tipping over. To do this, you must have a constant flow of information about where your body parts are in relation to each other, to objects around you, and to the force of gravity. The ears provide a key part of this information, continually letting you know whether you are upright or not.

The inner ear contains two kinds of balance-sensing structures that provide somewhat different kinds of information.

The saccule and utricle tell you the position of your head relative to gravity. These structures are lined with hair cells that come into contact with a jelly-like pad containing small stony grains called **otoliths**. When you tip your head, the otoliths move and press against the hair cells, which then send messages along nerves to the brain.

The three semicircular canals give information about movements and changes in position. Each semicircular canal is filled with fluid and lined with hair cells. Moving your head in any direction will set the fluid in one of the semicircular canals moving, excite its hair cells, and send messages to the brain.

Messages from the saccule and utricle tell the brain when you are tilted. The brain automatically sends messages to the muscles that will set you right-side-up again. Messages from the semicircular canals signal the brain that you are about to fall off balance. The brain can make corrections ahead of time to keep you from falling. Spinning around rapidly in a merry-go-round or riding in a swaying car or boat can set the fluid in the semicircular canals sloshing around. This condition can produce confusing messages about your equilibrium (balance). The result may be dizziness and nausea, which is called sea sickness, air sickness, car sickness, or simply motion sickness. Some people seem more likely than others to suffer from motion sickness, but there are safe drugs that can prevent this unpleasant condition.

▶ HEARING PROBLEMS

We tend to think that a gradual loss of hearing is a normal part of getting old. Hearing loss is actually the result of damage to various parts of the ear, the nerves, or the hearing centers in the brain. It is important to detect and treat hearing loss in babies and young children as early as possible, so that speech can develop normally.

An accident, an infection, or a very loud noise such as a dynamite blast can tear the eardrum. Small tears usually heal, but large ones can leave permanent damage. A torn (ruptured) eardrum does not vibrate when sound waves hit it, and so it does not transmit sounds into the inner ear. Infections can also produce scarring of the eardrum, making it less sensitive to sounds.

An inflammation of the middle ear can result from an infection or allergy. Commonly referred to simply as an "ear infection," this condition is more accurately called **otitis media**. The membranes swell and fluid accumulates in the middle-ear cavity. There is some loss of hearing, but it returns to normal when the inflammation clears up. Otitis media is common in children and can be treated with antibiotics to clear up the infection. Other medications can dry up the excess fluids and shrink the swollen membranes. Another form of treatment involves inserting a tiny tube into the eardrum to drain the fluid from the middle-ear cavity. Otitis media can be serious if it is not treated. Not only can the inflammation

damage the ear structures and produce a loss of hearing, but the infection might spread through the sinuses into the brain.

A form of middle-ear deafness that may occur in old people is **otosclerosis**, the formation of bony growths on the tiny ear bones, fusing them together. Normally the hammer, anvil, and stirrup, which link the eardrum with the oval window, are joined together rather loosely so that they can jiggle when the eardrum vibrates. When the bones become fused into a stiff bridge, with the footplate of the stirrup firmly anchored to the oval window, they can no longer jiggle. Thus they cannot transmit the sound vibrations. Most cases of otosclerosis can be treated surgically, by removing the footplate of the stirrup, replacing the bones with an artificial part, or making a new window into the inner ear.

A hearing aid is a device containing a tiny microphone worn in the ear. Hearing aids amplify sounds so that they can be heard by many suffering from hearing loss. But hearing aids do not help people with damage to the cochlea or to the nerves or brain centers involved with hearing.

The tiny hair cells in the organ of Corti are very delicate. Loud noises can damage them, resulting in a temporary or even a permanent loss of hearing. Ear protectors that muffle sounds can help to protect the ears from damage when a person is working with noisy machinery. Amplified music, such as that at a rock concert, is often loud enough to damage hearing if the ears are not protected. Loud music played through earphones attached to stereo equipment or portable tape recorders and players may also damage hearing.

Researchers are working on "bionic ears" that can be implanted in a person's ear. A miniature electronic device breaks down the electrical signals of a microphone into frequencies, and thin wire electrodes stimulate nerves in the cochlea. So far, though, these artificial ears do not work as well as natural ears.

ALVIN SILVERSTEIN
College of Staten Island, CUNY

VIRGINIA SILVERSTEIN
Co-authors, *Human Anatomy and Physiology;*
The Sense Organs; The Story of
Your Ear; Wonders of Speech

EARLY CHILDHOOD EDUCATION. See KINDERGARTEN AND NURSERY SCHOOLS.

EARHART, AMELIA (1897–1937?)

World-famous aviator Amelia Earhart was the first woman pilot to fly solo across the Atlantic Ocean. She is chiefly remembered as a tragic heroine, who disappeared in 1937 without a trace while attempting a round-the-world flight.

Amelia Mary Earhart was born in Atchison, Kansas, on July 24, 1897. When she saw her first airplane at the age of 11, she commented that it looked like an orange crate. Years later she took up aviation as a hobby while living in California, earning her pilot's license in 1922.

In 1928, while working in Boston, Amelia was chosen to be the first woman to become a passenger on a flight across the Atlantic Ocean. The book she later wrote about her experiences, *Twenty Hours Forty Minutes: Our Flight in the Friendship*, was published by George Palmer Putnam, whom she married in 1931.

A woman of great ambition, Amelia was determined to be the first woman to fly solo across the Atlantic Ocean. She accomplished her goal in 1932, with a flight from Newfoundland to Ireland. In 1935 she set another record when she became the first person to fly from Hawaii to California.

In June 1937, the world watched as the famous pilot and her navigator, Frederick J. Noonan, set off from Miami, Florida, to attempt the first round-the-world flight near the equator. On July 2, after setting out on the most dangerous leg of the journey—from New Guinea to Howland Island in the Pacific—their plane vanished. President Franklin D. Roosevelt sponsored a massive 17-day sea-and-air search for the two lost adventurers, but it resulted only in an official finding of "lost at sea."

Many theories have arisen concerning Earhart's fate. The most enduring one suggests that she and Noonan were captured by the Japanese and mistakenly executed as spies. In 1991, on an atoll southeast of Howland Island, an aluminum map case was found that might have belonged to Earhart, but it could not be positively identified. The mystery surrounding her disappearance remains unsolved.

ANITA LARSEN
Author, *Amelia Earhart: Missing, Declared Dead*

EARP, WYATT (1848–1929)

Wyatt Berry Stapp Earp, a frontiersman, gunfighter, and lawman, is largely remembered for his involvement in the famous shootout at the O.K. Corral, which took place in Tombstone, Arizona, in 1881. He was born on March 19, 1848, in Monmouth, Illinois. As a young man, he drove stagecoaches, worked on the railroads, hunted buffalo, and eventually became a policeman. In 1876 he served as chief deputy marshal of Dodge City, a booming Kansas cattle town.

In 1879, Earp and his brothers, Virgil and Morgan, moved west to Arizona. Wyatt became a deputy sheriff of Pima County, and later, as a deputy United States marshal, he guarded stagecoaches for Wells, Fargo & Company, an overland mail business that specialized in transporting gold and silver from western mining towns.

In Tombstone, Wyatt, his brothers, and their friend John H. "Doc" Holliday became involved in a feud with the Clantons, local cowboys and probable outlaws. This conflict, whether personal or political, was part of the Earps' effort to enhance their influence in Tombstone. On October 26, 1881, the opponents met at the O.K. Corral. After exchanging gunfire, Billy Clanton and two of his associates, Tom and Frank McLaury, were killed. Morgan Earp was later murdered, and Wyatt killed three other men in retaliation.

Wyatt Earp eventually settled in California, where he died on January 13, 1929. The question of whether he should be considered a heroic frontiersman or a ruthless killer is still disputed.

ELLIOTT WEST
University of Arkansas, Fayetteville

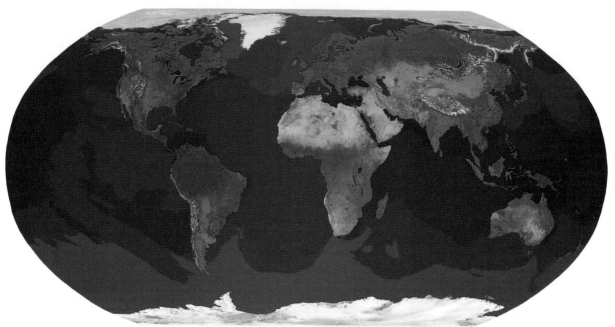

EARTH

The Earth is a great globe of rock surrounded by air. About 71 percent of the Earth's surface is water, which lies in basins in the rock, forming oceans, seas, and lakes. The remaining 29 percent of the Earth's surface is land.

The Earth's air, water, rock, soil, and plant and animal life interact with one another continuously, and as a result, the Earth is constantly changing. The planet is very different today from when it was first formed, and it does not look the same as it did several million years ago or even 100 years ago. Furthermore, it will continue to change far into the future.

To learn about the Earth and how it is changing, scientists study its surface, its air, its oceans, and its interior. The general term for the study of the Earth is **earth science**. This includes several related sciences such as geography, geology, geochemistry, geophysics, meteorology, oceanography, paleontology, and ecology. Geography is concerned

with the surface of the Earth, especially as it relates to human activities. Geology deals with Earth's history and composition. Geochemistry and geophysics deal with the chemical and physical properties of the Earth and its rocks, air, and oceans. Meteorology is the study of the air and weather. Oceanography is the study of the Earth's oceans. Paleontology deals with the history of life as it has developed on the Earth. Ecology is concerned with the ways in which plants and animals interact with the environment.

▶THE EARTH'S PLACE IN THE SOLAR SYSTEM

The Earth is the third planet from the sun in the solar system. Its average distance from the sun is about 93 million miles (150 million kilometers). Earth's only satellite, the moon, is about 240,000 miles (386,400 kilometers) away.

Accurate, cloud-free pictures of the Earth were developed from data collected by space satellites orbiting the Earth. They show the oceans and continents of our planet—as we often see them, on a map (*above*), and from space, as part of a rotating planet making its 365-day orbit of the sun (*left*).

The Earth's Motions in Space

The most northerly spot on the Earth is called the North Pole, and the most southerly spot is the South Pole. Imagine a line connecting the North and South poles through the center of the Earth. This imaginary line is the axis on which the Earth rotates, or spins.

The Earth rotates on its axis from west to east, which makes the sun appear to rise in the east and set in the west. The Earth makes one complete rotation on its axis about every 24 hours, or one Earth day. As each part of the Earth faces the sun, it is in daylight; as it faces away, it is in darkness. At any one time during an Earth day, about half of the planet has daylight, while the other half is in darkness.

As the Earth rotates on its axis, it also travels around the sun in an elliptical (oval) **orbit**, or path. One trip around the sun takes about 365 days, or one Earth year. This is called the planet's period of revolution. During the Earth's revolution around the sun, it travels about 590 million miles (950 million kilometers). While rotating on its axis and orbiting the sun, the Earth is also traveling with the sun as the entire Milky Way galaxy turns like a giant rotating disc.

Light and Heat

As the Earth orbits the sun, it receives energy from the sun in the form of light and heat. All parts of the Earth, however, do not receive the same amount of the sun's energy. One reason is that the Earth is round. Near the Earth's equator, the sun's rays are concentrated on a small area. Nearer the poles, the sun's rays reach the Earth at a greater angle and spread out over a wider area. Therefore the amount of heat received is less. At the poles, the angle of the sun's rays is even greater, so the rays spread out even more and these areas receive very little heat.

The Shape of Planet Earth

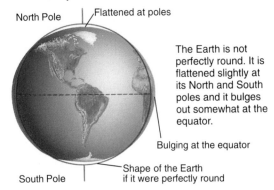

North Pole

Flattened at poles

The Earth is not perfectly round. It is flattened slightly at its North and South poles and it bulges out somewhat at the equator.

Bulging at the equator

South Pole

Shape of the Earth if it were perfectly round

Another reason that heat from the sun varies from place to place has to do with the Earth's axis. This axis is not at right angles to the sun's rays—it is tilted. As a result, the warmest time of the year (summer) in the Northern Hemisphere occurs when the North Pole is tilted toward the sun. That is when the greatest number of direct rays from the sun strike this part of the planet. The coolest part of the year (winter) in the Northern Hemisphere occurs when the North Pole is tilted away from the sun and more slanted rays strike this part of the Earth. The seasons are just the opposite in the Southern Hemisphere.

▶THE EARTH'S SIZE AND SHAPE

The amount of matter that makes up the Earth is called its mass. The Earth's mass is about 6.6 sextillion tons. The planet's diameter is 7,923 miles (12,751 kilometers).

The Earth is shaped like a ball, but it is not perfectly round. Years ago, the English scientist Isaac Newton (1642–1727) correctly predicted its shape—a sphere slightly flattened at the poles with a bulge at the equator. The circumference of the Earth at the equator is almost 25,000 miles (about 40,000 kilometers).

The Earth's round shape and tilt on its axis cause the amount of heat and light it receives from the sun to vary from place to place. In December the concentration of the sun's rays over areas of the Southern Hemisphere makes days longer and temperatures warmer there, while days in areas of the Northern Hemisphere become shorter and cooler. In June these conditions are reversed. In September and March, when the sun's rays are more concentrated over the equator, days and nights become more equal in length in areas of both hemispheres.

December 21

Earth

Equator

September 21

June 21

Earth's axis

North Pole

March 21

South Pole

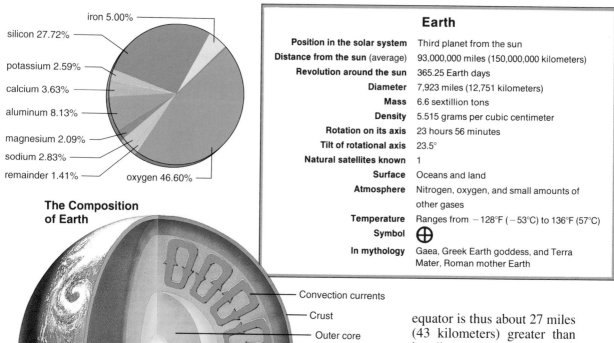

iron 5.00%

silicon 27.72%

potassium 2.59%

calcium 3.63%

aluminum 8.13%

magnesium 2.09%

sodium 2.83%

remainder 1.41%

oxygen 46.60%

The Composition of Earth

	Earth
Position in the solar system	Third planet from the sun
Distance from the sun (average)	93,000,000 miles (150,000,000 kilometers)
Revolution around the sun	365.25 Earth days
Diameter	7,923 miles (12,751 kilometers)
Mass	6.6 sextillion tons
Density	5.515 grams per cubic centimeter
Rotation on its axis	23 hours 56 minutes
Tilt of rotational axis	23.5°
Natural satellites known	1
Surface	Oceans and land
Atmosphere	Nitrogen, oxygen, and small amounts of other gases
Temperature	Ranges from −128°F (−53°C) to 136°F (57°C)
Symbol	⊕
In mythology	Gaea, Greek Earth goddess, and Terra Mater, Roman mother Earth

Convection currents

Crust

Outer core

Inner core

Upper mantle

Mantle

From space the Earth's surface features are partially hidden by clouds in the atmosphere. Convection currents in the mantle, thought to result from the intense heat in the core, may be responsible for the movements of the tectonic plates that make up the Earth's crust.

Gravity and Centrifugal Effect

Two phenomena account for the shape of the Earth: gravity and centrifugal effect. The Earth's gravity attracts things toward it; the nearer an object is to the center of attraction, the greater the pull of gravity. At the same time, however, the Earth's rotation creates an outward push, known as the centrifugal effect, that pushes things away from the planet's center. The faster the rotation, the greater the centrifugal effect.

The inward pull of gravity tends to make the Earth spherical, but the centrifugal effect tends to make it bulge at the equator. Why is this? The surface of the Earth at the equator must cover a greater distance during one rotation than it covers in places nearer the poles. As a result, the centrifugal effect is greatest at the equator, and it causes that part of the planet to bulge. The Earth's diameter at the equator is thus about 27 miles (43 kilometers) greater than its diameter measured from pole to pole. The planet's mountains, valleys, and other features also add to its irregular shape. Despite these irregularities, the Earth appears perfectly round when seen from outer space because the differences are so small compared to the planet's size.

▶INSIDE THE EARTH

The surface of the Earth, the oceans, mountains, rivers, rocks, and soil, is just a covering. A rocky interior lies beneath it. The Earth is made up of three main layers —the crust, the mantle, and the core.

The topmost layer of the planet is the **crust**, which consists of solid rock. The thickness of this crust ranges from only about 3 miles (5 kilometers) under the oceans to an average of 22 miles (35 kilometers) under the continents. The crust contains two basic types of rocks. Most rock under the ocean basins is basalt, which is much like the rocks of the upper mantle. Beneath the continents, the crust is made up mostly of granite. Because granite is not as heavy as basalt, the continental crust floats on top of the mantle, which is made up mostly of the heavier basalt rock. The roots of the continents, however, extend down into the mantle, much as the lower part of an iceberg extends beneath the water.

The lower boundary of the crust is known as the **Mohorovičić discontinuity**, or **Moho** for short. Named after a Yugoslav scientist who discovered it in 1909, the Moho separates the crust from the layer beneath it, which is known as the **mantle**. The mantle, which reaches a depth of about 1,800 miles (2,900 kilometers), is also made of solid rock. But because of the great heat and pressure at these depths, the rock of the mantle is not perfectly rigid. Over long periods of time, it may yield to stresses, and it can even flow very slowly.

The innermost part of the Earth is the **core**, which is about 4,200 miles (6,700 kilometers) in diameter. This core consists mostly of iron with lesser amounts of nickel and other elements. The inner core is believed to be solid, while the material of the outer core behaves like a liquid.

The Earth's Magnetism

The Earth behaves like a huge magnet. Like every magnet, it has a north magnetic pole and a south magnetic pole. These magnetic poles are not precisely at the Earth's geographic poles, but they are near them. Over time, the magnetic poles slowly shift position, and scientists keep track of their exact locations.

Scientists think that the Earth's magnetism is caused by the circulation of molten rock in the planet's outer core. As this molten material moves, it may generate electrical currents that, in turn, create a geomagnetic field on the surface of the Earth that spreads out into space. This field is called the **magnetosphere**.

▶ THE EVER-CHANGING EARTH

The surface of the Earth is constantly changing, and it has been changing since the planet was first formed. Some changes are noticeable over short periods of time. Others, such as the formation of mountains, occur too slowly for humans to notice.

Changes in the Earth's surface are the result of interactions between external and internal forces. External forces, such as weather and climate, erode, or wear away, portions of the Earth's surface. Snow forms glaciers that erode away mountains and gouge out valleys. Rain swells rivers, allowing them to carve canyons and carry sediments to the oceans. Ice breaks rocks into tiny fragments that are carried away by rain or wind. Internal forces, which originate deep within the Earth, gradually raise up mountain ranges, form volcanoes, and move large sections of the Earth's crust and upper mantle.

The Earth's Plates

Scientists have determined that the crust and the uppermost part of the mantle are made up of several large sections, or plates, and a number of smaller ones. These plates move about very slowly on the Earth's surface, gradually shifting position over millions of years. As they move, they may slide by each other, move apart, dive beneath one another, or collide head-on. The idea that these plates are moving and are interacting with each other at their boundaries is known by the term **plate tectonics**.

Water in the form of rainfall and rivers carved out the famous Guilin Hills of China, the remains of a limestone landscape almost completely eroded away by water. The ground level of the region was once at the tops of these hills.

The ancient seabed of the Tethys Ocean has been found on the crest of Mount Makalu (*left*), which stands on the border of Nepal and Tibet and is one of the highest peaks in the Himalayan Mountains.

Some changes in the Earth's surface are caused by years of snowfall, which in areas such as Glacier Bay, Alaska (*right*), form glaciers that erode rock and soil and gouge out valleys in great mountains.

When neighboring plates move apart, the space between them, called the **spreading center**, is immediately filled by new crust formed of molten rock from the underlying mantle. This process of plate separation and steady addition of new crust is the way ocean basins have formed. **Convergent boundaries** are places where one plate dives beneath another. The deepest parts of the oceans, the **oceanic trenches**, mark these places, which are also known as **subduction zones**. When two plates carrying continents collide, the force slowly thrusts up great mountain ranges. The Himalayas and the Alps were formed this way, as were the Appalachian Mountains more than 300 million years ago. In some places, two plates slowly slide past each other. This is called a **transform boundary**.

Plates moving across the Earth's surface and diving back into the interior form part of a huge **convection** system, which may extend through the entire mantle. To imagine what this convection system is like, consider a pan of soup heating on a stove. As the soup at the

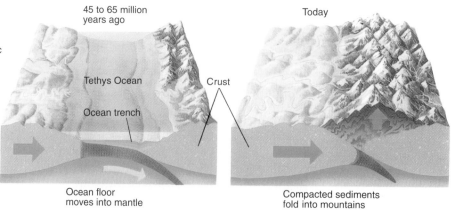

Great mountain ranges can be formed when moving pieces of the Earth's crust, called tectonic plates, crash into one another. The Himalayas in Southern Asia were formed when the Australian Plate, while moving north and finally crashing into the Eurasian plate, forced the floor of the Tethys Ocean into the Earth's mantle. The ocean floor was covered over while sediment built up, became compacted, and was violently folded and thrust upward to form mountains.

45 to 65 million years ago

Tethys Ocean

Ocean trench

Ocean floor moves into mantle

Today

Crust

Compacted sediments fold into mountains

material produces a convection current. Something similar takes place in the Earth, although the material of the mantle is not a liquid but a very hot solid rock that, under great pressure, flows very slowly.

Mountain Building

All of the Earth's great mountain ranges have formed at plate boundaries. The longest range—about 30,000 miles (50,000 kilometers) long—is under the Atlantic, Indian, and Pacific oceans. This undersea range, which lies nearly 2 miles (3 kilometers) below sea level, marks the place where new plates are forming as hot material from the mantle is pushed upward and old plates are pushed apart.

Other mountain ranges, such as the Himalayas in Asia and the Alps in Europe, mark the places where different plates converge, forcing one to dive beneath the other and lifting up parts of the crust in the process. Rock in the colliding crust may be either bent or broken. When rock in the crust is lifted up and bent, it creates what are known as **folds**. When rock in the crust breaks and moves along a line of fracture, it produces **faults**. The motion along faults is what produces earthquakes.

bottom of the pan warms, it becomes lighter and rises. The soup cools when it reaches the surface and may form a skin. The soup skin travels across the top, like a plate on the Earth's surface, and dives back down at the edge of the pan. The circulation of the rising hot soup, the rigid skin, and the returning cold

The Earth's crust is broken into many plates called tectonic plates. The major plates and some smaller ones are outlined below. They move very slowly in the directions shown by the arrows, carrying along continents and ocean floors lying on top of them.

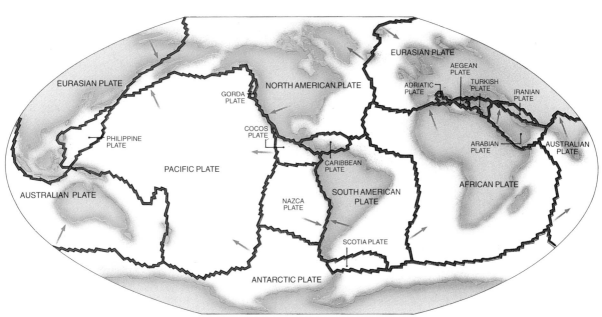

Earthquakes

Movement at the Earth's plate boundaries is rarely steady. Where the plates meet, rocks at the boundaries often adjust to the strain by bending or slipping quietly. Sometimes, however, they stick and stop moving. If this happens, great strains build up in the rocks until they break. When the rocks break and the plates move along the fault that has been created, shock waves are sent out through the Earth. The shaking that accompanies the passage of these waves is called an **earthquake**. Most earthquakes occur near active plate boundaries. Some, however, occur far from these active plate boundaries, and others are generated by volcanic eruptions.

The San Andreas Fault in California runs along the boundary of two major plates in the Earth's crust—the North American and Pacific plates, which are slowly moving past one another.

WONDER QUESTION

How do earthquakes help scientists learn about the Earth's interior?

Scientists learn a great deal about the Earth's interior by studying earthquakes. When an earthquake occurs, vibrations spread out in all directions through the Earth's interior. These vibrations, called **seismic waves**, can be detected with an instrument called a seismometer. They travel at different speeds depending on the type of material they travel through and change direction as they go from one type of rock to another.

One point where seismic waves change direction is at the Moho, the lower boundary of the Earth's crust. Scientists have been able to find the bottom of the Earth's crust by observing and measuring this change. Another change occurs at a depth of about 1,800 miles (2,900 kilometers). At this depth, one type of seismic wave, the **P-wave**, slows down and changes direction, while another type, the **S-wave**, stops completely. Scientists know, therefore, that there must be a change in the material of the interior at that depth. This region marks the boundary between the mantle and the core. S-waves cannot travel through liquid. The fact that they stop shows that the outer core must be liquid. The P-waves continue, but they change speed and direction again at a depth of about 3,160 miles (5,100 kilometers) This suggests that they have reached a solid inner core.

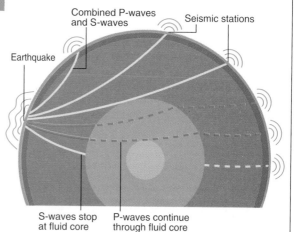

Studying the forces that cause devastating earthquakes helps scientists learn important information about the interior of the planet we live on.

The time that it takes seismic waves to pass through the Earth and reach measuring stations on the surface depends on how far the station is from the earthquake and the material through which the waves travel. When scientists record an earthquake, they compare the patterns of the waves and their travel times. From this information, they can calculate the path of seismic waves and make conclusions about the Earth's interior.

Volcanoes

Volcanoes are places where hot molten rock (lava), fragments of hot solid rock, and hot gas are pushed out of the Earth's interior in **eruptions**. Some eruptions, like that of Mount Pinatubo in the Philippines in 1991, are very explosive, violently ejecting lava, rocks, and gases within a short period of time. Others, such as Kilauea in Hawaii, gently push out streams of lava over the course of several weeks or longer. Volcanoes that have erupted in the last few hundred or thousand years are considered active and are likely to erupt again. Those that are inactive are said to be dormant.

Most active volcanoes are found near the boundaries of the Earth's plates. Many are located at the spreading centers of the mid-oceanic mountain ranges, but because they are deep in the ocean they are not well known. Volcanoes found at the convergent boundaries of oceanic or continental plates are much better known. A line of convergent boundaries around the Pacific Ocean forms what has been called the Ring of Fire. Many active volcanoes in the western United States, including Mount St. Helens, which erupted violently in 1980, form part of the Ring of Fire.

Volcanoes form in different ways. As tectonic plates move apart at spreading centers, the pressure on the underlying mantle is reduced. This causes the mantle to melt at shallow depths, and the rising molten rock erupts to form volcanoes. At convergent boundaries,

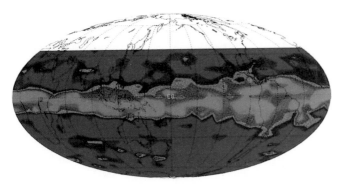

Continuous streams of red-hot lava flowed out of Mt. Kilauea in Hawaii (*top*) over several weeks in 1984, while a violent ejection of lava, rocks, and gases erupted out of Mt. Pinatubo in the Philippines on June 21, 1991 (*above*). A volcanic plume of sulfur dioxide from Mt. Pinatubo extended 15 miles (25 kilometers) above the Earth (*left*) and was tracked by the U.S. Upper Atmosphere Research Satellite (UARS).

Over time wind and chemicals in the air break down and wear away large outcrops of rock, often carving amazing shapes and deep canyons out of them such as these in Bryce Canyon, Utah.

expanding as it freezes and causing the rock to split into smaller pieces. Rainwater also mixes with carbon dioxide in the air, producing an acid that breaks down some rocks. As rain falls or the wind blows, loose grains of rock or soil are then dislodged and carried away to streams and rivers. In polar regions or high mountains, snow accumulates to form glaciers, or large rivers of ice, which grind up rocks and carry them away. As they flow, glaciers can level the planet's surface and change the shapes of its valleys and mountains. In the deserts, where there is little rain, wind erodes the land by carrying away sand in sandstorms and dust storms.

The process of deposition occurs as eroded materials from the land are carried away by rivers and deposited in the ocean. The greatest concentrations of deposited materials, or sediments, are found in deltas at the mouths of great rivers. As the process of plate tectonics continues, these layers of sediments may someday be lifted up to form new mountains. Numerous cycles of mountain building, erosion, and deposition have characterized Earth's history.

as the crust dives downward into the mantle, the mantle heats up and melting follows. The rising molten rock forms volcanoes like those in the Ring of Fire. A few volcanoes are found far from plate boundaries. These volcanoes, such as those in Hawaii, form as plumes of hot mantle rock rise to the surface through cracks or weakened areas in the plate itself.

Erosion and Deposition

As mountains are raised up by the processes of plate tectonics, other forces begin wearing them away as part of the process of erosion. The main forces of erosion are air, water, and wind.

The process of erosion works like this: Oxygen from the air combines with certain chemicals in rock, causing it to weaken and crumble. Rainwater seeps into cracks in rock,

The crust beneath our planet's oceans is constantly changing *(right)*. At oceanic ridges, magma from deep within the Earth rises and forms ranges of under-water mountains that extend all the way around the Earth. At oceanic trenches, the crust of a tectonic plate can sink below the crust of an adjoining plate and begin to melt as it reaches molten magma. During this process the adjoining plate may be thrust upward to form volcanoes or even islands that sometimes extend above the surface of the oceans.

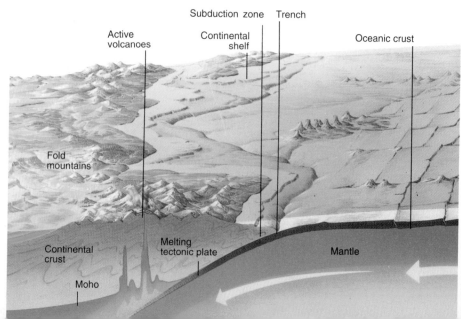

Active volcanoes

Subduction zone   Trench

Continental shelf

Oceanic crust

Fold mountains

Continental crust

Melting tectonic plate

Mantle

Moho

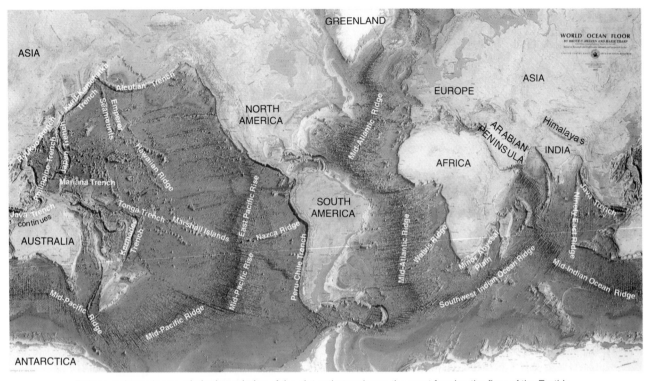

GREENLAND

WORLD OCEAN FLOOR
BY BRUCE C. HEEZEN AND MARIE THARP

ASIA

ASIA

EUROPE

NORTH
AMERICA

ARABIAN
PENINSULA

Himalayas

AFRICA

INDIA

Aleutian Trench

Kuril-Kamchatka Trench

Emperor Seamounts

Hawaiian Ridge

Mid-Atlantic Ridge

Java Trench

Mariana Trench

Java Trench
continues

SOUTH
AMERICA

Mid-Atlantic Ridge

Ninety-East Ridge

AUSTRALIA

Tonga Trench

Marshall Islands

East Pacific Rise

Nazca Ridge

Peru-Chile Trench

Walvis Ridge

Minor Abyssal Plain

Southwest Indian Ocean Ridge

Mid-Indian Ocean Ridge

Mid-Pacific Ridge

Mid-Pacific Ridge

Mid-Pacific Rise

ANTARCTICA

Ridges and trenches mark the boundaries of the plates that make up the crust forming the floor of the Earth's oceans. Trenches tend to be near land, while ridges are usually found in the midst of the oceans.

▶ THE EARTH'S OCEANS

People have always been fascinated by the oceans, but little was known about them until scientists mapped the ocean floors and studied ocean currents and other phenomena. Although they have learned a great deal, there is still much to learn.

The Earth's oceans are actually a huge continuous body of water encircling the planet. They occupy large ocean basins, which are low-lying areas of the Earth's surface. These vast ocean basins share a number of important features.

Spreading Centers

The largest features of the ocean basins are their spreading centers and the broad, gently sloping areas on either side. These are the places where tectonic plates are moving apart and new material is being added from the

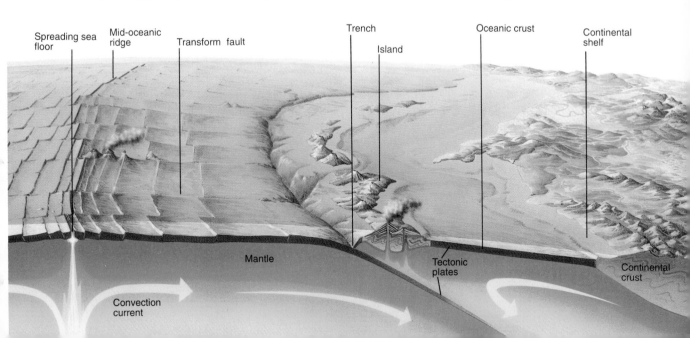

Spreading sea floor

Mid-oceanic ridge

Transform fault

Trench

Island

Oceanic crust

Continental shelf

Mantle

Tectonic plates

Continental crust

Convection current

Powerful waves are created as the wind blows over the surface of the Earth's oceans. Waves pounding on the shores of coastal areas change the land's shape — causing portions of the land to recede by eroding rocks and soil, and forming beaches and sandbars by depositing sediments.

Where rivers empty into seas and oceans, some of the clays, silts, and sands they carry with them may be deposited and, over time, form deltas. Such sediments deposited by the Blue Nile and White Nile rivers created the Nile Delta, which extends into the Mediterranean Sea and provides acres of fertile land for agriculture.

mantle below. One such spreading center, the Mid-Atlantic Ridge, lies in the middle of the Atlantic Ocean basin. This spreading center continues into the Indian Ocean and the Pacific Ocean, forming the longest mountain range on Earth. A few places along this giant undersea mountain range are marked by intense volcanic activity, which has created islands on the ocean's surface. The largest of these islands is Iceland.

Ocean Margins

Oceans have two main kinds of margin, or edge. In some areas of the world, the ocean bottom slopes gently up to land, forming a broad, shallow submerged area called a **continental shelf**. This type of ocean margin, which is known as a **divergent margin**, is especially prominent along the edge of the Atlantic Ocean near northwestern Europe and North America. Divergent margins mark places where continents have slowly moved apart over hundreds of millions of years as a result of plate tectonics. Along some divergent margins, great rivers have deposited sediments on the continental shelf, forming large deltas. In other places, rivers have cut deep underwater valleys through the continental shelf.

The other main type of ocean margin is a **convergent margin**. Convergent margins are areas where deep oceanic trenches lie close to

the land. They mark the places where portions of one tectonic plate are diving beneath another and where the plates are moving together rather than spreading apart. Convergent ocean margins have narrow continental shelves, and in many places the land rises steeply from the ocean shore to high mountain ranges.

Ocean Tides and Currents

The water in the oceans moves continuously. One type of movement is the tides, in which the levels of the oceans rise and fall each day. Tides are caused by the gravitational pull of the moon and the sun.

Ocean currents are another type of movement. Currents flow like great rivers in the ocean. The Gulf Stream in the Atlantic Ocean is one such "river." It flows northward along the east coast of North America and turns eastward to flow toward Europe.

Surface currents are driven mainly by wind blowing over the water. As the wind blows, it drags the top layer of water with it. This top layer, in turn, drags on the water beneath it, and that layer of water drags on still deeper layers until a large amount of water is moving. Once currents start moving, they tend to keep moving, although they are deflected (turned off course) by the continents. The movement of currents is also affected by the rotation of the Earth, which causes them to follow a curved path. The Earth's rotation causes currents to flow around the oceans in a clockwise direction in the Northern Hemisphere and in a counterclockwise direction in the Southern Hemisphere.

Ocean currents may be either warm or cool. Warm currents, which start in tropical regions, heat the air above them. Winds carry this warm air to nearby land, making the climate warmer. The Gulf Stream is a warm current

that helps keep northern Europe warmer than it would otherwise be. Cool currents, which start near polar regions, bring cooler air and cooler climates to nearby land areas. The Peru Current in the Pacific Ocean is a cool current. It cools the coasts of Chile and Peru.

In recent years, strong currents have been discovered beneath the main surface currents.

Hydrothermal gas escaping from within the Earth through deep ocean vents (*right*) indicates possible volcanic activity or movements in the ocean floor. Instruments used to measure heat levels of escaping gas can also be seen in this photo of an active vent on the Pacific Ocean floor.

Surface currents formed by wind patterns flow through all of the Earth's oceans (*below*). These currents are warm or cold depending on where they begin, and they affect the climates of continents near which they flow.

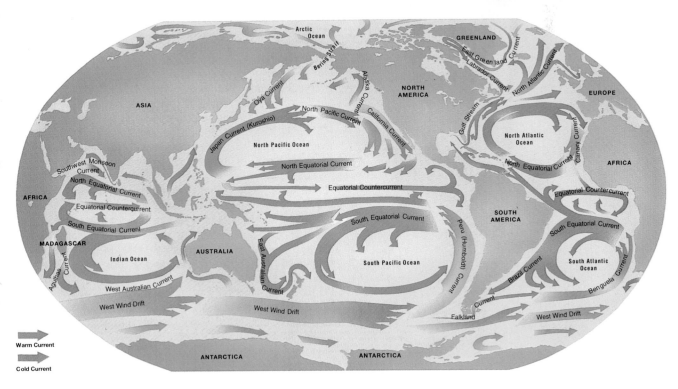

The Earth's Atmosphere

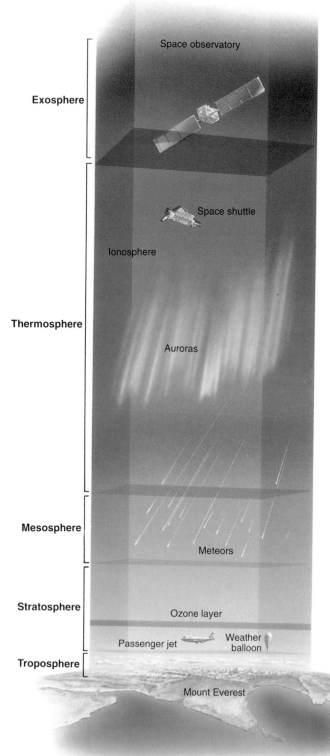

Exosphere

Thermosphere

Mesosphere

Stratosphere

Troposphere

Space observatory

Space shuttle

Ionosphere

Auroras

Meteors

Ozone layer

Passenger jet

Weather balloon

Mount Everest

These deep currents, which often move in the opposite direction of the currents above them, are called countercurrents. Scientists are studying these currents and hope to learn more about them and how they affect the circulation of water in the oceans.

The Ocean Water

The water in the oceans helps store heat from the sun, and this has an effect on weather and climate. Unlike land, which heats up quickly when the sun shines on it and cools off quickly at night, the oceans heat up slowly and cool off slowly. The water in the oceans can thus absorb and hold large amounts of the sun's heat. In winter, when the land becomes very cold, the ocean is warmer because of the heat stored in its water. As this heat is released, it warms the air above the ocean. Winds then blow this air over the land, which helps to warm the land. Scientists have calculated that the temperature of the Earth's surface is warmed by about 12°F (7°C) because of heat stored in the oceans.

▶THE EARTH'S ATMOSPHERE

Surrounding the Earth are layers of air called the atmosphere. This atmosphere is made up of several gases, including nitrogen (about 78 percent), oxygen (about 21 percent), and small amounts of water vapor and gases such as helium, hydrogen, argon, krypton, neon, and xenon. Air also contains small particles of dust.

The atmosphere is essential to life on Earth. It contains the oxygen we breathe. It acts as a shield to prevent some of the sun's harmful rays from reaching the Earth's surface. Like a blanket, it holds in some of the sun's heat that reaches the Earth's surface, preventing extreme changes in temperature between night and day.

The atmosphere is held around the Earth by gravity. The weight of the outer layers of atmosphere compresses the air near the surface, making the atmosphere densest near the ground. Near the upper edge of the atmosphere, the weight of the gas pressing down is small, so the atmosphere there is very thin. While about one half of the atmosphere is squeezed into the first 3½ miles (5.5 kilometers) above the Earth's surface, the thin outer edges of the atmosphere reach far out into space.

This satellite photograph of cirrus clouds in the sky above Egypt indicates the presence of jet stream winds in the Earth's atmosphere. The jet stream—a band of fast-moving winds that circles the planet—helps bring warm air toward the Earth's poles and cold air toward its equator. In this photo you can also see portions of the Red Sea and the Nile River.

The Layers of the Atmosphere

The atmosphere has several different zones, or layers. The layer of atmosphere nearest the Earth's surface is called the **troposphere**. The wind is the troposphere in motion. As it moves, the circulating air becomes warmer or cooler, drier or moister, depending upon changing conditions on the Earth's surface. Changes in the troposphere are what cause weather.

The **stratosphere** is the layer of atmosphere just above the troposphere. The air in this layer moves up and down very little. Instead, it remains in thin layers, or strata, and is thus said to be **stratified**. The lower regions of the stratosphere are very cold. At higher altitudes, however, the air becomes warmer because a layer of ozone there absorbs most of the sun's ultraviolet rays and keeps them from reaching the surface of the Earth. This is fortunate for life on Earth because too much ultraviolet radiation can be deadly.

Above the stratosphere is the **mesosphere**, where the temperature drops again. The layer above the mesosphere is the **thermosphere**. This layer has great differences in temperature, ranging from below freezing at the bottom to 2200°F (1200°C) or more at the top. An important region within the thermosphere is the **ionosphere**. In this region, atoms and molecules of gas are bombarded by radiation from the sun and broken into electrically charged particles called **ions**. Radio waves are reflected off the ionosphere, making long-distance radio communication possible on Earth. Much of the dangerous radiation from the sun, such as X rays and cosmic rays, is absorbed in the ionosphere. If all of these rays reached the Earth's surface, life would be possible only below water and in other protected environments.

The outermost layer of the Earth's atmosphere is called the **exosphere**. This is the least dense part of our atmosphere. It is also the area where the atmosphere of the Earth merges with the vacuum of interplanetary space.

The Earth's atmosphere is one of the things that makes the planet special. No other planet in the solar system has an atmosphere that can support life as we know it. Scientists debate whether human activities, such as the burning of oil and coal, might change the Earth's atmosphere and affect our climate, making the planet less suitable for life. So far as we know, life as we experience it cannot exist on other planets, which is a reminder of how fragile and remarkable our planet is.

KEVIN BURKE
Department of Geosciences
University of Houston

See also ATMOSPHERE; EARTH, HISTORY OF; EARTHQUAKES; EQUATOR; GEOLOGY; OCEAN; OCEANS AND SEAS OF THE WORLD; PLANETS; SOLAR SYSTEM; VOLCANOES.

EARTH, HISTORY OF

When did the Earth form? How did it form? What was it like when it was first formed? These questions have fascinated people for centuries.

Scientists trying to find answers to these questions think that the Earth is about 4.5 billion years old. This estimate is based on their study of rocks from three sources—the Earth itself, the moon, and meteorites, rocks that have fallen to Earth from space. All of these rocks contain radioactive atoms, which break down at a steady, known rate and act like radioactive "clocks," indicating how much time has passed since the rocks were formed.

are considered together, they indicate to scientists that all of the planets, including Earth, most likely formed at about the same time.

Since its formation, the Earth has undergone great changes. Mountains have formed and then worn away, and oceans have taken their place. Sediments in rivers and oceans have turned into rock, and some of this rock has been raised up to form new mountains. Many life-forms have evolved and then died out, leaving behind only a fossil record of their existence. The Earth's history is written in its rocks and in the fossils that the rocks contain. Rocks tell of the great changes in the geography, the climates, and the life-forms of planet Earth from prehistoric times to today.

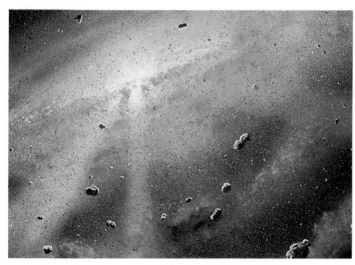

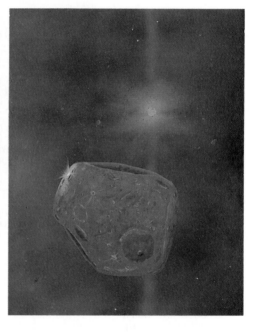

Clouds of dust and gas particles once orbited our sun. As the particles collided with one another, they stuck together, forming bodies called planetesimals (*above*). Over millions of years of collisions, the planetesimals grew larger and larger (*right*), eventually reaching the sizes of the planets (*far right*).

Because so much geological activity, such as erosion, takes place on our planet, scientists think that none of the rocks that existed at the earliest stages of the Earth's formation have survived. The oldest rocks that have been studied and dated come from sites in Greenland, Canada, and Australia and are about 3.9 billion years old. Chemical tests on samples of such old rocks, however, suggest that the Earth itself formed much earlier. Furthermore, in studying meteorites and rocks from the moon, scientists have discovered that the meteorites and the moon probably formed about 4.5 billion years ago. When all of these factors

▶ **HOW THE EARTH FORMED**

Geologists (scientists who study the Earth's physical changes), astronomers, and other scientists work together to study how the Earth was formed. The ideas they develop are called hypotheses. A hypothesis is an interpretation based on evidence that has been observed and studied.

The most widely accepted hypothesis about how the Earth formed is the **accretion** hypothesis. Accretion refers to the formation of a body by the accumulation of many smaller bodies. Scientists think that after the sun was formed, about 4.55 billion years ago, it was surrounded by a disk-shaped cloud of dust and gases. As these particles of dust and gas orbited the sun, they collided with one another and stuck together. As more and more particles stuck together, they began to form bodies called **planetesimals**. In time, these planetesimals grew in size and formed the Earth and other planets.

During its early history, the Earth was struck many times by nearby planetesimals. These collisions, together with radioactivity and other processes, heated the primitive planet, causing most of the material in it to melt. As this material melted, the elements in it began to separate and flow to different parts of the planet. The heaviest element, iron,

snowfields, and deserts. Fossil evidence shows that no substantial plants or animals existed before about 3.5 billion years ago.

The Atmosphere. Evidence suggests that the Earth's early atmosphere was also very different from what it is today. The atmosphere today consists mostly of nitrogen and oxygen gases. Scientists hypothesize that the early atmosphere consisted mostly of carbon dioxide gas and steam, with very little oxygen. They base this hypothesis on various kinds of evidence. Oxygen itself is a very reactive gas. This means that it reacts or mixes with other elements, such as iron, and is depleted or lost in the process. In fact, oxygen would not last long in a planet's atmosphere unless it was

During its early history, the Earth was covered with huge craters caused by collisions with planetesimals, meteorites, and other matter from space (*left*). As a result, much of the Earth's surface may have looked like this barren, rocky landscape (*below*).

flowed to the center. Depending upon their weight and density, other elements floated to the surface or to other levels. As these materials separated and moved, they formed the Earth's three basic layers: an iron and nickel **core** in the center, a thick surrounding rock layer of intermediate-density rocks called the **mantle**, and a thin surface layer of lighter rock called the **crust**. These three zones have been detected by studying waves that pass through the Earth's interior during earthquakes.

The Earth's Early Environment

The Earth's early environment was very different from what it is today. There were no plants or animals, and landscapes consisted of barren plains, eroded valleys and hillsides,

constantly resupplied. Scientists also base their hypothesis on the fact that volcanoes, which must have been common on the early Earth, emitted large quantities of carbon dioxide and steam. For supporting evidence, they also look to Earth's neighbors, Mars and Venus, which have atmospheres of carbon dioxide. Scientists think that the early histories of these three planets were similar and that the differences today are the result of differences in each planet's development. During the Earth's history, the development of plants, which absorb carbon dioxide from the air, use it in the process of making food, and then release oxygen back into the atmosphere, spurred the growth of oxygen in our atmosphere and keep it in constant supply.

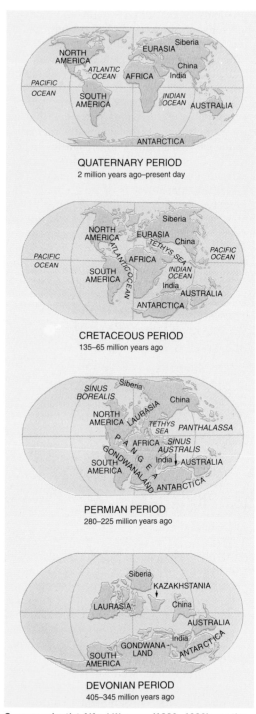

QUATERNARY PERIOD
2 million years ago–present day

CRETACEOUS PERIOD
135–65 million years ago

PERMIAN PERIOD
280–225 million years ago

DEVONIAN PERIOD
405–345 million years ago

German scientist Alfred Wegener (1880–1930) was the first to suggest that the Earth's continents drift across its surface. Years later, others worked out the process of plate tectonics, showing how pieces of the Earth's crust, called plates, are moving from one place to another. Maps such as these illustrate how over millions of years the Earth's continents split apart into different shapes and locations as they moved with the Earth's plates.

The Continents. Over the course of millions of years, forces deep within the Earth have slowly pushed huge sections of the planet's crust from one place to another. Such movements of the Earth's surface are called **tectonic motions**, and the pieces of crust that are being moved are called **plates**. The process by which these plates are moved is called **plate tectonics**. Since this process sometimes moves entire continents from one place to another, it is sometimes also known as **continental drift**.

In recent years, scientists have discovered many different plates and plate movements. By studying deposits of ancient rocks and measuring the properties of the deposits, such as their magnetism, age, and the types of minerals and fossils they contain, scientists have been able to construct maps showing the locations of continental landmasses hundreds of millions of years ago. They have also been able to show how the Earth's landmasses have changed during its long history.

▶**LIFE ON EARTH**

People have always wondered how life originated on Earth. Scientists do not have a complete answer to this question, but they do have a general theory about when and how life began and how it has developed.

Paleontologists, the scientists who study fossils, have found fossil evidence of microscopic algae and bacteria in deposits of rocks dating from about 3.5 billion to 2 billion years ago. Since these early forms of life probably developed from even simpler organisms, paleontologists hypothesize that life must have developed even earlier. Today scientists think that simple one-celled organisms first developed about 3.8 billion years ago, and perhaps even earlier.

The Building Blocks of Life

The development of the life-forms we know about depends on the ability of carbon atoms to join together to form very large complex molecules or combinations of atoms. Two of the most important complex molecules are amino acids and proteins, substances that are the building blocks of life. (For more information about living organisms, see the article LIFE in volume L.)

Scientists have learned that amino acids can form in many environments and could have formed in the Earth's early oceans. They have

PERIOD	Geological Timescale

CENOZOIC ERA
65,000,000 years ago–present

Quaternary
Humans learned to grow plants, raise animals, and use metals. Modern times.

Modern humans developed. Woolly rhinos and mammoths appeared and then died out. Glaciers covered much of the Earth.

Tertiary
Ocean and land life resembled that of modern times. Primitive humans appeared.

Apes developed in Africa and Asia. The Alps and Himalayas had formed by the end of this period.

Primitive apes first appeared. Climates were mild.

Primitive horses, camels, monkeys, and other new mammals appeared. Grains and grasses developed.

Small mammals developed. Climates varied.

Domestic animals

Primitive humans

Apes

Monkeys

Grasses

MESOZOIC ERA
240,000,000–65,000,000 years ago

Cretaceous
Dinosaurs reached their peak and died out. Fruit trees and flowering plants developed. North America's inland sea drained, and the Rocky Mountains formed.

Jurassic
An inland sea formed in North America. More dinosaurs developed, and the first birds appeared.

Triassic
The first dinosaurs and first small mammals appeared.

Flowering plants

Dinosaurs

Birds   Small mammals

PALEOZOIC ERA
600,000,000–240,000,000 years ago

Permian
Cone-bearing trees appeared. Climates changed, and glaciers covered many areas. The Appalachian Mountains formed.

Pennsylvanian/Mississippian (Carboniferous)
The Coal Ages. Plant growth in swampy lowlands laid the foundations of later coal deposits. The first reptiles appeared, and giant insects developed.

Devonian
The Age of Fish. On land, large fern trees and other plants developed. The first amphibians appeared.

Silurian
Animals and plants moved onto the land.

Ordovician
Seas spread across much of North America. Shellfish were plentiful.

Cambrian
Life was restricted to the seas. The first vertebrate, a small fish, appeared.

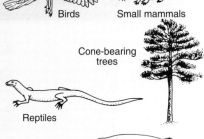
Cone-bearing trees

Reptiles

Amphibians

Fish

Ferns

Shellfish   Trilobite

Precambrian Time 4,550,000,000 (billion)–600,000,000 years ago

Earth's atmosphere gained oxygen. Multicelled life-forms developed, including algae and soft-bodied Ediacaran animals. Single-celled organisms developed. Chemical processes formed large molecules. Earth's surface and oceans formed. Earth formed.

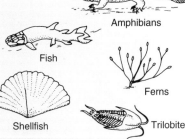
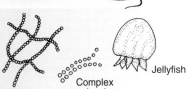
Jellyfish

Cyanobacteria   Complex molecules

also found that carbon-based molecules in water can combine to make cell-shaped structures. Many scientists think that life formed on our planet when natural processes occurring on the Earth many millions of years ago began building up concentrations of complex carbon-bearing molecules in the planet's oceans. Some of these molecules combined into cell-sized structures and reproduced to form simple microscopic living organisms such as blue-green algae.

Life then slowly evolved, or developed, into more complex life-forms. By about 2.5 billion years ago, there was abundant plant life in the oceans. This plant life had an important effect on the Earth's environment. As part of their life cycle, plants absorb carbon dioxide from the atmosphere and give off oxygen. By about 2.2 billion years ago, oxygen had become an important part of our planet's atmosphere.

Precambrian Time

The portion of Earth's history during which life first began to develop is called Precambrian time. It lasted from about 4.5 billion years ago, before any life existed, to about 600 million years ago. It is divided into two eons, the Proterozoic (between the Cambrian and 2.5 billion years ago) and the Archean (older than 2.5 billion years ago). During this time, life-forms slowly developed in the oceans, but no life could exist on land with the dense carbon dioxide-rich atmosphere.

After life first began in the oceans of the Precambrian, it slowly evolved from the simplest to more complex organisms. Fossils of the oldest-known complex multicelled organisms have been found in Australia, the former Soviet Union, and Canada. These organisms included sponge-like creatures and other soft-bodied animals. They were assigned to a new period, the Ediacaran, in 2004.

Toward the end of the Precambrian, organisms began to develop hard protective shells. Such life-forms began appearing on the floors of Earth's shallow oceans about 542 to 488 million years ago. These fossils are important to scientists because they mark the beginning of an amazing proliferation of life on the floors of the Earth's oceans.

Fossils from the Precambrian are very rare, and those that do exist are tiny and poorly developed. This is not true for the millions of years that followed. During the "Cambrian Explosion," numerous life-forms evolved. Many fossils have been found from this time onward. The best-studied fossil sites include the Burgess shale beds near Banff, Canada. By studying fossils, scientists piece together the history of life on the planet.

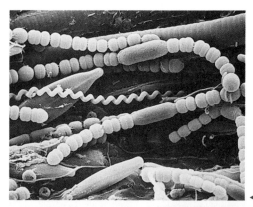

Scientists think that cyanobacteria, simple microscopic marine organisms, were among the earliest forms of life. Between 700 and 600 million years ago, more complex soft-bodied organisms slowly evolved. About 542 to 488 million years ago, life-forms with hard shells, such as brachiopods and trilobites, became abundant in the oceans.

◀ Cyanobacteria

▲ Brachiopod fossils

Trilobite fossils ▶

Scientists have classified the last 600 million years of the Earth's history into three general eras. Each is characterized by the type of life that was dominant during that era—sea creatures, reptiles, and mammals. These three eras are further divided into different geologic periods according to the major life-forms found in the fossils of each period. These fossils provide clear evidence of the dramatic changes in life that occurred from one period to the next. (See the Geological Timescale Chart in this article for a summary of each geologic period.)

The Paleozoic Era

The era that began about 600 million years ago is called the Paleozoic era. (The word "paleozoic" comes from two ancient Greek words meaning "early" and "life.")

During the Paleozoic era, which spans about 360 million years, life first emerged from the oceans and began to develop on the land. By the end of the Paleozoic era, life was teeming on both land and in the seas.

The first period of the Paleozoic era is the Cambrian period. The most well-known creatures from this period are trilobites, small hard-shelled creatures that resemble horseshoe crabs. Abundant fossils of trilobites were originally found in an area of Great Britain called Cambria, for which this geologic period is named.

During the next period, the Ordovician period, life was still limited to the seas, but different types of marine life, including shellfish, corals, and fishlike vertebrates (animals with backbones), began to develop. The following Silurian period is significant because it marks the first appearance of substantial plant and animal life on land. The earliest living things on land were probably simple plants, such as mosses, and the earliest land animals seem to have been centipedes and spiderlike creatures. As the first forms of life began appearing on land, life was blossoming in the oceans, too.

The Devonian period, which began about 405 million years ago, has been called the Age of Fishes because the Earth's seas were dominated by fish, including fearsome 30-foot (9-meter) sharklike fish and fish with massive bony plates. The seas were also filled with invertebrates (animals lacking a backbone) and seaweed. The Devonian period also marks the proliferation of plant life on land. Toward the end of this period, about 360 million years ago, forests of ferns and asparaguslike plants covered much of the Earth's surface. This abundance of plant life led to an important development. In the seas, there was intense competition for food among the numerous types of fish. On land, however, there was no competition for food because there were no land animals. Scientists think that mutations, or genetic changes, gradually allowed certain types of fishlike creatures to spend short periods of time out of water, foraging for plant food on land. This led to the development of the first amphibians about 360 million years ago. (Amphibians are vertebrates that live part of their lives on land and part of their lives in water.)

The Mississippian and Pennsylvanian periods of Paleozoic time have been called the Coal Ages, or the Carboniferous periods. During these periods, the Earth's climate was hot and moist, and most of its landmasses were low, heavily forested, swampy areas. As trees and plants died, they became buried in swampy sediments. Over long periods of time, these plant remains turned into coal, forming massive coal deposits in many regions of the Earth. It is still not uncommon to find fossil imprints of leaves and tree stems in coal.

An important milestone in animal evolution began around 300 million years ago: the development of animals that could survive entirely on land without returning to the oceans. These were the early reptiles. Unlike fish and insects, who lay eggs with soft outer layers, reptiles lay eggs with hard shells. This characteristic made it possible for reptiles to lay their eggs on land, where the shells created protected, moist environments in which babies could grow.

During the Permian period, which ended about 250 million years ago, conifers, or cone-bearing trees, appeared. By the end of the period, large areas of the Earth were covered with forests of conifers and ferns filled with insects, amphibians, and small reptiles. At this time, the Earth's land and climate were changing as well. Tectonic forces were creating new mountains and oceans, and in some parts of the world, glaciers covered the land.

The Great Dying

About 240 million years ago, a great disaster occurred. For some reason, about 90 percent of all species of life on Earth died out within a few million years. This event is sometimes called the Great Dying, and it abruptly ended the Permian period and the whole Paleozoic era. The cause of this disaster is one of Earth's great mysteries. Some scientists think that animals may have died out because of drastic climate changes. Some hypothesize that intense volcanic activity, caused by continental drift, may have released large quantities of deadly volcanic gases. Still others think that a large asteroid may have struck the Earth, blasting debris around the planet that blocked the light of the sun and affected the planet's climate. Whatever happened, it led to a whole new era of geologic history, one in which huge animals dominated the Earth.

The Mesozoic Era

This new era of geologic history is called the Mesozoic era. (The word "mesozoic" comes from two ancient Greek words meaning "middle" and "life.") Many life-forms got a new start in the Mesozoic era. Reptiles, which had been small and obscure in the Paleozoic era, dominated the Earth's landmasses. The Mesozoic era is often called the Age of Dinosaurs because these reptiles were the largest, most powerful, and most fearsome animals of the time. Although dinosaurs were the dominant animals, small mammals also began to appear. These early mammals, however, were timid, mouselike creatures dwarfed by the huge reptiles that roamed the Earth.

The Mesozoic era, which lasted from about 240 million to 65 million years ago, is divided into three periods—the Triassic, Jurassic, and Cretaceous. These three periods are marked by somewhat different species of dinosaurs and other creatures.

The Triassic period was marked by the appearance of the first true dinosaurs—the "terrible lizards." The period also saw the development of new types of invertebrates in the sea, as well as huge seagoing reptiles and the first tiny mammals on the land. In the Jurassic period, new types of reptiles evolved, including large flying reptiles and huge plant-eating dinosaurs, some of which were almost 100 feet (30 meters) long. Meat-eating dinosaurs also lived in this period, feeding on plant-eating dinosaurs and other animals. The first birds also appeared in the Jurassic period. The Cretaceous period was the peak of dino-

How do geologists learn about the history of planet Earth?

Geologists learn about Earth's history by studying rocks. One type of rock they study is called sedimentary rock. This type of rock formed when sediments—eroded fragments of older rocks—were deposited in layers on the surface of the Earth over millions of years. Some sedimentary rocks contain fossils, the imprints or remains of plants and animals that lived when the sediments were deposited.

Sedimentary rock strata

Unless particular layers of sedimentary rocks have been disturbed by movements of the Earth, the lower layers of the deposit were formed before the upper layers. This means that fossils in lower layers are older than fossils in upper layers. By carefully studying the fossils in different rock layers, or strata, geologists can learn the order in which those plants and animals lived on the Earth. By studying the sediment in each strata, they can also learn how and where the rock formed. For example, some sediments contain bits of seashells, indicating that they formed at the bottom of oceans. This type of observation can then give scientists clues about the environments or habitats in which these ancient animals and plants lived.

Unfortunately, the Earth's rock record is not always easy to read. The planet's surface has been changed many times by erosion and other forces. As a result, its rocks and fossils are like pieces of a giant jigsaw puzzle. Geologists have learned to recognize the pieces and fit them together, but many pieces are missing. Nevertheless, scientists continue to find clues that help fill in the gaps and create a more complete and accurate history.

saur development. Many different dinosaurs, including some with horns and bony armor, roamed the Earth. New plants, including fruit trees and flowering plants, also appeared at this time. These plants provided food for small mammals and other plant-eating animals.

The End of the Dinosaurs

Like the Paleozoic era before it, the Mesozoic era also ended abruptly, about 65 million years ago. At that time, 75 percent of the animal species on Earth, including all dinosaurs, died out within about a million years or less. Some scientists think they know what may have happened. In the 1980's, geologists found a unique layer of soil about an inch or so thick at many sites throughout the world. This thin layer of soil contains dust from asteroids, small pieces of once-melted rock, mineral crystals subjected to violent pressure, and amounts of soot that could only be the result of fires. This evidence suggests that about 65 million years ago a large asteroid, about 6 miles (10 kilometers) in diameter, hit the Earth, blasting dust into the upper atmosphere and hot debris around the planet. The hot debris touched off worldwide forest fires, while the dust blocked sunlight for months, killing many plants that served as food for animals. Without food, many animals, especially the larger ones, could not survive.

Scientists found support for this theory in the late 1980's when they discovered the remains of an asteroid impact crater, about 110 to 190 miles (180 to 300 kilometers) in diameter, hidden under sediments on Mexico's Yucatan Peninsula. Scientific studies indicate that this crater was formed about 65 million years ago—the same time that many animal species died out. Scientists think that this crater may be the site of the explosion that led to the ending of the Mesozoic era. More evidence for this theory came in 1998, when researchers studying ocean mud samples found a small piece from what they believe was the asteroid that struck Mexico.

The Cenozoic Era

With the end of the dinosaurs, the Cenozoic era began. (The word "cenozoic" comes from two ancient Greek words meaning "recent" and "life.") This era has lasted for the past 65 million years, and it continues today. The most important development during the Cenozoic era was the emergence of mammals, and it has often been called the Age of Mammals.

Scientists have divided the Cenozoic era into two periods, the Tertiary and the Quaternary. And these periods have been divided into smaller divisions of time called epochs, which are characterized by different developments in mammal evolution.

In the first epoch, the Paleocene, tiny mammals were common. Gradually, genetic mutations produced many new and larger types of mammals, each adapted to their own particular environment. During the Eocene and Oligocene epochs, early horses, camels, elephants, whales, and monkeys first appeared. The Miocene epoch saw the spread of apes throughout Asia and Africa and the emergence of other mammals such as bears, seals, and raccoons.

About 2 to 4 million years ago, during the Pliocene epoch, apelike creatures in Africa developed larger brains and began making crude tools out of wood and stone. Although primitive humans had appeared by the end of the Pliocene epoch, modern humans did not develop until the Pleistocene epoch. The epoch we live in now is the Holocene epoch, and it has been characterized by the growth and spread of human civilization.

Earth's History Continues

Most of Earth's changes have occurred very slowly. In fact, when change is rapid, such as at the end of the Paleozoic and Mesozoic eras, the results can be catastrophic to life. While the Earth itself continues to change slowly, human beings are beginning to realize that their activities can cause the environment of the Earth to change very rapidly. Just since the early 1900's, for example, the burning of fossil fuels has added large amounts of carbon dioxide to the Earth's atmosphere. Scientists are trying to determine just how significant such events can be to the planet. Taking steps to preserve the heritage of the Earth's long, eventful history may be necessary to ensure that the planet continues to be a safe habitat for human beings.

WILLIAM K. HARTMANN
Author, *The History of Earth*

See also CONTINENTS; DINOSAURS; EARTH; EVOLUTION; FOSSILS; GEOLOGY; ICE AGES; LIFE; MINERALS; MOUNTAINS; ORES; PREHISTORIC ANIMALS; PREHISTORIC PEOPLE; ROCKS; SOLAR SYSTEM.

Bulldozers run on tracks instead of wheels. A wheel only touches the ground in one small area, but a track touches a much wider area. This helps it climb steep hills and work in rugged terrain without slipping. Tracks are also used by tanks.

EARTH-MOVING MACHINERY

At the construction site of any new building, bridge, or road, the roar of powerful earth-moving machinery can be heard. Snorting bulldozers level trees and push large piles of earth from place to place. Power shovels thrust their digging buckets into the ground, scooping up huge loads in one stroke. Scrapers gouge earth from the ground's surface and swallow it. Dump trucks grind their way up and down dusty slopes as they carry away material heaped into them by power shovels or loaders.

Earth-moving and excavation work would be much more difficult than it is already without these and other machines. For thousands of years the moving of earth was done by people using only their muscles, hand tools, and horse-drawn wagons. Today large earth-moving machines are capable of loading and hauling more than 100,000 pounds (45,000 kilograms) of earth.

Most earth-moving machines do one kind of job. Excavators dig into the earth. Loaders pick up big loads of earth from one spot and drop them into another—often into dump trucks. Haulers, such as dump trucks, carry loads of earth away from where it was excavated. Some earth-moving machines do more than one job. For example, scrapers can dig earth and haul it to another place.

▶EXCAVATING MACHINES

Excavating machines can loosen and remove earth from the ground by digging and pushing. The choice of which excavating machine to use for a job depends on the amount and type of soil to be removed and how deeply the machine must dig to remove it.

Bulldozers. A bulldozer is a heavy, powerful tractor with a large steel blade attached at the front. The blade, which is attached to steel arms extending to the front of the bulldozer, can be set to dig into the ground for excavating. However, bulldozers are frequently used for pushing earth and rock on the ground surface. They are also used for grading. A strong steel tooth, or ripper, attached to the rear of a bulldozer can be used to rip up and loosen rock. Two bulldozers can work side by side to push a large amount of earth at one time. Often they work with, and assist, loading machinery.

Power Shovels. A power shovel is an excavating machine, generally mounted on crawler tracks, with a toothed scoop or bucket attached to the end of a long, movable steel arm called a **boom**. The digging action of a power shovel is toward the front and away from the machine. Power shovels operate their buckets with cables and are used mainly for excavating in strip-mining. A major variation of the power shovel is the hydraulic excavator. (Many earth-moving machines use hydraulic cylinders to move their digging and lifting parts. These cylinders can exert great force, allowing machines to lift and move huge loads. For more information, see HYDRAULIC AND PNEUMATIC SYSTEMS in Volume H.)

Hydraulic Excavators. A hydraulic excavator is an excavating machine of the power shovel group. Many hydraulic excavators are mounted on pivoting platforms. This kind of platform enables the cab and arm of the excavator to be turned in a complete circle. There are two types of hydraulic excavators, distinguished by digging action.

Hydraulic excavators that have their digging action toward the front of the excavator are commonly called **front shovels**. Although their digging action is similar to that of the power shovel, hydraulic excavators are typically smaller and easier to maneuver. Like the power shovel, they are used mostly in situations where the earth is to be taken from an area in front of, or above, the excavator.

Hydraulic excavators that have their digging action toward the back of the excavator are referred to by several names, such as backhoe, hoe, backshovel, or pullshovel. They are primarily used to excavate below the natural ground surface, as in digging trenches or pits for basements, and for general excavation that requires precise control of depths. Backhoes are often used to dig trenches for sewer lines or gas pipelines. A large backhoe can dig to depths of up to 30 feet (9 meters).

Draglines. A dragline is an excavating machine used on ground that is too soft or water-

Dragline excavators are among the largest earth-moving machines. Some can scoop up more than 30 tons of earth in a single bucketful.

logged to support an excavating machine. The bucket of a dragline is cast or projected to the ground ahead of the arm supporting it. The bucket fills with earth and possibly water as it is pulled back toward the machine by a cable. Water can drain from waterlogged earth through small holes in the bucket. The bucket empties when its front end is lowered. Draglines are especially useful for excavating the side slopes of rivers, shaping waterway channels, dredging, and building levees (high riverbanks for flood control).

Trenching Machines. A trenching machine consists of a series of toothed buckets that rotate one after another in a circular motion. Empty buckets rotate into the trench and fill as they rotate out of the ground. The buckets generally empty onto a conveyor that deposits the material along the edge of the trench. Trenching machines are commonly used to dig

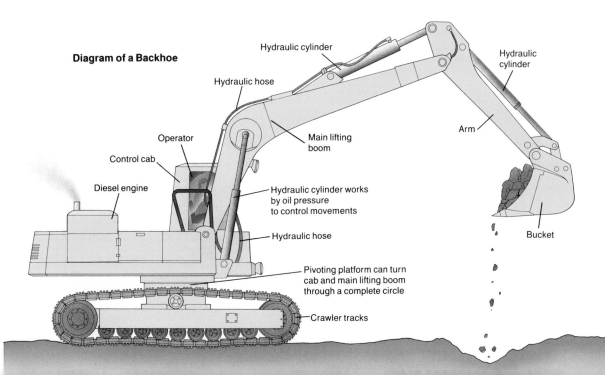

Diagram of a Backhoe

- Hydraulic cylinder
- Hydraulic hose
- Hydraulic cylinder
- Operator
- Main lifting boom
- Arm
- Control cab
- Diesel engine
- Hydraulic cylinder works by oil pressure to control movements
- Hydraulic hose
- Bucket
- Pivoting platform can turn cab and main lifting boom through a complete circle
- Crawler tracks

Left: With its blade lowered, a scraper's open-fronted box will fill as it moves forward.
Right: A wheel loader empties earth into a dump truck.

relatively narrow trenches, such as those into which underground electric cables, telephone lines, and television cables are laid. After the cables are laid in the open trench, a bulldozer covers them by pushing the excavated earth back into the trench.

▶ SCRAPERS, GRADERS, AND COMPACTORS

A scraper can scrape down a level area and haul earth. It is a wheel-mounted, open-fronted box, or "bowl," with a hinged bottom that can be lowered to scrape up a layer of earth. During the loading operation of a scraper, the bottom of the bowl opens at the front edge, allowing earth to enter it as the scraper moves slowly forward. The bottom of the bowl closes when fully loaded. Earth can then be hauled in the bowl to the area where it is to be unloaded. A load of earth can be spread across a broad area by lifting the bowl slightly and opening the bottom as the scraper moves forward.

Scrapers are among the largest of the earth-moving machines. Some scrapers are pulled by either crawler type or wheel-type tractors, while others are self-propelled by single or dual engines that develop as much as 950 horsepower. The size of a scraper is designated by the capacity of its bowl. Some have capacities greater than 40 cubic yards (30 cubic meters). Scrapers are used to scrape down, haul, and uniformly distribute earth for roads, airports, dams, canals, and levees.

Graders. A motor grader is a high-bodied, wheeled tractor under which a long, horizontal leveling blade is mounted between the front and rear wheels. The blade can be hydraulically tilted or turned to a desired position. Motor graders are important in road construction, where they are used to uniformly spread and shape earth that has been excavated elsewhere and deposited by hauling equipment such as trucks and scrapers.

Also important in road construction is **compacting machinery**. Earth that has been excavated and transported to another location is deposited in a loose condition. Compacting equipment is used to compress the earth into a dense condition to increase its strength. Compacted earth is especially important for roadways and airports where heavy loads will travel over the ground. There are two types of compacting machines: steel-wheel rollers and rubber-tire rollers.

▶ LOADERS AND HAULERS

Loaders are earth-moving machines that pick up earth that has been excavated by other machines and place it into trucks or tractor-pulled wagons. A bucket is attached to long steel arms that extend to the front of the loader. Its movements are controlled by a series of hydraulic cylinders. A loader with crawler tracks resembles a bulldozer, except that it has a broad bucket instead of a blade. Wheel loaders operate on rubber tires. They are faster and easier to maneuver than those mounted on crawler tracks.

Loaders may work with **dump trucks**, wheeled vehicles that can haul excavated materials great distances. A dump truck carries a large box on its frame into which earth is loaded. The load of earth is dumped out by hydraulically tilting the box. Giant dumpers have capacities of up to 200 tons, although smaller, more maneuverable dump trucks are most commonly used.

GAROLD D. OBERLENDER
Author, *Earth Moving and Heavy Equipment*

See also BUILDING CONSTRUCTION; DREDGES.

EARTHQUAKES

When people think of earthquakes, they often picture the ground cracking open, roads and bridges buckling and breaking apart, buildings collapsing, and people being injured or killed. Such disasters frequently result from earthquakes, although many earthquakes are so small that people can barely feel them. What causes earthquakes? Why are some earthquakes worse than others? These and many other questions have been answered by seismologists, the scientists who study shaking motions of the Earth.

Earthquakes are natural events on planet Earth. They occur as part of the geological processes that form the Earth's mountains, oceans, valleys, and plains. During the last hundred years or so, scientists have learned a great deal about these processes, including the causes of earthquakes, how to measure them, and where they occur. In learning about earthquakes, scientists have learned much about the Earth itself.

▶CAUSES OF EARTHQUAKES

An earthquake occurs because of geologic forces inside the Earth. These forces build up slowly and eventually become so strong that they cause rocks to break underground. When this happens, tremendous energy is released suddenly in the form of motion that spreads out in all directions from the break, causing the ground to shake and move. This sudden release of energy and movement is what makes an earthquake so destructive.

There are two parts to the story of what causes earthquakes. The first concerns how forces in the Earth build up. The second explains why the ground breaks with a sudden motion rather than a slow shift.

When the Earth was first formed, radioactive materials, such as uranium, potassium, and thorium, began to decay naturally in the planet's interior. This process of radioactive decay slowly heated up the rocky material deep inside the planet. Since heat attempts to rise, this heated material has been moving slowly toward the Earth's surface. The movement is very slow—less than an inch or so each year. But over hundreds of millions of years, this slow movement adds up to distances of thousands of miles.

Deep inside the Earth, where temperatures are very high, the heated rocky material is flexible, so it moves slowly and steadily. Nearer the Earth's surface, however, the rocky material becomes cooler and more brittle, and it cannot move so easily. The slow, continual movement of material deep in the interior builds up and exerts stronger and stronger forces on the brittle rocks near the surface, making them move as well. For an earthquake to occur, the rocks nearer the surface have to

On September 19, 1985, an earthquake of magnitude 8.1 caused strong ground shaking in an area of Mexico City, where about 500 structures such as this collapsed concrete building were severely damaged or destroyed. The earthquake caused more than 8,000 deaths in Mexico and left an estimated 30,000 injured and 50,000 homeless.

California's San Andreas Fault marks the boundary between two tectonic plates in the Earth's crust that are sliding past one another. A sudden slip that forced the movement of more than a 248-mile stretch of the fault caused the San Francisco earthquake of 1906.

When rock breaks along a fault, the pieces of rock will move by sliding past each other if the force is great enough. The motion may occur in a series of jerks, each one of which is an earthquake. In a large earthquake, the rock along the fault may move several feet in only a few seconds.

Over tens of millions of years, such geologic forces have caused massive changes in the Earth's landscape, as millions of earthquakes have moved large chunks of the planet's surface hundreds of miles. This process has changed the shape and location of the continents and oceans over the Earth's long history, and it continues to do so today.

▶SEISMIC WAVES

The sudden release of energy from an earthquake sends out several different shaking movements, or seismic waves. (The word "seismic" comes from a Greek word for "shaking.") Some of these seismic waves travel over the surface of the Earth and are called surface waves. Others, called body waves, travel down through the Earth's deep interior before returning to the surface.

Surface Waves

If you throw a stone into a calm pond, it creates a short splash and then ripples spread outward for a much longer time. Something similar happens in the Earth when there is an earthquake. When rocks slip past each other along a fault, the initial movement is over very quickly. However, the energy that is released causes ripples, called surface waves, that spread outward. These waves gradually get weaker the farther they travel, until they eventually die out.

Seismic surface waves travel at speeds ranging from about 1 to 3 miles (1.6 to 4.8

break suddenly—just like a dead stick that breaks suddenly when it is bent too far.

People do not usually think of the ground as something that can break. But if you take a small piece of rock and squeeze it strongly enough in a metal vise, it will crack or crumble. An earthquake is like that cracking rock, but on a much larger scale. Often a break occurs in a place that has broken before, on what scientists call a **fault**—a break in the Earth's surface between two blocks of rock that have moved past each other.

Many types of faults have been classified by geologists. Normal and reverse faults are among those that have vertical movements. Various types of strike-slip faults have horizontal movements, and oblique faults have both vertical and horizontal movements.

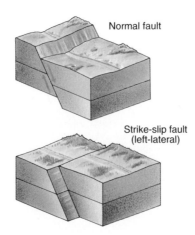

Normal fault

Reverse fault

Strike-slip fault (left-lateral)

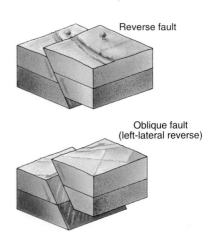

Oblique fault (left-lateral reverse)

kilometers) per second. The surface waves from small earthquakes usually go unnoticed except by sensitive instruments. But people who experience a large earthquake often describe a swaying or a rolling motion, which is the characteristic motion of seismic surface waves.

Body Waves

A seismic wave that travels through a material rather than over its surface is called a body wave. There are two basic types of seismic body waves: **sound waves** and a type of shaking called **shear waves**. Everyone knows that sound travels through the air, but did you know that sound can also travel through water and even through solid rock? Sound waves are the fastest type of seismic wave. Shear waves travel slower than sound but a little faster than surface waves. Because sound waves and shear waves are usually the first two types of seismic waves to arrive at any point after an earthquake, they are called P-waves and S-waves, from the Latin for "first" (*primus*) and "second" (*secundus*).

P-Waves. The faster of the two types of body waves is the P-wave, or sound wave. When an earthquake occurs, sound waves travel through the interior of the Earth rather than over the surface. A sound wave is created in air, water, or rock as particles of material press rapidly together and then pull apart. The sound wave travels through the material as a series of squeezes and stretches. At the Earth's surface, sound waves travel through rock at about 3 miles (4.8 kilometers) per second. Deep inside the Earth, however, the speed can

Surface waves travel at a range of speeds and spread out as time goes on. Surface waves spreading away from an earthquake source are shown as they appear 20 minutes after an earthquake occurs (*right*) and an hour later (*far right*). The waves are a rippling motion of the Earth's surface. Their height is exaggerated here.

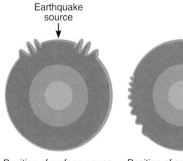

Position of surface waves, 20 minutes after an earthquake

Position of surface waves, one hour after an earthquake

An earthquake generates P-waves that spread through the Earth's interior just like sound waves spread through the air in a room when someone claps their hands. One diagram (*top*) shows the position of a P-wave after 5 minutes, when it has spread downward through the mantle and begun to travel in the fluid core. Another (*bottom*) shows its position after 10 minutes, when it has traveled almost to the center of the Earth.

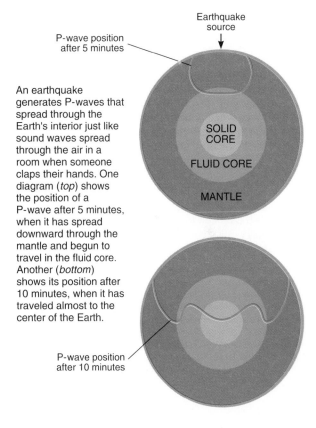

These diagrams show: the path of an S-wave through the Earth's interior from a deep earthquake source to a distant seismometer (*right*); the paths for two different reflections, labeled sS and SS, that an S-wave can make (*middle*); and the paths for two more reflections— ScS, the reflection from the fluid core, and sScS, the double reflection from the Earth's surface and then its core (*far right*).

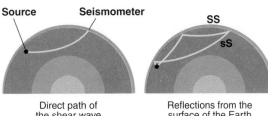

Direct path of the shear wave

Reflections from the surface of the Earth

Reflections from the Earth's core and surface

be almost three times faster. P-waves also travel at different speeds depending on the type of material they pass through. Within the Earth they travel fastest in the region at the bottom of the Earth's mantle. Within the fluid core they travel much more slowly. Diagrams on page 35 show how a P-wave travels through the Earth after an earthquake. P-waves reach everywhere around the Earth after about 20 minutes.

S-Waves. The slower type of body wave, the S-wave, or shear wave, can be described in this way. Imagine that you have tied one end of a rope to a post and are holding the other end. When you shake your end of the rope from side to side, a shaking motion, like a wriggling snake, travels along the rope. S-waves are a similar type of shaking motion. With S-waves, material in the Earth is actually moving sideways to the direction that the wave is traveling. S-waves cannot travel in liquid; they can travel only in solid material. Therefore, when S-waves reach the fluid part of the Earth's outer core they stop or are reflected back, or they convert to P-waves in the core. The shaking motions of S-waves are usually much larger than the motions of P-waves.

Probing the Earth's Interior. The major layers of the Earth—the crust, mantle, and core—have been known to seismologists since the early 1900's. These scientists have also discovered that the Earth must have both a solid inner core and a fluid outer core composed mainly of iron. Our modern view of the Earth's interior is based on millions of measurements of the time it takes body waves to travel through the Earth. It is also based on knowledge of how the speed and direction of body waves are affected by substances of different densities, such as rock and molten iron.

▶**MEASURING SEISMIC MOTION**

The instruments that measure seismic waves are called **seismometers**, and the records they make are called **seismograms**. By studying seismograms, seismologists can determine where an earthquake occurred. By studying seismograms over many years, they have also determined in what regions of the world earthquakes are likely to occur. Over the Earth's long history, forces deep within the planet have moved huge sections of the Earth's crust from one place to another. These sections are called **tectonic plates**, and the process by which they are moved is called **plate tectonics**.

Earthquakes, seismologists have discovered, generally happen along the boundaries of the tectonic plates in the Earth's crust that are moving apart, that are moving past one another horizontally, or that are moving toward one another in a process that forces one plate deep into the Earth. (See EARTH, HISTORY OF in Volume E and GEOLOGY in Volume G.)

In the 1989 Loma Prieta earthquake, seismic waves caused extensive damage in San Francisco and Oakland, California, particularly to structures built over landfill. The rippling and collapse of sections of this freeway interchange caused several deaths when the upper deck dropped and crushed cars on the lower level.

There are many different types of seismometers, but the principle behind all of them is very simple. They all measure the distance that the ground moves either vertically or horizontally as a result of some seismic motion. Seismic motion can be measured in two basic ways. One way is with a weight suspended from a spring. Vertical motion can be measured by noting changes in the distance between the bottom of the weight and the base of the frame before the ground shakes and while the ground is shaking. A second way to measure seismic motion is with a weight on a

▶ LOCATING AN EARTHQUAKE

Thousands of seismometers are now operating at stations all around the world. Each is quietly waiting and "listening" for the seismic waves of a distant or a nearby earthquake. When an earthquake occurs somewhere on Earth, many of these seismometers will record the motions of the sound waves, shear waves, and surface waves that are produced. By measuring the size of these waves and the times at which they reach each seismic station, seismologists can determine where the earthquake occurred and how large it was.

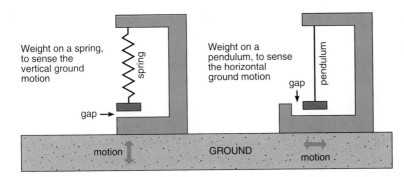

Seismometers (*left*) work by measuring a gap between a suspended weight and a frame that moves with the ground when an earthquake occurs.

A seismogram (*below*) is a record of how the ground moves at a particular place—in this case, at Palisades, New York, during an earthquake on November 30, 1992. The largest waves shown here are surface waves, which last for several minutes.

pendulum that can swing sideways. Using this method, horizontal motion can be measured by noting changes in the distance between the side of the weight and the sides of the frame before and while the ground is shaking. In practice, seismologists often use a weight on a spring to measure vertical motions plus an east-west swinging pendulum and a north-south swinging pendulum to measure horizontal motions. All three systems are needed because the ground can move in any direction during an earthquake.

Seismometers must be very sensitive because the seismic motions from distant earthquakes are often very small. A medium-sized earthquake in Alaska, for example, will produce a ground motion in New York of less than one millionth of an inch when the P-waves arrive. If sensitive seismometers are placed in a large city or near an ocean beach, traffic or ocean waves produce vibrations that will interfere with the detection of distant earthquakes. In areas that are seismically active, strong-motion seismometers are often used. These instruments can measure very intense seismic motions that would cause sensitive seismometers to go off the scale.

November 30, 1992, North Atlantic Ocean, Magnitude=5.7, Depth=10 km, Distance=3,461 km

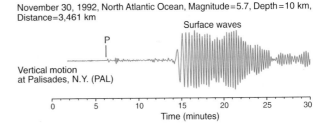

One way seismologists can locate the source of the waves—the place where the earthquake occurred—is to interpret all the seismic motions recorded at each station and to backtrack along the path the motions traveled to find the common point from which all the seismic waves originated.

Another way to locate an earthquake is to study more than one type of seismic wave, taking into account the fact that different waves travel at different speeds. Both P-waves and S-waves, for example, start out at the same time like runners in a race. P-waves travel faster, however, and the farther they travel, the greater the time difference between when they arrive at a seismometer and when the S-waves arrive. By measuring this time difference, seismologists can tell how far

A Short Version of the Modified Mercalli Intensity Scale

I. Not felt except by a few people under especially favorable circumstances.

II. Felt by only a few persons at rest, especially on the upper floors of buildings.

III. Felt quite noticeably indoors. Vibrations are like the passing of a truck.

IV. Felt indoors by many, outdoors by a few. Dishes, windows, doors disturbed; walls make cracking sounds.

V. Felt by nearly everyone; many people are awakened. Some dishes, windows, and other objects are broken.

VI. Felt by all; many people are frightened and run outdoors. Some heavy furniture is moved. Damage is slight.

VII. Everybody runs outdoors. Negligible damage in buildings of good design and construction; considerable damage in poorly built or badly designed structures. Noticed by people in cars.

VIII. Considerable damage in ordinary buildings; heavy damage in poorly built structures. Chimneys, monuments, and walls fall. Heavy furniture is overturned.

IX. Great damage to many buildings; many are shifted off their foundations. Conspicuous cracks in the ground. Underground pipes are broken.

X. Most masonry and frame structures are destroyed. Rails are bent. Large landslides on river banks and slopes.

XI. Few, if any, masonry structures remain standing. Bridges are destroyed. Broad fissures open in the ground. Underground pipelines are completely out of service.

XII. Damage is total. Seismic waves are seen on ground surfaces. Objects are thrown upward into the air.

away the earthquake is from each station. They can then locate the source of the earthquake by studying the different times at which the waves reached different seismic stations.

The place on the Earth's surface where an earthquake occurs is called the **epicenter**. This will usually be the place where the shaking is strongest. The place where the seismic waves actually originate is called the **hypocenter**. Lying below the epicenter, the hypocenter is the place where rock actually breaks along a buried fault. It is quite rare for an earthquake to occur on a fault that breaks through to the surface of the Earth. However, such surface faulting does sometimes occur—for example, in parts of California. Most earthquakes occur in the Earth's crust only a few miles below the surface. But about 10 percent of all earthquakes are deep, occurring more than 60 miles (about 100 kilometers) below the surface. Some hypocenters are as deep as 450 miles (about 700 kilometers).

▶ THE SIZE AND FREQUENCY OF EARTHQUAKES

Seismologists use three different ways to describe earthquake shaking and earthquake sizes. **Intensity** refers to the strength of shaking motions and the damage they can do. The intensity of shaking varies from place to place for the same earthquake, and seismologists use an **intensity scale** to describe the strength of seismic motions at a particular location. To describe how big the earthquake itself is, seismologists refer to the **magnitude**, as measured on a **magnitude scale**, which compares the sizes of different earthquakes. Alternatively they use the **seismic moment** of the earthquake, which is a way of describing an important combination of physical conditions at the earthquake source.

Earthquake Intensity

More than a hundred years ago, when people began studying earthquakes scientifically, they needed a practical way of describing the strength of an earthquake's shaking motions. They began by describing the pattern of damage to buildings and making maps to show different levels of damage at different places.

Seismologists call this approach the study of earthquake intensities. Today they usually work with twelve different damage zones, using what is called the modified Mercalli Intensity Scale. Each zone is assigned a Roman

The force of S-waves moving from deep within the Earth to its surface can be greatly intensified at the surface when both the initial wave and its reflection are added together. These buckled railroad tracks reflect the severe ground shaking and deformation that resulted during a 1976 earthquake in Tangshan, China.

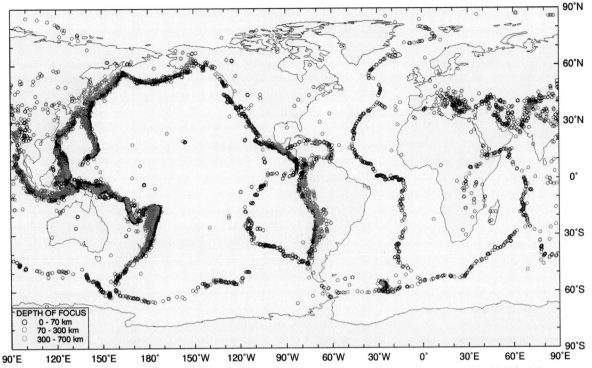

DEPTH OF FOCUS
○ 0 - 70 km
○ 70 - 300 km
○ 300 - 700 km

This map shows the location of more than 10,000 of the largest earthquakes that occurred from 1977 to 1992. Most occurred at the boundaries between tectonic plates and resulted from the motions of the plates.

numeral, and each of the descriptions corresponds to a particular intensity of shaking.

After an earthquake, seismologists make intensity maps based on people's experiences and the types of damage that have occurred. By referring to old newspaper accounts and personal diaries, it is even possible to make intensity maps for past earthquakes.

Intensity and damage from an earthquake can be abnormally high in certain places because of the type of soil or surface. Areas with soft sedimentary layers of material are more susceptible to severe damage from shaking than surrounding areas of harder rock. Extensive damage is likely to occur in landfill areas where sandy material has been dumped into a lake or a bay to create a surface upon which buildings are constructed. Buildings in these areas should be specially strengthened.

The intensity scale describes the strength of seismic motions in different places; it does not tell whether the earthquake that caused the motions was large or small. Shaking at intensity III, for example, could occur near the epicenter of a small earthquake or at a great distance from a large earthquake.

Earthquake Magnitude

In the 1930's, the American seismologist Charles Richter (1900–85) studied thousands of seismograms of earthquakes that had oc-

curred in southern California. He realized that it would be useful to have a numerical scale for comparing the size of earthquakes that went beyond describing them as just large or small. Richter knew that he would have to take two things into account in devising such a scale: the distance from the epicenter and the great difference in size of ground motion between small and large earthquakes.

The result of Richter's work was a method of assigning magnitude that we know today as the Richter scale. It is based upon a measurement of the size of the largest wave recorded on a certain type of seismometer that was commonly used in Richter's day. He took account of the distance from the epicenter by finding how to make a correction to the actual measurement so that he knew how big the seismic waves would be at a distance of exactly 100 kilometers (about 60 miles) from the epicenter. He took account of the great difference in size of ground motion for different earthquakes by using a scale on which an increase by one unit (for example, from magnitude 7 to magnitude 8) meant an increase in earthquake shaking by a factor of ten. Thus a magnitude of 8 is 100 times greater shaking

Notable Earthquakes

Earthquakes cause devastation in many ways. Shaking of the land can destroy buildings and trigger landslides. Shaking of the ocean floor can cause a **tsunami**, a special kind of water wave. (For more information, read the article TSUNAMIS in Volume T.)

San Francisco, California: April 18, 1906

A magnitude 8 (M8) earthquake was caused by a horizontal slip of several yards between the Pacific and North American tectonic plates. The slip affected more than 248 miles (400 kilometers) of the San Andreas Fault, to a depth of about 6 miles (10 kilometers). But it was also easily visible at the surface. Many brick buildings collapsed immediately. Many wooden frame buildings were destroyed by the fires that burned for days afterwards. Over 3,000 people in the area died.

Kanto, Japan: September 1, 1923

Because Japan sits atop four tectonic plates, it is one of the world's most earthquake-prone countries. In 1923, a devastating M7.9 earthquake struck the Kanto region, which includes the cities of Tokyo and Yokohama. After the earthquake, many fires broke out. About 140,000 people died.

Chile: May 22, 1960

An M9 earthquake was caused by a fault slip of about 66 feet (20 meters) between the Pacific and the South American tectonic plates. The fault surface was so large—more than 620 miles (1,000 kilometers) long and about 124 miles (200 kilometers) wide—that we associate this earthquake with an entire country. Few instruments measured the very long surface waves. But the available records showed that the shock made the whole Earth "ring" like a gigantic bell for days.

Tokyo, Japan

than a magnitude of 6, and a million times greater than a magnitude of 2. He took 0 (zero) on his scale as the smallest earthquake he cared to work with at that time—100 million times smaller than an earthquake of magnitude 8. Very small earthquakes are rated up to about 2.5 on the Richter scale. Moderate earthquakes rated up to magnitude 5 can cause minor damage. Earthquakes of magnitude 6 and higher are major earthquakes that can cause widespread damage and loss of life.

Today there are many different magnitude scales in addition to the Richter scale, all based on ways of measuring the sizes of different seismic waves on different seismometers. The largest earthquakes on these scales range up to about magnitude 8 or 9. Using sensitive instruments, seismologists have detected earthquakes as small as magnitude –3 or –4. An earthquake with magnitude of –3 is 1,000 times smaller than magnitude 0, the smallest number on the original Richter scale.

Seismic Moment

Seismologists often prefer to describe the size of an earthquake in terms of the physical conditions at the earthquake source itself rather than in terms of the shaking it produces. To do this, they use **seismic moment** rather than magnitude. The seismic moment of an earthquake is determined from three factors. The first factor is the distance that rock slides along a fault surface after it breaks. This distance is called the **fault slip.** The second factor is the area of the fault surface that is actually broken by the earthquake. And the third factor is the measurement of how rigid the rocks are near the broken fault. All solid materials have a rigidity that can be measured. For example, a strong rock such as granite is usually more rigid than a softer rock such as sandstone, which can be broken easily.

We determine the seismic moment of an earthquake by multiplying together the fault slip, the fault area, and the rigidity. The seismic moment describes the essential combination of physical quantities that really matters at the earthquake source and that determines how strong the seismic motions will be.

In the greatest earthquakes, the fault slip can be many feet and the fault area can be thousands of square miles. In the smallest

Anchorage, Alaska: March 27, 1964

An M8.5 earthquake occurred when the Pacific tectonic plate slipped about 42 feet (13 meters) beneath the North American tectonic plate. The slip occurred beneath the seafloor just south of the port of Anchorage, which was destroyed. Many seismometers around the world were knocked off scale for hours. When recording resumed, it was clear that the whole Earth was ringing at exactly the same frequencies as for the great Chilean earthquake. Large amounts of water were almost immediately moved up or down several yards because the main fault surface that broke was beneath the ocean floor. This seafloor motion caused a tsunami that traveled all over the Pacific Ocean.

Tangshan, China: July 27, 1976

An M7.5 earthquake occurred in eastern China, about a hundred miles from Beijing, in a coal-mining area where thousands of people worked underground day and night. About 240,000 people died. In this part of the world, the boundary between tectonic plates is not clearly defined. Rather, it

Anchorage, Alaska

appears as if a region millions of square miles in extent is deforming, or changing shape, not by a steady process but by earthquakes.

Banda Aceh, Indonesia: December 26, 2004

When the edge of the India plate slipped beneath the edge of the Burma plate, a buildup of stresses was released, producing an M9 earthquake with two kinds of motion: strike-slip faulting (slip parallel to the fault) and thrust faulting (slip perpendicular to the fault). The earthquake, which was centered off the coast of Indonesia, shook the seafloor, producing a devastating tsunami that reached shorelines along Indonesia, Thailand, Sri Lanka, India, and even distant Africa. The tsunami's waves, which rose as high as 35 feet (10.5 meters), caught most people unaware. Estimates of the death toll ranged between 156,000 and 178,000.

Northern Pakistan: October 8, 2005

An M7.6 earthquake affecting northern Pakistan and Kashmir resulted from the same forces that have produced the highest mountains in the world, including the Himalayas. The Indian tectonic plate, which is moving north at a rate of about 1.6 inches (4 cm) each year, passes beneath and lifts the Eurasian plate. This action gradually raises mountains in the region. It also triggers earthquakes. A month after the earthquake, deaths numbered at least 79,000. Sending aid was hard because of the remote and rugged terrain.

measurable earthquake, on the other hand, the fault slip might be as small as a fraction of an inch and the fault area may be only a few square feet. If the rigidities are about the same, the largest seismic moment is a trillion times larger than the smallest.

Earthquake Frequency

Different-sized earthquakes occur with greater or lesser frequency depending on the magnitude. Seismologists have discovered that for each increase of one magnitude, there are generally about ten times fewer earthquakes. Considering the world as a whole, there are approximately 10,000 earthquakes of magnitude 4 or greater each year. Thus there are only about ten earthquakes of magnitude 7 or greater each year.

▶ EARTHQUAKE PREDICTION

Although seismologists know that certain regions are more earthquake-prone than others, they do not know for certain just when an earthquake will occur. Today much of the effort of earthquake prediction goes into studying the geology of the Earth and examining historical records of particular regions to determine exactly where and how often earthquakes occurred in the past. This information can then be used to make rough estimates of what to expect in the future in that same region. Such studies lead seismologists to think that there is between a 10 and 50 percent probability that a major earthquake will strike California within a person's lifetime.

Most earthquakes do little harm, but a few can cause great destruction and loss of life. Engineers study each major earthquake to learn how to build safer buildings, dams, and bridges so that destruction and loss of life can be reduced. Seismologists and other scientists continue their studies to learn more about what happens at the earthquake source and to discover more about the interior of the Earth.

PAUL G. RICHARDS
WON-YOUNG KIM
Lamont-Doherty Earth Observatory of
Columbia University, New York

See also EARTH; EARTH, HISTORY OF; GEOLOGY; MOTION.

EARTH SCIENCE. See EARTH; EARTH, HISTORY OF; EXPERIMENTS AND OTHER SCIENCE ACTIVITIES (Earth Sciences); GEOLOGY.

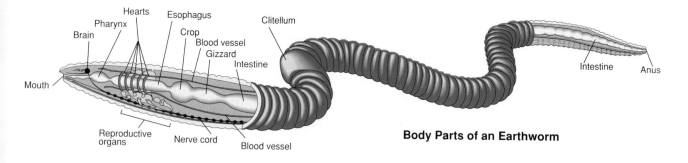

Brain · Pharynx · Hearts · Esophagus · Crop · Blood vessel · Gizzard · Intestine · Clitellum · Intestine · Anus · Mouth · Reproductive organs · Nerve cord · Blood vessel

Body Parts of an Earthworm

EARTHWORMS

Earthworms, often called night crawlers or angleworms, are segmented worms belonging to the group of animals called **annelids**. The word "annelid" comes from the Latin word *anellus,* which means "small ring," and refers to the many rings, or segments, that make up the worm's body.

The earliest earthworms lived on earth more than 80 million years ago. Today more than 6,000 species occur worldwide. About 200 species are found in North America.

Most earthworms live in warm, moist soil, although some are occasionally collected from streams and lakes. Earthworms usually remain near the surface of the soil, but they have been known to burrow as deep as 20 feet (6.1 meters) during periods of dryness or during the winter months.

The most noticeable feature on an earthworm's pinkish brown body is a swelling, called the **clitellum**. The clitellum is located near the worm's front end, or anterior, and plays a role in reproduction.

The common earthworm has about 150 segments, although some may have as few as 50 or as many as 500 segments. Small species of earthworms may measure less than 1 inch (2.5 centimeters) in length. One giant species living in Australia is more than 11 feet (3.4 meters) long.

Four groups of hairs, called **chaetae**, are found on all but the first and last segments of an earthworm. The chaetae assist the worm in movement by clinging to the walls of the burrow as the earthworm pushes and pulls itself along. A bird usually struggles to pull an earthworm out of the ground because the chaetae help hold the worm in its burrow.

Earthworms often are observed crawling outside their burrows at night but rarely during the day. This is because they are sensitive to light and excessive loss of moisture. A slimy mucus produced by specialized cells helps protect against moisture loss and keeps the skin moist. Earthworms have no eyes, but tiny organs sensitive to light are present near the ends of the worms. They also have no ears, but earthworms respond rapidly to even the slightest vibrations in the soil. Earthworms do not have lungs. They absorb oxygen through the thin, moist outer layer of skin.

Earthworms feed on leaves, dirt, and other organic matter (remains of living things). Waste is pushed out through the anus. A worm may eat and discard its own weight in food and dirt each day. Earthworms are often found on sidewalks and driveways after a heavy rain because water fills their burrows.

Earthworms are valuable to gardeners and farmers because they transform organic matter in the soil into rich nutrients used by plants for growth. They also change the texture and structure of the soil, increasing the availability of air and water to the roots of plants.

Earthworms, like all annelids, are **hermaphroditic**: Each individual has both female and male reproductive organs. Earthworms cannot fertilize themselves, however, and must pair up with another earthworm of the same species to reproduce. Young earthworms mature in about six months and may live as long as ten years.

Although all pieces of an earthworm may wriggle for a while when cut up, only the anterior (front end) will survive. The other pieces soon die.

MARK J. WETZEL
Illinois Natural History Survey

EASTER

Easter Sunday is the day on which Christians celebrate the **Resurrection** (return to life) of Jesus Christ. Christianity was founded on the belief that Jesus, a Jewish religious teacher, was the Son of God, that he was executed by the Romans about 2,000 years ago, and that 3 days after his death, he was resurrected. Christians believe that Jesus' resurrection means that they will also be resurrected after death. Therefore Easter is celebrated in church services with joyful music and symbols of new life such as flowers and new clothes.

Easter is believed to have taken its English name from *Eostur,* an ancient North European festival celebrating the return of spring. The French word for Easter, *Pâques,* the Italian *Pasqua,* and the Spanish *Pascua* all came from the Hebrew word *Pesah,* a Jewish feast celebrated on the night of the first full moon in the spring season. The feast of Pesah (in English, Passover) marks the freedom of the ancient Israelites from the Egyptians, who had enslaved them.

▶ THE EASTER SEASON

In most Christian churches, Easter falls sometime between March 22 and April 25. It falls on the first Sunday after the first full moon following March 21, the vernal equinox (the time in spring when day and night are of equal length). The date of Easter Sunday was established by the church council of Nicaea in A.D. 325. The Eastern Orthodox churches determine the date of the holiday in a slightly different way. Thus Easter in these churches may on occasion fall later than April 25.

Before Easter, many Christians observe a period of prayer and penitence (regret for wrongdoing). During this 40-day period, which is called **Lent,** they may fast (not eat certain foods) and give up some pleasures. Lent begins on **Ash Wednesday,** so named because ashes are a symbol of penitence. In some churches Ash Wednesday is observed with a service at which the priest or minister marks the foreheads of the members of the congregation with a cross of ashes to symbolize penitence.

The last week before Easter is **Holy Week.** It begins on **Palm Sunday,** which marks the entry of Jesus into Jerusalem through streets his followers had strewn with palm leaves.

On Easter, Christians celebrate Jesus' resurrection. This painting shows Jesus stepping from the tomb. The guards have been struck unconscious by an angel.

Holy Thursday is the day of the Last Supper, Jesus' Passover meal with his disciples. **Good Friday** is the day of Jesus' crucifixion (execution by being nailed to a wooden cross). Its name may refer to the belief that Jesus' death was good for Christians, or it may be a version of God's Friday. Many Christians attend a church service from noon until 3:00 P.M. on Good Friday, to recall the last three hours of Christ's suffering on the cross. The day before Easter, called **Holy Saturday,** is often observed with an evening candlelight service.

On Easter morning the resurrection is celebrated, often with a sunrise service. The Lenten period of fasting is over, and many Christians gather with family and friends for a festive meal after the church services.

In some churches the Easter season continues through **Ascension Day** (40th day after Easter) and **Pentecost** (50th day after Easter). Ascension Day celebrates the ascent (rising) of Jesus into Heaven. Pentecost commemorates God's sending of the Holy Spirit to Jesus' disciples to inspire and strengthen them for the task of preaching Christianity.

DECORATING EGGS

To prepare eggs for decorating, hard boil them for 20 minutes and then cool them. Or, you can poke a hole in each end of a raw egg with a large needle and then gently blow out the contents. Rinse out the inside of a blown egg and drain it dry before decorating.

You can dye your eggs with store-bought dye, food coloring dye, or even homemade dye. To use food coloring, mix 20 drops of coloring and one teaspoon of vinegar in a half cup of very hot water. A yellowish brown homemade dye can be made by boiling onion skins barely covered with water for one hour. Red or blue dye can be made by crushing berries with a small amount of water and straining them through a paper towel.

Batik-like eggs are done by drawing on the egg with crayon before dyeing. To make "stained-glass" eggs, crisscross the eggs with heavy lines using a black marker and then fill in each space with a different color marker.

Eggs can also be decorated patchwork style by gluing on squares of fabric, tissue, or wrapping paper. Sequins, glitter, and stickers can lend a festive touch.

Turn eggs into animals or people using markers and cut paper. Display your egg characters on paper collars or spray-can caps.

Broken egg halves can be filled with Easter grass and chicks made from cotton balls. Or, they can be turned into tulips by adding a pipe-cleaner stem. Save crushed egg shells to glue on cardboard to make a mosaic picture.

Happy decorating!

▶ **EASTER CUSTOMS AND SYMBOLS**

Before the season of Lent, people in many parts of the world have parties and parades. These celebrations are called Mardi Gras or Carnivals (see HOLIDAYS in Volume H).

Pagan festivals celebrating spring included fire and sunrise celebrations. Both later became part of Easter celebrations. In the Middle Ages people gathered on Easter to pray as the sun rose and then went in procession to their churches. Their candles' flames came to symbolize the light of Jesus Christ.

The new clothes worn on Easter Sunday are a symbol of new life. The custom comes from the Easter Sunday baptism of early Christians, who were led into church wearing new robes of white linen. The present-day Easter parade has a parallel in the Middle Ages, when people walked about the countryside on Easter, stopping to pray. Nowadays people walk in Easter parades to show new spring hats.

The lamb, one of the symbols of the Christian Easter, originated in the ancient Hebrew Passover. God had ordered the Israelites to smear the doors of their houses with the blood of a sacrificed lamb. Thus the angel of death would know their houses from the Egyptians' and spare the Jewish first-born sons. The paschal (Passover) lamb became identified by Christians with Christ, whom they called the Lamb of God. This is a reference to Jesus' death as a sacrifice, like that of the lamb.

One of the best-known Easter symbols is the egg, which has symbolized the return of spring and renewed life since ancient days. The egg is said to be a symbol of life because in living creatures life begins in the egg. The Persians and Egyptians colored eggs and ate them during their new year's celebration, which came in the spring.

In North America and some European countries, children enjoy hunting for Easter eggs, which they believe were hidden by the Easter Bunny or the Easter Hare. The hare, a close relative of the rabbit, was the symbol of Eostre, the ancient pagan goddess of spring.

Other Easter symbols include the sun, which stands for good fortune; the rooster, fulfillment of wishes; the deer, good health; and flowers, love and charity.

Reviewed by MSGR. JOHN PAUL HAVERTY
Blessed Sacrament Church,
Staten Island, New York

EASTERN ORTHODOX CHURCHES

Most Christians in Eastern Europe and the Middle East worship in Eastern Orthodox churches. The Eastern Orthodox Church is one of the three major **confessions** (branches) of Christianity. The other two major confessions are the Roman Catholic Church and the Protestant churches. The Eastern Orthodox churches have more than 80 million members worldwide. They include Russians, Serbs, Romanians, Greeks, Bulgarians, Albanians, Ukrainians, Carpatho-Russians, Syrians, and others. The word "orthodox" means "right believing."

History

In the beginning all Christian communities were united. Christian communities were founded by Jesus' apostles and the men they chose in each city to aid them. Some of these men, later called bishops, in turn ordained other bishops and priests. The custom of passing knowledge and authority from one generation to the next in this way is called the **apostolic succession.**

Because the Christian Church began in the days of the Roman Empire, its divisions were based on the division of the empire into **dioceses**. Each diocese was headed by a bishop. The bishops of large cities were called patriarchs and were especially powerful. The early Christian Church had five patriarchs—one at Rome, one at Alexandria, one at Antioch, one at Constantinople, and one at Jerusalem. The Church was ruled by an assembly of bishops and patriarchs called the **Ecumenical Council.** The council met seven times between A.D. 325 and A.D. 787.

Gradually the Roman Empire split into the Western Empire, which was ruled from Rome, and the Byzantine Empire, with its capital at Constantinople. In 1054 the Patriarch of Rome, who was the pope and leader of Western Christians, separated from the other patriarchs. Thus, the Christian Church divided into Eastern and Western branches. This separation is called the **great schism**. The Eastern branch became the Orthodox Church, and the Western branch became the Roman Catholic Church.

Today the Orthodox Church is a confederation of many national churches. The largest of these are self-governing, meaning they have the right to choose their own heads. They include the churches of Constantinople (in Istanbul, Turkey); Alexandria and Sinai (in Egypt); Antioch (in Damascus, Syria); Jerusalem (in Israel); Moscow (in Russia); the republic of Georgia; Serbia and Montenegro; Romania; Bulgaria; Greece; Cyprus; Albania; Poland; and the Czech Republic and Slovakia. There are nine national branches of the Orthodox Church in the United States. They are Albanian, Bulgarian, Carpatho-Russian, Greek, Romanian, Russian, Serbian, Syrian, and Ukrainian.

How Orthodox Christians Worship

There are priests, bishops, nuns, monks, and ordinary worshipers (lay people) in the Eastern Orthodox Church. Only men may become priests. Priests may be married, but bishops, monks, and nuns may not. Monasticism (that is, monastery and convent life) lies at the very heart of the Orthodox Church. It is organized on the guidelines that were set by Saint Basil the Great, who lived in the 300's.

Orthodox spiritual life is full of the joy of Easter. Every Sunday is considered a celebration of Christ's resurrection after death. The rituals include the **Eucharist**, known as the **Divine** or **Holy Liturgy**, and a number of other offices (services), such as marriage and baptism. "Eucharist" comes from the Greek word meaning "thanksgiving." "Liturgy" comes from a Greek word meaning "public service." For Orthodox Christians the Holy Liturgy is the highest expression of Christian worship.

Orthodox Christians are noted for singing, or chanting, their services, without instrumental accompaniment, and for displaying beautiful icons—religious pictures (sacred images) of Jesus, the Virgin Mary, and the saints. Orthodox Christians give these icons an important place in their worship, both at church and at home. They do not worship the actual pictures but the person or event pictured.

In the words of Saint Paul, the Church is "the house of God, which is the Church of the living God, the pillar and ground of the truth." The Church lives according to the teachings of the Old and New Testaments. Quotations from the Bible form the basis of Church services.

Eastern Orthodox churches, such as the Kremlin Cathedral in Moscow (*right*), are characterized by their many domes. Inside the churches are paintings called icons (*below*). An icon contains the sacred image of Jesus Christ, the Virgin Mary, or a saint and serves as a focus of prayer and devotion for Orthodox Christians.

The Orthodox Church uses three liturgies: the Liturgy of Saint John Chrysostom (which is used most often), the Liturgy of Saint Basil, and the Liturgy of Saint Gregory, also called the Liturgy of the Presanctified, because the bread and wine of the Eucharist have been consecrated (made holy) by the priests on the preceding Sunday. This liturgy is celebrated on Wednesdays and Fridays during Lent and on the first three days of Holy Week.

The Holy Liturgy has three parts. The first is the Office of the Preparation of the Elements (Office of Oblation), during which the elements (bread and wine) are prepared for use later in the Eucharist (Communion). The second is the Liturgy of the Catechumens. In early days people who wished to be baptized were called catechumens. They could attend only through this part of the service, which includes the reading of the Epistle and the Gospel (passages from the Bible), the sermon, and the great litanies. (**Litanies** are ritual prayers in which the congregation shares.)

The third part is the Liturgy of the Faithful. This is the mystical part of the service: the consecration of the bread and wine and the Communion of the faithful. "Faithful" means not simply a believer but a Church member who lives up to Church teachings. The Sacrament of Holy Communion, or the Eucharist, is the climax of all religious services in the Eastern Orthodox Church. Orthodox Christians believe that this sacrament was instituted by Jesus Christ at the Last Supper.

In addition to the Holy Liturgy, the Church has a range of other offices. Baptism and marriage are among the most important to the lay worshiper. In addition there are daily offices —groups of prayers, psalms, hymns, and Bible readings—to be said at set times.

Worshipers in the Orthodox Church are considered members of the family of Christ, the Church, which includes both the living and the dead. It is their privilege, as well as their duty, to attend the Holy Liturgy on every Sunday and feast day.

Because the Greek word for resurrection, *anesti*, literally means "to stand up," worshipers in Eastern Orthodox Churches usually stand during services. But the Church does not insist that they do this. They may cross themselves, kneel down, stand, sit, or pray at an icon. As long as they respect the great moments of the liturgy and do not disturb fellow worshipers, they may do whatever best expresses their love and worship. They participate with their whole being, so that every service is an act of praise.

The Orthodox Church in the United States

The first Orthodox Christians to reach North America were the Russian explorers who discovered Alaska in 1741. Two years later the first Christian was baptized on Alaskan soil. In 1794 seven monks from the Valaam Monastery on Lake Ladoga in Russia began missionary work. With the help of Russian settlers they founded the Russian Orthodox Church in America. That year they opened the first school for the Inuit and consecrated the first Orthodox Church, in St. Paul's Harbor, Alaska.

During the 1800's and early 1900's many immigrants came to the United States from Eastern Europe, Greece, and the Middle East. Except for the Russian mission, most churches were organized by the immigrants themselves (who were not in a position to set up seminaries). They were not founded by planned missionary work of Orthodox churches in Europe and the Middle East. Yet for more than a century most priests serving American Orthodox churches did come from overseas, where they were trained.

Because of two world wars and other upheavals, ties between the new churches in America and the old Orthodox churches of Europe and the Middle East could not be close. Thus the American churches grew up on their own, with a strong feeling of independence. Nevertheless, Orthodox Christians look forward to the day when all these national churches will join in one American Orthodox Church.

Sister ILEANA, PRINCESS OF ROMANIA
Author, *Meditations on the Nicene Creed*

See also BYZANTINE ART AND ARCHITECTURE; BYZANTINE EMPIRE; CHRISTIANITY, HISTORY OF; ROMAN CATHOLIC CHURCH.

EAST GERMANY. See GERMANY.

EAST INDIA COMPANY

European explorers of the 1500's returned from their voyages with tales of the wealth of the Indies. They brought with them strange spices and rich silks. Many merchants soon realized that great profits could be made in trade with India and the neighboring islands. But ships were expensive, and voyages were dangerous. Merchants raised the necessary money. They contributed to a common fund and shared in the profits.

The first East India Company was chartered in 1587 by a group of Portuguese merchants. Similar companies later were founded in England (1600), the Netherlands (1602), Denmark (1616), and France (1664). But of all the companies, the British East India Company became by far the largest and most successful.

In the early 1600's the British East India Company set up trading posts in India and Java to compete with the Dutch East India Company for European markets. Together the British and Dutch for the most part drove the Portuguese out of the East Indies.

After failing to gain control over the Dutch spice trade in Java, Sumatra, and Ceylon (now Sri Lanka), the British began limiting their activities to the Indian mainland, while the Dutch took control over the islands then known as the Dutch East Indies (now part of Indonesia). Soon the British controlled almost all of the trade between India and Europe and later the American colonies. England prospered and grew rich as a result of this expanding trade.

Along with economic power, the British East India Company acquired a great deal of political influence. It was even allowed to maintain a private army to enforce its power. In 1757 this army, led by Sir Robert Clive, fought against the French East India Company and drove the French out of India altogether. This victory secured England's dominant position in India.

The French East India Company was dissolved soon after, in 1769. The Dutch East India Company, which had reached the height of its success in the 1600's, was dissolved in 1799. The Danish East India Company was dissolved in 1845. The British East India Company controlled India until Indian troops rebelled in 1857. The bloody massacre known as the Sepoy Rebellion brought an end to the company's authority. The following year, the British government canceled the company's charter and took direct control over India.

Reviewed by RICHARD B. MORRIS
Columbia University

EAST INDIES. See INDONESIA; SOUTHEAST ASIA.

This picture of George Eastman holding a Kodak camera was taken on board a ship in 1890. The early Kodak cameras produced circular pictures.

EASTMAN, GEORGE (1854–1932)

George Eastman was an inventor and businessman who made photography one of the world's most popular hobbies. He started the company that makes the famous Kodak cameras and films.

Eastman was born on July 12, 1854, in Waterville, New York, where his father was the head of a business school. In 1860, the family moved to the nearby city of Rochester. The father died about two years later. Eastman had to quit school and go to work when he was 13. Even as a boy he was good at business. The first year he made $131. He supported himself, saved his money, and in a few years saved over $500.

In 1874, Eastman went to work in the Rochester Savings Bank as a bookkeeper. With his earnings, he supported himself and his mother. Some of his money was also spent on his hobby, photography.

In those days, taking pictures was not simple. Exposures were made on chemically treated glass plates instead of on film. Eastman went into business, making and selling a better kind of photographic plate.

In 1884, Eastman introduced flexible roll-up film. About four years later, the first of Eastman's Kodak cameras appeared. Loaded with film and ready to use, it sold for $25. Instead of fumbling with clumsy glass plates and tanks of chemicals, all the photographer had to do was push a button. The film could then be sent to the Eastman company for developing and printing.

Eight years later, Eastman brought out a camera that sold for only $5. Eastman's cameras made photography a favorite hobby of millions, and his company grew rapidly.

Eastman had many interests besides his company. At his Rochester home he grew flowers and other plants. He liked going hunting and camping, and he collected paintings by Van Dyck and Rembrandt.

Eastman never married, but his home was a gathering place for many friends. Especially popular were his Sunday evening dinners, usually followed by musical performances.

Eastman's love of music prompted him to found the Eastman School of Music, a division of the University of Rochester. He gave about $75 million to educational institutions, but he sometimes insisted that his identity be kept secret to avoid publicity. Eastman made large donations to the Massachusetts Institute of Technology, the University of Rochester, Hampton Institute, and Tuskegee Institute. He died on March 14, 1932.

JOANNE LANDERS HENRY
Author, *George Eastman: Young Photographer*

EAST TIMOR. See TIMOR, EAST (TIMOR-LESTE).

EASTWOOD, CLINT. See MOTION PICTURES (Profiles: Movie Stars).

ECHIDNA. See PLATYPUS AND SPINY ANTEATERS.

Exterior (*left*) and interior (*right*) of an early Kodak camera, such as the one that took the picture above.

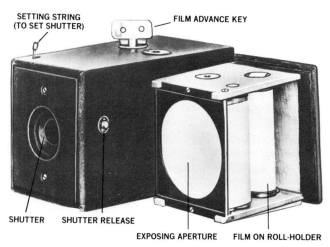

SETTING STRING (TO SET SHUTTER)

FILM ADVANCE KEY

SHUTTER   SHUTTER RELEASE

EXPOSING APERTURE   FILM ON ROLL-HOLDER

ECHO

It is a familiar experience to hear the sound of your voice reflected from a large, smooth surface, such as a rocky cliff. If you shout "Hello," the word returns to your ears a moment later. This is an echo.

An echo is a sound you hear that has been reflected (bounced back) from a hard surface. Although all sound waves can be reflected, only reflected sounds you can hear distinctly are called echoes.

For an echo to occur, the reflecting surface must be at least 55 feet (17 meters) away from the original sound. If the surface is closer, your brain cannot tell the difference between the original sound and its echo.

As the distance between a sound source and a reflecting surface increases, the echo takes longer to be heard. If you shout at a canyon wall ½ mile (0.8 kilometer) away, the echo takes almost 5 seconds to return.

You can estimate how far away a reflecting surface is by measuring how long an echo takes to reach you. Sound travels about 1,100 feet (335 meters) in a second. To be heard as an echo, a sound has to travel to the reflecting surface and back again. So in one second, it can travel about 550 feet (168 meters) each way. If you are standing in front of a large rocky cliff, shout "Hey!" and count the seconds until you hear "Hey!" as an echo. Multiply the number of seconds by 550 feet to find out about how far away the cliff is.

Echolocation

Some members of the animal kingdom use echoes to help them navigate. This is called echolocation. These animals include bats, shrews, dolphins, white whales, toadfish, and even tiny minnows.

Animals that use echolocation produce sounds far above the range of human hearing. (Humans can hear sounds that are between 20 and 20,000 vibrations per second.) Sounds above this range are called **ultrasonic**.

Bats, for example, send out high-pitched cries of about 90,000 vibrations per second. Sound reflections tell the bats where obstacles are and enable them to fly in completely dark surroundings.

Dolphins produce ultrasonic sounds of almost 200,000 vibrations per second. These sounds reflect from underwater objects to give dolphins the ability to "see" when waters are cloudy or dark.

Echo Devices

Mechanical and electronic devices make use of echoes as well. Sonar, which is short for *so*und *na*vigation and *r*anging, helps with the navigation of ships and submarines. In sonar, electronic pulses are converted to scanning sound beams, and the timed echoes give the distance and direction to the ocean floor or to other ships. Similar echolocation techniques use radio waves instead of sound to find objects in the air and outer space.

Ultrasonic sounds can penetrate the solid earth. Echoes bounce back from various interior layers, enabling geologists to search for oil and minerals.

Ultrasonic sound can safely penetrate the human body. The sound reflections from various types of body tissue are used to produce pictures of bones and internal organs. These pictures can help doctors diagnose problems.

People who are blind may become sensitive to reflected sounds. Because sounds arrive at slightly different times and volumes at each ear, the brain can interpret these differences to help locate walls or other barriers.

Echoes are even used in the sound recording industry. Electronic sounds can be repeated with the original sound to produce distinct echoes, like those you might hear in a canyon, or overlapping echoes, called **reverberation**, like those you might hear in an auditorium. Such electronic echoes are used in many commercial recordings.

LARRY KETTELKAMP
Author, *The Magic of Sound*

See also BATS; DOLPHINS AND PORPOISES; RADAR AND SONAR; RADIO ASTRONOMY; SOUND AND ULTRASONICS.

This photograph of the stages of a solar eclipse provides a striking view of the sun's corona—a large, bright halo that is revealed around a totally eclipsed sun.

ECLIPSES

More than 2,000 years ago, the Greek historian Herodotus related a tale of how a strange astronomical event once stopped a war between the ancient Lydians and Medes. As the armies fought, the light of the sun suddenly faded away in the middle of the day. Astonished by what they thought was a sign from the gods, the armies stopped fighting and made peace. If this story is true, the event the Lydians and Medes witnessed was an eclipse of the sun that probably took place in 585 B.C.

In an **eclipse**, light from one object in space, such as the sun, is blocked by another, such as the moon or the Earth. Two types of eclipses can be witnessed from the surface of the Earth: an eclipse of the sun and an eclipse of the moon.

An eclipse of the sun, or **solar eclipse**, occurs when the moon passes directly between the Earth and the sun. It can only occur at the time of a new moon and when the moon is in

the exact position between the sun and the Earth to block some of the sun's light from the Earth. (A description of the phases of the moon is in the article MOON in Volume M.) During a solar eclipse, the moon casts a shadow that races across a narrow strip of the Earth. To observers in the shadow's path, the moon briefly seems to cover the sun's disk. In an eclipse of the moon, or **lunar eclipse**, the moon passes through the shadow that the Earth casts out into space. During a lunar eclipse, which can only occur during a full moon, the Earth is positioned between the sun and the moon. As the moon enters the Earth's shadow, it grows dark because it is no longer lighted by the sun.

Both solar and lunar eclipses may be **total eclipses**, when the whole sun or the whole moon is darkened, or **partial eclipses**, when only part of the sun or the moon is darkened.

A solar eclipse does not occur every time there is a new moon, and a lunar eclipse does not happen every time the moon is full because the moon's orbit is tilted in relation to the Earth's orbit around the sun. Thus, when the moon is new and it passes between the Earth and the sun, its shadow usually misses the Earth, passing above the North Pole or below the South Pole. When the moon is full, it usually passes above or below the shadow cast by the Earth into space. As a result, eclipses occur only at times when the sun, the moon, and the Earth are aligned. These times, called **eclipse seasons**, occur about every six months and last about three weeks. The total number of solar and lunar eclipses that can take place in a year varies from two to seven.

▶ SOLAR ECLIPSES

A total solar eclipse occurs only when the moon moves between the sun and the Earth, casting a shadow that moves across the Earth from west to east, the direction that the moon moves in its orbit. The shadow can often move at a speed of more than 1,000 miles (1,600 kilometers) per hour. The central part of the shadow, called the **umbra**, is usually less than 167 miles (270 kilometers) in diameter. A larger area of partial shadow surrounding the umbra, called the **penumbra**, extends about 2,500 miles (4,000 kilometers) beyond it on all sides. Observers in the path of the penumbra will see only a partial eclipse, while observers in the path of the umbra will see a total eclipse.

Solar eclipses create striking effects, such as the one known as the diamond ring effect (*far right*). They also provide vital opportunities for astronomers to study the sun's atmosphere. Eclipses can reveal the solar flares that stream out of the sun's corona (*right*), releasing large amounts of energy that can disrupt radio communications on Earth, and the fiery prominences that erupt out of the sun's chromosphere (*far right*) and shoot solar gases far out into space.

When a total eclipse begins, at first only part of the sun is blotted out by the moon, as if a bite had been taken from it. Gradually, this "bite" increases until the sun's disk is completely covered. The period in which the sun is completely covered, called the period of **totality**, can last up to 7½ minutes, but it is usually shorter. As totality approaches, the sky grows dark and the temperature often drops. Just before totality, a tiny portion of the sun's surface is still visible peeking out from behind the moon, which is now surrounded by the bright glow of the sun's lower atmosphere. This effect is known as the "diamond ring" because of its appearance. At the moment totality begins, the brighter stars and planets become visible in the sky and the outer atmosphere of the sun, the **corona**, can be seen glowing like a halo around the blackened disk of the moon. After totality, the sun slowly reappears from behind the moon, and the sky gradually lightens. The total time that has

elapsed from the beginning to the end of the eclipse is about 90 minutes. Solar eclipses occur regularly, but the chances of seeing a total eclipse from any given place on Earth are small because the moon's shadow covers such a small part of the planet's surface. Total solar eclipses recur at the same location only once every 360 years or so.

Since the moon's orbit is elliptical, or oval, the moon's distance from the Earth changes as it travels in its orbit. Sometimes a solar eclipse occurs when the moon is too far from the Earth to cover the sun completely. Then, a bright ring of sunlight completely surrounds the dark disk of the moon, even when it is directly in front of the sun. This type of eclipse is called an **annular**, or ring-shaped, eclipse.

▶ **LUNAR ECLIPSES**

Lunar eclipses occur less frequently than solar eclipses, but they can be seen by more people. This is because a lunar eclipse can be

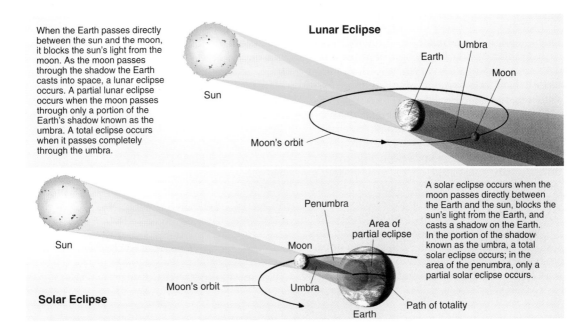

When the Earth passes directly between the sun and the moon, it blocks the sun's light from the moon. As the moon passes through the shadow the Earth casts into space, a lunar eclipse occurs. A partial lunar eclipse occurs when the moon passes through only a portion of the Earth's shadow known as the umbra. A total eclipse occurs when it passes completely through the umbra.

Lunar Eclipse

Sun

Earth

Umbra

Moon

Moon's orbit

A solar eclipse occurs when the moon passes directly between the Earth and the sun, blocks the sun's light from the Earth, and casts a shadow on the Earth. In the portion of the shadow known as the umbra, a total solar eclipse occurs; in the area of the penumbra, only a partial solar eclipse occurs.

Sun

Penumbra

Area of partial eclipse

Moon

Moon's orbit

Umbra

Earth

Path of totality

Solar Eclipse

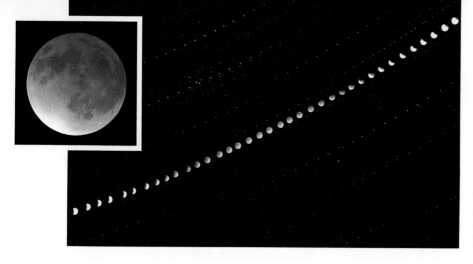

Time-lapse photography produced this photograph of the stages of a partial eclipse of the moon (*left*). Even when the moon is totally eclipsed (*inset*), it is still visible because sunlight reflected onto its surface by the Earth's atmosphere gives it a reddish glow.

seen from anywhere on the dark side of the Earth (that is, wherever it is night), as long as the moon is above the horizon.

A lunar eclipse begins when the moon enters the Earth's penumbra. There is little darkening, however, until the moon enters the Earth's umbra. The period of totality, when the moon is completely shaded by the umbra, may last more than an hour. Even during a total lunar eclipse, the moon may remain visible as a beautiful deep red disk, illuminated by sunlight that has been filtered and bent into the shadow by the Earth's atmosphere.

▶LEARNING FROM ECLIPSES

Astronomers observe eclipses in an attempt to understand and predict them. More than 3,000 years ago, astronomers in Mesopotamia recorded their observations of eclipses. In ancient China, two astronomers reportedly were put to death for failing to predict an eclipse accurately. The ancient Greeks confirmed the fact that the Earth is round by noting the shape of its shadow on the moon during lunar eclipses. The records of these astronomers have helped today's scientists predict eclipses with a high degree of accuracy.

Scientists have learned a great deal by studying eclipses. By photographing the positions of stars that become visible during a total solar eclipse, scientists have been able to confirm a prediction based on Albert Einstein's general theory of relativity—that light beams can be bent by the gravitational field of the sun. Eclipses have also helped scientists understand complex interactions between the sun and the Earth. For example, the Earth's upper atmosphere is very sensitive to ultraviolet and X-ray radiation from the sun, which interact with atoms of gas in the air, changing them into electrically charged particles called **ions**. The **ionosphere**, the layer of the Earth's atmosphere where this happens, reflects and bends long-distance radio waves and is thus important in radio communication. Eclipse studies help scientists understand how variations in the sun's radiation can affect the ionosphere and disturb communications.

Some eclipse studies have focused on obtaining a precise measurement of the sun's diameter because variations in its diameter may play an important role in long-term climate changes on Earth. Studies can also help scientists understand how changes in sunlight affect the Earth's weather patterns.

The study of the sun itself has also benefited greatly from the observation of eclipses. For example, scientists have learned about the existence of a narrow layer of the sun's atmosphere—the **chromosphere**—that lies near the solar surface. They have also learned that a much thinner, but extremely hot, layer of atmosphere—the corona—extends far out into space and actually engulfs the Earth and other planets. Within the corona are streams of rapidly moving particles and radiation known as the solar wind that affects the Earth's atmosphere. These and other discoveries reveal information about the sun and also increase our knowledge about other stars. Thus the solar eclipse produces both a magnificent visual spectacle and an important opportunity to study the natural world and the universe.

WILLIAM A. GUTSCH, JR.
Chairman, American Museum-
Hayden Planetarium

See also MOON; STARS; SUN.

ECOLOGY

The natural world is characterized by great beauty: fish-laden waters flowing over rocky streambeds, bison grazing on open grasslands, hot springs bubbling with microbes and minerals. Each of these settings is an ecological community. Ecology is the study of the interactions among living things, or organisms, and between organisms and their non-living surroundings. These interactions are complex and constantly changing. It is the role of the ecologist to try to explain how they change and why.

The word "ecology" comes from Greek words meaning "study of the home, or surroundings." Traditionally, there have been three major branches of ecology: population ecology, community ecology, and ecosystems ecology. While these branches are still important, the distinctions among them have blurred as ecologists learn that understanding nature requires knowledge in all of these fields.

Ecologists study relationships among living things and their surroundings. This farmland is an example of an environment that has been altered by humans.

▶ POPULATION ECOLOGY

Plant and animal populations are not the same in every environment, even when the kinds of organisms in the environment are the same. Population size may be large or small, depending on such factors as food and water resources. Interactions of the organisms with each other may influence population size and may be influenced by the terrain or by threats from predators. And the individuals may be more or less successful at producing offspring, depending on weather conditions, diseases, or other factors.

These features of plant and animal populations are studied by population ecologists.

They usually focus on a single species (kind) of plant or animal, trying to determine what factors influence the organism's behavior, population size, and reproductive success. Some factors are obvious, such as when a fire or flood suddenly limits population growth. Other factors are harder to identify. For example, subtle genetic traits can influence population growth as well, making some individuals more likely to survive climate changes or to escape from predators.

Some population ecologists even study extinct species. They are called **paleoecologists**. They rely on fossil evidence, including preserved genetic material, to reconstruct the history of extinct organisms and try to determine what caused a species to die out.

▶ COMMUNITY ECOLOGY

One of the oldest questions ecologists have tried to answer is, Why are there so many kinds of animals? Basically it is because different features in every environment support and maintain a variety of living things. And no two environments are exactly alike.

Community ecologists seek to understand how and why a specific environment is able to support its particular variety of plants and animals. (Variety of species is called **biodiversity**.) These ecologists study soils, waterways, forests, and other features. They have found that a varied environment allows many types

A number of articles in this encyclopedia cover topics relating to the environment. This article describes the relationship of living things to each other and to the environment. The article LIFE (Living Things and Their Environment) explores similar topics. Identifying and protecting our environment's resources are covered in NATURAL RESOURCES and CONSERVATION. The article ENVIRONMENT gives an overview of environmental problems. Individual articles on these problems include AIR POLLUTION; ENDANGERED SPECIES; HAZARDOUS WASTES; and POPULATION.

Natural disturbances, such as forest fires, will not permanently harm a healthy ecological system.

of organisms to survive. For example, ocean shorelines are rich in many species of marine invertebrates because there are many different habitats in these areas.

Research in community ecology also focuses on the interactions of predators and their prey. It examines **food webs**, the descriptions of how plants and animals are used for food by other organisms in their environment. Rarely is a food web as simple as, for example, a rabbit eating clover and a coyote then eating the rabbit. Food webs are usually quite complex. Ecologists are working to understand why some environments have more complex food webs than others. They also want to know whether the complexity of a food web affects the long-term health of a particular ecosystem.

▶ ECOSYSTEMS ECOLOGY

This branch of ecology is devoted to the study of the flow of nutrients, chemicals, and energy in an environment. These essential substances constantly move between living organisms and their non-living surroundings. For example, a tree uses energy from the sun to produce new growth each spring. The tree's roots draw nutrients and water from the soil. When the leaves fall off or the tree dies, the plant material decomposes on the forest floor, returning nutrients to the soil.

Ecosystems ecology is less about the study of one part of an environment, such as the forest floor, than the study of how material moves through the forest floor and how quickly. **Ecosystem functioning** is the term used to evaluate such natural processes as decomposition (the breakdown of dead plants and animals), production of new organic material, and nutrient movements.

Healthy natural environments are those in which natural processes continue uninterrupted. Many ecologists believe that if an ecosystem is functioning well, it can survive and recover from disturbances, such as floods or fires, faster and more completely than a poorly functioning ecosystem.

Restoration ecology is a related branch of ecosystems ecology. It is the science of helping damaged environments return to a healthy state. Its goal is to restore overall ecosystem functioning after a severe disturbance rather than to only replant lost trees or reintroduce missing animals. Many scientists now believe that environmental management should be based on ecosystem management, instead of being focused simply on a single, often endangered, species.

▶ CHANGES IN THE ENVIRONMENT

Early views of ecology focused on an idea called the balance of nature. The central belief was that all ecological systems were kept in a balanced, steady state by a natural system of checks and balances. We now know that ecological systems are constantly changing. Some systems experience predictable changes, but even they can be interrupted at unexpected times.

Some ecosystems may be relatively constant for long periods. But change will occur. New species may arrive, causing others to die out. Nutrients may be brought in by a flood or fire, benefiting some organisms but harming others. Or a disease may spread through a population, drastically reducing its numbers.

Ecologists distinguish between "normal" changes caused by natural environmental variation and dramatic changes that are usually due to human intervention. Normal changes, sometimes called natural disturbances, include hurricanes, fires, and floods. Although disruptive, they also provide benefits. A flood, for example, can help maintain coastal nutrient levels, plant productivity, and fish diversity. A healthy ecological system is not harmed by natural disturbances, so long as they are within certain expected bounds.

In contrast, human activity—such as clearing a forest or building homes along a shoreline—can cause dramatic changes leading to species extinction or the disruption of natural ecosystem functioning. For example, alterations in land use that double the frequency of floods and fires—or completely eliminate their occurrence—can cause irreparable damage to an ecosystem.

CURRENT RESEARCH

Increasingly, ecologists are studying environments both at the molecular level and at the whole ecosystem level, rather than just examining nutrient flow or plant and animal populations. For example, new techniques for genetic mapping allow ecologists to study how genetic factors influence a population's ability to disperse, or spread, into new and different environments.

One current area of great interest in ecology is the attempt to understand the influence of species on ecosystem functioning. There is evidence that some species may

Using mathematics, ecologists can break down complex ecosystems such as this lake environment into many small parts, each of which can then be analyzed.

have extremely important roles, while other species are of little consequence. For example, removal of a vital species may cause a dramatic drop in plant growth, affecting the entire food web. Loss of another species may have no effect at all.

Some ecologists argue that we know far too little about ecosystem processes to risk losing even a single species. In fact, there is research evidence suggesting that the productivity of an environment declines simply when the number of species is reduced. Further research in this area is especially important because of its impact on conservation efforts. Loss of biodiversity may not only mean loss of desirable species, it may mean harm to entire ecosystems.

RESEARCH TECHNIQUES

Field and laboratory experiments are an important part of ecological science. Researchers may count organisms to determine population size in a given area. They may measure differences among individuals of a species, such as fur thickness or leaf size, to understand how and why these differences appear. Some researchers alter an environmental condition and then measure and analyze an organism's response. The results from all such experiments are subject to statistical analyses. The goal is to understand, with as much certainty as possible, what factors are involved in making an ecosystem the way it is.

Mathematics is an important part of this type of research. For example, population biologists can use complex mathematical equations to predict a particular species' risk of extinction. Community ecologists use equations and statistical tools to study how environmental features affect biodiversity. And ecosystems scientists use sets of equations solved with computer programs to predict how nutrients will be used following changes in an environment's populations.

The power of mathematics in ecological science is that it allows the ecologist to break down very complex systems into many small parts and then to explore the role of each part. For example, an ecologist can ask how much influence a changing climate might have on a lake's production of new growth or on the amount of nutrients flowing into the lake. Answers to these types of questions are essential to environmental management and to better understanding how our natural world functions.

MARGARET A. PALMER
Ecology Program Director
National Science Foundation

Land is a limited resource in Hong Kong. Many families in its large population, faced with the scarcity of land, are forced to live on boats in Hong Kong harbor.

ECONOMICS

Why is it difficult to satisfy everyone's wants? Why are some people richer than others? Why do people sometimes have trouble finding jobs? Why do the prices of things increase? For centuries people have pondered these questions and many others like them. The science that deals with such questions is called economics, and the scientists who study these questions are called economists.

▶ SCARCITY, GOODS, AND SERVICES

One of the basic concerns of economics is the relation between resources and wants. More specifically, economists study how individuals and societies use limited resources to satisfy their needs and wants. Unfortunately, the earth does not have enough resources to satisfy everyone. If it did, everything would be available to everyone, and no one would be in need.

The problem of trying to meet unlimited wants with limited resources (such things as land, labor, and factories) is the most basic of all economic problems. Economists call it the problem of **scarcity**. There are simply not enough resources in any society to provide its people with everything they want. In a world of limited resources, only so many cars, shoes, electronic games, movies, bushels of grain, and other things can be produced in any given year. There will not be nearly enough of these things to satisfy everyone.

Although it is not possible to satisfy everyone's wants, most societies try to satisfy as much as possible through the production of economic goods and services. Economic **goods** are things of value that can be seen and touched, such as bicycles, automobiles, clothing, and television sets. Economic goods also include such things as factories, stores, machines, and tools. Economic **services** are things that have value but often cannot be seen or touched, such as entertainment, medical care, legal advice, and national defense.

▶ LAWS OF SUPPLY AND DEMAND

Perhaps the most basic laws in the science of economics are the laws of supply and demand. These laws play a major role in almost all economic issues.

The law of demand says that as the price of a good or service rises (and other factors remain unchanged), the demand for that item will fall. As the price of the good or service falls, the demand for the item will rise. In other words, people will buy more of an item if the price is low than if the price is high.

The law of supply is the opposite of the law of demand. It says that as the price of an item rises (and other factors remain unchanged), the supply of the item will rise. As the price of the item falls, the supply will also fall. It is only natural that as prices rise, the people providing goods and services will be willing to supply larger quantities of those goods and services.

The interaction of supply and demand determines the prices of goods and services. An increase in demand tends to make prices higher. A decrease in demand tends to make prices lower. Similarly, an increase in supply tends to make prices lower, while a decrease in supply tends to make them higher.

FACTORS OF PRODUCTION

The basic resources an economy needs for the production of goods and services are called factors of production. Economists usually divide the factors of production into three basic categories: natural resources, capital goods, and labor. Many economists add a fourth factor of production—entrepreneurship.

Natural Resources

Natural resources are things provided by nature, such as land, air, water, forests, oil, coal, iron ore, and other minerals. Natural resources are the starting point of all production. As such they represent the most basic limitation on how much any economy can produce. No matter how much labor, capital goods, and technological knowledge an economy has, it cannot produce goods without natural resources.

Capital Goods

Capital goods are human-made resources used for the production of other goods and services. Factories, machines, tools, and office buildings are all examples of capital goods. Such capital goods are necessary for using natural resources. For example, sawmills, chain saws, and other capital goods are needed to convert timber into usable products.

Labor

Labor, which is sometimes called human resources, is any kind of human effort used for production. For economists, labor includes not only physical work but also intellectual work and the use of human knowledge, talents, and skills. The work of truck drivers, factory workers, lawyers, doctors, and public officials are all examples of labor. Labor is essential to production because natural resources and capital goods are of no value unless they can be put to use by the work of people.

Entrepreneurship

Natural resources, capital goods, and labor must be combined and organized before production can take place. This process is known as entrepreneurship. An **entrepreneur** is a person who takes the initiative to bring the three factors of production together in order to produce a good or service. He or she provides money, time, and effort to buy raw materials, hire labor, and buy machinery to produce a particular good or service. In return, the entrepreneur receives a profit for his or her efforts. The cheaper the cost of producing the good or service, the greater the profit.

BASIC ECONOMIC QUESTIONS

In deciding how to use limited resources to satisfy people's wants, a society must consider three basic questions: What goods and services will be produced? How will those goods and services be produced? For whom will the goods and services be produced?

What Goods and Services Will Be Produced?

This is a difficult and complex question. A portion of a nation's limited resources must be used by the government to provide government services, including such things as national defense. The remaining resources are available for use in producing other goods and

Trees are a valuable natural resource. In this Arkansas forest, trees are cut and prepared for shipment to mills for the production of goods such as paper and lumber.

services. Some of these resources will be used to produce capital goods, such as factories, machines, and tools. The rest will be available for the production of consumer goods and services, such as food, medical care, bicycles, automobiles, and movies.

Consumer Sovereignty. In some countries the government decides how many, and what kinds of, consumer goods and services will be produced. But in the United States the people (consumers) decide what will be produced—a process called consumer sovereignty. People vote (with their money) for the goods and services they want produced. If consumers do not buy a product in sufficient quantity to make its production profitable, producers will discontinue making the product. If people demand more of a product than is available, production will be increased.

How Will Goods and Services Be Produced?

There is often more than one way to produce a particular good or service. For example, suppose a construction company has been hired to dig a large basement for a new building. The basement could perhaps be dug by fifty workers using shovels and wheelbarrows, or by one worker using a giant crane. The construction company, in competition with other companies for the job, must choose the most efficient and least costly method of digging the basement. In this case, it would probably mean using one worker and the giant crane rather than fifty workers equipped with shovels and wheelbarrows.

Competition forces producers to use the least costly methods of production. It allows consumers to buy goods and services at lower prices than would be possible if less efficient, higher-cost methods of production were used.

For Whom Will Goods and Services Be Produced?

No nation can produce enough goods and services to satisfy all its citizens' wants. It is necessary, therefore, to have some way of deciding who gets the things that are produced.

In the United States, goods and services are distributed on the basis of wealth. The people with the most money get the most goods and services. While this may be an efficient way of deciding who gets what, it is not necessarily a fair way. People with the most money may not be the most deserving or the ones with the

greatest need. Nor do they necessarily work the hardest. Some people who work very hard earn a small income. Although some wealthy people have worked hard to get their money, others have inherited much of it.

Providing Basic Goods and Services. If the distribution of goods and services were based entirely on personal wealth, some people might be without food, clothing, and shelter through no fault of their own. The fact that a person is willing and able to work does not guarantee that he or she will be able to find a good job. Some people are so disabled that they are unable to work. For these reasons, the United States government and private organizations sponsor various programs for the purpose of helping the very poor obtain some basic goods and services.

▶ KINDS OF ECONOMIC SYSTEMS

Every society has an organized set of procedures for answering the three basic economic questions. This set of procedures determines a nation's economic system. There are basically three kinds of economic systems in the world: traditional economies, command economies, and market economies.

Traditional Economies

In some rural, nonindustrial areas of the world, there is no national economy. Instead, there are many small economies centered around families or tribal units, each of which produces almost everything it consumes. In

The crops being harvested by the Otavalo Indian tribe are part of a traditional economy in Ecuador, South America.

these economies, the basic questions of "what," "how," and "for whom" are answered directly by the people involved. Because the answers to these questions are usually based on tradition, these economies are called traditional economies.

Command Economies

In some societies, answers to the three basic economic questions are determined by the government. Individuals have little control or influence over economic questions and issues. They are told what to produce, how to produce it, and what they will receive. Economies in which the government makes most or all economic decisions are called command economies. The economy of China is an example of a command economy.

Market Economies

In many Western societies, the answers to basic economic questions are determined primarily by individuals and businesses. Buyers and sellers in the marketplace have a great deal of economic freedom, and the economy functions largely through the laws of supply and demand. Because economic decisions are made by individuals in a free marketplace, such economies are called market economies. The economies of the United States, Canada, and Japan are examples of market economies.

Maintaining Freedom of Choice. There are steps a government sometimes takes to make sure the market allows consumers freedom of choice. The United States government has passed laws that require producers to give correct information about their products. Other laws forbid dishonest advertising. Still others try to equalize the uneven power of producers. For example, if one large producer provides almost all of a certain good or service, it is called a **monopoly**. If only a few large producers provide all of a certain good or service, it is called an **oligopoly**. Laws in the United States limit the power of monopolies and oligopolies so that they cannot control the market unfairly.

Mixed Economies

Almost no economies in the world are exclusively command or market economies that rely solely on free markets or on government decisions to answer basic economic questions. Instead, most major economies are mixed economies in which some decisions are made by individuals in the marketplace and others are made by the government.

Capitalism, Socialism, and Communism

Economies are also categorized on the basis of who owns most of the means of production (such as factories, natural resources, and machinery). Economies in which the means of production are owned primarily by individuals or private companies are called **capitalist** systems. The United States has a capitalist economic system. Economies in which the government owns some or all of the means of production are called **socialist** systems. There

The weavers in this carpet factory in Inner Mongolia, China, (*top*) work in a command economy. The variety of vegetables in this Idaho supermarket (*left*) is one result of the market economy in the United States.

is a great variation among socialist systems. In some socialist systems, the government may own only certain key industries, such as steel or energy. In others it may own almost everything. A **communist** system is a type of socialist system in which the government controls virtually all industries and makes all economic decisions.

Economic Goals

Every society tries to attain certain economic objectives. Four goals that are fundamental to all economic systems are efficiency, equity, stability, and growth.

Efficiency. Because of the problem of scarcity, it is very important that limited resources be used as efficiently as possible. This means that all workers who want to work should be able to get jobs, and other productive resources should be fully utilized. This is not always the case. Sometimes business activity slows down, and factories and workers become idle. During such times, the government may make decisions in an attempt to stimulate the economy and get it running more efficiently again.

Full utilization of productive resources is only one part of efficiency. In addition to producing the largest possible output with available resources, an economy should also be producing combinations of goods and services that best meet the preferences of the people.

Equity. Equity refers to economic fairness or justice, and it involves the distribution of a society's total production of goods and services among its citizens. The question of who gets how much is determined primarily by the distribution of income among the members of

WONDER QUESTION

What is the amazing "invisible hand"?

Consider life in a major city with millions of inhabitants who require huge amounts of various goods and services to meet their wants and needs. Do people lie awake at night worrying that the goods and services they need might be unavailable when they need or want them? In market economies such as the United States, people take it for granted that the things they need or want will be available. But if you think about it, the fact that most things are usually available when people want them is a remarkable accomplishment.

Suppose you live in a city in the United States and decide that you want to have fish, broccoli, and sliced tomatoes for dinner. Even though you may not have purchased these items for months, you can be almost certain that you will find them at the nearest supermarket. The fish may have come from a faraway ocean or lake and the broccoli and tomatoes from a distant farm and shipped to your local supermarket at just the right time for eating. None of the many people involved in producing and marketing these products knew you were going to want them on a particular day, yet they were there at the very time you needed them.

As amazing as it may seem, there is no government agency, business, or individual respon-sible for ensuring that the economic needs and wants of people are met. It is the American economic system—its market economy—that sees to it that products of the right type and in the right quantity are available when most people want them. Some economists say that the economy works like an "invisible hand" in meeting the needs of the people.

The principle of the invisible hand was first reported by the economist Adam Smith in 1776 in his book *Inquiry Into the Nature and Causes of the Wealth of Nations*. Smith said that in a market economy, if individuals were allowed to pursue their own self-interests without government interference, they would be led, as if by an invisible hand, to achieve what is best for the society. The idea of letting economic problems work themselves out with no government interference is known as *laissez-faire*, a French term meaning "let do" or "let things alone." Although the U.S. economy today is very different from the type of economy described by Adam Smith, the principle of the invisible hand still applies to some extent.

Businesses work to maximize their profits, workers seek higher wages, and consumers attempt to get the maximum value for their money. To maximize their profits, businesses must provide the goods and services that most consumers want at the right time and in the right places. In this way, the American economy operates as if it were regulated by an "invisible hand."

society. Those with the most income get the most goods and services.

Most societies try to achieve an equitable distribution of income. It is important to understand, however, that equitable means "fair" or "just," not "equal." What seems fair and just to some people may seem unfair and unjust to others. The terms "fair" and "just" involve value judgments, and there is no scientific way of determining what is a fair or just distribution of income.

Stability. A goal of every society is to achieve price stability for its goods and services. This does not mean that all prices should be fixed. It means that the average level of prices should be stable. When average prices rise substantially, an economy experiences what is known as **inflation**. Inflation can be very harmful to a society. If average prices fall substantially, it is known as **deflation**, which can also be harmful to an economy.

Growth. Another goal of every society is economic growth—an increase in the quantity of goods and services produced per person. If economic production does not grow when the population is growing, the standard of living will decline. If production grows at the same rate as the population growth, the standard of living will remain constant. If production grows more rapidly than the population growth, the standard of living will rise.

▶ECONOMIC PROBLEMS

All nations face many economic problems, including the inability to satisfy all wants, unemployment, inflation, recession or depression, budget deficits and a national debt.

Inability to Satisfy All Wants

Because all nations have limited resources and unlimited wants, they all face the problem of scarcity. There is no way to eliminate this problem, but certain things can be done to increase the production obtained from a given amount of resources. One way to increase production, and thus narrow the gap between limited resources and unlimited wants, is to increase **productivity**—to produce more goods and services with less material and in shorter time. Increased productivity results in increased output per person.

One way to achieve greater productivity is through specialization. Both individuals and nations can become more productive by spe-

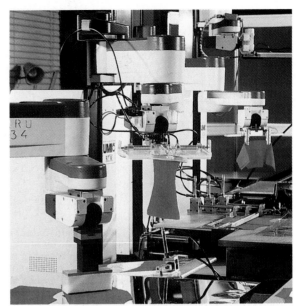

The "robots" in this garment factory in the United States are programmed to sew pieces of fabric into articles of clothing.

cializing in the production of the things they can produce most efficiently.

Another way to increase productivity and economic output is through the use of new technology. New machines and new techniques have played a very important role in increasing economic productivity throughout history. They continue to do so today.

Unemployment and Inflation

Unemployment and inflation are both very serious problems for a nation. Unemployment, of course, means that people who could be productive are out of work and are not contributing to the health of the economy.

Inflation causes a decline in the purchasing power of money, which means that consumers can purchase less with the money they have. The most commonly used measure of the inflation rate is the **consumer price index**. This measure, sometimes referred to as the "cost-of-living index," is used to determine the average increase in the prices of goods and services commonly purchased by consumers. Unemployment and inflation are interrelated in such a way that efforts to reduce one usually makes the other worse.

Recession or Depression

A period of reduced economic activity and increased unemployment is called a recession.

Adam Smith

John Maynard Keynes

Adam Smith (1723–90) is generally considered to be the founder of economics. Born in Scotland, Smith became a professor of logic and moral philosophy at the University of Glasgow at age 28. His studies led him to the conclusion that people always act in their own best interest. He argued that if individuals were allowed to pursue their interests free from government interference, they would promote what was best for society as a whole.

Smith revolutionized economics with the publication of *Inquiry Into the Nature and Causes of the Wealth of Nations* (1776). Because of the ideas in this book, Smith is given credit for promoting the economic freedom, the industrialization, and the prosperity that characterized the Western world during the 1800's.

John Maynard Keynes (1883–1946), a British economist, revolutionized economic thinking in the 1900's. With the publication of *The General Theory of Employment, Interest and Money* (1936), Keynes became one of the most influential economists of all time. In this book, he set forth a theory that became known as Keynesian economics.

Keynes argued that insufficient spending in an economy can cause continued high unemployment. He thus argued that government should use its powers to tax and spend to influence the nation's level of spending. By the 1950's, Keynesian economics had become the dominant economic theory in the Western world. By the 1960's, Keynes's ideas had become the basis for economic policy in the United States and in most other Western nations.

Paul Samuelson (1915–), the first American to receive the Nobel prize for economics (1970), is one of the world's best-known economists. During his career, which includes a professorship at the Massachusetts Institute of Technology, Samuelson has produced an extraordinary range of scientific economic work. His first book, *Foundations of Economic Analysis* (1947), helped break new ground by making economics a more precise and scientific discipline.

Samuelson has been a leading supporter of Keynesian economics and a leading critic of the economic theory of monetarism—the idea that control of the

Economists define recession as a period when the gross national product (GNP)—the total market value of all goods and services produced during a year—is declining and unemployment is rising. If the gross national product, or GNP, falls to a very low level and remains there for a prolonged period while large numbers of people are unemployed, the situation is called a depression. Depressions are times of severe economic crisis for every nation.

Budget Deficits and the National Debt

Most countries prepare an annual national budget—a plan outlining income and spending for the nation. Any time a government spends more than its total revenue, or income, it has a budget deficit. One of the most serious

During a severe recession or depression when large numbers of people are out of work, the lines at unemployment insurance offices get very long. These are times when such people need help in supplying basic needs such as food and shelter for their families.

Paul Samuelson

Milton Friedmman

John Kenneth Galbraith

money supply is the primary determining factor of a nation's economic performance. He believes the government should use its power to tax and spend in order to influence spending and control unemployment and inflation.

Milton Friedman (1912–), a recipient of the Nobel Prize for economics (1976), is a well-known contemporary economist. A critic of Keynesian economics, he is a leading spokesman for monetarism. Friedman opposes the use of monetary policy (changes in credit availability and interest rates) and fiscal policy (changes in government taxing and spending) to influence spending. Instead, he favors a policy designed to increase the money supply by a given amount each year.

Friedman is also known for his opposition to government intervention in the economy. He feels that many government programs designed to help the disadvantaged or to protect consumers do more harm than good. His consistent support for free markets is reflected in the titles of his books, *Capitalism and Freedom* (1962) and *Free to Choose* (1980).

John Kenneth Galbraith (1908–), a Canadian-American economist, is best known for his skillfully written books and his challenges to conventional thinking. In *The Affluent Society* (1958), he critiqued a postwar America that chose to consume more and more goods rather than to invest in areas, such as education, that would benefit society as a whole. Galbraith's other books include *The New Industrial State* (1967), *The Age of Uncertainty* (1977), *The Voice of the Poor* (1983), and *The Good Society* (1996). Born in Canada, Galbraith became a U.S. citizen in 1937. He was a professor of economics at Harvard University from 1948 until he retired in 1975. He served three American presidents, including as U.S. ambassador to India (1961–69).

problems facing the United States in recent years has been its large budget deficit. Throughout the 1980's and into the early 1990's, the United States government had annual deficits averaging approximately $200 billion. That figure more than doubled, to over $400 billion, in 2004.

When a government borrows money to finance a deficit, it causes an increase in the national debt. In early 1981, the national debt of the United States reached $1 trillion. It had taken the nation more than two hundred years to accumulate this first $1 trillion of debt. By 1991 the national debt had more than tripled, to $3.7 trillion. By early 2005 that figure had more than doubled, to $7.8 trillion. Many economists see the rapid rise in the national debt and the huge budget deficits of recent years as very serious problems.

▶ **CAREERS IN ECONOMICS**

About half of all economists work in government agencies at the federal, state, and local levels. They collect and analyze information about economic conditions and about possible changes in government economic policies. They and other economists often utilize **econometrics**—the application of mathematical analysis to the development of economic theory. This analysis can show relationships between different forms of economic activity and help predict the results of applying different economic policies.

Many other economists work for private businesses, such as insurance companies, banks, investment companies, manufacturing firms, economic research firms, and management consulting firms. Also, many economists teach and often do research at colleges and universities.

The amount of training required to become an economist depends on the type of job. A college or university bachelor's degree with a major in economics is adequate for many entry-level jobs. Most jobs for economists, however, require advanced training, with either a master's degree or a doctorate in economics.

ALLEN SMITH
Author, *Understanding Economics*

See also BANKS AND BANKING; DEPRESSIONS AND RECESSIONS; INDUSTRIAL REVOLUTION; INDUSTRY; INFLATION AND DEFLATION; LABOR-MANAGEMENT RELATIONS; TAXATION; TRADE AND COMMERCE; UNEMPLOYMENT AND UNEMPLOYMENT INSURANCE.

ECUADOR

Ecuador is a small country in South America. It is located on the western coast of South America, facing the Pacific Ocean. It borders Colombia on the north and Peru on the east and south. Ecuador is crossed by the high Andes mountains and lies on the equator. The country takes its name from the Spanish word for equator. Ecuador's territory also includes the Galápagos Islands in the Pacific Ocean.

▶**THE PEOPLE**

Origins. About 80 percent of Ecuador's people are Indians or mestizos. Mestizos are people of mixed Indian and European (mainly Spanish) ancestry. About 10 percent of the people are of Spanish descent. Many of these trace their origins to the Spaniards who ruled Ecuador for nearly three hundred years, from the 1500's to the early 1800's. Blacks and people of mixed black ancestry make up another 10 percent of the population. The blacks are descendants of slaves brought from Africa during the period of Spanish colonial rule.

Where the People Live. Slightly more than half the people live in rural (country) areas. The remainder live in urban areas (cities and towns). Most of the population is concentrated in two geographical regions: the highlands of the Andes mountains, or *sierra*, and the Pacific coastal lowlands, or *costa*. Each region is dominated by a major city. Quito, the capital, lies in the *sierra*. Guayaquil, the largest city and chief seaport, is situated on the *costa*.

Most Indians historically have lived in the rural areas of the Andean highlands. Ecuadorians of Spanish descent live mainly in Quito, Guayaquil, and other cities. Some mestizos live in rural areas, but others have moved to the cities. Most blacks live in the northern part of the Pacific coastal region.

Language, Religion, Education. Spanish is the official language of Ecuador. Indian languages, particularly Quechua, are spoken by some Ecuadorian Indians. Most of the people are Roman Catholics.

Education is free and required by law for all children between the ages of 6 and 14. In practice, however, many Ecuadorian children, especially in the rural areas, do not complete their required schooling. In recent years the government has made progress in increasing the number of children attending school. About 85 percent of the population 15 years of age and older are literate (able to read and write). Ecuador has a number of universities. The largest is the Universidad Central de Ecuador (Central University of Ecuador), located in Quito.

Way of Life. Life in Ecuador strongly reflects its history and geography. The country's upper social class consists of whites of Spanish ancestry. These include the large landowners and the relatively few wealthy businessmen. The landowners are the oldest ruling

group. Most operate large haciendas, or plantations, in the *sierra*. The businessmen live mainly in Guayaquil and other cities of the *costa*, the most rapidly growing region.

Ecuador's small middle class includes office workers in the cities, government employees, and professional people. At the lowest social level are the Indians of the *sierra*, the rural mestizos, and the blacks. Most highland Indians and many mestizos have traditionally worked on the large mountain haciendas. They received little money. But they were allowed to live on and cultivate small plots of land of their own.

The Indians of the Andean highlands have been the most reluctant to leave their ancestral plots of land. Many of the mestizos who have migrated to the cities work in factories or as shopkeepers, laborers, or servants.

▶ **THE LAND**

The mainland of Ecuador consists of three distinctive regions: the coastal lowlands (*costa*), the Andean highlands (*sierra*), and the *Oriente*, or eastern region. The Galápagos Islands form a fourth region.

Coastal Lowlands. The coastal lowlands extend from the Pacific Ocean to the Andes

Opposite page: The majority of Ecuador's people are of Indian or of mixed Indian and European (mestizo) ancestry. The Indians traditionally lived in the highlands of the Andes mountains. Most work on large mountain haciendas (plantations) and also cultivate small plots of their own land.

Right: Quito, Ecuador's capital, lies in the Andean highlands, at the foot of Cerro Pichincha, an extinct volcano. The two ranges of the high Andes run through the center of Ecuador, dividing the country into three topographical regions: the coastal plain, Andean highlands, and the thinly populated eastern region.

mountains and make up about one quarter of Ecuador's area. The region varies from about 7 to 125 miles (11 to 200 kilometers) in width. Its vegetation ranges from dense tropical forests in the north to open grasslands to the south. The coastal region includes a rich agricultural area, where most of Ecuador's commercial crops are grown. The region's major river systems are the Esmeraldas in the northwest and the Guayas, which flows into the Bay of Guayaquil in the south.

Andean Highlands. The backbone of Ecuador is formed by two parallel rows of peaks of the Andes. These lie in the center of the country and stretch for about 425 miles (680 kilometers) from north to south. The highest peak, Chimborazo, rises to 20,577 feet (6,272 meters). The second highest, Cotopaxi, at 19,344 feet (5,896 meters), is the world's highest active volcano.

The valleys and plateaus between the two rows of mountain peaks are Ecuador's most fertile areas. The Andean highland region oc-

cupies an additional one quarter of Ecuador's territory. Most of the population was concentrated here until recent times, when increasing numbers of people began to settle in the coastal lowlands.

The Oriente. The *Oriente* lies to the east of the Andean highlands and is part of the great Amazon River basin. It is the country's largest region, with about one half of its total area, but it is only thinly populated. Most of its people are Indians. The *Oriente* is covered with thick tropical rain forests. Its rivers are part of the Amazon River system. The region is important economically because of its extensive petroleum deposits.

The Galápagos Islands. The Galápagos Islands are a group of islands and numerous islets, lying about 600 miles (965 kilometers) west of the coast of Ecuador. They are a province of Ecuador, officially known as the Archipiélago de Colón. The islands, which are scattered over a wide area of the Pacific, have a total land area of about 3,000 square miles

The Galápagos Islands of Ecuador are famed for their unique animal life, including the giant Galápagos tortoise (*below*). One of the world's largest land turtles, it may weigh 500 pounds (227 kilograms) or more. The islands took their name from the Spanish word for "tortoises."

What were the enchanted islands?

Las Islas Encantadas—the enchanted or bewitched islands—was the name that Spanish sailors gave the Galápagos Islands when they were first discovered in 1535. The Spaniards were mystified by the desolate, volcanic islands, with their strange forms of animal life. They thought that the islands were not real, but only "shadows" of islands. Although the islands then were uninhabited, evidence later was found of earlier settlement by South American Indians.

The name Galápagos (from the Spanish for "tortoises") was adopted by mapmakers, based on descriptions of the many giant tortoises, or land turtles, found on the islands. The islands' other distinctive animals include rare flightless cormorants (fish-catching sea birds), penguins, land and marine iguanas (large lizards), and numerous species of finches and other birds.

The animals were of special interest to the British naturalist Charles Darwin, who visited the islands in 1835. The many varieties of finches, in particular, provided Darwin with a clue to his theory of evolution.

Since 1832 the islands have been administered by Ecuador, which first colonized them. They are a province of Ecuador, officially known as the Archipiélego de Colón. The dwindling number of animals on the islands are protected by the Ecuadorian Government.

(7,770 square kilometers). Their combined population is about 9,000. Only a few of the islands are inhabited.

The largest islands are Isabela (Albemarle), which occupies nearly half the total area; Santa Cruz (Indefatigable); Fernandina (Narborough); San Cristóbal (Chatham); San Salvador (James); and Santa María (Charles). The English names were given to the islands by British seamen who visited them in the 1600's and 1700's. The Galápagos Islands are famous for their unusual animal life, which includes the giant Galápagos tortoise.

Climate. Altitude, or distance above sea level, is the strongest influence on Ecuador's climate. The higher the altitude, the lower the temperature. The coastal lowlands, the lower western Andean slopes, and the *Oriente* generally have a warm, tropical climate. The climate grows much cooler in the highland valleys. Above 12,000 feet (3,700 meters) it is continually cold, and the higher Andean peaks are snow-covered all year long. Rainfall is heaviest in the *Oriente*, which may receive 100 inches (2,500 millimeters) or more of rain a year.

Natural Resources. Petroleum is Ecuador's most important mineral and its most valuable natural resource. The country's proven oil reserves amount to more than 1 billion barrels. Ecuador has small deposits of other minerals, including gold, silver, copper, lead, and zinc.

Forests cover more than half of the Ecuadorian mainland. The tropical rain forests of the coastal lowlands and the *Oriente* are an important source of timber. Some of the world's richest fishing grounds are found off the Ecuadorian coast. The many streams that rise high in the Andes are a potential source of hydroelectric power.

▶ **MAJOR CITIES**

Quito is Ecuador's capital, second largest city, and the country's cultural center. It is situated in the Andean highlands, at an elevation of more than 9,200 feet (2,800 meters). The city lies at the foot of Cerro Pichincha, an extinct volcano.

Quito was the site of an Indian city and served as the northern capital of the Inca Empire, before the arrival of Spanish conquerors, who founded the present city in 1534. The decisive battle of Ecuador's war of independence from Spain was fought near Quito in

Independence Plaza in Quito honors the heroes of Ecuador's struggle for independence from Spain. The building behind the plaza is the presidential palace.

1822. The city has been the capital of the Republic of Ecuador since 1830. The old part of the city has retained much of the architecture of the Spanish colonial period. Economically, Quito is a processing center for the agricultural products of the region.

Guayaquil is the largest city, main seaport, and manufacturing center of Ecuador. It is situated in the southern part of the coastal region, on the Guayas River, near the Bay of Guayaquil. The city was founded by the Spanish in 1535. Guayaquil's chief manufactured products are textiles, leather goods, refined sugar and other processed foods, and cement and other construction materials.

Other important cities include Cuenca and Machala in the Andean highlands, and the port city of Esmeraldas on the northern coast. Esmeraldas is the country's petroleum refining-and-shipping center.

▶ **THE ECONOMY**

Until the discovery of large petroleum deposits in the 1970's, Ecuador's economy was based largely on agriculture. Agriculture is still important economically, even though only about 10 percent of Ecuador's land is suitable for farming.

Agriculture. Farming and related activities employ about one third of the workforce. Bananas are Ecuador's most valuable cash crop, followed by coffee, cacao (from which chocolate is made), and sugarcane.

Beef and dairy cattle are also raised in the highland region. On the higher mountain slopes, sheep are grazed.

Fishing and Forestry. The waters of the Pacific Ocean off the coast of Ecuador abound in fish, particularly tuna. Most commercially caught fish is canned for export. Ecuador is also one of the world's leading suppliers of shrimp, most of which is exported frozen.

Ecuador is the world's major producer of balsa wood. Its forests also contain mahogany and other valuable hardwoods. Most of the country's forest resources, however, are still untapped.

Industry. Petroleum production and refining is Ecuador's most important industry. Petroleum accounts for at least half of the country's exports by value, and a decline in world oil prices can have a severe effect on the economy. A 300-mile (480-kilometer) pipeline carries oil from the *Oriente* across the Andes to the port of Esmeraldas, where it is refined and shipped abroad.

Ecuador's chief manufactured goods are processed foods and other agricultural products, textiles, and shoes and other leather

products. One of the country's traditional industries is the manufacture of Panama hats, so named because at one time Panama was the main distribution center for the hats.

Left: Petroleum is the mainstay of Ecuador's economy. Most of the country's petroleum is produced in the eastern region. *Below:* Bananas, the most valuable export crop, are grown chiefly in the coastal region.

They are woven from fibers made from the leaves of the jipijapa tree.

▶ **GOVERNMENT**

Ecuador's government is based on a 1998 constitution. The president, who is the head of state and government, is elected to a 4-year term of office and is not eligible for immediate re-election. The legislature is the one-house National Congress. Most representatives are elected on a national basis and serve 4-year terms. The remainder are elected on a provincial basis, also to 4-year terms. Ecuador has 22 provinces. Each is headed by a governor appointed by the president.

▶ **HISTORY**

As early as A.D. 1000, Indians of the Andean highlands had established a kingdom at Quito. In the late 1400's, the Quito Kingdom became the northern part of the Inca Empire, which fell to the Spanish conquistador (conqueror) Francisco Pizarro in the 1530's. One of Pizarro's lieutenants, Sebastián de Benalcázar, completed the conquest in Ecuador, founding a new city at Quito in 1534. Slaves were imported from Africa as laborers in the tropical coastal region.

Independence. In the early 1800's, Ecuadorians fought under Simón Bolívar as part of a widespread struggle for the liberation of the Spanish colonies in South America. The defeat of royalist troops by Antonio José de Sucre at the Battle of Pinchincha, near Quito, in 1822 freed Ecuador from Spanish rule. After independence, Ecuador joined Bolívar's Republic of Gran Colombia, which also included what are today the nations of Colombia, Venezuela, and Panama. (See the biography of Bolívar in Volume B.)

Republic of Ecuador. In 1830, Gran Colombia fell apart and Ecuador declared itself a separate republic. General Juan José Flores became its first president.

A revolution in 1895, led by General Eloy Alfaro Delgado, began a period of liberal government. A new constitution, framed in 1906, provided for the separation of church and state. Measures were taken to establish greater freedom of speech and worship. Social reforms to benefit the Indians also were enacted.

After 1911 the trend toward liberal government faded, and the next nine years were marked by civil war. Between 1925 and 1948, Ecuador was governed by 22 heads of state, none of whom succeeded in completing his term of office.

Recent History. From 1934, Ecuador's dominant political figure was José Maria Velasco Ibarra. Velasco served as president of Ecuador five different times. Four times he was deposed by the armed forces—the last time in 1972. Following Velasco's final fall from power, the country was governed by the military, who ruled by decree. A new constitution paved the way for a return to an elected civilian government in 1979. Successive governments faced periodic protests by labor unions and by Indians opposed to the exploitation of their homelands.

In 1998, Jamil Mahuad Witt won the presidential election. In the same year, he and Peruvian president Alberto Fujimori signed a peace treaty that settled a long-standing border dispute between the two countries. But Mahuad's popularity quickly waned. Within a year, disastrous weather conditions combined with plunging oil prices and a huge national debt led to a complete financial collapse.

In January 2000, thousands of Indians seized the Congress building in Quito and demanded Mahuad's resignation. When he refused, Mahuad was overthrown by the military in a bloodless coup, and Vice President Gustavo Noboa Bejarano was elevated to the presidency. Later in the year, in a desperate attempt to stabilize the economy, the new government adopted the U.S. dollar as its official currency.

In 2002, Lucio Gutiérrez Borbúa, a former army colonel who had taken part in the 2000 coup, was elected president. But in 2005, Congress ousted Gutiérrez himself from office on charges of trying to control the supreme court. He was succeeded by his vice president, Alfredo Palacio González.

HERBERT L. RAU, JR.
Author, *Geography of South America*
Reviewed by ALFREDO PAREJA DÍAZCANSECO
Universidad Central de Ecuador

EDBERG, STEFAN. See TENNIS (Great Players).

EDDINGTON, SIR ARTHUR STANLEY. See ASTRONOMY (Profiles).

EDDY, MARY BAKER. See MASSACHUSETTS (Famous People).

EDELMAN, MARIAN WRIGHT. See WASHINGTON, D.C. (Famous People).

Inventor Thomas Edison made important discoveries in such fields as electric lighting, sound recording, motion pictures, and telegraph and telephone technology.

EDISON, THOMAS ALVA (1847–1931)

Whenever you turn on a light or listen to the phonograph, you are enjoying one of the inventions of Thomas Edison. Indeed, it is difficult to go through a day without using an Edison invention. Edison probably invented more things than any other person in history.

Thomas Edison was always curious. As a boy he read every book he could and loved to tinker with machinery. He even set up a chemical laboratory in his cellar. But sometimes his curiosity went too far. For example, he once talked his friend Michael Oates into drinking a mixture that made gas bubbles in order to see if it would make Michael fly like a gas-filled balloon. Michael got sick, and young Edison got a whipping from his father. As Edison got older, he became more careful with his experiments, but he never stopped being curious about the world around him.

In his lifetime Edison received 1,093 patents in the United States alone—more than anyone before or since. He helped us communicate better through improvements to the telephone and telegraph. He brought music into our homes with his invention of the phonograph. He lit our houses with electricity by designing and building the first indoor electric lighting system. He helped develop new transportation such as electric streetcars and automobiles. He invented the electric storage battery now used in gasoline-powered vehicles and for many other purposes. He even invented waxed paper in which food can be wrapped to retain its freshness.

Edison's Boyhood

Al Edison—as he was called as a boy—was born in Milan, Ohio, on February 11, 1847. He was the youngest of seven children born to Sam and Nancy Edison. When Al was 7, the family moved to Port Huron, Michigan.

Al was often sick when he was a child. He had frequent ear infections that often kept him home from school. Eventually he became deaf in one ear and remained hard of hearing his whole life.

Even when Edison was in school, he did not do well. He was too independent to follow the rules and had a hard time making friends. His teachers thought he was a problem, but Al's mother knew he was very bright. She thought he might do better at home. She had had some experience teaching, and she eventually did take him out of school and teach him at home.

In those days most people only stayed in school through the sixth grade. So when Edison took a job at age 12, few people were surprised. He sold newspapers and candy on the Grand Trunk Railroad. He printed a small newspaper, *Paul Pry,* which became very popular along the railroad line. He proved he was a good business manager and also found time to continue his experiments in a chemical laboratory he had set up in the baggage car.

The train went from his home in Port Huron to Detroit every day. In the big city he met all kinds of people and educated himself through reading books in the Detroit Free Library.

In 1862, Al saved 3-year-old Jimmy Mackenzie from being run over by a moving boxcar. Jimmy's father, a station agent and a telegrapher, was so grateful for this heroic deed that he agreed to give Edison telegraph lessons as a reward for saving his son. Telegraphers were in great demand in those days, so this skill enabled Edison to find work almost anywhere he chose to go. His experience convinced him that he wanted to improve how the telegraphs worked, rather than just operate them.

The First Inventions

Edison began his profession as an inventor in Boston, where the latest work in electricity was being carried out. Here other inventors such as Samuel Morse and Alexander Graham Bell worked on their inventions.

In October, 1868, Edison introduced his first major invention—the vote-recording machine. This machine would allow legislators to record their votes instantly. But some politicians did not think this was a good idea. If votes were instantly recorded, there would be no time for some legislators to try to get others to change their minds and their votes.

This experience taught Edison a valuable lesson. An invention must be something people want. Edison was a practical man, and he vowed that all of his future inventions would be things people would want to buy.

Edison's invention business was not very successful, although he did invent an improved stock ticker. A stock ticker receives transmissions by telegraph wires. It provides information about transactions on the stock exchange. Edison's ticker could print letters of the alphabet as well as numbers. Still, business in Boston was difficult. He moved to New York City in May 1869, hoping for more opportunities there.

He found a good job, but he knew that he did not want to work for someone else. By the end of 1869, he and a partner had set up Pope, Edison, and Company. They designed and sold new telegraphic equipment. The partnership broke up, but Edison's inventions had brought him enough money to set up a telegraph manufacturing shop and laboratory in Newark, New Jersey. There he met Mary Stillwell, an employee, and married her in 1871. They had three children.

Edison's own inventions and the work he was doing for big companies such as Western Union gave him the money to do something he had always wanted to do. In Menlo Park, New Jersey, in 1876, Edison built his "invention factory." He was the first person to go into the business of making inventions. He was so successful that he became known as "the Wizard of Menlo Park."

The Menlo Park Years

Menlo Park was a business and research center. Edison brought together a group of loyal men who called themselves "muckers." They called Edison "the old man," although he was only about 30 years old at the time. He was not an easy boss to work for, but the men were happy with the exciting work they were

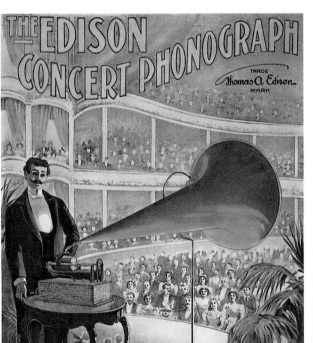

Edison's first great invention was the phonograph, the first machine able to record and play back sound. *Below:* Edison displays his invention during a visit to Washington, D.C. *Left:* An advertisement suggests that hearing a phonograph is as good as being at a concert.

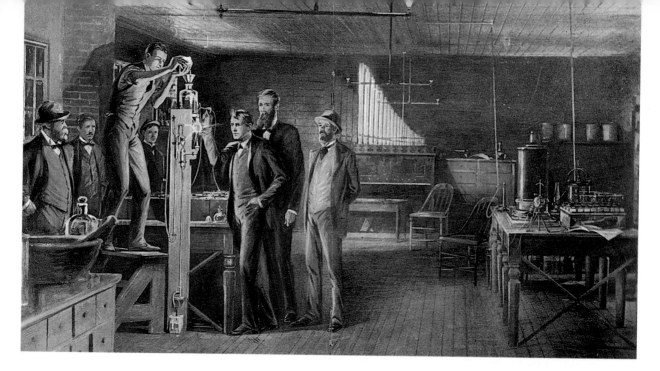

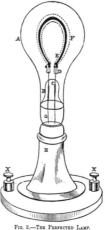

In his "invention factory," Edison (*above*, third from right) and his associates keep watch to see how long the first successful light bulb will burn. It lasted for forty hours. *Right:* A diagram of a later bulb shows its main parts. Air had been pumped out of the bulb, creating a partial vacuum. The filament was made of carbonized cardboard and was a great improvement over earlier filaments.

Fig. 3.—The Perfected Lamp.

doing. They worked together as a team to produce many important inventions. One of the first inventions at Menlo Park was an improved telephone transmitter, which allowed people to hear more clearly.

The most original invention of those years was the phonograph. This first phonograph machine did not play on a disc but on a waxed cylinder. For the first test of the machine, Edison recited "Mary Had a Little Lamb" and played it back, amazing everyone.

Edison was very proud of the phonograph. He told a reporter, "I've made a good many machines, but this is my baby, and I expect it to grow up to be a big feller and support me in my old age."

The Electric Light

Edison is best remembered for the invention of the light bulb. He was not the first to invent an electric light bulb, but he was the first to develop a complete indoor electric lighting system. Before this people did not have any way to use a bulb. There were no sockets, no switches, no insulated wires, and no central source that produced electricity. Edison's great achievement was to make electric lighting practical. By 1879 he had made a long-burning lamp, and in 1882 he built a complete lighting system on Pearl Street in New York City. In the 1880's, electric lighting and power systems were built across the United States and in many other countries.

The Businessman-Inventor

Success did not make Edison's life easy. With each invention, he had to face the claims by other inventors that their ideas were just as good as his. There were disagreements over patents, and these often had to be settled in court. Although this made the business of selling inventions difficult, Edison continued his research. Many more inventions came out of Menlo Park.

After inventing the light bulb, Edison had to become more of a businessman than inventor. He had to oversee many companies that he had set up to manufacture and sell his new discoveries.

Following the death of his wife, Mary, in 1884, Edison spent less time at Menlo Park. In 1886 he met and married Mina Miller. They moved into a new home near the new laboratory and manufacturing center that Edison had built in West Orange, New Jersey. Edison had three more children in this second marriage.

Edison continued to develop new inventions and products at West Orange, although he had some financial losses and a fire that destroyed several of the buildings.

Edison and a member of his staff, William K. L. Dickson, developed a motion picture camera and projector. The world's first motion picture studio was built at West Orange, and many famous entertainers and actors came to perform. Edison's company is thought to have produced the first motion picture to tell a story. This was *The Great Train Robbery*, made in 1903. It was 8 minutes long.

Anything electric raised Edison's curiosity. His work on the storage battery was not as glamorous as the electric light, the phonograph, or motion pictures, but it was very important. With a good storage battery, electrical equipment could have its own source of power, and automobiles could run safely and quietly. Edison never was able to get the electric car to replace the gasoline car, but he developed a battery that could be used over and over again. Other people carried on experiments with the storage battery, and today there are many types of batteries that can be used for such devices as flashlights, toys, radios, and portable televisions.

Edison gradually began to let others run his many businesses. He began to spend more time with his family and to travel. He had become a celebrity and was welcomed and given awards by many nations. His friends included other successful inventor-businessmen such as Henry Ford and Harvey Firestone.

Thomas Edison continued to work in his laboratory, trying to find ways to improve older inventions and to create new products. On October 18, 1931, he died, at the age of 84. His employees and associates remembered him as a man who worked hard and demanded hard work of those around him. He was a great believer in solving problems through careful study and determination. He said, "There is no such thing as genius. What people choose to call genius is simply hard work."

MARTIN MELOSI
Author, *Thomas Alva Edison and the Business of Invention*

EDMONDS, SARAH. See CIVIL WAR, UNITED STATES (Profiles: Union).

EDMONTON

Edmonton, the capital city of the Canadian province of Alberta, is located on the North Saskatchewan River, about 200 miles (320 kilometers) east of the Rocky Mountains. Traditionally referred to as the "Gateway to the North," Edmonton has played a key role in developing the rich agricultural and mining regions of the great Canadian northwest.

Nearly half of Edmonton's prosperous economy is based on the production, refining, and transportation of oil, coal, and natural gas. Other important goods produced there include meat, packaged foods and beverages, chemicals, metals, and machinery.

Edmonton supports a wide variety of cultural and educational institutions, including art museums, opera and ballet companies, a symphony orchestra, the University of Alberta, and the Northern Alberta Institute of Technology. It is also home to the West Edmonton Mall, the world's largest shopping center and indoor amusement park. This 123-acre (49-hectare) complex features more than 800 shops and a water park with an ice-skating rink and 23 water slides. Edmontonians also support several professional sports teams, including the Edmonton Oilers in the National Hockey League.

Fort Edmonton was settled in 1795 by the English Hudson's Bay Company. This fur-trading post expanded with the arrivals of the railroads (beginning 1891) and the Klondike gold rush (1898). The city was incorporated in 1904 and became the provincial capital the following year. Today Edmonton is Canada's largest city in area, covering approximately 260 square miles (670 square kilometers). More than 782,000 people live within the city limits; 954,000 live in the greater metropolitan area.

GARY POIGNANT
The *Edmonton Sun*

Elementary school students respond to a teacher's question during class. Although education can occur anywhere, most takes place in a traditional classroom setting.

EDUCATION

Education, the process of teaching and learning, can be formal or informal. Formal education generally consists of specific instructional activities conducted in a classroom or other institutional setting, while informal education includes all other learning experiences.

Education is important for many reasons. It helps people learn the skills they need to survive and perform day-to-day tasks. It makes life easier and more enjoyable. It also allows society as a whole to advance, to organize itself, to produce goods and services, and to transmit cultural traditions and knowledge from one generation to the next. Education plays an important role in democracy as well, since citizens must be well informed to vote responsibly.

▶ **EDUCATION AROUND THE WORLD**

In most industrialized countries, formal education is compulsory (required) and free, although educational systems vary. In other countries—primarily developing nations—formal education is not always available, and many people never learn to read or write. In large developing countries such as China and India, children may go to school for a few years, but many do not attend beyond adolescence.

In the United States, Scotland, Canada, South Africa, Australia, New Zealand, and Scandinavia, educational systems are organized similarly. In these countries most of the students go to public elementary and secondary schools.

Secondary schools include academic schools for college-bound students and vocational schools for those who want to learn a trade. Comprehensive high schools that serve both groups—most common in the United States—are becoming more common in these other countries as well.

Students in England, France, Italy, and Germany who are between 11 and 13 come to a fork in the road. Those who are planning to hold certain kinds of jobs (secretary or auto mechanic, for instance) go directly to a vocational school. Those planning to go to college attend schools that focus on academics. At one time, students who went to college were generally from wealthy or socially prominent families. Today, however, more students from other social and economic backgrounds are attending as well.

Some educational systems include work-study programs. In China, for example, students may attend classes and also work in factories or on farms.

Most African countries have western-style educational systems. These were originally introduced by Christian missionaries and by European governments that had established colonies there. In many areas, there is a need for more schools and teachers.

In Russia, all children go to school for eleven years, but only a small percentage pass the examinations enabling them to go on to universities. Studies are combined with work experience, and while in high school, students may also attend technical and trade schools. A number of schools teach gifted children.

In Japan, schools are organized as they are in the United States, with nursery schools, kindergartens, elementary schools, junior and senior high schools, and universities. The main difference is that Japanese secondary schools and universities are ranked from best to worst, and students compete to enter the best schools. A student's entire professional career may be largely determined by how well she or he does in this competition, which begins in elementary school.

Chinese education is still limited in poor rural areas. But the Chinese say that almost all school-age children are in school. There are also thousands of part-time schools for older people who want to make up the education they missed. In addition, there are schools that have work-study programs, which allow young people to get technical training while they also work part-time in factories and on farms.

Although the educational systems in many Latin American countries have improved, most still face difficulties. These include poverty and lack of transportation in rural areas, as well as language barriers. There are large native Indian populations in the Latin American countries, and many different languages are spoken. Because of this, many children go to school without knowing their country's official language.

The lack of a common language is also a problem in many African countries, as well as in India, the Philippines, Israel, and even some sections of the United States. In the

Philippines, for example, elementary school classes are conducted in the local dialect, but pupils going on to secondary schools must also learn the official dialect, plus English. In Israel, about 200 different languages are spoken, so all schoolchildren must be taught Hebrew, the official language. In the United States, schools in some areas have many Spanish-speaking children who must learn to speak English. Often these students are first placed in transition classes with Spanish-speaking instructors.

Whether they live in rural or urban areas, most U.S. students are transported on the familiar yellow school bus.

▶ EDUCATION IN THE UNITED STATES

Every state requires children to stay in school from about age 5 to age 16, 17, or 18, depending on the state. Most students attend public schools; only about 12 percent attend private schools. Graduation from high school (usually at age 17 or 18) is strongly encouraged, and more than 80 percent of young adults are high school graduates.

The quality of education among public schools can vary; there is often a significant gap between mostly affluent suburban schools and schools in poorer urban and rural communities. But in recent years, higher standards have been set for public schools that have helped raise achievement levels and literacy and high school graduation rates.

Most schools are organized by graded classes in a "ladder" system, beginning with preschools and elementary schools, followed by middle and junior high schools and high schools. At the top level are schools of higher education—two-year community colleges and four-year colleges and universities. In most schools, advancement from one grade to the next is based on student performance, although some students are promoted despite poor achievement because of concern they will fall even further behind.

There are also other kinds of schools, including those that prepare students for jobs such as cooking or truck driving. Some schools help students prepare for tests required for professional licenses in fields such as real estate and carpentry. Many night

Adult education classes have become popular in many communities, particularly among older adults. Courses are usually offered on a wide range of subjects.

schools run by local colleges or school systems teach newly arrived immigrants to speak English. There are also adult education classes on many other subjects.

Public Schools. In the United States, most of the money to support public schools comes from local and state taxes. The federal government also provides some funds, but no more than 10 percent. Some large U.S. corporations also contribute funds for public schools. This money has been used for dropout prevention programs, student scholarships, teacher training, educational research, and other programs.

Each state has the power to regulate its schools, although control over individual schools goes to local school districts. There are nearly 16,000 local school districts in the United States. They range from large city school districts with dozens of schools to small-town or rural districts that have only one school for all children. Many states have laws that allow several school districts within a county to form a single district.

In each public school district, a school board or committee of local residents oversees the operation of the schools. In many places these school board members are elected; in some cities they are appointed. School boards make many decisions concerning local schools. They determine school policies; approve the hiring of staff, including teachers, principals, and others; and approve and gain public support for annual school budgets. They also select a school superintendent to oversee the daily operation of the school system.

As the result of local control, there may be differences between various districts. In some, for instance, there are no kindergartens for 5 year olds. The grade levels may be divided differently among elementary schools, middle schools, and junior high and high schools. Some districts may have vocational programs for students with special interests, such as agriculture.

Although local control has its advantages, it can also have drawbacks. Some less affluent school districts do not have as much money as others to pay for education. Other districts may not be managed well. Local control also makes it difficult to raise standards throughout a state.

Private Schools. Private schools are funded chiefly by tuition and by donations from individuals and organizations. People who pay tuition for private education also pay taxes to support public schools. In the United States, all taxpayers are required to support public schools even though some may not use them. Recently, however, federal and state tax funds have supported some programs at private schools.

Some private schools are run by religious groups. These schools (sometimes called parochial schools) provide religious education in addition to other subjects. Many other private schools are independent and not associated with any other organization or religious group.

Private schools appeal to some parents because they may offer innovative programs or teaching methods, smaller classes, or stricter discipline than public schools. It is easier for them to expel disruptive students. Like public schools, most private schools teach a standard **curriculum**, or group of subjects.

▶ HISTORY OF EDUCATION

Education began long before there were schools. In ancient times, people taught their children what they needed to know for survival. The earliest schools we know about were in Mesopotamia and Egypt about 2000 to 1000 B.C. Systems of writing taught in these schools were very difficult, and most people never learned to write. Those who did usually became scribes—highly respected, well-paid professionals who wrote letters and kept accounts for others.

In Egypt there were higher levels of education for a few young men who were going to be priests, government officials, architects, or doctors. The remarkable work of ancient Egyptian engineers can still be seen today.

Another ancient people, the Hebrews, had a long tradition of education. They set up formal schools where every boy, rich or poor, could be taught the language, religion, and history of the Jews. This was probably the first time in history that formal education was provided for rich and poor alike. As with other early schools, however, girls were not allowed to attend.

In China, education changed little from the time of Confucius (about 500 B.C.) to the 1900's. Almost every village and town had an elementary school. Families who could afford the fees sent their boys to learn reading and writing. The boys also memorized long passages from the writings of Chinese philosophers.

There were few schools beyond the elementary level. A gifted student, however, might attend a university, and a few boys—usually those who were wealthy—continued their studies on their own. If they became very learned, they might be able to pass the examinations given by the imperial government. A young man who passed these could then become a high government official. Anyone was allowed to take the examinations. Sometimes even the son of a poor family might learn enough to pass.

Scribes were among the few people in ancient Egypt who learned to read and write. They were highly paid to write letters and keep accounts for others.

In ancient India, only a few people could improve their lives through education. From early times, the people of India had been divided into classes, or castes. At the top were the Brahmins, and at the bottom were the outcasts (or untouchables), who had no rights at all. The castes between included soldiers, business people, and farmers. The sons of a businessman had to follow their father's trade. They could not move up and become soldiers or Brahmins. They were allowed to learn whatever was needed for that business, but nothing else. Only the Brahmins got a complete education.

The Brahmins went to a twelve-year school called a parishad. There they learned about the Hindu religion as well as poetry, philosophy, astronomy, and medicine.

Education in Ancient Greece. People in the Western world today owe many of their ideas to the ancient Greeks. The Greek city-states, of which Athens was the greatest, are the starting point of Western civilization. While the Chinese, the Hindus, and the Hebrews all saw education as a means of preserving traditions, the people of ancient Athens sought new knowledge.

Athens had the first democratic government, although only free men had a voice in it; slaves and women were excluded. But they were the first people to have self-government and freedom of thought. In Athens, the ideal education was to prepare a boy for this freedom. They believed every young man should be well-rounded and should try to excel in all

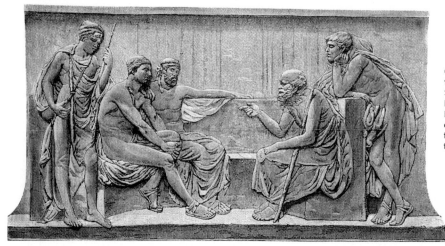

One of history's most famous teachers was Socrates (center), who lived in ancient Greece. He taught by asking questions, a technique that became known as the Socratic method.

things. In primary school boys learned reading, writing, arithmetic, and singing. They also did exercises and learned boxing, wrestling, broad jumping, high jumping, and discus throwing. As they grew older, they learned by being part of the life around them.

Athens also had one of the world's most famous teachers—Socrates (470?–399 B.C.). Socrates did not lecture his students, as other teachers might, but instead asked questions that made them think. What is a good government? What is the difference between right and wrong? What is the difference between beauty and ugliness?

Once the student had given an answer, Socrates would ask more questions—a technique that became known as the Socratic method. As this continued, the student might see that his facts had been wrong or his arguments unclear. A special kind of conversation, which we still call a Socratic dialogue, followed. One of Socrates' students, Plato, wrote down many of these dialogues.

Education in Athens changed somewhat in the 300's B.C. Followers of the philosophers Plato (427?–347 B.C.) and Aristotle (384–322 B.C.) set up formal schools where young men studied philosophy, mathematics, music, language, and literature. These continued to draw students for hundreds of years, even after Athens was a conquered city.

Another kind of school that became popular in Athens was called a school of rhetoric. Its main purpose was to teach public speaking. Many students also studied philosophy and literature.

The Schools of Ancient Rome. The Romans conquered the Greeks on the battlefields, but the Greeks conquered the Romans in the schoolrooms. Before Rome became large and powerful, a Roman father taught his sons whatever he knew. This may have included some reading, writing, and a trade. This simple form of education changed as more and more Roman citizens began to have Greek slaves. Many Greek slaves were far better educated than their Roman masters. They began teaching the masters' children. Some of the slave-teachers were given their freedom, and they set up schools where groups of boys were taught.

In the ludus, the Roman primary school, boys—and sometimes girls—learned reading, writing, and arithmetic. The secondary schools were for boys only. The teacher was called a grammaticus, and the schools were known as grammar schools. The students learned Greek, as well as Latin grammar and literature.

The Romans also had schools of rhetoric, copied from the Greeks. The rhetor, or teacher, tried to make his students expert in argument, logic, law, and public speaking. Originally these schools were intended to prepare young men for political leadership. But when Rome changed from a republic to an empire, training for political leadership was almost useless. The schools of rhetoric in the later empire taught the young men to speak and write elegantly, but little else.

Many Roman youths went to Greece for higher education. Even in conquered Greece, education continued to thrive. The greatest library of the ancient world was in Alexandria, a Greek-ruled city in Egypt. In Athens and Rhodes there were also learned teachers of philosophy, architecture, medicine, and other sciences.

Schools of the Middle Ages. Most of Europe and the lands around the Mediterranean Sea had been united under the rule of Rome. A network of roads connected the Roman Empire. There was a single official language, Latin, and a single code of laws. Most citizens were able to read and write.

When the Roman Empire began to crumble, this unity was destroyed and many schools closed. By the early Middle Ages, few people had any formal education. Even kings were illiterate (unable to read and write).

Religious leaders then began running schools. Jews who had settled in Italy, France, Spain, and North Africa began schools that taught their children to read and write Hebrew and to understand the Talmud, the book of Jewish law. The Christian Church founded schools in cathedrals and monasteries throughout Europe.

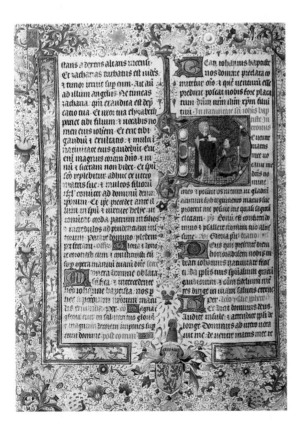

During the Middle Ages, books were rare and costly because they were copied and illustrated by hand. Only the wealthy could afford them.

At church schools in eastern Europe, students learned Greek. In western Europe, they learned Latin, no matter what language they spoke. Thus all educated people could understand one another. A scholar in Italy and one in Ireland could write or speak to each other in Latin.

Books were rare and valuable because they had to be copied by hand. When barbarians attacked a city, learned people picked up their books and fled for safety to another part of Europe. In the 400's many escaped from France and England to Ireland. Later, when England was safe, many scholars gathered at the Cathedral School in York in northern England. When Charlemagne (742?–814) brought peace to France in the 700's, he sent to York for teachers.

Charlemagne was so interested in education that he established a school in his palace. He ordered all the cathedrals and monasteries in his empire to set up schools. These were to be open to anyone, even the sons of serfs (the peasants who worked the land). In some parts of his empire there were schools in every parish, but many children did not go to school because they had to work. After Charlemagne's death many of his schools were closed.

The child who did go to school in the Middle Ages learned little except reading, writing, and the teachings of the church. If he continued his education beyond the elementary level, it was usually in order to be a priest or a monk who copied books in the monastery library. The good student was the one who could memorize the book and copy a page without making any mistakes.

The Impact of Islam. While the monasteries in northern Europe were preserving Christian teachings and some learning from the past, a new prophet, Mohammed (570?–632), arose in the Middle East. He began a religion about 620, called Islam, which emphasized belief in a single god (Allah). Islam eventually dominated the Middle East and northern Africa.

Before the year 800, Mohammed's followers, called Muslims, had pushed across to Spain. Among them were learned men who

Muslims, followers of Islam, greatly valued education. During the Middle Ages, each Muslim place of worship (mosque) had a free school for boys.

umes. They welcomed books and scholars of all religions and all countries. Because of this freedom, knowledge grew in Spain while it shrank in the rest of Europe.

The Universities of the Late Middle Ages. Gradually the people of northern Europe realized how much knowledge they were missing and began traveling more. Many went on pilgrimages to Jerusalem and the surrounding area, known as the Holy Land. These travelers discovered ancient Greek writings that western Europe had forgotten. They found Arabic writings on science that were far better than their own. Some saw the great schools in Baghdad, Alexandria, and Córdoba. As western European cities grew larger and richer, people began to want libraries and schools such as those they had seen on their travels.

In some cities, such as Paris, the cathedral school grew until it became a university. In other cities, students and professors began universities without the help of the church. The professors formed a group called a collegium. The students formed another group called a guild. The collegium and the students' guild made the rules for the university.

Students learned by disputation, a formal argument that is like a debate. The teacher

had traveled and studied in many places. They brought with them much knowledge from the East. They knew the mathematics of India. They also knew the science and philosophy of Greece. The monks of northern Europe had copied and preserved mostly the books approved by the Christian Church. The Muslims had knowledge that had been lost to the rest of Europe.

Each Muslim place of worship (mosque) had a school where boys could learn reading and writing. These schools were free, and most Muslim boys attended. The children of the rich went on to boarding schools.

The Muslims were especially interested in science and medicine. They taught the works of the Greek scientists. Beyond that, they were interested in using science to make life richer and more comfortable. They made paper and steel. They taught the Spanish how to grow and use new crops: rice, sugar, and cotton. They built observatories to study the stars. Their physicians and surgeons were the most scientific and skillful in the world.

The first true universities of western Europe were in Spain—at Córdoba, Seville, Toledo, and Salamanca. Some of them had libraries of several hundred thousand vol-

Oxford University in Oxford, England, was founded in the 1100's. It remains one of the world's most prestigious universities.

would read a difficult passage from a book. The student would decide what he thought it meant and make arguments to prove his point. Other students and the teacher would then try to tear these arguments apart. Something like this still takes place in modern universities, when students write theses and then defend them.

Most of the material studied in the universities was from the Greek writings that had been found by travelers. Aristotle's writings were the most important. Scholars took his explanation of the physical world and combined it with Christian beliefs about how the world was made.

The Renaissance. The next period of history, called the Renaissance, was a time of renewed interest in learning and the arts of ancient Greece and Rome. It also marked the beginning of science as we know it. At this time, people also discovered many new things. They began to observe and study the physical world, inventing such instruments as the telescope and the thermometer.

At the beginning of the Renaissance, most books were still written in Latin, the language of scholars. However, most of the common people did not speak Latin and so did not read. With the invention of the printing press in the mid-1400's, however, books became easier to produce and writers began writing in their own languages. As a result, more people learned to read, and knowledge and ideas spread much faster.

Also during the Renaissance, many kinds of primary (or elementary) schools began to appear in Europe. The Protestant churches often had schools in each parish and the Roman Catholic Church built more schools as well. In 1559, the German state of Württemberg organized the first school system with a primary school in every village. In other German states, in the Netherlands, and in Scotland, governments also founded primary schools. In some English villages, women taught reading and writing to children in their homes for a small fee. These were called dame schools. In England many large schools were established by wealthy nobles as a charity.

Few students went beyond primary school. Those who did were usually the sons of wealthy families. Their education was very similar to that of wealthy boys in the days of the Roman Empire. They learned Latin and Greek. After they had mastered grammar, they learned how to speak and write with elegance. These skills were the mark of the upper social classes.

Teachers at these schools were often strict and harsh. Most did not care whether the students understood what they were studying. They wanted them only to memorize the books and keep quiet. The wisest scholars knew that this kind of education was cruel and made students dislike learning. Here and there some teachers tried to make school more interesting and pleasant. One Czech teacher, John Amos Comenius (1592–1670),

With the invention of the printing press in 1440, books became easier to produce. As a result, knowledge spread faster and more people learned to read.

wrote schoolbooks for young children and put pictures in them—a startling new idea.

Early Schools in America. In Massachusetts, a law adopted in 1647 required every town of at least 50 families to have an elementary teacher and every town of 100 families or more to have a Latin grammar school. This marked the beginning of American public education. Other New England colonies passed similar laws. New Englanders who settled the West took this idea with them. New England elementary schools were public schools, built by the town. Some tax money was used to run them, although parents who could afford

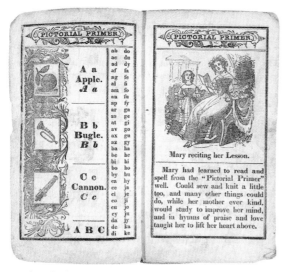

In colonial America, many children learned their lessons from primers. These schoolbooks included rhymes, prayers, and pictures.

fees had to pay them. Puritan beliefs, considered an important part of a child's education, were also emphasized at these schools.

In other colonies, such as New York and Pennsylvania, other churches (Roman Catholics, Baptists, and so on) wanted their religious beliefs taught in school. Since it was almost impossible to set up public school systems with tax money collected from everyone, each church ran its own schools.

In the southern colonies the governments sometimes ran schools for poor children whose parents could not afford church school. Some wealthy colonists gave money to set up schools, particularly for orphans. In colonial elementary schools children learned reading, writing, and arithmetic. They learned their letters from a hornbook—a thin board with a piece of paper fastened on it. On the paper were the alphabet and two or three prayers. Over the paper was a thin sheet of horn like a plastic cover.

A child's first real book was called a primer. The most famous was the *New England Primer*. It had a picture for each letter of the alphabet and a short rhyme to be memorized. It also included the

During the 1700's, Swiss educator Johann Pestalozzi developed new teaching methods designed to make learning more interesting for children.

Lord's Prayer and the catechism, a statement of religious beliefs. Once they had finished the primer, the children went on to read the Bible.

After three years of elementary school most children were finished with formal education. They were then expected to help their parents in the shop or on the farm. A boy might be apprenticed to a tradesman, to live in his house and learn his trade.

A few boys went on to Latin grammar school to become ministers, doctors, or lawyers. These schools were much like those in Europe. Students learned how to read, write, and speak Latin and possibly some classical Greek. They had much less instruction in science, history, mathematics, and English than students do now.

The Enlightenment. Big changes in education began during the 1700's, a period known as the Enlightenment. A French writer of the time, Jean Jacques Rousseau (1712–78), published a novel called *Émile*. This described the ideal way to raise children. Rousseau said children should not be forced into learning but should be gently led to learn practical things and develop their natural talents.

One of Rousseau's readers was a young Swiss man named Johann Heinrich Pestalozzi (1746–1827). Pestalozzi wanted to help the poor and believed that even the neediest and least talented children could learn and grow mentally. He brought together a group of homeless children on his farm and began teaching them according to Rousseau's ideas. He also had several schools but most failed for lack of money. Despite this, his teaching methods became famous. He gave the small-

est children blocks with letters on them, to put together words. The children began the study of geography by making a clay model of a river valley near the school. They learned history by dressing up as famous characters and acting out past events. Pestalozzi made learning so interesting that his students' progress astonished all who saw them.

Benjamin Franklin wanted to reform education. He started a new kind of school called an academy.

New Kinds of Schools. Although the harsh Latin grammar school continued for some time in Europe and the American colonies, new kinds of schools were also beginning. In England the Dissenters, religious groups outside the Church of England, set up schools in which Latin was only one of many subjects. In their schools the children learned geography, history, economics, arithmetic, and modern languages, such as French and Italian. They even learned practical subjects, such as surveying and shorthand. In Germany the newer kind of school was called a Realgymnasium. It offered subjects that were closer to real life and also emphasized the sciences.

During the 1750's Benjamin Franklin (1706–90) started a school in the American colonies called an academy. There, English replaced Latin. Franklin thought students should be able to read and speak their own language perfectly. He also thought they should learn another modern language. The academy taught history, natural science, mechanics, and drawing. Students also learned about other countries. The academy was the beginning of the modern American high school, although it would be another 175 years before all Americans could receive such education.

Other early leaders of the United States also wanted to reform education. Thomas Jefferson (1743–1826) said that in a country where the people have the right to vote, everyone should be educated. Jefferson suggested a state system of public education, separate from any of the churches, supported by tax money. But his own state, Virginia, refused to carry out his plan.

In the 1800's many European countries established state-supported elementary schools. Some also provided free secondary schooling.

France and Prussia led the way in these efforts. In these countries, public schools were seen as a way of increasing national unity.

In the United States there were a number of leaders who fought to get tax money for the schools. One was Daniel Webster, who said in 1837, "Open the doors of the school houses to all the children in the land. Let no man have the excuse of poverty for not educating his offspring." Other leaders included Horace Mann (1796–1859) in Massachusetts, Henry Barnard (1811–1900) in Connecticut and Rhode Island, and Thaddeus Beecher (1792–1868) in Pennsylvania. They believed that there should be a system of "common schools," which would give all children an elementary education.

Like Thomas Jefferson, these leaders thought it better to have one system of public schools, separate from the churches. They also wanted laws that would make education compulsory for all children. At that time farm families often kept the children at home to work in the fields. In cities and towns, poor children often worked all day in factories.

It is hard for a student of today to realize what a struggle it was to get free public schools and to make sure that all children at-

The one-room schoolhouse was a feature of American education for many years. In these schools, students of all ages and levels were taught by one teacher.

A kindergarten teacher helps a student with his lessons. Kindergarten as we know it today was introduced by German educator Friedrich Froebel in the 1800's.

tended. In the past, many people thought that poor children did not need to be educated. Many also thought that the government had no right to take tax money from one family to educate another family's children. And many poor families wanted their children to work because they needed the money.

Massachusetts, with its long history of interest in education, was ahead of all the other states. Yet even in this state, there was not always enough tax money to keep the schools going, and parents sometimes had to pay for their children's education. In 1827, however, Massachusetts passed a law requiring that schools be funded entirely by tax money. Not long after this, other New England states passed similar laws.

Most of the Middle Atlantic and Southern states did not have free public education until after the Civil War. The midwestern states did better. Wisconsin set up free public schools in 1848, Ohio in 1853, and Iowa in 1858. The federal government helped the midwestern states start their school systems. It gave the states free land, which could be sold to provide funds for schools. Before the end of the 1800's, common schools had been set up in all the states. In most places children learned the same things and used the same texts. These included Noah Webster's blue-backed speller, the McGuffey *Readers*, and Ray's *Arithmetics*.

Extending Education. As tax-supported common schools—which came to be known as elementary schools—became more widely accepted, some educational leaders began ef-

forts to educate children who were younger and older than elementary-school age. Friedrich Froebel (1782–1852) in Germany started the idea of kindergarten, a word that means "children's garden." Froebel made toys and wrote songs for preschool children that helped them learn as they played. Froebel felt that young women got along better with little children and trained many to be kindergarten teachers. (Before his time, all teachers had been men or older women— usually widows who had to work.) Some who had studied under Froebel started private kindergartens in the United States. The first public-school kindergarten opened in St. Louis, Missouri, in 1873.

Secondary Schools and Colleges. Secondary education also became available to more students during the 1800's. By 1850 there were about 6,000 academies like Benjamin Franklin's in the United States. Most were boarding schools, which drew students from a wide area. Most were for boys. There were some for girls, called female academies. At first the female academies taught only music, dancing, art, and embroidery. Later, girls were allowed to learn history, mathematics, and languages.

The first U.S. high school was established in Boston in the 1820's. Its aim was to complete "a good English education" for boys who did not expect to go to college. For a little while the academies and the high schools served two different groups. But this division of students did not last long. Since people had accepted the idea of free public elementary schools, it was not difficult to establish public high schools. By 1910, high schools were common in the United States. By the end of the 1800's, almost all states were providing higher education that was either free or at reduced tuition at state colleges and universities.

▶ TRENDS IN AMERICAN EDUCATION
Curriculum. Although the public school curriculum is usually set by the state, local school districts have some power to establish a curriculum that reflects their own needs and interests. Subjects offered by all schools normally include language arts (reading, writing, grammar, and vocabulary), mathematics, social studies, science, and health and physical education. In addition, many schools offer other subjects such as art, music, computer

A student solves a math problem at the blackboard as the teacher looks on. Mathematics is one of the subjects usually offered by all schools.

science, foreign languages, and family and consumer sciences.

Until recently, secondary schools often provided students with a choice among three basic programs, or tracks. The academic track prepared students to go to college. Those who followed the general track might plan to attend a technical school after high school. The vocational track included general education and training in specific job skills, such as those used in health care, clerical work, construction, and mechanics. However, the growing national concern about the poor reading and mathematics skills of many high school students has caused a number of districts to

cut vocational courses and emphasize academics for all.

Class Size and Makeup. In most public schools today, the average class size for all grade levels is 24 students. In the early 1980's, many states began trying to improve academic performance among students in public schools by reducing class size, but found it difficult because of the cost of hiring more teachers and building more classrooms. Cutting class size to about 15 students seemed to raise achievement, but few schools managed to do that.

Some schools organize students according to achievement; there are classes for average students, slow learners, and gifted students. This grouping method may be used for all subjects or only for selected ones. Some elementary schools are organized so that there are no grades, and children are grouped separately for each subject.

Many public school classes include children with disabilities. At one time, these children were placed in separate classes. In the special education program called **mainstreaming**, children with physical or mental handicaps are placed in regular classrooms where they can be taught with other children. In urban areas, however, many school districts also pay for private teaching of children with disabilities.

Students who are not fluent in English are more common in many classrooms as well.

WONDER QUESTION

Should students attend year-round school?

Although year-round school is common in some countries, it is still a new idea in the United States. But it is an idea that is becoming more popular, as evidence shows it can help boost student achievement.

In some ways, the term "year-round" is a little misleading, since students on this type of schedule have just as many vacation days as those on the traditional calendar. Instead of eight or ten weeks off in the summer, however, students on a year-round calendar have shorter, more frequent breaks.

Opponents of year-round school say it makes it hard for families to schedule day care or vacations. Also, it may be difficult to

coordinate sports events with teams from school districts on the traditional calendar. High school students can have a harder time finding full-time summer jobs or jobs that fit in with their breaks.

But advocates of year-round school say it helps students more easily retain what they have learned from one grade to the next. As a result, teachers do not have to spend time reviewing the previous year's lessons when students return in the fall. And for students who are struggling with certain subjects, there is no need to wait for summer school; remedial help is available sooner and usually takes less time.

At one time, students with disabilities were placed in special classes. Now, as part of a program called mainstreaming, many are taught with other students.

As immigration laws changed, public schools that previously had mostly non-Hispanic white and African-American students became much more diverse. By the year 2000, most students in many urban schools were Hispanic. There were also more Asians.

Because of this, many schools have developed bilingual programs for students whose first language is not English. These bilingual and English as a second language (ESL) programs help students progress in other subject areas while they become more fluent in English.

Computers and Technology. Although books remain one of the primary tools for teaching, other tools are used as well. These include audiovisual aids such as maps, slides, films, videotapes and videodiscs, and audiocassettes. Some teachers also use closed-circuit television to provide or enhance in-

Many classrooms now have computers. Students use them to learn basic computer skills and to access educational materials.

struction or use programs broadcast by educational television stations.

Computers are used increasingly in classrooms. Students learn how to use keyboards, software and the Internet, as well as the basics of a computer workplace. They also use some computer programs to help improve skills in reading, writing, and math.

A number of different teaching tools are used to provide **programmed**, or individual, instruction for students. Programmed instruction involves dividing the material to be learned into small bits. Students study and learn the bits of information at their own pace and review material as needed. Programmed instruction can be done with computers, books, CD's, and other aids. It allows a student to advance slowly or rapidly—whichever is best for the individual.

Academic Standards and Tests. Setting higher standards for public schools and assessing students and schools with standardized tests became important in the 1990's and 2000's after political leaders became troubled by poor achievement, particularly in low-income areas. Researchers comparing the test scores of students in the United States and other countries found that the United States lagged behind several countries in mathematics, science, geography, and history. Forty-nine states established specific academic standards, and all states began testing students to check their progress. Several require high school students to pass some of the tests for graduation.

With the signing of the No Child Left Behind law in 2002, the federal government required all states to test all public school children in the third to eighth grade annually.

States are required to identify schools that are not meeting their standards and give them special help.

Since the 1960's, the federal government has also been funding educational programs such as Head Start to help disadvantaged preschoolers prepare for formal schooling. Many of these children are from poor rural and urban areas.

Teacher Training. At one time all teachers had to have college degrees in education in order to teach. Critics of this system claimed

As the result of a new federal law, yearly academic testing is now required for all U.S. public school students in third through eighth grade. These tests are used to measure student achievement and school performance.

that teachers should be more familiar with the subject matter than teaching methods. Today, many education schools and states require teachers to instead hold degrees in the subject they plan to teach, such as mathematics, science, or English.

States have also toughened teacher certification requirements to make sure new teachers have passed standardized tests in their subject areas, as well as tests of educational practice. Some states also offer financial rewards to teachers who win national teacher certificates. Those who earn these certificates must first pass rigorous exams.

Other Kinds of Schools. One approach to improving education is to allow greater choice of schools. Some districts have established **magnet schools**, which typically focus on a specific subject area such as the arts or science. Students in those districts are allowed to choose which magnet school they wish to attend. Many school districts also offer open enrollment, allowing students to choose any school in the district.

In the 1990's, some school districts began allowing the establishment of **charter schools**, which are public schools run without school district supervision. These are generally smaller than other public schools and may have smaller classes. Many charter schools require longer school days and longer school years. They also hire younger teachers willing to put in the longer hours and try different teaching methods.

Privatization of Education. Some people believe that public schools would be better if they were run as businesses. Proponents of this trend, called privatization, believe that if the goal of a company running a school is to make a profit, competition will force it to offer a superior product. Critics, however, claim that this does not always occur; privately run public schools have not been able to raise student achievement levels significantly. They also say that such schools do not serve students who cost more to educate, such as those with disabilities.

Vouchers. In some parts of the country, programs were created that allowed low-income parents to use government vouchers to pay part of the tuition if they moved their child to a private school. These programs, initiated in the 1990's, were criticized because some private schools are run by religious groups. Many people believed that allowing federal funds to be used for such schools would violate constitutional rules against supporting religion. But in 2002 the U.S. Supreme Court ruled that voucher programs were not unconstitutional.

Parent Participation. The federal government and several school districts have tried to increase parent participation in education by organizing parent groups in each school and asking parents to sign contracts promising their support for learning. Some schools also call parents in to the school if their children have not done their homework.

UNIFORMS AND PUBLIC SCHOOLS

School uniforms have always been required at many private schools. But recently some U.S. public schools have made them mandatory as well.

Advocates of uniforms (usually parents and school officials) say that students who wear them have fewer discipline problems and are able to concentrate more on schoolwork. They also claim uniforms help reduce peer pressure. When everyone dresses the same, they say, students worry less about their appearance.

Advocates believe uniforms can give students a distinct identity and status and can promote school spirit. In some areas they prevent gang members from wearing gang colors and emblems to school, so gang activity is reduced. They can also help school officials easily recognize outsiders who come into the school and thus improve safety.

Critics of uniforms say that strict dress codes discourage creativity. Clothes are one of the ways people express themselves and uniforms do not allow them to do that. They believe that as long as a student's clothing is clean, proper, and does not interfere with learning, it should not matter what he or she wears.

Opponents of public school uniforms also say that uniforms can create new problems. That is, enforcing a more restrictive dress code among students who oppose it can take time away from more important things—such as learning. Because of this, some public schools that had adopted uniforms no longer require them.

For many years, parents have also participated in parent-teacher organizations, which sponsor various school enrichment programs and offer regular parent programs on child development and education. In addition, many schools encourage parents to regularly volunteer time in their children's classrooms or assist with other school activities.

Homeschooling. Homeschooling is a form of education in which school-age children learn at home. Between 1.5 and 1.9 million children are currently homeschooled (about 3 percent of the school-age population), with this number growing by about 15 percent each year. Homeschooling is legal nationwide, but regulations vary from state to state.

Homeschooling methods range from highly structured "school-at-home" programs to "unschooling," which is unstructured, interest-based learning. Many families design their own study programs, often using a unit study approach that links all academic subjects around common themes. Some enroll in online or correspondence courses, purchase commercial curricula (pre-prepared lesson plans), or take part in learning cooperatives with other families.

Children taught at home usually take less time to complete required courses than those enrolled in public or private schools. But for homeschooling to be successful, parents must have the time and the skills to prepare and teach academic lessons daily.

School Violence. A rash of violent episodes in public schools, notably the murder of twelve students and a teacher at Columbine High School in Littleton, Colorado, in 1999, led to calls for better school security. As a result, a number of schools have introduced measures intended to reduce the factors leading to school violence. These include campaigns to discourage the use of offensive language and peer mediation programs that teach students how to settle their own disputes.

JAY MATHEWS
Education Writer
The Washington Post

EDUCATION, UNITED STATES DEPARTMENT OF

The Department of Education (ED) is one of the 15 cabinet-level departments in the executive branch of the United States government. Although U.S. schools are not controlled by the government, the ED tries to encourage high-quality education by establishing policies, developing educational programs, and providing financial aid to schools.

A secretary of education manages the department and serves as the president's chief adviser on educational matters. He or she is selected by the president with the approval of the Senate. The secretary is assisted by a deputy secretary, a general counsel, and three assistant secretaries.

Organization

The secretary is also responsible for the overall planning and operations of ten program offices, each headed by an assistant secretary or other officer.

The **Office for Civil Rights** assures equal access to education and promotes educational excellence through the enforcement of civil rights.

The **Office of Innovation and Improvement** makes grants to states, schools, and community organizations to further promising educational practices.

The **Office of Elementary and Secondary Education** promotes academic excellence, enhances educational opportunities, and helps improve the quality of teaching and learning by providing leadership, technical assistance, and financial support.

The **Office of Postsecondary Education** formulates federal education policy regarding colleges and universities in an effort to improve access to quality education.

The **Office of Special Education and Rehabilitative Services** supports the improvement of education for people with disabilities through special education, vocational rehabilitation, and research.

The **Office of Vocational and Adult Education** helps prepare young people and adults for postsecondary education, with a concentration on high schools, career and technical education, community colleges, and adult education and literacy.

The **Office for Federal Student Aid** administers the federal aid programs for college students.

The **Office of English Language Acquisition, Language Enhancement, and Academic Achievement for Limited English Proficient Students** leads the effort to promote quality education to students learning English.

The **Institute of Education Sciences** compiles statistics and conducts research to promote high-quality educational policies.

The **Office of Safe and Drug-Free Schools** administers, coordinates, and recommends policy for improving programs that promote drug- and violence-free schools.

History

A non-cabinet-level education research agency was established in 1897. Later named the Office of Education (EO), it became part of the Department of Health, Education, and Welfare (HEW) in 1953. In the 1960's, the EO began providing funds and direction to state-run schools, primarily to ensure that low-income and minority students would receive equal educational opportunities. The EO was then given the power to enforce laws prohibiting racial segregation in the schools and discrimination against women, minorities, and the disabled. Greater emphasis was placed on educational research and the development of model school curricula. This expansion led to the elevation of the EO to a cabinet-level department. The Department of Education began operating in 1980.

ED headquarters are located at 400 Maryland Avenue, S.W., Washington, D.C. 20202. Offices also are located in Boston, New York, Philadelphia, Atlanta, Chicago, Dallas, Kansas City (Missouri), Denver, San Francisco, and Seattle.

STEPHEN J. SNIEGOSKI
Author, *The Department of Education*

Secretaries of Education		
Name	Took Office	Under President
Shirley M. Hufstedler	1979	Carter
Terrel H. Bell	1981	Reagan
William J. Bennett	1985	Reagan
Lauro F. Cavazos	1988	Reagan, G. Bush
Lamar Alexander	1991	G. Bush
Richard W. Riley	1993	Clinton
Roderick Paige	2001	G. W. Bush
Margaret Spellings	2005	G. W. Bush

EDWARD

Edward is an ancient English name, derived from the Anglo-Saxon "Eadward," meaning "guardian of prosperity." During a period of one thousand years, eleven English kings have reigned (r.) under this name.

Edward I was a strong ruler who instituted administrative and legal reforms in England. He was also a great warrior, conquering Wales and temporarily dominating Scotland.

▶ EARLY KINGS OF ENGLAND

Edward the Elder (872?–924) (r. 899–924) was the son of the famous King Alfred the Great. Succeeding to his father's kingdom of Wessex (southern England) in 899, he successfully continued Alfred's counterattack against Viking invaders, launching a sustained and skillfully organized series of campaigns into Viking-held territory. By the time of his death he had reconquered all midland and eastern England, and was widely recognized as the most powerful ruler in Britain.

Edward the Martyr (963?–78) (r. 975–78), son of Edgar, first king of all England, succeeded his father while still a youth. Treacherously murdered three years later by retainers of his half-brother Aethelred "the Unready," he was later regarded as a saint and martyr.

Edward the Confessor (1004?–66) (r. 1042–66) was the next to the last Anglo-Saxon king of England. He was the son of Aethelred the Unready by his second wife, Emma of Normandy. Edward's ties to Normandy helped prepare the Anglo-Saxons for the Norman ways of life that were to be imposed on them after the Normans, led by William I, conquered England in 1066.

Edward's reign was troubled by threats from abroad and by opposition at home from the powerful nobleman Earl Godwin, who resented Edward's enthusiasm for Norman ways. That he weathered these storms proved him a determined and shrewd monarch, a fact that has been overshadowed by his reputation for great personal holiness. After his death, Godwin's son Harold briefly became king, only to be defeated by the Normans at the Battle of Hastings (1066) by William the Conqueror, Edward's chosen successor.

Popularly regarded as a saint in his own lifetime, Edward was officially canonized in 1161, and he became the special patron of English kings. His body is enshrined in the abbey he refounded at Westminster, which is still the coronation place of British monarchs.

▶ KINGS OF ENGLAND AFTER THE NORMAN CONQUEST (1066)

Edward I (1239–1307) (r. 1272–1307) was one of the most formidable of English medieval kings. Immensely strong and tall, he earned the nickname Longshanks (long legs). He was also known as the English Justinian because of his passion for legal reform.

Edward I, however, is chiefly famous as a soldier. His reputation was founded during his campaigns against the baronial rebels who threatened his father, Henry III. His greatest military achievement was the conquest of Wales (1277–84), which he secured by building an impressive series of new royal castles, including Caernarvon. His attempts to subdue Scotland gave him another nickname, Hammer of the Scots. Although initially successful, he was ultimately foiled by the tenacity of Scottish resistance under Robert I (the Bruce).

Increasingly stern and violent-tempered with age, Edward also had his softer side. His devotion to his wife, Eleanor of Castile (who bore him at least 15 children), is attested to by the magnificent Eleanor Crosses—twelve memorial crosses that mark the places where her body rested on its journey to Westminster Abbey for burial.

Edward's subjects came close to rebellion against the crippling taxation he imposed upon them to finance his wars. He left many problems unsolved when he died in 1307 while still campaigning resolutely against the Scots.

Edward II (1284–1327) (r. 1307–27) was the son of Edward I, whose fine physique he inherited. However, their characters could scarcely have been more different. He was born at Caernarvon Castle in Wales and in 1301 was made Prince of Wales, a title since held by most heirs to the English throne. His troubled reign was plagued by financial problems, famines and other natural calamities, and, most of all, baronial opposition. Edward's subjects disapproved of his unconventional enthusiasm for rustic crafts and sports and the attention he paid to his favorites at court. They also bitterly resented his failure in the Scottish wars, culminating in the Scottish invasions that followed his disastrous defeat at Bannockburn (1314). Discontent flared into open civil war in 1321. At first Edward held his own, but in 1326 he was defeated in a rebellion headed by his wife, Queen Isabella. Deposed (removed from the throne) and imprisoned, he was violently murdered a year later in Berkeley Castle, Gloucestershire.

Edward III (1312–77) (r.1327–77), the son of Edward II, was among the greatest of the English medieval warrior kings. He succeeded his murdered father, but his mother Queen Isabella and her lover Mortimer held all the power. In 1330, however, he threw off their control with a dramatic coup and seized personal power. He then set about restoring the shattered prestige of the English monarchy, beginning by launching a successful attack on Scotland (1333). His campaigns in France, which began the Hundred Years' War, proved still more triumphant. His armies won a series of victories at Crécy (1346), Calais (1347), and Poitiers (1356) so that by 1360, Edward controlled much of France. His successes were publicized by the tournaments and knightly displays he loved. In 1348 he founded the exclusive Order of the Garter to reward his captains. It still exists and is the oldest knightly order in Europe.

The later part of Edward's long reign was far less glorious. After 1369, English campaigns were inconclusive, financial crises pro-voked widespread discontent, and Edward himself was dominated by corrupt ministers and greedy favorites. His death in 1377 bequeathed to his grandson and successor, Richard II, a land threatened with turmoil.

Edward, the Black Prince (1330–76), the son of Edward III, was never king. Nevertheless, he was a knightly hero of the Hundred Years' War, winning several critical battles against the French. At 16 he fought at the Battle of Crécy (1346) and later commanded the victorious English forces at Poitiers (1356). His nickname, the Black Prince (not recorded until after his death), was apparently derived from the color of his tournament shield, which also bore the ostrich-plume badge since used by all princes of Wales. It still adorns his magnificent tomb in Canterbury Cathedral (Kent). The Black Prince died shortly before his father, whom his own young son succeeded as Richard II.

Edward IV (1442–83) (r. 1461–83), son of Richard, Duke of York, was the first Yorkist king of medieval England. At the height of the Wars of the Roses—a fight between the houses of York and Lancaster for the English throne—he seized the crown from the Lancastrian king Henry VI, and secured it by a great victory at Towton, near York. Edward was a handsome, charismatic figure, who was especially popular in the south of England. But his marriage to Elizabeth Woodville (1464), and the later rise of her numerous and greedy relatives, alienated his most powerful supporter, Earl Warwick "the Kingmaker" Allied with the Lancastrians and with Edward's disloyal brother the Duke of Clarence, Warwick eventually drove the king into exile in 1470, reestablishing Henry VI on the throne.

Five months later Edward returned to defeat both Warwick and the Lancastrian Queen Margaret in a brilliant whirlwind campaign (1471). Henry VI was then quietly murdered, and Edward's hold on power became more secure than ever. The second half of his reign (1471–83) brought welcome peace to England. However, Edward failed to reconcile the smouldering feud between his Woodville relatives and his brother Richard, Duke of Gloucester. He also neglected to make effective arrangements for the royal succession. Therefore, his sudden death at the age of 40 brought on crises that eventually led to the downfall of his house.

Edward III, who ruled England for fifty years, launched what became known as the Hundred Years' War (1337–1453). Edward's armies defeated the French at Crécy (1346), Calais (1347), and Poitiers (1356).

Edward V (1470–83?) (r. April–June 1483) was the tragically short-lived son of Edward IV. An intelligent boy, he technically succeeded his father in April 1483, when he was 12 years old. But in June, while journeying to London with his mother's Woodville relatives, he was seized by his uncle and "protector," Richard, Duke of Gloucester. Gloucester confined him in the Tower of London with his younger brother, declared him illegitimate, and deposed him. He then took the throne as Richard III. Neither of the so-called Princes in the Tower was ever publicly seen again. It was commonly believed at the time that Richard had them murdered.

Edward VI (1537–53) (r. 1547–53), the son of Henry VIII by his third wife, Jane Seymour, was his father's only male heir. A sickly, studious boy, he succeeded at the age of 10, but he never exercised personal power. Government during his reign was directed first (1547–50) by his uncle, Lord Protector Somerset, and later (1550–53) by the Duke of Northumberland.

With the approval of the boy-king, himself a devout Protestant, these ministers extended the religious Reformation begun by Henry VIII. Henry had claimed himself head of the English Church without effectively altering its Catholic beliefs. Under Edward its doctrines and practices became radically Protestant, centered on the Book of Common Prayer, which was published during his reign in English instead of Latin.

The enforcement of these religious changes, together with resentment of the government's economic policies, provoked several local uprisings, all ruthlessly suppressed. After Edward's death of tuberculosis, the Catholics reasserted themselves under his Catholic sister, Queen Mary I.

Edward VII (*left*) was related to so many European royal families, he was known as the "uncle of Europe." His grandson, Edward VIII (*right*), reigned less than one year. He gave up the throne and lived out his life as the Duke of Windsor.

▶ **KINGS OF ENGLAND, SCOTLAND, AND IRELAND**

Edward VII (1841–1910) (r. 1901–10) was the eldest son of Queen Victoria and her beloved Prince Albert. The strict upbringing they enforced on him backfired. Far from becoming the serious, moral prince they had hoped for, Edward reacted to his stern upbringing by turning into a determined pleasure-seeker. His relationship with his mother was therefore strained, and she rigidly excluded him from power. Many of his subjects disapproved of his socializing, gambling, and lady friends, though others followed him as a leader of fashion. He also had a passion for hunting on his Sandringham estate, and a stupendous appetite, which provided his unofficial nickname Tum-Tum. Yet he was genuinely pleasant and intelligent, and eventually became a popular monarch, who used his influence with related European royal families to maintain international peace.

Edward VIII (1894–1972) (r. 1936), the eldest son of George V, succeeded his father in January 1936 but was never crowned. Preferring to marry the twice-divorced Wallis Warfield Simpson (who by British law could never become queen), he abdicated (gave up the throne) in favor of his brother George VI (December 1936). Thereafter, he and his wife, titled the Duke and Duchess of Windsor, lived abroad.

Dr. Charles Kightly
Contributor, *The Illustrated Dictionary of British History*

See also ENGLAND, HISTORY OF.

Young King Edward VI, the only son of Henry VIII, strongly supported Protestant reforms in the Church of England. The English-language Book of Common Prayer was first published during his short reign.

Eels are fishes that have long, snakelike bodies and thick, slimy skin. Most eels do not have scales. The freshwater eel (*left*) travels thousands of miles to the middle of the Atlantic Ocean to reproduce. The adults die in the ocean, never returning to their homes in fresh water. Moray eels (*below*) can grow as long as 10 feet (3.1 meters). They have sharp teeth that can inflict serious wounds.

EELS

Eels are fishes with long, snakelike bodies and tapering or rounded tails. They have a blunt head with a small, rounded or slitlike gill opening. Like other fishes, they have backbones, live in water, and breathe through gills.

Eels have a long fin on the back (dorsal fin) and a long fin on the underside of the body behind the anus (anal fin). These fins are joined to a small tail fin, providing the eel with a continuous fin around its tail. Some eels also have fins on the sides of the body near the head (pectoral fins). The fins are supported by soft, flexible rays.

Most eels do not have scales. All shallow-water eels have a thick, tough slimy skin. These eels are slimy to the touch because of a heavy coating of protective mucus secreted (given off) by the skin. This covering helps protect the eel from injury as it moves through small crevices (cracks) in rocky areas and coral reefs or buries itself in sand or mud.

Most eels are smaller than 3 feet (1 meter) in length. Moray eels sometimes grow as long as 10 feet (3.1 meters). Many are a drab yellowish green or dark brown color, but snake and worm eels and some morays may be bright yellow or red with bold patterns of blotches, spots, bars, or white rings.

Eels have a particularly strong sense of smell. They locate prey, such as other fishes, insects, and worms, more by smell than by sight.

Eels swim with a motion similar to the motion of a snake on land. They flex the entire

body in a series of waves. The waves begin near the head and pass from side to side along the body toward the tail. This swimming motion is called the anguilliform mode of swimming and is used by all long, flexible fishes.

Most eels live in the ocean. They are found mostly in the coastal waters of warm seas. Only one family of eels lives in fresh water. But even they are hatched in the ocean and return to it when they are ready to spawn.

An eel goes through a unique early stage of development. When it hatches from an egg, it looks nothing like a small eel. Instead, it is a transparent ribbonlike creature called a **leptocephalus**, which means "thin head." After a year or more in this form, it changes into the form of an eel.

KINDS OF EELS

Eels are difficult to study, yet ichthyologists (scientists who study fishes) have described more than 600 species. Familiar types include freshwater eels, moray eels, congrid eels, and snake and worm eels.

Freshwater eels live in lakes and ponds and shallow coastal areas. These muscular-bodied eels are valuable food fishes. Morays have a thick body and daggerlike teeth. Congrids are like morays except that they usually have pectoral fins and stout, cone-shaped teeth. Most are nighttime predators that feed on a variety of marine animals. Morays and congrid eels are found in warm seas around the world.

There are more than 278 species of snake and worm eels. They are slender and round-bodied and live in warm, shallow water. They are difficult to study because they are active mostly at night and burrow tail-first into soft, muddy bottoms if disturbed.

LIFE CYCLE

The life cycle of the freshwater eels of Europe and North America is one of the most interesting of all fishes.

Adult freshwater eels are found in harbors, rivers, lakes, small brooks, and even isolated ponds. After ten years or more, the eels are ready to reproduce. Late one summer they begin to swim downstream toward the ocean.

Freshwater eels change form several times after they hatch from eggs. During one stage they are transparent creatures called elvers, or glass eels.

To reach their spawning grounds in the Sargasso Sea (a region with large patches of floating seaweed in the middle of the Atlantic Ocean), they may have to swim about 3,500 miles (5,600 kilometers).

Before the migration, the eels undergo amazing changes. They lose their dark color and become silvery. Their skin becomes thicker and fatter, and their eyes get huge. Their reproductive organs begin to mature.

As soon as the journey begins, the eels stop feeding. Their drive to reach the ocean is so strong that individuals living in isolated ponds may wriggle across stretches of meadow during the night when the grass is wet with dew.

We do not know just how the eels find their way through the Atlantic Ocean to the Sargasso Sea, but they gather there from both North America and Europe. When they arrive, the females lay their eggs and the males fertilize the eggs. Then the adult eels die.

In the spring, the larvae, or leptocephali (plural of leptocephalus), hatch from the eggs. They have long, needlelike teeth that help them feed on tiny organisms. The larvae drift and feed in the upper layers of the ocean for a year or more. During this time, they are carried northward by the Gulf Stream.

When the larvae reach the shallow waters near the continental coasts, they metamorphose (change) into **elvers**. An elver, sometimes called a glass eel, is a round, transparent creature about 2½ inches (6 centimeters) long.

Elvers swarm around the mouths of rivers and tend to swim into the currents. Some continue to swim upstream until they have reached smaller bodies of fresh water. Once they reach their new homes, the elvers feed and grow into adult eels. Then after ten years or more, it is time for them to set off on their own breeding migration to the Sargasso Sea.

EELS AND HUMANS

Eels are important food fishes. They are especially popular in Europe and Japan. Eels are most often caught with eel traps, nets, baited hooks, or eel pots.

Some eels, especially morays, snake eels, and congrids, can be dangerous to swimmers or divers. These species have powerful jaws and strong teeth and can inflict serious wounds if mishandled or attacked.

THOMAS A. MUNROE
Smithsonian Research Associate

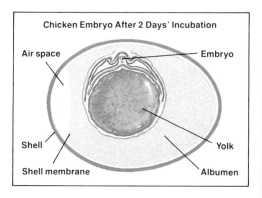

Chicken Embryo After 2 Days' Incubation

Air space — Embryo

Shell

Shell membrane — Yolk

Albumen

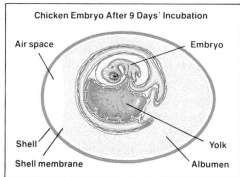

Chicken Embryo After 9 Days' Incubation

Air space — Embryo

Shell

Shell membrane — Yolk

Albumen

In a bird's egg, like the chicken egg in the diagrams, an embryo develops on the surface of the yolk. The photograph shows a moorhen chick struggling free of its eggshell.

EGGS AND EMBRYOS

When most people think of eggs, they picture the eggs of chickens or other birds. But bird eggs are just one type of egg. Most animals produce eggs of one sort or another.

This is because most animals reproduce sexually—that is, through the joining of male and female reproductive cells. (Many plants also reproduce this way. See PLANTS in Volume P.) An egg, or **ovum** (plural: ova), is a female reproductive cell, formed in the female's body. An egg develops into a new animal after it is fertilized by a male reproductive cell, or sperm. While it is developing, the new animal is called an embryo.

Egg production is amazing because every kind of animal has its own story. Some stories are familiar; others are very strange. The eggs of some animals are huge—the largest, the ostrich egg, may weigh 3 pounds (1.4 kilograms). Other eggs are smaller than the period at the end of this sentence. In each case, however, an animal's eggs and the way it produces them are perfectly suited to its way of life.

No matter how an animal produces its eggs, it must provide ways of nourishing and protecting the developing embryo. A chicken egg contains a ball of yellow yolk that is food for the embryo. The embryo begins as a cluster of cells on the surface of the yolk. (You can see the embryo in a fertilized egg as a tiny white spot on the yolk.) The shell and the **albumen** (egg white) provide protection. But only some kinds of eggs have shells, whites, and large yolks. Many eggs provide protection and nourishment in other ways.

▶EGG LAYING

Many animals that live in water, including corals and many fishes, release their eggs into the water before or soon after fertilization. The tiny eggs are covered with a layer of clear, jelly-like material that protects them and makes them hard to see as they drift along. Some fishes attach their eggs to stones or plants. Salmon and trout, for example, lay their eggs in the gravel of streambeds.

Salamanders wrap their eggs in water plants, while many insects lay their eggs on

leaves. Turtles, lizards, and snakes lay large eggs that look like birds' eggs but have soft, leathery shells that protect the developing embryo. In all these cases the eggs are left to develop on their own. Some kinds of animals carry their eggs with them. The male sea horse, for example, carries the eggs in a pouch, and some frogs and fishes carry eggs in their mouths.

Some animals give their eggs extra protection. Two groups of animals that do so are birds and mammals. Birds lay their eggs in nests and then sit on the nest to **incubate** the eggs (keep them warm until they hatch). Mammal embryos develop inside the mother's body. There they are nourished and protected until they are born as babies. This is called **live birth**. (A few insects, snakes, and fishes also bear live young.)

The platypus and the echidna of Australia are the only mammals that do not give birth to live young. The platypus lays its eggs in an underground burrow and incubates them there. The echidna carries its single egg in a pouch on its underside until the egg hatches.

▶SIZE AND NUMBERS OF EGGS

If a group of animals is to live successfully in a certain region, the adults must produce enough young animals to balance the number of animals that die. However, for most animals the great majority of eggs never hatch, and many young die before they are fully grown. This is particularly true of animals that shed their eggs into the water or lay them on land and leave them to develop on their own.

Therefore, animals that abandon their eggs lay huge numbers of eggs. This makes up for the ones eaten by other animals or for those that die when conditions become too extreme for the eggs to survive.

A single clam or oyster, for example, can produce up to several million eggs at one time. Each egg is about the size of a pinprick. The cod lays a million eggs in one spawning (egg-laying) season. Such large numbers ensure that at least some eggs will develop and grow into adults.

For some ocean animals, tiny eggs produced by the thousands have another purpose. Animals such as sea anemones, corals, and barnacles cannot move about, but their eggs are carried by currents to new areas, much as wind carries the seeds of plants.

The small eggs of some animals do not have enough yolk for the embryo to complete its development. The egg hatches as a **larva** (plural: larvae). A larva is generally quite different from the adult. For example, frog eggs, which are laid in fresh water, hatch into tadpoles that swim with wriggling tails and breathe with gills, like fishes. Tadpoles feed at first on plants and then on small water animals. This gives them the nourishment to grow legs and turn into adult frogs. Caterpillars are another sort of larva. They turn into adult butterflies and moths. (You can read more about the change from larva to adult in the article META-MORPHOSIS in Volume M.)

The large eggs laid by snakes and birds contain more yolk for growth, so the embryo can stay inside the egg longer and develop further.

An animal's eggs develop in a way that suits its way of life. *Facing page:* A frog's eggs (*left*) are laid in water and protected by masses of sticky jelly. A beehive (*right*) may contain thousands of eggs. They hatch into larvae, which stay in the hive until they develop into adults. *This page:* A red rat snake (*left*) lays eggs in a sheltered spot. Most snakes leave their eggs, but some stay with them. The young of mammals such as the cat (*below*) develop from fertilized eggs in the mother's body and are protected until birth.

The young animal is more like an adult when it hatches.

An animal can use only a certain amount of material and energy for making eggs. It can lay either a few large eggs or many small eggs. The general rule in the animal kingdom is that small eggs are produced in large numbers, while large eggs are few in number but well protected.

This rule does not hold true for mammals. Mammals produce a few very small eggs. But they do not need large yolks, whites, or shells because the mother provides nourishment and protection while the embryo develops inside her body.

▶ **HOW AN EGG BECOMES AN EMBRYO**

An embryo begins to develop as soon as the egg is fertilized. (In rare cases, the egg develops without fertilization. This event is called **parthenogenesis** and occurs in some insects, such as aphids and honeybees.) Every fertilized egg, large or small, is a single cell. Even an ostrich egg contains only a single cell, although the part of the egg that will develop into an embryo is a tiny fraction of the whole. Within the cell's nucleus, or center, is a set of chemical codes (called **genes**) that carry instructions for turning the egg into a living animal of the same type as its parents.

To become an embryo, the fertilized egg cell, or **zygote**, must become many cells. It does this by dividing. The single cell divides into two smaller cells by the process of **mitosis**. (You can read more about this in the article CELLS in Volume C.) Each of the two new

cells divides into two more cells, making four cells. The four new cells each divide, making eight cells, and so on, until there is a mass of cells that have formed a hollow ball, something like a tennis ball. The ball of cells is called a **blastula**. The dividing process thus far is known as **cleavage**.

Identical twins are the result of a single zygote splitting into two zygotes—and each half

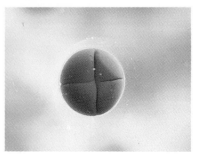

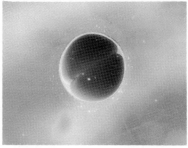

1. The egg cell is fertilized.

2. The cell divides, forming two cells.

3. The two cells divide, forming four cells.

In its early stages, cell division in the eggs of most animals follows the same basic pattern. First the egg is fertilized by a sperm cell (*above*). The cell then divides to form two cells. Each cell continues to divide, until the embryo has the form of a hollow ball. At this point it is ready to start taking shape as a tiny animal of the same kind as its parents.

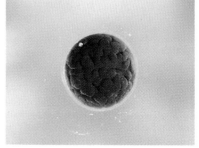

4. Division continues, forming eight and then sixteen cells.

5. The embryo reaches the hollow ball (blastula) stage.

developing into a complete animal. In humans and other animals this is an unusual event, but some animals regularly produce many identical embyros. The nine-banded armadillo gives birth to identical quadruplets (four offspring) from a single zygote. Some insects produce as many as 1,000 larvae from a single egg.

The next stage is for the blastula to fold and tuck itself in to make a two-layered or three-layered structure called a **gastrula**. The embryo is now ready to start taking shape as a tiny animal. This takes place through further cell division. As the number of cells increases, the cells also **differentiate**, or change into different types, such as muscle cells, liver cells, and bone cells. The body structures, such as bones, muscles, blood vessels, and skin, are formed as cells of various types come together. New cells are told what to become by chemical messages from surrounding cells. The messages are controlled by the embryo's genes.

As quickly as two days after fertilization, the embryo inside a chicken's egg has a heart that is pumping blood. As the embryo devel-

ops, it becomes more like the complete living animal. The limbs and internal organs become more fully formed and ready to work, even though growth continues after the animal is born. Only the animal's reproductive organs are not developed. These mature as the animal grows into adulthood.

The stages of an embryo's development are very similar in all animals, from a sea urchin to a giant whale. The more closely related the animals are, the more similar is the process. Only in the later stages of embryo development is it possible to distinguish the embryos of lizards, birds, and mammals.

The process of embryo development came into being many millions of years ago and has changed very little since then. Scientists have even found the fossilized eggs of long-extinct dinosaurs. But embryologists, scientists who study embryos, are only beginning to understand how this very complex and amazing process works.

ROBERT BURTON
Author, *Eggs: Nature's Perfect Package*

See also REPRODUCTION.

EGYPT

Egypt is a modern nation in an ancient land. The valley of the Nile, the river that runs like a ribbon through the length of the country, was the birthplace of one of the world's earliest civilizations. Reminders of Egypt's glorious past dot the landscape. The Great Pyramid at Giza was one of the wonders of the ancient world and is the only one that has survived. The giant statue known as the Sphinx —part human and part beast—has mystified and fascinated travelers for centuries. In ancient tombs, brilliantly colored wall paintings show the life of the Egyptian people as it was some 4,000 years ago.

Modern Egypt is the world's most populous Arab country and the second most populous nation in Africa, after Nigeria. Located at the northeastern corner of Africa, where Africa and Asia meet, it links the Muslim countries of southwest Asia with those of North Africa.

The Nile River (*below*) was the cradle of a great civilization 5,000 years ago. The Pharaoh (king) Tutankhamen (*left*) came to power more than 3,000 years ago. Today, the Nile is at the center of modern Egypt, providing water for crops and serving as a highway for traders and travelers.

▶ THE PEOPLE

The ancient Greek historian Herodotus called Egypt "the gift of the Nile." Almost all of Egypt's people live on less than 4 percent of the land, on the fertile soil that borders the Nile River. Most of the rest of Egypt is desert, inhabited largely by nomadic Bedouin. About half the people live in the countryside. The rest live in cities, which are rapidly growing in population.

About half of Egypt's people live in the many small villages near the Nile River. The camel at left powers a pump that brings up water to irrigate nearby fields.

Language. Arabic is the official language of Egypt. English and French are also spoken, mainly among the more highly educated.

Religion. Egyptians are predominantly Muslims. However, nearly 7 percent of the people belong to the Coptic church, an ancient Christian church that existed in Egypt before the arrival of the Muslims.

Education. All levels of public education in Egypt are free. Five years of primary and three years of secondary school are compulsory for all children. Three additional years of secondary school are needed for college.

Al-Azhar University in Cairo, established in the 900's, is considered by many people to be the oldest university in the world. Founded as a center for teaching Arabic literature and Islamic law and theology, it now includes technical subjects along with its traditional course of study.

Rural Life. The country people, or fellahin, live in thousands of small villages, which lie along the Nile River or amid a network of irrigation canals. The fellahin farm the land much as their ancestors did. Each village has a mosque (a Muslim house of worship), a few shops, and a religious school. Homes are simple, usually consisting of a one-story house of two rooms. A mud-brick fireplace is used for cooking and to supply heat when needed.

Both men and women work in the fields. The children tend the donkey or water buffalo and herd sheep or goats if the family is prosperous enough to own them. The staple foods are bread made from corn flour and a dish made of beans, called *ful*. Meat is usually reserved for special holidays.

Urban Life. Egyptian city-dwellers live in apartment houses, in private homes in suburbs, or in crowded tenement districts. The growth of factories near the cities has attracted a large number of unskilled laborers from the farms, who sometimes wear the tradition-

FACTS and figures

ARAB REPUBLIC OF EGYPT is the official name of the country.

LOCATION: Northeastern Africa (and Sinai Peninsula of southwest Asia).

AREA: 386,662 sq mi (1,001,449 km²).

POPULATION: 68,300,000 (estimate).

CAPITAL AND LARGEST CITY: Cairo.

MAJOR LANGUAGE: Arabic (official).

MAJOR RELIGIOUS GROUP: Muslim.

GOVERNMENT: Republic. **Head of state**—president. **Head of government**—prime minister. **Legislature**—People's Assembly.

CHIEF PRODUCTS: Agricultural—cotton, rice, wheat, corn, sugarcane, oranges, tomatoes, potatoes. **Manufactured**—Textiles, processed foods, steel products, fertilizers, refined petroleum and other petroleum products, cement, glass, consumer goods. **Mineral**—petroleum, natural gas, iron ore, salt, phosphates, coal.

MONETARY UNIT: Egyptian pound (1 pound = 100 piasters).

al dress of the fellahin. This consists of an ankle-length cotton robe, called a *gallabiyea*, and a skullcap or turban. Many city people, however, prefer to wear European-style clothing.

Adult members of city families return home from work for the main meal of the day, which is served at about two o'clock in the afternoon. The midday menu may include rice, vegetables, and lamb, broiled pigeons, fish, or poultry. Fruit is the most popular dessert. The meal usually ends with a tiny cup of strong, black Turkish coffee.

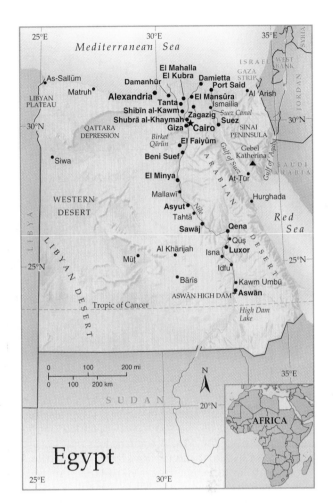

Egypt's cities are growing rapidly, as people from villages arrive to find jobs in factories. Cairo (*above* and *right*) is Egypt's capital, its largest city, and its economic and cultural center. Founded by Arab conquerors in the A.D. 900's, it is the largest city in Africa.

Egypt's growing economy includes the production of petroleum (*above*). Agriculture, once the most important sector of the economy, now employs nearly 30 percent of the workforce. Cotton (*left*) is the main commercial crop.

▶ THE LAND

Egypt is bordered by Libya on the west and by Sudan on the south. It is bounded on the north by the Mediterranean Sea and on the east by Israel and the Red Sea.

Land Regions. Egypt consists of four geographical regions: the Nile River valley and its delta (the fan-shaped plain at its mouth); the Libyan, or Western, Desert in the west and south; the Arabian, or Eastern, Desert in the east; and the Sinai Peninsula.

Originating in the heart of Africa, the Nile flows northward through Egypt for a distance of about 930 miles (1,500 kilometers), before emptying into the Mediterranean Sea. The Sinai Peninsula lies in southwest Asia and is the site of Egypt's highest mountain, Gebel Katherina (Mount Catherine), which rises to a height of 8,651 feet (2,737 meters). For more information, see the article NILE RIVER in Volume N.

The Suez Canal. Egypt's second most important waterway is the Suez Canal, which links the Mediterranean Sea with the Gulf of Suez, an arm of the Red Sea. Because it shortens ship travel time between Europe and Asia, the canal is one of the world's chief commercial waterways. The canal and the Isthmus of Suez are the traditional boundary between Africa and Asia. See the article SUEZ CANAL in Volume S.

Climate. Egypt has a generally warm, dry climate. Summers are hot. In the south, daytime temperatures may reach 110°F (43°C), although nights are cool. Winters are usually mild. Rainfall is limited and is heaviest on the Mediterranean coast.

▶ THE ECONOMY

Agriculture. Egypt's Nile Valley is one of the most intensively cultivated and productive farming regions in the world. Agriculture has declined in importance in recent years, but it still employs nearly 30 percent of the workforce. Cotton is the major export crop. Egypt is also an important producer of rice, wheat, corn, sugarcane, oranges, tomatoes, potatoes, and other vegetables.

Historically, Egyptian farmers depended on the yearly flooding of the Nile Valley to provide water for their crops. The Aswān High Dam and its reservoir, High Dam Lake (formerly Lake Nasser), now provide a more regular source of water for irrigation. The dam is also an important source of hydroelectric power.

Industry. Egypt has a growing industrial economy. The chief manufactured products include textiles, refined petroleum, steel products, cement, glass, fertilizers, processed foods, and a variety of consumer goods.

Mining is of increasing importance. Petroleum is the main export, along with cotton and textiles, although Egypt has smaller deposits of petroleum than some other Middle Eastern nations. Natural gas, salt, phosphates, iron ore, and coal are also produced.

Egypt's many ancient monuments have made tourism a traditional industry. Tolls for use of the Suez Canal and money sent home by Egyptians working abroad are additional sources of income.

▶CITIES

Cairo is Egypt's capital and largest city and the largest city in Africa. Situated on both banks of the Nile, it is Egypt's commercial and cultural center as well as the seat of government. See the separate article on Cairo in Volume C.

Alexandria, Egypt's second largest city, is a busy port on the Mediterranean Sea. Founded by Alexander the Great in the 4th century B.C., it was long a cultural center of the Mediterranean region. It was famed in ancient times for its Pharos, or lighthouse, and for its great library.

Giza, a suburb of Cairo, is the site of the University of Cairo. Nearby are the Great Pyramid of Khufu (Cheops) and the statue of the Sphinx. Port Said, situated at the northern (Mediterranean) end of the Suez Canal, is one of Egypt's principal ports. The ancient city of Luxor is one of the country's major tourist attractions. Its historical sites include the Temple of Luxor, the Temple of Karnak, and the Valley of the Kings.

For more information on the Pharos and the Great Pyramid, see the article WONDERS OF THE WORLD in Volume W-X-Y-Z.

▶GOVERNMENT

Egypt is a republic headed by a president, who serves a term of six years. The president appoints one or more vice presidents, the prime minister, and cabinet members. The legislature is the People's Assembly, elected for five years unless dissolved sooner by the president. The People's Assembly nominates the president, who then must be confirmed by popular vote. The National Shura Council, formed in 1980, serves as an advisory body.

▶HISTORY

Ancient Egypt. Egypt has one of the longest histories of any nation in the world. The valley of the Nile River was one of the birthplaces of civilization. Egypt's written history alone goes back almost 5,000 years, to the very dawn of civilization.

Although there is disagreement about early Egyptian dates, it is thought that Egypt came into being sometime around 3200 B.C., when a king named Menes (also called Narmer) united the cities of northern and southern Egypt under one government. Some of the most impressive structures known, including the great pyramids (tombs for the early Egyptian kings) and the Sphinx at Giza, were built before 2200 B.C. The largest of the pyramids was constructed by King Khufu, or Cheops, perhaps about 2600 B.C.

Around 1675 B.C. the Hyksos, an eastern people about whom very little is known, invaded Egypt and conquered the country, bringing with them the first horses and chariots ever seen in Egypt. By about 1500 B.C. the Egyptians had driven the invaders out.

The pharaoh Ramses II (reigned about 1292–1225 B.C.) built a tomb for his favorite queen, Nofretari. Its walls are decorated with figures of Egyptian gods. The falcon-headed figure with a solar disk (*center*) is Ra-Harakht, a form of the sun god Ra.

Around 1375 B.C., Amenhotep IV (later Akhenaten) became king of Egypt. He abolished the worship of the many ancient Egyptian gods and introduced worship of only one god. But after Akhenaten's death the believers in the old gods gained power again, and Akhenaten's reforms were disregarded.

Ramses II (1292–1225 B.C.) is best known for his monuments and temples at Karnak and for the temple he carved out of the cliffs on the bank of the Nile at Abu Simbel.

Decline of Egyptian Power. Around 1000 B.C., Egyptian power declined. Between this time and 331 B.C., Egypt was ruled in turn by the Libyans, Nubians, Assyrians, and Persians. In 331 B.C., Egypt was conquered by Alexander the Great. On Alexander's death one of his generals became ruler of Egypt, as Ptolemy I. The dynasty (ruling family) of the Ptolemies ended in 30 B.C., when Cleopatra, the last of the line, took her own life. Egypt then became a Roman province.

For the next 670 years Egypt has a succession of rulers appointed by Roman and Byzantine emperors. It also was ruled briefly by the Persians. Egypt became largely Christian during this period. For more information see EGYPT, ANCIENT in this volume.

The Arab Conquest: Muslim Egypt. In 640, Muslims (members of the newly formed religion of Islam) swept westward from the Arabian Peninsula and conquered Egypt. Muslims founded the city of Cairo in 969 and made it their capital. One of the most famous of the rulers of Egypt in this era was Saladin, who fought the Christian Crusaders at the end of the 12th century. Egypt has remained a Muslim country to the present day.

Mameluk and Turkish Rule. Egypt was ruled by the Mameluks from 1250 until 1517, when it came under the domination of the Ottoman Turks. In 1798 the French general Napoleon Bonaparte invaded Egypt. His expedition aroused European interest in Egypt and led to the discovery of the Rosetta stone, which provided a long-sought key to the ancient Egyptian's hieroglyphic writing. (For more information, see HIEROGLYPHIC WRITING SYSTEMS in Volume H.)

Mehemet Ali. Napoleon's troops were forced to withdraw from Egypt in 1801 by British and Turkish forces. In 1805, Mehemet Ali was made viceroy, or royal governor, of Egypt by the Ottoman sultan. Seizing power for himself, Mehemet Ali ruled until 1848, undertaking a remarkable program of reforms, modernization, and military conquest.

British Influence. Egypt's prosperity declined under Mehemet Ali's hereditary successors, who borrowed large sums of money from the British and French. In 1875 the British Government bought Egypt's shares in the Suez Canal, which had been built by the French and opened in 1869. To collect their debts, a British-French commission was established to oversee Egyptian fi-

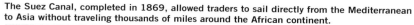

The Suez Canal, completed in 1869, allowed traders to sail directly from the Mediterranean to Asia without traveling thousands of miles around the African continent.

nances. A nationalist revolt in 1881–82 was put down by British troops, who occupied the country. In 1914, Egypt was officially declared a British protectorate.

Britain granted Egypt independence in 1922. But British interests remained uppermost, and during World War II (1939–45) Egypt and the Suez Canal were vital links in Britain's empire.

The 1952 Revolution: Nasser. After the war, discontent grew. Egyptians resented Britain's continued control of the Suez Canal. The government of King Farouk, who had come to the throne in 1936, was corrupt and inefficient. The military blamed the government for losing a 1948–49 war with the new nation of Israel. In 1952 a group of army officers began a revolt that overthrew the king, and, in 1953, established a republic. A leader of the revolt, Colonel Gamal Abdel Nasser, became Egypt's president in 1956.

Suez Crisis. In 1956, Nasser nationalized (took control of) the Suez Canal. When Israel was denied use of the canal, its forces attacked and occupied most of Egypt's Sinai Peninsula and the Gaza Strip. At the same time, British and French troops landed in the canal area. After the United Nations intervened, the three nations withdrew.

Attempt at Arab Unity. In 1958, Egypt and Syria formed the United Arab Republic. But Syria withdrew in 1961 because of political differences. Egypt changed its name to the Arab Republic of Egypt in 1971.

The 1967 War. The removal of United Nations forces in the Sinai at Egypt's request and Egypt's closing of the Gulf of Aqaba to Israeli ships led to war with Israel in 1967. Israel again invaded the Sinai, reaching the Suez Canal itself, and retook the Gaza Strip.

Sadat: War and Peace. In 1970, Nasser died and was succeeded as president by Anwar el-Sadat. Determined to regain the lost Sinai, Sadat, in 1973, launched an attack on Israeli positions on the east bank of the canal. Following a cease-fire, United Nations forces were again stationed in the area. Israel withdrew from the canal, which was reopened to shipping in 1975. Israel was allowed use of the canal for nonmilitary cargoes.

In 1977, Sadat visited Israel to discuss the question of peace in the region. His historic journey led to a peace treaty between Egypt and Israel, in which Israel agreed to a gradual

Gamal Abdel Nasser led a revolution that overthrew King Farouk in 1952 and established a republic. He served as president of Egypt until his death in 1970.

withdrawal of its forces from the Sinai Peninsula. A formal treaty was signed in 1979.

Mubarak as President. In 1981, Sadat was assassinated by opponents of his peace policies. His successor as president, Hosni Mubarak, supported the peace treaty. The last Israeli forces withdrew from the Sinai in 1982, and the area was returned to Egypt.

Mubarak was continually re-elected. As president, he restored Egypt to its position as one of the leaders of the Arab world. Egypt was formally welcomed back into the Arab League in 1989, ten years after it had been suspended for signing the peace treaty with Israel. During the Persian Gulf War (1990–91), Egypt provided one of the largest forces to the U.S.-led military coalition against Iraq. After the September 11, 2001, terrorist attacks on the United States, Mubarak worked to restart the stalled peace talks between Israel and the Palestinian Arabs. A staunch ally of the United States, he also cracked down on Muslim fundamentalists who opposed his government.

In 2005, the People's Assembly amended Egypt's constitution to allow multiple candidates to run for president in the fall. Nevertheless, Mubarak was re-elected to a fifth term by an overwhelming margin.

RUTH WARREN
Author, *First Book of the Arab World*

Reviewed by MONA N. MIKHAIL
Hagop Kevorkian Center for Near Eastern Studies
New York University

See also EGYPTIAN ART AND ARCHITECTURE; NASSER, GAMAL ABDEL; SADAT, ANWAR EL-; SUEZ CANAL.

The three monumental pyramids at Giza, built as tombs for the early pharaohs, are among the most famous symbols of ancient Egypt.

EGYPT, ANCIENT

One of the greatest civilizations of the ancient world thrived in ancient Egypt from about 3200 to 30 B.C. At the height of its power, ancient Egypt extended its influence along the banks of Africa's Nile River for about 1,000 miles (1,600 kilometers), reaching south to the ancient region of Nubia (present-day northern Sudan), east into the Sinai Peninsula, and north into present-day Israel and Syria.

▶ **LIFE IN ANCIENT EGYPT**

At the top of ancient Egyptian society was the king, or pharaoh, who was considered a god. Beneath him were the priests, who served in the temples, and the scribes, educated Egyptians who kept the accounts of the country's finances. Next were the craftsmen, who built temples, decorated tombs, and carved statues of the gods. At the bottom were the vast majority of the people, most of whom made their livings as farmers.

Housing. The basic Egyptian house for all but the very poor consisted of a high-walled rectangular enclosure with a door facing north, to take advantage of the prevailing breeze. Inside, a pool irrigated trees and shrubs that provided shade, and guests could be entertained on a roofed porch. In the rear were the rooms where the owner and his family lived.

Food. The diet of most ancient Egyptians consisted of fruits and vegetables, such as figs, grapes, onions, and beans; fish; and bread. Ducks, geese, and pigeons were also plentiful, but only the upper classes ate meat regularly because it was very expensive. Many spices, such as cumin, thyme, dill, and sage, were used to add flavor to the food. Beer, which may have been invented by the Egyptians, was a favorite beverage.

Language. The ancient Egyptians recorded their language with a hieroglyphic writing system. Egyptian hieroglyphs were pictures that represented either a concept (an ideogram) or a sound (a phonogram). For more information, see the article HIEROGLYPHIC WRITING SYSTEMS in Volume H.

Recreation. Favorite recreational pastimes included sailing and fishing on the Nile; hunting ducks in the marshes; and riding chariots to chase down rabbits and gazelles in

Egyptian mummies were often encased in ornate coffins. The ancient Egyptians were experts at mummification—the preservation of a body after death.

the desert. Hunting tools included bows and arrows, boomerang-like sticks, and harpoons. The Egyptians also loved banquets, where entertainment was provided by women musicians playing harps, lyres, and flutes.

Education. Most education centered on reading and writing, but very few ancient Egyptians could do either. Only the brightest children were selected to go to school so they could become scribes and obtain good jobs in the government. Priests were selected from among the best scribes and were sent to the House of Life, a kind of college where priests were trained.

Religion. The Egyptians were polytheists, meaning they believed in many gods, and this was central to their daily lives. Because no scientific principles were known that explained natural occurrences, they believed that almost everything had a supernatural cause. For instance, the Egyptians believed that each night the sun god, Re, made a dangerous journey past enemies who tried to prevent his reappearance in the morning.

The Egyptians believed in resurrection— that a person would rise again in the afterlife—so they mummified their dead. They treated, or embalmed, the bodies to preserve them and then wrapped them in linen strips. Osiris, the god of the dead, was depicted as a mummified man. For more information, see the article Mummies in Volume M.

Other Egyptian gods were depicted as animals. Horus, the god of the sky and protector of the pharaoh, was a falcon; Hathor, the goddess of motherhood, was shown as a woman

Ancient Egypt About 1450 B.C.

with the head of a cow whose horns encircled the sun; and Anubis, the god of embalming, was represented as a jackal.

Worshiping the gods was the job of the priests, and the temples were generally off limits to everyone else. Inside each temple, the priests tended to a statue of that temple's god. The statue was clothed, perfumed, and offered food. The average Egyptian saw the statue only during major festivals.

Economy. The economy of Egypt depended on the Nile River and was based on a barter system. The river overflowed its banks each year, depositing rich, black topsoil on the land. The fertile soil enabled farmers to grow an abundance of crops—more than enough to feed themselves. The surplus was vital for trade. For instance, if a farmer needed a bronze plow blade, he could trade grain or vegetables for it.

Farmers paid their income tax with grain, and the government then used the grain to pay the priests. The surplus food also enabled Egypt to sustain the first professional army in

The ancient Egyptians believed in many gods. This tomb painting shows the pharaoh Ramses III being blessed by Isis, the goddess of magic.

Agriculture in ancient Egypt depended on the rich soil surrounding the Nile River. The abundant crops grown were vital to the country's economy.

history, and that is why the country was able to control the Middle East for so long.

Government. The pharaoh was the supreme ruler of ancient Egypt, and he governed for life. He led the army in battle and ensured that divine order prevailed throughout the kingdom. Viziers, or prime ministers, were responsible for collecting taxes, overseeing the priesthood, presiding in the courts, and other administrative duties. The viziers appointed hundreds of other officials, creating the largest governmental bureaucracy in the ancient world.

Art and Architecture. Perhaps the greatest achievement of the ancient Egyptians was their art and architecture. Although the craftsmen did not view their creations as art, they produced some of the greatest masterpieces of sculpture, painting, and architecture the world has ever seen.

All Egyptian art and architecture had a function. Statues were produced for temples, paintings were done on tomb walls to ensure that the deceased would have a pleasant afterlife, and amulets were worn for protection. The Great Sphinx (a mythological creature with the body of a lion and the head of a human) at Giza is one of the largest sculptures ever made. It was carved during the 4th dynasty (2614–2502 B.C.) out of limestone.

The Egyptians were the first people to build in stone, and the ultimate examples of their skill are the monumental pyramids and temples that still exist along the Nile. The pyramids, including the Step Pyramid at Saqqara (the first stone building in history), the Bent Pyramid at Dahshûr (the angle of its sides were altered during its construction), and the three giant pyramids at Giza, were built as tombs for early pharaohs. Temples, such as Ramses II's at Abu-Simbel, were built to honor royalty and the gods. For more information, see EGYPTIAN ART AND ARCHITECTURE in this volume and PYRAMIDS in Volume P.

MAJOR GODS OF ANCIENT EGYPT

Amun: The king of the gods. He was depicted as a man wearing a crown of ostrich feathers.

Anubis: The god of embalming. He was depicted as a jackal or as a man with a jackal's head.

Aten: A sun god. He was represented by the image of a solar disk.

Bastet: The goddess of the east and of fire. She was depicted as a cat or as a woman with a cat's head.

Hathor: The goddess of motherhood. She was depicted as a cow or as a woman with a crown of two horns that encircled the sun.

Horus: The god of the sky and protector of the pharaoh. He was depicted as a falcon or as a man with a falcon's head.

Isis: The goddess of magic. She was depicted as a woman with a crown of two horns, between which was the sun.

Anubis, the god of embalming, was depicted as a jackal or a man with a jackal's head. In this painting, Anubis prepares a mummy for the afterlife.

Osiris: The king of the underworld and protector of the dead. He was depicted as a man wrapped as a mummy.

Re: Another sun god. He was depicted as the sun or as a falcon wearing a headdress of the sun.

Thoth: The god of writing and knowledge. He was depicted as a baboon or as a man with the head of an ibis.

Literature. Although few people were literate, Egyptian writers left a considerable body of literature. One mythological adventure, *The Shipwrecked Sailor*, tells of a sailor marooned on a magical island with a talking cobra. A love poem laments the separation of a young couple:

My love is on one side of the riverbank
I am on the other
And there is a crocodile on the sandbank.

▶ **HISTORY**

The history of ancient Egypt is divided into three major periods: the Old Kingdom, the Middle Kingdom, and the New Kingdom. There are other periods, but these are the most important.

Prior to the Old Kingdom, Egypt was composed of two distinct kingdoms: Upper Egypt in the south (surrounding the upper part of the Nile, which flows south to north) and Lower Egypt in the north (which included the Nile's delta at the coast of the Mediterranean Sea). About 3200 B.C. a king of Upper Egypt named Narmer conquered Lower Egypt, uniting the two kingdoms and establishing ancient Egypt's first dynasty.

The Old Kingdom (2686–2181 B.C.). The Old Kingdom began with the founding of the third dynasty. A strong central government was established with this dynasty, which enabled the Egyptians to build all the major pyramids during this period. It was also during the Old Kingdom that ancient Egypt's artistic standards, such the proper proportions for depicting the human form, were established. These rules were followed for centuries by later Egyptian artists.

The Middle Kingdom (2040–1782 B.C.). The Middle Kingdom was a period of stability and relative prosperity in ancient Egypt, but the pharaohs of this period did not have the wealth of those who ruled during the Old Kingdom. The pyramids of this time were built of mud brick with only an outer casing of stone. These pyramids did not survive as well as the earlier stone pyramids, and today they look like steep natural hills.

The New Kingdom (1570–1070 B.C.). The New Kingdom (the 18th through the 20th dynasties) is often referred to as Egypt's Golden Age because it was a period of great prosperity, great art, and great kings. Warrior pharaohs such as Thutmose III and Ramses II (the Great) conquered foreign lands and expanded Egypt's influence to its greatest extent.

During his reign, Akhenaten abolished the worship of all gods except Aten, a sun god. This change was very unpopular with the people of ancient Egypt.

Also during this time, a powerful female ruler, Hatshepsut, successfully ruled Egypt—not as queen but as king. But because she was a woman, Hatshepsut's name was never included in ancient lists of Egypt's pharaohs. The remains of her temple at Deir el-Bahri are one of the most impressive monuments of ancient Egypt.

Although Egypt was at its peak during the New Kingdom, it also suffered from internal turmoil during this period. The pharaoh Akhenaten abolished the worship of many gods and declared that there was only one god, Aten, a sun god. This was so unpopular with his people that Akhenaten had to move out of the capital, Thebes (present-day Luxor), and establish a new one in the desert at Akhetaten (present-day Tell el-'Amârna). Polytheism was re-established by Akhenaten's successor, Tutankhamen, whose tomb was found virtually intact in 1922.

Beginning about 1075 B.C., Egypt was invaded by Libyans, Assyrians, Nubians, and Persians, all of whom possessed superior armies and weapons. Alexander the Great conquered Egypt in 331 B.C. and the Greeks ruled Egypt until the death of Cleopatra VII in 30 B.C. After the Romans assumed control of Egypt from the Greeks, the ancient Egyptian civilization virtually disappeared.

BOB BRIER
Author, *The Daily Life of the Ancient Egyptians*

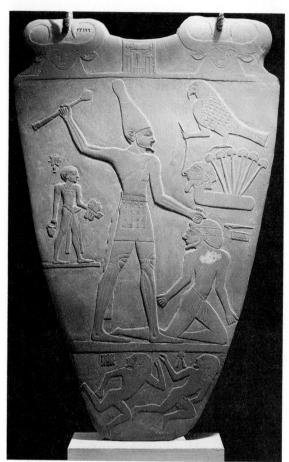

A carved tablet from about 3000 B.C. depicts the Egyptian king Narmer preparing to slay an enemy. The tablet records that Narmer united upper and lower Egypt.

EGYPTIAN ART AND ARCHITECTURE

For more than 2,000 years, Egypt was one of the richest and most civilized lands in the ancient world. Much of what we know about this great civilization has been learned from its art and architecture. In particular, the ruins of tombs and temples have provided a valuable record of Egyptian life.

The Egyptians were extremely religious, and their belief in life after death was an important part of their culture. They believed that, in order for the spirit to live on, the dead person's body had to be preserved, or mummified, and buried along with supplies of food and drink, tools and utensils, valued possessions—all the things the person had needed or enjoyed on earth. The higher the person's station in life, the more extensive the preparations for the afterlife. Kings and other wealthy persons had elaborate tombs built. Sculptures and wall paintings in the tombs were also created for use in the next life.

The gods, too, needed proper care. Their temples were built as great palaces, with stables, orchards and farmlands, and staffs of attendants. Daily rituals and seasonal festivals were pictured on the temple walls. Rulers prided themselves on what they had done to improve the shrines of the gods.

▶ **THE EARLY DYNASTIC PERIOD** (3000–2650 B.C.)

Egyptian history is usually divided according to the 30 dynasties (series of rulers of the same family) listed by an early historian. The first dynastic period began about 3000 B.C. with the legendary ruler Menes (also called Narmer), who united Egypt under one government and founded the capital city of Memphis.

A carved slate slab, or palette, made about 3000, shows Narmer, his raised arm holding a club, about to crush the head of his enemy. In the Narmer palette the human form is portrayed in a way that became standard in Egyptian art. The head and legs are shown from the side, while the eye and shoulders are shown from the front.

▶ **THE OLD KINGDOM** (2650–2150 B.C.)

The first great period of Egyptian civilization, called the Old Kingdom, began during the rule of King Zoser. The advances of the period were due mainly to Imhotep, the king's first minister. He was a skilled architect, statesman, and scholar. He was probably the architect of the famous Step Pyramid at Saqqara. The Step Pyramid was the first stone building in history and the first of the many pyramids to appear during the next 1,000 years.

The Step Pyramid was designed as a tomb for Zoser and members of his family. It was an unusual pyramid because of its broad terraces, or "steps." It consisted of seven rectangles, each rectangle smaller than the one beneath it. Within the rock was a well where the king was buried. He was surrounded by a maze of corridors and chambers that contained endless materials for his afterlife. More than 30,000 stone vessels—jugs, bowls, and vases—were buried in the chambers. This pyramid, about 200 feet (60 meters) tall, was the most important of a great number of buildings enclosed within a high wall. An entrance gate, a

The pyramid of Chephren rises behind the Great Sphinx at Giza. These huge monuments reflect the wealth of the pharaohs and the imagination and ingenuity of Egyptian artisans.

great court for the celebration of religious festivals, and a second tomb were built nearby. All these buildings were constructed from small blocks of limestone, a soft rock common to the region.

The form of the pyramid that we are familiar with developed quickly. The most important and famous pyramids are the three great pyramids at Giza, on the west bank of the Nile River. They were built between about 2660 and 2560 for the kings Cheops, Chephren, and Mycerinus. The pyramids were meant to house the pharaohs' bodies and serve as reminders of their almighty power.

Building the great pyramid of Cheops (2551–28) was a tremendous feat. The pyramid is so large that it could contain comfortably the entire Capitol building of Washington, D.C. The pyramid is made of about 2,300,000 blocks of finely cut limestone. These stones have an average weight of 2½ tons. The largest stones were cut and floated almost 700 miles (1,125 kilometers) down the Nile to the pyramid site. With only

the simplest of tools, the stones were dragged up earth ramps and set in place.

The pyramid, the tomb of the king, was only one part of a group of structures that formed the pyramid complex. Adjoining the pyramid on its eastern, or Nile, side was the pyramid temple, where the king was worshiped. From this temple a covered causeway led to the valley temple, which had access to the Nile. Clustered around the royal tombs or dug into the surrounding cliffs were smaller, flat-roofed tombs called **mastabas** that held the bodies of nobles. Though sometimes built of mud brick, the mastabas were more often of limestone. The sides of the buildings sloped inward. Within the long building only a small area was made into chapels for offerings and chambers to hold statues of the dead. Far below the surface a burial chamber was hollowed in the rock. After burial the shaft was filled with large stone blocks.

Parts of temples have been found, but only the temple dedicated to the sun at Abu-Gurab (near Giza) remains. It, too, was approached

Left: A statue of a scribe, or record keeper, has the calm, still pose typical of Old Kingdom sculpture. *Right:* Skillfully painted geese decorate a tomb wall at Medum.

by a long passageway and surrounded by a high wall. Unlike all other Egyptian temples, much of this temple was open to the sun. The most important part of the building was its great center court containing an altar and an **obelisk,** sacred symbol of the sun. An obelisk is a four-sided pillar tapering to a miniature pyramid at the top. Usually an Egyptian obelisk was made of one solid stone, often covered with writings of the kings' triumphs.

Sculpture and Painting. One of the earliest and most typical of royal Egyptian sculptures is a statue of the great Zoser found in his pyramid at Saqqara. This life-size statue shows the sitting pharaoh staring straight ahead. For a long time, only such calm poses were popular in Egyptian sculpture.

Many royal sculptures of hard stone were intended for the inside of a tomb of a king. But we can still see the remains of some public monuments. The outstanding example of these larger works is the Great **Sphinx** at Giza. A huge sculpture with a lion's body and a human head, the Sphinx was carved from the natural rock of the site. It is as high as a modern seven-story building.

Smaller, brightly painted limestone sculptures were also made for the tomb. They usually showed the owner as a youthful man. Minor members of the royal family and many nobles had statues made of red granite and other hard stones, but these were expensive. At all times throughout the Old Kingdom wood was used for statues. It, too, was brightly painted. The eyes were often inlaid, giving the statue a lifelike appearance. Most officials had several statues made for their tombs.

Wall carving, or relief sculpture—sculpture carved to stand out from a background—decorated the walls of the pyramid temples and tombs. Scenes from daily life—sports, crafts, hunts—were carved in rows.

Much less painting than architecture and sculpture remains from this period. The interior walls of the tombs of noblemen were lined with plaster and then painted. In many ways wall carvings were similar to paintings. In both, figures were placed on the walls in rows, one on top of the other. The carefully drawn outline was filled in with even, unshaded colors. In this way the painted wall carvings looked very flat, as though the figures were cutouts pasted to the wall.

▶**THE MIDDLE KINGDOM (2040–1640 B.C.)**

About 2150 the central Egyptian government seems to have fallen apart. Egypt once more became a series of separate states in great confusion. During this time little building or sculpture was done.

Eventually, about 2040, a central government was again organized under a strong king. King Mentuhotep II revived the architecture of the Old Kingdom. His tomb included a courtyard, terrace, temple, and the king's burial chamber at the end of a long passage that had been cut into the solid rock of the cliffs. The tomb had a highly original design that was copied centuries later for Queen Hatshepsut's famous temple. Though now badly damaged, Mentuhotep II's tomb is of great interest because it is the oldest remaining temple at Thebes, the chief city of the south.

With the rise of King Amenemhet I about 1991, Egypt entered one of its great periods.

Amenemhet returned to the tradition of using the pyramid as the royal tomb. His pyramid was constructed at El Lisht, not far south of Memphis. In general form his pyramid and those of his successors followed the Old Kingdom style—valley temple, passageway, upper temple, and finally the pyramid itself.

But the newer pyramids were smaller and poorly constructed. Instead of the great stone blocks used earlier, these Middle Kingdom pyramids were often built of mud brick covered with limestone. The limestone was always stolen, and the brick pyramids crumbled into huge mounds. And, despite efforts to protect them, the royal burial chambers in these pyramids were all robbed.

In this period the best tombs built by wealthy nobles were cut into great rock cliffs. The most famous are at Beni Hasan in Middle Egypt, on the east side of the Nile. The tombs have columned entryways and halls. The inside walls are covered with paintings and relief sculptures.

The sculpture of the Middle Kingdom was one of the greatest achievements of Egyptian art. The best works were the portrait sculptures of Sesostris III and Amenemhet III. For the first time in Egyptian history, kings were realistically represented as mortal men. These kings show the wear and tear of life; their faces are handsome but deeply lined, and they look sad and weary. Since they were thought of as god-kings, this realism was unusual. But only the faces were realistic; the bodies of these statues looked youthful, slender, and strong.

Huge statues of kings were produced at this time in granite and other hard stones. Some statues were so oversized that they could not fit inside the temples but had to be placed in the open air. Smaller royal statues were sometimes made in wood.

Some wood sculpture was done larger than life-size. Wooden models of boats and houses and even scenes of daily life were made to be placed in tombs for use in the afterlife. Statuettes of human and animal figures were made of ivory and semiprecious stones.

The sculpture ordered by the nobility was similar to royal work. Harder stones were used more than limestone. Figures were shown in several new positions. Perhaps the most important was the cube, or block, statue. A man (never a woman) was shown seated on the ground with his knees drawn up against his chest. His entire body was wrapped in a great cloak. The sculpture gives the impression of a head coming out of a great cube.

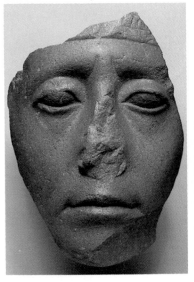

Left: A wooden model depicts a cattle inspection. Such models of everyday scenes were often placed in tombs. *Below:* This Middle Kingdom sculpture of Sesostris III is a realistic portrait of a world-weary ruler.

The temple of Queen Hatshepsut, built into the rock cliffs at Deir el-Bahri, dates from about 1470 B.C. Its terraces once held gardens of rare trees and plants.

▶ THE NEW KINGDOM (1550–1070 B.C.)

The Middle Kingdom came to an end with a series of foreign invasions. Soon after the beginning of the 16th century the last of the invaders were driven from Egypt. The new Egyptian kings were warriors, and they began conquering nearby states. Their conquests made Egypt the richest and most civilized power of the time, the ruler of a great empire. The empire was rich in gold, there were countless slaves, and money from tribute added to the wealth. This explains the richness of New Kingdom architecture.

One of the important changes in architecture was the disappearance of the pyramid. The pyramids had failed to protect the royal burial from robbery. Kings and queens were now buried in tombs cut deep into the rock cliffs at Thebes. Long corridors with relief sculpture and religious writing on the walls led to a hall with columns. There the royal mummy rested in a great stone coffin. The temples were built separately on the edge of the desert, facing the Nile. Even today their ruins are a beautiful sight.

The most beautiful of these is the temple of Deir el-Bahri. It was built about 1470 by the famous Queen Hatshepsut. A series of terraces was surrounded by colonnades and connected by ramps. This temple was built entirely of fine limestone. In contrast, the nearby temple of Ramses II was built (about 1250) entirely of sandstone—a coarse material that is easy to work with.

The latest—and best preserved—of these temples was constructed for Ramses III about 1180. Known as Medinet Habu, it is really a group of buildings and includes a palace, smaller temples, and houses for priests. It was surrounded by a great brick wall. The temple itself had two great courts that led to a dimly lit hall completely filled with columns. Behind the hall, which was called a **hypostyle** hall, was the sanctuary where the statue of the god was placed. This dark, innermost section of the temple was open only to the king and the priests.

Across the Nile at Karnak the temple of Amon-Re, the king of the gods, was rebuilt. It was enlarged into the largest temple ever known. Built mostly of sandstone, it was not constructed according to a fixed plan. Instead it was added to and changed by almost every king during the New Kingdom. Throughout the period Egyptian architects worked on a large scale. A long avenue of sandstone sphinxes connected the great temple at Karnak to a much smaller temple at Luxor, a few miles away.

The most spectacular building of the age is the famous temple of Abu-Simbel, cut entirely from the rock. It was built by Ramses II about 1250. Four huge seated statues of the pharaoh, each nearly 70 feet (21 meters) high, were carved in front of the temple. (About A.D. 1850 a traveler described standing on the lip of one of the statues and not being able to reach the eyebrows!) The inside plan of the temple copied the design of the usual Egyptian temple, on a smaller scale.

Private (or nonroyal) tombs of the New Kingdom were built all over the country. The major ones of the nobility were at Thebes and were rock-cut. They are more interesting for their decoration—reliefs and paintings—than for their architecture. As in all periods, the private homes were built of mud and then whitewashed. They were surrounded by gardens with pools of water.

Sculpture and Painting. Much sculpture has survived from the New Kingdom. No one knows the names of the artists because Egyptian artists never signed their works.

King Amenhotep III (1391–1353) was a great patron of the arts. Two gigantic statues, called the Colossi of Memnon, on the west side of the Nile at Thebes mark the site of his mortuary temple. The statues, which show the king seated on his throne, are more than 60 feet (18 meters) tall. But the king was not interested only in erecting huge monuments. The art of his reign is remarkable most of all for its elegance and variety.

Egyptian art was becoming more realistic, moving away from the standard ways of representing the human form. For example, a sculpture done late in Amenhotep's rule shows the king in foreign dress. Also, for the first time in the long history of Egyptian art, certain flaws of the ruler's body are clearly depicted. He is shown as a plump, aging man.

Statues became even more realistic during the reign (1353–35) of Amenhotep III's son Akhenaten (originally Amenhotep IV). Instead of worshiping many gods, Akhenaten worshiped Aten as the only god of Egypt. His belief may have had something to do with the revolution in Egyptian art. The statues of Akhenaten made early in his reign portrayed him with a long, thin face and a generally

Left: The temple of Ramses II at Abu-Simbel features four colossal statues of the pharaoh. Each is nearly 70 feet (21 meters) high. *Below:* A decorated box from the tomb of New Kingdom ruler Tutankhamen. One of the few royal graves to escape robbery, the tomb yielded many treasures when opened in 1923.

Left: A wall painting from a Theban tomb depicts a nobleman hunting waterfowl. *Right:* A new realism is seen in a carving of Akhenaten that shows the king's distinctive features.

weak body. It was a realistic—and shocking—way to represent the god-king of Egypt. His queen, Nefertiti, and his many daughters were also shown in this true-to-life and unflattering style.

Akhenaten created a new capital city at Tel el Amarna. A group of heads—some made of plaster—was found there in the studio of a sculptor. They were not engraved with names, but some of them were royal portraits. Among them was a famous limestone portrait of Nefertiti. In these heads the individual features of the person were shown. The great contribution of the brief period of Amarna art was the development of portraiture.

After the death of Akhenaten, rulers went back to the less personal and less realistic style of sculpture.

Relief sculpture in the New Kingdom shows great quality and originality. Many new subjects were introduced. For example, one temple relief depicts a voyage to Punt, with carvings of the incense trees, animals, and people of that distant land. In the same temple and also at Luxor, we find scenes of the birth of the king. Lively and long reliefs of the celebration of certain religious festivals can also be seen in temples.

Painting was more often used in tombs than relief sculpture. Painting in royal tombs was chiefly limited to outline drawings of religious rites. It was rather in the tombs of wealthy noblemen that the best pictures were painted. The paintings in Theban tombs were so fine that the New Kingdom has been called the Golden Age of Egyptian painting. As in earlier decorations, figures were painted in rows, one above the other. At the beginning of the period the figures were painted in bright colors on a sky-blue background. Later in the New Kingdom, as the style of painting grew freer and more natural, neutral or light-gray backgrounds were used in the tomb paintings.

A very important development took place in temple relief sculpture. To glorify the king, the courtyard walls were covered with complicated battle and hunting scenes. The large figures were brightly painted against white backgrounds.

▶ THE LATE PERIODS (712–332 B.C.)

The centuries following the close of the New Kingdom (11th to 8th centuries) produced little beyond a weak continuation of New Kingdom traditions. Egypt was divided into two or more nations much of this time.

This decline ended suddenly in the late 8th century with the Kushite conquest of Egypt. The Kushites had come into Egypt from the south and had long been under Egyptian influence. A revival of the arts took place in Thebes in the 7th century. Not much of the Kushite architecture survives in Egypt, but architecture in the Egyptian style survives in the Kushite homeland in the Sudan. There the pyramid was again used as the royal tomb. These late pyramids were midgets compared with the earlier Egyptian ones.

Between 664 and 525 the capital was moved to Saïs in the Delta (northern Egypt). No major architecture of the time survives. Even royal tombs of the period are unknown. The same is true for the period of Persian conquest (525–404). Dynasty XXX (378–341) was the last native dynasty of Egypt. It has left a few shrines and hard stone reliefs.

▶ **THE PTOLEMAIC PERIOD (332–30 B.C.)**

In 332 B.C., Egypt was conquered by Alexander the Great, the King of Macedonia. He founded a new capital city, Alexandria, on the Mediterranean coast. After Alexander's death in 323, Egypt fell to one of his generals, Ptolemy, who founded the Ptolemaic Dynasty. The Ptolemaic rulers governed Egypt for 300 years, carrying on the traditions of the pharaohs. Huge temples were constructed at state expense. Indeed, most of the surviving temples of Egypt belong to the Ptolemaic period. Famous ones remain at Edfu, Kom Ombo, and Dendera. They were built on the site of earlier temples, the remains of which were used in the new buildings.

In plan and general form these late temples show little difference from earlier work. But there were many changes in details. Sandstone remained the most common building material. Sandstone was soft and could be easily carved. On top of columns clusters of flowers were carved and brightly painted. The walls of the temples were covered with religious and mythological scenes.

The Ptolemaic rulers had themselves represented in many standing statues. In style these statues were similar to those of the ancient pharaohs. The results were often ordinary. The period also saw the production of many so-called sculptors' models—small limestone statues and reliefs of gods, parts of buildings, and parts of the human body.

Relief carvings cover the walls of Cleopatra's temple at Dendera. Egypt's artistic traditions continued through Cleopatra's reign but passed away under Roman rule.

The last Ptolemaic ruler of Egypt was Cleopatra VII, one of the most famous figures of ancient times. When her forces, combined with Mark Antony's, lost to Octavius Caesar (later Augustus) at the battle of Actium in 31 B.C., Egypt lost its independence and became a province of the Roman Empire. Although the Romans continued to create architecture in the old Egyptian style—at Philae and Dendera, for example—Egyptian art had lost its vitality, and the ancient traditions gradually passed away.

JOHN D. COONEY
Curator of Egyptian and Classical Art
The Cleveland Museum of Art

Reviewed by LAWRENCE M. BERMAN
Department of Ancient Art
The Cleveland Museum of Art

See also ANCIENT CIVILIZATIONS; OBELISKS.

EHRLICH, PAUL (1854–1915)

The pioneering work of German bacteriologist Paul Ehrlich laid the foundation for the science of chemotherapy (the use of chemical agents in treating disease). In 1908 he shared the Nobel Prize for physiology or medicine.

Ehrlich was born on March 14, 1854, in Strehlen, Silesia (now Poland). As a university student, Ehrlich paid more attention to his experiments than to his studies. He never received formal training in chemistry, but while in medical school, he discovered a chemical dye that could stain blood cells, making them more visible under a microscope. His work allowed other researchers to study and classify blood cells.

Ehrlich passed his medical exams in 1878 and continued his experiments. In 1881 he developed a way to stain the bacteria that cause tuberculosis so that they could be identified under a microscope. During a six-year period, from 1878 to 1883, Ehrlich made 37 important discoveries.

In 1890 Ehrlich joined the Institute for Infectious Diseases in Berlin. There he worked to establish the dosages for Emil von Behring's diphtheria antitoxin. As his work progressed, Ehrlich developed a theory that there were chemicals that could act as "magic bullets." That is, they could attack and lock up certain substances that cause disease without hurting the rest of the body. In 1909 he successfully developed the first specifically designed chemical cure for a disease. The compound, which he named Salvarsan, was able to cure the deadly disease syphilis in humans.

Paul Ehrlich wrote more than a hundred papers and received many honors in addition to the Nobel Prize. He died of a stroke on August 20, 1915, in Bad Homburg, Germany.

GAIL KAY HAINES
Author, *Micromysteries:
Stories of Scientific Detection*

EHRLICHMAN, JOHN. See WATERGATE (Profiles).

EICHMANN, ADOLF. See NAZISM (Profiles).

EIFFEL, ALEXANDRE-GUSTAVE (1832–1923)

Alexandre-Gustave Eiffel was one of the greatest engineers of modern times. He built the famous Eiffel Tower in Paris, France, the tallest building of its time.

Eiffel was born on December 15, 1832, in Dijon, France. After he graduated from the École Centrale des Arts et Manufactures in 1855, he began to specialize in constructing objects out of metal. Early in his career, he built a huge bridge over the Douro River in Portugal, as well as the Garabit Viaduct, which spanned a distance of 540 feet (165 meters) across the Truyere River in southern France. This bridge rose 400 feet (122 meters) over the stream below, making it the highest bridge in the world for many years.

In 1887, Eiffel began work on the Eiffel Tower, which was completed for the Paris Exposition two years later. This masterpiece of technology was the winner of a competition sponsored by the French government for the celebration of its 100th anniversary in 1889. When Eiffel submitted the plans for his 1,063-foot (324-meter) building, many people were skeptical. No building that tall had ever been erected—and certainly none had been built in the short time and with the small labor force that Eiffel proposed. Eiffel had such a deep understanding of how to work with metal, however, that he was brilliantly successful. The Eiffel Tower was not only a technological wonder, earning him the nickname "magician of iron," but it was also known for its beauty and it became the symbol of Paris. (A picture of the Eiffel Tower appears in the article PARIS in Volume P.)

This gifted engineer later helped design the locks for the Panama Canal, which are used to move ships from one end of the canal to the other, and the world's first laboratory of aerodynamics, which was located at Auteuil, outside Paris. Eiffel died in Paris, France, on December 28, 1923.

RACHEL KRANZ
Editor, Biographies
The Young Adult Reader's Adviser

Albert Einstein developed revolutionary theories about the physical realities of the universe, challenging ideas that had been held for more than two hundred years.

EINSTEIN, ALBERT (1879–1955)

There have been only a few scientists whose work has changed our total view of the world. One of these was Albert Einstein.

During his lifetime, Einstein set forth a number of theories about the physical world. These theories dealt with everything from the inside of an atom to the farthest regions of the universe. They showed that such things as gravity, energy, matter, light, space, and time are related.

Einstein used the most advanced kinds of mathematics to describe his ideas. These theories were so unusual that very few scientists could understand them at first. As the years passed, experiments, observations, and discoveries in many branches of science proved Einstein's work to be correct. The theories explained the bending of light by stars and other phenomena. Scientists also used his theories to unleash the power of the atom.

▶ EINSTEIN'S YOUTH

Einstein was born on March 14, 1879, in Ulm, Germany. A year later his family moved to nearby Munich, where his father ran a small factory that manufactured electrical supplies.

Albert was never very happy in school. He did not like to memorize facts and rules. He answered slowly because he was very thoughtful, and he asked difficult questions, which made his teachers think that he was trying to make trouble. However, young Einstein did learn what interested him. He was always good at mathematics and literature. In his teens he became very interested in popular science and started to wonder about the mysteries of the universe.

Einstein entered the Polytechnic Institute in Zurich, Switzerland, when he was 17. While there, he studied mathematics and physics. He stayed away from many lectures and so did not impress his professors, but he was actually studying very hard. When he graduated in 1900, he asked to be appointed as an assistant in the physics department but was refused.

▶ HIS EARLIEST THEORIES

After unsuccessful efforts at teaching, Einstein went to work in the Swiss patent office in Bern. He married Mileva Marić, a girl he had known in his student days in Zurich, and settled down in an apartment in Bern. Einstein's job was to check the technical descriptions in the applications for patents, and he found great interest in looking over the inventors' models. Because he worked so quickly, he found he had free time to follow his own thoughts. He was determined to discover some of the basic laws that would help him understand the universe.

In 1905, he published a series of articles setting forth some of his theories, including a theory of relativity. The ideas in these articles were so revolutionary that many scientists disagreed with them. But they all asked, Who is this man Einstein? And what is he doing in a patent office? By 1908, Einstein had received so much notice from other scientists that the University of Bern offered him a position. Soon scientists at other European universities were asking him to lecture. By 1913, he was invited to Berlin, then the leading center of scientific research.

When Einstein went to Berlin, he separated from his wife, who was also a physicist,

Einstein and Elsa aboard ship as they sail home after their first trip to the United States in 1921.

and their two children. In Berlin he lived not far from his cousin Elsa, a widow with two young daughters. They had known each other since childhood, and more than anyone else, Elsa understood the unusual nature and personality of her cousin. The two got along very well, and finally, in 1919, they married.

In the years following his first published article, Einstein had continued to work out his ideas. But he and his theories were known only to scientists. It was not until 1919, after World War I ended, that Einstein became known to the general public as a leading scientific thinker. In March of that year there was a total eclipse of the sun. This gave scientists their first chance to test one of Einstein's theories about light rays. It turned out that he had predicted exactly what took place.

▶ FAME AND THE NOBEL PRIZE

Einstein became an international figure. Most people still could not understand his ideas, but they recognized that he was a genius. Einstein was invited to lecture at universities all over the world. He was awarded the Nobel Prize for physics in 1921.

For the next ten years, Einstein lived in Berlin. Sometimes he went to other countries to give lectures. But in general he led a quiet life, working out his own ideas.

In the meantime many changes were taking place in Germany. In 1933, Adolf Hitler became dictator and headed the Nazi Party. The future looked bleak for German Jews. Aside from being Jewish, Einstein was in danger for criticizing German preparations for war. While traveling abroad, he decided not to return to Germany.

▶ EINSTEIN IN THE UNITED STATES

In 1933, Einstein accepted a position at the Institute for Advanced Study in Princeton, New Jersey. At the institute, Einstein continued to work on his scientific theories. Although his work cut him off from most people, he never lost touch with the problems of the world. Among other things, he aided Jewish scientists and students who were forced to flee Germany.

Then, in 1939, on the eve of World War II, some scientists came to Einstein to enlist his help. Fearful that Germany was making an atomic bomb, they wanted the United States to develop its own bomb. These scientists turned to Einstein because his theories suggested that there was a great amount of energy in atoms. This idea was the basis of the atomic bomb. They also thought the government would listen to Einstein because he was famous.

Einstein realized that an atomic bomb might be needed to protect the world from Nazi Germany. He did not participate directly in the development of the atomic bomb, but he wrote a letter to President Franklin D. Roosevelt, recommending that the bomb be built. However, as soon as World War II ended, Einstein urged that atomic energy be put to peaceful uses.

Einstein lived in Princeton more than twenty years. With his old sweaters and his long white hair, he was a familiar figure on the streets. In spite of his great achievements and fame, Einstein never lost his sense of humor. Once he had lectured for over an hour on his theory of time. He had discussed dozens of ideas about time. Suddenly he stopped and, with a pained look on his face, said, "I fear it is getting late. Does anyone know the time?"

Einstein died on April 18, 1955. Directly or indirectly, Einstein influenced many areas of the modern world—science, art, and philosophy. As one president of Princeton University said, he was "a new Columbus who sails alone across the uncharted seas of thought." In 2000, Albert Einstein was named Person of the Century by *Time* magazine.

Reviewed by MAE B. FREEMAN
Author, *Story of Albert Einstein*

DWIGHT D. EISENHOWER (1890-1969)

34th President of the United States

FACTS ABOUT EISENHOWER
Birthplace: Denison, Texas
Religion: Presbyterian
College Attended: U.S. Military
  Academy at West Point
Occupation: Army officer
Married: Mary ("Mamie")
  Geneva Doud
Children: John S. D.
Political Party: Republican
Nickname: "Ike"
Post Held Before
  Becoming President:
  Supreme Commander,
  North Atlantic Treaty
  Organization (NATO) forces
President Who Preceded Him:
  Harry S. Truman
Age on Becoming President: 62
Years in the Presidency: 1953-1961
Vice President: Richard M. Nixon
President Who Succeeded Him:
  John F. Kennedy
Age at Death: 78
Burial Place: Abilene, Kansas

DURING EISENHOWER'S PRESIDENCY
A truce agreement was signed (1953) ending the fighting in the Korean War. *Below:* The first nuclear-powered submarine, the U.S.S. *Nautilus,* was launched (1954). The U.S. Supreme Court declared racial segregation in public schools unconstitutional (1954). *Right:* The Salk polio vaccine, developed by Jonas E. Salk, was declared safe and effective (1955). The Soviet Union launched the first artificial satellite, Sputnik I, into orbit around the earth (1957). *Left:* The first U.S. artificial earth satellite, Explorer I, was launched by a Jupiter-C rocket (1958). The St. Lawrence Seaway, linking the Great Lakes with the Atlantic Ocean, was opened (1959). Alaska and Hawaii became the 49th and 50th states (1959). The laser was patented (1960).

EISENHOWER, DWIGHT DAVID. Before winning election to the presidency in 1952, Dwight D. Eisenhower had spent most of his adult life as an army officer, rising to the highest military rank, general of the army. Both as a general and as president, Eisenhower aroused an enormous affection in the people of the United States and indeed in people throughout the world. This was because in a time of national danger, of changing values and uncertainty, he possessed the virtues that most Americans feel represent the United States at its best. He was brave, kind, steadfast, idealistic, friendly, and so completely honest that even his political opponents never questioned his integrity.

▶EARLY YEARS

Eisenhower was born on October 14, 1890, in Denison, Texas, the third son of David and Ida Stover Eisenhower. His ancestors on his father's side had emigrated from Germany to Pennsylvania in 1732. The family name meant "iron axe" or "iron hitter." The boy was christened David Dwight Eisenhower. Later his names were accidentally reversed to Dwight David. This was agreeable to him, since he was called Dwight by his family.

Eisenhower was 2 years old when the family moved to Abilene, Kansas. Although his father never made more than $1,500 a year, he managed to save enough to buy a small house and a 10-acre (4-hectare) farm. The five Eisenhower boys worked the farm and raised almost all the food for the family. They had virtually no money, but they ate well. The boys went to the local school, where Dwight was nicknamed "Ike."

West Point. After he graduated from high school, Eisenhower went to work in a creamery, partly to enable one of his older brothers to attend college. When Dwight realized that the only chance of getting his own college education was to try for a free one, he took the competitive examinations for both the U.S. Naval Academy at Annapolis and the U.S. Military Academy at West Point. He placed first for Annapolis and second for West Point. He wanted to go to the Naval Academy, but he discovered that at 20 he was too old. At the Military Academy the age limit was 21.

Eisenhower entered West Point in 1911. His academic record was average. He stood 61st in a class of 164. But he was very popular. He was a big, powerful young man with a friendly grin. He was a star halfback on the football team until he hurt his knee. The knee bothered him the rest of his life.

▶MARRIAGE AND EARLY MILITARY CAREER

Upon graduation in 1915, Eisenhower was commissioned a second lieutenant in the 19th Infantry and ordered to Fort Sam Houston in San Antonio, Texas. There he met Mary (Mamie) Geneva Doud of Denver, Colorado, and fell in love with her. They were married in Denver in 1916, on the day that Eisenhower was promoted to first lieutenant.

World War I. Eisenhower was promoted to captain in 1917 and then served as an instructor at several Army training camps. With the United States involved in World War I, he sought active service in France. But he was too good at training troops, and in 1918 he was assigned to command the Tank Training Center at Camp Colt, Pennsylvania. He was quickly promoted to major (temporary), and by the war's end, in November, 1918, he held the temporary rank of lieutenant colonel.

Peacetime Years. The peacetime years were routine for Eisenhower. He went back to his regular rank of captain and served at Camp Meade, Maryland, and in the Panama Canal Zone. In 1924 he was promoted to major again. In 1926 he studied at the Command and General Staff School at Fort Leavenworth, Kansas, from which he graduated first in his class.

During the next few years Eisenhower served on the Battle Monuments Commission in France. He also attended the War College in Washington, D.C. He served under the assistant secretary of war from 1929 to 1933, when he was appointed to the staff of General Douglas MacArthur, who was then chief of staff of the Army. When MacArthur undertook the task of building a Philippine army in 1935, he asked Eisenhower to go along as his assistant. In the Philippines, Eisenhower had a major role in planning the defense of the islands. In 1936 he was promoted to lieutenant colonel.

▶WORLD WAR II

Eisenhower remained in the Philippines for four years. When World War II broke out in Europe in 1939, he was anxious to get home, for he foresaw that the United States must eventually become involved. He returned to the United States in December, 1939, and was assigned to the 15th Infantry as regimental executive officer. In 1941 he was promoted to colonel and made chief of staff of the U.S.

Third Army. Later that year he was promoted to brigadier general.

Pearl Harbor. On December 7, 1941, Japanese planes attacked U.S. bases at Pearl Harbor, Hawaii, bringing the United States into World War II. Eisenhower was promoted to major general in March 1942, and in April he was appointed to the position of chief of operations under Army Chief of Staff General George C. Marshall.

In May 1942, Marshall sent Eisenhower to England. That June, Eisenhower was chosen to command all U.S. forces in Europe. He was promoted to lieutenant general.

North Africa. When the Allied invasion of North Africa was agreed on, Eisenhower was given command of all British and U.S. forces. On November 8, 1942, the troops were successfully landed in Algeria and Morocco. However, the German Army in Africa reacted sharply, beginning six months of bitter fighting. Eisenhower had never commanded even a division in the field, and he had to learn the techniques of command while fighting. The Americans suffered an almost disastrous defeat at Kasserine Pass in Tunisia, before Eisenhower got hold of the situation and his raw American troops settled down. In February, 1943, he was promoted to full general. The British and U.S. forces, assisted by the Free French, defeated the Germans and their Italian allies in North Africa, taking more than 250,000 prisoners.

Italy and Supreme Commander. Allied forces under Eisenhower's overall command had occupied the Italian island of Sicily by the summer of 1943. In September, 1943, they landed at Salerno, on the mainland of Italy. In the winter of 1943, President Roosevelt, British Prime Minister Winston Churchill, and Soviet leader Joseph Stalin met at Teheran, in Iran, and agreed on plans for the invasion of France the following year. At the Cairo Conference, which followed, it was decided that Eisenhower was to be appointed supreme commander of the Allied expeditionary force. In January, 1944, Eisenhower arrived in England to take command. D-Day, the date for the Allied invasion of Normandy in western France, was set for June 5, 1944.

D-Day. On Saturday, June 3, the weather was bad. The invasion was postponed one day. Monday morning, June 5, at 4:00 A.M., forecasters said weather conditions might clear enough by Tuesday, June 6, to make the landings possible. Otherwise they must be put off for about three weeks. Eisenhower asked his generals for their opinions. Some were for going on, some for postponement. He got a final weather check; then he said the historic words: "O.K. We'll go ahead!"

By early September, 1944, Paris was liberated and the Germans were driven back to the borders of Germany. But the Allied armies had outrun their supplies and had to stop. This gave the Germans time to recover.

Opposite page, top: Eisenhower married Mary (Mamie) Doud in 1916, when he was a young first lieutenant. *Bottom:* As supreme commander of Allied forces in Europe during World War II, General Eisenhower addressed U.S. airborne troops just before the 1944 D-Day landing in Normandy. *Right:* Christmas Eve in the White House, 1960: President and Mamie Eisenhower are at center. At the far left are son John and his wife, Barbara Jean, with their children (from the left), Barbara Anne, David, Mary Jean, and Susan.

Above: Eisenhower was sworn in for a second term as president in 1957. At the right is Vice President (later President) Richard M. Nixon. *Right:* Eisenhower met with Soviet leader Nikita Khrushchev during Khrushchev's visit to the United States in 1959.

Battle of the Bulge. On December 16, 1944, the Germans launched their last great offensive, which became known as the Battle of the Bulge. German armored divisions almost succeeded in breaking through the thin, stretched-out Allied lines. In this dangerous position Eisenhower never lost his calm optimism. He made the necessary decisions to meet and counter the German attack. Then he took to his jeep and rolled over the snowy roads of France and Belgium to encourage the hard-pressed front-line troops.

Victory. When the Germans were stopped at the Bulge, Eisenhower, now holding the rank of general of the Army, proceeded with his plan for the conquest of Germany. His British and U.S. generals sharply disagreed about these plans. By tact, persuasion, and finally the assertion of authority, Eisenhower got them to work as a team. The British themselves said that no one but "Ike" could have kept such temperamental characters as British General Bernard Montgomery and U.S. General George Patton working in harmony. Their armies swept through Germany from the west while the Soviet Army attacked from the east. On May 7, 1945, the German High Command signed an unconditional surrender at Eisenhower's headquarters in a schoolhouse in Reims (Rheims), France.

▶**POSTWAR YEARS**

Eisenhower returned home to demonstrations of affection and enthusiasm by the American people. In November, 1945, he succeeded General Marshall as Army chief of staff.

Eisenhower retired from active military service in 1948. He published an account of his wartime experiences, *Crusade in Europe,* and in 1949 accepted the post of president of Columbia University.

Eisenhower returned to active duty in 1950, at the height of the Cold War with the Soviet Union. President Harry S. Truman appointed him supreme commander of the forces of the recently formed North Atlantic Treaty Organization (NATO), a defensive military alliance made up of the United States, Canada, and a number of European nations.

As early as 1947 both the Democratic and Republican parties had sought to make Eisenhower their presidential candidate. In the tradition of American military leaders, Eisenhower had never taken part in partisan politics. He firmly refused offers from both parties. However, by 1952, he had come to feel in tune with the principles of the Republican Party. He resigned his NATO command that year to campaign for the Republican presidential nomination.

PRESIDENT

Eisenhower easily won the Republican nomination on the first ballot. In the 1952 election, he defeated the Democratic candidate, Adlai E. Stevenson, by 442 to 89 electoral votes. Eisenhower's vice president was Richard M. Nixon, who was later to win election to the presidency himself.

First Term. As president, Eisenhower tried to lead the United States in a program of cooperation with all free nations and strong opposition to Communism. In this he relied heavily on the advice of his secretary of state, John Foster Dulles. Eisenhower was not completely successful, but he did have some notable achievements. The first of these was bringing an end to the fighting in the Korean War in 1953. His Atoms for Peace program assisted other nations in developing atomic energy for peaceful uses. The Southeast Asia Treaty Organization (SEATO) was set up in 1954 to prevent Communist aggression in Southeast Asia. (SEATO was phased out in 1977.) The President's integrity was seen during the 1956 Suez crisis, when he criticized three U.S. allies—Britain, France, and Israel—for their attack on Egypt after Egypt had nationalized (the state had taken control of) the Suez Canal.

Illness and Re-election. In 1955, Eisenhower suffered a heart attack but soon resumed his full activities. Twice more he was stricken with illnesses, once by an intestinal attack that required a major operation and later by a slight stroke. Despite his illnesses, he decided to run for re-election in 1956. Again his opponent was Adlai E. Stevenson. Eisenhower received 457 electoral votes to Stevenson's 73. His popular vote of nearly 35,590,000 was the largest ever received by a U.S. president up to that time.

Second Term. During his second term, President Eisenhower was even more heavily involved in foreign affairs. To help protect the nations of the Middle East from Communist aggression, Eisenhower in 1957 offered to send them military aid if they requested it. This proposal became known as the Eisenhower Doctrine. In 1958, under the terms of the doctrine, Eisenhower sent U.S. Marines to Lebanon to prevent a Communist takeover of its government. He also ordered ships of the U.S. Seventh Fleet to Taiwan to prevent a possible invasion, by the Communist Chinese,

of the islands of Quemoy and Matsu, which were held by the Nationalist Chinese.

The seizure by Cuba of U.S. property and the establishment of a Communist government on the island prompted Eisenhower to break relations with Cuba in 1961. The U-2 incident, in which a U.S. spy plane, the U-2, was shot down over the Soviet Union, was an embarrassment to the administration.

In 1954 the U.S. Supreme Court had handed down a historic decision, declaring the segregation of white and black children in public schools unconstitutional. Eisenhower had hoped for peaceful integration, but he did not hesitate to send U.S. military units to a Little Rock, Arkansas, high school in 1957, in order to enforce the law.

RETIREMENT

After leaving the White House in 1961, Eisenhower retired with Mamie to his farm in Gettysburg, Pennsylvania. One of the first acts of the new president, John F. Kennedy, was to restore Eisenhower to his rank of general of the Army. Eisenhower wrote several books, including *Mandate for Change* (1963) and *Waging Peace* (1965). He died on March 28, 1969, in Washington, D.C., and was buried in Abilene, Kansas.

ALDEN HATCH
Author, *General Ike*
Reviewed by JOHN S. D. EISENHOWER

IMPORTANT DATES IN THE LIFE OF DWIGHT D. EISENHOWER

1890	Born in Denison, Texas, October 14.
1915	Graduated from West Point.
1916	Married Mary (Mamie) Geneva Doud.
1918	Commander, Tank Training Center, Camp Colt, Pennsylvania.
1935–39	Assistant to General Douglas MacArthur in the Philippines.
1941	Chief of Staff, Third Army.
1942	Commanding General, American forces, European theater; Commander in Chief, Allied forces in North Africa.
1943	Supreme Commander, Allied Expeditionary Force.
1944	General of the Army.
1945	German Army surrendered, May 7.
1945–48	Chief of Staff, United States Army.
1948–50	President of Columbia University.
1951–52	Commander, NATO forces.
1953–61	34th president of the United States.
1969	Died in Washington, D.C., March 28.

ELEANOR OF AQUITAINE (1122–1204)

Eleanor of Aquitaine was the most influential woman of the Middle Ages and one of the few women of her time to exercise political power. She held many titles throughout her lifetime, among them countess of Poitou and Anjou; duchess of Aquitaine and Normandy; queen of France; and queen of England. She was also said to be the most beautiful woman of the age.

Eleanor was probably born near Bordeaux (in present-day France). Unlike most women of that period, she received some formal education. But more important, she was allowed to inherit the vast domain of her father, William X, duke of Aquitaine—lands that now make up about one-quarter of present-day France.

In 1137, shortly after the death of her father, Eleanor married the heir to the French throne. That same year her husband became King Louis VII and she became queen. She wielded strong influence over Louis and accompanied him on the Second Crusade to the Holy Land in 1147. Louis

and Eleanor had two daughters, Marie and Alix. But the couple grew apart, and in 1152 the marriage was annulled (declared invalid) by the Roman Catholic Church. Eleanor promptly married the future king Henry II of England.

When Henry became king in 1154, his and Eleanor's dominions stretched from Scotland to the south of France. With Henry, Eleanor had at least eight more children: William, Henry, Matilda, Richard, Geoffrey, Eleanor, Joanna, and John.

In 1173, Eleanor supported her sons in a rebellion against their father. When the rebellion failed, Henry placed Eleanor under house arrest, and she was held prisoner until he died in 1189. In her final years, Eleanor helped manage the realm for her surviving sons, King Richard I (the Lion-Hearted) and, after his death, King John. She retired to the abbey at Fontevrault (in Anjou), where she died on April 1, 1204, at the age of 82.

Reviewed by JEREMY BLACK
University of Exeter

ELECTIONS

An election is the democratic process of selecting one person from among a group of candidates to fill a political office or other position of responsibility. The word "election" comes from the Latin root meaning "to choose." The election process is accomplished by **voting**. The people who are qualified to vote are called the **electorate**. The electorate may vote on issues as well as for candidates. For example, they may vote on tax measures or changes in the law.

Elections may be decided (won) in a variety of ways. In many elections the winning candidate must win by a **plurality**—that is, receive more votes than any other candidate. In other elections a winning candidate must win by a **majority**—that is, receive more than half the total number of votes cast.

Elections may be held to select officers at any level of government. In the United States, for example, mayors, county supervisors, some judges and sheriffs, members of the state legislatures, members of the U.S. Congress, and the president and vice president of the United States are elected to office. However, in some countries with parliamentary forms of government, such as the United Kingdom, typically only the members of the county and national legislatures are elected.

▶ ELECTIONS IN DEMOCRATIC SOCIETIES

Elections are an essential political feature of democratic nations, such as the United States, Canada, Japan, Mexico, and the United Kingdom. Elections give people the

American political parties hold national conventions in the summer before a presidential election to choose the persons they want to run for president and vice president.

opportunity to choose their own leaders and to replace those whose actions have become unpopular. Elections thus serve as an important means of limiting the power of government leaders. By choosing among different candidates and political parties, voters also help give direction to their government. For example, by voting for a candidate who promises to improve local schools, voters show that education is important to them.

Requirements for Free, Democratic Elections

Five protections are necessary to safeguard a democratic election: (1) candidates and parties must be free to communicate with voters and campaign publicly; (2) any person meeting the minimum requirements (such as age or citizenship) must be allowed to run for office; (3) people must be allowed to vote in private to protect them from being intimidated (made fearful or threatened); (4) the votes must be accurately and fairly counted; and (5) any person meeting the minimum requirements of age, citizenship, and residence must be allowed to vote.

When elections are held in nondemocratic countries, these requirements may not be safeguarded. For example, candidates the government does not support may be attacked or forbidden from campaigning; citizens may fear punishment if they vote against the government; votes may be miscounted or even destroyed to ensure the victory of a particular individual; or certain groups may be prevented from voting, either by law or intimidation. In such cases, although the government may claim that a free and open election has taken place, the true desires of the people may not necessarily be reflected.

In countries that are neither fully democratic nor totally nondemocratic, elections may be held that are considered partially free and fair. For example, the government may allow opposition candidates and parties to run for office, but the government controls all the news media, so the opposition cannot get its message out to voters.

Most countries hold elections—even when it is apparent the elections are not free or fair—because an elected official is seen as having been given a mandate (bestowed with the authority) to lead or to represent the

CAMPAIGN FINANCING

To finance the high cost of campaigning, candidates for state and national offices must raise millions of dollars. The result is that politicians need to ask for money from wealthy individuals, businesses, unions, and special interest groups. Most of these contributors have political agendas, and many experts feel that the current system gives them too much influence in American politics. Over the years, the U.S. Congress has passed laws to control the flow of money into national election campaigns, including the Federal Corrupt Practices Act (1925); the Hatch Act (1939); the Federal Election Campaign Act (1971); and the McCain-Feingold campaign finance reform law (2002).

In 1975, the U.S. Congress established the Federal Election Commission (FEC) as an independent agency of the U.S. government to enforce federal election laws. The FEC also administers public funding of presidential elections.

International bodies, such as the United Nations, hold elections to select committee members and also to decide issues of global consequence.

electorate. In the modern age, elections are so essential to the appearance of lawful rule that even the most feared and cruel dictators will hold elections to try to prove to their own people and the outside world that their leadership is legitimate.

Many organizations in addition to governments hold elections. In the United States, political parties, labor unions, and a variety of associations—from local social clubs to business and political groups—choose their leaders through elections. Corporations choose their boards of directors by election, but with a special rule. Instead of each person casting one vote, stockholders have one vote for each share of stock they own.

▶ THE ELECTORAL PROCESS IN THE UNITED STATES

The national government establishes federal election requirements, and many of the states generally adopt the same rules and practices to reduce costs and avoid the complexity of having two different systems. For example, most states and cities hold their elections the same day as federal elections.

The electoral process begins with the selection of candidates and ends with the casting of votes on Election Day. For more information on voting procedures, see the article VOTING in Volume UV.

Selecting Candidates

Political parties, which are made up of groups of voters who share similar political views, are an important feature of the American political system. The two major parties—the Democratic Party and the Republican Party—nominate most of the candidates who run for public office in the United States. There are also minor parties, or third parties, which often promote a single cause or issue.

In most elections, each major party selects a candidate and supports him or her with money, advice, and publicity. For the major federal and state offices, including U.S. president, senator, representative, and governor, candidates appear on the ballot identified with a particular party. However, for judges and for many local government offices, candidates often run without any party identification. These are known as **nonpartisan** races.

Qualifications Necessary to Run for Office. Although they need not belong to a political party, candidates must meet certain minimum requirements to run for various offices. For example, according to the U.S. Constitution, to serve in the U.S. House of Representatives a candidate must have been a U.S. citizen for at least seven years, be a resident of the state (and usually the district) he or she will represent, and be at least 25 years old. To serve in the U.S. Senate, a candidate must have been a U.S. citizen for at least nine years, be a resident of the state he or she will represent, and be at least 30 years old. To become president of the United States, a candidate must have lived in the country for at least 14 years, be a natural-born U.S. citizen, and be at least 35 years old.

Nominating Procedures. A variety of nominating procedures are used to select candidates in the United States. Usually, any person who wants to run for an elective office must show that he or she has a minimum amount of public support. A potential candidate might have to collect a minimum number of signatures of registered voters to qualify to appear on the ballot.

For many elections (and that includes the most important national and state elections), the candidates from one party compete with each other in a **primary election** to determine who will represent the party. Primaries are usually held a few months before the general election.

Primary elections fall into two main categories: In a **closed primary**, only voters registered with the party can vote in that party's primary. More common is the **open primary**, in which voters can participate even if they are not registered with that party.

For some elected positions, candidates are chosen by party caucuses. A **caucus** is a gathering of voters from the same party at the local level which has the authority to select the party's candidates.

In the case of presidential nominations, states send representatives called **delegates** to each party's presidential convention. At the convention, the delegates agree on a final candidate and publicly demonstrate their support for that candidate.

Types of Elections

The most important election in the United States is the **general election**, when Americans vote for the president and vice president and members of Congress. It takes place on **Election Day** (the first Tuesday after the first Monday in November), which in some states is a holiday. State and local elections are also usually held that day.

Usually, if a candidate receives a majority of the votes in the general election, he or she is declared the winner. However, in a race where there may be three or more strong candidates, it is possible that no one will receive a majority of votes. In such a situation, a **runoff election** may be held several weeks later. The two candidates who received the most votes run against each other again, and the candidate who receives the majority of the votes is declared the winner.

There are several types of elections in addition to primary, general, and runoff elections. **Special elections** may be held to fill an office whose occupant has died, resigned, or been recalled. An issues election, called a **referendum**, may be held to decide whether to accept or reject a piece of legislation. A **recall election** may be held to decide whether an office holder should be removed from office.

THE IMPACT OF THE MEDIA ON ELECTIONS

Ever since television became part of daily life beginning in the 1950's, elections in the United States have become media events. In the past, political parties promoted their candidates by holding campaign rallies or by going door-to-door. While those activities still occur, today most of the money and effort are directed toward advertising the candidates on television and radio and in newspapers and other media. For example, in the 2000 presidential race between George W. Bush and Al Gore, about $1.5 billion was spent on the campaign, with about one-third of that used to buy advertising.

Televised debates can have a significant impact on voters. Many observers agree that the first televised presidential debates (below) in 1960 helped candidate John F. Kennedy (right) defeat Richard Nixon (left), in part because Kennedy looked robust and energetic, while Nixon appeared pale and nervous.

If the recall election succeeds in removing the elected official, the office may be filled by appointment by the president or governor or by a special election.

Frequency of General Elections

Under the American political system, general elections are held in early November. The choice of that time of year dates from the days when America was largely an agricultural society, and farmers were unable to take time to vote until the fall, after the harvests had been gathered.

In the United States, presidential elections are held every four years and congressional elections are held every two years (in even-numbered years). In congressional elections the entire House of Representatives and one-third of the United States Senate are elected.

There are state elections for governors and other statewide officers. The term of an American governor varies with the individual state—either two or four years. The state leg-

Voters in Algeria mark paper ballots and place them in boxes. The ballots are then counted by electoral officials.

islatures must also be elected at regular intervals. In addition, there are county, city, and even school-board elections, which are of vital interest to taxpayers and parents living in school districts. Local elections are held at various times during the year.

This round of federal, state, and local elections goes on in every community throughout the nation. No war or disaster has ever halted this vital function of the American electorate.

▶ ELECTORAL SYSTEMS IN OTHER COUNTRIES

In the United States, most candidates are elected in **single-member districts**. That is, two or more candidates run for office in one district, such as a congressional district. The person who receives the most votes wins. But in other democratic countries, such as Japan,

Germany, and Israel, a different system called **proportional representation** is used to elect the nation's parliament. Under proportional representation, if a party gets a certain proportion (percentage) of the vote nationwide, it gets that percentage of representation in parliament. In Israel, for example, if the Labor Party gets 25 percent of the votes cast, it will receive 25 percent of the seats in parliament. An advantage of this system is that it allows small parties to have more of a voice in government. On the other hand, if many small parties are more or less equally represented, it may be difficult to form a stable parliamentary majority to run the government.

▶ HISTORY

From the time of the ancient Hebrews and Greeks, people have fought tyranny for the right to choose their own leaders. The early kings of Israel were chosen, as were the generals of the ancient Greek armies. Xenophon's famous march across Asia Minor in 401 B.C. began with his election as captain by a band of Greek soldiers. The Greeks voted for their new leader while standing in the very shadow of the pursuing Persian armies.

The Teutonic tribes of Northern Europe elected the bravest members as their leaders. This habit of freely choosing their leaders was brought to Britain by the Anglo-Saxon conquerors some 1,500 years ago. As the British Parliament gradually gained power, elections became more frequent and regular, and gradually the number of people allowed to vote was increased.

In colonial America, election of church and public officials began shortly after the first colonists arrived. The institution of democratic self-government through elections became common in most of the American colonies. But until the 1900's, most election laws in the United States did not regulate the way the major parties selected the candidates to represent them in elections. Candidates would simply announce their intentions to run for office and distribute stickers with their names to the voters. These were pasted on the ballot on election day. After many years, political organizations began holding conventions in districts, wards, cities, counties, and states. In these conventions, tough political bosses often ruled with an iron hand and chose the party candidates themselves.

A direct primary system was first tried in Crawford County, Pennsylvania, in 1868. The voters in each party used ballots to select the nominees for the next election. For the first time this put the choice of candidates in the hands of the party members. Other states adopted the plan, and today direct primaries are used almost everywhere throughout the United States.

Reviewed by KAY J. MAXWELL
President
League of Women Voters of the United States

See also ELECTORAL COLLEGE; POLITICAL PARTIES; UNITED STATES, CONSTITUTION OF THE; UNITED STATES, GOVERNMENT OF THE; VOTING.

ELECTORAL COLLEGE

The citizens of the United States do not elect their president directly. When Americans cast their vote for a presidential candidate, what they are really doing is voting for an elector—a delegate who is pledged to vote for that same candidate. There are 538 such electors chosen in every presidential election. As a group they are known as the electoral college.

▶ **HOW THE ELECTORAL COLLEGE WORKS**

Each state has as many electors as it has members in the U.S. Senate and House of Representatives combined. The electoral college thus includes 535 electors from the states (one for each of the 435 members of the House plus one for each of the 100 senators)—plus another three to represent the District of Columbia—for a total of 538.

According to the U.S. Constitution, state legislators decide how electors will be chosen in their states. First, each political party in a state nominates a slate (list) of electors. These electors are usually pledged to support the party's nominee for president and vice president. In some states, electors are legally required to vote for their candidate.

On election day—the first Tuesday after the first Monday in November every four years—voters throughout the nation go to the polls to choose the electors in their states. In many states the names of the electors do not even appear on the ballot. The voters see only the names of the candidates for president and vice president. Nevertheless, voters who favor the Republican (or Democratic) candidate for president actually vote for the Republican (or Democratic) electors in their state. This voting of the people for electors is called the **popular vote**.

In 48 of the 50 states, the candidate who receives the most popular votes wins all that state's electoral votes. In Maine and Nebraska, the state's electoral votes can be divided among the candidates. To be elected president, a candidate needs a majority—or 270—of all the electoral votes in the country (one-half of the total number of votes plus one).

In most presidential elections, the winner is usually known by the morning following election day. However, election results do not become official until weeks afterward. The winning electors meet in their state capitals on the Monday after the second Wednesday in December. There they vote for president and vice president and send the sealed results to Washington. On January 6, the results are read in the presence of the entire Congress and the winner becomes official. Then, on January 20, the president-elect takes the oath of office as president of the United States.

▶ **PROBLEMS OF THE ELECTORAL SYSTEM**

Many people dislike the electoral college system. They think it is wrong for the winning party in a state to get all the electoral votes and the losing party none. The victor may win several large states by just a few popular votes. But even this small margin would win all the state's electoral votes. The opponent, on the other hand, may win large popular majorities in several smaller states with few electoral votes. This makes it possible for a person to lose the nationwide popular vote and still be elected president. This happened in the 2000 presidential race. Al Gore received half a million more popular votes than George W. Bush but lost the electoral college by a vote of 266 to 271 (see the feature accompanying this article).

Another criticism of the electoral college is that it negatively affects the campaign process. Because the votes that really matter—the electoral college votes—are counted by state, candidates will often pay a great deal of attention to some states and no attention to other states. For example, if a certain state is considered "safe," or sure to vote for one candidate, neither candidate will do much campaigning there. Consequently, fewer voters may go to the polls in those states.

▶ HISTORY

The Founding Fathers who drew up the Constitution in 1787 were not willing to allow ordinary citizens to vote for their president directly. Among other things, the founders were afraid that the people would not be well informed enough to choose wisely and would simply back candidates they knew from their own state. Rather, the founders believed that a selected group of electors should pick the president.

The founders thought that electors should be allowed to vote as they pleased. But during John Adams' term as president (1797–1801), political parties became much stronger than they had been before. The parties nominated candidates for president and vice president and then picked electors to vote for them. Electors were expected to vote for their party's choice, so in most cases the voting procedure merely became a formality. The person who received the most votes from the electors would become president. The one with the next highest number of votes would be vice president. That system endured until 1800, when Aaron Burr and Thomas Jefferson got exactly the same number of electoral votes and the system had to be changed. The Twelfth Amendment to the Constitution (ratified in 1804) clarified the electoral college procedure and provided that each elector would vote for one person for president and another for vice president.

Although today the electoral system is important, individual electors are not. But they can become significant if they go back on their pledges. For example, they may fail to vote for candidates they promised to vote for in order to press political points. They may vote for another candidate or someone who is not even running. Scholars call this the "faithless elector" problem. Such an incident happened in 2000, when an elector from Washington, D.C., who was pledged to Al Gore, abstained from voting to protest the District's lack of representation in Congress.

DAVID E. WEINGAST
Author, *We Elect a President*
Reviewed by KAY J. MAXWELL
President
League of Women Voters of the United States

CLOSE U.S. PRESIDENTIAL ELECTIONS

1800 Due to a technicality, the election of 1800 resulted in a tie between Thomas Jefferson and Aaron Burr, Jefferson's vice presidential running mate. After several months, the U.S. House of Representatives certified Jefferson as the winner, but the confusion prompted a clarification of voting procedures, which resulted in the Twelfth Amendment to the Constitution.

1824 Although Andrew Jackson won the popular vote in 1824, neither he nor his opponent, John Quincy Adams, won a majority in the electoral college. When the House finally chose Adams, Jackson became the first presidential candidate to win the popular vote but lose the election.

1876 Samuel Tilden won the national popular vote in 1876, but a close race in Florida swung the majority of electoral votes to Rutherford B. Hayes. A special congressional commission, voting along party lines, finally awarded the presidency to Hayes.

1888 Although Grover Cleveland, the incumbent president, won the national popular vote in 1888, Benjamin Harrison won the presidency with a majority in the electoral college.

2000 A stalemate in Florida held up the 2000 election results between Al Gore and George W. Bush for five weeks after the election. The U.S. Supreme Court finally intervened, settling the election in favor of Bush, even though Gore had won the national popular vote.

ELECTRIC GENERATORS

Think of the many comforts and conveniences made possible by electricity. Electricity runs washing machines, refrigerators, and vacuum cleaners. It lights houses. It runs radios, televisions, and computers. Electricity powers machinery, cools buildings, and carries voices over telephone lines. The list could go on for pages. But all these uses depend on a cheap and plentiful supply of electricity. Generators are used to make electricity cheaply in huge quantities.

The electric generator is a machine that converts mechanical energy into electrical energy. The source of mechanical energy needed to drive a generator is called the **prime mover.** Examples of prime movers include turbines and internal-combustion engines.

Every prime mover changes some kind of energy into mechanical energy. For example, when fossil fuels such as coal or oil are burned, the chemical energy stored in the fossil fuels is changed into heat energy. Heat turns water into steam and the steam drives a turbine, which is connected to an electric generator. In this way, the moving turbine becomes the source of mechanical energy needed to drive an electric generator.

Electric generators vary greatly in size. Some are smaller than the kind mounted next to a bicycle wheel for powering bicycle lights. Others are larger than a house.

▶DISCOVERY OF THE GENERATOR

In 1819, Hans Christian Oersted, a Danish physicist, noticed that the needle of a compass moved away from its normal north-pointing position when a wire carrying an electric current was brought near it. The effect was stronger when the current was increased. When the current in the wire was stopped, the needle again pointed north. Scientists already knew that a compass needle, which is a magnet itself, would move if another magnet was brought near it. By creating this effect with an electric current, Oersted had discovered that an electric current produces a magnetic field. A magnetic field is the area around a magnet or current-carrying wire where magnetic force can be detected.

An English scientist, Michael Faraday, heard of Oersted's discovery and wondered if the reverse would prove true. Could a magnetic field produce an electric current? Faraday experimented with magnets and wires and found that a magnet just lying still beside the wire would not produce an electric current. However, an electric current would be produced if a wire was moved quickly between the poles of a U-shaped magnet—that is, through its magnetic field. A current would also be produced if the magnet was moved and the wire held still. The electric current would flow as long as the magnet or the wire kept moving. Faraday's discovery in 1831—that a changing magnetic field could create, or **induce,** an electric current—makes possible the use of today's electric generators.

▶AC AND DC GENERATORS

There are two main types of generators: alternating current (AC) generators and direct current (DC) generators. AC generators produce **alternating current,** or electric current that reverses the direction in which it flows. DC generators produce **direct current,** or electric current that always flows in the same di-

Alternating Current Generator
Each time armature makes half turn, direction of current reverses

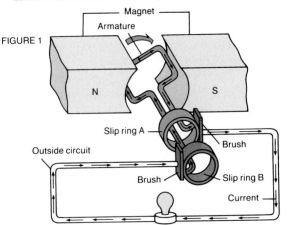

FIGURE 1

Direct Current Generator
Current always flows in same direction

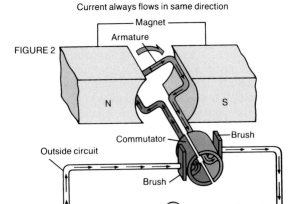

FIGURE 2

rection. Figure 1 shows a simple AC generator. The magnet remains still and the coil of wire, called the **armature,** rotates. Each end of the armature coil is connected to a metal **slip ring** that slides against a piece of carbon called a **brush.** The two brushes collect electricity induced in the armature as it rotates within the magnetic field. The brushes are connected to the outside circuit.

The magnet in Figure 1 induces an electric current to flow in a clockwise direction through the armature. During the first half of a complete rotation, one side of the armature coil moves upward through the magnetic field. At the same time the other side moves down. During this half of the armature's rotation the brush at slip ring A collects the current from the armature. The current flows through the outside circuit and is collected by the brush at slip ring B, where it flows back into the armature. In the second half of the armature's rotation the side of the coil that had previously moved upward now moves downward and the other side of the coil moves upward. This causes an opposite flow of the electric current through the armature, and thus through the outside circuit as well. During this half of the rotation, the brush at slip ring B collects the current from the armature, and the brush at slip ring A returns it to the armature.

Figure 2 shows a simple DC generator. It looks just like the AC generator in Figure 1 with one important difference. Each end of the armature coil is connected to one half of a single split ring instead of two separate slip rings. This split ring is called a **commutator.** The magnets still induce alternating current in the armature as it rotates. Each time the armature rotates half a turn, the current in the armature reverses direction. But at the moment the current in the armature reverses, the gap between the commutator pieces lines up with the brushes. In the next instant, each commutator piece connects with the opposite brush. In this manner, one brush always collects the current from the armature and the other brush always returns the current to the armature. Therefore, the current in the outside circuit flows in the same direction at all times.

The power of an electric current—that is, the amount of work it can do—depends on two things: the voltage and the amperage. **Amperage** is the measurement of how much current is moving through the wire. **Voltage** is the measurement of the force that is pushing the current through the wires. Three things determine the voltage a generator will produce:

(1) The strength of the magnetic field. The stronger the field, the greater the voltage.

(2) The number of coils of wire in the armature. The greater the number of coils in the armature, the greater the voltage.

(3) The speed of rotation. The faster the generator turns, the greater the voltage.

These principles are used in designing generators. Almost all generators have more than one magnet to make the field stronger. In addition, most generators use electromagnets instead of permanent magnets because electromagnets can be made stronger than permanent magnets. Most electromagnets consist of a coil of wire wound around an iron core. An electric current running through the coil produces a magnetic field. The iron core, which concentrates (strengthens) the magnetic field, is magnetized only as long as the current is flowing through the coil. Generators that use permanent magnets, or magnets that keep their strength for long periods of time, are sometimes called **magnetos.** A small DC generator can be used to supply current for the electromagnets of a whole series of large generators. (Power stations today usually have one small DC generator for each big AC generator.)

Unlike the simple generators shown in the diagrams in this article, generators for actual use are built with many coils in the armature. In many AC generators, especially the larger ones, the armature coils remain still and are arranged around the outside of rotating electromagnets. That is, the magnetic field moves instead of the armature coil. The reason for doing this is that the voltage induced in the armature is very high, while the voltage used for the electromagnets is much lower. If high-voltage current had to pass from a moving armature through the brushes and slip ring, it might cause harmful sparking and overheating. It is easier to use slip rings for the low voltage electromagnets and a permanent connection for the high voltage armature.

J. A. MASSINGILL
General Electric Company
Reviewed by GREGORY VOGT
Author, *Generating Electricity*

See also ELECTRICITY; ELECTRIC MOTORS; FARADAY, MICHAEL; MAGNETS AND MAGNETISM; POWER PLANTS.

Cities consume enormous amounts of electricity every day for such purposes as lighting, heating, and air conditioning. Electric power is so abundant and easy to use that we often forget how different life would be without it.

ELECTRICITY

Although no one has ever seen electricity, evidence of its presence is everywhere. It is used in nearly every home, office, and factory. We use it every day to provide lighting, heat for cooking and home heating, and cooling for refrigeration and air conditioning. Electricity provides power for elevators (so that people in skyscrapers do not have to walk up and down hundreds of stairs), power to run trains and subways, and power to operate electrical appliances, radio and television, and computers.

Scientists have learned that electricity is not just a form of power for human use. Physicists know that electrical forces bind atoms together to form all matter. Chemists know that electrical forces play an important part in all chemical changes. Biologists know that electricity carries messages through the nervous system of animals, including humans. The more we learn about electricity, the more amazing it seems.

▶WHAT IS ELECTRICITY?

Early experimenters thought that electricity was a mysterious force that appeared only in certain materials. Today we know that it is a part of all matter.

Electricity and Matter

All matter is made up of tiny particles called atoms. An atom is made up of even smaller particles. In the center, or nucleus, are one or more **protons**, particles with a positive electrical charge, and **neutrons**, particles with no electrical charge. In motion around the atom's nucleus are one or more **electrons**, tiny particles with a negative electrical charge.

An atom usually has exactly the same number of protons and electrons. The positive and negative charges balance each other, so altogether, the atom is electrically neutral.

Particles with different charges exert forces on one another. Particles with like charges (both positive or both negative) repel each other—push each other apart. Particles with opposite charges attract each other. This is the law of electrical charges.

ATOM

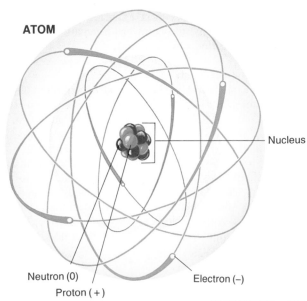

Nucleus

Neutron (0)

Proton (+)

Electron (−)

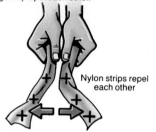

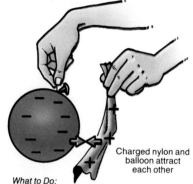
There are many ways to remove an electron from an atom or add an electron to it. In some kinds of atoms, electrons farthest from the nucleus are loosely held and can easily be set free. When that happens, the **free electron** has a negative charge, and the rest of the atom, called a **positive ion**, has a positive charge. Other kinds of atoms can easily attract and "capture" one or more extra electrons. When that happens, the atom has a negative charge and is called a **negative ion**.

Static Electricity

Long before we understood electricity in the atom, the Greek philosopher and scientist Thales (640?–546? B.C.) observed that amber (a yellow, plastic-like material) had a strange quality. If Thales rubbed the amber with a piece of woolen cloth, the amber would attract small, light materials such as lint and bits of dry leaves and cork. Thales believed that there was some unknown force in the amber. The Greek word for amber is *elektron*. In time, the mysterious force in the amber became known as electricity.

In the next two thousand years, experimenters discovered that some other substances, including glass, have properties like amber. You can easily repeat these early experiments. If you rub a glass rod or plate with silk, you will find that small pieces of dry paper jump to the glass and cling to it. A plastic comb run through dry hair on a dry day will also attract paper scraps.

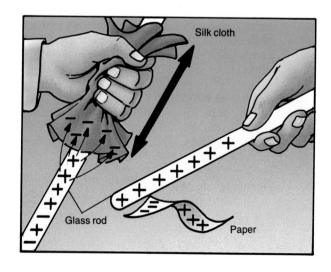

Silk cloth

Glass rod

Paper

Left: Lightning streaks across the sky or strikes the ground when a large amount of static electricity built up in a storm cloud discharges. *Right:* Benjamin Franklin proved in 1752 that lightning is electricity with his dangerous kite experiment.

We now know what gives materials these electrical qualities. Normally a piece of glass is electrically neutral. But when the glass is rubbed with silk, some of its free electrons are pulled away. The glass is left with some positive ions and has a positive electrical charge. We say it is charged with **static electricity**. It attracts the electrons in a nearby bit of paper. The electrons move toward the end of the paper nearest the glass, making that end of the paper slightly negative. Since opposite charges attract, the paper clings to the glass.

Running a plastic comb through your hair causes a similar effect. Some of the electrons in the hair are attracted to the plastic comb. The comb then has some negative ions and therefore has a negative electrical charge. When the comb comes near a bit of paper, it pushes electrons in the paper slightly away from the comb. The electrons move toward the side of the paper farthest from the comb. The surface of the paper nearest the comb then has a small positive charge, so it clings to the comb.

The box on page 136 has instructions for an experiment with static electricity.

Lightning

On a stormy summer day, positive and negative charges can build up in clouds. When the attraction between positive and negative grows large enough, a sudden burst of electricity can flow between clouds or from a cloud to the ground. This causes a flash of light—lightning —and the shock creates a great crashing sound —thunder. Lightning occurs when a large buildup of static electricity suddenly becomes a burst of electric current moving to another place.

The first person to prove that lightning is electrical was the American Benjamin Franklin (1706–90). In 1752, he conducted a now-famous experiment. During a thunderstorm he flew a kite. He tied a key in the string near his hand. When lightning struck the kite, the electrical charge followed the wet string down to the key. When Franklin moved his hand toward the key, a spark jumped to his hand and gave him a shock.

Franklin was lucky he lived to tell about his experiment—he did not fully understand how

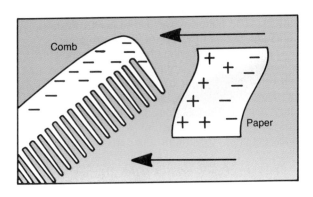

Comb

Paper

The nature of electricity was a mystery to early experimenters. *Far left:* The Italian scientist Luigi Galvani mistakenly believed that "animal electricity" made the leg of a dead frog twitch when touched by two metals joined together. *Left:* Alessandro Volta, another Italian scientist, found the source of the electricity. By layering disks of different metals, over and over, he was able to produce an electric current with a device called a voltaic pile.

powerful lightning can be. Never repeat this experiment. It could easily kill you and anyone standing near you.

Franklin put his discovery to practical use. He knew that electricity travels through metals, so he reasoned that a metal rod placed on top of a building and running down to the ground might protect the building from lightning. People laughed at his "lightning rods," but experience proved that lightning would strike the rods and part of the electrical charge would be carried to the ground through the metal without harming the building. Soon other people were protecting their buildings with lightning rods, too.

Creating a Steady Current

In the late 1700's, the Italian scientist Luigi Galvani (1737–98) found that the muscle of a dead frog would twitch if it came into contact with copper and iron that were touching each other at the same time. He believed that the muscle was the source of the electricity.

Alessandro Volta (1745–1827), another Italian scientist, showed that the electricity came from the combination of metals, not from the frog muscle. He showed that when two different metals come into contact, a positive charge is developed in one metal and a negative charge in the other. When a wire (or a frog's muscle) connects the two metals, a small electrical current flows through it. The frog's muscle, it turned out, was serving as a **conductor**, a substance through which electricity can pass easily.

Galvani's discovery about the frog muscle proved to be important to biology. It showed that electrical forces have something to do with an animal's control of its muscles. Later experimenters would learn that an animal's nervous system sends electrical messages to tighten or relax muscles.

Volta's discovery that two metals in contact could create an electric current led in a different direction. Using what he had learned about different metals, he created a **voltaic pile**—a device that could create a steady flow or **current** of electricity.

Volta used the idea of two metals. He made a stack of a silver disk, a zinc disk, and paper moistened in salt water, a silver disk, a zinc disk, and so on. When he ran a metal wire from the top of the pile to the bottom, a strong, steady current of electricity ran through the wire.

We know now that electricity in the voltaic pile comes from a chemical reaction that involves the silver, the zinc, and the salt water. Gradually the metals are changed by the chemical reaction, and when they are used up, the electrical current will end.

A few years later, Sir Humphry Davy (1778–1829), an English scientist, connected a number of voltaic piles together to produce even stronger current. We call his device a **battery**. The batteries we use today in flashlights and radios work on the same principles.

The early experimenters found that to create an electrical current, a path must be provided that runs in a circular route or **circuit**—from the source of electricity and back to it again. They learned that as long as this circuit is closed, or complete, current will flow. If a break occurs in the circuit, the current stops.

Measuring Electricity

The flow of electrons in an electrical circuit is something like water flowing through a hose. If you could look into the hose at one point, you would see that a certain amount of water passes that point each second. How much passes in a second depends on how much pressure is being applied—how hard the water is being "pushed." It also depends on how wide the hose is. The larger the force and the wider the hose, the more water passes each second.

In a similar manner, the flow of electrons in a wire depends on the electrical pressure being produced by the battery or generator and on the characteristics of the wire.

Current Flow. The flow of electrical current is measured in **amperes**, often called "amps." Amperage is a measure of how many electrons are passing a given point in a second.

Electrical Pressure. The pressure that is "pushing" electrons through an electric circuit is measured in **volts** and is called voltage. It is also called "electromotive force" (emf).

Resistance. Resistance is the opposition a material offers to the flow of electricity. It is measured in **ohms**.

Metals are good conductors of electricity—they offer little resistance to its flow. Some metals, such as copper, are especially good conductors. Pure water is a poor conductor, but when some substances, such as salt, are dissolved in it, it conducts electricity well.

Many other natural substances, such as most rocks and minerals, have so much resistance that they can scarcely be made to conduct electricity. These substances, and human-made substances such as glass and plastic, are such poor conductors that they are often used as **insulators** to protect people from accidental contact with an electrical current. Insulators are used to wrap metal wires that carry an electric current, for example.

The electrical resistance of an object is affected not only by what material it is made of, but also by its shape. A very thin copper wire has more resistance than a thick copper wire of the same length. A very long copper wire has more resistance than a short one of the same thickness.

Some materials can conduct an electric current under conditions that can be controlled. They are called **semiconductors**. The ability to control the flow of electric current is the

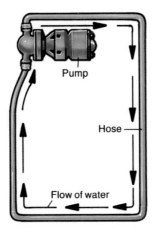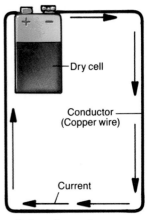

Left: A pump supplies the force that pushes water through a hose. *Right:* A dry cell supplies the voltage, or electromotive force, that pushes electrons through the wire and makes an electric current flow.

most important property of semiconductors and makes them useful in modern electronics. You can learn more about them in the article ELECTRONICS in Volume E and the article TRANSISTORS, DIODES, AND INTEGRATED CIRCUITS in Volume T.

Certain materials, called **superconductors**, lose all electrical resistance when cooled to very low temperatures. They have made it possible to create powerful electromagnets. One use for these magnets is in magnetic resonance imaging (MRI) scanners, which let doctors see detailed images of the inside of the brain and other body organs. New materials that are superconductive at high temperatures might one day be used to transmit electric power over long distances more efficiently.

Ohm's Law

The German scientist Georg Simon Ohm (1787–1854) made an important discovery about resistance. He studied the relationship between the amount of current that flowed through a wire (the amperage) and the amount of electromotive force that drove that current (the voltage). In the substances he tested, he found that if he doubled the voltage, the current would also double. If he cut the voltage in half, the current would be cut in half. Resistance remained the same when the voltage and current flow increased or decreased. This is called Ohm's law, and as a formula it can be written in three simple ways:

(1) $$\frac{\text{pressure}}{\text{(in volts)}} = \frac{\text{current}}{\text{(in amperes)}} \times \frac{\text{resistance}}{\text{(in ohms)}}$$

or

(2) $$\text{current (in amperes)} = \frac{\text{pressure (in volts)}}{\text{resistance (in ohms)}}$$

or

(3) $$\text{resistance (in ohms)} = \frac{\text{pressure (in volts)}}{\text{current (in amperes)}}$$

If you know the resistance of a particular electrical device and the voltage of the electrical supply, you can easily calculate how much current (amperage) is flowing through the system. For example, if you know that household voltage is 120 volts and is connected to a device with a resistance of 20 ohms, the current flow in the electric circuit is 6 amperes.

$$\text{amperes} = \frac{\text{volts}}{\text{ohms}}$$

$$\text{amperes} = \frac{120}{20}$$

$$\text{amperes} = 6$$

Electricity and Magnetism

Magnets—substances that attract iron and certain other metals—were known in ancient times. Centuries later, people discovered that a magnetic material floating on water would always point in the same direction—one end toward the north and the other toward the south. Sailors learned to use magnetic material to make compasses to help them navigate.

In 1820, Hans Christian Oersted (1777–1851), a Danish scientist, noticed that when a wire with an electric current came near a compass needle, the needle moved away from pointing north. This suggested to him that electricity and magnetism must be related.

About the same time as Oersted, the French scientist André Marie Ampère (1775–1836) also saw that electricity and magnetism must be much alike. The ends of a bar magnet are called its poles. One end is called the north pole and the other the south pole. The poles of magnets behave something like electric charges. The north pole of one magnet repels the north pole of another magnet. In the same way, one south pole repels another south pole. Two unlike poles—a north and a south—attract each other. This rule is much like the law of electrical charge.

Ampère discovered that if he passed an electric current through a coil of wire, the wire acted like a magnet. It had a north and south pole and could attract iron. This suggested more strongly than ever the relationship between electricity and magnetism. For more information on magnetism, see the article MAGNETS AND MAGNETISM in Volume M.

The English scientist Michael Faraday (1791–1867) imagined that there were "lines of force" stretching out into space from a

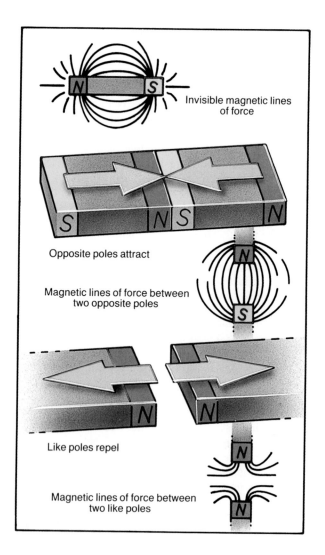

Invisible magnetic lines of force

Opposite poles attract

Magnetic lines of force between two opposite poles

Like poles repel

Magnetic lines of force between two like poles

magnet or from an electrical charge. He suggested that magnetic lines of force can push or pull on other magnets and certain metals without touching them. Similarly, an electric charge can push or pull another electric charge.

If an electric current running through a coil of wire can make a kind of magnet, Faraday asked, could a magnet help to create an electric current?

One day he pushed a bar magnet into a coil of wire. The coil was connected to a galvanometer, an instrument for measuring current. As he pushed the magnet into the coil, Faraday noticed a reading on the meter. When he held the magnet still, there was no reading. But as long as the magnet was moving, a current flowed in the wire. The same thing happened if Faraday moved a wire quickly between the two poles of a magnet.

Faraday reported that a suddenly changing magnetic field can create, or induce, an electric current in a conductor. This offered a new way of creating an electric current—the electric **generator**, which can turn the energy of a moving object into electricity with the help of a magnet. Faraday's discovery later became an important part of today's practical electrical systems.

Faraday showed that the process of an electric generator can be reversed. He constructed a model of an electric motor, in which electrical energy can be converted to mechanical en-

ergy. Electric generators and motors are discussed in more detail later in this article.

Electromagnetic Waves

Many scientists were intrigued by the work of Faraday and other experimenters in electricity. The Scotsman James Clerk Maxwell (1831–79) spent many years trying to understand more about electricity and magnetism. He wrote four famous mathematical formulas describing the basic electrical and magnetic forces and the relationships between them.

Above: The English scientist Michael Faraday is sometimes called the "father of electricity" because of his many important discoveries. *Left:* One discovery was that moving a magnet in a coil of wire produces an electric current in the wire (as shown by the galvanometer needle).

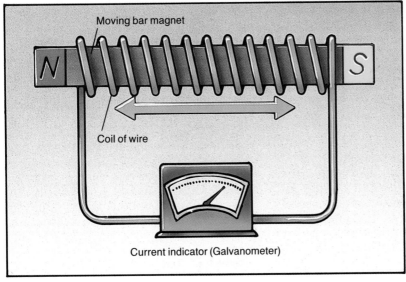

Moving bar magnet

Coil of wire

Current indicator (Galvanometer)

At the Hoover Dam on the Colorado River, huge generators change the energy of falling water into electricity, which is used by cities hundreds of miles away.

quantities, to transport it long distances, and to use it to produce light, heat, power, and new means of communication.

Producing Electricity

Generators. As people began to use electricity to light their homes and provide power for electrical appliances, engineers developed larger and larger plants to generate the power. These plants rely on the principle first discovered by Faraday—when a magnet spins inside a coil of wire, the magnet will induce an electric current. With the help of the magnet, a generator can turn mechanical energy into electrical energy.

In large generators, power to turn the magnets is often supplied by steam under high pressure. Coal or oil is burned to boil water and create the steam. The tremendous power of nuclear reactions can also be used to generate the heat needed to boil water and produce steam. Huge generators, many as big as houses, work around the clock producing electricity for our daily needs. For more information about generators, see the article ELECTRIC GENERATORS in this volume.

In mountainous territory or at large dams, the power of falling water can supply power to generate electricity. Such plants are called hydroelectric plants.

Generating huge amounts of electrical power causes various dangers to the environment. For example, burning coal or oil contributes to air pollution. Nuclear plants produce radioactive wastes that are difficult to dispose of safely. And nuclear fuels could be harmful if accidentally released into the environment. Construction of a major dam for hydroelectric power may flood thousands of square miles or change the flow of streams, killing plants and animals. Planners try to balance our need for electricity with the health of the environment.

Some sources of electricity offer fewer risks to the environment. "Wind farms" harvest steady winds, converting the energy of moving air into electrical energy. Solar cells convert sunlight directly to electricity. The surface of the cell is a thin wafer of specially treated silicon. Unfortunately, neither wind nor solar generators can produce large amounts of power at the present time.

Batteries. Batteries convert chemical energy into electricity.

Based on these formulas, Maxwell predicted the existence of **electromagnetic waves** that would travel at the speed people had measured for light. In fact, Maxwell said, light itself is an electromagnetic wave.

Maxwell's theory of electromagnetic waves was later proved and became an important step toward development of radio and television. Other forms of electromagnetic waves are microwaves, X-rays, and a form of radioactivity called gamma rays.

To learn more about uses of electromagnetic waves, see the articles MICROWAVES in Volume M, RADAR AND SONAR and RADIO in Volume QR, TELEVISION in Volume T, and X-RAYS in Volume WXYZ.

Making Electricity Practical

Until about 1830, electricity was an interesting scientific phenomenon, but it had no practical uses. Over the next century, practical inventors joined scientists in studying electricity. They found so many uses for it that they greatly changed the way people live.

Building on early discoveries, inventors found ways to produce electricity in large

A GLOSSARY OF ELECTRICITY TERMS

ALTERNATING CURRENT: An electric current in which the direction of flow reverses many times a second. *See also* DIRECT CURRENT.

AMPERE: The basic unit of electric current flow.

BATTERY: A device that converts chemical energy into electrical energy.

CIRCUIT BREAKER: A device used to protect electrical circuits. If a short circuit or other circumstance causes too much current to flow through a circuit, the circuit breaker opens a switch, thus breaking the circuit and ending the flow of current. *See also* SHORT CIRCUIT.

CONDUCTOR: A material, such as silver or copper, through which electricity will easily pass. A conductor offers little electrical resistance.

DIRECT CURRENT: An electric current which flows in a single direction. *See also* ALTERNATING CURRENT.

ELECTRIC CIRCUIT: The path along which an electric current flows, running from a source of electrical energy and back to it in a loop or circuit.

ELECTRIC CURRENT: A flow of electrically charged particles, such as electrons or ions.

ELECTRIC MOTOR: A device that changes electrical energy into mechanical energy.

ELECTRON: A tiny particle with a negative electric charge. Electrons are parts of all atoms.

FUSE: A device used to protect electrical circuits. If a short circuit or other circumstance causes too much current to flow through the circuit, the current causes a part of the fuse to melt, breaking the circuit and ending the flow of current. *See also* CIRCUIT BREAKER.

GENERATOR: A device that changes mechanical energy into electrical energy.

INSULATOR: A device or material that is a poor conductor of electricity. Wires are covered with insulating materials to prevent the leakage of electric current.

ION: An atom that has an electrical charge because it has gained or lost one or more electrons.

KILOWATT: A unit of electric power equal to 1,000 watts.

KILOWATT-HOUR: A measure of electrical energy generated or used. It equals the work done by a kilowatt of power in one hour.

OHM: The basic unit of electrical resistance.

RECTIFIER: A device that changes alternating electric current into direct current.

RESISTANCE: Opposition that a material offers to the flow of electricity. Materials that offer little resistance are called conductors. Materials that offer much resistance are poor conductors.

SEMICONDUCTOR: A material that is a poor conductor under some conditions and a good conductor under other conditions. This special electrical property makes semiconductors useful in creating electronic circuits for computers, television sets, and other devices.

SHORT CIRCUIT: A malfunction in an electrical system that allows current to flow against little resistance. A short circuit can cause wires to overheat and even start a fire. *See also* CIRCUIT BREAKER and FUSE.

SUPERCONDUCTOR: A material that, under special conditions such as very low temperature, offers almost no resistance to electric current.

TRANSFORMER: An electrical device that can increase (step up) or decrease (step down) the voltage of an alternating current.

VOLT: The unit of electrical pressure.

WATT: A measure of power, often used for measuring electrical power. *See also* KILOWATT and KILOWATT-HOUR.

Above: **Workers install panels of solar cells, devices that convert the sun's energy directly into electricity. It takes many solar cells to generate a useful amount of electricity.** *Right:* **Batteries produce electrical energy by means of a chemical reaction. In a flashlight battery (see cutaway), a chemical reaction between the central core, the surrounding paste, and the metal casing creates an electric current.**

Dry cell batteries are used to power small devices such as flashlights and portable radios. These batteries use many different chemical reactions to produce electric current. Flashlight batteries use a reaction between zinc and carbon. Other chemicals are used in longer-lasting alkaline and lithium batteries. Nickel cadmium batteries can be recharged many times before wearing out.

Storage batteries, also called wet cell batteries, are used in automobiles, and can be continuously recharged. Electricity from the battery operates lights, radio, and many other

Electricity travels to users through a complex network of power lines. High-voltage lines, hung on tall towers, transport electricity long distances. Where overhead power lines are not practical (through cities, for example), underground cables are used.

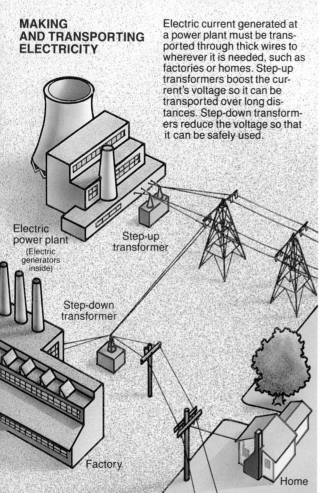

MAKING AND TRANSPORTING ELECTRICITY

Electric current generated at a power plant must be transported through thick wires to wherever it is needed, such as factories or homes. Step-up transformers boost the current's voltage so it can be transported over long distances. Step-down transformers reduce the voltage so that it can be safely used.

Electric power plant
(Electric generators inside)

Step-up transformer

Step-down transformer

Factory

Home

systems in the car. When the car is running, some of its mechanical energy runs a recharger, which reverses the chemical reaction in the storage battery, recharging it and extending its life. The recharging process is not perfect, however, and eventually the battery will need to be replaced.

Transporting Electricity

One of electricity's most important qualities is that it can be carried long distances through electrical wires. Electricity can be generated in one location and sent through a network of wires to homes, offices, and factories many miles away. Easy transporting of electricity depends on a number of important discoveries.

When people first tried to transport electricity from a large generator to homes, they ran into a problem. A generating plant could turn out electricity at very high voltages, but a household lightbulb or small appliance could only use electricity at low voltages. How could the voltage be lowered, or "stepped down" for household use?

The current generated in all early electrical experimentation was **direct current**—an electrical current that flows in one direction through a circuit. Unfortunately, experimenters could not find any convenient way to reduce or increase the voltage of direct current.

Then inventors discovered how to generate **alternating current**, which flows in both directions through a circuit, changing direction many times each second. The voltage of alternating current could be stepped up or down using a relatively simple device called a **transformer**.

Soon large electrical supply systems were using alternating current. It could be generated at high voltages, then stepped down for household use. For machines that require direct current, another device called a **rectifier** could turn alternating current into direct current.

Electricity for Heat and Light

Early experiments in electricity showed that if a high current is forced through a conductor that offers fairly high resistance, the conductor becomes warm. In other words, electrical energy can be changed into heat. Inventors soon made use of this fact to create electrical heaters and ovens. The most familiar use of heat from electricity is the electric toaster. When current runs through the toaster's coils, the coils become red hot.

Thomas Edison (1847–1931) saw that if he ran electric current through a substance that glows when it is heated, he could produce light from electricity. He experimented for years, and eventually he produced practical **incandescent lights**, lamps that give off light when a substance is heated until it glows. Such lights provided safe, inexpensive lighting for homes and factories. In fact, the first electrical systems were planned to provide home lighting. Today, incandescent light bulbs are still a major form of lighting.

Further experiments found other ways to produce light from electricity. In a tube holding certain gases, an electrical current excites electrons in the gases and causes the tube to glow. In a fluorescent light, for example, the excited gas produces invisible ultraviolet light. When it strikes a special coating on the inside of the tube, the coating glows, producing visible light. For more information on lighting, see ELECTRIC LIGHTS in this volume.

The Electric Motor

Electricity can also be converted to mechanical energy, as it is in an electric motor. When an electrical current is passed through a coil, it

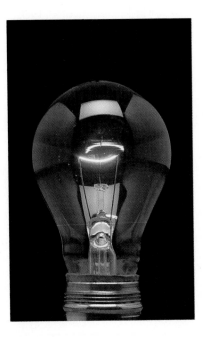

What makes an incandescent light bulb glow brightly? The coiled filament in an incandescent bulb is made of a very thin metal wire. Certain metals, such as tungsten, have a high resistance to the flow of electricity. When electricity flows through these conductors, heat is produced. A strong enough current will cause a filament to generate so much heat that it glows and produces light.

creates a magnetic field which can make a magnet spin. The spinning part may be connected to a drive shaft. Such motors are found in dozens of home appliances, such as clothes washers and dryers, refrigerators, and vacuum cleaners. To learn more about electric motors, see the article ELECTRIC MOTORS in this volume.

Electric motors have long been used to operate elevators. The electric elevator helped make tall buildings practical in large cities. Motors also powered pumps for lifting water to tanks on tall buildings. Without the pumps, tall buildings would have no water supply.

Heavy-duty electric motors soon replaced horses as the power to move trolleys in city streets. The trolleys got their power from wires strung overhead. The motors of some early automobiles were also powered by an electric battery, which was a quiet and clean source of power. But electric cars were slow and could run less than 40 miles (64 kilometers) before they needed to be recharged. Newer electric cars can travel much farther using longer-lasting rechargeable batteries.

Today very small electric motors are finding many uses in industry and everyday life. For example, an electronic wristwatch—with hands that show time on a dial—contains a tiny battery-powered motor that moves the hands. Even smaller motors no wider than a human hair have been built for special uses.

Electrical Communications

The first practical use of electricity was for communication. In the 1830's, inventors in Europe and the United States reasoned that a person might send a message by interrupting or varying an electrical current in ways that would make a code. A person receiving the message could decode the electrical impulses.

A practical system was perfected by the American Samuel F. B. Morse (1791–1872). It came to be known as the telegraph. Morse's telegraph made it possible for a sender to send a code of short dots and dashes (interruptions in the electrical current) which stood for letters in a message. The receiver decoded the dots and dashes and reassembled the message.

Soon telegraph companies were stringing wires on poles through cities and across the countryside. Railroads used the telegraph to send messages from station to station, and businesses soon learned to get "instant" information from distant markets or factories.

In the 1870's, Alexander Graham Bell (1847–1922) and others discovered a way to send the human voice on electrical wires. This was the beginning of the telephone system that connects almost every home and business in North America.

Late in the 1800's, others were experimenting with electromagnetic waves. They were trying to send messages through the air. This would enable ships to keep in communication with land. This new "wireless" communication became what we know as radio.

At first, only coded messages could be sent through the air. Soon, however, the Italian inventor Guglielmo Marconi (1874–1937) found a way to transmit voices. Within thirty years, radio was used not only for communication, but for home entertainment.

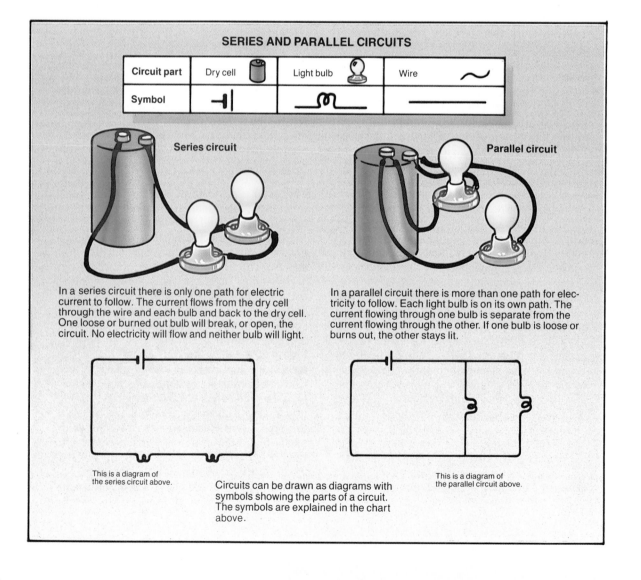

SERIES AND PARALLEL CIRCUITS

Circuit part	Dry cell	Light bulb	Wire
Symbol	⊣⊢	∿	─────

Series circuit

Parallel circuit

In a series circuit there is only one path for electric current to follow. The current flows from the dry cell through the wire and each bulb and back to the dry cell. One loose or burned out bulb will break, or open, the circuit. No electricity will flow and neither bulb will light.

In a parallel circuit there is more than one path for electricity to follow. Each light bulb is on its own path. The current flowing through one bulb is separate from the current flowing through the other. If one bulb is loose or burns out, the other stays lit.

This is a diagram of the series circuit above.

This is a diagram of the parallel circuit above.

Circuits can be drawn as diagrams with symbols showing the parts of a circuit. The symbols are explained in the chart above.

Household Circuits

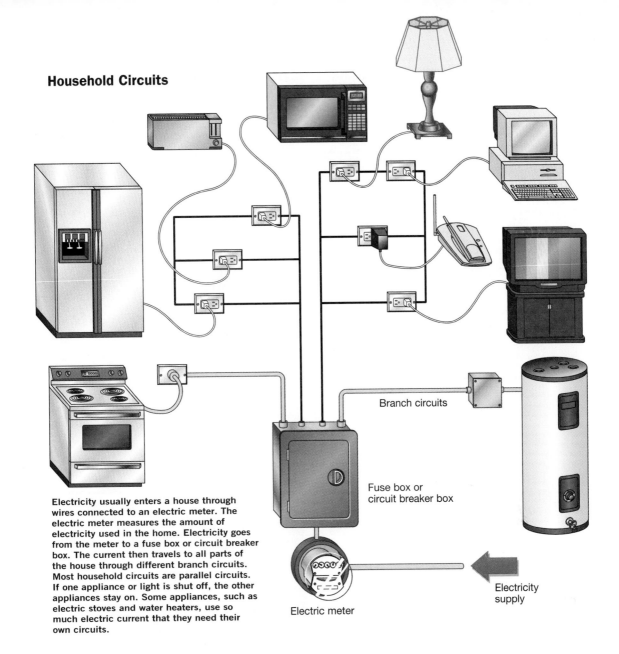

Branch circuits

Fuse box or
circuit breaker box

Electricity usually enters a house through wires connected to an electric meter. The electric meter measures the amount of electricity used in the home. Electricity goes from the meter to a fuse box or circuit breaker box. The current then travels to all parts of the house through different branch circuits. Most household circuits are parallel circuits. If one appliance or light is shut off, the other appliances stay on. Some appliances, such as electric stoves and water heaters, use so much electric current that they need their own circuits.

Electricity
supply

Electric meter

Inventors worked for decades to find a practical way of sending pictures, too. By the 1930's, practical television systems had been developed. In the 1950's, television became an important medium of home entertainment.

In the 1980's, the fax machine became a popular way of sending text and images over telephone lines. By the 1990's, vast amounts of computer data were being transmitted worldwide over networks such as the Internet.

For more information on electrical and electronic communication, see TELECOMMUNICATIONS and TELEVISION in Volume T.

Household Electricity

Most household current has an electromotive force of 110 to 120 volts. Some special circuits for air conditioning or major kitchen appliances such as electric stoves and ovens may have 220 volts. Parts of an everyday household electrical system illustrate much about practical electricity.

The Circuit. A household electrical circuit, like other circuits, has several important characteristics. First, the wire that carries the current follows a path that begins at the power source and returns to the power source. When-

Fuses and circuit breakers protect circuits from damage by stopping the flow of too much current. *Below:* These ten-amp fuses will "blow" if a current of more than ten amperes flows through them. *Right:* Circuit breakers, which switch off when a circuit carries too much current, have an advantage over fuses. They do not have to be replaced —they are simply switched back on.

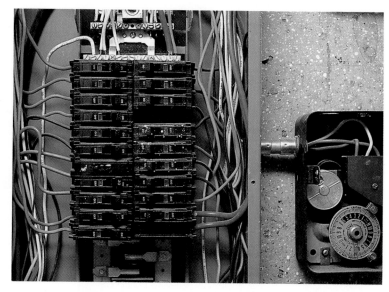

ever the circuit is complete (or *closed*), the current flows through it. Whenever the circuit is broken (or *open*), however, no current flows.

Second, the electrical current passes through one or more electrical devices—a light, appliance, or piece of electronic equipment. The device may use electricity to produce light, heat, or mechanical energy. In some devices (radio, television, computers), the electricity is used to display, record, or process information.

A circuit also has a switch or other control. A **switch** turns a light or appliance on and off —it closes or opens the electrical circuit. When you turn a light on, you are closing the circuit so that current can flow and cause the light to go on. When you turn the light off, you are breaking the circuit and ending the flow of current. If the light bulb burns out, this also breaks the circuit so that no current can flow. The bulb must be replaced before current will go through the circuit.

Safety Features. If a frayed wire or a faulty appliance causes a **short circuit**, a circuit with almost no resistance, current flow in the circuit suddenly increases. This causes the wires to heat and could cause an electrical fire. To prevent this possibility, most household electrical systems have **fuses** or **circuit breakers**.

A fuse is wired into a particular circuit. Current runs through the fuse, which has a section made of a material that heats and melts rapidly

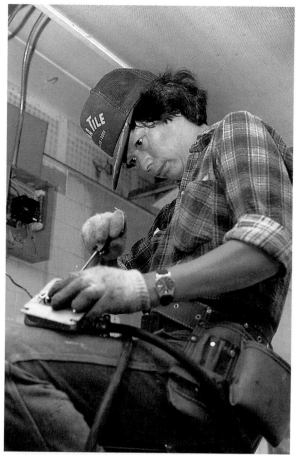

Electricians are specially trained people who install wiring in houses and factories. They also repair and maintain electrical equipment of many kinds.

SAFETY WITH ELECTRICITY

Like fire, electricity is a great helper and friend, but it can also be a dangerous enemy. Electrical accidents kill many people each year, often because simple electrical safety rules were not followed. Here are some of the most important.

AROUND HOUSEHOLD CURRENT

DO **NOT** handle or touch any electric appliance or light switch when you are in a bathtub or shower or when you are wet.

DO **NOT** put your finger in a light socket.

DO **NOT** change a light bulb when the light switch is on.

DO **NOT** plug in an electrical appliance that has a damaged cord.

DO **NOT** run electrical cords under rugs.

AVOID LIGHTNING

If caught out in a lightning storm:

DO find indoor shelter, or

DO get into a car or truck, or

DO squat down in a low-lying place.

DO **NOT** take shelter under a tree, and

DO **NOT** run across high ground.

AVOID POWER LINES

DO **NOT** climb electric poles or towers.

DO **NOT** climb trees near power lines.

DO **NOT** fly kites near power lines.

DO **NOT** go near fallen power lines after a storm or accident.

Suppose a live high-voltage wire has fallen across an automobile with people in it. They would be safe inside the car because the electric charges stay on the outside of the metal frame and no current flows through the passengers. But the rubber tires are good insulators, and this means that the entire frame of the car can be at high voltage. If you ever get caught in this way, do not step outside before the voltage is turned off. Otherwise, your body would conduct electricity from the auto to the ground. For the same reason, people on the ground outside must not touch the car.

when current above a certain amount passes through it. If the circuit is overloaded and the wires in the circuit begin to overheat, the fuse material melts and opens the circuit. The power goes off in the circuit, but the fuse has ended the danger of a fire.

If you replace that fuse with a new fuse, but have not repaired the defective cord or appliance, the new fuse will soon "blow," too, and the power will go off again.

A circuit breaker does the same job as a fuse. It is a switch that automatically opens if too much current is flowing through it.

Measuring Household Electricity. A basic measure of electric power is the **watt**, named for the Scottish scientist James Watt (1736–1819). One watt is the amount of power produced by one volt of electromotive force driving one ampere of current.

Various electrical devices require different levels of power to work properly. For example, the power rating of most light bulbs is printed on the glass bulb. A 100-watt incandescent light draws 100 watts of power from a household's electrical system. A 40-watt bulb of the same kind draws less power but gives less light. The watt is a very small unit of measure for most household uses. Often electrical power is measured in **kilowatts**. One kilowatt is equal to 1,000 watts.

Producers of electricity measure the amount of electricity used in a home, office, or factory in **kilowatt-hours**. A kilowatt-hour is the amount of work done by one kilowatt of power in an hour's time. The average American home uses about 850 kilowatt-hours of electricity in a month.

An electric meter measures the number of kilowatt-hours used by a consumer. It has a metal disk that turns at varying speeds—the more electricity used, the faster the disk turns. A meter reader from the electric company checks the meter each month to determine the customer's bill. Newer meters can automatically transmit readings to the electric company.

The box at left contains safety rules for anyone near electricity. If not handled properly, electricity can cause severe injury.

IRWIN MATH
Author, *Wires and Watts: Understanding and Using Electricity*

See also BATTERIES; ELECTRIC GENERATORS; ELECTRIC MOTORS; ELECTRONICS; MAGNETS AND MAGNETISM.

ELECTRIC LIGHTS

Toward the end of the day, as the sun sets and night begins to fall, we take for granted the electric lighting that enables us to continue working or playing in spite of the darkness. Today, most such lighting is provided by electric lightbulbs, called "lamps" by lighting engineers and designers.

Incandescent Lamps. Thomas Alva Edison and his assistants lit the first practical incandescent lamp in 1879. They had made a filament out of carbonized thread and mounted it inside a glass bulb from which the air had been removed. The ends of the filament were connected by wires to an electric generator. The inventors watched as that first lamp burned for 40 hours. In 1881, an African American inventor named Lewis Howard Latimer made incandescent lamps last much longer, using inexpensive carbon filaments. Latimer also invented a process for manufacturing these filaments more efficiently and a threaded wooden socket for his improved bulb.

The standard incandescent lamp of today is very similar in basic form to those first lamps. The important parts of an incandescent lamp are the bulb, the filament, and the base.

The bulb protects the hot filament from contact with the air, where it would combine with oxygen and burn. The bulb may be clear, but most are either acid-etched (finely scratched by acid) or coated on the inside with a powder. This helps diffuse (scatter) the light from the filament and softens the glare produced by the lamp. Most incandescent lamps are filled with nitrogen and argon gases, which help extend the life of the filament. Incandescent lamp bulbs are made in many shapes.

The filament is a thin, coiled wire made of the metal tungsten. Electricity flows through the filament when the lamp is switched on. The filament resists the flow of electricity. This resistance, which is like friction, causes the tungsten filament to glow almost white, reaching about 4670°F (2580°C). Filaments are made of tungsten because its very high melting point—6120°F (3380°C)—allows it to glow for many hours without melting or breaking. An incandescent lamp has a normal operating life of about 1,000 hours. Most incandescent lamps have screw-type bases that hold them in the lighting fixture and conduct electricity to the filament.

Incandescent lamps with built-in reflectors are directional light sources; that is, they project light as a beam in a single direction. There are two types of beams available. A spot lamp has a narrow beam and is generally used to highlight objects. A flood lamp has a wider beam and is used more for area lighting.

The **tungsten-halogen lamp** differs from an ordinary incandescent lamp in that it contains a gas mixture that includes a small amount of a halogen gas—usually iodine or bromine. As a standard incandescent lamp ages, tungsten evaporates from the filament and forms a black deposit on the inside of the bulb. Eventually one spot on the filament becomes so narrow that the filament breaks and the lamp burns out. In a tungsten-halogen lamp, the tungsten that boils off the filament is not deposited on the bulb wall. It combines temporarily with the iodine or bromine and is redeposited back on the filament. As a result, the life of a tungsten-halogen lamp is about twice that of a similar incandescent lamp. Because of the extremely high temperature at which the tungsten-halogen lamp operates, the bulb must be made of quartz rather than glass.

Fluorescent Lamps. In the late 1930's a long, tubular light source called a fluorescent lamp was introduced. A fluorescent lamp is made of a glass tube coated on the inside with a fluorescent powder called a phosphor. It produces light by passing electricity through a gas at very low pressure, thus causing the phosphor to glow, or *fluoresce*. The tube contains mercury vapor and a small amount of argon gas. Inside the tube, at each end, is a coiled filament called an electrode. When the lamp is switched on, electric current passes from the electrodes through the mercury vapor. This process produces invisible ultraviolet radiation. On striking the phosphor, the ultraviolet is changed into visible light.

Fluorescent lamps are more efficient and last longer (10,000 to 20,000 hours) than incandescent lamps. In addition to white, fluorescent lamp colors include blue, green, gold, pink, and red. Circular and U-shaped fluorescent lamps are available. Some compact fluorescent lamps are designed to be screwed into regular incandescent sockets.

Neon Lamps. Neon lamps are long tubes of light used for advertising, signs, and decoration. They work somewhat like a fluorescent lamp, but normally have no phosphor coating.

Many different kinds of electric lights are used for work and play. Powerful metal halide lamps illuminate sports stadiums at night (*right*); fluorescent ceiling and desk lamps are commonly used in offices (*below left*); and incandescent lamps serve most of our home lighting needs (*below right*).

Instead the light comes from a small amount of neon gas, argon gas, and mercury vapor inside the tube. Neon gives off orange-red light, argon a lavender light, and mercury vapor a blue light. Other colors are obtained by baking phosphors onto the inner tube wall and causing them to fluoresce.

High-Intensity Discharge Lamps. There are three kinds of high-intensity discharge lamps: the mercury-vapor lamp, the metal halide lamp, and the high-pressure sodium lamp. A **mercury-vapor lamp** consists of a bulb called a quartz arc tube mounted inside a larger glass bulb. Electricity is released in a short arc between two electrodes. Because the mercury vapor is under greater pressure than it is in a fluorescent lamp, no phosphor is needed. Visible bluish green white light is given off directly, rather than ultraviolet radiation first. Mercury-vapor lamps are used in landscape lighting.

The **metal halide lamp** is like the mercury-vapor lamp but contains chemical elements that produce a much more natural white light. Metal halide lamps are used for lighting roadways and shopping centers. They are also used for televised sporting events.

A **high-pressure sodium lamp** has a ceramic arc tube within a glass bulb. The yellowish white light from this kind of lamp is warmer in appearance than light from mercury-vapor or metal halide lamps. High-pressure sodium lamps are widely used in industrial lighting as well as for lighting gymnasiums, walkways, parking lots, and roadways.

JOSEPH B. MURDOCH
Author, *Illuminating Engineering:
From Edison's Lamp to the Laser*
Reviewed by PARVIZ FAMOURI
West Virginia University

See also EDISON, THOMAS ALVA; ELECTRICITY; LIGHTING; NEON AND OTHER NOBLE GASES.

ELECTRIC MOTORS

Electric motors are machines that change electrical energy into mechanical energy. They are used to do work in hundreds of ways every day. Electric motors drive machinery in factories. They turn the wheels of electric cars, and of robotic vehicles designed to explore Mars. They spin disks that store data in computers. In homes, electric motors provide power for air conditioners, refrigerators, washing machines, vacuum cleaners, videotape players, and other appliances that make life easier and more pleasant.

Electric motors come in many sizes and shapes. They can rotate or move back and forth (linear motion). Giant motors propel ships and locomotives. Linear motors propel and guide magnetically levitated (maglev) trains that float above their tracks. Very small, battery-powered motors turn the hands of some electronic wristwatches. Engineers have built even smaller motors—micromotors, or microelectromechanical systems (MEMS)—no wider than a human hair. Electric motors can be designed to do almost any kind of job.

▶ **WHAT MAKES ELECTRIC MOTORS RUN?**

Electric motors run by a series of magnetic pushes. Electricity and magnetism are closely related. Moving a wire through a magnetic field creates an electric current in the wire. Passing an electric current through a wire creates a magnetic field around the wire.

When an electric current is passed through a wire coil wound around an iron bar, the iron bar becomes magnetized. When the current is turned off, the bar loses its magnetism. This type of magnet is called an electromagnet because it is magnetic only while electric current is passing through the coil.

One basic fact about magnets is that like, or similar, poles repel each other (push each other away). If you try to put the two north poles or south poles of two magnets together, you will find that you cannot. This is the basic principle on which electric motors work. (For further information, see the articles MAGNETS AND MAGNETISM in Volume M and ELECTRICITY in this volume.)

The simplest electric motor has only two magnets. One of the magnets is an electromagnet mounted on a shaft that turns freely. This magnet is called the **armature**. The other magnet does not move. It is called a **field magnet**. The armature is located between the north and south poles of the field magnet.

When the armature is magnetized by passing electric current through it, the like poles of the armature and the field magnet repel each other, causing the armature to make half a turn. At that point, the unlike poles of the armature and the field magnet line up. To prevent the armature from coming to rest, the direction of the electric current is reversed. This causes the poles of the armature to switch places—the north pole becomes the south pole, and the south pole becomes the north pole.

At that moment, the poles of the armature and the field magnet become alike and again repel each other. The armature rotates another half turn. By reversing the direction of the current in the armature every half turn, the armature will rotate continuously.

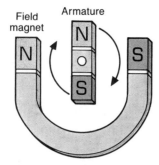

North and south poles of the field magnet attract opposite poles of the armature. The armature turns until the opposite poles line up.

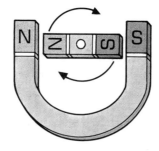

If the armature's poles are switched (north becomes south and south becomes north), like poles will suddenly be lined up. Since like poles repel each other, the armature is given a push.

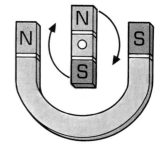

Armature poles are again in a position to be pulled toward the unlike poles of the field magnet. Through this process — over and over — the armature will turn continuously.

Electric motors range in size from very small to very large. *Below:* Small battery-operated electric motors power toy cars. *Right:* Large and powerful electric motors can propel high-speed passenger trains to more than 200 miles (320 km) per hour.

There are many types of electric motors, but all of them can be classified into two broad groups based on the type of electricity they use. They are direct-current (DC) motors and alternating-current (AC) motors.

▶ DIRECT-CURRENT MOTORS

DC motors operate on direct current, electricity that flows only in one direction. In addition to an armature and a field magnet, a DC motor has an important third part called a **commutator**. It is a device that reverses the flow of electric current every half turn of the armature. Without the commutator, the motor would not run.

A commutator is made up of two or more pieces of copper arranged in a circle. The commutator pieces, or segments, are separated by insulation so that current cannot jump from one piece to another. Each end of the armature is attached to a different piece of copper. Elec-

tric current is fed to the commutator by a conductor called a **brush**, which is wired to a source of electric power. Another brush, on the opposite side of the commutator, conducts current from the commutator back to the power source.

Direct-current motors are used mostly in trains, elevators, and other machines that must handle varying loads and run at varying speeds.

▶ ALTERNATING-CURRENT MOTORS

Most electric motors are AC motors because most of the world's generated electricity is alternating current. Alternating current continually changes the direction of its flow. It flows in one direction, then reverses and flows in the

SOME PARTS OF A DC MOTOR

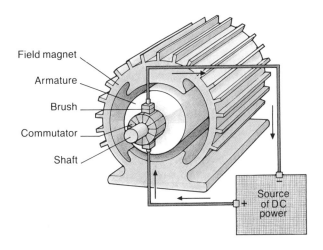

Field magnet
Armature
Brush
Commutator
Shaft

Source of DC power

− +

opposite direction. It does this many times a second.

Most motors that operate on alternating current do not have commutators. The moving part of an AC motor is commonly called a **rotor**. The stationary part is called a **stator**.

Because AC motors run at a constant speed, they are used in electric clocks, compact disc players, and other devices where exact speed is important. They also drive factory machinery, refrigerators, fans, vacuum cleaners, washers, and other machines and appliances designed to run at a steady speed. AC motors are more compact and cheaper to build than DC motors are. Some AC motors are now integrated in electronic devices called power conditioners to make them behave like DC motors.

▶**HISTORY**

Several scientific discoveries led to the invention of the electric motor. In 1820, Hans Christian Oersted, a Danish physicist, noticed that when an electric current ran through a wire, the needle of a compass near the wire moved. This showed that a magnetic field was being created around the wire by the current.

Soon after this the French scientist André Marie Ampère found that a coil of wire carrying an electric current acted like a magnet. This discovery led to the electromagnet, which is an important part of electric motors.

In 1821, English scientist Michael Faraday constructed a laboratory model of an electric motor. But many years of testing and experimenting were necessary before a practical electric motor was developed.

During the 1830's a Vermont blacksmith named Thomas Davenport constructed a number of battery-powered electric motors. He used them to power lathes, drills, and even a small electric locomotive and a printing press.

Unfortunately, Davenport and other inventors who built electric motors ran into a serious problem. There was no cheap and reliable source of electric power for their motors. Batteries, in addition to being heavy and clumsy, were very expensive. As long as batteries were the only source of current, the electric motor was doomed to be no more than a clever gadget. Not until a practical generator was built did electric motors become useful.

Scientists had been tinkering with devices to generate electric current without batteries since the early 1830's. Faraday had shown in 1831 that moving a coil of wire through a magnetic field caused an electric current to flow through the coil. An ancestor of the modern generator was demonstrated in 1832 by Hippolyte Pixii, a French inventor. But it took nearly forty years of experimenting before Zénobe Théophile Gramme, a Belgian engineer, developed the first practical generator in 1870. Gramme's dynamo (another name for a generator) was the first one that ran steadily without getting overheated.

The Gramme dynamo was an immediate success. But no one thought of using it to generate power for electric motors. Then, at the Vienna Exhibition of 1873, a careless workman hooked up the wires of a Gramme dynamo to another dynamo that was already generating electric current. To his amazement he saw the first dynamo whirl around like a pinwheel. It was, in fact, running as a motor.

The last great obstacle to overcome was the problem of whether to use AC or DC power. DC took the lead at first, because all the existing motors ran on DC. (Gramme's dynamo, like batteries, generated only DC.) Then in 1888, Nikola Tesla, an American engineer, invented a motor that ran on AC.

Electric motors brought about tremendous changes in factories. Before that time all the machines in a factory were usually driven by one gigantic steam engine, with belts and pulleys running to each machine. Factories were often noisy, inefficient, and dangerous.

By the beginning of the 1900's, electric motors were found everywhere in industry. Textile mills were among the first plants to change over. Then steel mills and other industries made the change from steam to electric power. Cities in America and Europe had begun installing electric streetcar lines in the 1880's. When electric washing machines and vacuum cleaners were invented, electric motors took their place as household servants as well as workhorses of industry.

Reviewed by T. J. MURRIN
General Manager, Motors and Gearing Division
Westinghouse Electric Corporation
and PARVIZ FAMOURI
West Virginia University

See also ELECTRIC GENERATORS.

ELECTROMAGNETS. See MAGNETS AND MAGNETISM.

ELECTRONIC COMMUNICATION. See TELECOMMUNICATIONS.

In an electronic music studio, a composer can use digital synthesizers and other sophisticated equipment to create musical sounds and assemble them into a finished composition.

ELECTRONIC MUSIC

Electronic music (or electro-acoustic music) is the name given to music that is produced or altered by electronic means. Since its beginnings in the early 1900's, electronic music has opened up vast new worlds of sound to composers and musicians.

Using today's advanced technology, one person can duplicate the sounds of an entire orchestra or create new musical sounds never heard before. This wide range of possibilities has made electronic music one of the most important and popular musical developments of the 20th century.

▶ ELECTRONIC INSTRUMENTS

All music is produced by sound waves traveling in an even, regular order from a vibrating object. (You can read more about sound waves in the article SOUND AND ULTRASONICS in Volume S.) A musician playing a traditional **acoustic** instrument produces sound waves by causing a vibration to occur in the instrument —by plucking the strings of a guitar, for example. In one kind of electronic musical instrument, such as the electric guitar, sound waves are produced in the same manner but are electronically changed. They are converted into electrical signals, **amplified** (made louder), and played through a loudspeaker.

In a second kind of electronic instrument, such as the electronic organ and the synthesizer, sound waves are produced, or generated, by electronic **oscillators**. These devices create variations in the electronic current, which are amplified and played through loudspeakers or headphones in order to be heard.

The first electronic instruments were invented in the late 1800's and early 1900's. Most used oscillators to generate sounds and were played with keyboards. They included the Telharmonium (1902), the Trautonium (1928), and the Ondes Martenot (1928). A few were designed to be played in new ways. For example, the Theremin (1919) was played by moving the hands through the air above the instrument.

Electronic instruments gained in popularity after 1935, when the first Hammond Organs were sold. Thereafter, electronic versions were made of many other traditional instruments. These instruments usually sound somewhat different from their acoustic relatives but can often be made to imitate an acoustic sound. It is also possible to amplify the sound of any acoustic instrument and use it in electronic music.

▶ STUDIO COMPOSITION

While some electronic music is played on instruments and can be performed much like other music, a great deal of electronic music is not "performed" in any traditional sense. Instead, the composer creates the sound material for a piece of music and assembles it into a finished work in a special studio. The composition is usually recorded on magnetic tape or on a computer floppy disk.

The original sound material may be recorded acoustic sound, electronically generated sound, or a combination of both. After selecting the sound material, the composer controls and changes it to produce the desired effect. The composer determines all the characteristics of a sound, including pitch, volume, duration, and timbre (sound quality). Studio technology is so advanced that composers face few limitations on their creativity. They can compose in ways that would not be possible using traditional instruments.

Several composers experimented with studio composition in the 1920's and 1930's. They used phonograph records and film sound tracks to record and manipulate sound. Few of these experiments resulted in finished compositions. One of the most influential early electronic music studios was begun by the French composer Pierre Schaeffer. In 1948 he composed five *Noise Studies* in the studios of the French National Radio in Paris. Soon, many other studios were established.

One of the earliest techniques for creating and altering musical sounds in an electronic music studio was tape manipulation. Later, composers began to experiment with computers and synthesizers.

Tape Manipulation. Composers can manipulate, or skillfully handle, magnetic recording tape to change the nature of the sound material that is recorded on it. Several techniques are used. **Tape loops** are made by splicing the ends of a tape together. When the loop is played, the same sounds are repeated continuously. Other **cutting and splicing** techniques can be used to remove part of a sound or join different sounds to each other. **Speed change** involves playing the tape back at a different speed. This alters both the speed and the pitch of the sound, making it lower and slower or higher and faster. **Direction change** is accomplished by playing the tape backward, reversing the sound information on the tape. **Tape delay** techniques allow the creation of echo and other time delay effects.

Computer Music. Computers are also used to generate electronic sound material and record and change acoustic sounds. In a typical computer music studio, the composer uses special programs to send instructions to the computer. These instructions are converted to a code the computer can understand, and the requested functions are performed. The finished data is translated into sound, and the music can be heard and recorded. Acoustic sound can also be coded, electronically altered, and converted back into sound.

Synthesizers. Synthesizers are often used to produce and play electronic music. As noted earlier, they use oscillators to produce sound waves electronically. Most synthesizers are operated with keyboards, but they also have other controls that can be set to produce the desired sound.

One of the earliest synthesizers was designed by RCA in the 1950's. It used a coding system similar to that used in early computers to store information.

The **analog synthesizer** was developed in the 1960's. It consists of many components, called modules. Each module has a special function for the production, control, or processing of sound. For example, sound generating modules include several types of oscillators that create different kinds of electronic sound waves. There are also white noise generators, which produce noises that sound like wind or radio static. These synthesizers are voltage-controlled. That is, all the properties of a sound signal, such as volume and pitch, are controlled by applying different levels of **voltage** (a measurement of electrical pressure). The Moog synthesizer, an analog synthesizer invented in 1964 by the American physicist Robert A. Moog, was the first commercially successful synthesizer.

A newer kind of synthesizer, called the **digital synthesizer**, uses digital technology to perform all the functions of analog synthesizers. (Digital technology uses a two-symbol, or binary, code to represent information. The binary code is the basic language used by digital computers to process and store information.) There is no need for individual modules, because the instructions necessary to create the desired functions are programmed into the synthesizer. As a result, digital synthesizers can be quite compact and easily used outside a studio setting. The Synclavier and other commercial digital synthesizers are popular with both professional and amateur musicians.

▶LIVE ELECTRONIC MUSIC

The simplest type of live electronic music is a performance by a musician playing an electronic instrument. Sometimes prerecorded electronic music is played in combination with a live performer. However, because the timing of the taped music cannot change, it has been difficult for live performers to play along with prerecorded sounds.

The development of more advanced technology has virtually eliminated this problem. Compositions can be recorded on floppy disks

Electronic music is often performed live. *Left:* One of the oldest and most popular electronic instruments is the electric guitar. *Below:* Newer electronic instruments have a traditional keyboard but use digital technology.

and played back in concert by computers. In a technique called score following, the computer can follow the tempo set by the musicians, allowing for more flexibility. It is even possible to improvise—change or create sounds on the spur of the moment—in a performance with synthesizers and computers.

▶ **NEW TECHNOLOGY**

The development of digital technology has added new dimensions to electronic music. Inexpensive digital synthesizers have made electronic music accessible to more people. Other equipment has increased the flexibility of the music. **Digital sound processors** alter the sounds of acoustic and electronic instruments to produce such effects as echo delay and reverberation. **Digital samplers** put a wide range of acoustic sounds at a musician's disposal. For example, a digital recording is made of a musician playing the violin. A sampling of the notes played can be used to produce an entire violin solo, or to duplicate the sounds of many violins playing together.

Another important technology is **Musical Instrument Digital Interface (MIDI)**. MIDI enables different types of synthesizers and samplers to be connected and controlled by a common source, such as a keyboard synthesizer or a computer. This has created an international system for conveying electronic music data. Instruments called **MIDI controllers** have the shapes and mechanical functions of such traditional instruments as pianos, guitars, or trumpets, but they do not make sounds themselves. Instead, they send MIDI data to electronic devices that generate and process sound. MIDI controllers allow musicians to use traditional playing techniques to operate any synthesizer or sampler.

The availability of digital synthesizers, MIDI, and other technology has greatly encouraged the spread of electronic music. In the film and television industry, for example, most music is now produced by electronic means. Often one composer using digital equipment can produce a finished score, eliminating the need for arranger, conductor, and orchestra. Although electronic instruments and techniques will not completely replace traditional methods, they will continue to change the way music is made and performed.

BARRY SCHRADER
Director, Electro-Acoustic Music Studios
California Institute of the Arts
Author, *Introduction to Electro-Acoustic Music*

ELECTRONICS

Electronics is a technology based on the motion of electrons, tiny particles of negative electrical charge. That technology has made possible many useful devices, from digital clock radios that wake us up in the morning to robotic space probes that explore distant planets. Electronics has also made possible the modern age of computers, telecommunications, and advanced medical technology.

▶ WHAT MAKES A DEVICE ELECTRONIC?

Electrons are a part of the building blocks of matter called atoms and are responsible for a material's ability to carry, or conduct, electricity. If hit by a burst of energy, an electron can escape its atom and become a free electron. Those bursts come mostly from the heat energy within a material. When a battery is connected across a block of material, an electrical pressure, or **voltage**, is created, causing free electrons to move through the block. This movement, called **current**, occurs at different rates depending on the material.

Materials, such as most metals, in which electrons need little energy to become free are called **conductors** because current flows through them easily. In other materials called **insulators**, such as glass, almost no current flows because the electrons need so much energy to escape that there are essentially no free electrons. Materials called **resistors** have a moderate number of free electrons. The smaller the resistance of a resistor is, the larger the current that can flow through it.

Electronic devices can be considered electrical, since they rely on currents, but they are different from what we normally think of as electrical devices, such as incandescent lightbulbs. Both types of devices can use conductors, insulators, and resistors. However, electronic devices can also use other materials and can control currents in ways simple electrical devices cannot.

Electrons in a Vacuum

The electronics era goes back as far as the late 1870's,

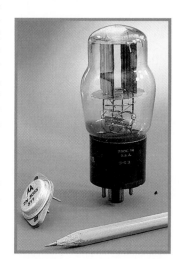

when English scientist Sir William Crookes discovered an interesting property of electricity. He sealed a small metal plate into each end of a glass tube, pumped nearly all the air out of the tube, and connected the plates to a voltage source. One plate, called the **cathode**, had a negative charge, and the other plate, called the **anode**, had a positive charge. When the voltage was strong enough, something surprising happened in the space between the cathode and the anode: It began to glow. Crookes had made an electrical current flow through a vacuum, creating the first electronic device—the **vacuum tube**.

Later, scientists realized that a small change in voltage between the cathode and anode can produce a great change in the amount of current that flows through the vacuum. If too little voltage is applied, most of the electrons cannot make it across the gap, and the current becomes very weak. If just enough voltage is applied, most of the electrons make it across the gap, and the current is much stronger. This function—controlling large changes in current with small changes in voltage—is the basis of all electronic devices.

One very important kind of vacuum tube is called the **cathode ray tube**, or **CRT**. Inside a CRT, the electrons (also called cathode rays) are directed so that they strike a screen with a phosphorescent coating, which

Top: Electronics has given us both useful and entertaining devices, such as the video game these boys are playing. *Left:* The large vacuum tube gave way to the much smaller and cheaper transistor, making modern electronics possible.

glows in the process. CRT's are used as television picture tubes, computer monitors, and other display devices.

Electrons in Semiconductors

You can still find other kinds of vacuum tubes in some very old radios and televisions, but vacuum tubes are no longer as important as they once were. Now most electronic devices are **solid state**, made from materials called **semiconductors**, most commonly silicon (one of the elements found in sand). Solid-state devices are generally smaller, faster, cheaper, longer-lasting, and more versatile than vacuum tubes.

Pure silicon is a poor conductor. However, when atoms of other elements are added to silicon in its crystal form, its electrical properties can change. If atoms of some elements are added, they increase the number of free electrons in the silicon. This type of silicon is called **n-type** because the free electrons have a negative charge. If atoms of other elements are added, a strong force is created that "steals" electrons from nearby silicon atoms. This type of silicon is called **p-type** because the missing electrons create positively charged "holes." When a voltage is applied, these holes appear to move through the crystal in the reverse direction of the free electrons.

In semiconductor devices, a **p-n junction** is similar in function to the gap between a cathode and anode in a vacuum tube. This junction forms where one region of a semiconductor has been made n-type and a neighboring region has been made p-type. If a positive voltage is applied at the p-type side and a negative voltage at the n-type side, a current flows because free electrons are attracted across the junction from the n-type side. If the voltage is applied in the opposite direction, the electrons are pulled back into the n-type region and no current flows.

▶ HOW ELECTRONIC DEVICES ARE USED

Many kinds of electronic devices can be made using semiconductors. (See the article

Vacuum tubes are still used in televisions (*above left*). But most electronic devices, such as portable stereos (*above*), are solid state. A smoke detector (*left*) has a solid-state device that can sense the presence of smoke and sound an alarm.

TRANSISTORS, DIODES, AND INTEGRATED CIRCUITS in Volume T.)

Signals and Controls

Some of the simplest electronic devices can detect signals or serve as on-off switches to control other devices. One example is a thermostat, which is used to control a house's air-conditioning or heating system. A thermostat uses a temperature-sensitive device that acts as a variable resistor, producing changes in current as the air temperature in the house changes. The thermostat also includes an adjustable device that is used to set the desired temperature. When the difference between the desired temperature and the air temperature is large enough, the thermostat uses an electronic switch to turn the air-conditioning or heating system on. When the desired temperature is reached, the system is turned off.

Other electronic devices sense and respond to all kinds of conditions—light or darkness, the presence of smoke or poison gases, or an intruder's motion. These devices can then respond automatically by switching on lights, alarms, appliances, or other machines.

Computers and Calculators

Among the most important uses of electronic switching today is in computers and calculators. (See the article COMPUTERS in Volume C.) In fact, everything that a computer or calculator does is based on tiny electronic on-off switches.

Computers and calculators perform their operations using the binary system of numbers, which has only two digits: 0 ("off") and 1 ("on"). Devices and information based on the binary system are called **digital**. Any number can be written as a string of 1's and

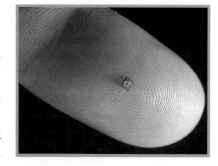

Modern computers are smaller and faster because of tiny chips, some slightly larger than a grain of sand, that can contain millions of transistors.

0's. Special codes can also be created in which numbers stand for the letters and symbols of any language or mathematical formula. By treating numbers, letters, and symbols as strings of 1's and 0's, computers can process just about any information in digital form.

The earliest calculating machines used mechanical or simple electrical switching devices. The first electronic computers used vacuum tubes. Compared to today's computers, they were very slow, more likely to break down, and very bulky—some occupying entire rooms. With modern solid-state devices, computers now have much faster, far more reliable, and incredibly smaller electronic switches. These advances have led to computers that can sit on top of a desk and perform operations requiring billions or trillions of calculations, without making a single mistake.

Electromagnetic Waves

Electronic devices are also important in producing electromagnetic waves, ranging from radio waves and microwaves to visible light and X rays.

Other electronic devices detect electromagnetic waves. Radio and television sets rely on electronics to transform the signals they receive into sounds and pictures. Night-vision devices detect invisible infrared light that comes from warm objects and convert it into images displayed in light we can see. Other light sensors, such as charge-coupled devices, detect visible light. These sensors are used in digital cameras to produce pictures that can be stored on disks or memory cards and displayed on computer screens or printed on paper. Other electronic sensors detect information carried on laser light in much the same way that radios pick messages out of radio waves.

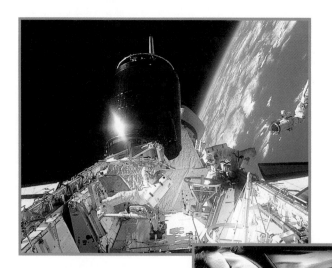

Above: Satellites, such as this one leaving a space shuttle, use electronics to send and receive vast amounts of information. *Right:* Some cars now have displays showing their positions on maps, using information sent by satellites.

Telecommunications

When electronic devices that produce and detect electromagnetic waves are combined with computers, many types of telecommunications devices are possible. (See the article TELECOMMUNICATIONS in Volume T.) Using this technology, information can be transmitted to communications satellites in orbit high above Earth and relayed to telephones, televisions, or computers virtually anywhere in the world. Light waves can carry massive amounts of information, through fiber-optic cables made of glasslike strands, from city to city. Information can also be carried to and from home computers over ordinary phone lines using electronic devices called modems.

The information can be numbers, words, sounds, pictures, videos, animations, or computer programs—anything you can think of. Thanks to electronics, nearly anyone in the world can share knowledge with anyone else.

Medical Electronics

Electronic devices are also being used in modern medicine to extend life itself. Some medical electronic devices can be implanted in the human body to detect electrical signals from a defective heart and correct them with tiny, well-timed electric shocks. Electronic hearing aids can help make up for a person's hearing loss. Scientists and engineers are working on implants that may some day bring sound to the deaf and sight to the blind by stimulating the auditory or optic nerves in the brain.

Other electronic devices probe the human body with different forms of energy. These devices send signals that change as they pass through the body. The signals are then detected and sent to computers. The computers produce images for medical experts to analyze. Because of electronic devices, ultrasound images can be taken of unborn babies inside their mothers. Magnetic resonance

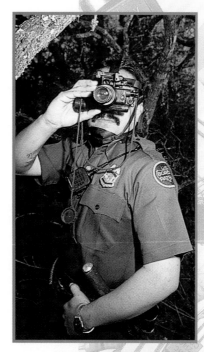

Left: A night-vision device uses electronics to convert heat energy given off by people, for example, into visible light. *Above:* A digital camera has sensors that can detect visible light and store a picture on a computer disk without using photographic film. *Below left:* A hearing aid uses electronics to amplify sounds.

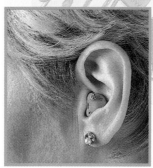

imaging (MRI) uses radio waves to produce pictures that tell us the condition of the brain and vital organs. For different information about those organs, doctors also have computerized axial tomography (CAT) scanners, which use X rays to see inside the body. Other advanced imaging instruments, such as positron-emission tomography (PET) scanners, give still more information.

Consumer Electronics

Perhaps the most familiar kind of electronic devices are consumer electronics—products that people buy for their everyday lives. We use these products when we watch a television show, play a video game, or tell the time of day on a digital wristwatch. Consumer electronics also let us enjoy music recorded on compact discs and performed live on stage by musicians playing electronic instruments. (See the article ELECTRONIC MUSIC in this volume.)

The Tomahawk cruise missile, used in the 1991 Gulf War, has advanced electronic circuitry that helps automatically guide it to its target.

Modern vehicles also have many electronic devices built into them. For example, electronic sensors can measure the gases in a car's exhaust. Those signals are sent to an onboard computer, which adjusts the way air and fuel mix together in the car's engine. As a result, the car uses less gasoline and produces less pollution. Other electronic devices sense crashes and inflate air bags to save lives. Some cars have electronics that can communicate with global positioning system (GPS) satellites to produce maps and directions to drivers' destinations.

Business and Industry

Modern businesses, offices, and factories could not function without electronic devices. Computers are on nearly every desk. Many workers even carry computers in pockets. Other electronic machines make copies and print documents. Computers control robots on assembly lines. Electronic mail, or e-mail, allows people to exchange messages over long distances in very little time. Cellular telephones and pagers keep people in touch almost any time and any place.

In stores, customers can pass through checkout lines much faster, thanks to electronic machines that use lasers to scan Universal Product Codes (UPC's)—special labels that identify the products. The scanner sends the codes to a computerized cash register that finds the price of each item and totals the cost of the entire order.

Even farming takes advantage of electronic devices. Satellite images can tell farmers whether their fields are growing as well as they should. Satellites can also provide farmers with weather and climate information.

Public Safety and Defense

Police officers, firefighters, and rescuers use electronic devices to keep people safe in their communities, and armed forces use electronics to defend countries. Ambulances carry compact medical electronic devices that can save lives at emergencies and on the way to hospitals. Soldiers and police use night-vision binoculars to find people. Satellite receivers help navigators on ships and planes find their way. Military satellites monitor places in the world where dangerous activity may be taking place. When it is necessary to go into battle, many nations have missiles with electronics to guide them to their targets.

▶ TRENDS IN ELECTRONICS

The major trend in electronics has been the development of devices that are increasingly smaller, faster, cheaper, and more versatile. Engineers expect that trend to continue for a long time. As electronic devices become smaller, they may eventually reach the size of just a few atoms. At that scale, they would act as **quantum mechanical** devices, which behave in more complex ways. These devices would be able to do things that conventional electronic switches cannot—for example, instantly performing many calculations all at the same time.

It is impossible to predict when such technology will become practical. But it is safe to say that for the foreseeable future, electronics will be changing as rapidly as it has in the past—and so will its impact on our lives.

ALFRED B. (FRED) BORTZ
Author, science books for children
STUART K. TEWKSBURY
Chairman, Department of Electrical and Computer Engineering, Stevens Institute of Technology

See also COMPUTERS; ELECTRICITY; ELECTRONIC MUSIC; LASERS; LIGHT; RADIO; TELECOMMUNICATIONS; TELEVISION; TRANSISTORS, DIODES, AND INTEGRATED CIRCUITS.

WONDER QUESTION

What is nanotechnology?

Many electronic devices are so small now that they are called microelectronic devices. "Micro" means "one-millionth" and refers to objects about a millionth of a meter in size. And electronic devices are getting even smaller. Engineers call this new technology nanotechnology. "Nano" means "one-billionth" and refers to objects one thousand times smaller than microelectronic devices. Nanotechnology may lead to computers with incredibly tiny circuits that are many times faster than current ones. It may also lead to extremely small medical devices that could repair damage inside individual cells in the body.

ELECTRON MICROSCOPE

An electron microscope is a scientific instrument that allows us to "see" objects so small that they cannot be seen in any other way. Electron microscopes have allowed scientists to see individual molecules and atoms for the first time.

Most microscopes, including those in schools and laboratories today, are **optical** microscopes. They use glass lenses to enlarge, or magnify, an image. A magnifying glass is a simple kind of magnifier. A microscope uses several lenses to magnify an image. As the number of lenses increases, the magnification increases. But there is a point at which the image becomes fuzzy and the fine details are no longer clear. The microscope's **resolution power**, its ability to produce a clear image of small details, decreases.

In the late 1870's, German physicist Ernst Abbe explained why there are limits to the resolution power of an optical microscope. A microscope uses visible light; and light, like radio waves, has a definite range of wavelengths. An optical microscope cannot produce an image of an object smaller than the length of the light wave. Abbe predicted the smallest object that could be seen would be about 2,000 angstroms (about $\frac{1}{250,000}$ of an inch). To see anything smaller, a wave of shorter length would have to be used.

In 1923, French physicist Louis de Broglie suggested that electrons, like light, travel in a wave. And the wavelength of electrons is much shorter than the wavelength of light. With a shorter wavelength, smaller objects could be "seen." Ernst Ruska, a German physicist, used De Broglie's discovery to design a microscope that used an electron beam instead of light to produce an image. By 1931, Ruska had produced a working model of the first electron microscope.

Types of Electron Microscopes

Several types of electron microscopes have been developed since Ruska's first model. Some are so large that they are housed in silos several stories high. Others are small enough to fit in the palm of a hand. Together, these instruments have given scientists a new look at the world around us.

Transmission Electron Microscope. Ruska's working model was a transmission electron

Viewed with an electron microscope, mold on a slice of bread, magnified 450 times, becomes a forest of slender stalks topped with rounded spore cases.

microscope (TEM). The transmission electron microscope works in much the same way as an optical microscope does. But it sends a beam of electrons, rather than light, through the object being viewed.

The object to be viewed must be very thin so the electrons can pass through it. Because air is too dense for electrons to pass through, the object must be placed in a vacuum chamber. A vacuum chamber has nearly all matter, including air, removed from it. A beam of electrons is focused on the object. Most of the electrons pass through the object; other electrons bounce off the object or are absorbed by it. The part of the beam that passes through the object is spread, or magnified, by magnetic lenses, which act in the same way as glass lenses in an optical microscope.

Finally, the beam strikes a fluorescent screen. The magnified image of the object can be seen on the screen of a television-like monitor. The beam of electrons may also be focused on a special photographic plate, creating a photomicrograph, a type of picture of the object.

The images formed by a transmission electron microscope are black and white like an X-ray picture. The parts of the object that scatter or absorb electrons appear dark; parts where electrons pass through are white. Although the transmission electron microscope can produce images of very small objects, the images are flat and do not show any surface detail. Computers can be used to translate the image information into a three-dimensional colored image.

Scanning Electron Microscope. In 1970, another electron microscope called the scanning electron microscope (SEM) was developed. The scanning electron microscope is used to study the smallest details on the surface of an object. It sees surfaces as your eyes do. The images, which are sharp and clear, look like three-dimensional photographs.

To produce an image, the sample is placed inside a vacuum chamber. An extremely fine beam of electrons is focused on the object. The beam travels, or scans, back and forth across the object from side to side. As each electron in the beam strikes a tiny area of the object, it smashes into the surface atoms and knocks loose a shower of electrons. The electrons knocked loose, called secondary electrons, are caught by a collector and used to form an image on a television-like monitor.

Scanning Tunneling Microscope. In 1981, fifty years after the first electron microscope was designed, a microscope that can produce an image a million times larger than the real size of an object was developed by Heinrich

The SEM image reveals the smallest surface details of this fierce-looking creature—a cat flea, shown 180 times its actual size.

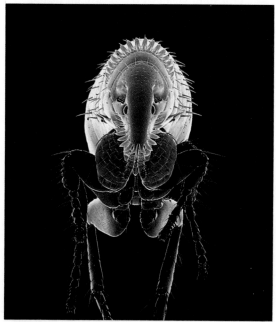

Rohrer and Gerd Binnig of IBM's Zurich Research Laboratory. The scanning tunneling microscope (STM) detects the smallest surface details of an object. With the STM, scientists can examine the structure and properties of individual atoms.

The scanning tunneling microscope works something like a phonograph stylus tracking a record groove. A sharp needle ending in a tip just one atom wide is lowered to within a few angstroms (billionths of an inch) of the object's surface. A small current is applied and electrons tunnel, or flow, between the needle and the surface of the object. The tunneling electrons create a current that changes as the gap between the needle and the surface changes. As the needle traces a hill, the gap narrows and the current increases; as it traces a valley, the gap increases and the current decreases. One line at a time, the tip travels across the surface. A computer measures the changes in the current and translates the repeated side-to-side scans into a minutely detailed picture of the atomic landscape. In the image, a hill is seen as white and a valley as dark. As with other computer-developed screen images, color can be added to emphasize important details.

The inventors of the scanning tunneling electron microscope shared the 1986 Nobel Prize in physics with Ernst Ruska, the designer of the first electron microscope. The electron microscope, only the fourth invention ever to have received the award, has been called one of the most important inventions of the 20th century.

Electron Microscopes and the Future

Scientists and researchers are finding many new uses for these powerful microscopes. As biologists get a closer look at how the body works and what happens when diseases attack, new treatments can be developed. Engineers examine metals and other materials to find new ways to make them stronger and longer lasting. And when the smallest parts of computers and other electronic products are viewed, defects can be found and new manufacturing techniques developed. Each day there are more discoveries and surprises as the once invisible world emerges.

BRYAN BUNCH
President, Scientific Publishing, Inc.

ELECTRONS. See ATOMS; ELEMENTS, CHEMICAL.

ELECTROPLATING

Electroplating is the process of coating, or plating, an object with metal by using an electric current. Things are given metal coatings to make them look better and to protect them from rust. Familiar examples of electroplated objects include gold-plated jewelry, silver-plated tableware (spoons, forks, knives), and chromium-plated automobile bumpers. The objects to be plated, as well as the plating materials, are usually metals.

To understand what happens during electroplating, you need to know something about atoms and the way they behave. Atoms are tiny particles that make up all matter. At the center of every atom is a **nucleus,** which has a positive electric charge. Spinning around the nucleus are negatively charged **electrons.** An ordinary atom has exactly as many positive charges as negative charges. All the charges balance, and the atom as a whole has a neutral electrical charge.

Suppose you upset the balance by removing or adding electrons. You will then produce an atom with a positive or negative electric charge. Such electrically charged atoms are called **ions.** An ion that has been formed by an atom's losing electrons will try to take on other electrons to regain its balance and once again become a neutral atom. When metal atoms become ions, they always lose electrons.

How are these laws of nature used in electroplating? To plate a spoon with silver, for example, the spoon is placed in a chemical solution that contains silver. The spoon is attached to the cathode, or negative terminal, of some source of electric current. A solid bar of silver is also placed in the solution. The bar of silver is connected to the anode, or positive terminal, of the same electric circuit. An electric current is then passed through the spoon, the silver bar, and the solution.

When the spoon is connected to the cathode of the electric circuit, it becomes loaded with extra electrons. Silver ions from the solution are attracted to the spoon. When they reach it, they take on electrons, lose their charges, and settle firmly on the spoon's surface. Bit by bit, a smooth, even silver coating is built up.

At the same time, silver atoms on the silver anode bar are losing electrons. These atoms thus become ions. They pass into the solution

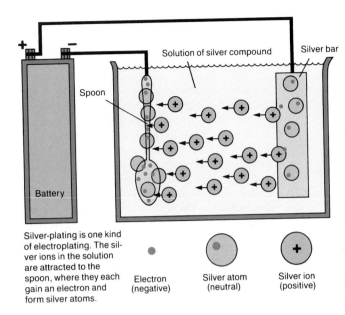

Silver-plating is one kind of electroplating. The silver ions in the solution are attracted to the spoon, where they each gain an electron and form silver atoms.

Electron (negative)

Silver atom (neutral)

Silver ion (positive)

and take the place of the ions that were deposited on the spoon. It is by this process that the silver bar slowly dissolves into the solution. This silver replaces the silver that has been deposited on the spoon from the solution.

In some electroplating processes the anode is not made of the metal that is being used for plating. Then all the metal for the plating must come out of the solution. When the metal ions in the solution are used up, new solution must be added.

Adding beauty or protection are not the only uses of electroplating. Electroplating done in reverse is called **electropolishing.** In this process the metal object is connected to the anode instead of the cathode, so that it loses a thin layer of metal instead of gaining one. This leaves a very smooth, bright surface.

A special type of electroplating called **electroforming** is used to reproduce delicate objects with many details. Printing plates and the master phonograph records from which copies are pressed are produced by electroforming. The metal is deposited as a thick coating, or shell, over a model of the object that is to be reproduced. When the shell is separated from the model, it forms a perfect metal copy of the model in reverse.

FRANKLIN D. YEAPLE
Editor, *Product Engineering*

See also ELECTRICITY.

ELEMENTS, CHEMICAL

Chemical elements are the basic substances out of which everything in the universe is made. Iron, aluminum, and sulfur are examples of some common elements.

Every element consists of tiny particles, far too small to be seen even through a microscope. These are called **atoms**. Every atom is made up of several types of even smaller particles. The three most important of these **subatomic particles** are the **proton**, the **neutron**, and the **electron**. In the very center of each atom is a tiny **nucleus**. All the protons and neutrons are packed into it. The rest of the atom is made up of electrons. (You can read more about the structure of the atom in the article ATOMS in Volume A.)

To save time and effort, chemists use a **chemical symbol** when referring to each chemical element. The symbol is based on the element's name, which is assigned by the International Union of Pure and Applied Chemistry (IUPAC).

Usually, the chemical symbol is made up of the first letter of the element's name, or of the first letter and one other. For instance, the chemical symbol for carbon is C, and the symbol for aluminum is Al. Sometimes the symbol is taken from the Latin name. For instance, the Latin word for iron is *ferrum*. Thus the chemical symbol for iron is Fe.

▶ ATOMIC NUMBER

Chemists have determined that every atom contains a particular number of protons in its nucleus. That is the atomic number of the atom. An atom with only 1 proton in its nucleus has an atomic number of 1. An atom with 4 protons has an atomic number of 4. Scientists have found 116 different elements, with atoms having up to 116 protons and many more neutrons in the nucleus. Some elements are not found in nature but are made from other elements by researchers.

All the atoms of a particular element have the same atomic number, but they are not always all identical. Sometimes the neutron number differs among the atoms of a particular element. There might be two different varieties of atoms in an element, or as many as 30. All would have the same number of protons but a different number of neutrons. These different varieties are called **isotopes**.

▶ ATOMIC WEIGHT

The weight of a particular atom depends on how many protons and neutrons it has. (Electrons are so light that they do not count in weight.) An isotope with more neutrons weighs a bit more than an isotope with fewer neutrons. The atomic weight of an element is the average weight of its different isotopes.

Chemists begin measuring atomic weights with an isotope of the element carbon. An atom of this isotope contains 6 protons and 6 neutrons. Therefore it has been decided to set the weight of this isotope at exactly 12.00000. The weights of all other atoms are compared with this. For instance, iron is made up of four different isotopes. The lightest one is 4½ times as heavy as the carbon atom; so this isotope's weight is 54. The other three isotopes are a little heavier and have weights of 56, 57, and 58. These different isotopes occur in iron in certain proportions. When the average weight is taken, it turns out that the atomic weight of iron is 55.845.

In the table that starts on page 170, the elements are listed alphabetically. Chemical symbols, atomic numbers, and atomic weights are given. You will notice that the atomic weight of carbon is 12.0107—not 12.00000, as given above. This is because carbon, like iron and the other elements, is a mixture of isotopes. When the average weight of these isotopes is taken, it turns out to be 12.0107.

▶ RADIOACTIVE ELEMENTS

Fully 81 of the elements are stable, having at least one isotope that never changes, if it is left to itself. A quantity of each of these elements is found in Earth's crust.

The remaining elements are **radioactive**, or unstable. The atoms of these elements are

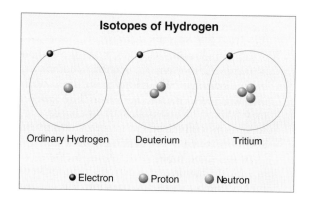

Isotopes of Hydrogen

Ordinary Hydrogen   Deuterium   Tritium

● Electron   ● Proton   ● Neutron

continually breaking down into simpler atoms with lower atomic numbers. But two of these elements, uranium and thorium, break down very slowly and are still present in Earth's crust, although they have been breaking down for billions of years.

That leaves more than 30 elements that break down so quickly, they are present in very small quantities on Earth—or are even entirely absent. Chemists know of them mainly through the samples prepared in the laboratory. But two of these elements, technetium and promethium, have been identified by astronomers as occurring in certain stars.

Ten of the chemical elements have been known since ancient times: carbon, sulfur, gold, silver, copper, iron, tin, lead, mercury, and antimony. No one knows when they were discovered or by whom. For other elements, the discoverer and the year of discovery are listed in the table beginning on page 170.

▶ **THE PERIODIC TABLE**

Atoms with different atomic numbers behave differently. Thus each element has characteristics, or **properties**, that are strictly its own and are not shared by other elements. Sometimes two elements are rather similar. For instance, nickel and iron are whitish metals that are attracted by magnets. Both are about equally hard, equally heavy, and equally difficult to melt. But iron rusts easily, while nickel does not. If fine pieces of iron are dissolved in acid, the acid will turn yellow. If fine pieces of nickel are dissolved instead, the acid will turn green.

On the other hand, two elements like iron and sulfur are very different. Iron is a whitish metal; sulfur is a yellow nonmetal. Iron is tough and hard; sulfur is brittle and soft. Iron will conduct electricity; sulfur will not. Iron can be magnetized; sulfur cannot.

For many years chemists tried to find some way of arranging the elements in a logical way. They wanted to group similar elements and to keep apart those that were not similar. This was finally accomplished.

The elements are first listed in the order of their atomic numbers. They can then be arranged in horizontal (side-to-side) and vertical (up-and-down) rows with similar elements lined up. Each horizontal row is called a period, so the arrangement is a **periodic table**, shown on pages 168 and 169.

WONDER QUESTION

What is the island of stability?

Most of the recently discovered "superheavy" elements are highly unstable: Their atoms break down into lighter atoms very quickly, often in fractions of a second. However, scientists believe an **island of stability**, a range of even heavier but stable elements, may exist. Elements in this range would have the largest numbers of particles called protons and neutrons in their atoms. These particles are thought to be arranged in "shells," each with a particular number of spaces for protons or neutrons. Atoms with a full shell, or "magic number," of protons or neutrons tend to be more stable. In 1999, a team of researchers from the Joint Institute for Nuclear Research in Dubna, Russia, and the Lawrence Livermore National Laboratory in California created an atom with 114 protons. Although the atom decayed quickly, it was stable for far longer than element 112, the next lightest superheavy then known. This discovery provided strong evidence that the island of stability does exist. By making such elements in the laboratory, scientists hope to learn more about the internal structure of atoms and to create new substances that could have unusual chemical properties.

In the periodic table, similar elements are often found in vertical rows. Lithium, sodium, potassium, rubidium, cesium, and francium have many similarities. They are found in the column on the extreme left. They are the **alkali metals**. The elements in the next column are beryllium, magnesium, calcium, strontium, barium, and radium. They are also similar. They are the **alkaline-earth metals**.

In the column on the extreme right are the **noble gases**: helium, neon, argon, krypton, xenon, and radon. In the column next to that are the **halogens**: fluorine, chlorine, bromine, iodine, and astatine.

In the middle of the table are groups of elements arranged in horizontal order rather than vertical. For example, there are the **transition metals**, which occur in a wide variety of minerals and form a wide variety of compounds, including many alloys. Transition metals include silver and gold, the best-known precious metals. Transition metals also include iron, cobalt, and nickel. These three might be referred to as the iron metals.

THE PERIODIC TABLE

In 1869 the Russian scientist Dmitri Mendeleev found that there was a beautiful order among the chemical elements. He arranged them according to their atomic weights. This was the first periodic table, and with it Mendeleev was able to describe a few elements that had not yet been discovered.

But Mendeleev's table was not complete. As the years passed and more elements were discovered, it became harder to find the right pigeonholes for the elements.

About 1913 the English scientist Henry G. J. Moseley arranged the elements in a new way. He found that if the elements were arranged according to their atomic numbers, the elements with the same properties fell in line. Moseley's table, which is the modern form, is shown here.

The elements in any vertical column have similar chemical properties. They behave chemically in much the same way.

Elements in some of the horizontal rows also have similar properties. The lanthanide elements, near the bottom of the table, are so similar that it is very hard to tell them apart.

Many chemists classify elements as either metals or nonmetals. These two groups are separated by a zig-zag line drawn above and to

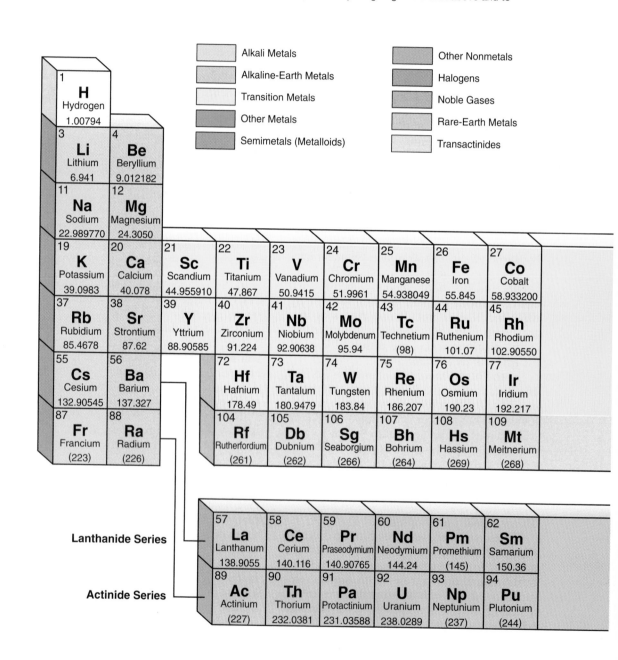

the right of aluminum, germanium, antimony, and polonium on the periodic table. Elements on the left side of this line are classified as metals, while elements on the right side are classified as nonmetals. Semimetals, or metalloids, fall roughly on either side of the line.

Hydrogen is generally grouped at the top of the first column in the table. However, this simplest of elements does not fall neatly into a single category. Hydrogen exhibits nonmetallic properties under ordinary conditions but some metallic properties at extremely high pressures.

Scientists continue to discover new elements. These are given temporary symbols and names until official ones can be assigned by the International Union of Pure and Applied Chemistry, usually in honor of a pioneering researcher. Elements 112 to 116, for example, have yet to be officially named, and so they are referred to by Latin words that stand for the digits in their atomic numbers.

Researchers create new elements by joining the nuclei of two existing elements using atom-smashing machines. However, because these atoms decay so quickly, scientists have yet to find out enough about their chemical properties to put them into well-defined groups. (See the Wonder Question that accompanies this article.)

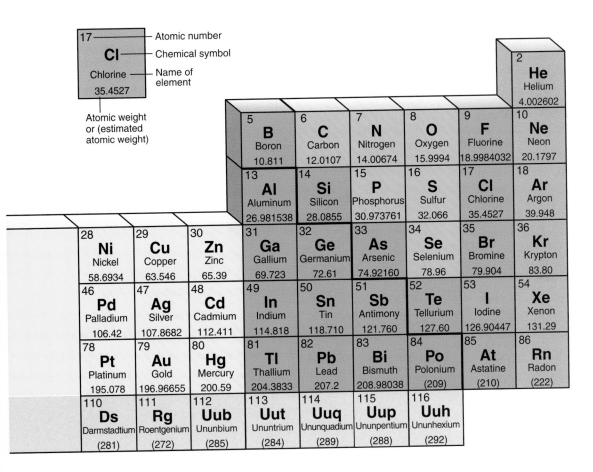

Under these in the table are six elements: ruthenium, rhodium, palladium, osmium, iridium, and platinum. They are enough alike to be lumped together as the platinum metals.

Lanthanum is a special case. Following it is a series of 14 other similar elements with atomic numbers from 58 to 71. They are usually listed separately under the table. At first the lanthanum group of elements was called the **rare-earth metals**. However, in the 1950's a second series of 15 rare-earth elements was found to be much like the first series. Each series was given a different name. The first begins with lanthanum; it is the **lanthanide series** of elements. The second set begins with actinium; it is the **actinide series**.

In one case a similarity runs diagonally (at an angle) across the table. Most elements are metals, and a number are nonmetals. There is also a group of elements with properties that fall between the metals and the nonmetals. These borderline elements have been called **semimetals**, or **metalloids**—boron, silicon, germanium, arsenic, antimony, tellurium, and polonium. Some chemists also group selenium and astatine among the semimetals. But many chemists simply group all elements above and to the right of aluminum, germanium, antimony, and polonium among the nonmetals and the rest among the metals.

Nearly all radioactive elements appear at the end of the table. Elements with atomic numbers over 83 are all radioactive. Two other radioactive elements are technetium and promethium (atomic numbers 43 and 61).

Until 1940 the element with the highest known atomic number was uranium (atomic number 92). Since then at least 24 elements past uranium have been made in the laboratory with the help of powerful machines that smash atoms together. They are synthetic, or artificially created, elements. The periodic table has a row of elements, with atomic numbers from 104 to 116, that are all synthetic. They are called the **transactinides**.

Scientists are trying to form still more elements with even greater atomic numbers in the laboratory. (See the accompanying Wonder Question, What is the island of stability?) New research methods and special equipment help chemists make discoveries that were not possible several years ago.

ISAAC ASIMOV
Author, *A Short History of Chemistry*

ALPHABETICAL TABLE OF ELEMENTS

Each of the 116 known chemical elements is described in the following section, which is arranged alphabetically. To help you match each chemical element with its position on the periodic table, a colored square (corresponding to one of the colored groups shown on the periodic table and listed here on the bottom of the page) has been placed beside each element. Some of the elements are covered in more detail in separate articles in this encyclopedia such as ALUMINUM; NITROGEN; and ZINC. An asterisk (*) before an entry indicates this. In addition, the index will help you find articles such as GASES; METALS AND METALLURGY; and RADIOACTIVE ELEMENTS that further describe many elements. See also ATMOSPHERE; ATOMS; CHEMISTRY; CHEMISTRY, HISTORY OF.

ELEMENT	SYMBOL	ATOMIC NUMBER	ATOMIC WEIGHT or (Estimated Atomic Weight)	DISCOVERER	YEAR DISCOVERED
Actinium	Ac	89	(227)	André Debierne	1899

A very rare radioactive element, the first of the actinide series in the periodic table. It glows slightly in the dark and is found in small quantities in uranium ores.

| *Aluminum | Al | 13 | 26.981538 | Friedrich Wöhler | 1827 |

A silver white metal. It is the third most common element in Earth's crust and the most common metal. Because it does not corrode (rust), it is used for kitchenware and for many items in the construction industry. A light metal, it is used a great deal in the construction of automobiles, railway cars, trucks, buses, and especially airplanes.

| Americium | Am | 95 | (243) | Glenn T. Seaborg and others | 1945 |

A synthetic radioactive metal of the actinide series. It does not occur in nature.

| Antimony | Sb | 51 | 121.760 | Element known since ancient times | |

A brittle white metal. Its compounds were used by the ancients. Its symbol is Sb, from its Latin name stibium. The addition of antimony strengthens soft metals such as tin and lead. Antimony is used in batteries.

| Alkali Metals | Rare-Earth Metals | Other Metals | Noble Gases | Other Nonmetals |
| Alkaline-Earth Metals | Transition Metals | Semimetals (Metalloids) | Halogens | Transactinides |

ELEMENT	SYMBOL	ATOMIC NUMBER	ATOMIC WEIGHT or (Estimated Atomic Weight)	DISCOVERER	YEAR DISCOVERED
Argon	Ar	18	39.948	Lord Rayleigh and Sir William Ramsay	1894

The most common of the inert gases. It makes up about 1 percent of the atmosphere. It is used to fill lightbulbs, because it does not react with the white-hot metal of the filament.

| Arsenic | As | 33 | 74.92160 | Albertus Magnus | 1250 |

A brittle gray semimetal, known to the alchemists of the Middle Ages. Most of its compounds are poisonous. They have been used as insecticides and, in wartime, as poison gas. Some have been used in medicines.

| Astatine | At | 85 | (210) | Emilio Segrè and others | 1940 |

A synthetic, highly radioactive halogen. It is not obtainable in nature.

| Barium | Ba | 56 | 137.327 | Sir Humphry Davy | 1808 |

A soft silver white alkaline-earth metal. Some of its compounds are used to give green colors to fireworks. An insoluble compound, barium sulfate, is sometimes taken internally to make the intestines visible to X-rays.

| Berkelium | Bk | 97 | (247) | S. G. Thompson and others | 1950 |

A synthetic radioactive metal of the actinide series. It does not occur in nature.

| Beryllium | Be | 4 | 9.012182 | Louis N. Vauquelin | 1798 |

A hard gray metal. Added in small quantities to copper, it makes the latter almost as hard as steel. It was once used in fluorescent lights, but its compounds are so poisonous that it is no longer so used.

| Bismuth | Bi | 83 | 208.98038 | Claude Geoffroy | 1753 |

A silvery metal with a reddish tint, probably known to alchemists of the Middle Ages. Mixed with other elements, it forms alloys that melt at very low temperatures. These alloys are used in fire sprinkler systems.

| Bohrium | Bh | 107 | (264) | G. Münzenberg, P. Armbruster, and others | 1976 |

A synthetic radioactive element that does not occur in nature. It is named after the Danish physicist, Niels Bohr.

| Boron | B | 5 | 10.811 | Joseph L. Gay-Lussac and Louis J. Thénard | 1808 |

A lightweight brownish semimetal. It is used in making glass that will resist temperature change. One of its compounds, borax, is a water softener and a household bleach.

| Bromine | Br | 35 | 79.904 | Antoine J. Balard | 1826 |

A red liquid halogen, with a choking odor. Its vapors are poisonous, and the liquid can cause serious burns. Its compounds are used in fire extinguishers and in medicines. It is found in considerable quantity in the solids dissolved in ocean water and is obtained from the sea.

| Cadmium | Cd | 48 | 112.411 | Friedrich Strohmeyer | 1817 |

A soft white metal. It is used in batteries and in nuclear reactors to absorb neutrons and slow down the reaction.

| Calcium | Ca | 20 | 40.078 | Sir Humphry Davy | 1808 |

A silver white alkaline-earth metal. It is found in bones and teeth, in eggshells, and in the shells of creatures such as clams and oysters. It is the fifth most common element in Earth's crust and is found in limestone and gypsum. Calcium compounds are used in mortar, plaster, cement, and concrete. They are also of importance in fertilizers.

| Californium | Cf | 98 | (251) | S. G. Thompson and others | 1950 |

A synthetic radioactive metal of the actinide series. It does not occur in nature.

| *Carbon | C | 6 | 12.0107 | Element known since ancient times | |

A black nonmetal occurring in a variety of forms, such as graphite (used in pencils), coal, charcoal, and soot. It also occurs as diamond, a transparent form of carbon, which is the hardest known substance. Carbon has the highest melting point of any element—about 6454°F (3550°C). Carbon dioxide makes up about 0.04 percent of the gas in the atmosphere.

| Cerium | Ce | 58 | 140.116 | Jöns J. Berzelius and Wilhelm Hisinger | 1803 |

A steel gray metal and the most abundant of the lanthanide series.

ELEMENT	SYMBOL	ATOMIC NUMBER	ATOMIC WEIGHT or (Estimated Atomic Weight)	DISCOVERER	YEAR DISCOVERED
Cesium	Cs	55	132.90545	Robert W. Bunsen and Gustav R. Kirchhoff	1860

A soft silver white alkali metal. It is the most active of the metals and melts at 83°F (28.4°C). .

Chlorine	Cl	17	35.4527	Sir Humphry Davy	1810

A greenish gas and one of the halogens. Because it kills bacteria, it is used (in small amounts) to purify drinking water. It combines with colored organic compounds and converts them into colorless ones; so it and some of its compounds are used as bleaches. The chloride ion in the compound sodium chloride, or ordinary table salt, is essential to life.

Chromium	Cr	24	51.9961	Louis N. Vauquelin	1797

A hard gray high-melting metal. Added to steel, it increases that metal's hardness. If enough is added, steel will no longer rust, and stainless steel is formed. Chromium can also be plated over metal to form a shiny surface that will not rust.

Cobalt	Co	27	58.933200	Georg Brandt	1735

A hard bluish white metal, resembling iron in its properties. For instance, it is attracted to a magnet. It forms very hard alloys with chromium and tungsten. Cobalt is one of the metals essential to life in trace amounts.

*Copper	Cu	29	63.546	Element known since ancient times	

A red metal. It is the best-known conductor of heat (at ordinary temperatures). Because it is also the second-best conductor of electricity (silver is first), its most important use is in electrical wiring. Copper can be beaten into shape easily, making it ideal for ornaments and artwork. It is one of the metals essential to life in trace amounts.

Curium	Cm	96	(247)	Glenn T. Seaborg and others	1944

A synthetic radioactive metal of the actinide series. It does not occur in nature.

Darmstadtium	Ds	110	(281)	P. Armbruster and others	1994

A synthetic radioactive element that does not occur in nature. It is named after the city of Darmstadt, Germany, where it was first produced.

Dubnium	Db	105	(262)	A. Ghiorso and others	1970

A synthetic radioactive element that does not occur in nature. It is named after the Russian city of Dubna.

Dysprosium	Dy	66	162.50	Paul E. Lecoq de Boisbaudran	1886

A soft silver metal of the lanthanide series.

Einsteinium	Es	99	(252)	A. Ghiorso and others	1952

A synthetic radioactive metal of the actinide series. It does not occur in nature.

Erbium	Er	68	167.26	Carl G. Mosander	1843

A metal of the lanthanide series. It is used in the manufacture of nuclear control rods.

Europium	Eu	63	151.964	Eugène A. Demarcay	1896

A metal of the lanthanide series.

Fermium	Fm	100	(257)	A. Ghiorso and others	1953

A synthetic radioactive metal of the actinide series with 18 known isotopes. It does not occur in nature.

Fluorine	F	9	18.9984032	Ferdinand F. H. Moissan	1886

A light yellow gas; the lightest of the halogens and the most active element known. The gas is dangerously poisonous. Small quantities of fluorine compounds in tooth enamel help to make the teeth resistant to decay. Fluorine is added to a city's water supplies to provide this decay-fighting protection.

Alkali Metals
Alkaline-Earth Metals
Rare-Earth Metals
Transition Metals
Other Metals
Semimetals (Metalloids)
Noble Gases
Halogens
Other Nonmetals
Transactinides

ELEMENT	SYMBOL	ATOMIC NUMBER	ATOMIC WEIGHT or (Estimated Atomic Weight)	DISCOVERER	YEAR DISCOVERED
Francium	Fr	87	(223)	Marguerite Perey	1939

A synthetic radioactive metal. It is the heaviest known alkali metal and is found in very small amounts in uranium ores.

| Gadolinium | Gd | 64 | 157.25 | Jean C. G. de Marignac | 1880 |

A metal of the lanthanide series. Gadolinium compounds are used in making the light-emitting phosphors in color television picture tubes.

| Gallium | Ga | 31 | 69.723 | Paul E. Lecoq de Boisbaudran | 1875 |

A silver white metal that melts at about 86°F (30°C) and thus is liquid on very hot days. This rare metal is found in Earth's crust in such various ores, rocks, and minerals as diaspore, sphalerite, bauxite, and coal.

| Germanium | Ge | 32 | 72.61 | Clemens A. Winkler | 1886 |

A brittle gray white semimetal that is used in transistors. One of its compounds, germanium oxide, is used in wide-angle camera lenses since it strongly bends, or refracts, light.

| *Gold | Au | 79 | 196.96655 | Element known since ancient times | |

A yellow metal. It is considered the most beautiful of all the elements, does not rust or tarnish, and is easily beaten into shape. It has been used in jewelry, ornaments, and artwork for thousands of years. Because of its rareness it has been used as money. Gold is also used in electronics, dental work, and medicine.

| Hafnium | Hf | 72 | 178.49 | Dirk Coster & Georg von Hevesy | 1923 |

A white metal very like zirconium in its properties. Because hafnium readily absorbs neutrons, it is used in reactors (especially in nuclear submarines) to control the neutrons produced in nuclear fission.

| Hassium | Hs | 108 | (269) | P. Armbruster and others | 1984 |

A synthetic radioactive element that does not occur in nature. It is named after *Hassias,* the Latin name of the German state of Hesse, where the laboratory in which the element was discovered is located.

| *Helium | He | 2 | 4.002602 | Sir William Ramsay | 1895 |

The lightest element except for hydrogen. Helium is safer than hydrogen for use in balloons and dirigibles because it cannot explode. Very small quantities of helium are present in the atmosphere. More is produced in the soil by the radioactive decay of uranium and thorium.

| Holmium | Ho | 67 | 164.93032 | Per T. Cleve | 1879 |

A metal of the lanthanide series.

| *Hydrogen | H | 1 | 1.00794 | Henry Cavendish | 1766 |

A colorless gas that is the lightest and simplest of the elements. It is the tenth most common element in Earth's crust. Stars like our sun are mostly hydrogen. Almost all organic compounds contain hydrogen as well. Hydrogen is thus essential to life. Its most important compound—water—is formed with oxygen.

| Indium | In | 49 | 114.818 | Ferdinand Reich & Hieronymus T. Richter | 1863 |

A soft silvery metal, used in the semiconductor industry and sometimes used in jewelry or in dental fillings. It is quite rare.

| *Iodine | I | 53 | 126.90447 | Bernard Courtois | 1811 |

A gray black solid and one of the halogens. It is quite rare and occurs more often in the sea than on land. It is essential to life in small quantities. Iodine is an active element; a solution of it in alcohol and water (tincture of iodine) will kill bacteria.

| Iridium | Ir | 77 | 192.217 | Smithson Tennant | 1803 |

A hard white metal of the platinum family, and the least active of the metals. Alloyed with platinum, it is used for standard weights because the alloy will not tarnish and thus change weight.

ELEMENT	SYMBOL	ATOMIC NUMBER	ATOMIC WEIGHT or (Estimated Atomic Weight)	DISCOVERER	YEAR DISCOVERED
*Iron	Fe	26	55.845	Element known since ancient times	

A whitish metal. In Latin it is called *ferrum,* which is why its symbol is Fe. It is more strongly attracted to a magnet than any other element is. Iron is the fourth most common element in Earth's crust. Earth's interior is thought to be composed mostly of molten (melted) iron. Iron plus carbon makes steel, which is much harder and stronger than iron itself. The greatest shortcoming of iron is the way in which it slowly turns into a crumbly rust. Iron is essential to life. It occurs in the body chiefly in the hemoglobin of the red blood cells.

Krypton	Kr	36	83.80	Sir William Ramsay and Morris W. Travers	1898

One of the inert gases, occurring in the atmosphere in very small quantities.

Lanthanum	La	57	138.9055	Carl G. Mosander	1839

A bluish white metal; the first of the lanthanide series. It is used in the manufacture of glass.

Lawrencium	Lr	103	(262)	A. Ghiorso and others	1961

A synthetic radioactive element and last of the actinide series. It does not occur in nature.

*Lead	Pb	82	207.2	Element known since ancient times	

A bluish white metal. In Latin it is known as *plumbum,* which is why its symbol is Pb. The chief use of lead is in storage batteries. Lead alloys are used in type metal and in solder. Some lead compounds are used as paint pigments. Lead is a dangerous cumulative poison (that is, small quantities build up in the body); its compounds should be handled with care.

Lithium	Li	3	6.941	Johan A. Arfvedson	1817

A soft white metal; the lightest of the alkalis and, in fact, the lightest of all metals. Some of its compounds have been found to be effective in treating illnesses such as bipolar disorders.

Lutetium	Lu	71	174.967	Georges Urbain	1907

The last of the lanthanide series of metals.

*Magnesium	Mg	12	24.3050	Sir Humphry Davy	1808

A light whitish alkaline-earth metal, the eighth most common element of Earth's crust. It combines with oxygen easily, burning with a brilliant white flame. It is used in flares, flashbulbs, and incendiary bombs. Its alloys with aluminum are important in airplane construction. It is obtained from solids that are dissolved in ocean water.

Manganese	Mn	25	54.938049	Johan G. Gahn	1774

A hard, brittle gray white metal and the twelfth most common element of Earth's crust. It is used mainly in the manufacture of alloy steel. It is one of the metals essential to life in small quantities.

Meitnerium	Mt	109	(268)	G. Münzenberg, P. Armbruster, and others	1982

A synthetic radioactive element that does not occur in nature. It is named after the Austrian physicist, Lise Meitner.

Mendelevium	Md	101	(258)	A. Ghiorso and others	1955

A synthetic radioactive element of the actinide series. It does not occur in nature.

Mercury	Hg	80	200.59	Element known since ancient times	

A silver white metal. It has the lowest melting point of any metal, about -38°F (-39°C), and thus it is liquid at ordinary temperatures. In Latin it is called *hydrargyrum* ("liquid silver"), which is why its symbol is Hg. An alternate English name is "quicksilver." Because mercury is a very heavy liquid ($13^1/_2$ times as heavy as water), it is used in barometers. It is also used in thermometers and in electrical switches.

Molybdenum	Mo	42	95.94	Peter J. Hjelm	1782

A very hard silver white metal, used mainly in the manufacture of alloy steel. It is one of the metals essential to life in small quantities.

	Alkali Metals		Rare-Earth Metals		Other Metals		Noble Gases		Other Nonmetals
	Alkaline-Earth Metals		Transition Metals		Semimetals (Metalloids)		Halogens		Transactinides

ELEMENT	SYMBOL	ATOMIC NUMBER	ATOMIC WEIGHT or (Estimated Atomic Weight)	DISCOVERER	YEAR DISCOVERED
Neodymium	Nd	60	144.24	Baron von Welsbach	1885

A faintly yellow metal of the lanthanide series. When it is combined with iron and boron, it forms the most powerful magnetic material known.

*Neon	Ne	10	20.1797	Sir William Ramsay and Morris W. Travers	1898

One of the inert gases, occurring in the atmosphere in very small quantities. It can be made to glow orange-red when an electric current is forced through it. Glass tubes containing this gas (and other inert gases) form the familiar neon lights.

Neptunium	Np	93	(237)	Edwin M. McMillan and Philip H. Abelson	1940

A synthetic radioactive element of the actinide series.

*Nickel	Ni	28	58.6934	Axel F. Cronstedt	1751

A hard whitish metal resembling iron. It is attracted by a magnet. The metal is used in coins, giving the U.S. 5-cent piece (the "nickel") its name. It is used in stainless steel. When plated over iron, it protects the iron from corrosion. When mixed with chromium, it can withstand extremely high temperatures. Scientists think that the molten core at the center of Earth is 10 percent nickel.

Niobium	Nb	41	92.90638	Charles Hatchett	1801

A gray metal. In the American steel industry it is usually called columbium and given the symbol Cb. It is used mainly in forming steel alloys. Its compound with carbon (niobium carbide) is very hard and is used for making cutting tools.

*Nitrogen	N	7	14.00674	Daniel Rutherford	1772

A colorless gas that makes up four-fifths of the atmosphere. It is inert and as a pure element is useless to most forms of life. Nitrogen compounds, however, are essential to life. Proteins and nucleic acids contain nitrogen. Plants tend to use up the nitrogen compounds present in the soil; so more nitrogen compounds are added as fertilizer. Nitrogen compounds are often explosive. Such substances as gunpowder, cordite, TNT, and nitroglycerin all contain nitrogen.

Nobelium	No	102	(259)	A. Ghiorso and others	1958

A synthetic radioactive element of the actinide series. It does not occur in nature.

Osmium	Os	76	190.23	Smithson Tennant	1803

A hard bluish white metal of the platinum family. It is the densest of all the elements—22.5 times as heavy as an equal volume of water.

*Oxygen	O	8	15.9994	Joseph Priestley	1774

A colorless gas. Oxygen is the most common element in the crust of Earth, making up nearly half of it. The ocean consists of hydrogen in combination with oxygen (water). And the air is one-fifth oxygen. Oxygen is an active element that combines easily with many other substances to yield energy. Gasoline, coal, paper, wood, and many other substances burn because they are combining rapidly with oxygen. Breathing draws oxygen into the body, where it slowly combines with our food to give us energy.

Palladium	Pd	46	106.42	William H. Wollaston	1803

A silver white metal of the platinum family, sometimes used in jewelry.

Phosphorus	P	15	30.973761	Hennig Brand	1669

A nonmetal, which may be prepared in various forms; yellow (called "white phosphorus"), red, or black. The yellow form is extremely poisonous. Phosphorus is the eleventh most common element in Earth's crust. It is found in the nucleic acids, which are the most important substances in living organisms. Phosphorus compounds (phosphates) are an important component of fertilizers. Phosphorus and some of its compounds unite easily with oxygen.

Platinum	Pt	78	195.078	Antonio de Ulloa	1735

A whitish metal with a high melting point. Quite rare, it is usually found in small quantities in nickel ores. It is heavier than gold and even less likely to corrode. It is important as a catalyst in a wide variety of chemical reactions, including those that in a catalytic converter (an automobile exhaust-system component) decompose harmful gases into harmless products. It is also used in chemical laboratories for equipment that must resist heat and chemicals.

ELEMENT	SYMBOL	ATOMIC NUMBER	ATOMIC WEIGHT or (Estimated Atomic Weight)	DISCOVERER	YEAR DISCOVERED
Plutonium	Pu	94	(244)	Glenn T. Seaborg and others	1940

A synthetic radioactive element of the actinide series. It is very rare. Plutonium can be made to undergo fission. It has therefore been used in nuclear weapons and nuclear reactors. It is extremely poisonous and is known to cause cancer.

Polonium	Po	84	(209)	Marie and Pierre Curie	1898

A rare radioactive element occurring in small quantities in uranium ore. It is extremely poisonous.

Potassium	K	19	39.0983	Sir Humphry Davy	1807

A soft silver white alkali metal, the seventh most common element in Earth's crust. It is an extremely active metal. Its compounds are essential to life, widely used in drugs, and an important ingredient in fertilizers.

Praseodymium	Pr	59	140.90765	Baron von Welsbach	1885

A silver yellow metal of the lanthanide series.

Promethium	Pm	61	(145)	J. A. Marinsky and L. E. Glendenin	1947

A synthetic radioactive metal of the lanthanide series. It is also found to occur in certain stars.

Protactinium	Pa	91	231.03588	Otto Hahn & Lise Meitner	1917

A radioactive metal of the actinide series. It is found in small quantities in uranium ores.

Radium	Ra	88	(226)	Marie and Pierre Curie	1898

A white radioactive alkaline-earth element, occurring in small quantities in uranium ores. It has strong radioactive properties. Its destructive rays have been used in treating cancer, but they can also cause cancer.

Radon	Rn	86	(222)	Friedrich E. Dorn	1900

A radioactive inert gas, formed by the breakdown of radium. It is the heaviest of the inert gases and is the only radioactive element that is a gas. It occurs naturally in the ground and sometimes seeps into buildings.

Rhenium	Re	75	186.207	Walter Noddack and others	1925

A white metal with a high melting point. It is very rare.

Rhodium	Rh	45	102.90550	William H. Wollaston	1803

A silver white metal of the platinum family. It is sometimes alloyed with platinum to make scientific instruments.

Roentgenium	Rg	111	(272)	P. Armbruster and others	1994

A synthetic radioactive element that does not occur in nature. It is named after the German physicist, Wilhelm Roentgen.

Rubidium	Rb	37	85.4678	Robert W. Bunsen and Gustav R. Kirchhoff	1861

A soft silver white alkali metal. One variety of its atoms is very weakly radioactive.

Ruthenium	Ru	44	101.07	Karl K. Klaus	1844

A hard, brittle whitish metal of the platinum family. It is combined with other metals to increase their hardness.

Rutherfordium	Rf	104	(261)	A. Ghiorso and others	1969

A synthetic radioactive element that does not occur in nature. It is named after the British physicist, Ernest Rutherford.

Samarium	Sm	62	150.36	Paul E. Lecoq de Boisbaudran	1879

A hard gray white metal of the lanthanide series. Combined with cobalt, it is strongly magnetic.

Scandium	Sc	21	44.955910	Lars F. Nilson	1879

A metal that resembles the lanthanides so greatly as to be found in the same ores. It is also found in stars.

Alkali Metals — Rare-Earth Metals — Other Metals — Noble Gases — Other Nonmetals

Alkaline-Earth Metals — Transition Metals — Semimetals (Metalloids) — Halogens — Transactinides

ELEMENT	SYMBOL	ATOMIC NUMBER	ATOMIC WEIGHT or (Estimated Atomic Weight)	DISCOVERER	YEAR DISCOVERED
Seaborgium	Sg	106	(266)	A. Ghiorso and others	1974

A synthetic radioactive element that does not occur in nature. It is named after the American physicist, Glenn T. Seaborg.

Selenium	Se	34	78.96	Jöns J. Berzelius	1823

A reddish nonmetal, similar to sulfur in properties. Selenium is considered a trace mineral; that is, small amounts are required in the diet to sustain the health of human beings and other animals. A gray metallic form exists, which conducts an electric current. The current increases when light falls on the gray selenium. This is why the substance is used in photoelectric cells, such as those used in meters that measure light.

Silicon	Si	14	28.0855	Jöns J. Berzelius	1823

A brown semiconducting nonmetal. It is the second most common element in Earth's crust, making up more than one-fourth of it. Tiny silicon chips are used in making integrated circuits, the heart of almost every computer. Silicon is also used in making transistors and solar batteries, to grind and polish other materials, and to make synthetic rubber.

*Silver	Ag	47	107.8682	Element known since ancient times	

A pure white metal. Silver and silver ore deposits are found throughout the world. Its wide distribution made it one of the first metals used by human beings. Silver is widely used for jewelry and for luxury tableware. Coins have often been made out of silver (with some copper added to make the metal harder). Silver is the best-known conductor of electricity at ordinary temperatures. Silver compounds are used in photography.

Sodium	Na	11	22.989770	Sir Humphry Davy	1807

A soft silvery alkali metal. It is the sixth most common element in Earth's crust. Sodium chloride (common table salt) is the most important of its compounds and is essential to life. Other common substances are sodium carbonate (soda ash), sodium bicarbonate (baking soda), sodium tetraborate (borax), and sodium hydroxide (lye). When heated, sodium glows with a strong yellow light that is sometimes used in lighting.

Strontium	Sr	38	87.62	Sir Humphry Davy	1808

A hard silver white alkaline-earth metal. Some of its compounds are used to give red colors to fireworks. A radioactive form of the element, strontium 90, is produced in the fallout of nuclear explosions.

Sulfur	S	16	32.066	Element known since ancient times	

A yellow nonmetal. It is also called brimstone. It is used in the production of sulfuric acid, the most important chemical in industry next to air, water, and salt. It is also used in the hardening (vulcanization) of rubber. And it is a component of gunpowder. Protein molecules contain small numbers of sulfur atoms, and so sulfur is essential to life.

Tantalum	Ta	73	180.9479	Anders G. Ekeberg	1802

A high-melting metal that resists corrosion. It is sometimes used for surgical wire or metal implants because it will not affect body tissues or fluids. Its compound with carbon (tantalum carbide) is very hard and is used for making cutting tools.

Technetium	Tc	43	(98)	Emilio Segrè and C. Perrier	1937

A synthetic radioactive element. It is the lightest element that does not exist in stable form.

Tellurium	Te	52	127.60	Baron von Reichenstein	1782

A gray white semimetal that is quite rare. Small quantities added to lead harden that metal.

Terbium	Tb	65	158.92534	Carl G. Mosander	1843

A soft, easily shaped metal of the lanthanide series.

Thallium	Tl	81	204.3833	Sir William Crookes	1862

A soft gray white metal resembling lead in some properties and the alkali metals in others. Its compounds are poisonous and have been used as rat killers.

Thorium	Th	90	232.0381	Jöns J. Berzelius	1828

A heavy white metal of the actinide series. It is slightly radioactive. Considerable quantities are found in Earth's crust. It can be converted into fissionable atoms. This means that thorium is a nuclear fuel.

Element	Symbol	Atomic Number	Atomic Weight or (Estimated Atomic Weight)	Discoverer	Year Discovered
Thulium	Tm	69	168.93421	Per T. Cleve	1879

A metal of the lanthanide series.

| *Tin | Sn | 50 | 118.710 | Element known since ancient times | |

A silver white metal with a low melting point. In Latin it is known as *stannum,* which is why its symbol is Sn. Thin layers of tin plated over iron will not react with acid foods; for this reason tin-lined "tin cans" have been used for food packaging. Tin is also used in alloys with low melting points, such as solder, as well as in pewter and bell metal.

| Titanium | Ti | 22 | 47.867 | William Gregor | 1791 |

A gray white metal that is the ninth most common element in Earth's crust. Because of its lightness and strength, it is used to make high-speed aircraft and missiles.

| Tungsten | W | 74 | 183.84 | Fausto and Juan J. d'Elhujar | 1783 |

A gray metal with the highest melting point of any metal—about 6150°F (3400°C). It is used to form the wires in electric light bulbs. Its German name is *Wolfram,* which is why its symbol is W. Tungsten is commonly used in alloy steels.

Ununbium	Uub	112	(285)	Heavy Ion Research Center, Germany	1996
Ununhexium	Uuh	116	(292)	JINR, LLNL[†]	2000
Ununpentium	Uup	115	(288)	JINR, LLNL	2003
Ununquadium	Uuq	114	(289)	JINR	1998
Ununtrium	Uut	113	(284)	JINR, LLNL	2003

All are synthetic radioactive elements, also referred to as elements 112, 113, 114, 115, and 116.
[†]JINR: Joint Institute for Nuclear Research, Russia; LLNL: Lawrence Livermore National Laboratory, United States.

| *Uranium | U | 92 | 238.0289 | Martin H. Klaproth | 1789 |

A silver white element of the actinide series. It is only slightly radioactive. One form, uranium 235, can be made to undergo nuclear fission, producing great quantities of energy. It was used in the first atomic bomb. Most uranium is another form, uranium 238. All forms of uranium can be used as fuel in nuclear reactors.

| Vanadium | V | 23 | 50.9415 | Nils G. Sefström | 1830 |

A gray high-melting soft metal used in alloy steels.

| Xenon | Xe | 54 | 131.29 | Sir William Ramsay and Morris W. Travers | 1898 |

One of the inert gases, occurring in the atmosphere in very small quantities.

| Ytterbium | Yb | 70 | 173.04 | Jean C. G. de Marignac | 1878 |

A soft silver-colored metal of the lanthanide series.

| Yttrium | Y | 39 | 88.90585 | Johan Gadolin | 1794 |

A grayish black metal related to the lanthanide series.

| *Zinc | Zn | 30 | 65.39 | Andreas S. Marggraf | 1746 |

A bluish white metal. The ancients alloyed it with copper to form the yellow alloy brass. Zinc is coated over iron to prevent corrosion, thus forming galvanized iron.

| Zirconium | Zr | 40 | 91.224 | Martin H. Klaproth | 1789 |

A white metal used in alloy steel. It is found in zircon, a semiprecious gem.

Alkali Metals
Alkaline-Earth Metals
Rare-Earth Metals
Transition Metals
Other Metals
Semimetals (Metalloids)
Noble Gases
Halogens
Other Nonmetals
Transactinides

Large ears, ivory tusks, and a long, flexible trunk are three of an elephant's distinguishing features. Another is its enormous size—elephants may weigh more than 8 tons.

ELEPHANTS

Elephants are the largest land animals in the world. You could never mistake an elephant for anything else. Observe one the next time you go to the zoo. There it stands—a mountain of flesh in a wrinkled suit of rough, gray hide. Its legs are like pillars. Its huge ears flap gently back and forth like wings. Out comes its long, flexible trunk as it begs for a peanut. It daintily picks up the peanut with the fleshy tip of its trunk. Then the huge beast tucks the tidbit into its mouth and rumbles with satisfaction. There is no other animal like it.

Elephants possess enormous strength. They also are highly intelligent and adaptable. For these reasons they have been tamed by people for thousands of years to be used as riding and work animals. They have good memories and seldom forget a trick or command once they learn it. In ancient times elephants were often used in battle. Today they are the stars of zoos and circuses all over the world.

▶ INDIAN AND AFRICAN ELEPHANTS

Most of the elephants you see in a zoo or a circus are Indian elephants (sometimes called Asian elephants). But sometimes you see an African elephant, too. You can easily tell the two apart by looking at their ears. African elephants have ears at least twice as big as those of an Indian elephant. But there are also many other differences between the two.

The Indian elephant has a bulging forehead and a back that is convex, or bowed out. The African elephant has a sloping forehead, and its back usually has a dip in it behind the shoulders. The trunk of the Indian elephant tends to be smoother than that of its African cousin. It has only one fingerlike lobe at the tip instead of the two lobes on the trunk of the African species.

On average, African elephants are bigger and heavier than Indian elephants. With the exception of some whales, African elephants are the largest animals alive today. They are between 9 and 13 feet (3 and 4 meters) high at the shoulder and may weigh up to 16,500 pounds (7,500 kilograms). Indian elephants are 8 to 9 feet (2.5 to 3 meters) high at the shoulder and may weigh up to 11,000 pounds (5,000 kilograms). Pygmy elephants are occasionally found in nature. These are unusually small individuals that may be no more than 5 or 6 feet (about 1.7 meters) tall as adults.

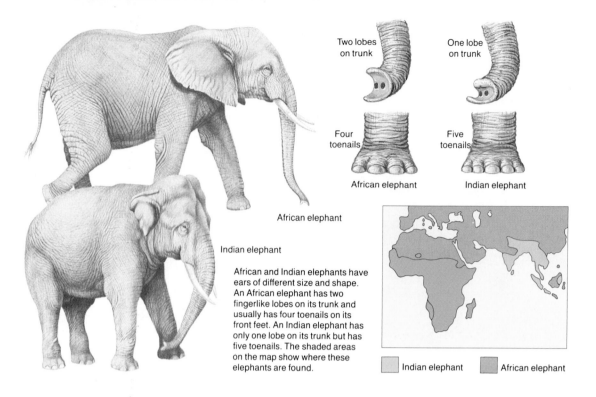

Two lobes on trunk

One lobe on trunk

Four toenails

Five toenails

African elephant

Indian elephant

African elephant

Indian elephant

African and Indian elephants have ears of different size and shape. An African elephant has two fingerlike lobes on its trunk and usually has four toenails on its front feet. An Indian elephant has only one lobe on its trunk but has five toenails. The shaded areas on the map show where these elephants are found.

Indian elephant   African elephant

Indian elephants live in Asia, roaming the forests of India, Sri Lanka, Myanmar, Malaysia, Sumatra, and Borneo. African elephants range over the forests, grasslands, and river valleys of Africa south of the Sahara. Some scientists divide Indian and African elephants into subgroups based on differences in appearance and on where they live. Evidence from genetic studies reported in 2001 suggests that African elephants should be considered two separate species—savannah elephants and forest elephants.

Both Indian and African elephants have all the toes of each foot enclosed in a single covering of skin. Only the toenails show. Indian elephants have five toenails on their front feet and four on their hind feet. African elephants may have one nail fewer on each foot.

As adults, both types of elephants have very little body hair. But their eyes are fringed with long lashes and their tails are tipped with clusters of thick, wiry hair.

Elephants require a great amount of food to nourish their huge bodies, and they feed many hours every day. Captive elephants may eat about 150 pounds (almost 70 kilograms) of hay in one day, as well as several bucketfuls of other food. In the wild, a big bull (male elephant) may eat up to 500 pounds (225 kilograms) of food a day. Ele-

phants drink between 20 and 40 gallons (75 and 150 liters) of water each day.

▶ THE USEFUL TRUNK

Aside from its large size, an elephant's most distinctive feature is its long trunk. Reaching almost to the ground, the trunk is formed by the very long nose and upper lip. It is needed not only for breathing but also for smelling, touching, feeding, and drinking. It can lift heavy objects, and courting elephants caress each other with their trunks.

To feed, the elephant uses its trunk to pick up all sorts of plant material—leaves, grasses, roots, bark, fruits, and vegetables. The elephant's trunk is strong enough to lift entire trees out of the ground. The elephant uses its trunk to strip the tree of leaves and bark and then to tuck the food into its mouth.

The trunk is also used for drinking. It is used to suck up water, which is then squirted into the mouth and swallowed.

To communicate with each other, elephants can make a loud, trumpeting sound with their trunks. This sound usually means anger or pain. A soft rumbling may be a sign of contentment. If trouble looms, an elephant often raps sharply on the ground with its trunk. This makes a booming sound that alerts the other members of the herd.

▶TUSKS AND MOLAR TEETH

Elephants are equally remarkable for their long, curving tusks. These extend out of the upper jaw on either side of the trunk. The tusks are enormously long teeth, which continue to grow throughout the elephant's life. They are made of bony material called ivory.

Among Indian elephants, only the males have long tusks, but both sexes of African elephants have them. They become visible when the animal is about 5 years old. Record African tusks have measured about 11 feet (3.4 meters) long and weighed about 300 pounds (135 kilograms). Indian elephants generally have somewhat smaller tusks.

Throughout history, elephants have been hunted for their ivory tusks. Big game hunters especially prized large tusks. In most countries today, killing elephants for their tusks is against the law. But illegal hunting, called poaching, still takes place.

The elephant's grinding teeth, or molars, are also unusual. During its long life an ele-

phant grows a total of 24 molars—six on each side of the upper jaw, and six on each side of the lower. But usually only eight teeth are in use in the mouth at any one time. When a tooth becomes worn down, it is pushed forward and out of the mouth by another tooth growing in behind it. In the Indian elephant the last and largest molar may be 1 foot (30 centimeters) long. When the last molars are worn down, the elephant can eat only soft plants. If it cannot take in enough food, it may die of starvation.

An elephant's trunk is the most versatile part of its body. The trunk is strong enough to lift and carry large logs (*below*). It can scoop up and toss dirt or dust (*right*), grasp objects as small as a peanut, and carry water to the elephant's mouth. When an elephant makes its trumpeting sound (*below right*), the sound is magnified by hollow regions inside the trunk.

A river, lake, or even a small water hole provides a gathering place for elephants. Daily mud baths help elephants keep cool and also help drive away bothersome insects.

▶ELEPHANT HERDS

An elephant herd may vary from 10 to 20 animals to 50 or more, most of whom are related. The herd has no permanent home but visits different food areas at different times of the year. During the dry season elephants migrate into the forests or stay close to a good supply of water. In the rainy season they wander out onto grassy plains. An elephant's top speed is about 25 miles (40 kilometers) an hour. Its ordinary gait is about as fast as a person can walk. And no elephant can jump.

The herd's seasonal migrations help prevent the destruction of all plant life in a particular region. Regrowth of grasses, bushes, and trees takes place after the herd of hungry animals moves on. The paths that elephants travel on —especially in the jungles of Asia—are wide clearings called elephant roads. Other animals, including people, often use these elephant roads for their own travel.

The leader of an elephant herd is usually an old cow (female elephant). Most of her followers are females with young in various stages of growth. Young males also travel with the herd, but adult bulls often travel alone. Many live apart from the herd but visit it frequently.

When two or more bulls join the herd at the same time, they are likely to fight each other. They push and strain at each other with their foreheads, often wrapping their trunks together like wrestlers. When one of them gains the upper hand, he may gore the other, drive him away, or even kill him.

Certain males are called rogue bulls. These are lone, ill-tempered individuals. Often they are suffering from toothaches or infected wounds. They are extremely dangerous to meet and may charge at sight.

A Day With the Herd

The daily life of an elephant herd often follows a routine. In the early morning hours the animals may travel to a nearby river. There they drink and bathe—snorting and rolling and squirting water over themselves. In spite of their huge size, elephants are excellent swimmers. At the river, elephants also are often seen covering themselves with mud to cool off and dusting their skin with dry soil.

After their morning baths the elephants feed for several hours. Then they pause in some shady area for a midday rest. As evening comes on, they sometimes go back to the river to drink again. Then they may feed far into the night before taking another rest period.

All of the adult elephants in a herd are constantly on the alert for danger. Because their eyesight is poor and their hearing only fair, they rely on a very keen sense of smell to warn them of danger. People are their chief enemies, but lions and tigers like a meal of baby elephant when they can get it. If a youngster is attacked, the rest of the herd rallies to its defense.

If a calf becomes stuck in mud or cannot go up a steep bank, the mother will push the calf with her forehead or pull it with her trunk. Adult elephants also help one another. If one is injured—say by a rifle wound—two other adults may station themselves beside the wounded one and help to hold it upright while it escapes.

▶LIFE CYCLE

Elephants may breed at any time of the year. When two are courting, they are very affectionate with each other. They wander about together and stroke each other gently with their trunks. But after they have mated, they gradually lose interest in each other.

The female carries her unborn young for 20 to 22 months, the longest period for any mammal. A newborn baby is generally about 3 feet (1 meter) high and weighs between 200 and 300 pounds (90 and 135 kilograms). Within an hour or so after birth, it can walk. Curling its little trunk out of the way, the baby nurses from one of two nipples near the mother's forelegs. Soon the baby is ready to travel with the herd. Several adult females usually help the mother during the birth and in looking after the youngster as it grows up.

At birth the baby is covered with a fairly dense coat of hair, but it loses most of this as it matures. Nursing for two years or more, the baby gradually learns how to eat solid foods. It becomes sexually mature when it is 10 to 15 years old. But it keeps on growing for a number of years after that.

Many people suppose that elephants live for hundreds of years. But their lifespan is much less than that. An elephant is old at 60 or 70.

▶PREHISTORIC ELEPHANTS

The ancestor of the elephants did not have a trunk. It did not have any tusks, either. This ancestor was *Moeritherium,* an animal the size of a big pig that lived in Egypt some 40,000,000 to 50,000,000 years ago.

As time passed, the order Proboscidea—elephants and their relatives—branched out. Many descendants of *Moeritherium* became larger and larger. They developed trunks and tusks, which helped them gather food.

During the last Ice Age (which began about 3,000,000 years ago), North America had elephants. These were the mammoths. Woolly mammoths roamed North America along with their near cousins, the imperial mammoths, which had tusks up to 16 feet (5 meters) long. Woolly mammoths and American mastodons lived in North America as recently as 8,000 or 10,000 years ago and were hunted by primitive people. But all mammoths and mastodons finally became extinct.

▶ELEPHANTS AND PEOPLE

Elephants have been tamed and used to serve the needs of people for at least 5,000 years. Their great size and strength has been put to use lifting large objects, carrying heavy loads, and even leading armies into battle.

Fossil remains show that modern elephants had strange ancestors like these, which lived in different prehistoric ages. The earliest was *Moeritherium (lower left),* which looked like a tiny rhinoceros.

Steppe mammoth

Hoe-tusker

Straight-tusked elephant

Imperial mammoth

Stegodont

Ancient Southeast Asian elephant

Plains mastodon

Highland mastodon

Moeritherium (The first elephant)

Ancestral shovel-tusker

Channel Islands dwarf mammoth

American mastodon

Woolly mammoth

Shovel-tusker

Tame elephants are used as beasts of burden and as riding animals. This costumed elephant in Sri Lanka is topped by a *howdah*, a special "car" for passengers.

To train elephants for this work, one handler, called a mahout, is assigned to each elephant. The mahout always stays with the same elephant. The mahout sits on the elephant's large neck and eventually teaches it to obey a number of different commands. It can be guided by a mere touch of the rider's foot behind the ear.

Famous Circus Elephants

The first elephant ever seen in modern America was brought into New York in 1796 by Captain Jacob Crowninshield, an American sea captain. He had bought it in Bengal, India, for $450. He sold it for $10,000. For the next three years the elephant was taken afoot through the country from Massachusetts to Georgia. Its travels gave many thousands of people their first sight of a real live elephant.

Another imported elephant was purchased in 1808 by Hachaliah Bailey, a New York farmer. He exhibited the elephant from town to town, adding other attractions along the way. Bailey and his elephant are often called the founders of the American circus.

The most famous circus elephant of all time was probably Jumbo—an immense African elephant that was the pride of the London Zoo. P. T. Barnum, who often presented odd attractions in his shows, took Jumbo to the United States in 1882. Jumbo was a sensation until he was killed in a train accident in 1885. But Jumbo's name lives on today—it stands for anything big or great of its kind.

Threats to Elephants

Elephants today are threatened somewhat by ivory hunters but more seriously by the gradual loss of their habitat. As more and more areas of Africa and Asia are being cleared for farming and human settlement, elephants have less area to roam to find the vast quantities of food they need every day.

Many elephants are now protected in national parks and reserves. Unfortunately, these are not large enough to allow herds to feed in one area and then move on to new areas while regrowth takes place. In their search for food, elephants have destroyed woodlands, grasslands, and even farmlands. Unless this problem is solved soon, Indian and African elephants may become extinct.

ROBERT M. MCCLUNG
Author, science books for children

Elephants were used in war against Alexander the Great in the 4th century B.C. In 255 B.C. the Carthaginians used war elephants (probably African elephants) in their campaigns against the Romans. Hannibal took elephants with him when he crossed the Alps and invaded Italy in 218 B.C. In time the Romans experimented with elephants in their own armies. Julius Caesar is reported to have put elephants into his battle legions.

Although heavy machinery is now coming into use, Indian elephants have long been part of the lumbering industry in India and Myanmar. (Indian elephants are easier to train than African elephants.) These strong animals push over partly cut trees with their foreheads. They pick up and carry heavy logs, which they support on their tusks and balance with their trunks.

ELEVATORS AND ESCALATORS

For centuries people have been thinking of ways to move heavy loads to higher places. As far back as 236 B.C., Archimedes developed a weight-lifting device operated by ropes and pulleys. Before him the Egyptians used hoists to build the Pyramids, the largest of which stands over 500 feet (150 meters) tall and has many building blocks weighing more than 200,000 pounds (90,000 kilograms) each. However, none of these early efforts were considered safe for lifting people because of one major flaw—when the hoisting rope broke, the lift fell.

It was not until 1852 that Elisha Graves Otis (1811–61) built a "safe" elevator. It was designed with a safety brake to prevent the hoist platform from falling even if the cable or rope holding it broke. A cable break caused spring-loaded bars on the elevator to snap out and hook onto the toothed guiderails in the elevator shaft. This locked the platform securely in place and prevented it from falling. Otis successfully demonstrated his invention at the 1854 World's Fair in New York City. With safety guaranteed, people were willing to ride in elevators. The safe passenger elevator was an important step in the development of tall, multistory buildings. First known as cloud-scrapers, and later called skyscrapers, these buildings would forever change the appearance of cities.

In 1857, Otis installed the world's first passenger elevator in a five-story New York City building. At that time, electric power was not widely available. Since few buildings had a source of power, Otis adapted a steam engine to power his elevators. The first electrically driven elevator was installed in a New York City building in 1889.

▶ HOW ELEVATORS WORK

There are three major types of elevators: gearless traction, geared traction, and hydraulic. The closed passenger car of a modern elevator rests inside a strong steel frame. The car and frame of an electric traction elevator are lifted and lowered within the elevator shaft by a large electric motor. Guide shoes or rollers on the car frame keep the car in place on the guide rails. Steel cables, or hoist ropes, are attached at one end to the top of the elevator car. They pass over a grooved drive sheave (pulley), which is connected to the electric motor. The hoist ropes are attached at the other end to a heavy weight called a counterweight. The counterweight slides up and down the elevator shaft on its own guide rails in the opposite direction of the elevator car. Because of this counterweight, which balances the full weight of the car and about half of its passenger load, the electric motor does not have to lift the full load of the car.

Gearless and geared traction elevators differ in the speed at which they travel and the amount of weight they can carry. Gearless traction elevators travel at speeds of 400 to 2,000 feet (120 to 610 meters) per minute and are used in buildings more than ten stories high. Geared traction elevators are slower than gearless traction elevators, usually traveling at speeds of 25 to 450 feet (7.5 to 105 meters) per minute. However, geared traction elevators can carry heavier loads—30,000 pounds (13,500 kilograms) or more.

Hydraulic elevators are used extensively in buildings of five stories or less. With speeds rarely exceeding 150 feet (45 meters) per minute, the advantage of the hydraulic elevator is that it does not need any overhead hoisting machinery. The elevator is mounted on a piston that is inside a cylinder extending into the ground to a depth equal to the height the elevator will rise. An electric pump forces oil into the cylinder, causing the elevator to rise. Valves release the oil when the elevator is to descend. Another form of hydraulic elevator is the "holeless" model. A plunger slides up and down on the side of the elevator, and no hole is required beneath the standard shaftway space.

Safety Devices. Today the typical elevator has a safety system made up of the following components: a speed-sensing device known as a governor; a clamping device, or safety, mounted under each end of the car frame that, when activated, grips the guide rail; a tension sheave (pulley) at the shaft bottom, or pit; and a steel governor (safety) rope. The governor rope makes a complete loop around the governor sheave and the tension sheave in the pit. Because the rope is fastened to and travels with the car, the governor sheave rotates at a speed corresponding to the speed of the car. If the hoist ropes break or the car overspeeds, the governor activates a device that grips the governor rope. The pull of the governor rope

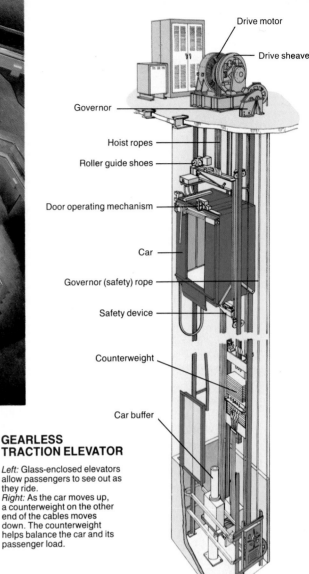

Drive motor

Drive sheave

Governor

Hoist ropes

Roller guide shoes

Door operating mechanism

Car

Governor (safety) rope

Safety device

Counterweight

Car buffer

GEARLESS TRACTION ELEVATOR

Left: Glass-enclosed elevators allow passengers to see out as they ride.
Right: As the car moves up, a counterweight on the other end of the cables moves down. The counterweight helps balance the car and its passenger load.

triggers the safeties, which apply clamping force to the guide rails and bring the car to a safe stop.

Safety devices are also built into elevator doors. When the doors open, the car is prevented from moving away from the landing. However, the car will keep itself level as the load changes due to passengers entering or leaving the elevator. A "safety shoe" mounted on the doors will prevent the doors from closing on passengers or objects in the doorway. The safety shoe will gently strike the object, retract, and cause the doors to re-open. Another safety feature is a light-ray device, which is often used along with safety shoes. This device causes a door reversal whenever the light ray is broken by a passenger entering or leaving the car.

All elevators are equipped with alarm buttons in case of an emergency. Many also have telephones that passengers can use to call for assistance.

Controlling the Elevator. In the 1950's, automatic elevators began to replace people known as elevator operators. Today microprocessors control many elevator functions, including speed and energy consumption. Today's elevators include braille buttons

and voice announcements of stops. Both features are helpful to those who have vision problems.

Under development are systems that respond to and can predict how and when people will be moving within a building. These systems assign elevator cars to destinations before actual demand and reduce passenger waiting times. Elevators of the future will be equipped with laser devices that scan a floor to "see" if passengers are waiting there. If so, the elevator will stop for them; if not, it will continue on.

Elevator Improvements and Designs. The increasing height of skyscrapers has led architects and engineers to design elevators that

How fast can the fastest elevators climb?

A high-speed elevator can climb faster than some airplanes. Some small, single-engine, propeller-driven planes ascend at the rate of 500 to 600 feet (150 to 180 meters) per minute. Taipei 101, a 101-story office building in Taipei, Taiwan, is the world's tallest building. It also has the world's fastest elevators. Ascending at 3,300 feet (1,000 meters) per minute, they can reach the 89th-floor observatory in just 39 seconds.

are faster and more efficient. If an elevator stopped on every floor of a 100-story building, it would take a very long time to reach the top. Thus, most skyscrapers designed today have sky lobbies—floors where people switch from express elevators to local elevators. Express elevators provide fast, nonstop service from the ground floor to the sky lobbies. Once at a sky lobby, passengers take local elevators to their desired floors. This decreases the amount of time people spend waiting for and riding the elevators. The Petronas Towers, the world's second tallest buildings, located in Malaysia, are 88 stories high. Each tower has a sky lobby on the 41st floor. With this design, the elevators take up only half the floor space that would be necessary for the same number of elevators running from the ground floor to the top floor.

Double-deck elevators are another way to move people efficiently in tall buildings. New York's Citicorp Tower has 20 double-deck elevators. The double-deck elevator consists of two elevator cabs, one on top of the other in a single car frame. The lower cab serves only odd-numbered floors, beginning at the ground, or first, floor. The upper cab serves only even-numbered floors. A double-deck elevator can handle twice as many passengers as an ordinary elevator.

Some elevators are enclosed by glass; called observation elevators, they enable passengers to enjoy the view as they ride. Glass-enclosed elevators are found in many hotels, malls, and landmarks, such as the Seattle Space Needle and the Eiffel Tower.

▶ ESCALATORS

Escalators are another way to move people from one level of a building to another. An escalator is essentially a set of moving stairs. Each step is connected to the next step by two heavy roller chains. These chains drive the steps in an up-and-down direction. Each step has axles with rollers on each end. The rollers rest on metal tracks inside a steel frame called a truss. The truss rests between two floors like a steeply slanted ladder.

The steps lie flat at each end of the escalator to make it easier for passengers to get on and off. As the steps travel up or down the escalator, they automatically rise so that they look like staircase steps. Near the end of the ride, the steps automatically flatten out again.

Hidden under the floor at the top end of the escalator is a set of sprockets. A sprocket is a wheel with projecting teeth, like the gear

ESCALATOR

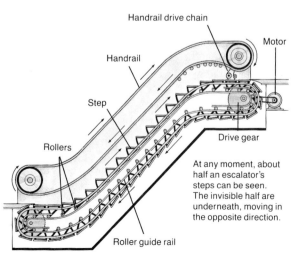

Handrail drive chain

Motor

Handrail

Step

Rollers

Drive gear

At any moment, about half an escalator's steps can be seen. The invisible half are underneath, moving in the opposite direction.

Roller guide rail

wheel of a bicycle. The teeth of the sprocket catch the links of the roller chain and drive it round and round, pulling the steps along their rails. The sprocket at the top end of the escalator is driven by an electric motor beneath the floor. The chains run over pulleys at the bottom. These pulleys steer the chains properly and keep them tight.

At each side of the moving steps is a protective wall called a balustrade. On top of the balustrade is a continuous handrail, made of a moving belt of rubber. It moves along with the steps, at the same speed and in the same direction. Handrails help passengers enter, ride, and exit the escalator.

The first escalator was patented in the United States in 1859, but no one used this invention commercially. However, a number of inventors developed escalators after 1890. At first escalators were crude and unsafe by today's standards. Most of them were not successful. In 1892 a patent was granted to Jesse W. Reno (1862–1947) for an "inclined elevator." A rider on Reno's escalator needed good balance. The flat-surfaced moving platform transported people upward at a 30-degree angle. Passengers needed to lean forward like skiers racing uphill. Because the handrail did not move, passengers had to keep moving their hands as they were carried up. Moving handrails and other safety features were added later. In 1899 an inventor who worked with the Otis Elevator Company built the first step-type escalator. He also coined the term "escalator," which is a combination of the Latin word *scala,* meaning "steps," and elevator.

Today's escalators all travel at about 100 feet (30 meters) per minute. The fastest escalators ever built ran at 180 feet (55 meters) per minute, slightly more than 2 miles (3 kilometers) per hour and slightly slower than an average walking pace. The world's highest escalator lifts passengers to a height of about 200 feet (60 meters), roughly equal to the height of a 20-story building. This escalator operates at a station of the Moscow Metropolitan Railway in Russia. Visitors to Hong Kong's Ocean Park can ride the longest outdoor escalator system in the world—750 feet (230 meters). The shortest escalator—a mere five steps—is tucked away in a private garden in Saudi Arabia. Spiral, or helical, escalators are a design breakthrough now being used in imaginative and elegant buildings.

Moving sidewalks are another way to move many people in public places such as airports, railroad terminals, and shopping centers. A moving sidewalk is basically a collapsed escalator where the flattened step treads move as a level or slightly inclined surface.

CYNTHIA DiTALLO
Otis Elevator Company

ELGAR, SIR EDWARD (1857–1934)

The great British composer Edward Elgar was born near Worcester, England, on June 2, 1857. His father was organist at St. George's Roman Catholic Church in Worcester, and Elgar learned a great deal by assisting his father at the organ and at rehearsals.

Elgar began composing when he was 12 years old. His first works showed talent, and he decided to go to London to study. Except for a few violin lessons, he learned to play and compose entirely without formal training.

In 1885, Elgar succeeded his father as church organist. His marriage four years later proved to be a very happy one. His wife had great faith in his ability and gave him encouragement when things went badly.

Gradually Elgar's works began to win a hearing. His first London success came in 1899 with the popular *Enigma Variations,* a charming set of musical portraits of Elgar's friends. This was followed by *The Dream of Gerontius,* a long religious composition for solo voices, chorus, and orchestra. Then came the *Pomp and Circumstance* marches. The first of these marches, used in the music for the coronation of King Edward VII, is Elgar's most famous piece. He also composed overtures, symphonies, concertos, and four pieces of chamber music.

Elgar was knighted in 1904, and he continued to prosper for many years. When his beloved wife died in 1920, Elgar was brokenhearted. He composed very little after that. He died at Worcester on February 23, 1934.

Reviewed by JON GILLOCK
The Juilliard School

EL GRECO. See GRECO, EL.

ELIJAH

Elijah was one of the bravest of the Bible's prophets. He was born during the 9th century B.C. in Gilead, a region of rough pasturelands. He wore garments of coarse haircloth and loved places of solitude—the wilderness and the mountains.

The kingdom of Israel, where Elijah lived, was governed by King Ahab and Queen Jezebel, the daughter of the King of Tyre. Jezebel was devoted to Baal, her pagan god, and determined to spread her religion throughout Israel. Because Ahab wanted to please her, he built her a temple in the city of Samaria.

Elijah fought against this pagan religion. He told Ahab that there would be no rain in the kingdom unless he, Elijah, commanded it. God told Elijah to hide himself by a brook and commanded ravens to bring him food morning and evening. Soon, without rain, the brook dried up. Then a terrible famine spread across the land.

Elijah went to Ahab and told him to send Jezebel's priests to an altar he had built on Mount Carmel. As a test they would call on Baal to send fire to burn up the offering. Elijah would call on God. The priests danced and shouted to Baal, but no fire came. Elijah prayed to God, and fire burned up the offering. The people then believed in God, and rain fell on the land. Jezebel was so angry that Elijah was forced to flee to Horeb (Mount Sinai), where he lived in a cave.

Elijah handed on his fight against cruelty and injustice to the prophet Elisha. They were talking together when a chariot and horses of fire appeared and separated them. Then, according to the Bible, Elijah disappeared, "taken up by a whirlwind into heaven."

Elijah was greatly loved by later generations. At the circumcision of a male child (a religious ceremony among the Jews) the Chair of Elijah symbolizes his presence. On Passover Eve he is represented at the dinner table by a cup of wine called the Cup of Elijah.

MORTIMER J. COHEN
Author, *Pathways through the Bible*

ELIOT, GEORGE (1819–1880)

Mary Ann, or Marian, Evans published her novels under the name George Eliot. She was born on November 22, 1819, in Warwickshire in England, where her father was the manager of a country estate.

Mary Ann was sent to boarding school when she was only 5, because her mother was sick. She was an ugly duckling of a child, plain and clumsy and very serious. "I don't like to play with children," she said. "I like to talk to grown-up people." She was very clever and read a great deal. Through her life she mastered many languages.

When Mary Ann was 16, her mother died and Mary Ann left school to look after her father. She continued her studies on her own, and her first published book was a translation from the German of D. F. Strauss's *Life of Jesus* (1846). After her father died, she moved to London and helped to write and edit *The Westminster Review*.

In 1854, Marian (as she now wrote her name) joined in a union with the writer George Henry Lewes. They were unable to marry be-

The English writer George Eliot, whose real name was Mary Ann Evans, wrote some of the outstanding novels of the 1800's, including *Adam Bede* and *Middlemarch*.

cause Lewes could not obtain a divorce from his wife. However, their common-law marriage proved to be a devoted and permanent relationship.

With Lewes' encouragement, Marian wrote a series of stories for *Blackwood's Magazine*, which she published as *Scenes of Clerical Life* in 1858. Her first novel, *Adam Bede*, appeared a year later and was a great success. Its hero was modeled on her father. Maggie Tulliver, the troubled heroine of her next novel, *The Mill on the Floss* (1860), was a portrait of her younger self. *Silas Marner* (1861) is the story of a lonely, bitter man and a child's love. George Eliot's most powerful novel, *Middlemarch* (1871–72), is about the complex life of an English country town. Her other novels were *Romola* (1863), *Felix Holt* (1866), and *Daniel Deronda* (1874–76).

Lewes died in 1878. In May 1880, Marian Evans married John W. Cross. She died on December 22, 1880.

Reviewed by JULIET MCMASTER
University of Alberta (Canada)

ELIOT, T. S. (1888–1965)

The poet, playwright, and literary critic Thomas Stearns Eliot was born on September 26, 1888, in St. Louis, Missouri. His father was a successful brick manufacturer. His mother was a writer.

Eliot's education began in 1898 at Smith Academy, a part of Washington University, which his grandfather had helped to found, in St. Louis. His first published poem appeared in the *Smith Academy Record* in 1905. He went to Harvard University in 1906, earning his B.A. degree in three years. He later studied philosophy at the Sorbonne in Paris and Oxford University in England.

In England, Eliot met the poet Ezra Pound, who admired Eliot's poem, "The Love Song of J. Alfred Prufrock," and sent it to *Poetry* magazine for publication.

Until 1925, when he joined the London publishing firm of Faber and Faber, Eliot taught school, wrote book reviews, and worked in the foreign exchange department of Lloyd's Bank. In 1922 he began his own magazine, *The Criterion*. When *The Waste Land* appeared in it in 1922, the poem's unusual style and somber outlook caused much discussion. Many of Eliot's later poems, like *The Waste Land*, were concerned with religious belief. His last long poem, *Four Quartets* (1943), describes the despair in the aftermath of war, but it is also deeply religious.

In 1927, Eliot became a British subject. He did not return to the United States until 1932, when he was invited to lecture at Harvard. His home remained in England.

Eliot also wrote plays in verse. They include *Murder in the Cathedral*, written for the

T. S. Eliot greatly influenced modern poetry and literary criticism. Widely honored for his original style, he received the Nobel Prize for literature in 1948.

Canterbury Festival of 1935, and *The Cocktail Party* (1950). His collection of children's poems, *Old Possum's Book of Practical Cats* (1939), was successfully adapted as the musical *Cats* in 1981.

In 1948, Eliot received the Nobel Prize for literature. He received many other honors before his death on January 4, 1965.

Reviewed by LINDA W. WAGNER
Michigan State University

ELIZABETH. See NEW JERSEY (Cities).

ELIZABETH I (1533–1603)

The 45-year reign of Elizabeth I, queen of England and Ireland (1558–1603), was one of the most exciting and prosperous periods in English history. During the Elizabethan age, as this period is now known, England became a major world power.

Elizabeth Tudor was born in Greenwich Palace on September 7, 1533. Her father, King Henry VIII, had broken with the Roman Catholic Church because the Pope would not allow him to divorce his first wife and marry Elizabeth's mother, Anne Boleyn. Henry then established the Church of England, making England a Protestant country.

When Henry died in 1547, Elizabeth's younger half brother ascended the throne as Edward VI. Her elder half sister, Mary, became queen when Edward died in 1553. Mary I, a Catholic, tried to re-establish Catholicism in England with the help of her Catholic husband, King Philip II of Spain. Because Elizabeth was a Protestant, Mary and Philip suspected her of encouraging plots to seize the throne with the help of Protestant supporters. They had Elizabeth imprisoned in the Tower of London. She was later released and sent away from court to live in the country.

When Mary died in 1558, her persecution of Protestants had earned her the name "Bloody Mary." So when the tall, redheaded Elizabeth arrived in London for her coronation in 1559, the people cheered her, hoping she would bring back peace and prosperity, which she did. She became enormously popular with her subjects, who affectionately called her "Good Queen Bess."

Elizabeth proved to be an extremely intelligent ruler and a skilled diplomat. She chose exceptional ministers to advise her, including Sir Francis Walsingham and her chief minister, Sir William Cecil (Lord Burghley), on whose counsel she relied for forty years.

Elizabeth re-established the authority of the Church of England with a group of laws signed in 1559. But she had to protect herself from the plots of those who sought to restore Catholicism by placing her Catholic cousin, Mary Stuart, the queen of Scotland, on the English throne. Because of these continuing religious conflicts, Elizabeth imprisoned Mary Stuart for 19 years and then reluctantly had her executed in 1585.

Elizabeth I of England was one of the most successful rulers in history. Under her able leadership, England prospered and became a major European power.

Elizabeth never married, although Philip II of Spain tried to woo her in an effort to regain control over English affairs. Failing this, in 1588 he sent a great fleet, known as the Spanish Armada, to conquer England. Spain was the most powerful kingdom in Europe at that time, yet the British fleet was able to destroy the Armada. This victory strengthened England's position in Europe.

Elizabeth's reign was an age of exploration. She supported efforts to establish a colony in the New World, the search for a northern sea passage around the North American continent, and Sir Francis Drake's voyage around the world. The period was also a golden age for English literature, when William Shakespeare, Edmund Spenser, and other great writers flourished.

When Elizabeth died on March 24, 1603, the line of Tudor rulers ended. By her wish, her kinsman, James VI of Scotland (Mary Stuart's Protestant son), succeeded her as James I of England, and England and Scotland were united.

Reviewed by DOROTHY MARSHALL
University College of South Wales

See also DRAKE, SIR FRANCIS; MARY QUEEN OF SCOTS; RALEIGH, SIR WALTER.

ELIZABETH II (1926–)

Elizabeth II, Queen of the United Kingdom of Great Britain and Northern Ireland, has worn the crown longer than any other British monarch since her great-great grandmother, Queen Victoria. Elizabeth became queen when her father, King George VI, died in February 1952. She was crowned in June 1953 at Westminster Abbey in London.

Elizabeth Alexandra Mary Windsor was born on April 21, 1926, to the Duke and Duchess of York. Her father, the second son of King George V, became king when his older brother, Edward VIII, abdicated (gave up the throne) to marry Wallis Simpson, an American divorcée, in 1936. Elizabeth's mother, Lady Elizabeth Bowes-Lyon, was the daughter of a Scottish earl. Elizabeth's sister, Princess Margaret Rose, was born in 1930.

In November 1947, Elizabeth married a distant cousin, Philip Mountbatten, the only son of Prince Andrew of Greece. Philip became a naturalized British subject and after his marriage was given the titles of royal highness and Duke of Edinburgh. The royal family's last name remained Windsor, but in 1960, Elizabeth decreed that her descendants would be called Mountbatten-Windsor.

Elizabeth and Philip have four children—Charles (born in 1948), Anne (1950), Andrew (1960), and Edward (1964). Charles, the eldest and heir apparent to the throne, was named Duke of Cornwall in 1952 and Prince of Wales in 1958. He and his wife, Diana, Princess of Wales (1961–97), had two sons, Prince William (born 1982), who is second in line to the throne, and Prince Henry (1984).

Buckingham Palace in London is the Queen's official residence. Windsor Castle, outside London, serves as the royal family's weekend residence. Vacations are spent at Balmoral Castle in Scotland and Sandringham House in eastern England.

The public duties of the British monarch are entirely ceremonial, but the queen takes them seriously. She sees state papers daily, and the prime minister visits her regularly. Although she is known as a well-informed participant in government business, her role obliges her to keep her political opinions to herself. She serves as a symbol of unity for the loose confederation of countries known as the Commonwealth of Nations.

Elizabeth II, queen of the United Kingdom of Great Britain and Northern Ireland, performs many ceremonial duties at home and abroad.

Elizabeth is "queen regnant" (head of state) rather than "queen consort" (wife of a king). Her duties at home and abroad as a representative of British interests keep her continuously busy. She has traveled widely. In 1986 she became the first British monarch to visit China.

Elizabeth has been criticized for being withdrawn from the people. But after the untimely death of Princess Diana in 1997, she made many efforts to make the royal family seem less remote and to demonstrate its purpose in the modern world. In 1992 she volunteered to pay an income tax on her yearly allowance. And in 1998, Elizabeth announced that she supported the position that the reigning monarch's eldest child, whether it be a boy or a girl, should succeed to the throne.

In 2002, the United Kingdom celebrated Queen Elizabeth II's Golden Jubilee, the 50th anniversary of her accession to the throne.

JERROLD M. PACKARD
Author, *The Queen and Her Court: A Guide to the British Monarchy Today*

ELK AND MOOSE

In the Rocky Mountain foothills, a male elk tilts back his large, pointed antlers and makes a loud, squealing sound called a bugle. At the edge of a pond in Maine, two male moose lock antlers and begin to shove each other. During mating season, displays like these help the males attract a female.

Elk live in North America, mostly in the western states and provinces. Moose live across the northern United States and in Alaska and Canada. But moose also live in parts of Europe, where they are called elk. One way to avoid confusion is to call North American elk **wapiti**. It means "white rump" in the Shawnee language.

Characteristics of Elk and Moose. Moose are the largest members of the deer family. Elk are the second largest. Males, or bulls, are bigger than females, or cows. A full-grown male moose may stand 7 feet (2 meters) tall at the shoulder and weigh 900 to 1,400 pounds (400 to 630 kilograms). An adult male elk weighs about 800 pounds (360 kilograms).

Adult moose have dark-brown coats; their young, called calves, are the color of a golden retriever. The shade of an elk's brown coat depends on where it lives, but all elk have a distinctive white rump. Males of both species grow a new set of antlers each spring.

Elk and moose eat mainly leaves, grasses, and twigs. In summer a male moose may gulp down 50 pounds (23 kilograms) of plant food a day. Moose often wade into ponds and duck underwater to eat water plants.

Elk and Moose and Their Young. Male elk are famous for their mating-season bugle calls in fall. Male moose give a similar call. The males of both species also dig wallows: They urinate in the dirt, then stomp around to splash the mixture on their legs. The odor attracts females. A male elk defends a harem, or group of cows; a male moose takes a single mate.

Females give birth in May to one or two calves. Mothers rear their young without help from the males. Newborn elk have white spots for camouflage. Their mothers hide them in tall grass and stay at a distance, visiting just to nurse. In a few weeks the calves are strong enough to join the herd. Newborn moose have no camouflage spots. They stay close to their mothers for a full year. In winter, mothers guide their calves to food.

A male, or bull, elk in Yellowstone National Park. Elk inhabit mainly western North America, while moose live across the northern reaches of the continent.

The Life of Elk and Moose. Elk live in herds and take turns watching for predators. Moose usually live alone. Elk that spend summers in the mountains avoid deep snows by migrating to lower elevations in winter.

Wolves, bears, and mountain lions prey on young moose and elk and sometimes attack feeble adults. Moose and elk sometimes suffer from deadly infections. Chronic wasting disease—a disease that attacks the animal's brain—was first reported in farmed elk in 1997 and has spread to wild herds.

Elk were once widespread in North America, but they were wiped out in the eastern states by the mid-1800's. Settlers killed them not just for meat, but also because they felt that their cattle had to compete with elk for grazing land.

Elk numbers increased in the 1900's, but much of the land that was once elk habitat is now occupied by humans. Setting aside sufficient habitat is a conservation challenge.

Settlers also wiped out moose populations in some eastern states. But in recent years moose have expanded their range back into New Hampshire, Vermont, and the Adirondack Mountains of New York. However, new dangers exist for moose, such as being hit by cars or trains, now that they often live fairly close to humans.

CYNTHIA BERGER
Science Writer

ELLINGTON, DUKE. See JAZZ (Profiles).

ELLISON, RALPH. See OKLAHOMA (Famous People).

EL NIÑO. See WEATHER (Wonder Question).

EL PASO

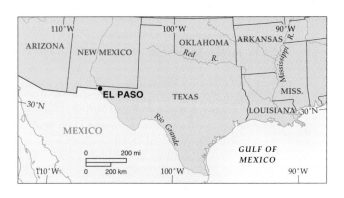

El Paso, in western Texas, is the fifth largest city in the state. Located on the north bank of the Rio Grande (Spanish for "great river"), across from the Mexican city of Ciudad Juárez, El Paso is an important port of entry from Mexico into the United States. Together with Ciudad Juárez, El Paso forms the largest international metropolitan complex on the United States–Mexico border.

Situated in the desert around the slopes of Mount Franklin, the city of El Paso covers 247 square miles (640 square kilometers). Its extraordinarily dry, sunny weather makes it a popular vacation resort. El Paso's population, which exceeds 560,000, is almost 77 percent Hispanic.

Because the city of El Paso is the seat of El Paso County and the home of Fort Bliss, the United States Army Air Defense Center, El Paso's most important industry is government. Also of major importance are tourism, manufacturing, and services. Irrigated farming became possible after the Elephant Butte Dam was constructed in 1916. Cotton became the area's principal crop.

El Paso's educational centers include the University of Texas branch at El Paso and El Paso Community College. The city also has many interesting museums and cultural attractions. Fort Bliss Replica Museum contains United States Army uniforms and weapons, dating from 1848 to 1948. The Wilderness Park Museum displays scenes of people living in a desert environment. An outstanding collection of European and Mexican colonial art is housed in the El Paso Museum of Art. Natural history exhibits and a planetarium are featured at the El Paso Centennial Museum at the University of Texas. The university also helps sponsor the dance company Ballet El Paso and the El Paso Symphony Orchestra, which performs regularly at the downtown Civic Center Plaza. El Paso's most popular outdoor attraction is its Sun Carnival, featuring the annual Sun Bowl college football game.

Europeans first discovered the El Paso area in 1581, when a Spanish expedition traveled through the pass between the Franklin and Juárez mountain ranges. They named this area El Paso del Norte ("the Pass of the North") because it led to the northern Spanish colony of New Mexico.

In 1848, the United States won the Mexican War. According to the Treaty of Guadalupe Hidalgo, Texas became part of the United States, and the Rio Grande became the international border between the two countries. El Paso del Norte, on the south bank, remained part of Mexico and was renamed Ciudad Juárez in 1888. The north bank was ceded to the United States, and a settlement there, then named Franklin, was incorporated as the City of El Paso in 1873.

W. H. TIMMONS
Professor Emeritus of History
University of Texas at El Paso

El Paso is a major port of entry into the United States from Mexico. The area once belonged to Mexico and still maintains close cultural ties to that country.

EL SALVADOR

El Salvador is the smallest in area of the Central American nations. But it ranks second in population, after Guatemala, and is the most densely populated country on the mainland of the Americas.

▶ PEOPLE

About 90 percent of the people are mestizo—of mixed European (mostly Spanish) and Indian ancestry. The other 10 percent is made up of Indians, Africans, and Europeans. Indians of Mexican origin compose about 3 percent of the Indian population; most reside in the village of Nahuizalco, where they retain many of their native customs.

Language. The official language is Spanish, although a few Indians speak Nahuatl, an Indian language.

Religion. Most of the people are Roman Catholics. But the number of Evangelical Protestants is growing. In the late 1990's about 15 to 20 percent of the population was Protestant; of that number, 75 percent was Pentecostal. Folk Catholicism—a mix of native and traditional beliefs—is also becoming more popular, most likely due to a shortage of ordained priests.

Education. School is compulsory through the primary grades, and about two-thirds of the children attend. About 70 percent of people age 10 and over can read and write.

Way of Life. For many years El Salvador has been dominated by a few families who own most of the good farmland. But most of the people are poor campesinos, or people of

Right: A girl picks coffee beans, one of El Salvador's leading exports. *Below:* The magnificent Izalco volcano is one of many across the country. Its numerous fiery eruptions gave rise to its nickname, the Lighthouse of the Pacific.

the fields. Some work on the large estates called *fincas*. Others farm small plots of land that they own or rent.

The typical diet of the campesino includes tortillas, beans, rice, bananas, and a little meat. For most Salvadorans life is hard. They are still suffering the effects of a civil war that raged from the late 1970's through 1991. More than 1 million people left the country between 1979 and 1986, most going to the United States. Furthermore, in rural areas, coffee and banana trees—which take years to mature—were destroyed by Hurricane Mitch in 1998 and caused people to move to the crowded capital city, San Salvador.

But the people have their pleasures. They enjoy religious festivals and ceremonies, and soccer and baseball are popular sports.

El Salvador

▶ **LAND**

El Salvador is bordered on the north and east by Honduras and on the west by Guatemala. The Pacific Ocean forms El Salvador's southern boundary. It is the only Central American country with no coastline on the Caribbean Sea.

El Salvador experiences many earthquakes. One of the most destructive occurred in 1991. There are also numerous volcanoes.

FACTS and figures

REPUBLIC OF EL SALVADOR (República de El Salvador) is the official name of the country.

LOCATION: Central America.

AREA: 8,124 sq mi (21,040 km²).

POPULATION: 6,100,000 (estimate).

CAPITAL AND LARGEST CITY: San Salvador.

MAJOR LANGUAGES: Spanish (official), Nahuatl.

MAJOR RELIGIOUS GROUP: Roman Catholic.

GOVERNMENT: Republic. **Head of state and government**—president. **Legislature**—Legislative Assembly.

CHIEF PRODUCTS: Agricultural—coffee, sugarcane, corn, rice, beans, oilseed, cotton, sorghum (a grain), cattle, dairy products, shrimp. **Manufactured**—processed foods, beverages, chemicals, fertilizer, textiles, furniture, light metals. **Mineral**—petroleum products.

MONETARY UNIT: Colón (1 colón = 100 centavos) and U.S. dollar (1 dollar = 100 cents).

Land Regions. El Salvador has three distinct geographic regions.

The Interior Highlands are made up of two mountain ranges that run the length of the country and include many volcanoes. The highest, Santa Ana, rises about 7,724 feet (2,354 meters) above sea level. The Izalco volcano has erupted so often that sailors called it the Lighthouse of the Pacific.

The Central Upland, where most of the people live, is a high plateau, averaging 2,000 feet (610 meters) above sea level. Located between the mountain ranges, it is covered with soil enriched by volcanic ash.

The Coastal Lowland is a narrow strip of land that runs along the Pacific coast. This area is hotter and less fertile than the highlands, and few people live there.

Rivers and Lakes. The longest and most important river flowing from the Central Upland is the Río Lempa. Dams were built on it to provide water for irrigation and to generate hydroelectric power.

Lake Ilopango, located in the crater of an old volcano, is the largest lake in the country.

Climate. In the Central Upland, the average high temperature is 90°F (32°C) and the average low temperature about 60°F (16°C). The Coastal Lowland is hotter and more humid. El Salvador has two distinct seasons—wet and dry. Rainfall is heaviest from May to October, while the dry season lasts from November to April.

Natural Resources. Fertile soil is considered a primary natural resource. El Salvador has few mineral resources. The petroleum produced is refined from crude oil imported from Venezuela. The country was once covered by tropical forest. But most of it has been cut down for firewood and homes, and soil erosion has become a serious problem.

Hunting and the destruction of the forests have almost eliminated many wild animals, and some are now endangered species. But snakes, parrots, and a few deer and monkeys can still be seen. Crocodiles inhabit many of the rivers. The coastal waters abound in shrimp, which are an important export.

▶ **ECONOMY**

Before the late 1970's, El Salvador was the most industrialized Central American nation. Some 15 percent of the labor force was employed in manufacturing. But the civil war reversed those gains. Today the economy relies almost entirely on the export of agricultural goods, particularly coffee. Two-thirds of the country's working-age people are either unemployed or underemployed.

El Salvador is an active member of the Central American Common Market (CACM), which was created in 1960. But that organization, too, has suffered setbacks from Central America's wars and civil strife.

Manufacturing. Despite its shrinking industrial base, El Salvador remains one of the more industrialized nations in Central America, selling many products to other Central American countries. Its most important products include processed foods, beverages, chemicals, fertilizer, textiles, and furniture.

Agriculture. El Salvador is one of the leading coffee producers in Latin America. Most of it is grown on *fincas* in the highlands. Other important agricultural industries include sugar, corn, rice, beans, oilseed, cotton, livestock, dairy products, and shrimp.

Trade. Most of El Salvador's exports include offshore assembly products, coffee, sugar, beef, textiles, chemicals, electricity, and shrimp. Main imports include raw materials, consumer and capital goods, fuels, foodstuffs, petroleum, and electricity. The United States is the country's main trading partner.

A woman carefully works on a "carpet" of colored sawdust in front of the national palace in the capital, San Salvador.

▶ **MAJOR CITIES**

Approximately 55 percent of the population lives in urban areas.

San Salvador, El Salvador's capital and largest city, is the center of the nation's commerce and industry, and home to CACM's headquarters. Its population is estimated at 400,000 for the city itself. About 1.75 million live in the city and its surrounding areas.

Santa Ana, the second largest city, has about 200,000 people. Located on the slopes of the Santa Ana volcano, the city is home to some fine buildings and churches. Santa Ana is a center of the coffee trade.

Nueva San Salvador, formerly Santa Tecla, is also a major coffee-growing district. From here one can see the nearby San Salvador volcano.

▶ **CULTURAL HERITAGE**

Art and Architecture. In northern El Salvador, artisans in the village of La Palma create colorful painted wood plaques and crosses. Ilobasco, northeast of San Salvador, offers decorated pottery and ceramics.

The architecture of the country varies. Styles include colonial, Spanish baroque, Renaissance, and neo-classical, seen especially in churches and government buildings. San Salvador has a more modern look, having been rebuilt after the 1854 earthquake.

Literature. Among the best-known Salvadoran writers are those who expressed political views through their work. Poet and novelist Claribel Alegría, known for *Ashes of Izalco* (1966) and *Luisa in Realityland* (1987), is known for her support of nonviolent resistance. Well-known political analyst and poet Roque Dalton authored works including *Miguel Mármol* (1972) and *Clandestine Poems* (1984).

▶ GOVERNMENT

El Salvador's most recent constitution was adopted in 1983. It calls for a president to serve as head of state and government. The president is elected (together with a vice president) for a term of five years and is not immediately eligible for re-election. If no presidential candidate wins a majority (more than half) of the vote, a runoff election is held. The legislature is the one-house Legislative Assembly. Its members are elected to 3-year terms.

▶ HISTORY

Early History. The earliest inhabitants of what is now El Salvador were Indians. Part of the great Maya civilization flourished there before the birth of Christ, and huge stone pyramids from that era can still be seen. The Maya were gradually replaced by Nahuatl-speaking Indians, related to the Aztecs of Mexico. These people, known as the Pipil, built great centers of population, including one called Cuscatlán, where Spanish conquerors later founded San Salvador.

The Spanish Conquest. Spanish forces under Pedro de Alvarado invaded the region from Guatemala in 1524. They overthrew Cuscatlán and after a fierce struggle defeated the Pipil. Because of the heroic resistance of the Indians, many Salvadorans today call themselves Cuscatlecos. Finding no gold or silver, most Spanish left the region. The few who settled built large plantations, using the Indians for forced labor. Spanish officials ruled El Salvador from 1570 until 1821.

Independence and Attempt at Union. In 1811 many Central Americans began to challenge Spanish rule. Perhaps their greatest leader was a Salvadoran priest, Father José Matías Delgado. El Salvador declared its independence from Spain in 1821 but could not preserve it alone and was forced to join a newly formed Mexican empire. When the short-lived Mexican empire was overthrown, Salvadorans played a major role in the creation, in 1824, of the United Provinces of Central America. But this federation, which also included Costa Rica, Nicaragua, Honduras, and Guatemala, had very little central authority and power and eventually fell apart. El Salvador left the federation in 1839 to become an independent state. Coffee soon became the mainstay of its economy.

The 1900's. In the early 1900's, the country continued to be dominated by the wealthy and powerful coffee planters, who controlled the government and determined the nation's presidents. The worldwide economic depression of the late 1920's, however, brought ruin to many small planters as the price of coffee fell by more than half. High unemployment, low wages, and the establishment of the dictatorship of General Maximiliano Hernández Martínez brought about an uprising in 1932. Most of the rebels were Indians and no match for the army. The revolt was crushed, and perhaps as many as 30,000 campesinos were put to death by the government. For more than 40 years thereafter, the government remained largely in the hands of the military.

The Maya inhabited El Salvador before the birth of Christ. Ruins from that era, such as this Maya sculpture, can still be seen today.

War with Honduras. In the 1950's and 1960's many thousands of Salvadorans crossed the border into Honduras seeking work, free land, or escape from repression. A long-standing border dispute between the two countries plus efforts by Honduras to reduce the presence of so many Salvadorans brought about the "Soccer War" of 1969, initiated by rioting between rival Honduran and Salvadoran fans at a World Cup soccer game. As a result of this short, bitter war, much of Central America's trade was hurt and thousands of Salvadorans were sent back home. Diplomatic relations between Honduras and El Salvador were not restored until 1980.

Civil War. Political unrest grew during the 1970's as people demanded that the government provide land and jobs for the poor. Leftist guerrillas tried to overthrow the government by blowing up bridges, railroads, power plants, and water systems. Right-wing extremists struck back with the use of "death squads." Beginning in 1979, El Salvador was torn apart by civil war, assassinations, and kidnappings, and thousands were killed.

In 1979 the president of El Salvador was overthrown and replaced by a junta (ruling council) composed of civilians and military officers but led by a civilian, José Napoleón Duarte. Duarte was a member of the moderate Christian Democratic Party. He attempted many reforms, including land reform. A program was initiated to break up the large *fincas* and redistribute the land to the campesinos. But the government faced so much resistance, both from the landowners and from Communist rebels, it could not act quickly. Thousands of campesinos remained landless. A new but limited land reform was part of the 1991 peace accord that ended the civil war.

Recent History. Duarte won the presidency in a runoff election in 1984, becoming the first freely elected Salvadoran president in more than 40 years. Duarte sought to make the economic and social changes for the country, while trying to satisfy the army and right-wing groups who opposed the changes. In the 1989 election, Alfredo Cristiani of the right-wing Nationalist Republican Alliance (ARENA) won the presidency by a wide margin. New attempts in 1990 to end the civil war failed, but an accord was reached in late 1991, and in 1992 a peace treaty was signed.

In 2001 a massive earthquake hit El Salvador, setting off landslides that blocked roads and buried houses in several towns.

The first elections since the end of the civil war were held in 1994. Armando Calderón Sol, the ARENA candidate, won the presidency. Francisco Flores Pérez, also an ARENA candidate, won the 1999 presidential election, but the opposition party took the most seats in the 2000 legislative elections.

In January 2001, ruinous earthquakes destroyed homes and crops. The lack of clean water and sanitation services led to increased disease, crime, and emigration. Bridges, roads, and a section of the Pan-American highway were damaged, slowing commerce and relief efforts. More than 1 million people lost their homes. Export agriculture, the nation's main source of income, also suffered.

In 2004, ARENA candidate Antonio (Tony) Saca was elected president.

MORTON D. WINSBERG
Florida State University

Reviewed by THOMAS M. DAVIES, JR.
Director, Center for Latin American Studies
San Diego State University

ELVES. See FAIRIES.

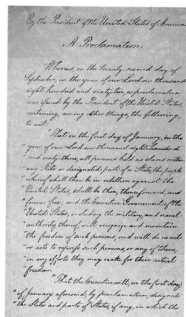

On January 1, 1863, President Abraham Lincoln, with the support of his advisers, proclaimed the slaves in the Confederate states to be emancipated, or "forever free." The Emancipation Proclamation was an important step toward ending slavery in the United States.

EMANCIPATION PROCLAMATION

On September 22, 1862, Abraham Lincoln, the President of the United States, issued a historic proclamation that changed the course of the Civil War and American history. He warned that unless the states of the Confederacy returned to the Union by January 1, 1863, he would declare their slaves to be "forever free." This famous document, which led to the abolition of slavery in the United States, is known as the Emancipation Proclamation because it emancipated, or freed, the slaves.

For a long while, Lincoln believed he had no legal right to free the slaves. In 1858, during his series of debates with Stephen A. Douglas, he had said that he did not intend to interfere with slavery where it already existed. He repeated this declaration when he took office as president in 1861. His priority was to save the Union.

After the Civil War broke out on April 12, 1861, Lincoln waged war against the Confederate states to restore the Union, not to put an end to slavery. Although there was an abolitionist movement in the North, most Northerners went to war because they did not believe that Southern states had the legal right to secede (withdraw) from the Union.

Lincoln Decides to Free the Slaves

By the summer of 1862, Lincoln was ready to change his policy. The war had been going badly for the North. A great Union drive against Richmond, costing thousands of lives, had failed. In the West the Union forces had slowed down after early victories. Long stretches of the Mississippi River were still in Confederate hands. Only a trickle of men answered the call for Union volunteers.

Lincoln reasoned that if slaves were offered their freedom, thousands would desert their masters. This would accomplish several goals for the North. First, the South would lose many of its laborers and have difficulty raising food and producing war materials. Second, the freed slaves could be brought into the Union armies to make up for the shortage of volunteers in the North. Third, a proclamation of freedom would help the Union cause in Europe. By making slavery a war issue, Lincoln made sure that the people of France and England, who believed in freedom and democracy, would no longer permit their governments to aid the Confederacy, which stood for slavery rather than liberty.

On July 12, 1862, the President urged the loyal slave-holding states—Missouri, Kentucky, Maryland, and Delaware—to free their slaves and promised them grants of money if they would do so. They refused. Lincoln then decided to make use of the broad powers of the presidency to act on his own authority during wartime.

On July 22, 1862, Lincoln called the members of his cabinet together and read them a proclamation of emancipation that he had written. The most serious objection to the document came from Secretary of State William H. Seward. Seward feared that because of recent Northern military defeats the proclamation might be looked on as a desperate measure, a "last shriek on the retreat." Lincoln agreed and put the document aside to await a victory.

In the Battle of Antietam (or Sharpsburg), on September 17, 1862, Union General George B. McClellan stopped Confederate General Robert E. Lee's invasion of the North. Antietam was not a clear-cut victory, but it was good enough for Lincoln's purpose. Five days later, on September 22, Lincoln called the Cabinet together again. He told the members that some time earlier he had decided to issue the proclamation as soon as the Confederate army had been driven from Maryland. "I said nothing to anyone," he admitted to the Cabinet, "but I made the promise to myself, and to my Maker. The rebel army is now driven out, and I am going to fulfill that promise." That same day a preliminary proclamation of emancipation was given to the country.

Effects of the Proclamation

The response to the proclamation was mixed. Abolitionists, who had long worked for the end of slavery, cheered the President's action. Many Northerners who had not objected to slavery in the beginning had come to see it as an evil. They too applauded. Yet thousands of men in the Union armies threatened to desert because they had enlisted to save the Union, not to free the slaves. Few did desert, however. In the South many saw the proclamation as an invitation to a slave uprising. Southerners became more determined than ever to win the war.

In the months following September 22, some people urged the President not to issue the final proclamation as he had promised. Many abolitionists pushed him in the other direction. There is no evidence that Lincoln ever considered backing down. The final proclamation was issued on January 1, 1863.

The Emancipation Proclamation did not in itself end slavery in the United States. In the first place, it did not apply to the four slave-holding border states of Missouri, Kentucky, Maryland, and Delaware, which had not seceded from the Union. Second, much of the territory to which the proclamation did apply was beyond the power of the Federal government, and therefore, at the time it was issued, it could not be enforced. Finally, even Lincoln doubted it would be held legal in peacetime.

Yet the Emancipation Proclamation was a turning point in the Civil War as well as a turning point in the history of the United States. During the last two years of the war, slaves left their masters by the thousands. Some 300,000 blacks joined the Union armies. In Europe, talk of supporting the Confederacy ended. Finally, on April 9, 1865, the Confederacy surrendered to the Union, ending the American Civil War.

On December 18, 1865, eight months after the war ended and President Lincoln was assassinated, the Thirteenth Amendment to the Constitution was ratified and slavery became illegal in the United States. Although Lincoln did not live to see his proclamation become law, he is remembered today as the Great Emancipator, the man who freed the slaves.

PAUL M. ANGLE
Author, *The Lincoln Reader*

EMBROIDERY. See NEEDLECRAFT.

EMBRYOS. See EGGS AND EMBRYOS.

EMERSON, RALPH WALDO (1803–1882)

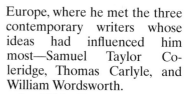

Ralph Waldo Emerson was among America's foremost poets and essayists. He was born May 25, 1803, in Boston, Massachusetts. His father, William Emerson, was a Unitarian clergyman and a stern but kindly man.

It was expected that Waldo would become a minister like his father, his grandfather, and his great-grandfather. Studies at Boston Latin School prepared him for Harvard, which he entered when he was 14. As the "president's freshman," he lived at the college president's house and ran errands in return for his room and board. He graduated from Harvard at 18, taking part in commencement exercises as class poet.

Emerson taught school before beginning theological studies. He was 26 when he finally became a minister in a Boston church. That same year he married Ellen Louisa Tucker, from New Hampshire. When she died less than two years later, he suffered deeply. Tragedy occurred again within a few years as two of Emerson's brothers, Edward and Charles, also died suddenly.

The people of Emerson's congregation loved him, but he was not happy. He realized that his ideas about religion were different from those of most people. Although urged to stay, he resigned in 1832 and traveled to Europe, where he met the three contemporary writers whose ideas had influenced him most—Samuel Taylor Coleridge, Thomas Carlyle, and William Wordsworth.

In 1834, Emerson went to live in Concord, Massachusetts. At first he lived in the Old Manse, a house built by his grandfather, who had been a chaplain during the Revolutionary War. Emerson wrote one of his best-known poems, "The Concord Hymn," in 1837 for ceremonies honoring the battles of Lexington and Concord.

Emerson gave lectures throughout the United States and in Canada, England, Scotland, and France. People liked to hear him so much that they sometimes had a brass band accompany him to his lectures. Young people, particularly, were devoted to him. He encouraged them to challenge ways of thinking that had been handed down from past generations and to trust themselves.

In his lectures, Emerson described a new world he believed to be possible and challenged established ways of thinking. Many of his lectures were reworked into essays—including the well-known *Self-Reliance*, *Experience*, and *Nature*—that influenced the thinking of other writers. Walt Whitman and Henry David Thoreau were both greatly influenced by Emerson's ideas.

Emerson was tall, dignified, and rather shy. Still, he welcomed the intellectuals who gathered in his home for discussions. In 1835, Emerson married Lydia Jackson. The couple and their four children lived in a big white house at the edge of Concord.

Emerson felt that his roots were in Concord, and he took an active part in the community. The day he died, April 27, 1882, the church bells of Concord tolled 79 times, for he would have been 79 in a few weeks.

Emerson was a great essayist, idealist, and poet. Some of his best writing and most original thinking appear in his *Journals*, which were published in ten volumes between 1909 and 1914. They provide the best biography of Emerson.

LOUISE HALL THARP
Author, *The Peabody Sisters of Salem*

EMIGRATION. See IMMIGRATION.

THE CONCORD HYMN

By the rude bridge that arched the flood,
Their flag to April's breeze unfurled,
Here once the embattled farmers stood,
And fired the shot heard round the world.

The foe long since in silence slept;
Alike the conqueror silent sleeps;
And Time the ruined bridge has swept
Down the dark stream which seaward creeps.

On this green bank, by this soft stream,
We set today a votive stone;
That memory may their deed redeem,
When, like our sires, our sons are gone.

Spirit, that made those heroes dare
To die, and leave their children free,
Bid Time and Nature gently spare
The shaft we raise to them and thee.

EMOTIONS

Everyone has feelings. Sometimes we feel happy and sometimes sad. If you made a list of all the feelings you have experienced, it might include anger, surprise, embarrassment, guilt, confusion, and even indifference. It could be a very long list. Taken together, the many feelings that people experience are called emotions.

For most of us, young or old, a smile is an outward sign of a happy feeling.

It is often possible to know when someone is feeling an emotion by the look on his or her face. For example, when people are happy, they usually smile or even laugh. When people are sad, they may show that feeling by crying. Babies, who are too young to talk, can still communicate their feelings with their facial expressions. This look on someone's face that communicates an emotion is called **affect**.

Emotion and affect are related to **mood**, which describes a person's overall emotional state. This relationship is similar to that between climate and weather. For example, it is much more likely to snow in colder climates, but that does not mean it could never snow in Florida. In the same way, it is much more likely for someone with a depressed mood to be sad and tearful, but that does not mean a person with a depressed mood could not smile or laugh on occasion. Compared with emotions, our moods last for longer periods of time. They also may influence how we experience the world.

▶ WHY DO WE HAVE EMOTIONS?

Our emotions help us organize our experiences. That is, the way we feel about something determines how much attention we give it, whether we will remember it, and how we will decide to deal with similar situations in the future.

For example, suppose you accidentally touched a hot stove. The feeling of pain in your finger would get you to take your finger away from the heat. You would then survey the situation, and perhaps feel angry at the stove, or at yourself for touching it, or at whoever left the stove on and did not tell you about it. Your brain would pay close attention to the circumstances surrounding this painful event, and the chances of accidentally touching that stove again would be reduced.

Emotions, attention, and memory are closely connected. The area of the brain mainly responsible for processing feelings and emotions is a structure called the **amygdala**. It is tightly linked to structures in the brain vital to memory processing, such as the **hippocampus**. (For more information see the article BRAIN in Volume B.)

When we feel emotions, particularly intense feelings such as fear or anger, our brains prepare our bodies to respond. The best known of the responses to strong emotion is the "fight or flight" response. When we are frightened, the brain signals the adrenal glands (which sit on top of the kidneys) to release a hormone called adrenaline into the bloodstream. Adrenaline makes the pupils of the eye enlarge so that we can take in more light. It makes the heart beat faster so that we can run if necessary. And it even releases sugar from fat stores in the body so that we will have energy. All these effects instantly prepare our body to pay at-

A roller coaster ride allows us to experience intense emotions without putting ourselves in real danger.

tention and to be fully able to respond to whatever challenge has made us fearful. The "fight or flight" response is important for survival and is seen throughout the animal kingdom.

HOW ARE EMOTIONS DETECTED?

There are differences among people in the way emotions are experienced and expressed. In part, we inherit a certain predisposition to experiencing emotions. This predisposition is sometimes referred to as **temperament**. One can detect differences in temperament even in babies. For example, some infants like to be held and some do not; some startle easily and others not.

In addition to genetic factors, our emotional response to situations or objects around us is influenced by our culture. For example, in a culture where snakes are worshiped, the emotional response to finding one in your house would probably be different than in a culture where snakes are not given divine qualities. Regardless of family background or culture, the human body's basic response to emotions is the same. People throughout the world smile when they are happy, and they cry when they are very sad.

Some medical conditions can alter a person's ability to experience or express emotions. In Parkinson's disease, facial expression can be quite limited due to reduced amounts of a brain chemical called dopamine. Although people with this disorder still feel emotions, it can be hard for others to tell just by looking.

Another neurological disorder that affects the perception of feelings is autism. Because of the way their brains process other people's facial expressions, people with autism have trouble reading others' emotions. As a result, they may anger or embarrass someone without meaning to. Imagine how hard it would be to figure out how to behave properly if you could not understand the emotional signals of people around you.

EMOTIONS IN ILLNESS

Occasionally the term "emotional disorder" is used to describe a mental illness. This is not completely accurate, because the affected person still experiences emotions. However, some disorders of mood or anxiety do influence how we feel. For example, the mood disorder called **major depression** refers to a condition characterized by a prolonged period of deep sadness, loss of interest in activities, loss of energy, trouble sleeping, and many other problems, including thoughts of suicide. In this condition, a person's feelings of sadness are not always related to what is happening in his or her life. Instead they may reflect abnormal brain function, which establishes an internal mood of generalized sadness. Similarly, a person with an **anxiety disorder** may worry about things that most people would be able to overlook.

People exposed to a life-threatening event, such as a severe earthquake or tornado, may be traumatized. The intensity of their emotions may so activate the brain that they later have unwanted memories of the event. They may go out of their way to avoid experiences that might remind them of the trauma. When such feelings are persistent for more than six months, the diagnosis of **post-traumatic stress disorder** is sometimes considered.

Whatever their cause, emotional problems are treatable. This is fortunate, because emotions are an important and constant part of our daily lives, and they strongly influence our behavior.

BRYAN H. KING, M.D.
Professor of Psychiatry and Pediatrics
Dartmouth Medical School

EMPHYSEMA. See DISEASES (Descriptions of Some Diseases).

Did you know that...

a lie detector tries to take advantage of the body's response to feelings?

If you are nervous, it is likely that you will perspire and that your heart will start beating faster. These responses may occur even if you can keep your face from showing that you are scared. A lie detector is a machine that records a person's heart rate and skin conductance (a sensitive measure of perspiration) as he or she is being questioned. If an experienced liar did not worry about being caught, it is less likely that the machine would detect anything significant. But if someone was quite frightened about being caught in a lie, a lie detector might capture the response. A lie detector cannot tell what is true, but it can pick up indicators of emotional responses that might be associated with the act of telling a lie.

ENAMELING

Enameling is the process of covering a surface with a hard coating, either decorative or protective. In art, enameling is a method of decorating an object by fusing colored glass onto its surface.

A metal or porcelain surface is covered with fine glass powder, which is sometimes mixed with oil or water, and then is fired (baked in a special oven). Under intense heat the powder melts and fuses with the metal or porcelain. The rich, glowing colors come from metallic oxides that are mixed into the glass powder. As the art developed, different methods were found to hold the powder in place.

Champlevé enamel is made by forming hollows in a piece of metal—by cutting, gouging, or etching (using acid that eats into the metal). The dug-out spaces are filled with opaque enamel, and the piece is fired. **Bassetaille** is a form of champlevé in which translucent enamel is used to fill hollows of different depths. Lighter shades are produced in shallow depres-

sions, and darker shades are produced where more enamel is deposited.

Cloisonné enamel is made with thin, flat wires, often of gold. These wires, or cloisons, are bent to form the outline of the design and are soldered onto a piece of metal. The cells, or spaces, formed by the wires are filled with layers of enamel, and the piece is fired.

In **plique-à-jour**, usually transparent enamel is used. It is layered into a framework of cloisons that rests on a metal background. After firing, the metal is removed. The finished piece looks like stained glass.

History. The art of enameling was first practiced by ancient peoples in Asia Minor and other eastern Mediterranean lands. But few examples of this early work have survived. Enameling techniques also appeared in lands conquered by the Romans, including England and Ireland.

During the Middle Ages, the art of enameling flowered in Constantinople (now Istanbul) and in Europe. Artisans produced beautifully decorated religious objects, as well as jewelry and crowns for the royal courts. Major centers of enameling grew up in Constantinople, in the Rhine and Meuse valleys of northwestern Europe, and in the city of Limoges, in France.

Painted enamels were a later development than either champlevé or cloisonné. In this technique, enamel is painted on a metal surface and is fixed by firing. Although the ancient Persians had a form of painted enamel, the technique did not become popular until the 1400's. The great center for painted enamels was Limoges. The leading Limoges artists were Nardon Pénicaud (1470?–1539?) and Léonard Limosin (1505?–77?) and their descendants and followers.

The art of enameling has been revived in modern times. Chemistry has made available a wider range of colors, but the techniques remain much the same as those used centuries ago by ancient peoples.

Reviewed by CHARLES T. LITTLE
Metropolitan Museum of Art

See also DECORATIVE ARTS.

This Chinese enamel vase was made in the early 1500's, during the Ming Dynasty.

ENCYCLOPEDIAS

Encyclopedias are among our most important learning tools. A good encyclopedia is a source of thousands of facts that you might otherwise find only by searching through many individual books.

The name "encyclopedia" comes from the Greek words *enkyklios paideia*, meaning "general education." Most people think of an encyclopedia as a book or set of books that gives information about all the important branches of knowledge. This kind of encyclopedia is called a **general encyclopedia**. A **specialized encyclopedia** gives information only about a certain branch of knowledge.

▶ **HOW AN ENCYCLOPEDIA IS PLANNED**

The first step in planning an encyclopedia is deciding who will use it. The publisher of *The New Book of Knowledge*, for example, wanted an encyclopedia to help young people with their school studies. This encyclopedia would also help its readers with after-school interests, such as sports or hobbies.

No encyclopedia could possibly include everything about all branches of knowledge. A publisher decides what to include based on the needs of those who will use the encyclopedia. The publisher of *The New Book of Knowledge* turned to many people who worked with children, including teachers, librarians, and counselors, for advice about what to include. Children were also asked about what interested them and what questions they would like answered in an encyclopedia.

The publishers then prepare an outline of the broad subjects that will be included. They also decide what part of the total space will be given to each subject. The broad subjects are then divided into parts, which will become the subjects of the encyclopedia's articles.

The content may be arranged in one of two ways—topical (according to main topics or branches of knowledge) or alphabetical (from A to Z). Most people prefer the alphabetical arrangement because they find it easier to use.

The number of volumes in an encyclopedia can vary widely. Multivolume encyclopedias that are arranged alphabetically may follow a **unit letter system** or a **split letter system**. In the unit letter system, all entries beginning with the same letter are in one volume. In the split letter system, the first volume may be marked "A to Arius," the second "Arizona to Bickell," and so on. A topical encyclopedia may group all the articles on a broad subject, such as literature, in one volume.

Many encyclopedias have a separate index volume, which provides an alphabetical "key" to all the information in the volume. The index is a valuable guide and should always be consulted when looking up a subject.

Cross-references also help the reader find information. Some cross-references guide readers to articles on subjects that may be known by more than one name. For example, if you look up Samuel Langhorne Clemens, the American author who wrote under the pen name Mark Twain, in *The New Book of Knowledge*, you will find a cross-reference directing you to the article TWAIN, MARK. Other cross-references guide you to related information in other articles. At the end of the article ASTRONOMY, for example, you will find cross-references to CONSTELLATIONS and other related articles.

The encyclopedia should be visually attractive to the user. To achieve this, artists and book designers establish the style and appearance of everything from the cover to the kind of type used. The planners also decide what part of the total space will be given to illustrations such as photographs, drawings, charts, graphs, and maps. These help the user understand the subject.

▶ **HOW ARTICLES ARE PREPARED AND REVISED**

While the encyclopedia is being planned, the publisher brings together editors to prepare the articles. Editors

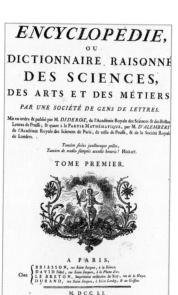

The title page of the famous reference work *Encyclopédie* (1751–80), edited by Denis Diderot and Jean d'Alembert.

are skilled at presenting information in a way that is interesting and understandable.

Once the encyclopedia is published, it must be kept up to date. There may be new developments in science and technology, new countries may be created, and governments may change. The articles must reflect these and other changes. Some articles must be completely replaced to keep them current, and new articles are added to keep pace with the needs and interests of the readers.

▶ ENCYCLOPEDIAS THROUGH THE AGES

The earliest known encyclopedias were written in Greece about 2,000 years ago. The philosopher Aristotle wrote summaries of the knowledge of his time. Speusippus, a nephew of Plato, recorded Plato's ideas on natural history and other subjects.

The oldest existing encyclopedia is the *Historia naturalis* ("Natural History"), produced by Pliny the Elder, a Roman, in the 1st century A.D. It is a vast collection of writings by many different authors on such subjects as geography, botany, zoology, and mineralogy. The *Etymologiarum libri XX*, written in Italy in the early 600's, was the first encyclopedia to have pictures accompany the text.

The Chinese produced many early encyclopedias. One, issued about the year 1400, contained more than 20,000 chapters. The first Arabic encyclopedia appeared in the 800's, and the first Persian encyclopedia in the late 900's.

Lexicon Technicum: or, an Universal English Dictionary of Arts and Sciences, published in England in 1704, was the first encyclopedia to alphabetize its articles as well as have them written by expert contributors. The English *Cyclopedia, or the Universal Dictionary of Arts and Sciences* (1728) was translated into French and enlarged to form the famous French *Encyclopédie* (1751–80), edited by Denis Diderot and Jean d'Alembert.

The *Encyclopaedia Britannica*, which first appeared between 1768 and 1771, has been published in the United States since the 1920's. A translation of a German encyclopedia, *Konversations-Lexikon* ("Dictionary Conversations"), was the basis of the *Encyclopedia Americana*, the first encyclopedia published in the United States. It first appeared between 1829 and 1833 and has been published ever since.

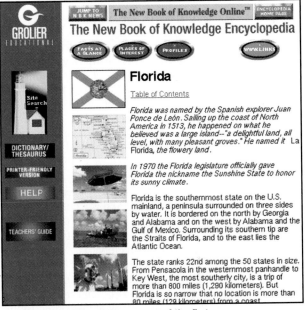

The New Book of Knowledge was one of the first encyclopedias on the Internet.

The first major encyclopedia for young readers was *The Children's Encyclopedia* (1908). In 1910 a version of this encyclopedia appeared in the United States as *The Book of Knowledge*. It was succeeded by *The New Book of Knowledge* in 1966. Several multivolume encyclopedias for older students are published in the United States. They include *Compton's Encyclopedia* and the *World Book Encyclopedia*.

The first electronic version of an encyclopedia was issued on CD-ROM in the late 1980's. CD-ROM's can contain the same information as a print set and may also include sounds and sophisticated animation.

Some encyclopedias, such as *The New Book of Knowledge*, are now also available on the Internet. These online encyclopedias have the same basic capabilities as those on CD-ROM's, but they are generally easier to use and can be updated continuously instead of just once a year.

Encyclopedias will continue to be a valuable learning resource. And with the growing use of computers in schools, libraries, and homes, encyclopedias will become even more available to more people.

SUE R. BRANDT
Former Executive Editor
The New Book of Knowledge

ENDANGERED SPECIES

Plants, animals, and other living things have developed, flourished, and vanished since the first flickerings of life. Sooner or later, every species, or kind, of living thing dies out because it cannot keep up with the natural changes in its environment. Yet, in recent times, many species have passed out of existence sooner than they would have naturally. Since the year 1600, more than 500 species of wild animals and plants have disappeared from the North American continent alone. At least 1,000 more are in trouble. Worldwide, scientists estimate that 20,000 species of plants are in danger of extinction, that is, dying out completely.

Scientists and conservationists have developed terms to pinpoint the species that are in danger of dying out. An **endangered species** is any species of animal, plant, or other living thing that will become extinct if nothing is done to stop the cause of its decline. Endangered species are in immediate danger of extinction. Species that are likely to become endangered in the near future are termed **threatened**. Other species that are not in immediate danger but that have small populations and so could move quickly toward extinction are called **vulnerable** or **candidate** species.

Some of the imperiled species are big and spectacular, like the black rhinoceros and elephant of Africa. Many more, however, are small and unfamiliar to most people. The little Moapa dace, a minnow about 3 inches (8 cen-timeters) long, lives only in about 2 miles (3 kilometers) of a Nevada river. It is endangered. So is the Madison Cave isopod, a tiny crustacean found only in one Virginia cave.

But no matter how small or unfamiliar, each species of living thing has its own special role in keeping the world of nature in balance. When one species becomes extinct, other species are affected. Just one plant may be food or shelter to more than 30 species of animals. Without that plant to feed or protect them, those animals may also die out.

▶CAUSES OF ENDANGERMENT

At one time, living things were primarily endangered by natural events such as the cold climate of the Ice Age or the geological changes caused by an earthquake or volcano. Now the greatest problems facing plants and animals—and people, too—are the human activities that harm the environment on which plants, humans, and other animals depend. Although many different human activities can threaten or endanger a species, the greatest problems occur because of habitat destruction. Illegal hunting and trading and introduction of new species can also cause serious problems.

Habitat Destruction

Plants and animals are adapted to their habitats. Some species can live in a variety of habitats, others can live in only a very specific type of habitat. Either way, if its habitat is destroyed, a species may not be able to find food or shelter, so it vanishes. This means that species such as the Moapa dace that inhabit only a very limited habitat are at great risk of extinction.

Habitat can be destroyed in many ways. As the human population increases, there is a greater need for food, places to live, fuel, and many other things. To meet these needs, tropical forests, wetlands, grasslands, and other

Loss of habitat through human activities, such as the clearing and development of land, is the greatest threat to living things.

natural areas are cleared, settled, and developed and their resources harvested for human use. In the process, habitats are destroyed.

Pollution can also harm habitats, sometimes killing species far from the source. Acid rain caused by pollution from factories in the United States falls on Canada, endangering the fish in northern lakes. Agricultural weed killers and insecticides have been washed by rain into many rivers, killing fish there. Predators that eat fish poisoned this way can also suffer.

The most dramatic effects of habitat destruction can be seen in tropical rain forests. These forests have the greatest diversity of plant and animal life. They are home to between 50 and 90 percent of the millions of species living on earth. Yet each hour, several thousand acres of tropical forest are destroyed. By conservative estimate, this destruction means that 50 to 150 species in the tropics become extinct each day!

Hunting and Trading

Ever since the first people appeared on the earth, they have used nature's resources. People have killed or collected animals and gathered plants for a variety of uses. Animal and plant products have been used for food, medicine, clothing, and shelter, among other things. But many species have been used to death.

In the early 1800's, 2 billion passenger pigeons lived in the United States. Because they were slaughtered for sport and food, by 1914 the last one had died in a zoo. Cheetahs, ocelots, tigers, and other wild cats have been killed for their skins. Several species of whales have been hunted to near extinction for their oil and blubber.

Although most of these animals now are protected by law, many still are poached, or hunted illegally. Animals such as the black rhinoceros and elephant, which are valued for their horns and tusks, have been drastically diminished in number by poachers. Penalties for people who illegally kill and trade wildlife have become much more severe in recent years.

Some species have dwindled because people viewed them as threats to livestock. Wolves have been wiped out of most areas in which they lived because they sometimes prey on domestic animals. In Central Asia, people have killed the endangered snow leopard because of its attacks on sheep and goats.

Wearing markers to identify it and a radio so it can be tracked, a captive-bred condor is released as part of an effort to re-establish condors in the wild.

Even if a living thing is not killed, taking it from the wild can endanger its species if it is rare. Many rare birds, including some parrots, have been caught for the pet trade. Some of these species are already menaced by the loss of their habitats. The combination of habitat loss and capture for commercial trade increases their risk of extinction.

Introduction of New Species

Sometimes native animals are endangered when a new species is introduced into a habitat. In 1820, people released rabbits in Australia that multiplied and became pests. Foxes, which prey on rabbits, were then introduced to control the rabbits. Instead, the foxes killed off native Australian marsupials. Foxes, cats, and dogs introduced into Australia have exterminated nine types of marsupials and endangered more than a dozen others.

Parasites and Diseases

Among the greatest threats to plants and animals are parasites, which include tiny organisms, worms, and insects that feed off other species. Some fungi and bacteria can also endanger plants and animals. For example, the fungus that causes Dutch elm disease has destroyed many populations of elm trees throughout Europe and North America. Sometimes certain algae can cause "red tides" in coastal waters, producing chemicals that kill many birds and fish.

The earth is home to many different kinds of plants and animals that are linked together in an intricate web of survival. Today, more than ever before, the great abundance and diversity of life is being challenged. Many factors are jeopardizing the delicate balance of nature. Presented here are just a few of the many plants and animals of the world that are having difficulty staying alive within their natural communities.

SMALL WHORLED POGONIA

FLORIDA PANTHER

GREENLAND

NORTH AMERICA

PACIFIC OCEAN

ATLANTIC OCEAN

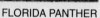

HUMPBACK WHALE

GALÁPAGOS HAWK

SOUTH AMERICA

ATLANTIC OCEAN

▶PROTECTING ENDANGERED SPECIES

People have hurt plants and wildlife. But people are also helping them survive. All over the world, conservation organizations, such as the World Wildlife Fund, Rainforest Action Network, and Friends of the Earth, are helping to conserve species and habitats. Such groups raise money to fund projects, maintain and publish lists of endangered species, and bring the plight of endangered species and habitats to the attention of policymakers and the public. The International Union for the Conservation of Nature and Natural Resources, based in Switzerland, coordinates endangered species conservation on a global basis.

National laws and international agreements have been established to protect endangered species. One such agreement, the Convention on International Trade in Endangered Species (CITES), bans trade in many rare species. In the United States, the federal Endangered Species Act lists and protects hundreds of species

BLACK RHINOCEROS

GIANT PANDA

SUMATRAN ORANGUTAN

TUATARA

EUROPE

ASIA

PACIFIC OCEAN

AFRICA

INDIAN OCEAN

AUSTRALIA

and habitats from activities that might harm them. The act was first passed into law in 1973.

Saving habitat is the cornerstone of protecting species. However, even if their habitat is saved, some species have too few members in the wild to repopulate. Many of these have been taken to zoos or parks and bred there. Within these captive-breeding programs, species are bred with the hope that offspring can be raised and then returned to the wild. Pro-

grams such as this, combined with laws, awareness, and commitment, will help maintain the delicate balance of nature that is necessary for the survival of all living things.

EDWARD R. RICCIUTI
Coauthor, *The Audubon Society Book of Wild Animals*

See also AMPHIBIANS; ANIMALS; BIRDS; CONSERVATION; FISHES; FISHING INDUSTRY; FUR; INSECTS; MAMMALS; PLANTS; REPTILES.

ENDOCRINE SYSTEM. See BODY, HUMAN.

Most of the energy on earth comes from the sun. Often, energy goes through many changes before it can be used. For example, the energy in the fuel for this jet can be traced back to plants that grew and took energy from the sun millions of years ago.

ENERGY

Energy is the ability to do work. However, to understand energy we must understand what scientists mean by "work." It might seem that it is work to try to solve a problem or to stand at attention for 15 minutes. But that is not "work" to a scientist.

In science, work is motion against resistance. Lifting a box against the pull of gravity is work, as is driving a nail into a board against the friction of the wood or winding a clock against the resistance of the spring.

In doing this work (or any other kind), energy is used up. Both work and energy are measured according to the distance an object is moved and the force that must be overcome to keep the object moving. Suppose a pound of iron is lifted 1 foot. Then 1 **foot-pound** of work has been performed and 1 foot-pound of energy has been used up.

Work can be done in various ways. Each way represents a different kind of energy. For instance, you can drive a spike into the ground against the resistance of hard soil by dropping a weight on it. It is the motion of the weight that does the work. (If you placed the weight very gently on the spike, nothing would happen.) The moving weight is said to have **kinetic energy.** ("Kinetic" comes from a Greek word meaning "motion.")

Suppose you hold the weight high above the spike. As soon as you let go, it starts falling and becomes capable of doing work. While you are actually holding it, however, the ability to do work is only potential. That is, the ability can exist in the future but does not in the present. A weight held high in the air possesses **potential energy.**

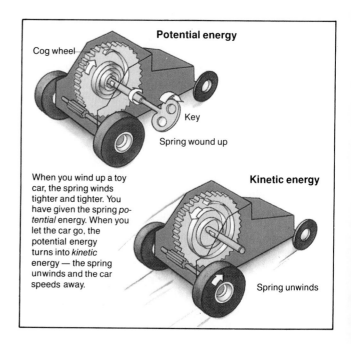

Potential energy

Cog wheel

Key

Spring wound up

When you wind up a toy car, the spring winds tighter and tighter. You have given the spring *potential* energy. When you let the car go, the potential energy turns into *kinetic* energy — the spring unwinds and the car speeds away.

Kinetic energy

Spring unwinds

In the same way, a rubber band that is stretched and held has potential energy. If the hold is released, the rubber band contracts. It possesses kinetic energy while it is contracting. Kinetic energy and potential energy can be lumped together as **mechanical energy.**

Imagine now that you have a corked glass flask with a little water at the bottom. On heating the flask, the water boils and begins to turn into steam. The steam pressure builds up as a kind of potential energy and then turns into kinetic energy when the cork flies out with a loud pop. The cork was moved against the friction of the neck of the flask (which was holding the cork in place). This motion against a force is work. The motion was caused by the heat that formed the steam. This is known as **heat energy.**

A magnet can lift a nail against gravity. Sometimes an electric current is passed through wires wound around an ordinary iron bar. This changes the bar into an electromagnet that will lift a nail against gravity. When electricity and magnetism do work in this way, they are known as **electric energy** and **magnetic energy.**

In any chemical compound there are attractions that hold atoms in place, against their own natural tendency to move about. This is a kind of potential energy, like that of a stretched rubber band. (All kinds of energy can be stored as potential energy.) If anything happens to break the attraction, the result can be an explosion, like that of dynamite. Atomic attractions represent **chemical energy.**

At the center of every atom is a nucleus. The nucleus is made up of smaller bits of matter called subatomic particles. The attractions that hold the subatomic particles together are even stronger than those that hold atoms in place. When these nuclear attractions are released, the result is a far more powerful explosion than that of dynamite. Atomic bombs owe the violence of their explosions to **nuclear energy.** (Sometimes nuclear energy is called **atomic energy** because it is obtained from atoms. But this is not a good choice of words because other forms of energy can also be obtained from atoms. For example, chemical energy also comes from atoms. But it comes from reactions outside an atom's nucleus. "Nuclear energy," therefore, is a more accurate name for the source of the atomic bomb's explosion.)

A fireworks display fills the sky with color, noise, and smoke as chemical energy is changed into light, sound, and heat energy.

Sound and light can be made to do work as **sound energy** and **light energy.** Rays of light, or light waves, are a form of radiation. Radio waves, heat, X rays, radar waves, and ultraviolet rays are other types of radiation. All these radiations, which are transmitted as waves, travel at the speed of light and represent **radiant energy.**

The radiant energy from the sun travels some 93,000,000 miles (150,000,000 kilometers) to the earth. Light from the sun that can be collected and converted into usable energy is called **solar energy.**

▶MEASURING ENERGY

One kind of energy can always be changed into another. Electric energy, for example, is changed into magnetic energy in an electromagnet. On the other hand, magnetic energy is changed into electric energy in a generator.

When wood is burned, the atoms in wood are pulled apart and combined with oxygen in the air. The new combinations contain less chemical energy than the old ones did. The energy left over appears as flame and is felt as heat. In this way chemical energy is turned into heat energy and light energy. Electricity can be changed into heat energy and light energy, as in an electric light. Kinetic energy can turn into heat through friction, as when a fire is started by rubbing one stick against another.

All kinds of energy are very easily changed into heat, which is the simplest and most basic kind of energy. Heat is measured in units called **calories.** A calorie is the amount of heat needed to raise the temperature of 1 gram of water (about $\frac{1}{28}$ ounce) 1 degree Celsius. One thousand calories is a **kilocalorie,** or simply Calorie, with a capital "c."

Because all other forms of energy can be changed to heat, energy is often measured in terms of heat. For example, the chemical energy in food is measured in kilocalories. However, food energy is most often expressed simply as "calories," even though "kilocalories" is meant.

▶ **THE CONSERVATION OF ENERGY**

Sometimes it looks as though energy disappears. If the heat under a kettle of boiling water is turned off, the water will slowly cool down to room temperature. What has become of the heat energy? It has not disappeared—it has just spread out through the air.

A bouncing ball hits the floor and rises again. But each time it falls short of the height it reached the time before. Finally it dribbles along the ground and stops. What has happened to its kinetic energy? It has not disappeared. Some of the kinetic energy was used in pushing the air aside as the ball moved. That part of the energy was turned into heat. The rest of the energy heated up the ball and the ground it struck. Slowly all the kinetic energy turned into heat, and that heat spread outward through the air and ground.

In all such cases, energy never disappears. It changes from one form to another and always ends up as heat. But it never disappears.

Furthermore, energy never appears out of nowhere. A weight at the top of a pile driver has a great deal of potential energy. (A pile driver is a machine that drives piles—long columns used to support buildings or other structures—into the ground.) But before the weight gained that energy, it had to be lifted upward. Energy from an internal-combustion engine did the work required to lift it. The chemical energy of the fuel burned inside the engine was turned into the potential energy of the weight.

Even the sun's radiant energy comes from somewhere. It is produced by combinations and breakups of subatomic particles deep inside the sun. Sunlight is an example of nuclear energy being changed into radiant energy.

In fact, it is a general rule that **energy may be changed from one form to another, but it is never created and never destroyed.** This is called the **law of conservation of energy.** It is also sometimes called the **first law of thermodynamics.** (Thermodynamics is the study of energy in all its forms.)

Still, energy has a tendency to even out. Heat spreads out in all directions, causing hot things to cool down. Whenever energy is changed from one form to another, or whenever energy is turned into work, some energy is changed into heat. The heat spreads out evenly.

When energy is spread out completely evenly, it cannot be turned into work. It is still there; it has not disappeared. But it cannot be used. This spreading out evenly and loss of available energy is called **entropy** by scientists. Every process occurring in the world leads to energy spreading out more and more evenly. Thus the amount of entropy in the universe is always increasing. This basic law of nature is sometimes called the **second law of thermodynamics.**

Fortunately, it will be billions upon billions of years before all the energy in the universe is spread out completely evenly.

▶ **ENERGY AND LIFE**

Living things make use of energy, too. A human being uses up thousands of kilocalories of energy every day. Even if a person just lies quietly in bed, the heart must beat and move the blood. The chest must lift as the person breathes, and so on.

This energy must come from somewhere. The law of conservation of energy is true for living things as well as for nonliving things. Energy cannot be made out of nothing.

Our energy comes from the chemical energy in food. Food contains substances in which many carbon atoms are attached to hydrogen atoms. This carbon-hydrogen attachment contains considerable chemical energy. In the body the carbon-hydrogen attachment is broken and both kinds of atoms are attached to oxygen atoms. (In this way carbon dioxide and water are formed.)

The carbon-oxygen and hydrogen-oxygen attachments contain far less chemical energy

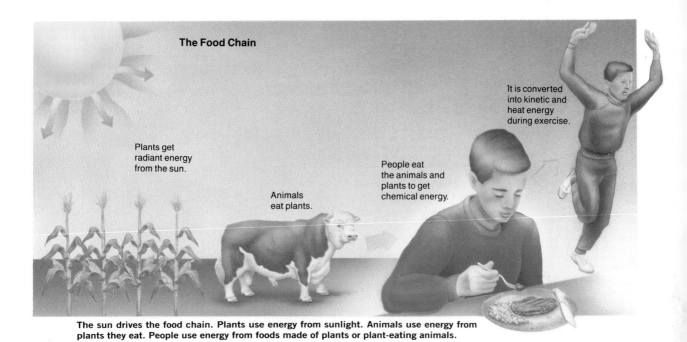

The Food Chain

Plants get radiant energy from the sun.

Animals eat plants.

People eat the animals and plants to get chemical energy.

It is converted into kinetic and heat energy during exercise.

The sun drives the food chain. Plants use energy from sunlight. Animals use energy from plants they eat. People use energy from foods made of plants or plant-eating animals.

than the original carbon-hydrogen did. The chemical energy left over is used to carry out the functions of the body. It is turned into other forms of chemical energy in building up our tissues. It is turned into kinetic energy when we move our muscles. It is turned into electrical energy in our nerves. It is turned into sound energy in our voice box.

In using energy we do not destroy it; we can only change it. We turn it into heat, which can radiate away as the infrared variety of radiant energy. To get rid of the heat even faster, we perspire. The liquid perspiration is turned into vapor by our body heat. In this way heat energy is turned into chemical energy, for water vapor contains more chemical energy than liquid water does. And when the vapor moves away, it carries that energy with it. On hot, muggy days, when the perspiration will not change into vapor, we become very uncomfortable. The reason is that we cannot get rid of the energy after we are through using it.

The Food Chain

All human beings eat food and make use of the chemical energy in it. All other animals do the same. Where does all the chemical energy come from and why doesn't all the food get used up? The answer is that new food is being formed as old food is used up. Green plants form the new food. Animals either eat the

plants or eat other animals that have eaten plants.

Chlorophyll, the green substance in plants, can absorb sunlight. When it does so, it changes the radiant energy of the sun into chemical energy. The chemical energy present in sunlit chlorophyll is used to combine carbon dioxide in the air with water from the soil. Starch and other complicated compounds are formed. These are high in chemical energy obtained from the sunlit chlorophyll. They make up the food on which people and all other animals live. In the process of forming this food, some oxygen atoms are left over. These are given off into the air by plants. The whole process is called **photosynthesis.**

Thus, plants use sunlight to form food and oxygen from carbon dioxide and water. And animals combine food and oxygen to form carbon dioxide and water again. Plants change the radiant energy of the sun into chemical energy, and animals change the chemical energy into kinetic and heat energy.

▶ SOURCES OF ENERGY

In prehistoric times people used only the energy their bodies obtained from food. Then, after they had learned to use fire, they changed the chemical energy of wood into heat and light. This enabled them to see at night, live in cold lands, cook food, and obtain metals

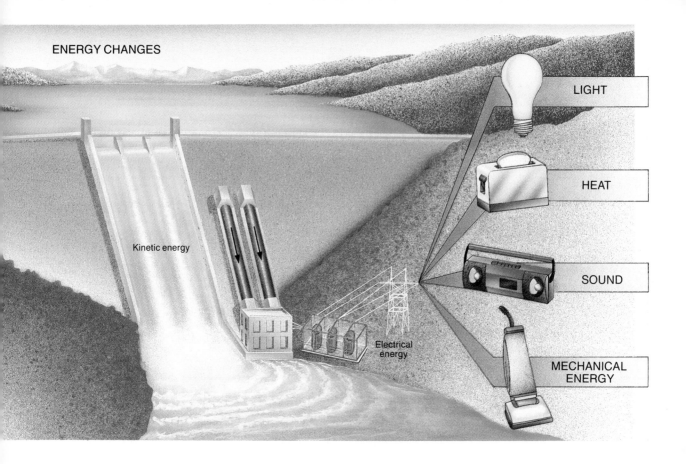

Kinetic energy

Electrical energy

LIGHT

HEAT

SOUND

MECHANICAL ENERGY

from ores. Without fire, there could have been no civilization.

The chemical energy in wood comes from the radiant energy of the sun because wood is formed by plant life as a result of photosynthesis. The energy in coal, oil, and natural gas also comes from the sun. Most scientists believe that these **fossil fuels** were formed from the remains of ancient plants and animals that fed on plants.

Ancient people learned to use the kinetic energy of the winds and flowing waters to drive windmills and waterwheels. Indirectly they were again using the sun's energy. Air rises when it is heated by the sun. As cold air moves in to take its place, we get a wind. The sun also heats ocean water, turning it into vapor, which rises into the atmosphere. The vapor condenses, falls as rain, and runs downhill in streams.

In the 1700's the chemical energy in fuels was put to use in steam engines to drive machines, locomotives, and ships. Steam supplied cheap energy on such a large scale that it began the Industrial Revolution.

Toward the end of the 1800's, internal-combustion engines were built in which liquid fuels such as gasoline were burned. These devices made automobiles and planes practical. In the 1800's, electric generators also were developed. Generators contain coils of wire. When these coils are turned at high speed by waterpower, engines, windmills, or other devices, electricity is produced. Electricity from generators is the world's major energy source.

In the mid-1900's, nuclear energy was produced by the fission (splitting) of atoms. But problems with nuclear energy plants have raised questions about the immediate expansion of fission as an energy source. Research is being done on nuclear energy from the fusion (union) of atomic matter. Because fusion can be fueled by elements found in common seawater, it has the potential of being an almost unlimited source of energy. But because fusion reactions are difficult to control, some scientists think that it will be many years before fusion becomes a useful energy source.

Energy from the sun can be gathered and converted to useful forms of energy. However, it has been difficult to produce such energy in large amounts and at low cost. Flowing or falling water has long been used by people as an energy source. Future use of water power will be limited by the often distant, hard-to-reach locations of large rivers and waterfalls. Wind power is practical only in areas that have strong and steady winds. Energy from the rising and falling tides, the motion of waves, and heat within the earth (geothermal energy) are all being looked at as possible future energy sources. While not an energy source itself, energy conservation is an important way of helping the earth's fossil fuel supply last as long as possible.

ISAAC ASIMOV
Boston University School of Medicine

See also ELECTRICITY; ENERGY SUPPLY; HEAT; LIGHT; NUCLEAR ENERGY; PHOTOSYNTHESIS; SOLAR ENERGY; SOUND AND ULTRASONICS.

ENERGY, UNITED STATES DEPARTMENT OF

The Department of Energy (DOE) is a federal agency that coordinates and carries out energy policies for the United States government. Its primary functions are to conduct research and development of energy-efficient technologies; improve energy production; improve the environment through the cleanup of energy facilities; ensure the safety and reliability of the nation's nuclear weapons stockpile; and to advance the nation in science and technology.

The DOE is one of 15 cabinet-level departments within the executive branch of the government. It is headed by a secretary, who is appointed by the president with the approval of the Senate.

Staff Offices

The secretary of energy is assisted by a deputy secretary, two undersecretaries, six assistant secretaries, and various other directors who administer the activities described below:

The **Office of Policy and International Affairs** develops national and international energy policies and coordinates departmental policy.

The **Office of the Departmental Representative to the Defense Nuclear Facilities Safety Board** oversees the interaction between the department and the Defense Nuclear Facilities Safety Board. It protects the health and safety of employees, the public, and the environment.

The **Office of Hearings and Appeals** reviews and issues the department's judicial orders and hears appeals to those orders.

The **Office of Economic Impact and Diversity** advises how energy policies and regulations affect minorities; oversees programs that assist small or disadvantaged businesses; and enforces department activities regarding equal opportunity and civil rights.

The **Support Office of the Secretary of Energy Advisory Board** advises the secretary on DOE issues and the nation's future needs for energy and security.

The **Office of Intelligence** provides intelligence on foreign nuclear weapons and nuclear materials and on global energy issues.

Energy Programs

The goals of the DOE's energy programs are to find the best ways to conserve and make use of available energy resources.

The **Office of Energy Efficiency and Renewable Energy** is responsible for increasing production and use of renewable energy sources, such as solar energy, alcohol fuels,

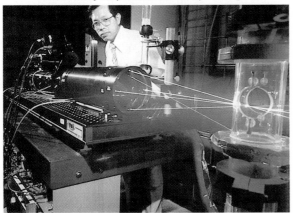

A U.S. Department of Energy scientist uses an argon laser to study air pollution caused by burning coal.

and wind. It also works to improve energy efficiency and conservation.

The **Office of Fossil Energy** conducts research and development with fossil fuels (coal, petroleum, and gas).

The **Energy Information Administration** (EIA) gathers information on worldwide production and use of energy resources.

The **Office of Nuclear Energy, Science, and Technology** manages nuclear energy research and development.

Nuclear Security Programs

The goal of the National Nuclear Security Administration (NNSA) is to strengthen the nation's security through the military application of nuclear energy and by reducing the threat from weapons of mass destruction. There are three offices within the NNSA:

The **Office of Defense Programs** directs the research and development of nuclear weapons and ensures the safety and reliability of the stockpiles. It also manages the wastes generated by that technology.

The **Office for Defense Nuclear Nonproliferation** keeps the DOE secretary informed on national security issues and directs the department's arms-control, nonproliferation, and nuclear-safeguard activities.

The **Office of Naval Reactors** directs the development and use of naval nuclear propulsion plants.

Environmental Quality Programs

These programs manage the handling and disposal of energy waste products to maintain a safe and healthy environment.

The **Office of Environmental Management** manages the risks associated with nuclear weapons. It directs waste management operations and environmental cleanup and restoration of department sites.

The **Office of Civilian Radioactive Waste Management** manages the federal program for the safe disposal of high-level radioactive waste and used-up nuclear fuel.

The **Office of Environment, Safety, and Health** is responsible for the safety and health of DOE workers and people living near DOE facilities.

The Office of Science

The Office of Science supports basic research in energy and in the biological, physi-

cal, environmental, and computational sciences. It operates many scientific facilities and supports ten national laboratories.

The Federal Energy Regulatory Commission

The Federal Energy Regulatory Commission (FERC) is an independent organization within the Department of Energy. The FERC regulates interstate sales of electricity and natural gas and sets natural gas prices and wholesale electric rates. It also regulates the interstate transmission of oil by pipeline.

The Power Marketing Administrations

Four administrations market and transmit federal hydroelectric power, each for a particular region. The **Bonneville Power Administration** covers the Federal Columbia River Power System along Oregon's northern border; the **Southeastern Power Administration** covers the southeastern states; the **Southwestern Power Administration** covers the southwestern states; and the **Western Area Power Administration** covers the central and western states.

History

The Arab embargo of oil shipments to the United States from 1973 to 1974 led to the establishment of the Energy Research and Development Administration and the Federal Energy Administration. In October 1977, Congress brought these administrations—along with such other agencies as the Atomic Energy Commission and the Federal Power Commission—under the administration of the U.S. Department of Energy.

DOE headquarters are located at 1000 Independence Avenue, S.W., Washington, D.C. 20585.

Reviewed by Office of Public Affairs
United States Department of Energy

Secretaries of Energy		
Name	Took Office	Under President
James R. Schlesinger	1977	Carter
Charles W. Duncan, Jr.	1979	Carter
James B. Edwards	1981	Reagan
Donald P. Hodel	1982	Reagan
John S. Herrington	1985	Reagan
James D. Watkins	1989	G. Bush
Hazel R. O'Leary	1993	Clinton
Federico F. Peña	1997	Clinton
Bill Richardson	1998	Clinton
Spencer Abraham	2001	G. W. Bush
Samuel Bodman	2005	G. W. Bush

ENERGY SUPPLY

Only 200 years ago, people's energy supply was made up almost entirely of wood and water. Wood was burned to heat homes and to cook food. Water was used to turn grinding stones. People had not yet discovered electricity or vast underground reserves of petroleum. There were no air conditioners or refrigerators, no automobiles or airplanes.

Today our energy supply consists mostly of fossil fuels (coal, petroleum, and natural gas) and nuclear fission. These in turn produce electricity for running machines, heating and cooling buildings, and many other jobs.

But these fossil fuels will not last forever. In the United States the inexpensive, easy-to-find petroleum is already almost gone. Any new large supplies will have to come from under the oceans or from the northern part of Alaska. A great deal of petroleum is known to remain in the countries bordering the Persian Gulf, but political differences between those countries and the United States can sometimes make this oil unavailable or very expensive for consumers in the United States. When the fossil fuels do run out, or become too expensive, what will take their place? What will produce the energy needed in tomorrow's world?

▶ WHAT DETERMINES ENERGY SUPPLY?

Several factors are important in determining energy supply. These factors also influence how much energy people use. Often one factor influences another.

Availability. People tend to use the sources of energy that are most plentiful and easiest to obtain. Coal and petroleum became important sources of energy because people found huge deposits of these substances that were easy to remove, or recover, from the ground. In contrast, the nuclear energy stored in hydrogen is not used because it is not available. Scientists have not yet been able to control the release of this energy.

Economics. When there is a large supply of something people need and it is easy to obtain, it is cheap. For example, until the early 1970's the United States had a great deal of easy-to-recover petroleum. It was sold for low prices, and people used it without thinking of cost. As the costs of a resource such as petroleum increase, people must study, develop, and use other resources.

Environmental Issues. The energy sources most used today have a variety of bad effects on our environment. The mining of coal can destroy land. Transporting oil across oceans has resulted in oil spills that kill ocean life. The burning of coal and petroleum produces air pollution. It may also contribute to acid rain, precipitation that contains chemical pollutants, and an increase in global temperature due to the "greenhouse effect." (The burning of coal and oil in homes and factories produces carbon dioxide, water vapor, and smoke. Carbon dioxide traps part of the earth's heat that would otherwise be radiated beyond the atmosphere. This is known as the greenhouse effect because the carbon dioxide

The Trans-Alaska Pipeline can carry up to 2 million barrels of oil per day. The pipeline runs almost 800 miles (1,300 kilometers) from oil fields near Prudhoe Bay on the Arctic Ocean to the ice-free port of Valdez on the Gulf of Alaska.

A huge bucketwheel excavator scoops tar sand from the Athabasca Tar Sands deposit in Alberta, Canada. Tar sand is a sandstonelike material rich in petroleum. The petroleum is separated from the tar sand and processed for use.

in the atmosphere acts somewhat like a very large glass greenhouse.) Nuclear fission creates dangerous radioactive wastes.

Laws have been passed to limit the bad effects. Coal mine operators, for example, must replace strip-mined soil. But restoring the land costs money. The cost is added to the price that people pay for coal. If the cost rises enough, another source of energy may become more economical.

Politics. Much of the money used to study energy sources comes from the government. If the government puts money into one area—nuclear energy, for instance—more research and development will be done there than in other areas.

Government laws and regulations also influence how we use energy. For example, cars and trucks use much more fuel to carry people and goods from one place to another than do railroads. But laws and government practices sometimes have encouraged the building and use of roads while doing little to encourage the building and upkeep of railbeds.

Local groups exert political pressure, too. People may protest the building of a power plant in their community or the drilling of an oil well in their offshore waters. A city may want to burn its garbage to produce electricity. The technology would actually save money and cause little pollution. But people who live where the plant could be built may fight its construction. They want and need energy, but they do not want a big plant and lots of garbage trucks in their neighborhood.

▶ **MAJOR ENERGY SOURCES**

Today, almost 90 percent of the world's energy supply comes from the burning of fossil fuels—coal, petroleum, and natural gas. A small amount comes from nuclear fission and water power.

Coal. Coal supplies about 28 percent of the world's energy and almost 23 percent of the energy used in the United States. More than half the electricity generated in the United States comes from burning coal, and the United States has larger known coal reserves than any other country. In spite of pollution problems, coal will continue to be an important fuel resource in the years to come.

Coal is obtained from either underground or surface mines, depending on the depth of the coal. Burning coal creates serious air pollution. In places where great amounts of coal are burned, as in power plants, antipollution devices can be used. These are expensive, however, and not completely effective. Some of these devices are known as ''scrubbers,'' because they help clean the smoke and exhaust gases coming from burning coal.

It may be cleaner to use coal by converting it first to a liquid or a gas, both of which can then be burned without expensive antipollution devices. They can also be used in fuel cells, which change the chemical energy of a fuel directly into electrical energy. At present, the making of liquid and gas fuels from coal is very expensive. Some processes for making gas from coal also require great amounts of water, which is not always available near coalfields.

Petroleum. The most widely used source of energy is petroleum. It supplies about 39 percent of the world's requirements and 43 percent of the United States' requirements. Much petroleum is also used for the chemicals it contains. These chemicals are used to make fertilizers, drugs, synthetic fibers, plastics, and many other products.

Like coal, petroleum creates environmental problems. Removing large quantities of petroleum from under the ground may cause the land to sink. Transporting petroleum may result in oil spills. Burning petroleum as gasoline or diesel fuel in cars and trucks causes smog and other kinds of air pollution.

Even in the United States there is a great deal of oil left in the ground. But much of it is difficult or impossible to remove with present technology or at a price people are willing to pay. Known reserves of petroleum that can be recovered are being used up rapidly. Oil companies are continually searching for new reserves and testing ways to remove hard-to-recover resources.

In the western United States—especially in Colorado, Utah, and Wyoming—there are immense deposits of rock called oil shale, from which oil can be extracted. The process requires huge amounts of water and may produce great mountains of waste rock. The world's largest deposits of tar sands, resembling sandstone, are found in Alberta, Canada. Oil has been successfully produced from these deposits on a large-scale, commercial basis. At present, however, the processes used to obtain oil from oil shale and tar sands are very expensive.

Natural Gas. Natural gas supplies more than 20 percent of the energy used by the world and more than 23 percent of the United States' energy. Deposits are usually found in the same areas as petroleum deposits. Many of the natural gas deposits in the world cannot be used at present because they are too far from consumers. In the future it may become necessary or economical to turn the gas into a liquid and ship it across the ocean in special refrigerated tankers.

Nuclear Fission. The breakdown, or fission, of uranium atoms supplies about 5 percent of the world's and 6 percent of the United States' energy requirements. The tremendous heat released by fission can be used to make steam to drive electric generators.

Early supporters of nuclear power believed that it would provide plenty of energy at low cost. But many problems have developed. The cost of building nuclear power plants has soared. There is great public concern about the possibility of a spread of radiation following an accident in a nuclear plant. As yet there is also no sure, safe way to dispose of the burned-out fuel, which is radioactive. And the supply of uranium on the earth, like the supply of fossil fuels, is limited.

Waterpower. About 7 percent of the world's and 4 percent of the United States' energy requirements are met by falling water that is used to generate electricity. There is no pollution, and the resource—water—is not used up. But there are not many places left where suitable dams can be built. For this reason we cannot expect waterpower to meet a large portion of our energy requirements.

▶ **ALTERNATE ENERGY SOURCES**

Some sources of energy either are not being used at present or are used only in a limited way. How useful they might be in the future is still not known. The following are brief descriptions of some promising sources:

Geothermal Energy. The interior of the earth is hot. Water seeping down deep into the earth is turned into steam. The steam can be piped

A vast supply of petroleum lies beneath the world's oceans. Wells bored by offshore drilling rigs provide new supplies of oil and natural gas. Setting up an offshore well is dangerous and expensive. But as inland reserves are used up, offshore resources become more important.

A solar furnace in the Pyrenees Mountains of France uses a curved wall of mirrors to focus the sun's rays toward a central receiving tower. The tower converts the heat from the sun's rays into electricity.

to homes for heating or to generating plants. Electricity produced in this way costs less than electricity from other sources. Little air or water pollution results.

Geothermal heat is now used in Iceland, Italy, New Zealand, and northern California, where natural reservoirs of hot water and steam are located. Efforts to drill deep holes and pump water down into the earth are being made in several places. At a place called The Geysers in northern California, geothermal steam is used to generate almost as much electricity as is used in the entire state of Maine.

Solar Energy. Energy radiated by the sun is free, nonpolluting, and limitless. The problem is to collect, use, and store this energy efficiently and economically.

Solar energy shows growing promise as a major source of energy for the future. Already, some 2 million Japanese buildings and thousands of buildings in the United States are using solar technology to heat rooms and water supplies. The concentrated energy from some large-scale systems is used to make steam to drive electric generators. Solar cells made of silicon and similar materials can be used to convert sunlight directly into electricity without having to use generators. These solar cells are now widely used for small applications such as calculators and watches. Research is aimed at making the cells cheaper and more efficient so that they can be used for large-scale electricity production.

Nuclear Fusion. Once scientists solve the problems with nuclear fusion, this may be a source of energy for thousands of years. Fusion is the union of hydrogen atoms to produce helium atoms. In the process, enormous

amounts of energy are released. Fusion produces little radioactive waste, and the oceans are an almost endless source of hydrogen atoms. But scientists have not been able to build a system that can contain and control the fusion process. Even optimists do not expect fusion to be available for energy needs for many years to come.

Wind Energy. Windmills have been used for hundreds of years to grind grain and pump water. More recently, they have powered small electric generators. Researchers are developing and testing large windmills—called wind generators—that could produce electric power on a large scale. Wind generators could be used in places that have fairly strong and fairly constant winds. At present, costs are high and the equipment needs to be improved.

Garbage Power. Trash and garbage can be processed to make gas and oil. They can also be burned to heat buildings or to make steam for generating electricity. European cities have been turning wastes into electricity for many years. This technology has particular appeal for big cities that produce large amounts of wastes. Such cities are running out of places to put all their garbage. Several cities in the United States are now burning their trash to make steam that is then used to generate electricity. The amount of electricity produced is small but important.

Tidal Energy. The daily rise and fall of the tides can be used to drive turbines for generating electricity. Tidal plants are hard to build because they must be in deep water. They also must be strong enough to withstand the pressure of enormous amounts of rushing water. These dams are very costly.

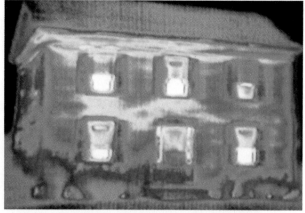

Just as a photograph (*left*) records light, a thermogram (*right*) records heat. The bright spots in this thermogram show areas where too much heat is leaking out of the house. Better wall and window insulation could keep more heat in and make the house less expensive to heat.

Ocean Thermal Energy Conversion (OTEC). OTEC is a process for converting the solar energy absorbed by tropical oceans into electricity. The electricity can be sent to shore by cable or used to do work on board a floating platform. If experimental programs are successful, OTEC may be commercially available in the near future.

▶WHICH WILL WE USE?

The field of energy supply is one of rapid change. New predictions of available supplies and of probable demands are continually being made. New ideas for developing alternate sources are continually being proposed. As these are tested, some prove to be unusable. Others need changes. Others may work—if the economics, politics, and environmental aspects are acceptable.

Probably we will depend on a variety of energy sources in the future. People in some places may use the wind as their primary energy source. In some coastal areas, tidal power may dominate. In other places, coal or petroleum will be used, and so on. Until then it is important that we conserve the supplies we have—to make them last as long as possible.

▶CONSERVING ENERGY

Everyone can help conserve energy. Energy conservation requires the actions of government, industry, and every individual.

One way to conserve energy is to use it more efficiently. For example, today's new cars travel nearly twice as far on a gallon of gasoline as those produced in the early 1970's. Heating and air conditioning systems, appliances, and other items can be designed to operate on less energy.

The people of the United States use more energy than any other people on earth. Some conservationists believe that they could cut personal (including home) energy use by one third without serious inconvenience. The following are some suggestions they offer for saving energy (and money as well):

Heating. Set home thermostats to 67°F (19°C) for heating and to 77°F (25°C) for cooling. Be sure all windows and doors are closed when heating or cooling a room or a house. In regions where winter temperatures are low, install storm doors and windows, as well as attic and wall insulation.

Appliances. Use washing machines, clothes dryers, and dishwashers only with full loads. An empty machine uses nearly as much energy as a full one. Turn off lights and appliances in empty rooms or when they are not needed. Install fluorescent lights. A 50-watt fluorescent light gives three times as much light as a standard 50-watt incandescent bulb.

Transportation. Keep in mind that a bus or train uses less energy per person than does a car. A car pool is a more efficient use of energy than is driving alone. Small cars are better energy savers than large ones. Bicycles are better than cars.

Everyone needs to ask: What am I doing to conserve energy? What more can I do—starting today?

MORRIS K. UDALL
Chairman, Committee on Interior
and Insular Affairs
U.S. House of Representatives
Reviewed by the U.S. DEPARTMENT OF ENERGY

See also COAL AND COAL MINING; CONSERVATION; ENERGY; ENVIRONMENT; NATURAL GAS; NUCLEAR ENERGY; PETROLEUM AND PETROLEUM REFINING; SOLAR ENERGY.

An electronics engineer assembles equipment for testing electronic components. Engineers help design and build many things, from tiny computer parts to huge buildings and bridges. Most engineers specialize in a particular branch of engineering.

ENGINEERING

Engineers invent, design, build, and produce most of the things that make up our modern civilization. Roads, bridges, dams, computers, automobiles, airplanes, telephones, and thousands of other items are the results of engineering.

Engineers design and run the factories that turn iron, coal, and other raw materials into useful things like automobile engines and plastics. They also plan ways to tame the forces of nature and put them to work for us.

Engineers have been important to every civilization, ancient and modern. Today they are more important than ever. Our society depends on science and technology to keep it running. There is so much work to be done by engineers that many of them are needed.

▶CONCERNS OF ENGINEERING

Engineers are involved in at least four major areas of concern—construction, materials, processes, and machines.

Construction. The earliest people who might be called engineers were those who learned how buildings, roads, and other large constructions could be built safely and efficiently. Ancient temples, Roman highways, and the cathedrals of the Middle Ages are a few of the works of these early engineers.

Today engineers help plan and build huge skyscrapers, dams, tunnels through mountains or under rivers, and majestic bridges. One of the largest engineering projects in history is the U.S. interstate highway system. It contains more than 42,000 miles (68,000 kilometers) of multilane highways and thousands of overpasses, bridges, and cloverleafs.

Materials. Early engineers were concerned with finding better building materials and improving the materials they had. Engineers today share these concerns. In recent years, they have developed new materials for building, for machines, and for many other uses. These include plastics, strong metal alloys, semiconductors, and special fuels for cars, planes, and rockets.

Processes. Engineers are also concerned with developing methods and systems to produce many kinds of goods. People have always looked for more efficient ways to produce the things they need. Engineers help develop new ways to manufacture goods. They design factories that make everything from automobiles and airplanes to such everyday items as canned goods and light bulbs.

Machines. Engineers design machines of many types. They also create mechanical systems such as those needed to generate, distribute, and use electricity. And they have designed thousands of new electronic devices, such as satellite relays for television and telephone transmission, photocopying machines, and a wide range of computers that help people store, interpret, and use information.

Because engineers work on such a wide variety of projects, various branches of engineering have emerged. In many of these special fields, the engineer may become involved in several areas of concern. To build a dam to produce hydroelectric power, for example, an engineer must know about materials, construction methods, the generation of electrical power, and the machines needed to accomplish the work.

▶ MAJOR BRANCHES OF ENGINEERING

In the past there were only two main branches of engineering—civil and military engineering. Civil engineers handled all the building projects for civilian use. These included roads, bridges, public buildings, canals, and aqueducts. Military engineers built fortifications for use during wartime.

New branches of engineering have been created as a result of the growth of scientific knowledge and the demands of an increasingly complex and industrialized society. Today the many branches of engineering are concerned with particular needs of industry and society. Below is an alphabetical list of modern engineering specialties.

Aerospace and Astronautical Engineers. Aerospace and astronautical engineers design and build aircraft and space vehicles. They may also work on the development of special vehicles, such as hydrofoil ships and deep-diving vessels for ocean research, that make use of some of the basic principles of aircraft design.

Agricultural Engineers. Agricultural engineers develop ways to increase farm production. They plan more effective ways of using soil and water and of processing and handling food. They also design farm machinery and equipment.

Architectural Engineers. Architectural engineers work closely with architects and other specialists in building construction. They help select building materials and design and assemble structures that are safe, efficient, economical, and attractive.

Biomedical Engineers. This specialty uses engineering methods to help solve medical and health-related problems. Biomedical engineers help develop tools and techniques used by doctors and hospitals. They must have knowledge of life sciences such as biology as well as of engineering.

Chemical Engineers. Chemical engineers are responsible for the processes and factories that produce plastics, synthetic fabrics, industrial chemicals, medicines, and many other materials that undergo chemical changes during their processing. They must be able to apply the principles of chemistry, physics, and engineering to their work.

Civil and Construction Engineers. Engineers in these specialties design and supervise the construction of a wide range of facilities—bridges, buildings, tunnels, highways, transit systems, dams, airports, water and waste treatment facilities, and more. Often an engineer will specialize in one or another of these areas. (A civil engineer is concerned mainly with public works, such as highway systems.)

Computer Engineers. These specialists design computers and computer systems. New designs are constantly being developed as computers become more powerful and affect more aspects of modern life.

Electrical Engineers. Electrical engineering is the largest of the engineering fields.

Two computer engineers work on a design for a computer printer. Computer engineering is growing in importance as computers affect more aspects of life.

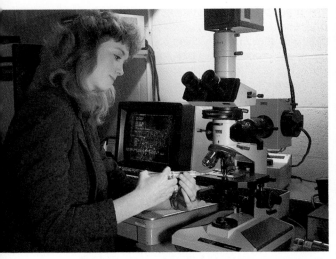

Engineers use sophisticated equipment in their work. *Above:* A chemical engineer uses a microscope to help analyze a sample of material. *Right:* With the help of a portable computer, these engineers carry on their work outdoors at a chemical plant.

Broadly, it is concerned with the use of electrical energy; but it is divided into many fields. These include solid-state electronics, information systems, automation, and electric power generation and distribution.

Industrial Engineers. Industrial engineers design, improve, and install systems used in manufacturing. To do this, they must bring together knowledge from many different fields —materials, machines and equipment, computers, energy use. They must also understand people, because people are an important part of any such system.

Marine Engineers. Along with naval architects and ocean engineers, marine engineers are concerned with the design of ships and other ocean vessels. They also design offshore structures and systems, which include oil platforms, artificial islands, and offshore harbor facilities.

Mechanical Engineers. Mechanical engineers design the engines and machines that provide power for manufacturing, transportation, and many other uses. These designs range from gasoline engines to rockets to kitchen food mixers. Mechanical engineers are also involved in the design of systems that use energy, such as air-conditioning systems.

Metallurgical Engineers, Mining Engineers, and Geological Engineers. These specialists are concerned in various ways with minerals and their use. Mining and geological engineers help find, extract, and process mineral ores. They may design mines, supervise the construction of mine shafts and tunnels, and devise ways of transporting the minerals. Metallurgical engineers find ways to extract and process various ores. In addition, they devise processes to refine metals and produce metal alloys.

Nuclear Engineers. Nuclear engineers help design and build power plants that use heat from nuclear fission to produce electricity. These specialists also work with companies that use radioactive materials in research or processing.

Petroleum Engineers. Petroleum engineers are involved worldwide in all aspects of the petroleum industry, from the location of petroleum in the ground through the refining process to the final delivery of petroleum products to their users. The importance of petroleum has made this a growing field in engineering.

▶THE TECHNICAL TEAM

Today many engineers work as part of a technical team. The team includes specialists from five occupational groups: scientists, engineers, technologists, technicians, and craftsmen and craftswomen. The work of the team is highly coordinated, and each member plays a special role.

The scientist is the team member most concerned with theory. Through observation and experimentation, scientists seek to understand why things happen. But many scientists also work to find specific uses for the knowledge developed through research.

Engineers bring extensive knowledge of science and mathematics to their work. But unlike scientists, they are always seeking practical solutions to specific problems. Engineers must be able to recognize conditions that need improvement and then use their knowledge and skills to find creative solutions.

Like engineers, technologists combine technical skills with scientific knowledge. But they are more likely to work on problems in organization and production than to develop entirely new designs. Engineering technicians work directly with equipment—assembling the parts of systems and testing the equipment, for example. Craftsmen and craftswomen are skilled specialists. They include such workers as electricians, welders, pattern makers, and precision machinists.

Each of these occupational groups requires certain training. Craftsmen and craftswomen, for example, generally learn their skills through intensive training programs and years of practice. A scientist generally earns a doctorate in some area of science, such as chemistry, physics, or one of the natural sciences. Engineers, technologists, and technicians acquire the knowledge and skills they need in various college programs.

▶TRAINING TO BE AN ENGINEER

No matter what their special field of work, all engineers need a knowledge of mathematics and physics. Most young people who are interested in becoming engineers begin studying these subjects early in high school. An interest in mathematics and physics is essential because every engineer must work with these sciences. Students preparing for engineering college should also study computer programming, chemistry, and other science subjects that are offered. A good command of language is important because engineers must be able to talk and write clearly.

An engineering degree usually takes four years to complete. With the rapid growth of technical knowledge, an increasing number of students continue to study for advanced degrees before going to work.

After finishing a year or two of college, an engineering student begins to concentrate in a special field. For instance, if the student wants to be an electrical engineer, many courses dealing with electronics, electrical machinery, and related subjects must be taken. If the future engineer wants to specialize in chemical engineering, more courses in chemistry will be essential.

Part of the student's time is spent in the classroom, and part is spent in the laboratory doing experiments. In some schools, students spend part of the year studying and part of the year working in their chosen field. This gives them the opportunity to apply their knowledge in practical situations.

Engineering technicians generally complete two years of college-level study. The courses are usually taken at a community college or a technical institute and lead to an associate's degree in technology. Engineering technologists are usually graduates of four-year college programs and earn a bachelor's degree in engineering technology.

▶HISTORY OF ENGINEERING

One of the oldest engineering projects in the world can still be seen in Egypt—the pyramids. The Great Pyramid—which was about 480 feet (145 meters) high, with a square base 755 feet (230 meters) on each side—was built about 2600 B.C. (It is smaller now because its outside covering of polished stone was removed for other uses.) The remarkable thing about the pyramids is that the Egyptians built them long before construction machinery was invented. All the cutting, hauling, and moving of the heavy stone blocks had to be done by human power. All historians who have studied the pyramids agree that the Egyptian engineers who planned and supervised the work did a remarkable job.

The Romans were the best engineers of the ancient world. They built some of the most durable roads ever made. A network of roads kept the capital in touch with outlying parts of the empire. The most famous Roman road is probably the Appian Way (Via Appia), which ran from Rome to the southeastern coast of Italy. This road, 350 miles (565 kilometers) long, was begun and partly completed about 310 B.C. by Appius Claudius Caecus, a Roman public official. Somewhat later, Gaius Flaminius, a Roman soldier and political

The Pont du Gard, near Nîmes, France, was built by the Romans in 19 B.C. to bring water to a Roman settlement. More than twenty centuries later, it still stands.

leader, built the Flaminian Way (Via Flaminia). It stretched from Rome northward to Rimini. The Romans also built large aqueducts to supply their cities with water. And Rome was full of magnificent public buildings, theaters, public baths, and arenas. The ruins of some of these structures can still be seen.

Information about the water supply of ancient Rome has come to us through the writings of Sextus Julius Frontinus, who had charge of the city's aqueducts. Vitruvius Pollio wrote a book on architecture that gives us most of our knowledge of Roman engineering. Apollodor of Damascus, a Greek engineer, built the bridge across the Danube that is pictured on Emperor Trajan's triumphal column in Rome.

After the Roman Empire fell, engineering suffered a decline. There were few highways, harbors, and aqueducts to compare with those of the Romans.

However, the cathedrals built in the Middle Ages stand as monuments to engineering skill. And medieval engineering is important because for the first time power was produced without human labor. Waterwheels, windmills, and animals (especially horses) provided the power to pump water, grind flour, and raise heavy loads.

During the 1600's and 1700's, engineering was reborn. Trade was increasing between towns and between different countries. Engineering projects were started to provide better transportation. France led the way in this work. The Languedoc Canal in southwestern France, which links the Atlantic Ocean to the Mediterranean Sea, was completed in the late 1600's. Its system of locks, tunnels, and aqueducts was the engineering marvel of the time. The canal, now called the Canal du Midi, is still in use.

The Industrial Revolution of the 1700's caused great changes in engineering. Until that time, engineers were mainly builders of military fortifications, roads, canals, buildings, or dams. The invention of the steam engine, which started the Industrial Revolution, gave engineers new tasks. From then on, engineers became scientific planners as well as builders. They developed better machinery to run textile mills, iron and steel plants, and other factories. Machinery was installed wherever it could be used to ease labor or to do new jobs. Engineers designed the machines and figured out ways to use them best.

New inventions added to the duties of engineers and created new kinds of engineering. Toward the end of the 1800's, inventors were hard at work. In a period of only 27 years, between 1876 and 1903, these important items were invented—the telephone, the phonograph, electric light, the gasoline automobile, the trolley car, photographic film, the motion picture projector, the wireless radio, and the airplane.

The explosion of knowledge in science and engineering continued into the 1900's. Invention and discovery became the result of teamwork, rather than of individual inventors, as in the past. Inventions such as the transistor, radar, jet engines, stainless steel, nylon, and microprocessors led to revolutionary changes in our society. The symbol of modern engineering achievement was the launching of astronauts to the moon.

Environmental preservation and the conservation of natural resources offer new challenges to engineers in the 21st century. The need for engineers continues to grow, as we try to solve many new technological problems and try to improve standards of living for everyone.

GEORGE S. ANSELL
Rensselaer Polytechnic Institute

Reviewed by GEORGE C. BEAKLEY
Arizona State University

See also TECHNOLOGY.

ENGINEERING DRAWING. See MECHANICAL DRAWING.

ENGINES

Engines are machines that convert some form of energy to mechanical energy. Mechanical energy is then used to do work. Engines are defined by the energy they convert. Windmills and waterwheels were some of the earliest engines, converting the energy of moving wind and water into mechanical energy. These types of engines are still being used to pump water and generate electricity.

Most other engines are heat engines—they convert heat energy to mechanical energy. Heat engines almost always burn a chemical fuel, such as wood, coal, oil, or gasoline, to produce the heat. There are many types of heat engines, including steam, gasoline, diesel, jet, and rocket engines.

▶ STEAM ENGINES

The first true engines were steam engines. All steam engines work for the same reason: Steam occupies more than 1,700 times as much space as the water from which it comes. When water turns into steam in an enclosed space, it exerts a force that is used to move parts of the steam engine.

Fuel to heat the water is burned outside the engine. (For this reason steam engines are called **external-combustion engines**—external means "outside," and combustion means "burning.") The water to make steam is heated in a boiler. Pipes direct the steam to the engine itself.

Early Steam Engines. Nearly 2,000 years ago, the Greek scientist Hero of Alexandria described an early steam engine called an aeolipile. It consisted of a hollow ball that spun around as steam escaped through two bent pipes attached to opposite sides of the ball. Why Hero's engine worked was not understood until Isaac Newton presented his laws of motion in 1687. Newton's third law states that **for every action there is an equal and opposite reaction**. Steam escaping from the pipes (action) pushed back on the pipes (reaction), causing the ball to spin. Engines that operate according to this principle are called **reaction engines**.

In 1629, Giovanni Branca, an Italian architect, developed a different type of steam engine. With this engine, a jet of steam struck paddles mounted on the rim of a wheel, causing the wheel to turn. An engine driven by the direct force of water, steam, or a gas is called an **impulse engine**.

In 1712, an English blacksmith named Thomas Newcomen built the first commercially successful piston-operated steam engine. (A piston is like a movable stopper that slides back and forth inside a cylinder, or chamber closed at one end.) It was designed to pump water out of flooded coal mines. During the mid-1700's, James Watt, a Scottish engineer, experimented with ways to improve the Newcomen engine. These improvements led to the invention of the **reciprocating steam engine**, in which steam was used to push a piston up and down (reciprocate). It was a relatively efficient engine that could be put to work for many different tasks. (For more information, see the article STEAM ENGINES in Volume S.)

Modern Steam Turbines. A turbine is simply a set of blades through which fluids or gases pass at high speeds. An impulse turbine works on much the same principle as a pinwheel, which spins rapidly when you blow on its blades. Branca's engine was an early example of a steam turbine.

A steam turbine changes the heat energy of steam into mechanical energy. High-pressure steam travels the length of a turbine engine and strikes a series of movable blades. These blades are mounted on and turn a central shaft. The spinning shaft provides the power to do work. Electric generators and most of the world's largest ships are powered by steam turbines. (For more information, see the article TURBINES in Volume T.)

Stirling Engine

The Stirling engine, invented in 1816 by the Scottish clergyman Robert Stirling, is also an external-combustion engine. However, it is not a steam engine. A Stirling engine has pistons that move up and down in cylinders containing hydrogen or helium gas. The gas constantly flows back and forth between a hot space at the top of the cylinder (created by an outside heater) and a cold space at the bottom of the cylinder. The gas expands in the hot part of the cylinder and contracts in the cold part. This cycle of gas expansion and contraction causes the pistons to move up and down. The Stirling engine can burn many types of fuels and produces almost no odor or smog-forming pollutants.

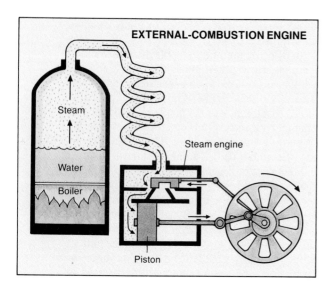

EXTERNAL-COMBUSTION ENGINE

Steam

Steam engine

Water

Boiler

Piston

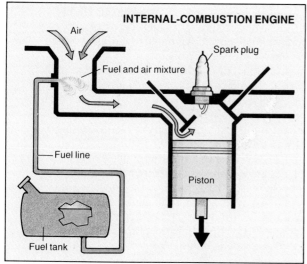

INTERNAL-COMBUSTION ENGINE

Air

Spark plug

Fuel and air mixture

Fuel line

Piston

Fuel tank

▶ **INTERNAL-COMBUSTION ENGINES**

An internal-combustion engine is a heat engine that burns fuel and air inside the engine itself. The fuel is broken up into tiny drops and mixed with air. When the mixture is ignited, the fuel and air burn to form violently expanding hot gases. The force of the expanding gases causes the working parts of the engine to move.

The principal types of internal-combustion engines are gasoline and diesel engines, which have pistons that reciprocate; the Wankel engine, in which gases turn a triangular rotor; and gas-turbine engines, in which gases drive a turbine rotor.

The **gasoline engine**, or spark-ignition engine, consists of one or more cylinders that contain pistons. A spark-producing device, called a **spark plug**, is placed in the wall of each cylinder. A mixture of gasoline and air is directed into the cylinder and is ignited by a spark. The resulting explosion gives the piston a very powerful push. The gasoline engine is the best known of all engines because it powers millions of automobiles, motorboats, lawn mowers, and other machinery.

The **diesel engine**, or compression-ignition engine, works like the gasoline engine. However, the diesel engine has no spark plugs. The fuel is ignited by being sprayed into very hot air. Diesel engines power most heavy trucks, buses, and locomotives. These engines are heavier, but more efficient, than gasoline engines. (For more information, see the article DIESEL ENGINES in Volume D.)

A very different internal-combustion engine, the **Wankel** engine, was invented in 1956 by German engineer Felix Wankel. It has a curved, triangular rotor that turns inside an oval combustion chamber. Each rotor face acts in the same way as a piston in a reciprocating engine. The engine is light and runs smoothly, but it is used in few cars. It requires complex engineering, and it burns as much fuel and emits as much pollution as many conventional engines. (For more information, see the article INTERNAL-COMBUSTION ENGINES in Volume I.)

As fuel prices rise, demand for more efficient car engines is growing. Alternatives include advanced diesel engines and **hybrids**. The new diesels are most efficient during highway driving. The hybrids, which combine an internal combustion engine with an electric motor, are most efficient in stop-and-go traffic. Both gas-electric and diesel-electric hybrids are being developed. These hybrids include electrical components that may prove useful in **fuel cell** vehicles. A fuel cell is a type of battery that may be used in a car instead of an engine. (For more information, see the article BATTERIES in Volume B.)

A **gas turbine** differs from a steam turbine in two ways. One is that a hot gas other than steam turns the turbine blades. The second is that the fuel is burned in a combustion chamber within the engine. The operation of the turbine depends on a compressor, which consists of rapidly spinning wheels with metal blades set in them. Great quantities of air are pulled in through the front of the engine. Then the air is compressed and forced into the combustion chamber. Fuel is sprayed into the compressed air and is ignited. The hot, expanding gases push against the turbine blades, causing them to spin rapidly. The turbine's spinning shaft can turn propellers or wheels, or run a generator.

Jet Engines

Jet engines develop power by forcing air through what appears to be a long cylinder. Hot gases rushing out the rear of the engine push the engine—and the aircraft—in the opposite direction. Thus jet engines are reaction engines.

A **turbojet engine** has four basic parts: a compressor, a burner, a turbine, and an exhaust nozzle. Air entering the front of the engine is compressed before reaching the burner, where it is mixed with fuel and ignited. As burning gases rush toward the rear of the engine, they push against and turn the turbine blades. The turbine in this case is used only to turn the compressor, which is mounted on the same shaft. Hot gases rush out the exhaust nozzle at the rear of the engine and the reaction force pushes the engine forward.

Turbojet engines power some of the fastest high-altitude aircraft, such as supersonic military planes. One drawback of the turbojet engine is that it has an enormous appetite for fuel at low altitudes and low speeds.

The **turboprop** engine was developed to solve the turbojet's shortcomings. It is similar to a turbojet, but the turbine also turns a shaft that drives a propeller. The turboprop combines the advantages of a propeller-driven aircraft (at low speeds and low altitudes) with the advantages of the turbojet.

A **turbofan** engine is a turbojet engine with a large, broad-blade fan located in front of the engine. A second turbine is used to drive this fan, which acts like a propeller. Most of the increased airflow created by the fan passes around the outside of the engine and helps produce the force that propels the aircraft. The rest of the air enters the engine, which operates like a turbojet. Turbofan engines are widely used on commercial airliners because of their quiet operation and fuel efficiency. (For further information on jet engines, see the article JET PROPULSION in Volume J-K.)

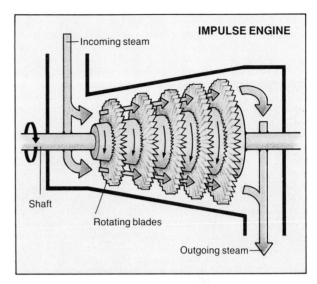

IMPULSE ENGINE

Incoming steam

Shaft

Rotating blades

Outgoing steam

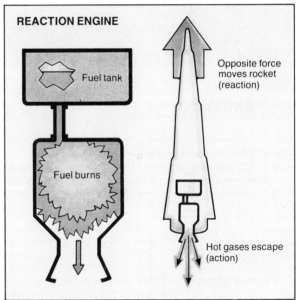

REACTION ENGINE

Fuel tank

Fuel burns

Opposite force moves rocket (reaction)

Hot gases escape (action)

A **rocket engine** is also a reaction engine. It consists of fuel storage compartments, a combustion chamber, and exhaust nozzles. Rocket engines use either solid or liquid fuels. Fuel burns in the combustion chamber and turns to a gas. Hot, expanding gas rushes at high speed out nozzles at the back of the rocket, pushing the rocket forward. Rocket engines can operate in space where there is no air because they carry their own oxygen supply. (For additional information, see the article ROCKETS in Volume R.)

JOSEPH W. DUFFY
Central Connecticut State University

Left: The houses of Parliament overlook the Thames River in London. *Above:* The Englishman at the left wears a bowler hat. The man at the right displays the traditional uniform of the Royal Hospital at Chelsea (Chelsea Pensioners), a home for old and invalid soldiers founded by King Charles II in the 17th century.

ENGLAND

England is the largest and most populous of the four parts of the United Kingdom of Great Britain and Northern Ireland. It is situated on the island of Great Britain, which lies off the northwestern coast of Europe. England shares the island with Scotland and Wales. Northern Ireland, the fourth division of the kingdom, is located on the smaller, neighboring island of Ireland.

▶THE PEOPLE

Population. England's population of more than 47,000,000 live in an area of about 50,362 square miles (130,441 square kilometers). This number of people in such a relatively small area (smaller than the state of Alabama) makes England one of the most densely populated regions of Europe. The great majority of its people live in cities or towns.

Origin. Most of the present-day English are descendants of the various peoples who settled or invaded England over a period of many centuries. They included the Celts (or Britons); Romans; such Germanic peoples as Jutes, Saxons, and Angles (from whom England takes its name); Danes and other Scandinavians; and Norman French.

In more recent times this mixture has been added to by immigrants from Great Britain's once far-flung colonial empire. Most of these newcomers are blacks, mainly from the West Indies, and Asians, chiefly Pakistanis and Indians.

Language and Religion. English developed from the language of the Germanic peoples, who first arrived in what is now England in the 5th century. The language was strongly influenced by the French of the 11th-century Norman conquerors. The English language spread around the globe with the growth of the British Empire. For more information on English, see the article ENGLISH LANGUAGE in this volume.

The Church of England is the established church. England also has large numbers of Roman Catholics; Methodists, Baptists, and members of other Protestant denominations; and the second largest Jewish community in western Europe. Freedom of worship is guaranteed to all the people.

▶THE LAND

William Shakespeare, England's greatest dramatist, described his country in this way:

> This precious stone set in the silver sea,
> Which serves it in the office of a wall
> Or as a moat defensive to a house. . . .

The "moat" of which Shakespeare wrote is the English Channel, which separates England from the coast of France, and the other surrounding seas. These waters have helped protect England against invasion ever since the Norman Conquest in 1066. Its position as an island nation also played a part in England's development into the world's leading seafaring and naval power, a role it held for almost two centuries.

The isolation that served to protect England in the past, however, is no longer possible. In 1994, the English Channel Tunnel was officially completed, linking Britain with the mainland of Europe. The 31-mile (50-kilometer) rail tunnel runs between Folkestone, England, and Calais, France.

Landforms. England is separated from Scotland in the north by the Tweed River, Cheviot Hills, and Solway Firth. The highest point in England is Scafell Pike, which rises to 3,210 feet (978 meters) in the Lake District of the northwest. The beauty of the Lake District has been praised by William Wordsworth and other English poets.

The most important mountains are the Pennine Chain, which runs from the Scottish border to central England. The country's longest rivers flow from the highlands to the sea. The Severn is in the west, and the Thames, which flows through London, is in the south. Other major rivers are the Humber, Tees, Tyne, Trent, Avon, Exe, Mersey, Cam, and Ouse.

Regions. East of the Pennines are moors (boggy, uncultivated land) and the Yorkshire coal mining and industrial areas. Lancashire, to the west, is the hub of the textile industry.

The Midlands region, around the southern edge of the Pennines, has traditionally been England's manufacturing center. To the east are the coastal lowlands, with green fields, farms, and fishing villages.

Southern England is rich in history and legend. The center of this region is the ancient city of London, the capital and largest city of the United Kingdom. Not far from London are Stratford-on-Avon, where Shakespeare lived, and the old cathedral town of Canterbury. Two of England's most famous universities, Oxford and Cambridge, are located in the south. See the separate article on London in Volume L.

A steep wall of chalk—the white cliffs of Dover—rises along the southeast coast. To

ENGLAND

A "green and pleasant land" was the way poet William Blake described the English countryside. Parts of England remain as Blake knew it in the 18th century.

Below: Factory towns, such as this one in Lancashire, grew up as a result of the enormous growth of British manufacturing in the 19th century, when England was workshop to the world. *Left:* Although its economy is mainly an industrial one, England also produces prize sheep and other livestock.

the southwest are the moors of Devon and the rocky cliffs of the Cornwall peninsula. At the tip of this peninsula is Land's End, the westernmost point of England.

Mineral Resources. Except for coal and oil and natural gas deposits in the North Sea, England has limited mineral resources. Some iron ore, lead, zinc, tungsten, and clays used in making pottery and china are also mined.

Climate. In spite of its northern latitude, England has a generally temperate climate. It is warmed by the North Atlantic Drift, an extension of the Gulf Stream. Winters are usually fairly mild, and summers are rarely very hot. Rain is abundant and falls evenly throughout the year.

▶THE ECONOMY

Industry. England was the birthplace of the Industrial Revolution, which began in the middle of the 18th century. The most important English industries traditionally have been the manufacture of cotton textiles, steel and steel products, and pottery and fine china. Today factories in England also manufacture synthetic fabrics, electronic equipment, automobiles, aircraft, and many other products.

Fishing was long an important industry but has declined in recent years.

Agriculture. Agriculture is highly mechanized, and only a small percentage of the population is engaged in farming. Much of England's food must be imported. The chief crops grown are barley, wheat, oats, potatoes, and apples and other fruits. The raising of livestock, including horses, cattle, sheep, and pigs, is especially important.

▶HISTORY

Wales was officially united with England in the 1500's. England (with Wales) and Scotland were united politically, as the United Kingdom of Great Britain, under the Act of Union in 1707. The Act of Union of 1800 joined Ireland to Great Britain. The present United Kingdom of Great Britain and Northern Ireland came into being after the partition (division) of Ireland in 1920–21. For more information, see the article ENGLAND, HISTORY OF, following.

DAVID C. LARGE
University of Reading (England)

See also UNITED KINGDOM; IRELAND; NORTHERN IRELAND; SCOTLAND; WALES.

ENGLAND, HISTORY OF

England is a very small country, not much bigger than the state of New York. Yet no one can fully understand the modern world without knowing some English history. The English worked out ideas of justice and obedience to law. Their democratic ideals and system of justice have spread to become the foundation for the laws and government of many nations, including those of the United States.

▶ EARLY HISTORY

The few people who lived in England during the Old Stone Age, about 12,000 B.C., were cave dwellers whose only tools were sticks and stones. Over several thousands of years, people from the mainland of Europe migrated to England, bringing with them more advanced skills. They made more efficient tools, first out of stone, then of bronze, and by 500 B.C., of iron. These early English people built places with enormous stones. The greatest of these, Stonehenge, may have been used for religious purposes or as an astronomical observatory.

Celtic Invaders Bring New Skills to England

In the 700's B.C., a group of people from central and western Europe called the Celts began invading England. Because their weapons were superior to those of the native people who lived along the English coast, the Celts drove the inhabitants inland and took their land. A group of Celts called the Britons eventually settled in areas that are now England and Wales. By the 1st century B.C. the Britons had learned to make houses from logs, tame horses for their war chariots, and raise sheep, cattle, and goats. They grew grain and made clay pots to store food and drink. The Britons also made beautiful bronze jewelry and magnificent weapons.

The Roman Conquest

While all this was happening in England, the Romans were building a mighty empire in western Europe. Some of the Gauls, another group of Celts, who lived in what is now France, did not like Roman rule. Sometimes they rose in rebellion against the Romans. As the Romans outnumbered them, the Gauls were usually defeated and often fled across the English Channel to live in England.

The Crown Jewels are symbols of the British monarchy. They include the Imperial State Crown (*left*); the royal orb (*below left*); and the royal scepter (*below*), which holds the Star of Africa, the largest cut diamond in the world.

Julius Caesar (100?–44 B.C.), the great commander of a Roman army, decided to invade Britain, too. In 55 B.C. and again the following year, Caesar led his army across the English Channel. It was not difficult for Caesar to defeat the Britons in battle, but he had neither the time nor the money to conquer Britain completely. In A.D. 43 another Roman, the Emperor Claudius, re-invaded the island. After many fierce battles the Romans defeated the Britons and established Roman rule. This was the beginning of a new period in British history.

The Romans Civilize England

The Romans were very clever and advanced people. They built forts in England to protect themselves against the more primitive tribespeople from the mountains of Scotland and Wales. Then they built roads. There had been no roads in Britain before the Romans came. The roads made a link between the forts so

Scientists believe that Stonehenge (*left*) on Salisbury Plain in Wiltshire, completed about 1100 B.C., may have served as an astronomical observatory. Hadrian's Wall (*right*), built in A.D. 128 to discourage invaders, marked the northernmost frontier of the Roman Empire.

that Roman soldiers could easily get to any place where the tribespeople might break through. But traders used them also, and towns were built for the first time along the roads.

Gradually Britons became used to Roman law and order and to paying taxes. In the towns wealthy people learned to speak Latin and to live the way the Romans did. For the first time in its history, that part of Britain that we now call England became a civilized land and part of the great Roman Empire. And as Christianity spread through the empire, it came to Britain. By the 300's, Christian bishops were presiding over churches in many parts of England.

Roman Influence Wanes

This happy state of affairs did not last. The Roman Empire was too big. There were too many wild tribes on the empire's frontiers for all the frontiers to be defended. The Roman soldiers were called back home, and the Britons were left to look after themselves.

Soon the Picts, who lived in what is now Scotland, swarmed over Hadrian's Wall, a fortification system the Romans had built to keep them out. In the 400's and 500's, fierce warriors came across the North Sea to raid the English coast. These new Germanic invaders were the Angles, the Saxons, and the Jutes. It was the Angles that named the southern half of the British island Engla-land.

The Britons fought hard and were not easily defeated. Legends have grown up about the

ANGLO-SAXON AND DANISH RULERS OF ENGLAND (838–1066)	
NAME	REIGN
Anglo-Saxons	
Egbert	828–839
Ethelwulf	839–858
Ethelbald	858–860
Ethelbert	860–866
Ethelred I	866–871
*Alfred the Great	871–899?
*Edward the Elder	899–924
Athelstan	924–940
Edmund I	940–946
Edred	946–955
Edwy	955–959
Edgar the Peaceful	959–975
*Edward the Martyr	975–978
Ethelred the Unready	978–1016
Edmund Ironside	1016
Danes	
*Canute	1016–1035
Harold I	1035–1040
Hardecanute	1040–1042
Anglo-Saxons	
*Edward the Confessor	1042–1066
Harold II	1066
*For more information, consult the Index.	

bravery of these last Romano-British leaders. One of them was the man whom writers and storytellers call King Arthur. However, by the 600's the invaders had conquered England and either killed or made slaves of many Britons. Others were driven into the mountains of Wales.

Gradually, the Roman influence in England began to wane. Many of the towns, roads, and homes the Romans had built fell into disrepair, crumbled, and decayed. Some of the ruins are still there to remind us that for over 400 years England was part of the Roman Empire.

But now England, separated from the rest of Europe, had to begin learning all over again. This is why the basis for English law and government is different from that of much of Western Europe. The Anglo-Saxons developed their own way of life, and all the conquerors and invaders that followed built on the Anglo-Saxon foundation. Even today, people speak of Britain's Anglo-Saxon tradition.

▶ ANGLES, SAXONS, AND DANES

By the beginning of the 700's there were seven kingdoms in England: Northumbria, Mercia, East Anglia, Essex, Wessex, Sussex, and Kent. Except perhaps for the Jutes, all the peoples in each of the kingdoms shared the same ideas on government and law. Each kingdom was ruled by a king, who depended on warriors, called thanes, to protect the kingdom and carry out justice. If the kingdom was too large for the king to oversee, he would appoint an officer called an ealdorman (later an earl) to represent him. Thanes and earls were given land and privileges in return for their services, and a share of the money they earned from their land went to support the king.

Before the 600's there were no written laws in England. Anyone suspected of wrongdoing was brought before a royal officer and a group of freemen (those who were not slaves) for justice. Most freemen were small farmers. They fought for their king when necessary and helped him carry out justice.

The Anglo-Saxons Are Converted to Christianity

When the Anglo-Saxons first came to England, they were pagans. But in 597, Pope Gregory I sent Saint Augustine as a missionary to Kent to convert its king, Ethelbert, to Christianity. Saint Augustine succeeded, and by the mid-600's most of the kingdoms in England had become Christianized.

Alfred the Great Holds Off the Danes

England was not united under one king until disaster threatened in the middle to late 800's. Fierce Norwegians and Danes raided the English coast, burning English monasteries, stealing treasures, and murdering monks. At first it looked as though all of England might be conquered. However, Alfred the Great (849–899?), the King of Wessex, managed to raise an army big enough to defeat the Danish leader, Guthrum. The two then decided to share England between them: Alfred took the southwestern half and Guthrum took the northeast, which was then named Danelaw.

A Saxon calendar dating from 1030 (*above*) illustrates what agricultural life was like in England during the Middle Ages. The popular legends of King Arthur (*below*) may be based on the life of a Celtic chieftain, who fought off Saxon invaders in the 6th century.

When Alfred died, he was succeeded by a series of kings, who by 955 had reconquered Danelaw. During the reign of Edgar the Peaceful (944–75), England for the first time was ruled by one king only.

The Danes Invade Again

England did not remain at peace for long. During the reign of Ethelred II (968–1016), the Danes began raiding England again. Ethelred II, who was nicknamed the Unready (meaning ill-advised), was no match for the Danes. In 1013 he fled across the English Channel to Normandy. England then became part of the kingdom of Denmark, and in 1016 the English barons accepted Canute of Denmark (995–1035) as their ruler.

Canute became a Christian and ruled England well. He was succeeded by his two sons, Harold I (1017–40) and Hardecanute (1018–42). When Hardecanute died without leaving an heir, the English barons invited Edward (1002?–66), son of Ethelred II, to return from Normandy to rule. In this way, the House of Wessex and the heirs of Alfred the Great were restored to the English throne.

▶WILLIAM OF NORMANDY CONQUERS ENGLAND

Because King Edward was a very religious man and a good friend of the church, he was known as Edward the Confessor. Unfortunately he had no children. When he died in 1066, the English had to choose a new king. Two men wanted the throne. One was Harold, who had been the leading earl in the kingdom under Edward. The other was William, Duke of Normandy (1027–87), a relative of King Edward.

In 1066, William, Duke of Normandy, conquered England by defeating the Anglo-Saxons at the Battle of Hastings. The battle was shown in the 11th-century Bayeux tapestry.

Harold was crowned, but William said that Harold had earlier sworn a solemn oath to support William's claims to the throne. The enraged William collected an army to invade England. Because Harold was also being attacked in the north by the Norwegian king, his position was difficult. He defeated the Norwegians, but he in turn was defeated by William, at the Battle of Hastings in 1066, thus ending the rule of Saxon kings. The English accepted William as their king, and he was crowned on Christmas Day in 1066. William the Conqueror became the first Norman king of England.

The Norman Conquest of 1066 is an important event in English history. Never again was England successfully invaded. Because William was both Duke of Normandy and King of England, the English then came under the influence of the Normans. The Normans brought England the feudal system, by which rulers granted land in exchange for military service.

The Reign of William the Conqueror

When William became king, he accepted the Anglo-Saxon laws and form of government. He meant to be a just, though strict, king. But the English thought him too harsh. They were used to the rule of the weaker Edward the Confessor, and there were rebellions against William. However, William was able to defeat his opponents.

In 1085, William I commissioned the **Domesday Book,** the first official public record of the kingdom's land holdings. To punish the rebels, William took away their land and gave it to his own nobles, who were called barons. Soon all the important people in both the church and government were French or Norman. Many of the Anglo-Saxon freemen became serfs and had to work for their Norman lords. French became the language of the king and his barons. English was spoken only by the common people.

▶MEDIEVAL ENGLAND

The years between 1066 and 1485, roughly the years of the period known as the Middle Ages, saw the laying of the foundation on which modern England was built. One of the most important questions examined during this time was how power was to be shared by the king and the barons. (At this time common people, who were mostly poor and unedu-

Left: In 1215, King John was forced to accept Magna Carta, which granted rights to the English barons. This document marked the first step toward constitutional law in England. *Right:* Edward I was the first English king to call together a parliament that included a Commons, or assembly of representatives from around the kingdom.

cated, had no power or say in their government.) Another important issue of the time concerned the church and how authority was to be shared by the pope and the king.

The Kings Extend Their Power

The early Norman kings were determined to make the royal courts more powerful than those of the barons. For in those days barons had their own strong castles; their own courts for their tenants; and their own fighting men.

To increase royal power, Henry I (1068–1135) and Henry II (1133–89) were anxious to make the royal justice the best in the land. They rewrote old laws and made new ones. Officials called justices were sent around England to hold courts to which all freemen could come. In this way the king's law became common to all parts of the country and so became known as the common law. Justices also levied taxes.

Although the barons were called to the royal council, the kings governed more and more through their own officials. The barons felt the king's power growing greater. The king also found ways to get money from the barons. When Henry II became king in 1154, he strengthened the royal power even more.

Magna Carta: The Barons Fight Back

Richard I (1157–99), known as Richard the Lion-Hearted, spent very little time in England because he went on the Third Crusade to drive the Muslims out of the Holy Land. But his brother John (1167?–1216) was particularly disliked by the barons. John was a capable ruler, and like Henry II, anxious to extend royal justice. But while he punished his barons for breaking the law, he often broke it himself.

The barons rose in full rebellion against John. With the help of Stephen Langton, Archbishop of Canterbury, they made a list of what they considered their most important rights and privileges, which they called *Magna Carta,* or the Great Charter. The barons presented it to John in 1215 and threatened to fight against him unless he agreed to its terms. This he was forced to do, and from then on it was clear that everybody, even the king, must obey the law. Magna Carta came to be the foundation of the legal rights of the English people.

The Beginning of Parliament

Even after Magna Carta, the struggle between the kings and barons continued. At Lewes in 1264, Simon de Montfort defeated Henry III (1207–72). He then summoned representatives from around the kingdom to join the barons in Parliament. But the following year, Henry's son, the future King Edward I, killed de Montfort at Evesham and reclaimed the throne.

Edward I (1239–1307) found it was easier to get the barons to co-operate if he asked, rather than demanded, their assistance. Edward needed a great deal of money, for in 1284 he conquered Wales, which until then had been independent. For a time he subdued Scotland, although the Scots were always rising against him. Edward had problems on the European continent, too. He was constantly fighting the French king to win back the lands of the early Norman rulers that had been lost by John.

To get money, Edward asked the counties and the towns to select men to come to Westminster Palace to discuss how to raise funds. Such a meeting came to be called a parliament. Although it was very different from England's Parliament of today, it was the first recognition of a representative assembly as a permanent part of government in England.

Medieval kings were always short of money, and gradually it became the custom that new taxes could only be granted by Parliament. Whenever new laws were needed, Parliament helped the king make them. By the reign of Edward III (1312–77), Parliament had two houses, the House of Lords, where the barons sat, and the House of Commons, where selected representatives met.

Throughout the Middle Ages the Commons had little independence. Commons was always under the influence of the king if he was strong, and of the barons if the king was weak. However, like the King's Privy Council (group of advisers), the Exchequer, and the royal courts of justice, Commons came to be thought of as part of the government.

Kings Versus Popes

The medieval kings were determined to assert their authority over the church. English rulers feared the power of the pope in Rome as much as they feared the power of the barons in England. Popes and kings quarreled mainly about how archbishops and bishops should be chosen, and when chosen, how independent they should be of the king. Kings and popes also disagreed about how much of the income of the churches should go to Rome and how much should go to England's royal treasury.

One of the best-known disputes between king and clergy happened during the reign of Henry II (1133–89). Henry II quarreled with Thomas à Becket (1118?–70), archbishop of Canterbury, over who had the final authority to punish clergy members who had been convicted of crimes: civil courts or church courts. In 1170, Becket was murdered in his own cathedral by four of Henry II's knights.

The Late Middle Ages

The earlier part of the Middle Ages was an exciting period. England was growing richer. Population was growing; farming methods were getting better; there was more money to build beautiful churches and monasteries; and the universities of Oxford and Cambridge were founded. But the latter half of the Middle Ages was not so prosperous. A series of terrible plagues—the first of which, the Black Death, occurred in 1348–49—killed more than one quarter of the population.

Left: In 1346 the English defeated the French at the Battle of Crécy, the first important battle of the Hundred Years War. *Right:* Edward, the Black Prince, was a great warrior who led his soldiers to victory over the French at Crécy (1346) and Poitiers (1356).

The Hundred Years' War

The Hundred Years' War is a name given to a long series of conflicts between the English and the French from about 1337 until 1453. The wars began when Edward III (1312–77) sent an army to France to claim the French throne. During his reign, England won many important battles, including Crécy (1346) and Poitiers (1356). Following the Treaty of Brétigny (1360) there was a brief period of peace. Henry V (1387–1422) renewed the conflict with France and won the Battle of Agincourt (1415). He finally became heir to the French throne by the Treaty of Troyes (1420). However, he died in 1422 and the fighting continued. In 1429, Joan of Arc helped save the city of Orléans from the British. They later captured her and burned her at the stake. The French continued to fight off the English, and by 1453 the English had lost all of its territory in France except Calais.

These wars were costly, and the heavy taxes needed to pay for them caused great discontent. In 1381 during the reign of Richard II (1367–1400), an uprising known as the Peasants' Revolt broke out. Led by Wat Tyler, the peasants fought against taxation and for the abolition of serfdom, a system that kept them in servitude to the landowning barons.

Richard III was a clever and able ruler. Shortly after Richard became king, his two young nephews, the sons of his dead brother Edward IV, mysteriously disappeared. Many people believe Richard had them killed (see Wonder Question). Richard himself was killed in 1485 by Henry Tudor, later Henry VII, at the Battle of Bosworth Field.

WONDER QUESTION

What Happened to the Princes in the Tower?

One of the many tragic stories surrounding London's ancient prison, the Tower, provides a dramatic incident in William Shakespeare's play *Richard III*. It tells how 13-year-old Edward V of England and his younger brother, the Duke of York, were smothered to death in 1483 on orders of their uncle, Richard III (1452–85), shortly after Richard had assumed the crown.

It was widely assumed that the murders had been carried out at Richard's orders. But many people doubted that they had ever taken place. In 1674 a wooden box containing the bones of two children about the age of the brothers was found under a stairway in the White Tower. Four years later Charles II (1630–85) ordered them reburied in Westminster Abbey. An examination by a royal commission in 1933 failed to make a positive identification. The bones remain in the Abbey, and the ancient legend persists.

The Wars of the Roses

Whenever the king was a child, there was always trouble. Rival barons tried to seize power to act in the king's name and to control the council in their own interests. Conditions were already bad when Henry V (1387–1422) died. When his infant son became King Henry VI (1421–71), the situation grew worse.

Henry VI, a descendant of Edward III and a member of the House of Lancaster, grew up a gentle young man, very much under the influence of his unpopular wife, Margaret of Anjou. Richard, the Duke of York, who was also descended from Edward III, decided to claim the throne for himself. This divided the barons into two camps: One supported the House of Lancaster (Henry VI), whose emblem was a red rose; the other group supported the House of York (Richard), whose emblem was a white rose. Richard, the Duke of York, was killed in the fighting. However, his son defeated Henry VI, probably had him murdered, and in 1471 became King Edward IV (1442–83).

Richard III, a Controversial King

Edward IV started to rebuild the royal power, but he died before his children grew up. He had appointed his brother, Richard, the Duke of Gloucester, as guardian of his two sons, the young Edward V (1470–83?) and his younger brother, the Duke of York.

Historians do not agree about the kind of man Richard was. He was an able soldier and administrator and had been loyal to his brother

In order to divorce the first of his six famous wives, Henry VIII broke away from the Catholic Church and made himself head of the protestant Church of England.

during his lifetime. After Edward IV died, however, Richard claimed Edward IV's marriage had not been legal, and therefore he, not Edward V, was the rightful heir to the throne. Because the country preferred an experienced man to a boy as king, Parliament recognized him as King Richard III (1452–85). His little nephews were placed in the Tower of London, which was then a palace as well as a prison. Soon the children disappeared and were never seen again.

Richard III did not remain king for long. In 1485, Henry Tudor, who had a weak claim to the throne through his mother, also a descendant of Edward III, returned from exile in France with an army and invaded England. He defeated and killed Richard III at Bosworth Field and so became Henry VII (1457–1509). Henry VII was first Tudor king (of the House of Tudor).

▶ **THE TUDOR ERA: ENGLAND COMES OF AGE**

Under the leadership of the Tudor kings and queens, England changed rapidly. The discovery of new trade routes and of the New World made people think differently. The invention of printing (1456) made it easier to spread new

ideas. Henry VIII (1491–1547), Henry VII's only surviving son, used the power and the treasure his father had gathered to create a new kind of monarchy.

Henry VIII Breaks with the Roman Catholic Church

The most important thing that Henry VIII did was to break away from the Roman Catholic Church. One reason for this break was the refusal of Pope Clement VII (1478–1534) to annul Henry's marriage to Catherine of Aragon. Henry knew how important it was to have a male heir. However, he had only one daughter, Mary (later Mary I), by Catherine. Catherine was his elder brother's widow, and it was not customary for Catholics to wed relatives by marriage. Henry decided to ask the pope to declare his marriage to Catherine invalid so that he could marry Anne Boleyn, a lady of the court. Henry loved Anne and hoped she could give him a son. When the pope refused, Henry persuaded Parliament to pass a series of acts between 1529 and 1536 to take away the pope's authority in England. He married Anne, dissolved the monasteries, seized their property, and declared that the king of England was head of both church and state.

But Henry still had no male heir, for Anne's child was a girl, the future Elizabeth I. Suspecting that Anne was interested in men other than himself, Henry had Anne beheaded. His next wife, Jane Seymour, had a son, later Edward VI (1537–53). Jane died in childbirth. After that, Henry VIII had three more wives. One he divorced, one he beheaded, and one outlived him.

Henry's quarrel with the pope was not the only reason for the break with Rome. The people, and even many of the clergy, disliked the way that the popes interfered with the Church of England and collected money from it. Some of the clergy and monks in England had lost the respect of ordinary people. The people hoped that if the king were head of the church he would reform it.

However, because there was no pope to tell people what they must believe, they disagreed as to the kind of church they wanted. After Henry VIII died in 1547 and Edward VI became king, the religious disagreements became much worse. Some people wanted services very much like the old Roman

Catholic ones; others hoped for a simpler, or, as they said, purer, service. For this reason these people later became known as Puritans. Their numbers included Thomas Cranmer, the Archbishop of Canterbury (1489–1556). In 1549 and 1552, Archbishop Cranmer issued new prayer books, which are still the basis of the services in the churches of the Anglican Communion (including the Episcopal Church in the United States). English, not Latin, was to be the language of the English Church.

Catholicism Returns Briefly Under Mary I

In 1553, England returned to the Roman Catholic Church. Edward VI died too young to marry. The Duke of Northumberland failed to get the Protestant Lady Jane Grey made queen instead of Mary Tudor (1516–58), Henry VIII's eldest daughter, who was still a Roman Catholic. Both Northumberland and the unfortunate Lady Jane were beheaded, and Mary became queen.

At first Mary I was popular because many people had disliked the new Protestant prayer books. But people came to hate her when she married Philip II of Spain (1527–98), persuaded Parliament to restore the pope's authority, and began to have men and women, including Archbishop Cranmer, burned at the stake for continuing to be Protestants. For this, they called her Bloody Mary. The English people blamed Mary for joining Philip II in his war against France and losing the port of Calais, England's last possession on the European continent. Therefore, many people rejoiced when Mary's half sister, Elizabeth, came to the throne on her death in 1558.

Elizabeth I Brings Back Protestantism

Elizabeth I (1533–1603) was a great queen who had to face enormous problems. She was only 25 when she came to the throne, and in those days nobody thought a woman could rule alone. Yet to marry a foreigner would be unpopular. If she married an English nobleman, she would make the rest of the nobles jealous. So she never married at all.

Philip II of Spain hoped that England would remain Roman Catholic and his ally. However, the English people disliked Spain and had been sickened by Mary's executions. Parliament, and especially the House of Commons, put pressure on Elizabeth to officially reject the pope. Because she depended on Par-

Elizabeth I, daughter of Henry VIII, was a wise and able monarch. During her long reign, England became a major world power with a prospering economy and a great navy.

liament to raise money, Elizabeth agreed. In 1559 a new prayer book was issued, and the English Church has since been Protestant.

England Versus Spain

Philip II of Spain and Elizabeth were becoming enemies. Philip had not wanted the English Church to become Protestant, and he was annoyed at the voyages of English explorers to the New World. Philip felt that the New World belonged to Spain and Portugal. As far as he was concerned, English sailors, like Sir Francis Drake, who had sailed as far as the California coast in his voyage of 1577–80, had no right to trespass in the New World.

Philip began to plot against Elizabeth and tried to make Mary Stuart, Queen of Scots (1542–87), queen in her place. Mary, descended from a daughter of Henry VII, was a Roman Catholic. Luckily for Elizabeth the Protestant Scots rose against Mary, and she was forced to flee to England. She remained there as a kind of guest-prisoner from 1568 to 1587. But when Mary became the center of plots against Elizabeth, the queen's ministers finally persuaded her that Mary must be

House of Normandy

*William I (the Conqueror)	Obtained the crown by conquest	1066–1087
William II (Rufus)	Third son of William I	1087–1100
Henry I (Beauclerc)	Youngest son of William I	1100–1135
Stephen	Third son of Adela, daughter of William I	1135–1154

House of Plantagenet (Anjou)

Henry II	Eldest son of Matilda, daughter of Henry I	1154–1189
*Richard I (Coeur de Lion)	Eldest surviving son of Henry II	1189–1199

KINGS OF ENGLAND AND LORDS OF IRELAND

John	Youngest son of Henry II	1199–1216
Henry III	Eldest son of John	1216–1272
*Edward I	Eldest son of Henry III	1272–1307
*Edward II	Eldest surviving son of Edward I	1307–1327
*Edward III	Eldest son of Edward II	1327–1377
*Richard II	Only surviving son of Black Prince, eldest son of Edward III	1377–1399

House of Lancaster

*Henry IV	Eldest surviving son of John of Gaunt, 4th son of Edward III	1399–1413
Henry V	Eldest son of Henry IV	1413–1422
Henry VI	Only son of Henry V	1422–1461

House of York

*Edward IV	Eldest son of Richard, Duke of York	1461–1483
*Edward V	Elder surviving son of Edward IV	1483
*Richard III	Youngest son of Richard, Duke of York	1483–1485

House of Tudor

Henry VII	Descendant of John of Gaunt	1485–1509
*Henry VIII	Only surviving son of Henry VII	1509–1542

KINGS AND QUEENS OF ENGLAND AND IRELAND

Henry VIII		1542–1547
*Edward VI	Only surviving son of Henry VIII, by Jane Seymour	1547–1553
*Mary I	Daughter of Henry VIII by Catherine of Aragon	1553–1558
*Elizabeth I	Daughter of Henry VIII by Anne Boleyn	1558–1603

*For more information, consult the Index.

executed for the sake of England's safety. She was beheaded in 1587.

Meanwhile Elizabeth had also been helping the Protestant Dutch, who were rebelling against Spanish rule in the Netherlands. Philip now decided to conquer England. In 1588 he sent a great fleet called the Spanish Armada to defeat England. Everybody thought that such a little country had no chance against mighty Spain. But the English ships and seamen were very good, and some of the Spanish ships were wrecked by storms while fleeing from them. England was saved.

The End of the Elizabethan Age

In 1603, Elizabeth died. During her reign, she had kept her country independent. With the help of her wise minister William Cecil (Lord Burghley) and his son Robert Cecil, she had ruled it well. England was growing richer. It had a great cloth-making industry and was developing its sea power, looking for markets in the New World as well as in Europe. More people had more time and money to take an interest in music, literature, and the theater. Men like William Shakespeare, Ben Jonson, and Christopher Marlowe were writing plays. Architecture flourished too because the nobles were building fine mansions rather than fortified castles.

Elizabethan England was an exciting place in which to live. However, many feared the day when Elizabeth would die, for the old queen had no heir. When Queen Elizabeth finally lay dying, she surprised many of her people by ordering that Mary of Scotland's son, James VI of Scotland (1566–1625), should become king of England. James, who had been brought up a Protestant, became James I of England. Scotland and England now had the same king.

During Elizabeth I's reign, Ireland, which had been semi-independent since Henry II's reign, had also been brought under English control. At last England, Wales, Scotland, and Ireland had the same ruler. But they did not have the same religion. Ireland remained Roman Catholic, and this was the cause of future trouble.

▶**THE STUARTS AND THE RISE OF PARLIAMENT**

The position of the Stuart kings (kings of James's family) was difficult, and the fact that they were autocratic made them unpopular. The Tudors, who had been faced with so many dangers, had worked closely with Parliament. The House of Commons in particular had grown in power. Now its members were increasingly critical of James I and his son Charles I (1600–49), especially on money matters. Prices had increased enormously since Tudor days, and government now cost more than it once had. Therefore, although the king had a large private income, he had to ask Parliament for more money. The Commons thought both kings were spending too much— to some extent they were—and there were continual quarrels over money.

Both kings also disagreed with the Commons over religion. The kings wished to control the church through the bishops. In 1611, James I had a new translation of the Bible created that became known as the King James Version. However, a growing number of Puritans wanted simpler services and fled to the New World in search of religious freedom.

Charles I Clashes with the Puritans

In Charles I's reign the quarrels over money and religion grew worse. Charles believed in the Divine Right of Kings—that God, not the people, had given him the divine right to rule. He chose as his archbishop of Canterbury William Laud (1573–1645). Unlike the Puritans, Laud did not want churches and services to be plainer but more beautiful, with choirs, organs, and special clothes for the clergy. To the Puritans, this seemed to be a return to Catholic customs. The members of the House of Commons, many of whom were Puritans, tried to influence Charles by keeping him short of money. Nevertheless, Charles sidestepped Parliament and raised money on his own, in part by increasing taxes on imported goods and by demanding forced loans.

On June 7, 1628, Parliament issued a **Petition of Right**, which they made Charles sign. In effect, it rejected the concept of the Divine Right of Kings and for the first time declared Parliament's authority over the monarch. It also made it illegal for the king to raise taxes without Parliament's permission; to quarter his soldiers in private homes; to imprison someone without just cause; or to use military force during peacetime.

Nevertheless, Charles continued to rule without the consent of Parliament, and in 1629 he decided to call no more Parliaments. By

Charles I was defeated by Oliver Cromwell in the English Civil War (1642–51). In 1649, Parliament found the king guilty of treason and beheaded him.

being very thrifty and keeping out of war, the king managed to rule without Parliament for eleven years. During his personal rule, Archbishop Laud relied on force and intimidation to defeat the Puritans, who continued to escape to the New World, where they hoped to find religious freedom.

The Short and Long Parliaments

Charles I's religious views were even more unpopular in Scotland than in England. When he tried to introduce a version of the English Book of Common Prayer there, the Scots rose in rebellion. This finally forced him in 1640 to call a Parliament to raise money to subdue the Scots. But Parliament refused to help the King until English grievances had been considered, and so Charles dissolved it after a few weeks. Since that time, it has been known as the Short Parliament.

But when the Scots invaded England, Charles was forced to call another Parliament. Led by the Puritans, who had come to be known as the Roundheads for their short-cropped hair, this so-called Long Parliament (1640–53) became one of the most important in English history. It declared that all the methods by which Charles I had raised money without parliamentary consent were illegal. Parliament even threatened to get rid of the bishops.

This last point divided the members because some of them wanted to keep the bishops. Some members of Parliament were beginning to think that they had taken enough power from Charles I and that a Parliament that could ignore the king would be as dangerous to liberty as a king who could govern without Parliament. This support enabled Charles I, in 1642, to raise an army, and Parliament formed an army, too. The armies fought a battle at Edgehill, beginning a civil war.

Cromwell's Parliament Puts Charles I to Death

The English Civil War was fought to decide whose will should prevail when king and Parliament disagreed. Many people chose sides for religious reasons or because they disliked the way Charles I had raised money without parliamentary consent. Many merchants and townspeople supported Parliament for this last reason. These merchants controlled the ports and the richer parts of the country, especially London. Parliament, therefore, could afford to spend more on its army than the king could spend on his.

At first Charles had a better army than Parliament, and the war went in his favor. But then a gentleman from Huntingdon called Oliver Cromwell (1599–1658) re-organized the parliamentary forces, and the King was badly defeated at Marston Moor (1644) and Naseby (1645). In 1646, Charles could struggle no longer and surrendered to his enemies.

Although defeated, Charles was still king, and since few people could imagine England without a king, Cromwell and Parliament tried for three years to reach an agreement with Charles. But when Charles encouraged the fighting to break out again, Cromwell decided that he could not be trusted. Those members of Parliament who disagreed with Cromwell were expelled, and the remainder, known as the Rump, put Charles I on trial and condemned him to death. He was beheaded in 1649.

The Restoration: The Stuarts Return

But although Cromwell and the army had executed the king, they soon found that it was easier to destroy the old government than to agree on a new one. They too quarreled over religion. The Rump wanted a Presbyterian Church like the Scottish Church. The army wanted a Congregational Church. Therefore, although Cromwell was made protector (ruler), he had a very difficult time. When Cromwell died in 1658, his son Richard was too weak to do his job. No one could agree on a new form of government, and in 1660 it was decided to ask Charles I's eldest son to become king as Charles II (1630–85).

The restoration of the king brought back the Stuart monarchy but not the wide powers taken away by the Long Parliament. Charles II found that he had to work with Parliament and sometimes give in to it against his will.

Charles II had no heir, and everyone knew that his brother James had become a Roman Catholic. One group of politicians, led by Lord Shaftesbury, pretended to have discovered a Roman Catholic plot (called the Popish Plot) to murder Charles II and make James king. Shaftesbury and his supporters attempted to persuade Parliament to keep James from becoming king. However, Charles II outwitted them, and Shaftesbury fled abroad. When Charles II died in 1685, James II (1633–1701) became king.

The Glorious Revolution and the Bill of Rights

People soon discovered that Shaftesbury had been partly right. James II tried to reconvert England to the Roman Catholic Church. He also tried to gain more personal power. Thus the leading politicians decided to ask William of Orange (1650–1702), the husband of James II's Protestant daughter Mary, for help against the King. William agreed. Louis XIV of France (1638–1715) was threatening the independence of William's own country, Holland, and William wanted England on his side. In 1688, William invaded England. James II, finding that even his army was deserting him, fled to France. Parliament then asked William and his wife, Mary, to be king and queen. But to safeguard English liberties and make sure that no future sovereign could be a Roman Catholic, Parliament insisted that William and Mary sign a Bill of Rights (1689). Some of its clauses were later used in the United States Constitution.

Because these changes took place fairly peacefully and by the authority of Parliament, the deposition of James II is known as the Glorious Revolution. In the future all English rulers had to learn to work with Parliament.

In 1793, French revolutionaries executed their monarchs, Louis XVI and Marie Antoinette. A commentary from that year explains why the English believed their brand of liberty was superior to that of the new French Republic.

THE CONTRAST 1793

BRITISH LIBERTY · FRENCH LIBERTY

RELIGION, MORALITY, LOYALTY, OBEDIENCE to the LAWS, INDEPENDANCE, PERSONAL SECURITY, JUSTICE, INHERITANC, PROTECTION of PROPERTY, INDUSTRY, NATIONAL PROSPERITY, HAPPINESS. | ATHEISM, PERJURY, REBELLION, TREASON, ANARCHY, MURDER, EQUALITY, MADNESS, CRUELTY, INJUSTICE, TREACHERY, INGRATITUDE, IDLENESS, FAMINE, NATIONAL & PRIVATE RUIN, MISERY.

WHICH IS BEST?

▶ ENGLAND IN THE 1700'S

The year 1689 was also an important date in England's relations with Europe. English trade was growing, and English merchants feared that if Louis XIV of France grew too powerful, he would threaten this trade. Therefore, when Louis supported James II for the English throne, England was prepared to support William III. England went to war against France. Peace was made at Ryswick in 1697, but in 1701 war broke out again. One cause of this was that Louis XIV's grandson had become king of Spain, and English merchants feared for their Spanish trade. Another was that when James II died (1701), Louis XIV recognized James II's son, James Edward Stuart (1688–1766), whom the English call the Old Pretender, as rightful king of England.

The war that began in 1701 was known as the War of the Spanish Succession. It lasted until 1714. In this war England became known

PRIME MINISTERS OF ENGLAND SINCE 1721

Name	Party	Years	Name	Party	Years
*Sir Robert Walpole	Whig	1721–1742	Earl of Derby	Conservative	1866–1868
Earl of Wilmington	Whig	1742–1743	*Benjamin Disraeli	Conservative	1868
Henry Pelham	Whig	1743–1754	*William E. Gladstone	Liberal	1868–1874
Duke of Newcastle	Whig	1754–1756	Benjamin Disraeli	Conservative	1874–1880
Duke of Devonshire	Whig	1756–1757	William E. Gladstone	Liberal	1880–1885
Duke of Newcastle	Whig	1757–1762	Marquess of Salisbury	Conservative	1885–1886
Earl of Bute	Tory	1762–1763	William E. Gladstone	Liberal	1886
George Grenville	Whig	1763–1765	Marquess of Salisbury	Conservative	1886–1892
Marquess of Rockingham	Whig	1765–1766	William E. Gladstone	Liberal	1892–1894
*William Pitt the Elder (Earl of Chatham)	Whig	1766–1768	Earl of Rosebery	Liberal	1894–1895
			Marquess of Salisbury	Conservative	1895–1902
Duke of Grafton	Whig	1768–1770	*Arthur J. Balfour	Conservative	1902–1905
Frederick North (Lord North)	Tory	1770–1782	Sir Henry Campbell-Bannerman	Liberal	1905–1908
Marquess of Rockingham	Whig	1782	*Herbert H. Asquith	Liberal	1908–1915
Earl of Shelburne	Whig	1782–1783	Herbert H. Asquith	Coalition	1915–1916
Duke of Portland	Coalition	1783	*David Lloyd George	Coalition	1916–1922
*William Pitt the Younger	Tory	1783–1801	Andrew Bonar Law	Conservative	1922–1923
Henry Addington	Tory	1801–1804	Stanley Baldwin	Conservative	1923–1924
William Pitt the Younger	Tory	1804–1806	James Ramsay MacDonald	Labour	1924
William Wyndham Grenville, Baron Grenville	Whig	1806–1807	Stanley Baldwin	Conservative	1924–1929
			James Ramsay MacDonald	Labour	1929–1931
Duke of Portland	Tory	1807–1809	James Ramsay MacDonald	Coalition	1931–1935
Spencer Perceval	Tory	1809–1812	Stanley Baldwin	Coalition	1935–1937
Earl of Liverpool	Tory	1812–1827	*Neville Chamberlain	Coalition	1937–1940
George Canning	Tory	1827	*Winston Churchill	Coalition	1940–1945
Viscount Goderich	Tory	1827–1828	Winston Churchill	Conservative	1945
*Duke of Wellington	Tory	1828–1830	*Clement Attlee	Labour	1945–1951
Earl Grey	Whig	1830–1834	Sir Winston Churchill	Conservative	1951–1955
Viscount Melbourne	Whig	1834	Sir Anthony Eden	Conservative	1955–1957
*Sir Robert Peel	Tory	1834–1835	*Harold Macmillan	Conservative	1957–1963
Viscount Melbourne	Whig	1835–1841	Sir Alec Douglas-Home	Conservative	1963–1964
Sir Robert Peel	Tory	1841–1846	Harold Wilson	Labour	1964–1970
Lord John Russell (later Earl)	Whig	1846–1852	Edward Heath	Conservative	1970–1974
Earl of Derby	Tory	1852	Harold Wilson	Labour	1974–1976
Earl of Aberdeen	Peelite	1852–1855	James Callaghan	Labour	1976–1979
Viscount Palmerston	Liberal	1855–1858	*Margaret Thatcher	Conservative	1979–1990
Earl of Derby	Conservative	1858–1859	*John Major	Conservative	1990–1997
Viscount Palmerston	Liberal	1859–1865	Tony Blair	Labour	1997–
Earl Russell	Liberal	1865–1866	*Consult the Index for separate biographies.		

KINGS AND QUEENS OF ENGLAND SINCE 1603

KINGS AND QUEENS OF ENGLAND, SCOTLAND, AND IRELAND

House of Stuart

*James I (VI of Scotland from 1567)	Son of Mary, Queen of Scots, and great-great-grandson of Henry VII of England	1603–1625
*Charles I	Only surviving son of James I [Commonwealth declared, 1649; Oliver Cromwell, Lord Protector, 1653–1658; Richard Cromwell, Lord Protector, 1658–1659]	1625–1649
*Charles II	Eldest son of Charles I	1660–1685
*James II (VII of Scotland)	Second son of Charles I	1685–1688
*William III and Mary II	Grandson of Charles I; eldest daughter of James II	1689–1694
*William III (Mary II died 1694)		1694–1702
Anne	Second daughter of James II	1702–1707

KINGS AND QUEENS OF GREAT BRITAIN AND IRELAND

Anne		1707–1714

House of Hanover

*George I	Great-grandson of James I	1714–1727
*George II	Only son of George I	1727–1760
*George III	Grandson of George II	1760–1801

KINGS AND QUEENS OF UNITED KINGDOM OF GREAT BRITAIN AND IRELAND

*George III		1801–1820
*George IV (regent from 1811)	Eldest son of George III	1820–1830
*William IV	Third son of George III	1830–1837
*Victoria	Granddaughter of George III	1837–1901

House of Saxe-Coburg-Gotha

*Edward VII	Eldest son of Victoria	1901–1910

House of Windsor

†*George V	Only surviving son of Edward VII	1910–1927

KINGS AND QUEENS OF UNITED KINGDOM OF GREAT BRITAIN AND NORTHERN IRELAND

George V		1927–1936
*Edward VIII	Eldest son of George V	1936
*George VI	Second son of George V	1936–1952
*Elizabeth II	Elder daughter of George VI	1952–

†Changed name to Windsor from Saxe-Coburg-Gotha during World War I to symbolically break all ties with Germany.

*For more information, consult the Index.

---

as a great military nation, largely because of the leadership of John Churchill, Duke of Marlborough. By 1713, France was glad to make peace with England at Utrecht. It was a profitable peace for England. It got possession of Gibraltar and Minorca, which strengthened control over the Mediterranean, and Nova Scotia, which gave the English a foothold against the French in Canada. France and Austria made peace the following year.

Good Years Under Anne

William III and Mary had no children. Mary's sister, Anne (1665–1714), became queen of England when William died in 1702.

Because of her admirable character, Anne was known as Good Queen Anne, and the years of her reign were truly good ones for England. Under the Stuarts, England had established colonies in North America and the West Indies and had set up the powerful East India Company. By the end of Anne's reign, England was one of the greatest colonial and trading countries in the world. At home political unity was strengthened by the Act of Union in 1707, in which Scotland and England agreed to share the same parliament. Previously they had had the same ruler but separate parliaments. Scots had not been permitted to trade with the English colonies. Now Scotland was represented in both the House of Commons and the House of Lords, although it still kept its own laws and its own Presbyterian Church. England and Scotland together became known as Great Britain.

Hanover Kings

It had been arranged by the Act of Settlement (1701) that if Anne left no heir, the throne should go to the descendants of James I's daughter Elizabeth, who ruled the state of Hanover in Germany. None of Anne's children survived her, thus in 1714 the prince of Hanover became George I (1660–1727).

As foreigners the Hanoverians were not popular. Most of the English would have preferred James II's son, the Old Pretender, as king if he had agreed to become a Protestant. However, because he refused, they had to put up with George I, who was 54 years old and spoke no English; at least, however, he was a Protestant. His son was George II (1683–1760). George II was followed by his grandson George III (1738–1820), during whose

George III (*left*) was king of England at the time of the American Revolutionary War (1775–83). Lord Nelson's naval victories over the French and Spanish fleets at the Battle of Trafalgar in 1805 (*right*) proved that Britain was the undisputed ruler of the seas.

reign the American colonies became independent. George I and George II cared more for Hanover than for England, but George III was truly interested in ruling England.

Political Developments

In the 1700's the monarch (king or queen) still had great responsibilities but could no longer have ministers or a foreign policy that Commons disliked. Therefore the need for a chief, or prime minister, to help manage Parliament increased. The prime minister and the other most important ministers made up the cabinet.

Naturally members of Parliament often differed over policy. By the end of the 1700's, they were beginning to divide into two parties, Whigs and Tories. The Whigs usually supported the Hanoverian kings.

England Begins to Build an Empire

In the 1700's, Britain became a great imperial power. Its chief rival was France, and there were frequent wars between them. This long series of wars began with the War of the Spanish Succession (1701–14) and ended with the terrific struggle between England and post-revolutionary, Napoleonic France. Although Napoleon briefly was able to dominate Europe, England's position as an island once again came to her aid. Admiral Horatio Nelson saved England from invasion by his sea victory at Trafalgar in 1805. In the end it was an allied force of Prussians and British under the Duke of Wellington that finally defeated Napoleon at Waterloo in 1815.

During the wars with France, Britain gained Canada and increased its hold on the West Indies and on trading posts in Africa. The East India Company, defeating French traders, strengthened British control of India. Even after the American colonies had won their independence, Britain still had an immense empire. During the course of protecting the empire, England became a great naval power, and British merchant ships could sail safely all over the world.

The Industrial Revolution Begins

The growing trade meant that England needed more goods to export. This made manufacturers anxious to find quicker ways of making things and farmers eager to grow more food. This development was especially important in the second half of the 1700's, when the population of England increased rapidly. In 1700 it was perhaps more than 5 million; in 1801, when the first census was taken, it was about 9 million; by 1850 it was double that of 1801. England's main industry was cloth making, but coal mining had developed in Elizabeth's reign and cotton manufacturing had done so in the 1600's. Because there was no electric power, most things were handmade.

Then in the second half of the 1700's, great changes began to take place. Machines were invented to spin and later to weave. James Watt discovered how to drive these machines by steam power. Others learned how to use coal as a fuel to make iron. Coal was cheaper than wood, and because England was so small, wood was in short supply anyway.

The Industrial Revolution began in England in the mid-1700's. England quickly became the world's leading producer of iron and coal (*above*), and people began pouring into the cities in search of jobs. Many found work in factories, which required long hours of hard work for very low wages. Even young children (*left*) had to go to work, and often under dangerous conditions.

Much money was spent on making canals and better roads, and by 1830 the first commercial railways had been developed. People and goods could now move easily, and as a result towns grew bigger. The towns were full of smoky factories, for Britain had become the workshop of the world. Although these changes took more than a hundred years, they had such an immense impact that this period is known as the Industrial Revolution.

▶ **THE VICTORIAN ERA: ENGLAND REACHES THE HEIGHT OF ITS POWER**

After the reigns of George IV (1762–1830) and William IV (1765–1837), their niece Victoria (1819–1901) became queen. She was only 18, but in her early years on the throne she was helped by her Prime Minister, Lord Melbourne (1779–1848). In 1840 she married Prince Albert of Saxe-Coburg-Gotha (1819–61), a wise and patient young man. After this marriage, the name of the royal house changed from Hanover to Saxe-Coburg-Gotha.

Widespread Discontent Produces Reform

In the early 1800's, England was enormously wealthy and prosperous, yet there was much suffering and discontent among English working people. Parliament had to pass laws to prevent women and children employed in factories from being horribly overworked. Public health acts had to be passed to clean up the unsanitary towns. Middle-class people, such as merchants, became unhappy. As they grew wealthier and increased in number, they thought that the old way of electing members of Parliament did not give them their rightful share in government.

By 1830 the ruling class feared that they might have to face a joint revolution of the workers and the middle class. To divide their critics, they allowed reformers in Parliament to pass the Reform Bill (1832). This bill won over the middle class to the side of the government by giving them a greater share in elections. This was the beginning of a more democratic form of government. In 1867 a second reform bill gave the vote to many town workers. Then in 1870 a start was made toward providing public education for those too poor to pay. In 1884, Parliament gave the rural workers a vote. But women did not get the vote until 1918, and then only if they were over 30. Finally in 1928 everyone over 21 who was of sound mind and not a criminal got the vote. Today England is a complete political democracy.

Peace and Prosperity

In contrast to the 1700's, the 1800's were comparatively peaceful years for England. The other European nations were busy with their own problems. The New World and Europe bought all the woolen and cotton cloth and all the coal and iron England could produce. England no longer had to depend on its empire for markets and also had no need to fight to gain new colonies or to protect old ones. Things were going so well that England became a supporter of free trade (trade without tariffs). No other country could produce the

During the 64-year reign of Queen Victoria (*left*), Great Britain reached the height of its colonial power. In 1905 the Prince and Princess of Wales (*right*), later King George V and Queen Mary, visited India, which was considered the jewel of the British Empire.

goods England had to sell more cheaply than England could. England also wanted to keep the price of raw materials and food for its own people as low as possible. So it cut tariffs and encouraged its English-speaking colonies to become self-governing.

Imperialism in Asia and Africa

The problem of governing the non-English-speaking parts of the empire was more difficult. The English believed that parliamentary government was the right form of government for advanced people. But they did not think that their African dependencies, or India, had enough experience and Western education to run their countries democratically.

After 1871, when Germany became a united and more powerful country, England began to think that it too must increase overseas possessions. Once again it seemed important to English people to have an empire. When in 1857 part of the Indian army had mutinied against British rule, it was felt that British India could no longer be ruled jointly by the East India Company and the British Government. Therefore, in 1858, Parliament took over the full responsibility. Then in 1875, Benjamin Disraeli (1804–81), who was Prime Minister and a favorite of Queen Victoria, bought for England a large block of shares in the Suez Canal, which controlled the

shortest route to India. A year later Queen Victoria assumed the title of Empress of India.

In Africa, England was responsible for Cape Colony, which it had conquered from the Dutch in the Napoleonic Wars. England was also partially responsible for the Transvaal and the Orange Free State. These were two semi-independent states, which the Boers —the original Dutch settlers in Cape Colony —founded in the wilderness in the 1830's. In the 1880's, England, acting through chartered trading companies, got control of Nigeria, Rhodesia, and Kenya. Other European countries, such as Germany, France, Belgium, and Portugal, who also had vast African territories, were very jealous of England's new possessions.

The Boer War

The situation became even more difficult when gold was discovered in the Transvaal. Finally war broke out between the Boer republics and the British. The Boers were defeated after a tough struggle, and England took over the Transvaal and the Orange Free State. The European nations were angry with England over its defeat of the two small states. Not all the English people had approved of the Boer War either, and so in 1906 the Transvaal received self-government. In 1910 the Union of South Africa was formed.

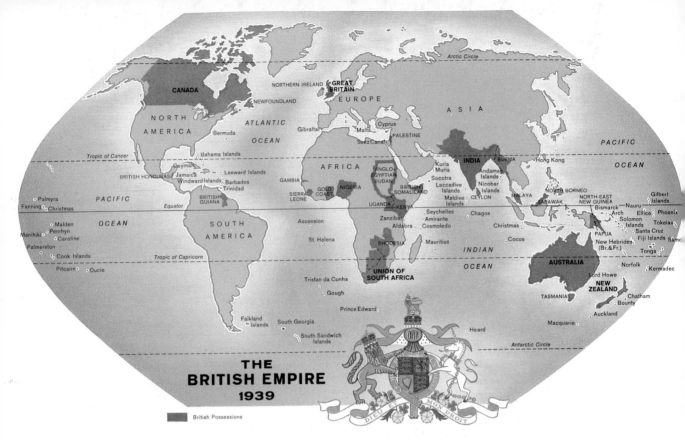

THE
BRITISH EMPIRE
1939

■ British Possessions

In 1939, the year World War II broke out in Europe, Great Britain's possessions covered much of the globe. It was said, "The sun never sets on the British Empire."

Trouble in Ireland

During Victoria's reign Ireland also became a great problem for English politicians. Since the reign of Elizabeth I, Ireland had been under English rule, although there was a separate Irish parliament at Dublin. Before 1829, though, no Roman Catholics could be elected to Parliament. Because the majority of Irish people were Roman Catholics, this made for a difficult and unhappy situation.

Finally William Pitt the Younger (1759–1806), who was prime minister, decided that the only solution would be for Ireland to give up its parliament and send representatives to a united Parliament in London as Scotland did. Reluctantly Ireland consented, and in 1801 the Act of Union was passed.

But Pitt's solution never worked well. The Irish soon came to feel that English politicians did not understand Ireland's needs and gave too little time to them. After the terrible famine in 1845 and 1846, when the potato crop failed and many Irish starved, this bitterness grew worse than ever. Many Irish people emigrated to the United States in search of new jobs. By 1870, Ireland was demanding a large measure of home rule, or self-government.

William Gladstone (1809–98), who was prime minister, came to think that this was the only solution, but Parliament would not support him. Much was done during the 1800's to meet Irish wishes. The Roman Catholics no longer had to pay money to the Protestant Church, and laws were passed to help the Irish. But nothing would now content Ireland but home rule. At the end of the century, no solution had been found.

▶ENGLAND IN THE 20TH CENTURY

When Queen Victoria died in 1901, she was succeeded by her eldest son, Edward VII (1841–1910), whose reign became known as the Edwardian Era.

By the time Edward VII became king, monarchs no longer could choose their own ministers or decide policy. They still had a great many duties to perform and documents to sign, but they had little real power. The prime minister had become the true leader of the government.

The New Political Parties

During the 1800's, politicians had slowly formed two parties. In the early part of the century, these were still called Whigs and Tories. By the second half of the century, their names were changed to Liberal and Conservative. The Liberals stressed the need for progress. The Conservatives, though not against change, were anxious to conserve what they thought best in the past. Sir Robert Peel in the first half of the century and Benjamin Disraeli in the second half were the most important Conservative prime ministers, and William Gladstone, the most famous Liberal prime minister.

By the 20th century, working people had come to feel that neither party really understood or cared enough about their needs and interests. Thus they formed a third party, which they called the Labour Party. In the Parliament in 1906 it only had 29 members in the House of Commons. Then in the 1920's, after World War I, the Liberals split into rival groups and the two biggest parties became the Labour Party and the Conservative Party. This is still true today.

World War I

Although Edward VII did not have much power, he was charming and interesting. English society became much livelier after the somber rule of his mother, Queen Victoria.

But trouble was brewing abroad. Both Edward VII and his ministers thought it wise to make friends with France, for Germany was jealous of England's empire and its navy. There was a danger of the two countries drifting into war. This eventually is what happened, although the causes of World War I are very complicated and concern other countries besides England and Germany. The war broke out in 1914, when George V (1865–1936) was king, and lasted until 1918. Germany was very strong, and England and its allies had enormous numbers of their men killed and wounded before Germany was defeated. In this struggle the colonies supported Britain. The United States joined England, too, after German submarines sank ocean liners and freighters with American passengers on board. For the first time all the English-speaking people were fighting together.

Peace was made by the Treaty of Versailles in 1919. An attempt was made to try to prevent future wars by setting up an organization called the League of Nations. The league was a failure, however. In 1933 a new leader named Adolf Hitler (1889–1945) took control of Germany. He was determined to make Germany a military power again.

World War II

For a while the British Prime Minister Neville Chamberlain (1869–1940) thought he could keep the peace by making certain concessions to Hitler. At the Munich conference in 1938, Hitler was allowed to take over the German-speaking Sudetenland, a section of Czechoslovakia. Hitler was not satisfied with this for long. He soon attacked Poland. England tried to help the Poles, fearing that Hitler would win control of all Europe and attack England, too. In 1939 war broke out between Germany and England, with France, again, as England's ally. The next year Chamberlain resigned and Winston Churchill (1874–1965) became prime minister.

Germany invaded France and forced it to make peace. England was in a very dangerous position, as German planes were able to bomb English cities and towns from French bases. Then in 1941, Germany attacked Russia, and Japan attacked the United States.

World War II marked the first time since 1066 that England's being an island did not save it from direct attack. Although England was not invaded, enemy planes did great damage in London and other cities. Fighting with Germany stopped in May, 1945, and Japan surrendered in August of the same year.

During the Battle of Britain (1940–41), when the Germans repeatedly bombed London, Prime Minister Winston Churchill boosted morale by visiting damaged areas.

Every year in June, the nation hosts an official birthday celebration for the queen. Gathered together in 1989 were (from left to right) Princess Margaret; Prince Harry; Prince William; Diana, Princess of Wales; Charles, Prince of Wales; Queen Elizabeth II; and Philip, Duke of Edinburgh.

The Empire Falls

The 1900's brought great changes to Britain, both at home and abroad. After World War II, the British Empire began to collapse, as almost all of its former colonies became independent nations. India, often called the crown jewel of the British Empire, received its independence in 1947.

One by one, Britain's African colonies were granted independence, beginning with Ghana in 1957. One of Britain's great achievements was helping to end the bitter civil war in Rhodesia. Under British supervision this former colony became the independent nation of Zimbabwe in 1980. Britain now directly governs only a few small colonies belonging to the Commonwealth of Nations, including Bermuda, the Cayman Islands, the Falkland Islands, and Gibraltar.

Foreign Affairs

Britain has strong ties with the rest of Western Europe. It has been a member of the North Atlantic Treaty Organization (NATO) since that organization was founded in 1949. In 1973, Britain joined the European Economic Community (now the European Union). And in 1979, Britain sent elected representatives to the European Parliament.

Britain is an active member of many other international organizations, including the United Nations, the Council of Europe, and the Organization for Economic Cooperation and Development.

Life in Britain Today

After the Labour Party won the election of 1945, Britain became what is called a welfare state. Since then the people have been receiving free medical, hospital, and dental care. A program called national assistance helps the poor get good housing, food, and clothing. In addition, since 1975, women have had equal rights with men where jobs and wages are concerned.

Since World War II there have been periods of widespread unemployment that have led to racial tensions between people born in Britain and the Asians and Africans who have migrated there in search of jobs. Immigration laws have been tightened, making it more difficult for people from former British colonies to settle in Britain.

The Monarchy in Recent Times

George V died before World War II broke out. He was succeeded by his son, the popular young King Edward VIII (1894–1972). But Edward was never crowned. Instead he gave up the throne to marry an American divorcée, Wallis Warfield Simpson. As the Church of England does not approve of divorce, Edward abdicated the throne and was given the title Duke of Windsor. He was succeeded by his brother George VI (1895–1952). When George VI died in 1952, his daughter Elizabeth Alexandra Mary became Queen Elizabeth II (1926–). Elizabeth's husband, Prince Philip, was named Duke of

Conservative leader Margaret Thatcher, Britain's first female prime minister, served from 1979 to 1990.

In 1997, newly elected prime minister Tony Blair posed with his wife outside 10 Downing Street, the official residence of all British prime ministers since 1735. His Labour Party won an unprecedented second term in 2001 and a third in 2005.

The world was shocked and saddened by the death of Diana, Princess of Wales, on August 31, 1997. Mourners paid tribute to the People's Princess, as she was known, leaving a sea of flowers outside Kensington Palace, her London home.

Edinburgh. Their eldest son, Charles, Prince of Wales (1948–), is heir to the throne. He has two sons by Diana, Princess of Wales (1961–97): William (1982–) and Henry (Harry) (1984–).

Charles married Lady Diana Spencer on July 29, 1981. The marriage ended in divorce in 1996, although Diana remained a favorite among the people. She died on August 31, 1997, in Paris. In 2005, Charles married Camilla Parker Bowles (1947–), who became Duchess of Cornwall.

Modern Politics

In 1979, Margaret Thatcher, leader of the Conservative Party, became the first female prime minister in British history. The Conservatives were returned to power in 1983 and 1987. Thatcher resigned in 1990, having served longer than any other prime minister in the 1900's. She was succeeded by John Major, another Conservative, who struggled to solve the nation's economic problems.

But in 1997, the Labour Party swept the general elections, and its progressive leader, Tony Blair, became prime minister. Later that year, in landmark referendums, the peoples of Scotland and Wales voted to establish home rule (their own legislatures) to oversee local affairs. They continue to be represented in the national Parliament, which remains responsible for their foreign affairs, defense, and social security.

With its landslide re-election in 2001, Blair's Labour government became the first to win two successive terms.

After September 11, 2001, the United Kingdom became a leader in the global war

on terrorism. The United Kingdom was second only to the United States in the number of troops sent to fight the Iraq War in 2003.

In 2005, Blair and his Labour Party were returned to power for a third term. However, their majority was significantly reduced, largely due to opposition to the war.

Reviewed by DON M. CREGIER
University of Prince Edward Island

See also BOER WAR; COMMONWEALTH OF NATIONS; CRIMEAN WAR; EAST INDIA COMPANY; HUNDRED YEARS' WAR; IMPERIALISM; INDUSTRIAL REVOLUTION; IRAQ WAR; MAGNA CARTA; PARLIAMENTS; REVOLUTIONARY WAR; UNITED KINGDOM; WAR OF 1812; WORLD WAR I; WORLD WAR II; and articles on individual British kings, queens, prime ministers, and military figures.

ENGLISH ART AND ARCHITECTURE

Throughout its history, English art has been influenced by that of the rest of Europe. But England has also made its own unique contributions to world art. In architecture, the English version of the Gothic style produced churches of great beauty; later English archi- tects captured the spirit of the Italian Renaissance style and transformed it to suit English needs. Perhaps most influential was the great era of English painting that began in the 1700's. This period set new standards for landscape painting and established watercolor as an important artistic medium. In the 1800's and 1900's, individual English artists continued to have an impact on international movements and trends.

▶CELTIC, ROMAN, AND ANGLO-SAXON ART

English art begins with the stone carvings and metalwork created by early Celtic tribes. The objects that survive show a love of decoration. Helmets, swords, and household goods were patterned with coils and spirals based on animal forms.

In A.D. 43, Britain was conquered by the Romans. They built fortified cities such as Londinium (London) and Aquae Sulis (Bath), which they joined by a network of paved roads. Roman engineers and craftsmen used techniques and materials from the Mediterranean to build elaborate palaces and temples, decorated with mosaic pavements and marble sculpture. Later, the Romans introduced Christianity to Britain.

After the Romans left Britain in the 400's, the country was invaded by northern European tribes, among them the Angles and Saxons. They were followed by Vikings from Scandi-

Left: The Book of Kells, an illuminated manuscript from Ireland, is a masterpiece of Celto-Saxon art. *Below:* The White Tower (center) of the Tower of London was built by William I to fortify his new capital city.

navia. From this mixture of cultures, a period of Celto-Saxon art emerged of even greater decorative richness. Much of it was portable treasure such as enameled gold jewelry set with precious stones. Objects discovered in the royal ship burial at Sutton Hoo and other sites suggest that both Christian and pagan religions were practiced.

During the 600's, missionaries arrived in Britain to strengthen Christianity there. They came from Rome and from monasteries in Ireland and Scotland. From the monasteries came the art of illuminating manuscripts. Gospels and other devotional books were copied by hand and beautifully decorated. The Book of Kells, an Irish manuscript of 760–820, is one of the best examples of this high point of Celto-Saxon art. Its richly colored illuminations interlace figures, animals, and birds with geometric designs.

▶ THE NORMAN PERIOD

In 1066, William of Normandy invaded England from northern France. He chose London as his capital and fortified it by building the Tower of London on the foundations of the old Roman fortress. William proceeded to subdue his new kingdom by installing Norman barons as feudal lords in different parts of the country. They built imposing castles on high ground as signs of their authority and as defensive strongholds for the small armies they commanded. Cathedrals such as the one at Ely had a similar purpose. Both types of buildings were solidly constructed, using heavy rounded columns and semicircular arches. These features are typical of a style of architecture called Romanesque, then popular throughout Western Europe.

▶ THE GOTHIC STYLE

By the end of the 1100's, the Romanesque style began to give way to a lighter and more delicate form of cathedral building known as the Gothic style. The Gothic style began in France and later spread to the rest of Europe. Heavy rounded columns were replaced by clusters of slender piers (pillars), and the walls were pierced by larger windows with pointed arches. Panels of stained glass in the windows were supported by delicate stone carvings called tracery. Toward the end of the 1400's the Perpendicular style developed in England. It was an even more elaborate version of

Canterbury Cathedral, begun about 1070 and completed about 1400, includes characteristics of both Romanesque and Gothic architecture.

Gothic, with wider ceiling arches spanned by fan vaulting (a modified form of tracery).

Many cathedrals took a long time to build and often reflect changes in style. Canterbury Cathedral, for instance, was begun about 1070 as a Norman church. By the time it was finished, about 1400, it was truly Gothic.

In this period were built many parish churches, still a familiar sight throughout the English countryside. A typical parish church has a long central aisle with north and south side aisles. Above the main entrance at the western end is a square tower or belfry, often topped by a pointed spire.

The roofs of English churches were made of timber and were often decorated with carved angels and painted moldings. Sculpture was used more and more to decorate churches. Saints were made to look lifelike and natural.

It was during the Gothic period that painting first became important in England. Panels and altars in churches were decorated with religious paintings. As in sculpture, painted figures were lifelike and natural. Manuscript decoration was more popular than ever before.

►TUDOR ART

When the Protestant Reformation came to England in the 1500's, church art was forbidden or destroyed, and the medieval period of art was over.

A style of architecture named for the Tudor kings developed in England during this time. King Henry VII (reigned 1485–1509) and King Henry VIII (reigned 1509–57) had much to do with the development of English art and architecture. The Tudor style of architecture combined characteristics of English Gothic with features of the Italian Renaissance style.

The main feature of Tudor architecture was the half-timber style. Wooden frames were filled with plastered panels, and the open timber roofs were painted in gold and bright colors. Tudor manor houses contained rooms of different sizes to reflect their different uses: summer and winter parlors, private dining rooms, and, in some cases, as many as forty bedrooms. Outside, a formal garden, often planted with herbs, surrounded the manor house.

In the 1500's the German-born painter Hans Holbein the Younger was the most important artistic figure in England. In 1532 he became court painter to King Henry VIII. In addition to the fine portraits he painted, he designed tapestries and royal robes. He also was sent on trips to other countries to paint portraits of possible brides for Henry.

►THE ELIZABETHAN AGE

Elizabethan portrait painters continued the traditions established in England by Holbein and his followers. They were rivalled in importance by the limners, painters of the miniature portraits that were in great demand at

Above: Little Moreton Hall, Cheshire, is an outstanding example of Tudor architecture. Its exterior consists of a wooden framework filled in with plaster, a technique known as half-timber construction.

Right: A miniature portrait of Sir Walter Raleigh is full of detail despite its tiny size. The artist, Nicholas Hilliard, made many such portraits for members of the royal court to exchange as keepsakes.

the court of Queen Elizabeth (reigned 1558–1603). Nicholas Hilliard was the Queen's limner, and he also designed medals for his royal patron.

During the Elizabethan Age, architecture showed the influence of the Renaissance. An early Elizabethan house was shaped like an E or an H with the entrance in the center. It had a great hall and broad staircases and terraces. Doorways, fireplaces, and staircases were decorated. The roofs were sloping and gabled. Later the plan of the house became square. The sloping roofs became flat. Roman columns decorated the outside, and more furniture filled the inside. As cities grew, brick was used instead of timber. Timber was growing too expensive and was proving to be a fire hazard.

►THE AGE OF THE STUARTS

In 1619 the Banqueting House in the royal palace of Whitehall was destroyed by fire.

Left: A portrait of Charles I by Anthony Van Dyck, a Flemish artist who greatly influenced English portrait traditions. *Above:* St. Paul's Cathedral, London, is the masterpiece of English architect Christopher Wren.

James I of the house of Stuart (reigned 1603–25) commissioned his architect Inigo Jones to rebuild it. Jones was one of the few Englishmen to have visited Italy and to have studied in particular the work of the great Italian architect Andrea Palladio. The Banqueting House that Jones completed in 1622 shows how strongly he favored the classical style of the Italian Renaissance. The building's influence on later English architecture cannot be overestimated.

During the reigns of James I and his son Charles I (reigned 1625–49), painters in England became aware of what was going on in the courts of Europe. The royal family began to form a fine collection of Italian paintings and became active patrons of British artists. They also persuaded important foreign artists to work at the English court. The Flemish painter Peter Paul Rubens was the leading European artist of his day. As a mark of respect, Charles I knighted Rubens and asked him to paint the canvases that decorate the ceiling of the banqueting hall at Whitehall. Anthony Van Dyck also was Flemish. In 1633 he was in-

vited by King Charles to settle in England. Van Dyck became the most outstanding figure in English art since Holbein. He established a painting tradition that has been reflected in English court portraiture ever since.

Political disturbances after 1642 led to civil war and the overthrow of the monarchy (rule by kings and queens). Royal support of the arts was ended until the monarchy was restored in 1660. Under the new king, Charles II (reigned 1660–85), Sir Peter Lely revived court portrait painting in the style of Van Dyck. Charles also began to remodel Windsor Castle with the help of painters from France and Italy. He employed the woodcarver Grinling Gibbons to create ornate carved wall panels, fireplace mantels, and other works.

The most important artistic figure associated with the court of Charles II was the architect Christopher Wren. In 1666, a great fire swept through London, and Wren was chosen to rebuild many of the buildings that had been destroyed. His greatest work is St. Paul's Cathedral (1675–1710), with its massive dome and beautifully decorated interior.

▶THE 18TH CENTURY

A style of architecture popular in the early 1700's was named for Queen Anne (reigned 1702–14). Queen Anne houses, built of brick, were boxlike in shape and had canopied doors and sashed windows. The Georgian style that followed was named for the kings who reigned from 1714 to 1830: George I, II, III, and IV. The Georgian style was even simpler than the Queen Anne style. Like the 17th-century English architect Inigo Jones, Georgian architects were greatly influenced by the Italian classical style.

The outstanding architects of the period were Robert Adam and his brother James. Between 1768 and 1772 the Adam brothers designed and built in London the Adelphi, a complex of townhouses beside the river Thames. There and elsewhere they succeeded in giving a sense of spaciousness to row houses built on narrow lots. Much of their work, as at Syon House in Middlesex, consisted of interior remodeling; they are noted for the delicate ornamentation with which they decorated the walls and ceilings of rooms that were oval, square, or round in shape. The Adam brothers also designed the furniture for many of their buildings.

A Golden Age of English Painting

The 1700's marked the beginning of a great period in English painting that lasted for more than a hundred years. Perhaps more than any other artist, William Hogarth helped to begin this period. Hogarth specialized in paintings and prints that attacked the folly and vice of the age. For example, *The Rake's Progress* (1735), a series of eight paintings, shows a rich but foolish young man going from one wrongdoing to the next, and finally ending in ruin. Hogarth was also successful in pressing for copyright laws to protect artists, and his essay *Analysis of Beauty* (1753) made an important contribution to art theory.

In 1768 the Royal Academy of Arts was founded in London with Sir Joshua Reynolds as its first president. Scholar, writer, teacher, and painter, Reynolds became a spokesman for the new, typically English kind of art that was developing. A trip to Italy in the mid-1700's had a great impact on Reynolds' art. He was also influenced by the work of Rubens. Reynolds combined these and other influences to create the English portrait in the "Grand Style," as he put it. He often included references to ancient legends in his formal portraits.

Signing the Marriage Contract, by William Hogarth, is the first in a series of six paintings entitled *Marriage à la Mode* (1745). Like other works by Hogarth, the paintings comment humorously on the customs and morals of the period.

Right: The Hay Wain (1821) is by John Constable, a leading English landscape painter. His best-known works are tranquil views of the English countryside.

Below: Sir Joshua Reynolds painted this self-portrait in 1773. As first president of the Royal Academy, he helped set a new standard for English art.

Another important portrait painter of the period was George Romney. Romney had studied in Rome and brought to his portraits the classical influence of ancient Greece and Rome.

Thomas Gainsborough was another outstanding painter of the same period. Gainsborough was one of the original members of the Royal Academy. His portraits, such as the famous *Blue Boy* (1770), are distinguished by fine brushwork and delicacy of color. Gainsborough is also recognized for his importance as a landscape painter.

English landscape painting shows the countryside for its own sake, not merely as a background. Many early landscape painters, like Thomas and Paul Sandby, trained as military artists. They were taught to make very accurate representations of what they saw. Others, like the Welsh painter Richard Wilson, were influenced by their travels to Italy and by the way artists of the 1600's such as Claude Lorrain had painted the Italian countryside. As a result, Wilson often altered the appearance of the countryside in his paintings to conform to his ideals.

The poet William Blake engraved and hand colored his own books. He printed from a single copperplate the text and illustration of each page before painting it. His style is linear, flat, and full of movement, and the pictures at first glance may appear strange. It is important to remember that Blake trained as an engraver but rejected many of the conventions of the day to develop his own artistic ideas.

▶CONSTABLE AND TURNER

By the end of the 1700's, landscape painting in Britain had reached a new level of importance as artists and writers focused on the

J. M. W. Turner painted *The "Fighting Téméraire" Tugged to Her Last Berth* (1838) as a commentary on the decline of sailing ships. The painting shows Turner's gift for capturing the effects of light on sea and cloudy skies.

beauties of nature. Like Blake, the young John Constable reacted against the academic tradition he found when he went as an art student to London. In 1802 he turned his back on the capital and returned to his native Suffolk to pursue what he described to a friend as "natural painture."

Constable found beauty in the ordinary life of farm, field, and woodland. His fresh approach resulted in delightful landscapes like *The Hay Wain* ("wain" means wagon). This painting later influenced the French painters known as the impressionists.

Unlike Constable, J. M. W. Turner grew up in London. Poor and unsociable, he began his career working as a draftsman. By the time he was in his mid-20's, he had become a member of the Royal Academy. His paintings reveal his interest in changing atmosphere and in the fleeting effects of light. The clouds seem ready to burst, trees appear to sway in the wind, and water seems almost to sweep off the canvas. Turner produced a great number of watercolors as well as oils.

England is a wet, green country. Clouds in the windswept sky change quickly from gray to white, from fluffy to thin. The climate and character of the landscape are well expressed in watercolor, a medium that flowered in England during the 1800's.

Turner was probably the best-known master of watercolor in England. But Turner himself singled out his boyhood friend Thomas Girtin, who died in 1802 at the age of 27. "Had poor Tom lived, I would have starved," was Turner's comment.

Two other artists who captured in watercolor the changing light and winds of the English countryside were John Sell Cotman and David Cox. Early in his career Cotman painted flat washes of color in simple shapes. Later he added material to his water paints to make thick, opaque colors.

▶THE VICTORIAN AGE

During Queen Victoria's reign (1837–1901), Britain emerged as the world's foremost industrial nation. But many people were critical of the society in which they lived, and many saw in art and architecture opportunities for social change.

When Augustus Welby Pugin published his essay *Contrasts* in 1837, he compared his own times unfavorably with the Middle Ages. His efforts, along with those of the great critic and writer John Ruskin, helped to promote the Gothic Revival as a reformist style. With Sir Charles Barry, Pugin was responsible for the design of the Houses of Parliament, one of the first important public buildings in Britain to look back toward medieval rather than classical architecture. Others followed, including London's Law Courts, designed by George Edmund Street.

In 1848 a group of artists formed the Pre-Raphaelite Brotherhood. Led by Dante Gabriel Rossetti, John Everett Millais, and Ford Madox Brown, they looked back to the art before the age of the Italian Renaissance painter Raphael. Other English artists began to imitate the work of painters of the Middle Ages, using jewel-like color and carefully drawn detail. Sir Edward Burne-Jones began his career as an assistant of Rossetti and developed into an important symbolist painter.

William Morris was one of the most talented men in England, a fine poet as well as an artist. He believed that the everyday objects that surround us should be made beautiful. In 1861 he founded a company to make stained-glass windows, furniture, wallpaper, and fabrics after his designs and those of his artist friends. Later he started the Kelmscott Press. One of his greatest accomplishments was an edition of Chaucer's *Canterbury Tales*. Morris beliefs formed the basis of the arts and crafts movement, which later spread to the rest of Europe and the United States.

▶THE 20TH CENTURY

To recapture the spirit of the Edwardian era (1901–10), it is necessary only to look at the romantic country houses built by the architect Sir Edwin Lutyens and the fashionable portraits painted by John Singer Sargent. (Sargent, an American, lived in London for many years.) They reflect a world of wealth and privilege that changed forever after World War I (1914–18).

The English art world had begun to undergo changes early in the century with the introduction of modern art movements. Walter Richard Sickert returned to London from Paris in 1905 to found the Camden Town Group of painters, who produced realistic depictions of everyday life. In 1910 the artist and critic Roger Fry arranged the first large-scale exhibition in London of work by the French postimpressionists. The impact was felt immediately by a new generation of students at the Slade School of Art, who rapidly aligned themselves with the modern movements. Of these, the vorticists, led by Percy Wyndham Lewis, were perhaps the most important in establishing a London-based group of abstract artists.

For a brief period in the 1930's, London competed with Paris as the center of the European art world. Artists and architects fleeing repressive governments settled in England. Among them were the German architect Walter Gropius, the Russian sculptor Naum Gabo, and the Dutch painter Piet Mondrian. This internationalism was reflected in the publication of the art journal *Circle* in 1937. The journal was a survey of international constructivist art, a popular modern art movement.

Two influential British figures were the painter Ben Nicholson and his wife, the sculptor Barbara Hepworth. During the bombing of London in World War II, they moved to the village of St. Ives, in Cornwall. There they established an artists' colony that was continued by a younger generation of artists, including the painters Roger Hilton and Peter Lanyon.

A page from an edition of the works of Chaucer published by William Morris' Kelmscott Press. Morris, a poet and artist, helped revive interest in fine design.

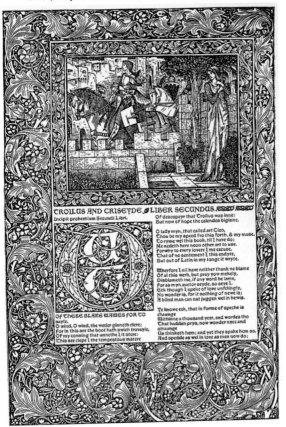

Left: *A Bigger Splash* (1967) by David Hockney depicts a scene in California, where the artist lived after 1964. *Above:* In his bronze sculpture *Reclining Figure No. 4* (1954–55), Henry Moore used simple, rounded forms to portray a human figure.

Francis Bacon based his *Study for Portrait V* (1953) on a famous portrait by Velázquez but distorted the image to produce a disturbing effect.

Internationalism has been the keynote of English art since 1945. Many English artists have lived and worked in other countries. The towering achievement of the sculptor Henry Moore is recognized worldwide. His works, with their curved shapes and interplay of solids and space, greatly influenced his contemporaries. Anthony Caro taught sculpture and created his welded metal works in both England and the United States. The earth artist Richard Long worked with the natural landscape to create innovative outdoor artworks in Europe, North and South America, Africa, and elsewhere.

Among painters, Francis Bacon gained an international reputation for his extremely powerful and often disturbing images. David Hockney, who moved to California in 1964, is perhaps the best known of the English artists who have settled abroad. His paintings, photographic collages, and other works show his mastery of different styles and mediums.

DUNCAN ROBINSON
Director, Yale Center for British Art
HERBERT B. GRIMSDITCH
Fleetway Publications, England

See also ARCHITECTURE; DECORATIVE ARTS; PAINTING; SCULPTURE.

ENGLISH LANGUAGE

In William Shakespeare's day, English was spoken by only about 5 million inhabitants of England. Today, some 400 years later, English is used by an estimated 700 million people worldwide. Of these, more than 300 million speak English as their native tongue. Most native English speakers live in the United States, Great Britain, South Africa, Canada, Australia, Ireland, and New Zealand. In many other countries, including the Bahamas, Ghana, India, Nigeria, and the Philippines, English is given special status.

English is truly a world language. It is the main language used in international trade, diplomacy, and scientific research. Most of the world's mail and computer data are written in English. English is also the language of air traffic control.

▶ DEVELOPMENT

When Julius Caesar invaded Britain in 55 B.C., he found a Celtic population—the ancestors of the present-day Irish, Scottish, and Welsh—that had lived on the island for hundreds of years. The Romans later conquered the Celts and occupied Britain from A.D. 43 to 410. Their language, Latin, had little effect on Celtic speech, and neither tongue had much influence on English, the language that succeeded them. A few Roman and Celtic place names survived and were later adopted into English. For example, the influence of the Latin word *castra*, meaning "camp" or "settlement," can be seen in the names of many English cities, including Manchester, Dorchester, and Lancaster. The terms *crag* ("steep, rugged rock") and *combe* ("valley") are Celtic words.

The ancestor of present-day English was brought to the British Isles in the 400's, after the Romans had left. Members of three Germanic tribes, the Angles, Saxons, and Jutes, migrated to England and subdued or absorbed the Celtic population. From the name of the largest group, the Angles, came the name England ("land of the Angles"). The language of the invaders became known as English.

English gradually was established in Britain, absorbing influences from later invaders: Scandinavians beginning about 750, and the Norman French in 1066. In fact, English became the world's most "absorbing" language:

It has coined words or borrowed them so freely from other languages and cultures that it now possesses the world's largest vocabulary, close to 500,000 words.

The history of the English language is divided into three major periods: Old English (450–1100), Middle English (1100–1500), and Modern English (1500 to the present).

Old English

The language of the Germanic tribes, called Old English or Anglo-Saxon, was the foundation of modern English. It was related to the ancestors of modern German, Dutch, and the Scandinavian languages. Examples of Old English are preserved in manuscripts going back to the 600's. (However, these written records reflect the literary language and not the everyday speech of the people.) Perhaps the most famous Old English poem is the heroic epic *Beowulf*, which celebrates the battles of a Danish king against a dragon and a monster named Grendel. The excerpt from *Beowulf* on page 266 shows that Old English, like a foreign language, must be translated for the modern reader.

Old English was very different from the English we use today. Its nouns and adjectives were **inflected**, that is, they had different endings to show how the word functioned in a sentence. Even the simple Modern English word *the*, which never changes, had a number of variations in Old English to indicate if the word it was used with was masculine or feminine, singular or plural, and so on.

Two events influenced the development of Old English. The first was the spread of Christianity in England during the 500's and 600's. Old English gained many new words from Latin, the language of the Church. They include *candle*, *chalk*, *dish*, *master*, *monk*, and *psalm*. However, a number of Old English words were used to express Christian concepts, including *god*, *heaven*, and *hell*.

The second influence was a series of invasions by Scandinavian people during the 800's and 900's. The Old English vocabulary was enriched by such Scandinavian words as *skin*, *skirt*, and *sky*. In addition, two important pronouns came into the language: the plural *they* and the feminine *she* replaced the native forms *hie* and *heo*. The new pronouns were much easier to distinguish from one another and from the masculine pronoun *he*.

Middle English

In 1066, William of Normandy invaded England from northern France and defeated the English army at the Battle of Hastings. William and his followers occupied England, bringing their language with them. The Norman dialect of French became the new language of the royal court.

Norman French, or more correctly, Anglo-Norman, was the official language of government in England for 300 years. But it never replaced English, which was still spoken by most of the people. The Norman rulers found that they had to learn English to communicate with the common people. French influence on the English vocabulary was small at first, limited to a few functional words like *castle* and *prison*. However, in the 1100's, the rate of borrowing increased. Many of the borrowed words have to do with areas in which French influence was strong: government and law (*prince*, *reign*, *court*), the military (*army*, *soldier*, *lieutenant*), the arts (*sculpture*, *romance*, *tragedy*), and science (*surgeon*, *anatomy*). However, the core of the vocabulary remained English, including such everyday words as *mother*, *father*, *home*, and *bread*.

The addition of French words gave English speakers the ability to express shades of meaning. For example, the French words *beef*, *veal*, *venison*, *mutton*, and *pork* refer to meats for the table, while the native English words *cow*, *calf*, *deer*, *sheep*, and *pig* are used to indicate the animal on the hoof.

When England was separated from Normandy in 1204, Anglo-Norman was cut off from its source and began to fade away. English then gradually regained its status as the language of government and culture, as well as the speech of the common people. By the 1300's, English was flourishing at the royal court and in the provinces, although the influence of French on the vocabulary would never be reversed.

Besides gaining words from French, the English of the period underwent another change. It became less inflected. Adjectives no longer changed forms to agree with their nouns, and nouns had only singular and plural forms, just as they do today. The excerpt from the Prologue to Geoffrey Chaucer's *Canterbury Tales*, written in the late 1300's, looks very much like modern English.

Modern English

The Modern English period is often said to have begun in 1500, shortly after the first printing press was introduced into England. Early Modern English did not completely resemble today's English. The excerpt from Shakespeare's *Hamlet*, reproduced in the original spelling of the 1623 edition, shows the similarities and differences.

Modern English differs from Middle English in pronunciation. Over a period of a hundred years or more, a series of changes occurred in the pronunciation of English vowels. Modern English differs in grammar as well. It continues the Middle English trend toward simplification of inflections, though it makes up for this loss by becoming more complex in its rules for syntax, or word order.

The invention of printing helped to **standardize** written English, that is, to establish commonly accepted spelling and usage of words. The publication of grammar books and dictionaries beginning in the 1700's also helped to standardize English. However, it took more than 200 years to reduce variations in spelling, and English usage still remains the subject of strong debate.

The Growth of Modern English. England became a world power beginning in the 1600's, colonizing areas in Africa, Asia, the Pacific, and North America. As the British Empire spread, so did English.

In turn, English was enriched by words from the colonies. For example, American English took many words from American Indian languages, especially words for native plants and animals unfamiliar to the English colonists. *Moose*, *skunk*, *squash*, and *woodchuck* are all of Indian origin. So are many American place names.

As English spread, it developed distinct varieties, and each nation where English is used has established its own standard. In the United States, for example, vocabulary, usage, and spelling are different from that of England. Americans say *elevator*, *apartment*, and *fries*, while the English prefer *lift*, *flat*, and *chips*. In the 1920's, American English was popularized in England through Hollywood films, to the distress of some in England who feared their language would be corrupted. The Australian greeting *G'day* was spread abroad in the 1980's through film and television. Of particular interest to scholars today are the varieties of English that have become established in Africa, Asia, and the West Indies.

The development of American English has been influenced by the many ethnic groups that make up the population of the country. A small sampling of common words illustrates the impact of these groups on the American vocabulary: *rodeo* from Spanish, *kindergarten* from German, *pizza* from Italian, *klutz* from Yiddish. Black English, which shows the influence of West African languages, has contributed many words and expressions. Some, like *jazz*, are of unknown origin. Others, like *soul*, give new meanings to existing words.

Today, English, like all living languages, continues to grow and change. Old words are discarded and new ones coined or borrowed. Rapid developments in technology are reflected in the language, and some technical terms also work their way into ordinary English speech: It is common now to talk of *lasers*, *software*, and *meltdowns*. New words come from many other sources as well, from slang to fashion to sports. Speakers of English continue their efforts to improve the language. Most recent has been the move to put an end to sexism in English usage by using terms that could apply to both men and women—firefighter instead of fireman, for example. And while English remains a borrowing language, it has become a lender as well. French, German, and Japanese borrow freely from English —so freely that the French government, for one, has tried to make the use of English words illegal in France.

It is likely that English will remain the world's most important language for some time to come. There are no major competitors waiting to take over. However, no language situation is ever permanent. Greek, Latin, and French lost their worldwide influence, and there is no reason to suppose that English will retain its present status forever.

DENNIS BARON
Author, *Grammar and Good Taste: Reforming the American Language*

ENGLISH LITERATURE

English literature had its beginnings with works written in about the 6th century. These early works were written in a language that few today would recognize as English. Called Old English, or Anglo-Saxon, it was the language of England for a long time before the Norman Conquest in A.D. 1066 and for some 100 years afterward.

Gradually Old English changed into Middle English, the language in which Chaucer's works are written. Middle English, too, is different from modern English. Yet in it one finds many of the elements of the English language as it is now written and spoken.

By the time of Queen Elizabeth I's reign (1558–1603), English was spoken and written basically as it is today. In all the centuries since, the English language has undergone gradual changes.

▶OLD ENGLISH LITERATURE

The study of English literature usually begins with the Anglo-Saxon epic poem *Beowulf*. From the names of historical persons mentioned, we can place the time of its story around the 6th century. The only manuscript of *Beowulf*, written down sometime in the 10th century, is preserved in the British Museum in London.

The setting of *Beowulf* is not England but Denmark. The poem tells how the great feasting hall of King Hrothgar, the Dane, is raided repeatedly by Grendel, a frightful sea monster. Beowulf comes from Sweden to aid Hrothgar. He slays Grendel and, in an undersea struggle, also kills Grendel's equally dangerous mother. In later years Beowulf, king of his own land, dies in the act of killing a fire dragon that is menacing his people.

Although ancient pagan myths lie beneath the story, Beowulf is a Christian epic. Its hero-king stands for Christian virtues. He lives his life and goes to his death in devoted service to other people. References to biblical stories are frequent in Beowulf, and Grendel is said to be descended from Cain, the first murderer.

Other poems from the Old English era, some perhaps older than *Beowulf,* include *The Wanderer* and *The Seafarer*. Like *Beowulf* they are by unknown authors. *The Wanderer* relates the sorrowful journeyings of a man driven from his home after the death of his

The legends of King Arthur and his knights of the Round Table have inspired many famous works of English literature, from the Middle Ages to the present day.

lord. The second is thought to be a dialogue between a youth and an old sailor; it talks of the hardships and joys of seafaring life. Other Old English works, such as *The Battle of Maldon,* deal with war.

The names of two Old English writers known for their poetry have come down to us. Caedmon, in the 7th century, wrote a creation hymn, of which only a few lines survive. He was said to have been an ignorant shepherd suddenly inspired, through visions, to sing praises of the creation. The poet Cynewulf lived into the early 9th century. Several works are known to be his.

King Alfred (849–99?) is an important figure in Old English literature and the only monarch England has honored as "the Great." Alfred's interests went beyond his duties as a ruler and warrior. He pursued learning to a degree unusual for his time.

A foundation stone of English history is *The Anglo-Saxon Chronicle*. The *Chronicle* gives the events of English history from the Roman invasion of Britain in 54 B.C. to the middle of the 12th century. It was begun by Alfred, or under his direction, although it included some still earlier chronicles. The King also made or directed the translation from Latin to Old English of many important religious, philosophical, and historical books from Europe. These translations did much to advance learning in the kingdom.

Nearly two centuries earlier there lived a historian-monk known as the Venerable Bede (673–735). It was he who quoted the lines of Caedmon's hymn that have come down to us. Bede also wrote in Latin the earliest major prose work in England, the *Church History of the English People* (731). Alfred had the history translated into Old English. After Alfred's time two more writers arose from within the church: Wulfstan, who died in 1023, and Aelfric, who died about 1020. Their work is entirely religious.

▶ MIDDLE ENGLISH LITERATURE

The Middle English period, generally defined as 1100 to 1500, sees the true beginning of the great heritage of English literature.

Latin was for a long time the language of learning. Because of this, many works of the Middle English period were first written in Latin. Scholars, historians, and churchmen particularly favored Latin. Such was the case with the monk Geoffrey of Monmouth (1100?–54), who wrote *History of the Kings of Britain.* So much of the work is legend that it may be called romance as well as history. It is especially important as an early source of the legends of King Arthur and his court. For centuries the characters in the Arthurian legends have been more than mere characters. They represent the courtly ideals of chivalry, courage, nobility, and virtue.

Indirectly derived from Geoffrey's Latin history is the *Brut* (Brutus) of Layamon, written about 1205. It contains the first accounts in English of Arthur, as well as of King Lear and Cymbeline, both of whom became the subjects of later writers, most notably Shakespeare.

Two other romances related to Arthur are among Middle English masterpieces. *Sir Gawain and the Green Knight* (14th century) is a superb poem of unknown authorship. It tells how on a certain New Year's Day a green-clad knight appears in King Arthur's court and challenges anyone to match him blow for blow with a battle-ax. The knight is to receive the first blow. Gawain accepts the challenge and strikes off the stranger's head. The Green Knight calmly picks up his severed head and, before riding off with it, tells Gawain to meet him at an appointed place one year later to receive the return blow. The tale relates Gawain's strange and fearsome adventures in carrying out his promise.

Le Morte Darthur ("The Death of Arthur") (1469–70) is a prose work by Sir Thomas Malory (died 1471). His great work, adapted from French stories and other sources, was written while Malory was in prison. One of his sources was an obscure (not well known) 14th-century epic poem, *Morte Arthure.*

Malory's book is the most complete single collection of the stories of Arthur and the knights of the Round Table. It has inspired widely different works. These include Tennyson's poems *The Idylls of the King,* which appeared between 1859 and 1885, and T. H. White's novel *The Once and Future King* (1958).

Le Morte Darthur has another historic distinction. It was among the earliest books printed in England on the press of the first English printer, William Caxton (1422?–91).

Quite a different kind of major 14th-century work is *Piers Plowman.* The poem is a **moral allegory**, a story told to teach or explain something. William Langland (1332?–1400?) is usually credited with writing *Piers Plowman,* but some scholars regard its authorship as unknown.

The mixture of languages in these centuries is reflected in the works of John Gower (1325–1408). His *Mirour de l'Omme* ("Mirror of Man") (1377?) is in French. *Vox Clamantis* ("The Voice of One Crying") (1382) is in Latin. And his most famous work, *Confessio Amantis* ("The Lover's Confession") (1390?), in spite of its title, is in English.

Chaucer

By far the greatest name in Middle English literature is that of Geoffrey Chaucer (1343?–1400). This poet was also an experienced man of the world. He enjoyed the favor of three kings—Edward III, Richard II, and Henry IV —and held many responsible posts in government. In his youth he served in the French wars and was taken prisoner. His duties for the Crown took him to Italy, which was a source for many of his later tales.

Chaucer was a productive poet of such merit that he is named in that trio of English poetry giants: Chaucer, Shakespeare, and Milton. Among his works are *The Parliament of Fowls* and *The Legend of Good Women,* both supposed dream visions, written between 1372 and 1386. His *Troilus and Criseyde,* of the same period, is a romance of the Trojan War.

His masterpiece is *The Canterbury Tales* (1387?). In the Middle Ages it was a common device of storytellers to gather together a series of tales loosely related in some way. Chaucer joins a group of travelers at the Tabard Inn, on the bank of the Thames River in the Southwark section of London. They are all bent on a pilgrimage to Canterbury Cathedral, to the tomb of the martyred Saint Thomas à Becket. Urged by the host of the Tabard, who accompanies them, the pilgrims agree to tell tales to lighten the journey.

Chaucer did not complete his total design, but there are 24 tales, most of them with brief prologues, or introductions. The General Prologue itself is a remarkable performance, setting the scene and introducing all the pilgrims with vivid character sketches.

Chaucer is a storyteller of genius. Like Shakespeare after him, he drew his stories from many sources. To all the stories he brought fresh vision. In event and in character, then, they became Chaucer's own, expressed with superb poetic craft. *The Canterbury Tales* abound in lusty humor but touch many other moods and styles. His characters—the knight, nuns, priests, landowner, scholar, miller, housewife, civil and church officials, farmer, and many others—represent a cross section of medieval life.

Every human type is known to him. He admires some and holds others in disregard. Yet both his admirations and dislikes are lightened with the grace of humor and deep understanding of humanity. Dryden, the 17th-century translator, poet, and critic, said of Chaucer's work, "here is God's plenty."

Middle English Drama

Religious drama, an important part of Middle English literature, was not created for reading. It grew out of the life and faith of the era. The origins of drama are bound up with worship. In the Middle Ages few could read. One of the ways the Christian story and the lessons of the Bible could be brought to the people was by simple dramatic scenes. In time these dramas spread from within the church building to the streets and public squares. Dramas were especially popular at important seasons of the Christian year. When the plays were put on outside, they were often presented on a procession of wagons. On each wagon, called a *pagyn,* a scene was acted. From *pagyn* comes the word "pageant."

Certain guilds—as groups of merchants and laborers called themselves—performed certain biblical stories. Plasterers presented the creation. Shipwrights had charge of building Noah's ark, and water carriers provided the flood. Goldsmiths fitted out the three kings for the Nativity.

These dramas, based on saints' miracles and the biblical miracles, were called **miracle plays.** The performance of several great cycles, or groups, of the plays became an annual event in England and Europe. Different towns' guilds presented their own cycles, and texts from several towns have been preserved. From York comes a cycle of 48 dramas that

A portrait of Geoffrey Chaucer appears on this hand-copied page from *The Canterbury Tales.* The tales portray lively scenes of medieval English life.

cover the whole of biblical history. Perhaps the most widely read of all is the *Second Shepherds' Play,* a drama about the Nativity from the town of Wakefield.

Another type of play was the **morality**, a form of allegory. In this kind of allegory each character represents a social type or a certain character trait. The greatest allegorical morality play is *Everyman* (15th century), which shows the summoning of Everyman by Death. When Everyman seeks friends to go with him, Fellowship, Beauty, Strength, and other such companions all abandon him. Only Good Deeds enters with him into the grave.

▶EARLY 16TH CENTURY

The 16th century was an exciting time for literature. The first half of the century saw the development of new literary forms and styles, which would reach full bloom in the second half of the century during the long reign of Elizabeth I.

Early in the century Sir Thomas More (1478–1535) wrote a remarkable book, *Utopia* (1516). Its title comes from the Greek word meaning "nowhere." It tells of a journey to an imaginary island named Utopia, where an ideal form of society exists. From Plato to modern times certain writers have created imaginary perfect societies. More's book has placed a word in our vocabularies and given the name to all literature of this kind, which has since been called Utopian.

Another prose writer of this period was Roger Ascham (1515–68). *The Schoolmaster,* his principal work, published after his death, is a criticism of educational methods.

Among the poets of the early 16th century, Sir Thomas Wyatt (1503–42), with the Earl of Surrey (1517–47), established the **sonnet**, a 14-line poem, as an English verse form. It was adopted from an Italian tradition but became a major form in all English poetry that followed.

The theater of pure entertainment grew, replacing the religious shows of the Middle English period. Two of the best early nonchurch, or secular, plays were **farces**—funny plays filled with ridiculous happenings. Nicholas Udall (1505–56) wrote *Ralph Roister Doister* (1553?); John Still (1543–1608) is believed to have written *Gammer Gurton's Needle* (1566?); Thomas Norton (1532–84) and Thomas Sackville (1536–1608) wrote the *Tragedy of Gorboduc* (1562).

▶THE ELIZABETHAN AGE

Elizabeth I reigned from 1558 to 1603, a period that saw new strengths and glories for England. This was due partly to Elizabeth's intelligence and force of character and partly to the flow of historical events. England became the leading sea power. It sent explorers to make settlements in the New World. It experienced a burst of literary brilliance that began slowly and reached a peak with the achievement of William Shakespeare.

The earliest writer clearly belonging to this era is John Lyly (1554?–1606). Although he wrote a number of plays, his name lives because of a single prose work, *Euphues: The Anatomy of Wit* (1578). It has been called the first English novel, but its form differs greatly from that of later novels. There was a sequel in 1580, *Euphues and his England.* Lyly's works launched a fashion for an ornate, flowery style of writing. The style came to be known as **euphuism**.

Elizabethan Poets

Sir Philip Sidney (1554–86) was a courtier as well as a man of letters. He was a master of the sonnet, and some of his finest work is in the series called *Astrophel and Stella,* published five years after his death.

Some Elizabethans wrote for the love of writing, not for gain or as a means of earning a living. For Shakespeare, Marlowe, Jonson, and other great writers, their work was indeed a livelihood. But the knights and courtiers, such as Wyatt, Surrey, Sidney, and Raleigh, were gentlemen-poets. They wrote for their own pleasure and that of their friends. The courtier poets developed a highly formal kind of verse. Musical and clever in style, it is characteristic of 16th-century writing.

Edmund Spenser (1552?–99) is the greatest of the early Elizabethan poets. His masterpiece is the long poem *The Faerie Queene,* published in two parts in 1590 and 1596. The poem is many things. It is a tale of knighthood and of a valiant champion against evil. It is a moral allegory. It is also a tribute to Queen Elizabeth. The form of the poem is both beautiful and complex. Spenser invented a rhyme pattern that he used in 9-line stanzas, or groups of verse, called the **Spenserian stanza**, which was later used by many English poets.

Spenser, like Sidney, wrote a **sonnet sequence**—a group of sonnets united by one theme. The sonnets that make up *Amoretti* are lovely, as is the wedding song *Epithalamion*. Both were published in 1595. The earlier *Shepheardes Calender* (1579) had shown at once that Spenser was a major poet.

Sir Walter Raleigh (1554?–1618) played a part in the history of the New World as the founder of the earliest Virginia colony, Roanoke, in 1585. He also wrote some excellent lyric poetry. He was a friend of Spenser's and composed a sonnet of tribute, published with *The Faerie Queene*. Among his prose works are *Discovery of Guiana* (1596) and *History of the World* (1614).

Michael Drayton (1563–1631) is best remembered for the popular and splendid "Ballad of Agincourt," written in memory of Henry V's triumph in France. Drayton produced a large body of poetry—historical, religious, and pastoral. **Pastoral poetry** deals with rural people and scenes. Drayton wrote lyric poetry as well. Two other lyricists of the period were Thomas Campion (1567–1620) and Sir Edward Dyer (1543?–1607).

Shakespeare and Other Elizabethan Dramatists

More than any other form of literature, drama flourished in this age. It contained the greatest of the poetry, although the plays were written to be performed. Their preservation in print, somewhat a matter of chance, was our great good fortune.

The stage of this time had come far from the wagons or crude platforms of the medieval miracle plays. The greatest Elizabethan theater was the famous Globe. There many of Shakespeare's plays were given between its opening in 1599 and its burning in 1613. It was a high building that Shakespeare described as shaped like a "wooden O." Playgoers paid 3 pennies to sit in the covered balconies that were one above the other. For a penny spectators stood in the uncovered ground area called the pit.

Like William Shakespeare (1564–1616), many of the playwrights were actors also. They drew their plays' plots from a common stock: historical and classical stories, romances, and farces. Of all Shakespeare's plays, only one, *The Tempest*, is original in the modern sense. Many hands sometimes patched and reworked lesser plays. The early *Henry VI* plays of Shakespeare are probably a doctoring up of other scripts rather than his

work alone. His great plays, however, are truly his. To these he brought an unmatched genius for stagecraft, poetry, and insight into human character. The genius served him in comedies and tragedies alike. These masterful plays have dominated English-speaking stages ever since they were written. They have been translated into every major language.

Shakespeare's plays fall into categories, or classes. He excelled in each kind. The tragedies include *Romeo and Juliet* (1595), *Hamlet* (1602), *Othello* (1604), *King Lear* (1605), and *Macbeth* (1606). Among the comedies are *The Taming of the Shrew* (1596), *A Midsummer Night's Dream* (1595), *As You Like It* (1599), *Twelfth Night* (1600), and *The Tempest* (1611). Shakespeare's chronicle plays, based on English history, include such masterworks as *Richard III* (1595), *Richard II* (1595), *Henry IV*, parts I and II (1597–98), and *Henry V* (1599). *Julius Caesar* (1599) and *Antony and Cleopatra* (1607) are outstanding tragedies on classical themes.

The greatness of the plays should not overshadow Shakespeare's other poetry. *Venus and Adonis* (1593) and *The Rape of Lucrece* (1594), two brilliant narrative poems, retell two classical stories. Then there are his 154 sonnets. These, dealing primarily with many moods of love, overshadow all the other sonnets of the time.

Shakespeare, who went to London from Stratford-on-Avon as an actor, pursued his two careers with immense success. He became one of the partners who owned the Chamberlain's Men, a company of actors. In his later years, having prospered greatly, he retired to Stratford. He died there on April 23, 1616.

This bustling age of theater had many playwrights. A few were men of considerable talent. Others had less. After Shakespeare, Christopher Marlowe (1564–93) holds second rank. "Marlowe's mighty line" was Ben Jonson's tribute to the poetic power of this fine dramatist. Had he lived longer, Marlowe might have made an even greater contribution to English literature. As a result of a quarrel, he was stabbed to death in a tavern brawl.

He left four major works. These show what might have come in the maturity of a man so gifted. *The Tragical History of Dr. Faustus* (1589) is the best known but not necessarily the best of his works. It is still often played. *Tamburlaine the Great* (1587), his first play, concerns the rise and fall of the ruthless conqueror Tamburlaine. *The Jew of Malta* (1590), popular in its time, is a cruder treatment of a theme Shakespeare handled more gracefully in *The Merchant of Venice.* Marlowe's last play, *Edward II* (1592), has great merit. It is a chronicle play, similar to but not the equal of Shakespeare's *Richard II.*

Thomas Kyd (1557?–95?) wrote several plays, notably the immensely popular *Spanish Tragedy* (1586?). Darkly melodramatic, it is the prime example of the revenge play. A terrible vengeance for some wrong is the mainspring of the story. *Hamlet,* too, is a revenge play. But Shakespeare's genius carries it to heights of drama and depths of character far beyond ordinary melodrama.

Robert Greene (1560?–92) wrote novels and romances in the manner of Lyly, as well as poems and plays. Jealous of those who prospered more than he, Greene savagely attacked Shakespeare in his autobiographical pamphlet, "Groatsworth of Wit bought with a Million of Repentance" (1592). His comedy, *Friar Bacon and Friar Bungay,* published two years after his death, is the only one of his plays that is much read.

The plays of Thomas Middleton (1570?–1627) and John Marston (1575?–1634) are rarely performed today, but they have historical interest. *The Duchess of Malfi* by John Webster (1580?–1625?) is often revived, as is *The Shoemaker's Holiday* of Thomas Dekker (1572?–1632?). Francis Beaumont (1584–1616) and John Fletcher (1579–1625) jointly wrote *The Knight of the Burning Pestle* (1608) and other plays. Very often two or more men collaborated in writing a play. As a result, the threads of authorship of many minor plays are much entangled.

Like Marlowe, Ben Jonson (1573?–1637) ranks directly after Shakespeare. Jonson wrote many plays and many **masques**—poetic entertainments with elaborate pageantry, for production at court or at great estates. His best plays are his comedies, especially *Every Man In his Humour* (1598), *Volpone* (1606), *The Silent Woman* (1609), *The Alchemist* (1610), and *Bartholomew Fair* (1614).

Jonson, a devoted friend of Shakespeare's, was his guest at New Place, in Stratford, near the time of the great playwright's death. Jonson was among those who helped preserve Shakespeare's plays in print. For the First

The poet and playwright William Shakespeare is England's greatest poet and dramatist. His plays are among the best-loved works of the English language.

Ben Jonson, a friend of Shakespeare's, wrote popular comic plays and was England's first official poet laureate.

Folio of the plays, published in 1623, Jonson wrote "To the Memory of My Beloved, the Author Mr. William Shakespeare." In this fine memorial poem occurs the line, "He was not of an age, but for all time!"

From 1619 to 1637, Ben Jonson was England's **poet laureate**, a court official who wrote poems for special occasions and received a yearly fee. Earlier poets had been called laureates, but Jonson was the first officially appointed to that office.

▶EARLY 17TH CENTURY

Literature cannot really be divided into exact periods. Any such divisions actually overlap and blend into one another. Thus the late Elizabethans are also Jacobeans. This term comes from the Latin form of the name of King James I, Jacobus. With his reign, beginning in 1603, the Scottish family of Stuarts took over the Tudors' throne.

The King James Bible

A permanent monument of English literary style commemorates James's name. He ordered the translation of the Holy Scriptures known as the King James Bible (1611). This was not the first English translation. It owed a

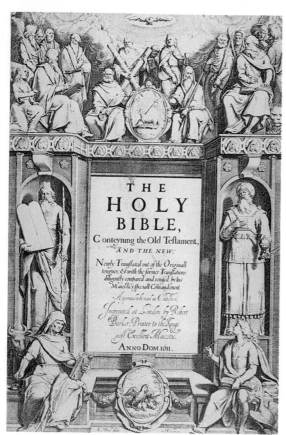

The first edition of the King James translation of the Bible was printed in 1611. Its stately language still influences writers of English.

debt to the earlier versions done by William Tyndale (1492?–1536) and Miles Coverdale (1488–1568). There was also the Bible of the English College at Douai, France, which is still the chief English text used by Roman Catholics. There have been many translations since, yet the King James Version will probably never be matched for majesty of language. For many generations it exerted a greater influence on style and standards of taste than any other single work in English.

Essays and Other Prose

The *Essays* of Francis Bacon (1561–1626) made popular in English a literary form widely practiced afterward. The essay is generally regarded as the invention of the French writer Michel de Montaigne (1533–92). Bacon was a public figure and statesman of importance under both Elizabeth and James, rising to the high post of lord chancellor. A scandal ended his public service in 1621. He devoted the rest of his life to literature and scholarship. The

Novum Organum (1620), written in Latin, sets forth a new method of approaching knowledge. *The New Atlantis* (1627) is a study in political philosophy. These are representative of a large body of Bacon's work. Yet it is the most informal and casual of his works, the *Essays,* that is read most often.

In 1621, Robert Burton (1577–1640) published *The Anatomy of Melancholy.* This unusual work is part medical lore, part philosophy. It is one of the important reflections of 17th-century knowledge and thought.

Sir Thomas Browne (1605–82) was a physician who studied science at great universities on the continent. He was also a man of letters. The most important of his works is *Religio Medici* (1643). Written many years before its publication, it was intended for circulation among his friends. *Religio Medici* examines the questions that Browne's medical science posed to his religion. Great beauty of spirit shines in the book, which calmly faces mysteries that yield no ready answers.

Cavalier and Metaphysical Poetry

Among the poets of this time, some were light-spirited, courtly, romantic lyricists of the kind found among the Elizabethans. Some supporters of King Charles I were clever poets who came to be known as the Cavalier poets. Robert Herrick (1591–1674), Sir John Suckling (1609–42), and Richard Lovelace (1618–58) are among these.

Another group of poets, many of whom also wrote in the lighter fashion, developed a new vein of poetry. These poets rebelled against artificial, worn-out subjects such as nymphs, shepherdesses, and fauns. The more thoughtful poets still kept all the frills of poetic form and style, adding more of their own. But they added new philosophical and religious themes that probed into man's nature and problems. A number of the poems are highly complex. Eighteenth-century critics termed such work metaphysical, meaning that it was subtle, puzzling, and often difficult to understand. The critics were not being complimentary. Yet the metaphysical poets have grown in importance.

The chief voice of this poetic movement was John Donne (1572–1631), whose excellent poetry showed only one side of his talents. A complex and worldly man, Donne became an Anglican priest and was the favorite preacher of both James I and Charles I. In an age of fine prose writing, Donne's religious prose is outstanding. He wrote sermons, meditations, and devotions. Another leading writer of devotions was Jeremy Taylor (1613–67).

Four other metaphysical poets deserve mention. The most important is George Herbert (1593–1633). Almost all his verse of a religious nature is included in the collection *The Temple* (1633). Richard Crashaw (1612?–49), Henry Vaughan (1622–95), and Thomas Traherne (1636?–74) also wrote poetry in the fashion of Donne.

▶ REVOLUTION AND RESTORATION

Midway through the 17th century, England felt a kind of earthquake. A force called Puritanism shook the land. It affected not only religion and politics, but literature as well.

Since the time of Henry VIII there had been a movement in England to reform the Church of Rome, which led to the creation of a separate Church of England. But there were some who wanted to simplify worship far more, to purify it, they believed. These people, known as Puritans, were opposed to crosses, images, robes, incense, and sometimes even music.

The Church of England did not look kindly on these people who wanted to change the church. As a result, some of the Puritans left England, sailed across the Atlantic, and settled in New England. There they could worship as they pleased. In their old country they left behind complex religious and political questions. At last the questions flared into open war between King Charles I and Parliament. Charles, defeated by Oliver Cromwell's forces, was tried by Parliament and beheaded. From 1653 until his death in 1658, Cromwell, actually a dictator, ruled England as lord protector. In 1660 the late king's son returned to England and ascended the throne as Charles II. This return to monarchy (rule by kings and queens) is called the Restoration.

John Milton

The literary giant of the century, John Milton (1608–74), was much bound up in these events. His literary talents showed themselves in early works. The twin poems "L'Allegro" and "Il Penseroso" present two different views of life—that of the lively man and that of the thoughtful man. The masque *Comus* was presented in 1634. "Lycidas" honors the memory of a dead friend. But religious and

The poet John Milton ranks with Chaucer and Shakespeare as a giant of English literature. Blind after 1652, Milton composed his greatest works in his mind and then dictated them to his daughters.

political disputes also interested Milton, and he wrote many pamphlets on these subjects. The most famous of them is *Areopagitica* (1644). The title comes from the Areopagus, a Greek place of debate. *Areopagitica* gives one of the most eloquent of all pleas for freedom of the press.

Milton took the side of Parliament in the Civil War and wrote pamphlets supporting the king's execution. During the protectorate he served as Latin secretary to Cromwell, composing many state documents in that language.

When Charles II came to the throne in 1660, Milton's position was endangered. He was heavily fined. Three things helped save his life. He was a famous poet, his friends used their influence, and he had been totally blind since 1652. Much of his state work, and the major poems yet to come, were done under the handicap of blindness. By astonishing powers of concentration he composed in his mind and then dictated.

During his retirement from public life he produced his masterpieces: the epic *Paradise Lost* (1667); its sequel, *Paradise Regained* (1671); and the poetic tragedy *Samson Agonistes* (1671).

John Dryden

The poet of this period who ranks next in importance to Milton is John Dryden (1631–1700). As a poet and dramatist Dryden had popular success. As a critic he came close to being literary ruler of the latter part of his century. He was named poet laureate in 1668 but later lost the honor for political reasons. His total output, including translations, is huge.

Representative are *All for Love* (1678), a tragedy about Antony and Cleopatra; the comedy *Marriage-à-la-Mode* (1673); the critical study *Essay on Dramatic Poesie* (1668); and the satire *Absalom and Achitophel* (1681).

Dryden excelled at a form of verse called the **heroic couplet**. (A couplet is a pair of rhyming lines within a poem that often contains a complete thought.) The heroic couplet was so named because some English writers used it in an effort to match the heroic verse of Latin and Greek classics. From the later writers' efforts to create "new classics" comes the expression **neoclassicism**.

John Bunyan

A third major figure remains in the 17th century, standing outside the main literary currents. He is John Bunyan (1628–88).

Early in life he joined a Baptist church, a nonconformist group outside the Church of England. Arrested in 1660 for preaching without a license, he spent twelve years in prison for his religious beliefs. There he began writing. Both his autobiography, *Grace Abounding to the Chief of Sinners,* and *The Holy City: Or, The New Jerusalem* appeared in 1666. During a later, shorter prison term Bunyan wrote *The Pilgrim's Progress from this world, to That which is to come* (1678).

This most famous religious allegory, usually called simply *Pilgrim's Progress,* describes a dream. Christian, the pilgrim, flees from the City of Destruction. He encounters many difficulties, dangers, and temptations in such places as the Slough of Despond, Doubting Castle of the Giant Despair, and Vanity Fair. While traveling he meets such persons as Mr. Worldly Wiseman, Faithful, and Good-Will. At last he reaches the Celestial City.

Pilgrim's Progress is a powerful tale with deep meaning. For years it was, along with the Bible, a staple in Christian homes, especially on the American frontier. It has been translated into more than 100 languages. A second part of *Pilgrim's Progress* describes the later journey of Christian's wife and children. Bunyan's other works, on similar themes, are *The Life and Death of Mr. Badman* (1680) and *The Holy War* (1682).

Diarists

Two diarists left valuable and lively records of the 17th century. The better known and more entertaining of these is Samuel Pepys (1633–1703). He moved in prominent circles and held a high post in the admiralty. His honest records of his own private weaknesses are amusing. More important, we learn much from him about politics and public events. Pepys gives vivid accounts of many dramatic happenings, among them the great fire that destroyed most of old London in 1666. The diary of the scholarly John Evelyn (1620–1706) does this also, but Evelyn's diary, not so lively as Pepys's, is less widely read. It is nevertheless a document of equal historical importance. Neither man, of course, wrote with the intention of publication.

▶ 18TH CENTURY

Eighteenth-century English literature is marked by a shift from the mood and tone of 17th-century literature. For one thing, a second great political disturbance took place in the late 17th century. This was the Revolution of 1688. King James II tried to make Catholicism the official religion of England. After a struggle, he was forced to give up the throne and withdraw to the Continent. Both of the English political parties, the Whigs and the Tories, offered the throne to Prince William of Orange and his wife Mary as co-monarchs. They ruled together from 1689 until 1694, when Mary died. William then ruled alone until his death in 1702.

Intellectual activity sets the 18th century apart. It was an age of wit, when great importance was placed on clarity of expression and the power of reason. It was an age of skepticism, when thinking people questioned previously accepted beliefs. Conversationalists and letter writers flourished in literary circles and gathered in London clubs. The first important dictionary of the language was produced. **Satire**, a form of writing that ridicules human vices and follies, expressed the spirit of the time. Many satirical comedies were written for the theater. Satire also found a powerful means of expression in a form that came to full growth in the 20th century—the novel.

Drama

The restoration of the monarchy in 1660 ushered in a great theater revival. **Restoration drama** possessed stored-up energy, for the Puritans had closed all theaters, holding them to be immoral.

The Beggar's Opera (1728) was a play by John Gay with musical numbers based on popular ballads. Its tale of thieves and cutthroats was really a satire of the British government. This scene from an early production was painted by artist William Hogarth.

Freed from Puritan control, the theater seemed to go out of its way to be frivolous and scandalous. Restoration comedies were **comedies of manners**, often called drawing-room comedies. In these plays characters patterned after high-society types sometimes behaved badly. They found themselves in foolish situations. The comedies, sparkling with witty dialogue, shocked some people. Laughter returned to the theater, and by the second half of the 18th century the comedy of manners had reached its highest point.

All Restoration drama was not comical. Among the writers of serious plays were Dryden and Thomas Otway (1652–85). Otway's best-remembered tragedy is *Venice Preserved* (1682). Comedies, however, dominated the age. History credits Sir George Etherege (1635?–91?) with beginning the period of Restoration comedy. Following his lead were William Wycherley (1641–1716), Sir John Vanbrugh (1664–1726), William Congreve (1670–1729), and George Farquhar (1678–1707). Congreve's *The Way of the World* (1700) and Farquhar's *The Beaux' Stratagem* (1707) are outstanding.

John Gay (1685–1732) wrote one of the great popular successes of his time, *The Beggar's Opera* (1728), a play with ballads. Its tale of cutthroats and highwaymen was really a satire of the government of Sir Robert Walpole, the British prime minister.

Walpole's anger at satires by Gay and other playwrights led to the passing of the Licensing Act of 1737. All theaters except Covent Garden and Drury Lane were closed, and all plays were subject to censorship by the government. These restrictions hurt the vitality of the English theater. Many of the best dramatists turned to other forms of literature.

Late in the century, drama revived again with the works of Oliver Goldsmith (1730?–74) and Richard Brinsley Sheridan (1751–1816).

Goldsmith's most successful play was the comedy *She Stoops to Conquer* (1773). He enjoyed esteem as a literary figure of varied talents. His *Vicar of Wakefield* (1766) is one of the best of the 18th-century novels. Two long poems—*The Traveller* (1764) and *The Deserted Village* (1770)—show still another of Goldsmith's abilities.

Sheridan was not yet 24 when the first of his two greatest plays, *The Rivals* (1775), was produced at Covent Garden in London. In 1777, Sheridan's other enduring masterpiece, *The School for Scandal*, made its appearance. It is still very much alive in the theater.

Poetry

The outstanding poet of the first half of the 18th century was Alexander Pope (1688–1744). Crippled early on by poor health, he was a man of great creative energy. His volume of work is huge. As poet, critic, and all-around man of letters he rivaled the earlier Dryden. Pope wrote most of his poetry in rhyming couplets. His poems include *The Rape of the Lock* (1712–14), which is a special kind of satirical poem called **mock-heroic**. That is, it makes fun of other poems that deal with heroes' brave deeds. The hero of *The Rape of the Lock* merely snips off a lock of a woman's hair. Two notable essays in verse are the *Essay on Criticism* (1711) and the *Essay on Man* (1733–34), a philosophical poem.

Pope also wrote verse translations of Homer's *Iliad* and *Odyssey*.

Good but lesser poets of the time include James Thomson (1700–48), best known for *The Seasons* (1726–30) and the patriotic song "Rule, Britannia." William Collins (1721–59) left a small body of fine verse. His "Ode to Evening" is an excellent nature poem. Among the works of William Cowper (1731–1800) is the popular humorous ballad "John Gilpin." The ballad tells of a "linen-draper bold" whose borrowed horse ran away with him on his 20th wedding anniversary. Thomas Gray (1716–71) wrote one of the most quoted of English poems: *Elegy Written in a Country Churchyard.*

Scotland produced a much-loved poet, Robert Burns (1759–96), who wrote in Scottish dialect. Among his many poems are "Tam O'Shanter," "To a Mouse," and "To a Louse." Among his songs are "Comin' thro' the Rye" and "Auld Lang Syne." He remains the beloved folk poet of Scotland.

In the 18th century William Blake (1757–1827) stands alone, different from every other writer. Son of a stocking maker, he did not go to school but was apprenticed to an engraver and became a master of that art. Educating himself, he developed into a mystic and visionary. He saw and imagined things no one else could see or imagine. His poetry has special forms and deep meanings all its own. Blake illustrated much of his own work, as well as the Bible and other writings. His art is as fascinating and sometimes puzzling as his poetry. His most famous poem, "The Tiger," comes from *Songs of Experience* (1794). Another remarkable collection of poems is *Songs of Innocence* (1789).

Prose

A master of the satirical form in prose was Jonathan Swift (1667–1745). A native of Ireland, Swift became a priest in the Anglican Church and later was made dean of St. Patrick's Cathedral in Dublin. He spent a number of his early years in England, and he was interested in English politics all his life. Often this interest found expression in savagely eloquent pamphlets, particularly about British policies toward Ireland. His pamphlets and other writings on politics and religion, his letters and poems—these alone would assure Swift a place in literature.

Yet he is best known as the author of *Gulliver's Travels* (1726), a fanciful account of four imaginary voyages. The first voyage is to Lilliput, the land of tiny people, and the second to Brobdingnag, the land of giants. In simplified versions the stories of these two voyages appeal to children. Yet the whole of Gulliver's adventures form the most bitter and hard-thrusting satire in the English language. It touches every vice, folly, and mere weakness of mankind. *Gulliver's Travels* reaches a powerful climax in its fourth part. The human race, represented by filthy creatures called Yahoos, is shown as inferior to a noble breed of thinking, talking, high-minded horses known as Houyhnhnms.

The essay flourished in the 18th century. Two men did much to advance it. Joseph Addison (1672–1719) and Sir Richard Steele (1672–1729) published and wrote for two popular journals featuring the informal essay. *The Tatler* appeared three times a week from 1709 to 1711. *The Spectator* appeared from March, 1711, to December, 1712, and was

"The Tiger" is a poem from William Blake's *Songs of Experience* (1794). Trained as an engraver, Blake often hand-lettered, illustrated, and printed his own poems.

revived again for some 80 issues in 1714. *The Spectator* contained many delightful sketches about the views and activities of a fictitious country gentleman, Sir Roger de Coverley.

Johnson and Boswell. Perhaps the central figure of the 18th century is Samuel Johnson (1709–84). He was a superb critic, a poet, a dictionary maker, and possibly the world's most famous conversationalist.

That we know so much of Johnson's intellect and abilities is mainly due to one man, James Boswell (1740–95). Boswell's *Life of Samuel Johnson* (1791) is one of the greatest biographies in any language or time. During their long friendship, Boswell kept journals of conversations he and others had with Johnson. Partly by drawing on these records, Boswell brings his subject to life. Nearly 200 years later we can almost hear Johnson's voice.

Boswell, a Scottish lawyer and man of the world, was long regarded as a mere follower of Johnson. In recent years a vast collection of Boswell's letters, journals, and other papers has turned up in a series of great literary finds. Several volumes of the journals have been published. They reveal the source of much of the *Life of Samuel Johnson*. In addition, the journals give so rich a portrait of the 18th century that they make Boswell a major figure in his own right.

As for Johnson, after years of work he published his famous dictionary in 1755. He is known for his poems *London* (1738) and *The Vanity of Human Wishes* (1749). Between 1750 and 1760 his essays appeared in his twice-weekly publication, the *Rambler*, and in the *Idler*, a regular section he wrote for a newspaper. *Rasselas, Prince of Abissinia*, a romance, appeared in 1759. *Journey to the Western Islands of Scotland* (1775) is an account of travels with Boswell.

An important part of Johnson's greatness was his literary criticism. He produced a long series of *Lives of the Poets* (1779–81) and critical studies of Shakespeare (1765) that are still of value.

The Novel

The 18th century saw the flowering of the novel. Some trace this form of fiction back to Lyly's *Euphues*. Some term Bunyan's *Pilgrim's Progress* a novel. But most often the English novel is thought to have had its real beginning in the works of five men whose ca-

Samuel Johnson (*left*) strolls with his biographer James Boswell in this caricature. Johnson compiled the first important dictionary of the English language.

reers overlapped: Defoe, Richardson, Fielding, Sterne, and Smollett.

Daniel Defoe (1660–1731) led an active life as a journalist and political pamphleteer. More than once his opinions carried him into prison. He wrote many books, including the novels *Moll Flanders* (1722) and *Roxana* (1724). His *Journal of the Plague Year* (1722) is written as a factual firsthand account of England's great plague of 1664–65. Actually it is a fiction built on other reports, for the author was about 4 years old when the plague struck. Defoe's first and greatest novel appeared in 1719. This was *Robinson Crusoe*, a famous tale of shipwreck and solitary survival.

Samuel Richardson (1689–1761), a printer by trade, wrote the novel *Pamela: or, Virtue Rewarded* (1740–42). A story with a moral, it is told through letters written by its heroine— a device often used in early fiction. Novels made up of letters are called **epistolary novels**. Two later Richardson novels, *Clarissa* (1747–48) and *Sir Charles Grandison* (1753–54), are also in the epistolary form.

Henry Fielding (1707–54) was a successful dramatist until the Licensing Act of 1737 caused his plays to be banned. Today, his fame rests on his novels. *Joseph Andrews* (1742) is a satire on the plot and sentiment of *Pamela* and also owes a debt to the Spanish classic of the previous century, *Don Quixote*. Fielding's masterpiece is *Tom Jones* (1749), a memorable work rich in humor and social satire. Like some other leading novels of the period, it is a **picaresque novel**. This type of story relates the wanderings and adventures of a *pícaro* (Spanish for "rogue").

Laurence Sterne (1713–68) was a decidedly worldly priest of the Church of England. A by-product of his fondness for travel is his *Sentimental Journey* (1768). His place as a novelist rests on *Tristram Shandy* (1759–67), a work that shocked many and was both notorious and popular.

Tobias Smollett (1721–71), a Scot, worked as a surgeon both in the Navy and in London. His chief novels are *Roderick Random* (1748), *Peregrine Pickle* (1751), and *Humphry Clinker* (1771).

Toward the end of the 18th century a new form of the novel emerged. **Gothic novels** were tales of horror and the supernatural. Horace Walpole (1717–97) wrote one of the earliest—*The Castle of Otranto* (1764). In 1794 the best of the Gothic novels appeared, *The Mysteries of Udolpho* by Ann Radcliffe (1764–1823).

▶**THE ROMANTIC PERIOD**

Roughly the first third of the 19th century makes up English literature's romantic period. The era was an unsettled one for England. War with France had begun in 1793 and continued until 1815. The Industrial Revolution was changing England from a rural society to a nation of factories. Perhaps in response to these and other events, romantic writers broke with the 18th-century belief in the power of reason. Instead, they placed their faith in the imagination and the emotions.

Poetry

The chief form of expression for the romantic movement was poetry. Certain 18th-

English Literature Time Line

Consult the index to find biographies of the writers listed on this time line.

Sir Walter Raleigh with his son

1387? *The Canterbury Tales* by Geoffrey Chaucer (1343?–1400)

1516 *Utopia* by Sir Thomas More (1478–1535)

1590 *The Faerie Queene* by Edmund Spenser (1552?–99)

1592 *Edward II* by Christopher Marlowe (1564–93)

1597 First edition of *Essays* by Francis Bacon (1561–1626)

1602 *Hamlet* by William Shakespeare (1564–1616)

1614 *History of the World* by Sir Walter Raleigh (1554?–1618)

1633 Collected poems of John Donne (1572–1631) published by his son

1667 *Paradise Lost* by John Milton (1608–74)

1678 *All for Love* by John Dryden (1631–1700)

London, about 1500

Christopher Marlowe

John Donne

THE Tragicall Historie of HAMLET Prince of Denmarke

century poets had shown signs of romanticism, and William Blake can be considered one of the earliest romantic writers. But it was not until 1798 that two poets published a volume of poems that has been called romantic poetry's "declaration of independence."

Wordsworth and Coleridge. The volume of poems was *Lyrical Ballads*, and its authors were William Wordsworth (1770–1850) and Samuel Taylor Coleridge (1772–1834). The poems in the collection have many characteristics typical of romantic poetry. Wordsworth's verses, for example, are about country scenes and country people and show his love for nature. The famous "Lines Composed a Few Miles Above Tintern Abbey" appeared in *Lyrical Ballads*.

Representative of Wordsworth's other work is the long autobiographical poem *The Prelude,* which was not published until 1850, and such shorter poems as "My Heart Leaps Up When I Behold" and "I Wandered Lonely as a Cloud," also called "Daffodils." Wordsworth's poetry varies widely. Some is written in plain language, and in other poems the style is complex.

Both Wordsworth and his good friend Coleridge were distinguished for writings on criticism and principles of poetry. Coleridge's major work of this sort is the autobiographical *Biographia Literaria* (1817). The most famous of his poems, "The Rime of the Ancient Mariner," appeared in *Lyrical Ballads*. Coleridge is also well known for the unfinished "Kubla Khan" and "Christabel."

Byron, Keats, and Shelley. Three poets brought the romantic movement to its height. George Gordon, Lord Byron (1788–1824), traveled widely in Europe, part of the time an exile because of scandals related to his per-

1712–14 *The Rape of the Lock* by Alexander Pope (1688–1744)

1719 *Robinson Crusoe* by Daniel Defoe (1660–1731)

1726 *Gulliver's Travels* by Jonathan Swift (1667–1745)

1755 *A Dictionary of the English Language* by Samuel Johnson (1709–84)

1786 *Poems* by Robert Burns (1759–96)

1789 *Songs of Innocence* by William Blake (1757–1827)

1798 Poems by William Wordsworth (1770–1850) appear in *Lyrical Ballads*

1812–18 *Childe Harold's Pilgrimage* by Lord Byron (1788–1824)

1813 *Pride and Prejudice* by Jane Austen (1775–1817)

1817 *Endymion* by John Keats (1795–1821)

1819 *Ivanhoe* by Sir Walter Scott (1771–1832)

1820 *Prometheus Unbound* by Percy Bysshe Shelley (1792–1822)

Robinson Crusoe

Jane Austen

Percy Bysshe Shelley

English countryside, about 1750

sonal life. At the age of 36 he died of a fever in Greece, where he had gone as a volunteer to fight for Greek independence. His many works include the partly autobiographical *Childe Harold's Pilgrimage* (1812–18). *Don Juan* (1819–24) owes its title and parts of its story to the old legend of the great lover. Byron retells the story in the form of satire. In the dramatic poem *Manfred* (1817) the hero sells himself to the Prince of Darkness.

John Keats (1795–1821) came from origins as plain as Byron's were aristocratic. His father kept a livery stable. It is fortunate that Keats's genius showed itself early, since he died of tuberculosis in Rome at the age of 25. Keats was superb at pictorial poetry—painting a picture with words. His art is nowhere greater than in the two poems "Ode on a Grecian Urn" and "Ode to a Nightingale." The opening line of *Endymion* (1817) is one of the best known in English poetry: "A thing of beauty is a joy forever."

Percy Bysshe Shelley (1792–1822), like Byron, had a controversial personal life. His second wife, Mary Wollstonecraft Shelley (1797–1851), is remembered as the author of the celebrated book *Frankenstein* (1818).

Shelley's writing has a wide range. The lovely musical quality of his work appears in the fine verses of "Ode to the West Wind" and "To a Skylark." *Defence of Poetry* (1821) upholds the place of imagination and love in the arts. Two dramas, *The Cenci* (1819) and *Prometheus Unbound* (1820), are among Shelley's outstanding work. The long poem *Adonais* (1821) is a beautiful lament written on the death of Keats. A month before his 30th birthday, Shelley drowned while sailing in the Mediterranean. His ashes lie in the same Roman cemetery where Keats is buried.

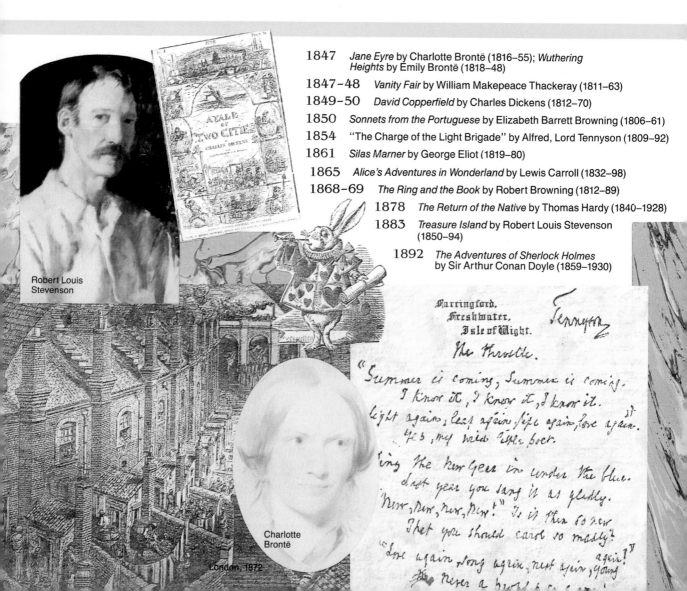

1847   *Jane Eyre* by Charlotte Brontë (1816–55); *Wuthering Heights* by Emily Brontë (1818–48)

1847–48   *Vanity Fair* by William Makepeace Thackeray (1811–63)

1849–50   *David Copperfield* by Charles Dickens (1812–70)

1850   *Sonnets from the Portuguese* by Elizabeth Barrett Browning (1806–61)

1854   "The Charge of the Light Brigade" by Alfred, Lord Tennyson (1809–92)

1861   *Silas Marner* by George Eliot (1819–80)

1865   *Alice's Adventures in Wonderland* by Lewis Carroll (1832–98)

1868–69   *The Ring and the Book* by Robert Browning (1812–89)

1878   *The Return of the Native* by Thomas Hardy (1840–1928)

1883   *Treasure Island* by Robert Louis Stevenson (1850–94)

1892   *The Adventures of Sherlock Holmes* by Sir Arthur Conan Doyle (1859–1930)

Robert Louis Stevenson

Charlotte Brontë

London, 1872

The Novel

The two outstanding novelists of the period wrote in very different styles.

Sir Walter Scott (1771–1832) helped popularize a type of romanticism different from that of Byron, Keats, and Shelley. Most of Scott's themes came from medieval lore and the history of his native Scotland. *Waverly* (1814), *The Heart of Midlothian* (1818), *Ivanhoe* (1819), and *Kenilworth* (1821) are but a few of his widely read novels. Scott established the form of the historical novel and influenced the development of fiction throughout Europe and the United States. He also wrote popular narrative poems, including *The Lay of the Last Minstrel* (1805) and *The Lady of the Lake* (1810), and produced many biographical, critical, and historical works.

The novels of Jane Austen (1775–1817) differ greatly from those of Scott. She is often called the last of the 18th-century novelists because of her controlled, almost flawless style. Austen excelled at a form of writing called the **novel of manners**. Novels of this type present in detail the manners and customs of a particular social class. Austen is considered to be one of the greatest of all English novelists, and her works continue to attract devoted admirers. Her novels include *Sense and Sensibility* (1811), *Pride and Prejudice* (1813), *Emma* (1816), and *Northanger Abbey* (1818).

Nonfiction

Essayists and other writers of nonfiction in the romantic period include William Hazlitt (1778–1830) and Charles Lamb (1775–1834). Hazlitt's most valuable collection of prose writings is *Table Talk* (1821). Lamb is best remembered for the delightful humor and

1895   *The Importance of Being Earnest* by Oscar Wilde (1854–1900)

1898   *The War of the Worlds* by H. G. Wells (1866–1946)

1900   *Lord Jim* by Joseph Conrad (1857–1924)

1901   *Kim* by Rudyard Kipling (1865–1936)

1912   *Pygmalion* by George Bernard Shaw (1856–1950)

1922   *The Waste Land* by T. S. Eliot (1888–1965)

1932   *Brave New World* by Aldous Huxley (1894–1963)

1949   *1984* by George Orwell (1903–50)

1954   *Under Milk Wood* by Dylan Thomas (1914–53)

1973   *The Honorary Consul* by Graham Greene (1904–91)

1984   Ted Hughes (1930–98) named England's poet laureate

George Bernard Shaw

London World War II

T. S. Eliot

Drawing by Kipling for his *Just So Stories*

grace of his *Essays of Elia* (1823–33). Elia was Lamb's pen name. With his sister Mary he wrote the charming children's book *Tales from Shakespeare* (1807). Thomas De Quincey (1785–1859) was both a critic and an essayist, known for his polished style. It was a book, however, that first brought him notice. This was *Confessions of an English Opium Eater* (1822), in which De Quincey tells of his struggle with the drug.

▶VICTORIAN LITERATURE

The romantic period shades gradually into the Victorian age, which takes its name from Queen Victoria. She came to the throne in 1837 and reigned until 1901. The romantic spirit did not disappear, but it ceased to be a clearly leading influence. Historical and philosophical writing continued to flourish along with poetry and fiction. At the same time, satire and protest against evils in society became strong elements. The later years of the period saw modern kinds of realistic writing and some authors who showed a new, deeper understanding of character.

Victorian England was mighty: its empire circled the globe. Industry became a major influence on English life. In Europe it produced much revolutionary unrest, and the basic socialist beliefs of Karl Marx were launched in 1848. Although Marx wrote his revolutionary book *Das Kapital* (1867) in London, England was able to keep its society stable and morality seemingly strict. Yet from the literature of the Victorian age we discover how many things stirred under the surface.

Nonfiction

Ideas were pursued in many fields. Thomas Babington Macaulay (1800–59) had a career in Parliament. He wrote some poetry, notably *Lays of Ancient Rome* (1842). His fame rests on his *History of England* (1849–61) and many essays, written in a masterly prose style.

In nonfiction a notable group follows Macaulay. Thomas Carlyle (1795–1881), Scottish historian and philosopher, influenced American literature through his friendship with Ralph Waldo Emerson. *Sartor Resartus* (1833–34), Latin for "The Tailor Re-Tailored," is an account of Carlyle's spiritual life. John Henry Newman (1801–90) is one of the foremost writers on religion and education. John Stuart Mill (1806–73), philosopher, historian, and student of government, wrote the great essay *On Liberty* (1859) and his *Autobiography* (1873). John Ruskin (1819–1900), the century's leading critic of art and architecture, was interested in economics as well. A rich style brightens such works as *Modern Painters* (1843–60) and *The Stones of Venice* (1851–53). The nonfiction of Matthew Arnold (1822–88) touches on many areas—social relations, science, religion, and literature. Early in his career Arnold wrote poetry, of which "Dover Beach" is a good example.

Walter Pater (1839–94) loved the beauty of perfect art, and many of his prose pieces are appreciations of what he found best in art and literature. *Marius the Epicurean* (1885) is his only novel. Thomas Henry Huxley (1825–95), a teacher and biologist, helped popularize science with *Man's Place in Nature* (1863) and other essays. The century was rocked by Huxley's friend Charles Darwin (1809–82). His *On the Origin of Species* (1859) and other books expressed theories about the origin of the human race that shocked many people.

Poetry

Alfred, Lord Tennyson (1809–92), who was made England's poet laureate in 1850, has been called the voice of Victorian England. Many of his works deal with the important issues of his age. Tennyson reflects the Victorian concern with moral codes in his retelling of the King Arthur legends in *The Idylls of the King* (1859–85). *In Memoriam* (1850), an expression of personal grief, also explores the question of religious faith in a changing world. *The Princess* (1847) examines the issue of women's rights. England's role in the Crimean War inspired the patriotic poem "The Charge of the Light Brigade" (1854).

While Tennyson enjoyed great popularity, Robert Browning (1812–89) was more admired than understood. Victorian England found his poetry "difficult," although that cannot be said of "The Pied Piper of Hamelin," his poem for children. *The Ring and the Book* (1868–69) is Browning's longest and most ambitious poem. Browning created a new poetic form, the **dramatic monologue**, in which a single character speaks and gives the background, setting, and action of an important occasion in his or her life.

The poet Elizabeth Barrett Browning (1806–61) was the wife of Robert Browning.

Her best work is in the collection known as *Sonnets from the Portuguese* (1850).

A group of poets and artists rebelled against the poetry and painting of the Victorian age. They called themselves the Pre-Raphaelite Brotherhood. Their aim was a closer attention to nature and a return to the spirit and methods of Italian painters before the time of Raphael (1483–1520). Dante Gabriel Rossetti (1828–82) led the group. To his poems, like "The Blessed Damozel," he gave a richness of language, color, and detail. Christina Rossetti (1830–94), Dante Gabriel's sister, was in sympathy with the Pre-Raphaelites, as was Algernon Charles Swinburne (1837–1909). Christina Rossetti's "Goblin Market" is a fairy tale in poetic form. Swinburne wrote dramas and criticism as well as poems. His collection *Poems and Ballads* (1866) caused a sensation when it appeared.

Many objected to the Pre-Raphaelites. Among those who defended them was the poet and designer William Morris (1834–96). Through his writings, as well as through his designs for furniture, fabric, books, and other useful objects, Morris tried to bring beauty into all aspects of English life. He also worked to bring about social change.

Other poets active during Queen Victoria's reign deserve mention. Edward FitzGerald (1809–83) gained lasting fame with a single work—*The Rubáiyát of Omar Khayyám*. FitzGerald's first version of the old Persian poem appeared in 1859. The poetry of both Gerard Manley Hopkins (1844–89) and Francis Thompson (1859–1907) reminds one of the metaphysical poetry of the 17th century. Hopkins' work has had a wide influence on modern poetry.

Drama

Oscar Wilde (1854–1900) possessed a wealth of talents. He was a poet of distinction ("The Ballad of Reading Gaol"), story writer ("The Happy Prince"), and novelist (*The Picture of Dorian Gray*) (1891). Perhaps most important of all, he was a playwright. His writing for the theater ranged from the poetic drama *Salomé* (1894) to a series of sparkling, witty comedies such as *The Importance of Being Earnest* (1895). In the theater of this time other playwrights were William Archer (1856–1924), Sir Arthur Wing Pinero (1855–1934), and Henry Arthur Jones (1851–1929).

Fiction

The Victorian period was the great age of the English novel. Many writers turned their talents to all kinds of prose fiction: tales of adventure, novels of social commentary, fantasies, and many other forms. Most Victorian novels are lengthy and draw the reader into a world full of memorable characters and events.

Thackeray and Dickens. Two figures tower over the Victorian novel. William Makepeace Thackeray (1811–63) was a master of satire, a critic of what he thought false in life. Most of his characters and plots come from upper- and middle-class life. *Pendennis* (1848–50) and *Henry Esmond* (1852) are notable novels, but Thackeray's masterwork is *Vanity Fair* (1847–48). Its heroine, Becky Sharp, is one of the immortal personalities of English fiction.

In the creation of memorable characters, however, Thackeray is topped by Charles Dickens (1812–70). After a boyhood of poverty, partly reflected in his own favorite book,

The stories of Charles Dickens are filled with colorful characters. Bob Cratchit and Tiny Tim, from *A Christmas Carol*, are among the most familiar figures in literature.

David Copperfield (1849–50), Dickens became a man of wealth through his books and his public readings from them, both in England and the United States. His novels combine a rare comic gift—especially in *Pickwick Papers* (1836–37), his earliest success—and a power to reduce his readers to tears. Some of his books, such as *Oliver Twist* (1837–39) and *Nicholas Nickleby* (1838–39), reflect Dickens' anger at debtors' prison, harsh treatment of children, and other social ills.

The Brontës. England has few more fascinating literary families than the Brontës. Charlotte, Emily, and Anne, three daughters of an Irish-born clergyman, grew up at Haworth parsonage, in Yorkshire. This remote region of bleak moors greatly influenced the imagination of the sisters. They first wrote poems and later turned to novels.

Anne Brontë (1820–49) was the least talented novelist of the three. Her chief work is *Agnes Grey* (1847), the story of a girl's experience as a governess. Charlotte Brontë (1816–55) produced *Jane Eyre* (1847), an exciting novel that contains elements of Gothic and romantic fiction. The one novel of Emily Brontë (1818–48), *Wuthering Heights* (1847), is a masterpiece of English literature.

The adventure stories of Robert Louis Stevenson appeal to readers of all ages. *Treasure Island* (1883) is an exciting tale of pirates and buried treasure.

Anthony Trollope (1815–82) gained wide popularity with his realistic books about English life. One series is called the Barsetshire Novels. *Barchester Towers* (1857), like the others of the series, concerns itself with life in the cathedral town of Barchester.

Eliot, Meredith, and Butler. George Eliot (1819–80), whose real name was Mary Ann Evans, combines great narrative power and depth of thought. As a scholar and philosopher her powers outreach those of Dickens and Thackeray. *Adam Bede* (1859), *The Mill on the Floss* (1860), and *Silas Marner* (1861) give expert pictures of the working class and their experiences. *Middlemarch* (1871–72) presents the problem of a young girl trapped by the will of her dead husband.

George Meredith (1828–1909) was an essayist, poet, and novelist. His novels stand out for their psychological studies of character and their grasp of social problems. Meredith's *Ordeal of Richard Feverel* (1859) deals with a father-son relationship and the son's crises throughout life. *The Egoist* (1879) is another worthwhile Meredith novel.

Samuel Butler (1835–1902) invented an ideal state—Erewhon—for the purpose of criticizing a real one—England. (Erewhon is an anagram of ''nowhere.'') Butler's *Erewhon* (1872) and *Erewhon Revisited* (1901) are in the tradition of More's *Utopia* and part of Swift's *Gulliver's Travels*. Butler's most enduring work is a partly autobiographical novel, *The Way of All Flesh* (1903).

Stevenson, Carroll, and Kipling. Robert Louis Stevenson (1850–94) died far from his native Scotland, on the South Sea island of Samoa. Poor health had driven him there. Both as a poet and storyteller he wrote for readers of all ages. *A Child's Garden of Verses* (1885) is a nursery classic. The adventures in *Treasure Island* (1883) and *Kidnapped* (1886) thrill readers young and old. Stevenson was a master of the short novel. His most famous one, *The Strange Case of Dr. Jekyll and Mr. Hyde* (1886), is a fascinating tale of the good and evil in one man.

An Oxford lecturer in mathematics, Charles Lutwidge Dodgson (1832–98), is known to most of us as Lewis Carroll. *Alice's Adventures in Wonderland* (1865) and *Through the Looking-Glass* (1872) remain lasting favorites. *The Hunting of the Snark* (1876) is a nonsense poem of mock-heroic adventure.

Yet another writer for young and old is Rudyard Kipling (1865–1936). India during the days of British rule serves as background for many of his poems, stories, and novels. It is interesting that he wrote *The Jungle Book* (1894) and *Second Jungle Book* (1895) during the two years he lived in America. These stories for children, like the *Just So Stories* (1902), are marvelous for their color, action, and detail. Kipling is also known for the lively poetry of *Barrack-Room Ballads* (1892) and the finest of his novels, *Kim* (1901).

Thomas Hardy. Thomas Hardy (1840–1928) lived well into the 20th century but did his major work as a novelist in the 19th century. Representative of his work are *The Return of the Native* (1878), *Tess of the D'Urbervilles* (1891), and *Jude the Obscure* (1896). These books fall into the prose group that Hardy called novels of character and environment. They offer powerful, realistic studies of life. Although Hardy ranks high as a novelist, we should not overlook the fact that he was a first-class poet. As a prose writer he is the last of the 19th century. As a poet he belongs to the 20th.

Other Victorian Novelists. The century was rich in other novelists. Edward Bulwer-Lytton (1803–73) was popular for such historical romances as *The Last Days of Pompeii* (1834). Charles Reade (1814–84) wrote *The Cloister and the Hearth* (1861). Charles Kingsley (1819–75), poet, novelist, and controversial essayist, wrote *Westward Ho!* (1855) and *Hereward the Wake* (1865). William Wilkie Collins (1824–89), with *The Woman in White* (1860) and *The Moonstone* (1868), pioneered the mystery thriller novel. The work of George Gissing (1857–1903) shows signs of the rise of realism in the novel. Sir Arthur Conan Doyle (1859–1930) developed the mystery story into the modern detective story and made the personality of Sherlock Holmes immortal.

▶ **1900 TO WORLD WAR II**

Many traits of Victorian literature carried over into the 20th century until World War I began, in 1914. But new ideas were mixed with old to follow the changing times.

Poetry

Robert Bridges (1844–1930) broke away from the tradition of Victorian poetry with experiments in new meters and verse forms. In

Sherlock Holmes (*right*) is the hero of detective stories by Arthur Conan Doyle. Holmes solves baffling crimes through brilliant use of deduction.

his lyric poems Bridges is at his best. The poetry of A. E. Housman (1859–1936) is written in a simple, uncluttered style. His first volume of poems, *A Shropshire Lad,* appeared in 1896.

The poems of Walter de la Mare (1873–1956) show great imagination, and his lyrics for children appeal to adults as well. *Peacock Pie* (1913) contains some of his best stories and verses for young readers. John Masefield (1878–1967) published *Salt-Water Ballads* in 1902 and is best known for his poems and ballads about the sea.

The gifted poet Rupert Brooke (1887–1915) died during World War I. His *Collected Poems* (1918) shows that he was a writer of rare promise.

The leading poets of the 1920's and 1930's moved further away from the old forms. Dame Edith Sitwell (1887–1964) was a brilliant experimenter who wrote poems heavy with rich language and unusual rhythms. One of her better-known works is *Façade* (1922).

No 20th-century poet has had as great an influence as T. S. Eliot (1888–1965). Both the United States and England claim this writer, born in St. Louis, Missouri, but a British subject after 1927. With "The Love Song of J.

Alfred Prufrock" (1917) and *The Waste Land* (1922) Eliot made a complete break from the romantic poetry of the past. He became a spokesman for all those who were saddened by the falseness and harshness of 20th-century civilization.

Robert Graves (1895–1985) first attracted attention with poems describing the horrors of World War I. He wrote many more volumes of poetry during his long career. Also noteworthy are his historical novels *I, Claudius* and *Claudius the God* (both 1934).

Three leading poets of the 1930's shared an interest in the teachings of Karl Marx, and their poems of that period were concerned mainly with social and political issues. C. Day Lewis (1904–72) published *From Feathers to Iron* in 1931. W. H. Auden (1907–73) received the 1947 Pulitzer Prize for the *The Age of Anxiety*, a long dramatic poem. *Collected Poems 1928–1953* by Stephen Spender (1909–95) was published in 1955.

The Welsh poet Dylan Thomas (1914–53) was a major influence on English poetry. His works include *Collected Poems, 1934–1952* (1953) and the play *Under Milk Wood* (1954).

Nonfiction

Sir Max Beerbohm (1872–1956) was a master of the parody, a humorous imitation of serious writing. His literary criticism is also first-rate. V. S. Pritchett (1900–97), a later critic, also excelled in this form.

The great statesman Sir Winston Churchill (1874–1965) was also a noted historian. He received the Nobel Prize for literature for his history *The Second World War* (1948–53). Arnold Toynbee (1889–1975) centered his attention on broad views of world history. His twelve-volume *Study of History* was published between 1934 and 1961.

Lytton Strachey (1880–1932) revived the art of honest biography with his *Eminent Victorians* (1918) and *Queen Victoria* (1921). Hesketh Pearson (1887–1964) continued the fine tradition of English biography.

Fiction

Of novelists active during the first half of the 20th century, few are more impressive than Joseph Conrad (1857–1924). Polish-born, Conrad was in his twenties before he knew any English. After becoming a British subject, he wrote brilliant novels in his adopted tongue. Among them are *Lord Jim* (1900) and *Nostromo* (1904).

Some of the novels of H. G. Wells (1866–1946) focus on political and social problems. Others, like *The War of the Worlds* (1898), are forerunners of today's science fiction. John Galsworthy (1867–1933) received the Nobel Prize for literature in 1932. His group of novels, *The Forsyte Saga* (1906–21), traces the shifting values of an upper-middle-class English family.

The novels of E. M. Forster (1879–1970) concern themselves with personal relations. In his most notable book, *A Passage to India*

In *The War of the Worlds*, Martians invade the Earth. Written by H. G. Wells in 1898, the book is one of the earliest works of science fiction.

Polish-born Joseph Conrad (*left*) wrote masterful novels in English, a language he learned as an adult. Virginia Woolf (*near right*) experimented with new forms for the novel. James Joyce (*far right*) used stream of consciousness and wordplay in creating the revolutionary novel *Ulysses*.

(1924), Forster examined the relationships between Englishmen and Indians. G. K. Chesterton (1874–1936) was an all-around man of letters—poet, novelist, essayist, playwright, biographer. In Father Brown he created one of modern fiction's best-known detectives. Plays, short stories, and novels made W. Somerset Maugham (1874–1965) one of the most popular of English writers. He is a superb storyteller. His autobiographical novel, *Of Human Bondage* (1915), is considered his masterpiece.

New generations of fiction writers followed. They experimented with new forms and made use of new insights into character as modern psychology developed. They challenged old ideas about life and art.

James Joyce (1882–1941) is regarded as one of the leading writers of modern times. He introduced startling new forms into the novel. He made major use of **stream of consciousness**, a style of writing in which the free flow of language reveals a person's thoughts, feelings, and memories. *Ulysses* (1922) gives a striking, detailed picture of one day in the lives of two fictional Dubliners, Leopold Bloom and Stephen Dedalus.

D. H. Lawrence (1885–1930) felt that society forced too many rules on people and kept them from living a full, natural life. Lawrence's forceful writing on daring themes shocked many. *Sons and Lovers* (1913) is one of his finest novels.

In some ways the work of Aldous Huxley (1894–1963) resembles that of Joyce and Lawrence. Huxley experimented with form and criticized society. *Point Counter Point* (1928), a witty satire, lashes out at British upper-class society of the 1920's. *Brave New World* (1932), another satire, pictures a future world that depends too much on science.

Early works of Evelyn Waugh (1903–66) were witty, satirical novels somewhat similiar to Huxley's. Later books, such as *Brideshead Revisited* (1945), are more serious. *Animal Farm* (1945) and *Nineteen Eighty-Four* (1949), by George Orwell (1903–50), express criticism of a dictator-controlled state.

Virginia Woolf (1882–1941) experimented constantly, always refining her special form of writing. She was less interested in plot than in probing people's characters, experiences, and feelings. Many consider *The Waves* (1931) her best novel. Katherine Mansfield (1888–1923) was a founder of the modern short story. In *The Garden Party* (1922), each story captures a single emotion or dramatic event.

Drama

Of all the prominent writers active both before and after World War I, George Bernard Shaw (1856–1950) looms as the giant. His comic talents and immense output probably earn this brilliant Irishman the rank of leading English-language playwright after Shakespeare. His wit and satire have held the stages of the world in such plays as *Man and Superman* (1903), *Major Barbara* (1905), *Pygmalion* (1912), and *Saint Joan* (1923). To Shaw, nothing was sacred. Marriage, religion, and parenthood received the same acid treatment as social snobbery and politics.

The Scottish-born playwright Sir James M. Barrie (1860–1937) was more in tune with the Victorian age. His sentimental comedy *What Every Woman Knows* (1908) is evidence of that fact. Barrie's great gift for fantasy makes *Peter Pan* (1904) a lasting favorite.

During the 1890's, Oscar Wilde had brightened the English stage with his comedies of manners. In the 1920's the plays of W. Somerset Maugham repeated Wilde's success.

English writers of the later 20th century included the novelists Graham Greene (*left*) and Doris Lessing (*near right*) and the poet Ted Hughes (*far right*). Greene's novels frequently deal with moral questions, while Lessing's often explore the role of women. Hughes was England's poet laureate from 1984 until his death in 1998.

Noël Coward (1899–1973) carried the comedy of manners form still further with *Private Lives* in 1930 and *Design for Living* in 1932. Terence Rattigan (1911–77) showed a talent for comedy in *French Without Tears* (1936) and for drama in *Separate Tables* (1954).

T. S. Eliot's genius for poetry made *Murder in the Cathedral* (1935) an outstanding verse play. Christopher Fry (1907–2005) delighted audiences with the witty verse play *The Lady's Not for Burning* (1948).

▶ **LATER 20TH CENTURY**

A number of gifted writers active after World War II (1939–45) added to the quality of English fiction. A series of novels, *Strangers and Brothers* (1940–70), by Sir Charles Percy Snow (1905–80), is a valuable record of English social history. Elizabeth Bowen (1899–1973) was a brilliant stylist whose novels show the influence of Virginia Woolf. The books of Graham Greene (1904–91), such as *The Heart of the Matter* (1948) and *The Honorary Consul* (1973), concern problems of the spirit.

Some modern novels deal with the potential for evil in human nature. Two examples are *Lord of the Flies* (1954), by William Golding (1911–93), and *A Clockwork Orange* (1962), by Anthony Burgess (1917–93).

During the 1950's a group of writers examined the lives of working-class people discontented with England's social system. These "angry young men" included the novelists Kingsley Amis (1922–95) and John Braine (1922–86) and the playwright John Osborne (1929–94).

Muriel Spark (1918–) created works of social satire. Another keen observer of 20th-century life was the novelist and philosopher Iris Murdoch (1919–99). Anthony Powell (1905–2000) provided a view of post–World War II England in his series of novels *A Dance to the Music of Time* (1951–75). Other outstanding novelists include Margaret Drabble (1939–), Doris Lessing (1919–), and John Fowles (1926–2005).

Noteworthy modern poets include Ted Hughes (1930–98), named poet laureate in 1984; Philip Larkin (1922–85); Donald Davie (1922–95); and the Irish poet Seamus Heaney (1939–).

A revival of English drama occurred in the 1950's, beginning with John Osborne's *Look Back in Anger* (1956). Another acclaimed dramatist is Harold Pinter (1930–), who won the Nobel Prize for literature in 2005. His plays, such as *The Homecoming* (1965) and *Betrayal* (1979), demonstrate a mastery of dialogue. Impressive younger playwrights include Peter Shaffer (1926–), author of *Equus* (1973) and *Amadeus* (1979); Tom Stoppard (1937–), author of *Travesties* (1974) and *The Real Thing* (1983); and David Hare (1947–), author of *Plenty* (1978) and *The Blue Room* (1995).

The second half of the 20th century saw the decline of England as a world power. Yet English language and literature continue to have a strong influence on the rest of the world. Today, English-language literature is enriched by the work of writers in Ireland, the United States, Canada, Australia, and New Zealand, as well as in South Africa, Nigeria, India, and other areas where English is spoken. For all these writers, and for their readers, the literature of England remains a valuable heritage.

EDMUND FULLER
Author, *Man in Modern Fiction*

See also AMERICAN LITERATURE; CANADA, LITERATURE OF; IRELAND, LITERATURE OF.

ENGLISH MUSIC

The music of England has always been similar to that of the rest of Europe, but it also has its own special qualities. Several English musical creations, including the anthem and the brass band, have become well known around the world. The influence of English music has been especially evident in the United States and Canada—until the mid-1800's, most music there was based on English traditions.

▶ THE MIDDLE AGES

Little is known of music in England before A.D. 597, when conversion to Christianity began. One of the practices introduced with the new religion was the singing of **chants** (also called plainsong), religious vocal music with Latin words. At first, chants were sung without any harmony or instrumental accompaniment. Then, about the year 1000, monks began to chant in two-part harmony. Over the years, more complex harmony was developed, both in sacred and secular (nonreligious) music. The 13th-century round, "Sumer is icumen in," is a later example of full harmony. It combines six voices, each singing a different part, in a way that was far in advance of developments elsewhere in Europe.

John Dunstable. The first English composer of major importance was John Dunstable (1390?–1453). He wrote mainly church music to be sung to Latin texts. Full harmony and a variety of rhythm play an important part in his style. Dunstable spent part of his career in France, where his music was widely imitated.

▶ THE REFORMATION

By the late 1400's, the choral music sung in English churches had reached a high point of richness and complexity. This changed after 1534, when King Henry VIII (reigned 1509–47) broke with the Church of Rome and established a separate Church of England. The break was part of a worldwide movement, known as the Reformation, that was aimed at reforming the Roman Catholic Church.

As a result of the Reformation in England, church services became very simple and were conducted in English instead of Latin. New music was needed for the new English texts. English composers developed the **anthem**, originally a musical arrangement of part of a psalm and later a longer piece.

In the 1700's many English composers wrote chamber music for small groups of players. In this painting the Prince of Wales joins his sisters in an informal concert.

The Puritans, a group of extreme reformers, thought that only simple music should be sung in church. They did not use harmony in their religious songs. Despite Puritan disapproval, Queen Elizabeth (reigned 1558–1603) encouraged the use of choirs and organs in her own chapel and in the 26 cathedrals of England and Wales. Elizabeth also allowed composers to continue writing Latin church music. Those writing in Latin included two of England's greatest composers, Thomas Tallis (1505–85) and William Byrd (1543–1623). Byrd remained a Catholic but also wrote music with English words for use in the Anglican (English) church.

▶ THE GOLDEN AGE OF ENGLISH MUSIC

A great flowering of music occurred in England from about 1590 to 1630. This was also the age of Shakespeare, England's greatest literary figure, and a period of national power.

Madrigals, Balletts, and Ayres. After 1590 many English composers wrote madrigals, a form of vocal music that originated in Italy. Madrigals were written for small groups of singers, each singing a separate part. In the best madrigals the music reflects the strong, often sad emotions expressed by the words. Outstanding composers of madrigals included William Byrd, Thomas Morley (1557?–1602), John Wilbye (1574–1638), and Thomas Weelkes (1576–1623).

A more cheerful form, also from Italy, was the ballett, a song with a lively dance rhythm. Balletts had two or more verses and a refrain of nonsense syllables, such as "fa-la." Another type of song was the ayre (or air), in which a single voice carried the main tune, accompanied by lute, viols, or other voices. The most famous composer of ayres was John Dowland (1563–1626). Others were Thomas Campion (1567–1620), who wrote the poetry as well as the music for his songs, and Orlando Gibbons (1583–1625).

Instrumental Music. Many composers wrote music for the virginal, a popular keyboard instrument of the period. Three composers, Byrd, Gibbons, and John Bull (1563?–1628), were especially important in this area. Similar music was written for the lute, by John Dowland and many others.

Music for consorts (a group of instruments played in concert) was written by many composers, among them Byrd and Gibbons. The most popular type of consort was made up of viols of different sizes. Viols were bowed stringed instruments that preceded today's instruments of the violin family.

▶ **CIVIL WAR TO RESTORATION**

The years 1642 to 1660 were unsettled ones for England. Disagreements between Parliament and the King led to civil war and the overthrow of the monarchy (rule by kings and queens). Under the Puritans, who were in power during these years, the royal court ceased to exist, the theaters were closed, and cathedrals no longer held elaborate services. These had been three important employers of professional musicians.

The restoration of the monarchy in 1660 brought about another productive period in English music. Court music now included an orchestra of violins. Cathedral music was reestablished, and the theaters were reopened. Wine- and coffee-drinking clubs for men were formed, and members sang **catches** and **glees,** unaccompanied songs for three or four voices.

Henry Purcell. The Restoration period produced one man, Henry Purcell (1659–95), who is considered the greatest of all English composers. During his short life he produced superb examples of music for the church, the theater, the club, and the home. He was particularly gifted at setting English words to music.

Purcell composed a large number of anthems for the chapel royal, some with accompaniment for strings and many with passages for solo voices. His deeply moving setting of the Burial Service is one of the gems of English church music. He also wrote songs for the voice and harpsichord, most of which were originally sung in the course of a play. His other theater music included choruses, dances, and songs for such plays as *King Arthur* (1691) and *The Fairy Queen* (1692). His only true opera—in which all the words of the drama are sung—is *Dido and Aeneas* (1689). Written for performance by students at a girls' school, it is still considered the greatest English opera.

▶ **THE GEORGIAN PERIOD**

The period from 1714 to 1830 is called Georgian after the kings who reigned during that time: George I, II, III, and IV. In the Georgian period England became a great world power. London attracted large numbers of foreign musicians, and their influence overshadowed that of native English musicians. Italian opera, established in London in 1705, became the most fashionable of all musical entertainments for the upper classes.

George Frederick Handel. The most famous composer in England in the period was the German-born George Frederick Handel (1685–1750). He settled in London in 1710 after training in Italy. At first Handel composed mainly Italian operas. But after 1732 he turned more and more to English-language **oratorios,** choral works based on biblical stories. The most successful of all Handel's oratorios, the *Messiah* (1741), is based on passages from the Bible that tell the story of Christ. Handel excelled at writing ceremonial music for royal occasions. He also wrote concertos, chamber music, and pieces for harpsichord.

Other Georgian Composers. Handel's success with the English public was so tremendous that he was long regarded as the foremost national composer. But there were some fine English-born composers, including Maurice Greene (1695–1755) and John Stanley (1713–86). Samuel Wesley (1766–1837) wrote important Latin church music, symphonies, and organ music.

A unique theater piece was *The Beggar's Opera,* produced in 1728. It was not a real opera, but a play with 69 popular songs inserted. Created by the poet John Gay, *The Beggar's Opera* was a fierce and witty attack on the corruption of England's rulers. The "ballad opera" became a standard form of entertainment in England.

The London Piano School. The pianoforte, the first keyboard instrument that could produce a range of loud and soft sounds, was invented in 1709 by an Italian. But the instrument did not become popular until the 1760's, when London manufacturers began to take the lead in improving its quality. London became a great center for piano music.

Muzio Clementi (1752–1832), an Italian composer, settled in England in 1766 and was the founder of the London Piano School, an influential group of composers. Two of his pupils, John Baptist Cramer (1771–1858) and John Field (1782–1837), also made important contributions to piano music. Cramer developed the piano study (*étude*), and Field originated the nocturne, another type of piano composition.

▶**VICTORIAN MUSIC**

During the reign of Queen Victoria, from 1837 to 1901, music continued to play a large part in English life. Large-scale choral festivals were held in vast halls such as the Crystal Palace (built in 1851). Brass bands were developed, and there was an increase in concerts of symphonic and chamber music. The music hall, a stage variety show, was popular with working-class people.

More and more churches began to use choirs and organ music in their services. In a revival of Anglican church music, Samuel Sebastian Wesley (1810–76), the son of Samuel Wesley, wrote powerful anthems full of romantic color.

Gilbert and Sullivan. Many operas were written by Victorian composers, but the only ones with lasting fame are 13 operettas (light operas) with words by William Schwenk Gilbert (1836–1911) and music by Arthur Seymour Sullivan (1842–1900). The Gilbert and Sullivan operettas, which include *H.M.S. Pinafore* (1878) and *The Mikado* (1885), contain memorable tunes and some of the wittiest dramatic writing since *The Beggar's Opera*.

▶**THE 20TH CENTURY**

Britain entered the 20th century as the leader of a great empire. The music of Edward Elgar (1857–1934) expressed the might and grandeur of the nation. The song "Land of Hope and Glory," adapted from one of Elgar's five *Pomp and Circumstance* marches, was played at the coronation of Edward VII in 1902. It is Elgar's best-known tune. Elgar's other compositions include the *Enigma Variations* (1899), which shows his command of orchestral writing, and *The Dream of Gerontius* (1900), a religious choral work.

The English Musical Renaissance. Elgar and his contemporaries Hubert Parry (1848–1918) and Charles Villiers Stanford (1852–1924) began a trend that has sometimes been called the English musical renaissance. They halted the long-standing tendency of the English to prefer the music of foreign composers.

Frederick Delius (1862–1934) and Gustav Holst (1874–1934) were English-born composers of foreign descent. Like Elgar, they were masters of the orchestra, and each is best known today for an orchestral work—Delius for *On Hearing the First Cuckoo in the Spring* (1912) and Holst for *The Planets* (1916).

More completely national in his approach was Ralph Vaughan Williams (1872–1958), who based his style largely on English folk songs and the music of the Golden Age (1590–1630). During his long life he composed nine symphonies, several operas, many choral works, and a large number of songs.

Modern Composers. The founder of modern English music was Benjamin Britten (1913–76). His style was quite modern but remained thoroughly English. Like Purcell, who was one of his heroes, Britten was skilled at setting English words to music. Britten wrote fine songs and orchestral pieces, but his most important works are operas on English subjects. He used children's voices in such works as *Let's Make an Opera* (1949).

Other important composers of Britten's generation include William Walton (1902–83) and Michael Tippett (1905–   ). Of later composers, Thea Musgrave (1928–   ) was a noted opera composer; Peter Maxwell Davies (1934–   ) specialized in music for schoolchildren; and Andrew Lloyd Webber (1948–   ) composed popular musicals, including *Jesus Christ Superstar* (1970) and *Cats* (1981).

NICHOLAS TEMPERLEY
University of Illinois
Author, *The Music of the English Parish Church*

St. Thais (*above*), made in the 1500's by Parmigianino, and the 1936 *Nymphe Surprise II* (*right*), by John Buckland-Wright, show different engraving styles.

ENGRAVING

Engraving is the process of cutting a design into a hard surface. Any hard surface that can be cut may be used, but metal and wood are the most common. In ancient times, decorations of all kinds were engraved on metal vessels. This use of the engraving process is one that has continued throughout history.

In the 1400's, in both Italy and Germany, a method of printing from engraved metal was invented. The name of this printing process—in which a print is made from ink forced into the grooves on a sheet of metal—is **intaglio**.

In intaglio printing, artists work on plates of zinc or copper. With sharp, pointed tools called **burins**, they "draw" on the plate by cutting into it. The areas that are not cut into, or engraved, will be white on the print. Lightness and darkness are achieved in a number of ways. One way is called **cross-hatching**. Little parallel lines are engraved and crossed by another set of parallel lines. Many such lines placed close together produce a darker area, while fewer lines spaced more widely will create a grayer area. Shading can also be controlled by lines that do not cross, or simply by thicker lines.

After artists cut their drawings into the plates, they rub the plates with thick, creamy ink. Next they wipe the plates with a special cotton pad, called a tarlatan pad, removing ink from the surface but not from the grooves. The plate is then covered with a piece of damp paper and soft felt blankets, and run through a printing press under great pressure. The top roller of the press exerts pressure on the blanket, forcing the paper into the grooves to absorb the ink. When the paper is removed from the plate, the drawing appears on the paper as a mirror image of the plate design.

At any point while working on a plate, the artist may want to see what the creation looks like. So the artist "pulls" a **proof** (sample copy) from the press. When the artist is satisfied with the plate, the artist prepares an **edition** (a certain number of copies printed from one plate).

Wood engraving became popular in the 1500's. The side (cross grain) rather than the top of a plank of hardwood is cut with engraving burins. Wood engravings are not printed by the intaglio method, however. The print is made from ink on the part of the surface that has not been engraved. A wood engraving can appear as white lines on a black background or as fine black lines on a white background.

The development of engraving led to more advanced intaglio printing methods. By the 1700's, etching, with its great variety of techniques, overshadowed engraving.

Reviewed by JOHN SPARKS
The Maryland Institute, College of Art

See also ETCHING; GRAPHIC ARTS.

A philosopher explains the solar system in this 1766 painting. The thinkers of the Enlightenment believed that the universe operates according to predictable natural laws.

ENLIGHTENMENT, AGE OF

The Enlightenment was the most important intellectual and social movement in Europe and America in the 1700's. The thinkers who were part of this movement shared a belief that people could improve themselves and their world through the use of reason. So powerful was their dedication to reason that historians often call the Enlightenment the Age of Reason.

The thinkers who defined the values and ideals of the Enlightenment were a varied group. In France, where many of them lived, they became known as the *philosophes* (a French word meaning "philosophers"). They did not agree on all points, but many of them shared a belief in liberty and justice for all people and championed "the rights of man." This was a revolutionary idea in a day when nations were ruled by monarchs and common people had few rights. Today, when we speak of "human rights," we are expressing the ideals of the Enlightenment.

▶ THE IMPACT OF SCIENCE

The Enlightenment built on a foundation of earlier ideas. The thinkers of the 1700's found inspiration in the scientific discoveries of the 1600's. For example, they were impressed by Isaac Newton's theory of gravity, which showed that the world operated according to physical laws. They were also influenced by the English philosopher Sir Francis Bacon. Bacon was optimistic about human progress. He believed that people, using science and mathematics, could fully understand the world. Knowledge would give them the power to control and use nature for their own benefit.

By the 1700's, educated Europeans and Americans accepted these views. They assumed that the behavior of the universe and everything in it, including people, was rational, regular, orderly, and predictable. The *philosophes* compared the universe to a giant mechanical clock and thought of God as the "Great Clockmaker." God had created the universe and set it in motion, but even God had to obey the laws of physics and mechanics. It was, therefore, only a matter of time before people would be able to unravel and explain all the mysteries of creation. The purpose of the Enlightenment, wrote the German philosopher Immanuel Kant, was to bring "light into the dark corners of the mind."

Profiles

Consult the Index to find more information in *The New Book of Knowledge* about the following people associated with the Enlightenment: Francis Bacon, René Descartes, Galileo, David Hume, Immanuel Kant, Gottfried Wilhelm Von Leibniz, John Locke, Isaac Newton, Jean Jacques Rousseau, Baruch Spinoza, and Voltaire.

Comte de Buffon

Montesquieu

Denis Diderot

Pierre Bayle (1647–1706), born in Carla-le-Comte, France, was a philosopher who had a great influence on later thinkers of the Enlightenment. In his *Historical and Critical Dictionary* (1697) and other works, Bayle used irony and humor to condemn superstition and criticize tradition and authority. Persecuted by French authorities for his political and religious views, he spent much of his career outside France, in Switzerland and Holland. He is regarded as the father of Rationalism.

Cesare Bonesana, Marchese di Beccaria (1738–94), born in Milan, Italy, concentrated on reforming legal systems. His treatise on criminal justice was published when he was just 26, and it is still influential. Beccaria opposed the torture, secret trials, and harsh punishments of his day. He wrote that severity of punishment should match the severity of the crime. He was the first writer to oppose capital punishment (the death penalty).

Jeremy Bentham (1748–1832), born in London, was an English philosopher. The son of an attorney, Bentham was schooled for a career in law and government. But he was more interested in the principles of law than its practice. He is best known for his theory of utilitarianism, which held that the goal of all laws must be "the greatest happiness of the greatest number." He was also a pioneer of legal and prison reforms.

Georges-Louis Leclerc, Comte de Buffon (1707–88), born in Montbard, France, was a naturalist. In 1739, he became keeper of the Jardin du Roi (the royal botanical garden), where he began to catalog the French royal natural history collections. This project grew into his lifework—a multivolume account of all nature. Buffon completed 36 of the planned 50 volumes in his *Histoire naturelle* before his death. The work was widely read and influenced ideas about the history of Earth, biological classification, and vanished species.

Denis Diderot (1713–84), born in Langres, France, was coeditor of the *Encyclopédie*, one of the best-known works of the Enlightenment. Diderot studied law,

▶ VIEWS OF SOCIETY

The *philosophes* were not only interested in understanding nature and the universe. They studied government and society to discover how to improve them. The *philosophes* were thus more than philosophers. They were closer to what we think of as sociologists, political analysts, and social critics.

One of the most important *philosophes* was the Frenchman Jean Jacques Rousseau. Rousseau believed that society was corrupt and that nature was innocent. His ideal was the "noble savage," a person who lived free of the artificial expectations of society. Rousseau's ideas did not fit very well with the rational, scientific outlook of the Enlightenment. Other *philosophes* criticized his views as sentimental and unrealistic.

Unlike Rousseau, most thinkers in the 1700's believed that people had to work to cre-

Artists, authors, and philosophers gathered regularly at Madame Geoffrin's famous salon in Paris in the 1700's. Such gatherings gave people a chance to exchange ideas.

but his real interests were literature, philosophy, and mathematics. He earned a living by writing, teaching, and translating. Diderot began work on the *Encyclopédie* in 1745, with the mathematician Jean le Rond d'Alembert (1717–83) as coeditor. Besides making their own contributions to the work, the editors gathered material from some of the leading thinkers and scientists of the time.

Thomas Hobbes

Marie-Thérèse Rodet Geoffrin (1699–1777), born in Paris, France, was a patron of the *philosophes*. The daughter of a servant, she married a wealthy manufacturer and became one of the most celebrated hostesses in Paris. From 1749 to 1777, artists, writers, and thinkers gathered at her salon at the Hôtel de Rambouillet to exchange ideas. She also supported the creation of the *Encyclopédie*, which expressed many of the era's important ideas.

Thomas Hobbes (1588–1679), born in Westport, England, was a scholar and political theorist. Hobbes studied classics at Oxford University. He believed that mathematics and science were the surest paths to greater human knowledge. But Hobbes was a pessimist where human nature was concerned. He thought that people would live in peace and security only if they agreed to be ruled by an absolute sovereign. His political ideas, outlined in *Leviathan* (1651) and other works, stand in contrast to those of more liberal thinkers of the Enlightenment.

Julien Offroy de La Mettrie (1709–51), born in Saint-Malo, France, was a physician and philosopher whose ideas helped pave the way for modern theories of human behavior. A French military surgeon, La Mettrie came to believe that human thought and other abilities were based entirely on physical processes. He expressed this view in *Natural History of the Soul* (1745), *Man a Machine* (1747), and other works. His ideas shocked religious leaders. La Mettrie was forced to leave France for Holland, and later left Holland for the court of Frederick the Great in Germany.

Charles-Louis de Secondat, Baron de La Brède et de Montesquieu (1689–1755), born near Bordeaux, France, was a philosopher whose political ideas had great influence. He spent much time in Paris, where he was at the center of intellectual activity. Montesquieu studied the sciences throughout his life, but he is best known for his political theories. His first important work, *Persian Letters* (1721), was a satirical critique of French society. His most important work was *The Spirit of Laws* (1748), a huge survey of the principles of law and government. Among the ideas he developed was the separation of powers into legislative, executive, and judicial branches of government. This idea was later adopted by the authors of the U.S. Constitution.

La Mettrie

---

ate happiness. The best way to do so was by making others happy. The happy and virtuous person was useful and helpful to others. This philosophy of **utilitarianism**, or usefulness, was set out by the Englishman Jeremy Bentham. Bentham measured the "utility," or usefulness, of any act of legislation according to its ability to produce "the greatest happiness of the greatest number" of people.

Many of the important ideas of the Enlightenment were contained in a work called the *Encyclopédie* (*Encyclopedia*). Published in 17 volumes during the 1750's and 1760's, the *Encyclopédie* expressed such ideas as tolerance of diversity, devotion to freedom, and commitment to progress. The editors, Denis Diderot and Jean d'Alembert, were critical of religion, which they thought promoted intolerance and superstition. Instead, they devoted attention to subjects such as agriculture and science. These subjects, they believed, were more likely to promote happiness and progress.

▶ **GOVERNMENT REFORM**

The writings of the English philosopher John Locke had a strong influence on ideas about government during the Enlightenment. Locke wrote that people should agree to be governed for their own benefit, to protect their lives, property, and freedom. He also held that educated people, given the right to speak freely and to hear opposing views, would act in the best interests of society.

Many of the *philosophes* believed that all people had "certain unalienable rights"—that is, rights they could neither give away nor lose. This idea formed the basis of both the American and the French revolutions. The great documents of those revolutions, the American Declaration of Independence (1776) and the French Declaration of the Rights of Man and of the Citizen (1789), expressed this principle.

The French thinker François-Marie Arouet, better known as Voltaire, championed freedom of thought and freedom of expression. He criticized the governments of various European countries and the Roman Catholic Church because he believed they stifled freedom, using threats of violent punishment to intimidate people. Voltaire urged tolerance and justice for all who did not follow established standards and practices in politics and religion. He was among the *philosophes* who believed that government should represent the people.

Other thinkers believed that strong rulers could improve society if they embraced reforms. Such rulers were known as **enlightened despots**. The rulers of several kingdoms in central and eastern Europe, such as Prussia, Austria, and Russia, tried to strengthen their realms by making them more efficient and more productive. To accomplish this task, they adopted many of the *philosophes'* ideas. The *philosophes* generally applauded the efforts of the enlightened despots because they believed these rulers encouraged freedom and progress. However, the rulers were often more interested in increasing the power of their governments. The enlightened despots were almost always more despotic than enlightened. As a result, they almost always disappointed the *philosophes*.

The limits of enlightened despotism were illustrated in a trip that the Russian empress Catherine the Great took to see how her people lived. Everywhere she went, Catherine found clean villages, well-built houses, fat cattle, and cheerful peasants. But everything she saw was part of an elaborate stage set organized by her favorite minister, Count Grigori Aleksandrovich Potemkin. (The term "Potemkin Village" is still used to describe a false spectacle.) When Catherine's *philosophe* friends, such as Voltaire and Diderot, chided her for participating in such false displays, she replied: "You write on paper. I write on human flesh." She meant that it was easy to propose reforms but harder to govern.

▶ ECONOMIC FREEDOM

England saw dramatic economic progress during the 1700's, and English thinkers expressed some of the most important economic ideas of the Enlightenment. The English practiced free enterprise; that is, people were allowed to earn a living with a minimum of interference from the government. In *An Inquiry Into the Nature and Causes of the Wealth of Nations* (1776), Adam Smith ar-

gued that government should not interfere with rational people who pursued their economic self-interest. Their efforts would not only produce individual wealth, but also increase general prosperity and social welfare. This principle is known as laissez-faire, a French phrase that means "let it be."

Earlier, in his work *The Fable of the Bees* (1723), Bernard Mandeville had made much the same point. In Mandeville's fable, the government of the beehive forces the bees to live more virtuous lives, and the economy collapses. Without greed and selfishness, the bees have no incentive to work gathering honey. The moral of the fable is that "private vices," such as greed, breed "public virtues," such as prosperity and social happiness.

▶ A MODEL OF ENLIGHTENMENT

Benjamin Franklin, who played a key role in the founding of the United States, embodied many of the values of the Enlightenment. He was involved in some of the most important philosophical and political debates of the day. Franklin promoted toleration, condemned prejudice and superstition, curbed unchecked political power, and celebrated reason. Along with other thinkers of his day, he questioned traditional values, beliefs, and institutions in the hope of improving society.

At the same time, in the spirit of utilitarianism, he carried out many useful projects. He founded a library and a fire department. He devised better ways to drain swamps and clean streets. And he invented many helpful items, from bifocal eyeglasses to an improved wood-burning stove. When friends criticized Franklin for concerning himself with such apparently insignificant matters, he told them that "human felicity [happiness] is produced not so much by great pieces of good fortune that seldom happen, as by little advantages that occur every day." Franklin believed that small, gradual acts of improvement increased human happiness.

The ideas expressed during the Enlightenment had far-reaching effects. They helped bring about not just reform but revolution. Some of these ideas were questioned in later years, but they helped shape modern society.

MEG GREENE
Contributing editor, *History for Children*

See also FOUNDERS OF THE UNITED STATES.

ENTREPRENEURSHIP. See BUSINESS.

ENVIRONMENT

In the broadest sense, environment is the surroundings in which a living thing grows, reproduces, and dies. Environment includes the earth, the water, the air, and all factors that help or hurt a living thing's chances of surviving. The condition of the environment helps determine if food is available, whether a living thing will live long enough to reproduce, and whether it will be able to produce healthy young.

Human beings have made many changes in the environment. They have cut down forests and planted crops in their place. They have hunted some animals and learned to raise others. Human inventions have put smoke and dangerous chemicals into the air, have polluted lakes and streams, and have worn out or damaged parts of the earth. These human-caused environmental problems have endangered not only humans, but also most other living creatures.

Environmentalists are people who have become concerned about such problems. They are looking for ways in which humans can live and prosper without harming the environment for future generations.

▶ RESOURCES AND WASTES

In every environment, the substances that make up all living things are used and re-used continually. For example, plants use carbon dioxide and water in the presence of sunlight to make their own food. During this process, plants release oxygen, the gas that animals must have for breathing. Animals exhale carbon dioxide, which is then available to be used by plants.

As plants grow, they take minerals from the soil. Some plants are eaten by animals. When the animals die, their bodies decay and minerals are returned to the soil where they can be absorbed again by other plants.

This article explores the interaction of human beings with their environment. It examines the many types of wastes, or pollutants, that harm the environment.

Several separate articles examine environmental pollutants in greater detail. These are ACID RAIN; AIR POLLUTION; HAZARDOUS WASTES; and WATER POLLUTION. Articles on ECOLOGY and LIFE describe the interrelationship of all living things in the environment. The resources we have on earth and how to best protect them are covered in the articles NATURAL RESOURCES and CONSERVATION.

Humans adapt to many different environments. *Top:* Desert people live near scarce water at an oasis. *Center:* Farmers in a crowded country use even steep hillsides for farming. *Bottom:* Along the seashore fishermen catch many kinds of food from the sea.

Left: As population increases and more people live in cities, we must produce more food, clothing, shelter, and energy. Increased needs place new strains on the environment. *Opposite page:* Insecticides sprayed on crops help to increase food production. But when insecticides are carried by wind or water runoff to rivers and lakes, they may poison useful insects, fish, and other forms of life, including people.

These substances—carbon dioxide, water, oxygen, and minerals—are examples of both resources and wastes in the environment. Although considered wastes by one organism, some substances are important resources to another. Because of this, there is a natural balance between resources and wastes. Each is important in the continuous cycle of life on earth.

Human beings also use resources in their environment and create waste. Unfortunately, as we have attempted to provide for our growing population, we have upset the balance of resources and wastes. Wastes are now being produced faster than they can be re-used. These wastes are no longer resources. Instead, they are considered pollutants because they are damaging to the environment. And the faster our population grows, the more pollutants are produced.

▶RESOURCES FOR A GROWING POPULATION

Between 1950 and 1990, the earth's population more than doubled, from 2.5 billion people to more than 5 billion. This enormous increase is called the population explosion. Many experts believe it is the greatest danger facing humankind.

Will there be enough food for so many people? Even today, more than one half of the people in the world do not have enough to eat. Agricultural experts have developed new kinds of rice and wheat plants that yield bigger crops per acre. These cereal grains can keep more people from being hungry, but they do not contain all the proteins necessary for good health and proper growth. Cattle and poultry provide these proteins, but they must be nour-

ished on grain that is scarce. Fish also provide protein, but some experts believe that overfishing and pollution have already dangerously reduced the number of fish.

Can anything be done to feed a doubled world population? Ways will have to be found to obtain more protein from the sea, by using plants now found in the oceans and by growing others. Synthetic (artificial) chemical foods must be manufactured. Yields of present crops will have to be increased tremendously. The way that food is now distributed will have to be changed. If mass hunger is to be avoided, the nations with sufficient food will have to make sacrifices to help the underfed countries.

A doubled population means a greater drain on the world's limited resources. Lumber is needed to provide decent housing. So are iron, copper, aluminum, and other metals. Vehicles to carry people and goods require tremendous amounts of metals. Some of these metals are already scarce.

A doubled population will need more electricity. Water power, which now generates about one third of the world's electricity, is limited because there are only a limited number of rivers that can be dammed. Coal, oil, and gas are used to make steam to provide about two thirds of the electricity generated today. The supply of coal seems adequate, but oil and gas supplies are being used up rapidly. No one can be sure how long these resources will last in the face of a vastly increased demand. A small amount of electricity is now produced by using nuclear energy, but the use of nuclear reactors presents problems of pollution by radioactivity.

A doubled population means that more land will be needed to raise food. More land will also be used for building roads for the increased number of vehicles.

Biologists are concerned with the many tensions that arise from overcrowding. They feel that the population should not grow beyond the capacity of the earth to house people in some comfort. Some scientists believe that even today the number of people is close to the limit that the earth can support. Many countries have begun family planning programs. In these programs people are urged to limit the number of their children. Some experts fear that these voluntary programs will not be effective enough, and that laws limiting the size of families may be needed.

▶ **WASTES THAT HARM THE ENVIRONMENT**

Finding enough resources to provide for the needs of all people is only part of the challenge we now face. Protecting the environment from harmful wastes is another part. Some of the most serious pollutants are described below.

Water Pollution

Fertilizers. Fertilizers are materials added to the soil to help plant growth. They may be organic or inorganic. An organic fertilizer is one that was once alive or that comes from a living thing. Fish meal and animal manures (wastes) are examples of organic fertilizers. Inorganic, or chemical, fertilizers are mined or made in a chemical factory.

When inexpensive chemical fertilizers became available, farmers added them freely to the soil. This resulted in great harvests, but the excess fertilizer drained away and was carried down into ponds and lakes. There it stimulated the growth of algae. (The green scummy growths floating on ponds are one form of algae.) Algae filled the lakes, crowding other plant and animal life.

The huge masses of algae died. As they decayed, they used up the oxygen in the water. This killed off many fish and other water animals. In time, slimy, foul-smelling mats of dead algae and fish floated on lakes that once served as a source for drinking water, swimming, and fishing.

This is an example of the delicate balance that exists between a resource and a waste. Fertilizer properly used is a resource that produces better crops. Used too freely, it becomes a waste that pollutes the environment.

Detergents. The invention of detergents provided people with a powerful new cleaning agent, but widespread use beginning in the 1940's caused environmental problems. Early detergents were **non-biodegradable**—that is, they could not be broken down into simpler chemical substances by bacteria. When household waste water flowed from sewers into streams and lakes, masses of foaming detergent piled up. Biodegradable detergents were developed, but they contained phosphates, chemicals that stimulated algae growth in streams and lakes. This problem has been somewhat solved by reducing the amounts of phosphates in most detergents.

Sewage. The most serious water pollutant, as far as public health is concerned, is sewage. This water, collected by sewer pipes, carries many types of waste, including the wastes from the human body.

Left: Each year about five million tons of oil end up on the ocean's surface where it kills many kinds of marine life. This spill in the Gulf of Mexico has actually caught fire. *Below:* Clean-up measures, such as these floating oil booms fixed in place with stakes, can keep an oil slick from spreading.

The solid wastes from the body contain large numbers of bacteria and viruses. Most of these are harmless, but disease-carrying organisms can also be found. If these get into drinking water they may cause widespread sickness, or epidemics.

For thousands of years all communities dumped their sewage into nearby water. The flowing water diluted the sewage. Bacteria broke down the wastes into simpler substances. But as the population increased in cities and towns, flowing water alone was not enough to dispose of the increased amounts of sewage. Sewage-treatment plants were built. Most of these plants remove the solid materials and harmful organisms from the sewage. The remaining water is dumped into a stream or lake.

Oceans, which cover about 70 percent of the earth's surface, have not escaped pollution. Sewage sludge—the solid material remaining after sewage is treated—is dumped at sea. In studies made in one ocean dumping area, no living things could be found. Effects of ocean-dumped sludge sometimes can be seen in the form of animal poisonings thousands of miles away from the dump site. In addition, wastes from mines, factories, and refineries are sometimes dumped directly into the ocean, or they reach it through rivers.

Water pollution can be ended by building advanced sewer systems, sewage-treatment plants, and installations to keep industrial wastes and fertilizers from entering the water.

The cost will be enormous, but the result will be water that is clean enough to again be used for drinking, swimming, and fishing.

Oil. Oil is now a common ocean pollutant. It may get into the water when an oil tanker springs a leak or sinks. Drilling for oil offshore has also caused pollution. The thick, sticky oil floating on the water coats and kills fish, birds, seals, and other living things. It spoils beaches and coastal waters, making them useless for swimming.

Agencies of the United Nations are conducting studies of ocean pollution and planning ways to deal with the problem. If the oceans of the world are to be saved, the nations of the world must act together to save them.

Pollution By Synthetic Chemicals

To make the environment a better place for people to live, scientists have developed a wide variety of new chemicals. Some of these are pesticides that reduce crop damage and control diseases. Other chemicals are used to insulate electrical equipment, produce many kinds of plastics, increase food supplies, create new products, and improve health.

Almost all new chemical substances were once viewed as modern miracles. Chemical insecticides and herbicides are cheap, easy to use, amazingly effective, and long-lasting. New plastic materials are so versatile and unique that they have found their way into many aspects of manufacturing and daily life.

However, synthetic substances also have created serious, long-term environmental problems. Many synthetic substances are non-biodegradable. This means that there are no micro-organisms able to break them down and thereby recycle their chemical components.

Plastics litter our highways and beaches because they are non-biodegradable. Sea turtles, birds, fish, and other organisms that are unfortunate enough to become tangled in plastics—or to eat them—often die.

Certain chemicals found in common pesticides not only kill the intended pest but may also accumulate in the bodies of any other organisms that come in contact with the substances. As these poison chemicals build up in the body, unintended victims perish. They may become weakened and succumb to disease, predation, or may actually die as a direct effect of the chemical. For example, some birds of prey, such as ospreys and eagles, are known to accumulate insecticides in their bodies. This interferes with their ability to produce strong eggs and healthy chicks.

When scientific studies indicate that specific chemicals are dangerous or harmful to humans, the U.S. Government limits or bans their use. Unfortunately, these banned chemicals are often used extensively in other countries. No matter where such harmful chemicals are used, they flow into rivers, lakes, and oceans and create significant environmental damage.

Smog obscures the skyline of New York City. In and around the world's large cities, smog is an irritating and sometimes deadly part of modern life.

Air Pollution

A great deal of energy is needed to run the factories of modern industrial nations. Automobiles, trains, planes, and buses need energy, too. Nearly all of this energy is produced in the same way—by burning fuels. The burning produces wastes. Some of the wastes get into the air, causing air pollution. Government officials in the United States estimate that 200 million tons of these wastes enter the air each year—one ton for each person in the country!

A curtain of smog often hangs over big cities. It irritates the eyes, throat, and chest. The word "smog" is a combination of the words smoke and fog, but smog itself is a mixture of many more ingredients. It begins with some of the pollutants from burning: soot, carbon monoxide, hydrocarbons, and oxides of nitrogen and sulfur are among them. Some of the pollutants react with one another to form new irritating substances. Energy is needed for the reactions, and it is supplied by the light of the sun. The resulting mixture is **photochemical smog**. ("Photo" means light.) It can be deadly.

In London, Tokyo, Los Angeles, Denver, and other cities, a weather condition called a temperature inversion allows smog to hang

over the city for several days at a time. Many people become ill, and the death rate among elderly people and people with lung disorders climbs rapidly.

At least half of the pollutants in the air come from the engines of motor vehicles. As they burn fuel, they give off carbon monoxide and other hazardous gases as wastes. Carbon monoxide is a colorless, odorless gas and a deadly poison. The amount of carbon monoxide that an engine gives off can be reduced by special devices designed to make the engine burn the fuel more efficiently.

Automobile manufacturers are working on experimental cars run by electricity or other means that will reduce pollution. State and city governments in various parts of the world are working to decrease automobile and truck pollution. Mandatory emissions tests are used to identify polluters, and laws require owners to make appropriate corrections reducing harmful emissions. Some city planners believe that central city areas should be kept free from automobile use.

Motor vehicles are not the only air polluters. Coal and oil, used to heat homes and factories and to generate electricity, contain small amounts of sulfur. When the fuels are burned, sulfur dioxide, a poisonous gas, is produced. It is irritating to the lungs. Some cities have passed laws that allow coal and oil to be burned only if their sulfur content is low.

Power plants that produce electricity usually burn fuel. The fuel is used to create steam for running electricity-producing turbines. About half of the unwanted sulfur dioxide and nitrogen oxides in the atmosphere come from fuel burned for this purpose.

Acid Rain

When sulfur and nitrogen oxides react with water vapor in the atmosphere, the rain (or snow) that falls to earth is more acidic than normal. This is known as acid rain. Acid rain is harmful because it changes the balance of both land and water environments. It especially weakens forests because normal plant growth decreases. Lakes become lifeless because insects, amphibians, fish, and aquatic plants are poisoned by acids.

Acid rain is specifically harmful to environments that are "downwind" from the industrial sources of sulfur and nitrogen oxide pollution. In many industrialized countries, large sections of forest are radically affected by acid rain. Some land areas are actually becoming completely deforested.

Human environments also are affected. Acid rain deteriorates stone, concrete, marble, and metal structures. Human health can be affected because people with respiratory diseases suffer from increased symptoms in acid environments. When acid rain enters water supplies, it can affect the health of the people who use the water.

Acid rain can be reduced or eliminated by burning fuels that have a low sulfur content. Devices that remove sulfur and nitrogen oxides from the exhaust of burning fuels also can help solve the problem of acid rain.

Rain Forest Destruction

Air pollution problems are made worse by the destruction of tropical rain forests. Each year many thousands of acres of rain forest are cleared for farming, animal grazing, lumbering, and building.

The great number of plants in a rain forest absorbs enormous amounts of carbon dioxide gas. As rain forest trees are cut and can no longer absorb this gas, carbon dioxide in the atmosphere increases and helps create what is called the **greenhouse effect**.

The greenhouse effect occurs when carbon dioxide traps certain kinds of radiation and heat close to the earth's surface. This results in increases in worldwide temperatures, changed weather patterns, increases in sea level, and other serious modifications of the world environment.

Opposite page: Dead and dying trees on the hills of the Black Forest in West Germany are stark evidence of acid rain. *Right:* The enormous amount of solid waste that human activity generates each year has long-lasting effects on the environment. Some man-made materials may take decades or centuries to decay.

Rain forests must be saved if the greenhouse effect is to be reversed. To accomplish this, some conservation organizations are buying and preserving large areas of rain forest. In some countries rain forests are promoted as tourist attractions. In some cases this has proven to generate more needed income than farming or lumbering while at the same time preserving an essential natural resource.

HOW YOU CAN PROTECT THE ENVIRONMENT

- Cut down on electricity use. Turn off unneeded lights. Do chores by hand instead of using an electrical appliance. Limit the use of air conditioners.
- Conserve heating fuels by setting the household thermostat a few degrees lower. Wear sweaters to keep warm. Set the thermostat even lower at night.
- Travel to school or work on foot, on a bicycle, in a car pool, or in public transportation, if possible. Avoid frequent trips with only one or two people in the family car.
- Buy products, especially foods, that are enclosed in minimal packaging. Try to avoid packages that are made of plastic or styrofoam, which are non-biodegradable. Buy soft drinks in returnable bottles or cans, and be sure to return them.
- Collect household trash such as glass bottles, newspapers, metal, and used motor oil. Deliver these items to a recycling center. Encourage your friends and neighbors to do the same.
- Consider a career in environmental protection, such as marine biologist, toxic wastes analyst, environmental lawyer, or wildlife manager.

Thermal Pollution

A significant amount of air pollution is caused by the fuels burned in power plants. But another type of pollution, called thermal (heat) pollution, is also caused by power plants. Both fuel-burning and nuclear power plants use huge amounts of cold water to cool the steam coming from the turbines. As a result the water is warmed. When this warm water is returned to rivers or ocean harbors, it may stimulate the growth of weeds. It may also kill fish and their eggs, or interfere with their growth.

Physicists are studying new ways of generating electricity that may be less damaging to the environment. In the meantime, many power plants are being modernized to give off less polluting material. Also, engineers try to design and locate new power plants to do minimum damage to the environment.

Solid Waste Pollution

As cities grow, the problem of what to do with solid waste material grows too. Solid waste includes litter, garbage, paper, old automobiles and tires, rubble from demolished buildings, as well as toxic industrial wastes and infectious medical wastes.

What should be done with all this refuse? Formerly the answer was to take it to the city dump or incinerator. But now many cities have run out of dumping space. Refuse can be disposed of by burning it in incinerators, but this causes air pollution.

Dumping into marshes, bays, or even the ocean causes water pollution. Ocean dumping

Workers sort through mounds of beverage cans at a community recycling center. The metal will be processed and used again.

is responsible for deaths of rare and endangered species, such as sea turtles and whales. Some beaches and shellfish beds are frequently closed to the public so that these destructive pollutants do not harm people.

Researchers have suggested many solutions to the problem. Nearly all of them will cost more than our present methods for disposing of refuse. Some materials, such as paper, glass, and metals, can be separated from the refuse, then processed for re-use. This method, called **recycling**, would also help to save some valuable resources. Experiments have been made in reducing certain solid wastes to compact bricks for building materials. Packages and containers made from materials that will decay after use can be used in place of "non-returnable" glass and aluminum containers.

▶ENVIRONMENTAL PROTECTION ORGANIZATIONS

Various organizations and government agencies have been formed to protect and help improve environmental quality. In 1970, the U.S. Environmental Protection Agency (EPA) was created to protect land, air, and water environments from pollution. It is the EPA's responsibility to form policies that help create a balance between human activities and the ability of the environment to support life. The EPA also enforces federal laws that pertain to air and water quality, solid waste management, and the control of toxic substances, pesticides, noise, and radiation.

Hundreds of other environmental organizations throughout the world also promote environmental quality. Organizations such as Friends of the Earth, the Audubon Society, Greenpeace, World Wildlife Fund, and the Nature Conservancy are committed to preserving, restoring, and carefully using the earth's natural resources. These and other groups help operate wildlife sanctuaries, provide environmental education services, conduct research on endangered plant and animal species, and encourage governments to pass environmental protection laws.

Other environmental organizations have a more limited scope and purpose. The New England Wild Flower Society, for example, promotes an appreciation and protection of native New England plants through research and education. Friends of the Sea Otter is a group that seeks to protect and maintain a healthy population of southern sea otters along the California coast.

▶THE FUTURE OF OUR ENVIRONMENT

Putting the environment into better order will not be cheap or easy. The environmental damage is worldwide. Working out the solutions will require planning on an international level. People will have to think over some hard questions. Are we willing to limit population? Are we ready to pay the staggering costs of ending air and water pollution? Are we ready to make less use of automobiles and electric power if that is part of the price?

The answers to questions like these must be "Yes." Rachel Carson, one of the first scientists and writers to warn of the dangers of pollution, once wrote, "No organism in biological history has survived for long if its environment became in some way unfit for it. But no organism before man has deliberately polluted its environment."

MATTHEW J. BRENNAN
Brentree Environmental Center
Reviewed by JOEL H. MEISEL
Center for the Environment
Southern Connecticut State University

See also ACID RAIN; AIR POLLUTION; ALGAE; CONSERVATION; DETERGENTS AND SOAP; ECOLOGY; ENERGY; FERTILIZERS; HAZARDOUS WASTES; LIFE; NATURAL RESOURCES; POPULATION; SANITATION; WATER POLLUTION.

ENZYMES

Enzymes are complex molecules that act as **catalysts** for chemical change in all living things. This means that enzymes speed up the chemical change but are not changed themselves. Enzymes are something like machines in a factory. They take in raw materials and put out finished products very rapidly. Like machines, enzymes are not used up in the manufacturing process. They can repeat a particular process many thousands of times.

Some enzymes can make chemical changes take place billions of times faster. For example, a chemical change that might take years without an enzyme takes only one hundredth of a second when an enzyme is present.

Every living thing contains thousands of different types of enzymes, each specialized for just one particular chemical change. Enzymes are found inside every living cell and also in blood, saliva, and other fluids. When you eat a cookie or a potato, the enzymes in your saliva speed up chemical changes that break down the starch into smaller molecules that can be absorbed and used by your body.

Enzymes can also be used outside living organisms. Because they are such good catalysts, enzymes are used in manufacturing processes such as fermentation, leather tanning, and the production of cheese.

What Are Enzymes Made of?

Enzymes are proteins. All proteins are made up of substances called amino acids that are chemically linked to each other to form long chains. The smallest enzymes contain only a hundred or so amino acid units, while large enzymes may have thousands. Enzymes may also contain atoms of metals, such as iron.

How Enzymes Work

Every enzyme first **binds**, or attaches, to the molecules it is going to help change. Once attached, the enzyme speeds up the chemical change that the molecule will undergo.

For example, proteins dissolved in water eventually break up into amino acids. Hydrogen and oxygen atoms from the water attach chemically to nitrogen and carbon atoms in the protein. An enzyme can give the hydrogen and oxygen atoms quick, direct pathways to their target atoms. The enzyme makes the chemical action take place much more quickly.

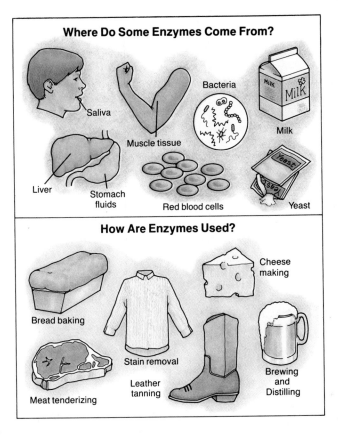

Where Do Some Enzymes Come From?

Saliva — Muscle tissue — Bacteria — Milk — Liver — Stomach fluids — Red blood cells — Yeast

How Are Enzymes Used?

Bread baking — Cheese making — Stain removal — Meat tenderizing — Leather tanning — Brewing and Distilling

The Control of Enzymes

No one would build a machine that cannot be turned on and off. In living systems, enzymes also need control. One such control is called **inhibition by-product**. For example, when starch molecules are broken down into sugar, the sugar (the product of the chemical change) binds to part of the enzyme. This prevents starch molecules from binding with the enzyme. If the sugar is later used up, the enzyme is free to bind starch again.

Hormones, another type of chemical in living things, can also act as control substances. They bind to the enzyme and cause it to change shape. If an enzyme has the wrong shape, it cannot take part in a chemical reaction. Controls such as these make it possible for the chemical changes in living organisms to occur when and where they are needed.

RONALD BRESLOW
Columbia University
Author, *Enzymes: The Machine of Life*

EPIDEMICS. See PUBLIC HEALTH.

EQUAL RIGHTS AMENDMENT. See WOMEN'S RIGHTS MOVEMENT.

EQUATIONS. See ALGEBRA; CHEMISTRY.

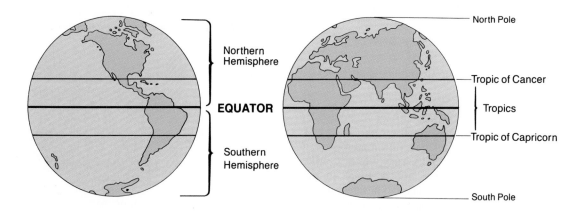

EQUATOR

Long ago, sailors often celebrated crossing the equator with elaborate ceremonies and outrageous merrymaking. Crew members and passengers crossing the equator for the first time were urged to pay tribute to King Neptune. Although the celebration began according to rigid tradition, it often degenerated into a rowdy festival of pranks and horseplay. Even today, crossing the equator is celebrated by passengers on some cruise ships.

The equator is an imaginary line circling Earth, almost 25,000 miles (40,000 kilometers) long, midway between the North and South poles. Its name comes from the Latin word *aequare*, meaning "to make equal." The equator divides Earth into two halves, the Northern Hemisphere and the Southern Hemisphere. It is also midway between the tropics of Cancer and Capricorn.

As a line on a map or globe, the equator passes through the countries of Ecuador, Colombia, and Brazil in South America; Gabon, Congo, the Democratic Republic of Congo, Uganda, Kenya, and Somalia in Africa; and Sumatra, Borneo, and other islands in the Pacific Ocean.

Climate Near the Equator

Many areas near the equator are hot and wet and covered with dense forests known as rain forests. These lush forests are so thick that cutting a path only a few yards long may take hours. (For more information, see the article RAIN FORESTS in Volume Q-R.) The Democratic Republic of Congo, a country located in equatorial Africa, contains such a climate. The rain forest there has an average daytime temperature of about 90°F (32°C). The air is humid, or heavy with moisture.

Other areas near the equator are highland or mountainous areas. Because of their higher elevations, these areas generally have cooler climates. It is possible for a highland area near the equator to be 10 to 20 degrees cooler than the lowland areas nearby. Two examples are Quito, Ecuador, and Nairobi, Kenya. People living in these cities, even though near the equator, enjoy many cool, springlike days. Yearly rainfall near the equator is heavy, often ranging from 60 to 100 inches (150 to 250 centimeters).

It is always summer near the equator. The rays of the sun shine more directly on the equator throughout the year than anywhere else on Earth. This region receives the same amount of sunlight all year long. Days and nights are approximately 12 hours each.

Determining Geographic Locations

The equator is the beginning point from which geographical positions are measured. The imaginary lines of latitude are shown on maps and globes as lines or circles parallel to the equator. Latitude is measured in degrees, with the equator considered to be zero degrees (0°). Any point north of the equator is said to be located in north latitude; any point south of the equator is said to be located in south latitude. Quito, Ecuador, is located almost on the equator (0°); New Orleans, Louisiana, is located at about 30° north latitude; and Brisbane, Australia, is located at about 27° south latitude.

No one can see the equator—it exists as an actual line only on maps and globes. Sailors know they are at the equator by the position of the North Star—it will appear to be on the northern horizon.

ANN BRISCOE NERO
Author, *Essential Skills in Geography*

EQUATORIAL GUINEA

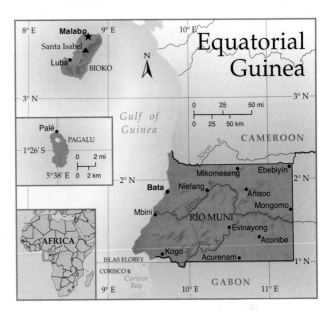

Equatorial Guinea

Equatorial Guinea is a small nation on the west central coast of Africa. It is made up of Río Muni, a region on the mainland, and five islands in the Gulf of Guinea—Bioko (the largest), Corisco, Elobey Grande and Elobey Chico, and Pagalu. A former Spanish colony, Equatorial Guinea became independent in 1968.

People. The largest ethnic group among Equatorial Guinea's roughly 523,000 people is the Fang, who live mainly in Río Muni. They are forest dwellers who live primarily by hunting and fishing. There are also settlements of other African peoples along the coast. The Bubi, the original inhabitants of Bioko, are chiefly farmers who grow crops to feed themselves. The basic food crops are cassava (a starchy root) and sweet potatoes.

Young girls in a village in Equatorial Guinea, where the climate is always hot and humid and the majority of people live in rural areas.

Spanish and French are the official languages, but the people of Equatorial Guinea also speak African languages, especially Fang and Bubi. Most of the people are Christian, mainly Roman Catholic. The influence of traditional African religions varies throughout the country.

Land. Most of Río Muni consists of tropical rain forest, with high plateaus in the central and eastern regions. Its main river is the Mbini. Bioko has densely forested mountains and a coastline that is high and rugged in the south. The most important town in Río Muni is Bata.

Economy. Equatorial Guinea's economy is based on the production of oil and natural gas, which brings in more than 90 percent of earnings from exports. The country also exports cacao beans, timber, and coffee. There are known but still largely untapped deposits of gold, uranium, and manganese.

Oil and natural gas were discovered in the 1990's, and growing world demand for these has sparked Equatorial Guinea's rapid economic growth. Most of the people, however, remain poor.

Major Cities. Malabo, the capital and largest city, is home to 95,000 people. It lies on the northern tip of Bioko.

FACTS and figures

REPUBLIC OF EQUATORIAL GUINEA (República de Guinea Ecuatorial) is the official name of the country.

LOCATION: West central coast of Africa.

AREA: 10,831 sq mi (28,051 km²).

POPULATION: 523,000 (estimate).

CAPITAL AND LARGEST CITY: Malabo.

MAJOR LANGUAGES: Spanish, French (both official), Fang.

MAJOR RELIGIOUS GROUP: Christian (Roman Catholic).

GOVERNMENT: Republic. **Head of state**—president. **Head of government**—prime minister. **Legislature**—House of People's Representatives.

CHIEF PRODUCTS: Agricultural—rice, cassava, bananas, palm oil, coffee, cacao, timber. **Mineral**—petroleum, natural gas.

MONETARY UNIT: C.F.A. franc (1 C.F.A. franc = 100 centimes).

History and Government. The first European to visit Bioko was the Portuguese explorer Fernão do Pó in the late 1400's. Portugal retained Bioko until 1778, when it was ceded to Spain. Spain first began to colonize Río Muni in 1843. The two territories were later united as Spanish Guinea. In 1959 they were made overseas provinces of Spain. Renamed Equatorial Guinea, the region was granted home rule in 1963 and independence in 1968. Under the Spanish, the territory developed public services, including health care and education, especially on Bioko.

The country's first president, Francisco Macías Nguema, named himself president for life in 1972. Under his repressive rule, the economy, schools, and health services collapsed. In 1979 Macias was overthrown in a military coup led by his nephew, Lieutenant Colonel Teodoro Obiang Nguema Mbasogo. Macias was executed, and Obiang Nguema became president. He was re-elected in 1989, 1996, and 2002, although his opponents claimed he won these elections through fraud.

Equatorial Guinea's constitution provides for a president elected every seven years and a House of People's Representatives elected every five years. In practice, almost all power is centered in the president.

Reviewed by GAIL M. GERHART
Columbia University

ERASMUS (1467?–1536)

The Dutch scholar and priest Desiderius Erasmus was the leading figure of the Renaissance in northern Europe. Erasmus was born about 1467, probably in Rotterdam. Both his parents died when he was in his teens. Erasmus had been sent to the famous St. Lebwin's school in Deventer, Holland, where he began to develop a witty writing style and to acquire the knowledge of the classics that in time would make him "the prince of humanists." (A humanist is one who studies human life and achievements.)

In 1487, against his wishes, Erasmus was sent to a monastery. He was ordained a priest in 1492 and later continued his studies at the University of Paris, France. In 1497 he visited England, where he made important friends, including the English humanist Thomas More. In 1506 he went to Italy. There the great printer Aldus Manutius of Venice published Erasmus' *Adagia (Adages)*, a vast collection of wise sayings and anecdotes from classical authors. The book established Erasmus' international reputation as a humanist.

After returning to England in 1509, Erasmus wrote his most famous book, *The Praise of Folly*. In this book, as in his later *Colloquies* (1518–33), he satirized the life and religious practices of his time. In 1516 he published an edition of the Greek New Testament, and later a new Latin translation. In the same year, Erasmus' edition of the *Letters* of St. Jerome appeared. This was followed by editions of the works of other church leaders.

These works were regarded with suspicion by conservative Catholic theologians. They accused Erasmus of supporting Martin Luther, whose attacks on the church had begun in 1519. Erasmus himself disagreed with Luther. He believed that the church should be reformed from within. But controversy continued to surround Erasmus until his death in Basel on July 12, 1536.

J. K. SOWARDS
Author, *Desiderius Erasmus*

See also MORE, SIR THOMAS; RENAISSANCE.

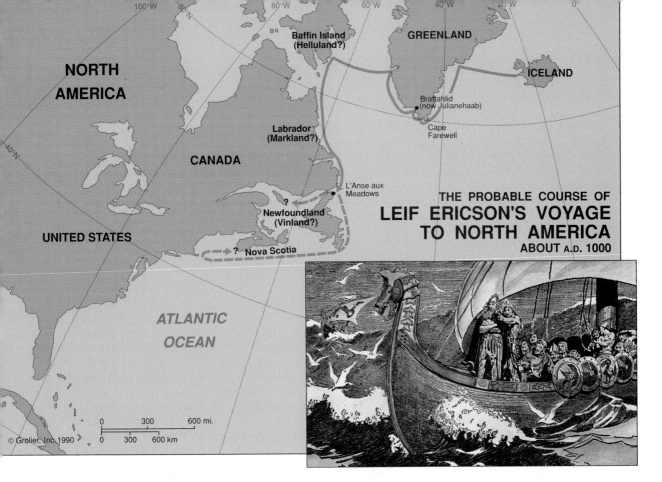

THE PROBABLE COURSE OF
LEIF ERICSON'S VOYAGE TO NORTH AMERICA
ABOUT A.D. 1000

© Grolier, Inc. 1990

ERICSON, LEIF (LIVED ABOUT A.D. 1000)

Almost 500 years before Christopher Columbus made his first voyage to the New World in 1492, the Vikings had "discovered" America. The tall, fair-haired Vikings, who lived in what are now Norway, Denmark, and Sweden, were fierce warriors and skillful sailors. In their long, swift ships they sailed far from their own countries to settle many new lands, including Iceland and Greenland. About the year 1000, a small group of Vikings landed on the northern coast of North America. Their leader was Leif Ericson.

Most of what we know about Leif Ericson comes from the old Icelandic sagas (stories). One such story is called *Eric's Saga*. The red-bearded Eric had been outlawed from the Iceland colony for killing several men in a fight. About the year 985, Eric took his family and settled in southern Greenland. With him was his young son Leif.

Leif grew up in Greenland. When he reached adulthood, he visited Norway, where he became a Christian. He sailed for home intending to convert the Greenlanders to his new faith.

Here the old stories begin to disagree. According to one account, on his return voyage to Greenland, Leif was blown off course and landed by mistake in North America. However, according to a more widely accepted story, Leif had heard of a new land from a fellow Greenlander, Bjarni Herjulfson. Many years earlier, Bjarni had seen a strange land on the horizon. Leif set out to explore this new land and to perhaps find wood, which was scarce in Greenland.

Leif followed Bjarni's old route and sighted the lands Bjarni had described. Leif went ashore at places he called Helluland, Markland, and Vinland. Many historians believe these places might have been places in Canada we now call Baffin Island, Labrador, and Newfoundland, respectively.

With his crew of 35 men, Leif stopped in Vinland for the winter. There it is said they found wild wheat and grapevines growing on fertile land and large salmon swimming in the lakes and streams. The name Vinland comes from one of two words in Old Norse and means either Wineland or Meadowland.

The following spring, Leif returned to Greenland with what is believed to be a cargo of timber and wild grapes. On the return voyage, he saved the lives of 15 men who had been shipwrecked on a reef. Because of his successful voyage and rescue, Leif became known as "Leif the Lucky."

Shortly after Leif returned to Greenland, Eric the Red died. Leif became the leader of his colony and continued his work to Christianize Greenland. He died about 1020.

Leif never went back to Vinland. For hundreds of years, the world knew nothing of the Viking discoveries in North America. Then in the early 1960's a Norwegian explorer found the ruins of a Viking settlement in L'Anse aux Meadows, Newfoundland. Little was left but the remains of a house and a fireplace. But scientists proved that the ruins date from about A.D. 1000. Many believe the discovery might have been Leif Ericson's house.

Reviewed by KENNETH S. COOPER
George Peabody College

See also VIKINGS.

ERIC THE RED

Eric the Red was a Viking chieftain who discovered and colonized Greenland in the late A.D. 900's. Most of what we know about him comes from *The Saga of Eric the Red* and *The Tale of the Greenlanders*, two Icelandic stories that were written sometime before the 1300's.

According to these centuries-old legends, Eric the Red was born Eric Thorvaldsson in Norway, but no one knows exactly when. He was called Eric the Red because he had fiery red hair. As a young boy, Eric journeyed to Iceland with his father, Thorvald, who was exiled from Norway for killing some men in a fight.

Eric grew up in Iceland and later married Thorhild, with whom he had three sons, Thorvald, Thorstein, and Leif. But Eric's life was not peaceful. Like his father, he possessed a quick temper and a ready sword. Continuous quarreling and his own acts of manslaughter forced him to move frequently from settlement to settlement. Around 982, he and his followers were declared outlaws and were banished from Iceland for three years.

Eric left Iceland with his young family and several friends. They sailed west in search of a large island a Viking explorer had reportedly sighted one hundred years earlier. After traveling about 450 miles (700 kilometers), the voyagers saw land, but it was surrounded by ice-choked waters. So they wintered on a smaller sheltered island nearby.

The following spring, Eric and his party landed at three or four places on the large island we now know as Greenland. They finally settled at a desirable spot on the southwestern coast, just north of the present district of Julianehaab, and named their new home Brattahlid. For the next two years, they explored the west coast of the island.

Eric returned to Iceland in 985 to attract settlers to his new homeland, which he had mischievously named "Greenland" to make the place sound inviting. His scheme worked, for the following year Eric returned to Greenland with 14 ships and about 350 potential settlers. Two colonies were immediately established. Osterbygd, the eastern settlement, was founded near Brattahlid on the southwest coast. Vesterbygd, the western settlement, was founded about 200 miles (320 kilometers) farther up the west coast.

About the year 1000, Eric's son, Leif, returned to Greenland from Norway to convert the Greenlanders to Christianity. Eric remained devoted to the Norse gods, but his wife, Thorhild, adopted the new faith and built the first Christian church in Greenland.

Leif soon decided to seek out a land that legends claimed lay even farther to the west and he offered Eric command of the expedition. But while riding to embark on the ship, Eric's horse stumbled and injured its leg. Eric interpreted this accident as a bad omen and decided to remain in Greenland, where he died soon thereafter.

CASS R. SANDAK
Author, *Explorers and Discovery*

See also ERICSON, LEIF; VIKINGS.

ERIE. See PENNSYLVANIA (Cities).

ERIE, LAKE. See GREAT LAKES.

The Erie Canal stretched across New York State and linked Lake Erie to the Hudson River.

ERIE CANAL

On November 4, 1825, Governor De Witt Clinton stood on the deck of the packet boat *Seneca Chief* and solemnly poured a keg of Lake Erie water into New York Bay. Cannons boomed. Fireworks exploded. Thousands of New Yorkers cheered the "marriage of the waters." Now New York State was united by an inland waterway from New York City to Lake Erie and the other Great Lakes.

For nine days after its official opening on October 26th, Clinton had led a parade of four boats along the canal. The *Seneca Chief*, carrying the governor and other officials, was the first boat through the canal. The remaining boats carried two little Indian boys and western animals—eagles, wolves, raccoons, a black bear—to New York City. In towns along the canal, bands played, church bells rang, and townsmen cheered the governor. Tar barrels burned like giant torches above the narrow waterway.

Governor Clinton died only three years later. He lived long enough, though, to see his prayer for the canal answered. But he was not to know in his lifetime how successfully the Erie Canal would serve New York State and the United States as a nation.

The Erie Canal was the first great canal built in the United States. About 100 years earlier, the surveyor Cadwallader Colden had suggested a waterway along the Mohawk Valley from Lake Erie to the Hudson. The idea died because there was no need for such a channel at that time. In the 1780's President George Washington again urged an inland canal system. By then the United States greatly needed canals.

The rich farmland of the Northwest Territory (Ohio, Illinois, Indiana, Michigan, and Wisconsin) was shut off from the Atlantic by mountains and wilderness. President Washington foresaw that settlements in these far places would have to be joined to the eastern states by a better means of transportation.

First the United States built turnpikes like the Philadelphia and Lancaster Turnpike. These were toll roads for stagecoaches and wagons. But freighting by turnpike was too expensive. Because of the cost Philadelphians could buy coal from faraway England more cheaply than from nearby Virginia. For what it cost to ship a ton of goods from England, merchants in the United States could move the ton only 30 miles.

Rivers were still the cheapest highways, and boats were the cheapest haulers of freight. It was too expensive to transport goods from the Western frontier farms overland by wagon to the East coast. So farmers in Ohio and Illinois sent their wheat and other products on barges down the Ohio and Mississippi rivers to New Orleans. From there these cargoes were shipped to cities along the Atlantic coast and to Europe. New York City became envious of the valuable Western trade that New Orleans was attracting.

De Witt Clinton, the mayor of New York City, believed that his city could become the nation's richest port. The Hudson River was already a great water highway. The Mohawk Valley was a natural passage for part of the way between the Hudson River and Lake Erie. Why not build a canal there?

It was a wild vision. Digging such a canal would be a tremendous job and cost a frightening amount of money. Many people thought the plan was insane and called the canal ''Clinton's Big Ditch.'' But Clinton believed in it. He led the fight to build the canal. In 1812 he tried to get help from the federal government but failed. In 1817, Clinton, who was by then the governor of New York, persuaded the state legislature to pass a $7,000,000 bill to pay for the Erie Canal. New York would do the work alone.

Building the Canal

Construction of the Erie Canal began on July 4, 1817, in Rome, New York. Small contracting companies were hired to work on different sections. Strong laborers cut trees and cleared a canal track 60 feet (18 meters) wide. Others worked with pick and shovel in deep wet mud. Yankee ingenuity made up for the lack of tools. Soon mule-drawn bulldozers cleared the land, and makeshift hoists pulled stumps.

Although Americans had built a number of short canals around river rapids or to connect rivers, they had never built a canal like this one. Engineers learned on the job. They had to invent machines, materials, and new methods as they went along. An army of workers attacked the wilderness with axes and scrapers and strange new plows. In eight years they dug a great ditch from Albany to Buffalo.

The cost of building the Erie Canal was high in lives as well as money. Clouds of mosquitoes tortured the diggers. Many of them died from the malaria and cholera they caught in the swamps. Falling trees crushed other workers. Dynamite exploded too soon. Fights broke out between immigrants from rival home towns in Europe.

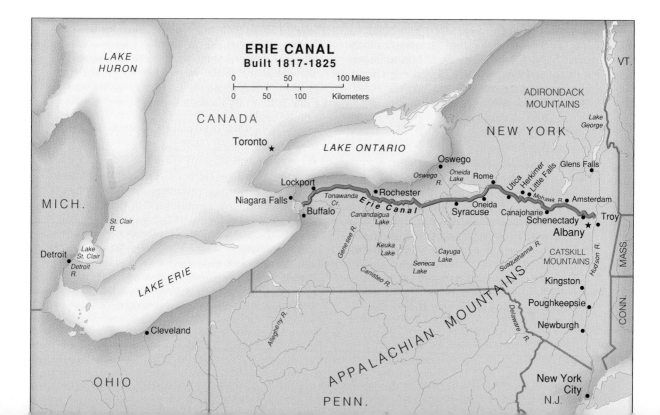

The canal was opened section by section. In 1819 the 15-mile (24-kilometer) stretch from Rome to Utica was completed. Four years later boats ran from Utica west to Rochester. In the same year the canal reached its eastern end at Albany. The backwoods village of Buffalo was finally chosen as the spot where the canal should strike through to Lake Erie. Finally in 1825 the canal was finished.

The Erie Canal was 363 miles (584 kilometers) long, 42 feet (12.8 meters) wide at the surface, and 4 feet (1.2 meters) deep. Because Lake Erie was 571 feet (174 meters) higher than the Hudson River, the canal contained more than 80 locks that were built to raise or lower vessels. Boats paid tolls to use the canal. Traffic was so great that in about ten years tolls more than repaid the cost of building the canal.

Before the canal was built, freighting a ton of goods from Buffalo to New York took 20 days. By canal it took six to eight days. Midwestern farmers could now send wheat, pork, and timber directly East to the eager buyers in New York. From the West, fur traders shipped pelts. Barges returned from Manhattan loaded with salt, textiles, and factory goods that Western farmers needed. As many as 50 boats a day left Albany. Once, between 60 and 70 boats waited in line at the locks, though the locks worked day and night.

Canal Boats

The first Erie Canal boats were flat barges up to 80 feet (24.5 meters) long, 15 feet (4.5 meters) wide, and 3½ feet (1 meter) deep. Horses, then mules, plodding along the banks pulled the boats forward. Journalist Horace Greeley said they traveled "a mile and a half an hour for a cent and a half a mile."

Line boats (freighters) were slow and uncomfortable, but they carried people at cheap rates. Packet boats, luxuriously fitted for passengers, had faster horses, cost a little more, and made slightly better time. But at best it took nearly five days to travel by canal packet from Buffalo to New York City. Unlike many rivers, the Erie was a sluggish ditch without snags or rapids.

The men who lived and worked on the Big Ditch and its boats called themselves "canawlers." They were a rowdy, boisterous lot. Many songs and stories grew out of canal life. People made fun of its calm waters by singing,

We were forty miles from Albany,
Forget it I never shall,
What a terrible storm we had one night
On the E-ri-e Canal.

The Canal's Effect on Cities

Along the canal, villages like Rochester and Albany grew overnight into busy ports. The Great Lakes, reaching almost halfway across the country, formed a vast natural extension to the canal. Few people had lived in that region before. Now frontier outposts like Buffalo, Detroit, and Cleveland turned into bustling cities. In Ohio, Cleveland became a trade crossroads. Trade poured east, and settlers streamed west. The West offered cheap, fertile land on the frontier. Timber waited in vast forests, and beaver streams tempted fur traders.

By 1847, Albany's canal business was greater than the New Orleans traffic from the whole Mississippi River system. Philadelphia suffered as New York stole its place as the Atlantic's main port. Other states, trying to copy New York's success, started building canals feverishly. The canal era had begun. By 1850 one could travel by canals and rivers all the way from New York City to New Orleans.

Railroads had been developing at the same time as the canals but took about ten years longer to overcome their engineering problems. By the mid-1800's the "iron horse" was replacing the canal barge as America's main freight carrier.

Many canals were abandoned because of railroad competition. But the Erie Canal continued. Engineers enlarged it many times. By 1882 the canal had brought New York State more than $121,000,000, and it was made toll-free.

History proved Governor Clinton and his supporters were justified in fighting for their canal. The Erie Canal opened the Great Lakes country and turned its log-cabin trading posts into cities. It tied the Middle West to the East. Above all, it turned New York City into one of the world's most important cities and America's greatest port.

Today the Erie Canal is part of the New York State Barge Canal. Completed in 1918, this new canal continues to provide a vital transportation route between the Atlantic ports and the Great Lakes.

Reviewed by CARL CARMER
Author, *The Hudson*

ERITREA

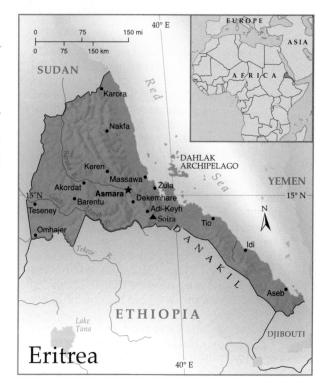

Eritrea

Eritrea is a nation situated in northeastern Africa. Formerly a province of Ethiopia, it gained its independence in 1993, after nearly thirty years of civil war.

Eritrea's neighboring countries are Sudan on the northwest, Ethiopia on the south, and Djibouti on the southeast. On the north, Eritrea is bounded by the waters of the Red Sea. Eritrea's location, dominating the southern part of the Red Sea, is of strategic importance. Tankers carrying oil from the Middle East to Europe by way of the Suez Canal regularly pass through this waterway.

The People. Eritrea's largest ethnic group consists of Tigreans (a people also found in Ethiopia), who speak Tigrinya, a Semitic language. The Tigreans of the southern highlands are Christians; those living to the north and west of the highlands are Muslims. In the southern part of the coastal plain live the Saho and the Danakil, who speak Afar. Other languages spoken include Arabic and Italian, a reminder of the era when Ethiopia was a colony of Italy (1935–41).

The Land. Eritrea's landscape is made up chiefly of a large coastal plain and a high plateau and mountain range in the interior. The Danakil, a large desert region, lies in the southeast. The climate varies with elevation. The coastal region is very hot and dry, while the interior plateau is cooler. Temperatures in the Danakil often reach 120°F (50°C). Rainfall is scanty, and frequent drought makes it difficult to grow crops.

Left: About half of Ethiopia's people are ethnic Tigreans. *Below:* High, arid plateaus cover a large area of Eritrea's interior region.

The country has few natural resources. The only known minerals are salt and small deposits of gold and copper. However, the Red Sea is rich in fish, particularly red snapper and tuna, and holds the potential for an important Eritrean fishing industry.

The Economy. Eritrean agriculture once produced wheat and other grains, coffee, cotton, corn, tobacco, dates and other fruits, peppers, and tomatoes. But Eritrea and its economy have been devastated by the struggle for independence, by a post-independence border war with Ethiopia, and by drought. Its cities and ports have been damaged by Ethiopian bombing, and its farms have suffered from wartime neglect.

Major Cities. Asmara is Eritrea's capital, commercial center, and largest city. It once had many ornate buildings that were constructed during the period of Italian colonial rule. But Asmara and other cities have been damaged by Ethiopian bombing attacks.

Massawa is the second largest city and chief Red Sea port. Assab, Eritrea's other port city, features an oil refinery. At independence, Eritrea agreed to give now-landlocked Ethiopia access to the sea through Eritrean ports. But since 1998, Ethiopia's imports and exports have been routed through Djibouti, depriving Eritrea of the customs duties that once provided a major source of income.

History. Eritrea's recorded history dates back to at least 3000 B.C., when the pharaohs of Egypt engaged in commerce with local Eritrean leaders on the Red Sea coast. Eritrea was also part of the empire of Aksum, the first Ethiopian state, which flourished from about A.D. 300 to 500. After Ethiopia went into decline around 900, Eritrea remained for centuries largely independent of foreign influence. But beginning in the 1500's, the region was dominated by the Ottoman Turks, then by Egypt, and once again by Ethiopia.

Italy's role in Eritrea began in 1885, with the occupation of Massawa. The Treaty of Wuchale (1889) with the Ethiopian emperor Menelik II gave Italy control of much of Eritrea, and in 1890 it was proclaimed an Italian colony. Britain took control of Eritrea in 1941, during World War II. In 1952, it was given the status of federation with Ethiopia, with control over its own affairs.

Eritrea's annexation by Ethiopia in 1962 marked the beginning of the struggle for independence. This was carried out first under the banner of the Eritrean Liberation Front (ELF), and after 1970, under the authority of the Eritrean People's Liberation Front (EPLF). The war ended in 1991 with the defeat of the Ethiopian army and the fall of its government.

The new Ethiopian government and the EPLF agreed to have Eritrea remain linked to Ethiopia until 1993, when an election was held to determine Eritrea's future. Eritreans voted overwhelmingly for independence, which was proclaimed on May 24, 1993.

Eritrea's post-independence recovery was shattered by a costly border war with Ethiopia that began in 1998. After an Ethiopian offensive drove hundreds of thousands of Eritreans from their homes, the two sides signed a peace treaty in 2000. The border was officially determined in 2002.

Government. A provisional government consisting of the top leaders of the EPLF took power in 1991. Isaias Afewerki, its secretary general, was named president by the provisional National Assembly. A new constitution approved in 1997 created a strong presidential regime. The president is now elected by the legislature for a 5-year term.

PETER SCHWAB
Author, *Ethiopia*

See also ETHIOPIA.

FACTS and figures

STATE OF ERITREA is the official name of the country.

LOCATION: Northeastern Africa.

AREA: 45,405 sq mi (117,600 km²).

POPULATION: 4,300,000 (estimate).

CAPITAL AND LARGEST CITY: Asmara.

MAJOR LANGUAGE: Tigrinya.

MAJOR RELIGIOUS GROUPS: Christian, Muslim.

GOVERNMENT: Republic. **Head of state and government**—president. **Legislature**—National Assembly.

CHIEF PRODUCTS: Agricultural—sorghum, cotton, teff (a grain), citrus fruits. **Mineral**—salt.

MONETARY UNIT: Nafka (1 nafka = 100 cents).

EROSION

Erosion is the process of wearing down, breaking up, and carrying off from the land soil and rock materials. It is a gradual and continuous process caused by wind, rain, waves, streams, and glaciers.

Erosion by Wind

The wind is an erosive agent. It picks up large quantities of dust, sand, and silt and carries them over great distances. In deserts, the wind piles the sand in high dunes. During dry seasons in other parts of the world bare lands are easily eroded by the force of the wind. Along beaches the winds move sand and silt out to sea or inland. Depending on the strength of the wind, airborne materials may be moved hundreds of miles.

The northeast tradewind of West Africa, known as the **harmattan,** carries airborne soils out over the Atlantic. The hot wind out of North Africa, known as the **sirocco,** carries dust across the Mediterranean into southern Europe. In France the rain may be stained with reddish dust from the sirocco. Because of its color it is known as *pluie de sang,* ''rain of blood.''

Erosion by Water

When rain strikes the ground, erosion begins. Where trees and other plants shield the soil and hold it securely in place with their roots, the rain may not displace much of it. But soil barren of plants may be quickly eroded.

During rainfall, water collects and runs downhill under gravity's pull. At first the runoff is in the form of sheets and can cause what is known as **sheet erosion.** If this runoff meets irregularities in the ground's surface, it may separate into channels of swiftly moving water. As this rushing water cuts deeper into the ground, it carries more soil away and leaves gullies behind. Runoff is eventually channeled into streams and rivers. Erosion caused by streams and rivers is called **stream erosion.** The amount of erosion caused by a stream is determined by how much water the stream carries and the speed at which it travels. A fast-running stream is more erosive than a slow-moving one.

The moving water causes rocks, pebbles, and sand to slide, bounce, and roll along the

The surface of the earth may be changed by unusually heavy rains. The runoff from heavy rainstorms and flash floods can cut into the ground to form erosion gullies.

stream bottom. This action widens and deepens the stream channel. Over many thousands of years this kind of erosion can create steep-walled gorges and canyons hundreds of feet deep. The Grand Canyon in Arizona was created by the cutting action of the Colorado River.

As the speed of a stream or river slows, the rocks, sand, and silt carried by the water settle out, or are deposited. The deltas of the Nile, the Volga, the Hwang Ho, the Mississippi, and many other rivers are made up of the material dropped by the rivers. In addition, large quantities of sediment are carried out to sea by rivers and deposited along the shores of the continents.

Erosion by Glaciers

In the glacial periods of the past the erosive work of moving ice was more important than it is today. Glaciers eroded the land they moved across and deposited rocks, boulders, sand, and gravel (glacial debris) far away. The water from the melting glaciers moved the finer materials forward toward the sea.

In high latitudes and high mountain regions the erosive action of glaciers goes on today.

As an alpine glacier flows from the mountains to a valley, it carves a U-shaped channel. The glacier picks up loose rocks and plucks pieces from the bedrock over which it passes. The rocks become embedded in the ice and act as cutting tools, scratching and gouging the bedrock. Some rocks are crushed and crumbled to dust, polishing rather than scouring the surface over which a glacier moves. The rate of glacial erosion depends on the thickness of the ice as well as the rate at which it travels.

Continental glaciers exist today in Antarctica and Greenland. Similar glaciers once covered much of the northern United States and Canada, northwestern Europe, and the southern tip of South America. The direction of their movement is shown by striations (scratches), grooves in the rocks, and by deep basins now occupied by lakes. The Great Lakes in the United States and Canada, the Finger Lakes in New York State, the Baltic Sea in Europe, and many long, narrow lake basins were deepened by glacial erosion.

Erosion by Waves

Where the land meets the sea, waves and currents cut away the land and move the materials to other places. During storms, high sea waves may change the shoreline many feet in a single day. The materials loosened by waves may be carried out to deeper waters by the undertow. The longshore currents may move sand and fine gravel and build up new bars and beaches. These may be destroyed by the next storm.

Seashores are favorite resort areas. Many people build cottages and homes along the seashore. These coastal areas may show little or no change for many years. But occasional storms such as the hurricanes of the Caribbean area and the Atlantic and Gulf coasts of the United States may cause great damage and change the coastline by erosion and deposition (depositing soil elsewhere).

Controlling Erosion

Wind, water, and glaciers can cause natural erosion. Erosion brought about by people's misuse of land is called **accelerated erosion**. By cutting down trees, breaking the sod, overgrazing the land, and cultivating fields, people speed up the rate of erosion. Topsoil that has been loosened by plowing is easily eroded by water and wind. In a heavy down-

As wind blows sand from one side of a dune to the other, the whole dune advances with the wind. Fences prevent sand dunes from shifting with the wind.

pour or violent windstorm, this top layer, about 6 to 8 inches (15 to 20 centimeters) thick, may be carried away.

To prevent or reduce erosion, farmers use conservation practices that will save the soil for future generations. Soil erosion can be reduced by plowing across a slope and planting in parallel rows. All parts of a row are on the same level, or contour. The troughs (shallow depressions) and ridges formed by contour plowing trap and channel runoff. Sloping fields are sometimes terraced to retain moisture and prevent soil erosion. A terraced hill looks similar to a large staircase, with the terraced planting areas forming the "steps." Rows of trees planted between fields serve as windbreaks to prevent wind erosion. Grass, shrub, and tree roots help protect shoreline dunes from wind erosion. Where natural vegetation is sparse, grass can be planted. Fences are also useful for controlling the movement of sand dunes. Seawalls may be used to control beach erosion.

GUY-HAROLD SMITH
Formerly, Ohio State University

See also AGRICULTURE (Land Management).

ESCALATORS. See ELEVATORS AND ESCALATORS.

ESCHER, M. C. (1898–1972)

The Dutch artist Maurits Cornelis Escher was famous for his prints that fooled the eye and intrigued the mind. His work is unique in modern art.

Born on June 17, 1898, in Leeuwarden, the Netherlands, Escher first studied architecture at the School for Architecture and Decorative Arts in Haarlem. While there, he became more interested in printmaking. In 1924, Escher married Jetta Umiker and the couple settled in Rome, Italy. In 1935, political turmoil forced the Eschers to move first to Switzerland and then to Belgium. In 1941 they moved to Baarn, the Netherlands.

While he lived in Italy, Escher often depicted Rome and the Italian countryside in his art. Afterward, his interest shifted from landscape to what he described as "mental imagery." These new works were partly inspired by tiles he found on Moorish architecture in Granada, Spain. Escher used the tiles' flattened patterns of interlocking shapes, replacing the abstract Moorish decorations with recognizable figures (such as fish, birds, and reptiles). The woodcut *Day and Night* (1938) was one of his first works to demonstrate this technique. Escher also used this technique in his famous *Metamorphose III* (1967–68), which features a series of interlocking shapes and figures that continually change over the woodcut's 23-foot (7-meter) length.

Other prints by Escher depict buildings and staircases that appear to be realistically drawn but are actually optical illusions (such as in the lithographs *Belvadere*, 1958, and *Ascending and Descending*, 1960), and flat, two-dimensional drawings that seem to transform into three-dimensional objects. An example of this type of print is the lithograph *Drawing Hands* (1948), in which two hands appear to rise off the paper as they draw each other.

Escher gained international fame beginning in the 1950's. Magazine articles were written about him, and he lectured about his art. Escher made his last print (the woodcut *Snakes*) in 1969, and he died on March 27, 1972, in Hilversum, the Netherlands.

GREGORY D. JECMEN
Assistant Curator
Department of Old Master Prints
National Gallery of Art

ESKIMOS. See INUIT.

ESPIONAGE. See SPIES.

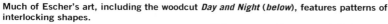

Much of Escher's art, including the woodcut *Day and Night* (*below*), features patterns of interlocking shapes.

ESSAYS

So many different types of writing can be called essays that it is not easy to say just what an essay is. The best way to define an essay is to note what is true of most essays.

First of all, an essay is about a single subject. It does not skip from one subject to another. It is usually written in prose, and it is usually short, although some essays are long enough to be small books.

The length of an essay is really a matter of common sense. An essay that is too long may turn into a treatise. A treatise is like an essay because it "treats" a certain subject, but it does so on a larger scale. Unlike an essay, a treatise usually attempts to say all there is to say about a subject.

The word "essay" is a verb as well as a noun. To essay is to attempt, to test, or to try out. Today the term "essayist" means a writer of essays. It used to mean any person trying out any kind of experiment or new venture. This older meaning gives a clue to the essay's most important quality—it is personal. It is the work of one person testing thoughts or trying out some idea. Essayists express their own points of view. That is why many essays are written in the first person, which means the writer uses the pronoun "I."

If all the points mentioned above are kept in mind, it is possible to define an essay as a short, usually prose composition that is personal in tone and discusses a single subject without trying to cover it completely.

History of the Essay. The essay can be traced back to its beginnings more clearly than most types of writing. A French writer, Michel de Montaigne, gave the essay its form as well as its name. In 1580 he published a collection of personal, informal writings on a wide range of topics. He called these writings *essais* ("attempts").

Montaigne's essays greatly influenced English writers, particularly Francis Bacon, a philosopher and statesman who was the first of the great English essayists. Bacon's *Essays* were first published in 1597. The new form of writing was extremely popular in England, and the essay became one of the glories of English literature.

Many English writers of the 1700's were masters of the essay form. Joseph Addison and Richard Steele published essays written

French author Michel de Montaigne established the essay as a literary form in 1580 with the publication of writings he called *essais*, or "attempts."

by themselves and others in the periodicals *The Tatler* and *The Spectator*. Samuel Johnson contributed essays to his own periodical, *The Rambler*, and wrote a series of essays called *The Idler* papers (1758–60). Jonathan Swift used satire to criticize England's treatment of the Irish in his essay *A Modest Proposal* (1729). Alexander Pope's *Essay on Criticism* (1711) and *Essay on Man* (1734) were written in verse form rather than prose. Pope, like other leading essayists, perfected the use of short, witty statements called **epigrams**. An example is "To err is human, to forgive divine."

In the 1800's, Charles Lamb wrote humorously about everyday life in *Essays of Elia* (1823). He and a later English writer, Robert Louis Stevenson, were masters of the essay's most informal style. Other noted English essayists of the 1800's were William Hazlitt and Thomas B. Macaulay. One of the most distinguished essayists of the 1900's was T. S. Eliot, an American who became a British citizen.

His works include *The Sacred Wood: Essays on Poetry and Criticism* (1920). Another modern English writer, George Orwell, was a skilled writer of political essays.

The United States has produced many fine essayists, notably Benjamin Franklin, Washington Irving, Ralph Waldo Emerson, Henry David Thoreau, and Edgar Allan Poe. The 1900's saw many more outstanding American writers working in the essay form, including James Thurber, E. B. White, Flannery O'Connor, James Baldwin, John Updike, and Susan Sontag.

There are many good essayists writing in all the major literary languages. The form can be used for so many purposes that it is popular everywhere. It may inform, instruct, advise, or entertain. Some essays express the writer's most personal thoughts as they explore the deep questions of life.

The versatile American essayist Susan Sontag wrote on many diverse subjects, including philosophy, politics, photography, and illness.

The essay's special role is to provide a form in which people can explore their own thoughts. Essayists try at all times to express their ideas in writing that has a certain style and ease. The traditional essay is "literary." But the best qualities of an essay—clarity, wit, and good writing—may also be found in newspaper and magazine editorials and in commentaries by television newscasters.

EDMUND FULLER
Author, *Man in Modern Fiction*

ESTIMATION. See ARITHMETIC.

In this excerpt from a 1740 essay, Benjamin Franklin compares the Native Americans to the English colonists. Franklin's essay makes the point that although different cultures may have different values and ways of life, one culture is no less "civilized" than another.

Savages we call them, because their manners differ from ours, which we think the perfection of civility; they think the same of theirs. . . .

The Indian men, when young, are hunters and warriors; when old, counselors; for all their government is by counsel of the sages [wise persons]; . . . Hence they generally study oratory, the best speaker having the most influence. The Indian women till the ground, dress the food, nurse and bring up the children, and preserve and hand down to posterity [future generations] the memory of public transactions. These employments of men and women are accounted natural and honorable. . . . Our laborious manner of life, compared with theirs, they esteem slavish and base [lacking value]; and the learning, on which we value ourselves, they regard as frivolous and useless. An instance of this occurred at the Treaty of Lancaster, in Pennsylvania, . . . 1744, between the government of Virginia and the Six Nations [a group of Iroquois tribes]. After the principal business was settled, the commissioners from Virginia acquainted the Indians by a speech, that there was at Williamsburg a college, with a fund for educating Indian youth; and that, if the Six Nations would send down half a dozen of their young lads to that college, the government would take care that they should be . . . instructed in all the learning of the white people. It is one of the Indian rules of politeness not to answer a public proposition the same day that it is made; . . . they show it respect by taking time to consider it, as of a matter important. They therefore deferred their answer till the day following; when their speaker began, by expressing their deep sense of the kindness of the Virginia government, in making them that offer; "for we know," says he, "that you highly esteem the kind of learning taught in those Colleges, and that the maintenance of our young men, while with you, would be very expensive to you . . . . But you, who are wise, must know that different nations have different conceptions of things; and you will therefore not take it amiss, if our ideas of this kind of education happen not to be the same with yours. . . . several of our young people were formerly brought up at the colleges of the northern provinces; . . . but, when they came back to us, they were bad runners, ignorant of every means of living in the woods, unable to bear either cold or hunger, knew neither how to build a cabin, take a deer, or kill an enemy, spoke our language imperfectly, were therefore neither fit for hunters, warriors, nor counselors; they were totally good for nothing. We are however not the less obliged by your kind offer, though we decline accepting it; and, to show our grateful sense of it, if the gentlemen of Virginia will send us a dozen of their sons, we will take great care of their education, instruct them in all we know, and make *men* of them. . . ."

ESTONIA

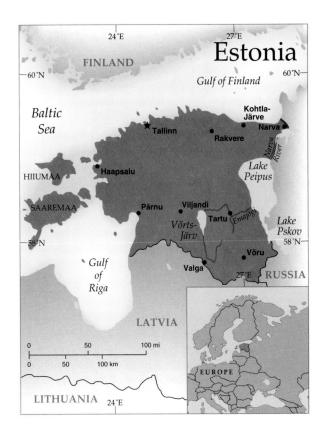

Estonia is the smallest and most northerly of the three Baltic States, which also include Latvia and Lithuania. Situated on the northeastern edge of the Baltic Sea, Estonia is bordered by Latvia on the south, the Russian Federation on the east, and the Gulf of Finland on the north. Like the other Baltic states, Estonia was formerly a part of the Soviet Union, before gaining its independence as a result of the Soviet breakup in 1991.

The People. Estonians belong to the Balto-Finnic branch of the Ugro-Finnic family of nations. Their language is closely related to Finnish and more remotely to Hungarian, or Magyar. This linguistic closeness to Finnish made it possible for Estonians to pierce the Iron Curtain imposed by the Soviet Communist government, by listening to radio and television broadcasts from Finland.

During the years of Soviet rule, the proportion of Estonians in the population declined from 88 to 62 percent. This was due to the deliberate policy of the Soviet government, which encouraged Russian immigration. Ethnic Russians now make up about 30 percent of the country's population. Other nationalities include Ukrainians, Belarusians, and smaller numbers of Germans and Latvians.

In religion, the great majority of Estonians traditionally have been Lutherans. Eastern Or-

thodox Christians are the second largest in number, followed by Baptists. But even though Estonians celebrate Good Friday as a national holiday, the influence of religion has much diminished. Religious observance is respected and increasing in favor, but for many years Estonia has been the least religious of the Baltic societies.

Way of Life. Estonian families typically are small, although family ties are strong. The tra-

Windmills and grazing sheep present a peaceful scene on Saaremaa, the largest of the islands that make up part of Estonia's territory. The flat or gently rolling terrain is typical of Estonia's landscape, which was formed by the action of glaciers during the Ice Age.

Estonians have long shared a love of choral singing. A national song festival, held every fifth year in Tallinn, the capital, is widely attended.

dition of wedding celebrations lasting several days, once common among country people, has disappeared. However, the love of choral singing, popular in Latvia and Lithuania as well, has remained strong. A national song festival is held every fifth year in Tallinn, the capital. A recent one, in which some 30,000 singers participated, was attended by nearly 300,000 people—almost one third of the entire nation.

Estonians possess a disciplined work ethic, but they are also a sociable people who enjoy sports, gardening, and other recreation. Chess, basketball, and soccer are especially popular. Estonian athletes participating in the Olympic Games have won gold medals in wrestling and weight lifting, and during the years when they competed under the flag of the Soviet Union, they contributed to many Soviet victories.

The Land and Climate. Estonia's landscape is made up chiefly of flat or rolling plain, with occasional hills. The land is crossed by thousands of rivers and lakes. Most of the rivers, however, are short and few are navigable, or usable by ships. The largest, the Emajõgi, flows into Lake Peipus, which forms most of Estonia's eastern border with the Russian Federation. Nearly 10 percent of Estonia's land consists of islands in the Baltic Sea, the largest of which are Saaremaa and Hiiumaa.

About 40 percent of the land is covered with forests. Estonia has more valuable mineral resources than the other Baltic States. In addition to limestone and clays, they include large deposits of phosphates (used in making chem-

ical fertilizers) and oil shale. The oil extracted from the shale makes Estonia nearly self-sufficient in energy.

The climate is variable. January temperatures average about 20°F (−7°C) inland, with some of the coastal waters icebound for several months of the year. Summers are mild, with July temperatures ranging from 60 to 65°F (15 to 18°C). Rainfall averages 24 to 28 inches (610 to 710 millimeters) a year.

Cities. Once mainly rural, Estonia now has more than 70 percent of its people living in cities. Tallinn, the capital and largest city, has a population of about 500,000. It is an industrial center and an ice-free port on the Gulf of Finland. Tartu, the second largest city, is the site of Tartu University, founded in 1632. Other imporant cities are Narva and Kohtla-Järve in the northeast.

The Economy. Estonia's economy is based chiefly on industry, which accounts for slightly more than 60 percent of its gross national product (the total value of its goods and services). Light industry, including the manufacture of textiles, footwear, leather products, and processed foods, is especially important. Estonia also produces various kinds of machinery, electronic equipment, chemicals and petrochemicals (derived from oil), and paper.

Agriculture, although it employs only about 12 percent of the workforce, is relatively well

FACTS and figures

REPUBLIC OF ESTONIA is the official name of the country.

LOCATION: Northeastern Europe, on the Baltic Sea.

AREA: 17,413 sq mi (45,100 km²).

POPULATION: 1,500,000 (estimate).

CAPITAL AND LARGEST CITY: Tallinn.

MAJOR LANGUAGES: Estonian (official); Russian.

MAJOR RELIGIOUS GROUP: Christian (Lutheran, Eastern Orthodox, Baptist).

GOVERNMENT: Republic. **Head of state**—president. **Head of government**—prime minister. **Legislature**—Riigikogu (State Assembly).

CHIEF PRODUCTS: Agricultural—wheat, rye, barley, potatoes, flax, meat and dairy products. **Manufactured**—textiles, footwear, leather products, processed foods, machinery, electronic equipment, chemicals, petrochemicals, paper. **Mineral**—phosphates, oil shale, limestone, clays.

MONETARY UNIT: Kroon (1 kroon = 100 cents).

developed. The major crops are wheat, rye, barley, potatoes and other vegetables, and flax (from which linen is made). Raising beef and dairy cattle is an important sector of the agricultural economy. The coastal waters support a significant fishing industry.

Early History. The ancestors of the Estonians arrived in the Baltic region from the east in ancient times. In the early 1200's the Estonian tribes in the south were conquered by Germans, including the crusading Teutonic Knights, while the north came under the rule of Denmark. During this period the Estonians were converted to Christianity. Two revolts in the 1200's and 1300's failed to shake off foreign rule. Estonia came under Swedish rule in the 1600's, but it fell to the expanding Russian Empire in the early 1700's, although the provinces long remained under the control of the German nobility.

Russian and Soviet Rule. A national awakening in the 1800's enabled Estonians to resist both German and Russian cultural domination. After the overthrow of the Russian czar in 1917, the Provisional Government granted Estonians political self-rule. But when the Bolsheviks (Communists) seized power, Estonia declared full independence, on February 24, 1918. A struggle against Soviet Communist forces, which had occupied one-third of the new republic, as well as German troops, ended with a peace treaty in 1920, under which the Soviet Union accepted Estonian independence.

Estonia enjoyed 22 years of independence before it fell, along with Lithuania and Latvia, to the Soviets. This came about as a result of a non-aggression pact between Nazi Germany and the Soviet Union signed in 1939, just before the outbreak of World War II. In 1940, Soviet troops occupied Estonia, a pro-Communist government was installed, and Estonia was made a Soviet republic. The government and economy were organized according to the Soviet model, with political power in the hands of the Communist Party. Religion and Estonian culture were both suppressed. An estimated 30,000 to 80,000 Estonians were deported. Many others perished in prisons or labor camps.

Except for its occupation by invading German troops from 1941 to 1944, Estonia remained a part of the Soviet Union until it regained its independence in 1991.

Tallinn, Estonia's capital, largest city, and chief port, lies on the Gulf of Finland. The old part of the city, shown here, dates from the 1300's.

Independence. Change came about after Mikhail Gorbachev rose to power in the Soviet Union in 1985 and began a series of political and economic reforms. In 1988, Estonians seeking freedom from Soviet control organized the Popular Front. In 1991, Estonia proclaimed its independence, just a few months before the Soviet Union collapsed.

Government. Estonia's government is based on a constitution adopted in 1992. The legislative body is the Riigikogu, or State Assembly, whose 101 members are elected to 4-year terms. Along with local government officials, the Riigikogu elects a president to serve as head of state for a 5-year term. The president then nominates a prime minister to head the government. In 2001, Arnold Ruutel was elected president, succeeding Lennart Meri, who had served since 1993.

Estonia joined both the North Atlantic Treaty Organization (NATO) and the European Union (EU) in 2004.

V. STANLEY VARDYS
University of Oklahoma
Coeditor, *The Baltic States in Peace and War*

See also LATVIA; LITHUANIA.

The technique of aquatint was used to create these etchings. *The Letter* (1891) by Mary Cassatt, *left*, was printed using several color plates. *The Sleep of Reason Produces Monsters* is one of *The Caprices*, a series of etchings published by Francisco Goya in 1799.

ETCHING

Etching is a process used by artists to make several copies of a drawing. The copies are printed from a metal plate on which a drawing has been etched (eaten in with acid). Invented in Germany in the 16th century, etching is probably used more by artists than any other print making method. It allows greater freedom than most other methods, because drawing on an etching plate is much like drawing with an ordinary pencil on paper. Such artists as Rembrandt, Goya, and Whistler were great etchers as well as great painters.

Prints that are made from an etched plate are called etchings. An **edition** refers to the number of etchings made from one plate: often an edition is from 10 to 50 prints, but it can be fewer or many more. To make an etching, the artist uses a metal plate of copper or zinc. The plate is covered with **ground,** an acid-resisting substance made of asphalt, varnish, and beeswax. When the ground dries,

the artist draws on it with an etching needle. This tool can be made of any pointed instrument—a key, a dentist's pick, or a sewing needle taped to a stick. In drawing, the artist scratches the ground away from the plate, exposing the metal. The plate is then placed in a bath of acid. The acid eats away at the exposed metal but cannot affect the plate where it has been covered with ground. The longer the plate is left in the acid, the deeper the grooves become. The darkness of the lines depends on the depth of the grooves. If some lines are to be light and some dark, the artist removes the plate from the bath after a moment or two, covers with ground the lines that are to be printed light, and puts the plate back.

Sometimes, while working on a plate, the artist will want to see what has been done so far. To make a **proof** (sample print), the ground is removed from the plate with **solvent,** a liquid that dissolves wax or varnish. A loose, creamy ink is then dabbed over the plate, filling the etched grooves. The ink is wiped off the surface of the plate with a dry, stiff piece of fabric called tarlatan. The plate is covered with a slightly damp sheet of paper and soft felt blanket and is run through a printing press. The great pressure of the press forces the paper into the grooves to absorb the ink. If the artist decides that the plate needs more work, new lines can be added by covering the plate with ground.

Aquatint is an etching process by which solid areas of grays and blacks can be created. The artist wraps crushed **resin**—a brittle, natural substance that looks somewhat like small yellow rocks—in a piece of cloth. The resin bag is held over the plate and is tapped gently, forcing grains of resin through the fabric and onto the plate. The plate is then heated. Heating causes the grains of resin to melt and stick to the plate. When the plate has cooled, it is dipped in the acid bath. The acid eats into the plate in between the grains of resin. The artist removes the plate and uses varnish to cover the areas that are to be light gray. Then the plate is put into the bath again. This process is repeated several times until the plate makes a print with a variety of grays. By using different kinds of fabric for the bag, the artist can also vary the texture of the grays. Aquatint can also be used to make colored etchings. A different plate is used for each color.

When petroleum jelly or **tallow** (animal fat) is added to regular ground, a soft ground that never dries is formed. A line scratched through soft ground is not as sharp as a line cut through regular ground; instead it is soft and fuzzy. The artist can place a piece of paper over the soft ground and draw on the paper with a pencil. The ground under the pencil lines sticks to the paper, so that when the paper is removed, the metal is exposed under the drawing. The remaining steps are the same as in hard-ground etching. By using several different kinds of pencils and differently textured paper, the artist can create lines of great variety.

Very few printmakers today limit their prints to one process. The many etching and engraving methods are frequently combined with excellent results.

Reviewed by JOHN SPARKS
The Maryland Institute, College of Art

See also ENGRAVING; GRAPHIC ARTS.

ETHER. See ANESTHESIA.

MAKING AN ETCHING

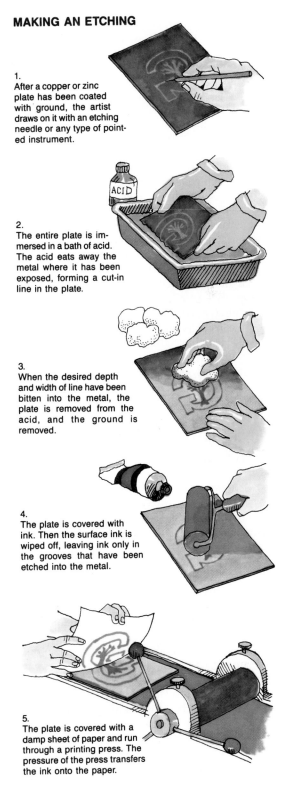

1.
After a copper or zinc plate has been coated with ground, the artist draws on it with an etching needle or any type of pointed instrument.

2.
The entire plate is immersed in a bath of acid. The acid eats away the metal where it has been exposed, forming a cut-in line in the plate.

3.
When the desired depth and width of line have been bitten into the metal, the plate is removed from the acid, and the ground is removed.

4.
The plate is covered with ink. Then the surface ink is wiped off, leaving ink only in the grooves that have been etched into the metal.

5.
The plate is covered with a damp sheet of paper and run through a printing press. The pressure of the press transfers the ink onto the paper.

ETHICS

Ethics is the branch of philosophy that concerns itself with the rights and wrongs of human behavior. Many people think of ethics as a series of simple, clear-cut rules such as "Do not tell lies" or "Do not kill." However, ethics is concerned with more than the rules themselves. It also suggests when and how the rules should be used. It helps us decide how to act when two or more different courses of action seem equally right.

The word "ethics" comes from the Greek word *ethikos*, meaning custom or character. The Greek philosopher Aristotle (384–322 B.C.) first used the word to describe the careful examination of human behavior in the light of moral principles. However, it was another Greek thinker, Socrates (469–399 B.C.), who earlier separated ethical considerations from other philosophical issues. Socrates saw ethics as a means of judging what was, and was not, moral. He believed that if he could understand what makes some types of conduct right and others wrong, he could help people learn to lead better lives.

Socrates may have been the first to make a formal study of ethics, but he was not the first to weigh what we today would call ethical issues. People have been doing that since the dawn of civilization.

▶DEVELOPING ETHICAL SYSTEMS

All human groups, no matter how small or simply organized, must agree to follow certain rules and standards. One standard might be honesty. Unless the members of a group can trust each other, the group will fall apart. Other rules might have to do with how work and responsibilities are shared or the way group members make decisions. Together, the rules and standards add up to a moral code.

Sometimes one part of a code seems to contradict another. A code that requires strict honesty might also say that people must not hurt other people's feelings. Not hurting a person may mean telling a "little white lie." But how big can "little" be? How serious must a fib be before it is bad enough to outweigh the good done by sparing someone's feelings? Answers to questions like these require us to make ethical judgments.

Over the ages, men and women have worked out systems for making such judgments. Some of these systems are rooted in the teachings of Socrates, Aristotle, and later philosophers. The German philosopher Immanuel Kant (1724–1804) wrote that people should never take any action that they would not be willing to see everyone take. For example, they should not lie under any circumstance—not even to save a life—because doing so would mean accepting the idea that everyone else has an equal right to lie. Kant's ethical system calls for human beings to do good for its own sake, rather than in the hope of earning a reward.

Some systems do allow for rewards. That reward may be happiness, for the individual or for the larger society. The English philosopher Jeremy Bentham (1748–1832) said that the ethical course is always the one that ensures the greatest amount of good for the greatest number of people. If telling a lie benefits a hundred people, while the truth benefits only fifty, Bentham would say that the lie is ethical.

Other ethical systems grow out of religious belief. However, ethics and religion are not the same, any more than ethics and moral rules are. Ethics goes beyond the beliefs and practices of any single religion to that which unites all religions—the human desire to live by universal standards of right and wrong.

In the Judeo-Christian tradition, those standards are summed up in the Golden Rule: "Do unto others as you would have them do unto you." Other religions express the same idea in different words. For Muslims, true belief means wishing for everyone what one desires for oneself. Members of the Hindu faith say, "Do naught unto others which would cause you pain if done to you."

Some ethical standards are embodied in laws and legal codes. Laws, however, do not offer a choice. They simply tell people they must not do certain things, like steal or kill, and that if they do, they will be punished. Laws are enforceable ethical judgments.

Smaller groups within a society may adopt ethical systems of their own. Members of the medical profession agree to live and work according to established ethical standards. Lawyers, business people, and others also have professional codes of ethics. Students at many schools and colleges are asked to obey honor codes aimed at preventing cheating or other unethical behavior.

PERSONAL ETHICS

Each individual develops his or her own ethical standards, usually by combining ideas from various ethical systems. These personal standards are the codes people turn to first when they face a moral dilemma.

Such dilemmas occur commonly in daily life. Suppose you see a friend cheating on a math test. How you react will depend on the ethical standards you decide to apply.

In your personal code of ethics, loyalty to a friend may rate so high that you will keep silent. Your school's honor code or the teacher's classroom rules, on the other hand, may require that you report any cheating. If you choose to be guided by either, you will turn the cheater in. Then again, you might use the teachings of your religion as a guide. No matter how you resolve your dilemma, and no matter what standards you use to do so, you have made an ethical judgment.

People have to make such judgments frequently. Someone may have to choose, for example, between defending an unpopular person or cause and simply going along with the crowd. A babysitter might have to decide whether to lie to a child in order to get that child to do as its mother wishes. A person whose religion forbids the eating of pork may be offered bacon at a friend's house. Should she refuse it? Or should she eat it so as not to seem rude?

ETHICS AND SOCIETY

Broader ethical issues also confront us as individuals and as a society. Among those being debated in American society today are legalized abortion (ending an unwanted pregnancy), capital punishment (the death penalty), and euthanasia (the right to die). Should these practices be permitted? People disagree, and the ethical discussion begins.

One group in the abortion dispute argues that an unborn fetus is not yet a separate person able to survive outside the mother's body. They argue that the woman's right to make her own medical decisions is more important than the fetus's right to live. Those opposed to abortion respond that from the very start, a fetus is a human being with full human rights, including the right not to be killed. Another part of the argument concerns the reasons for abortion. Some think it should be forbidden unless the mother's life is in danger; others would extend the right to victims of rape or incest. Some would permit it "on demand."

Capital punishment presents its own ethical problems. Supporters of the death penalty believe that it prevents crime. They also say that some crimes, such as murder, are so terrible that a person who commits them deserves to die. Opponents argue that it is wrong to kill anyone, even a criminal. They point out that there is no evidence that capital punishment leads to fewer crimes. Further, they say, the death penalty is not always enforced fairly. The social position of the accused, the skills of the attorneys, the location of the trial—all can affect the severity of the sentence.

Before the era of modern medicine, euthanasia was not an issue. Little or nothing could be done to prevent the death of a very old or sick person. Today the life of a person with an incurable illness can be prolonged, but it may be a life filled with pain and suffering. Some people believe that a person in this situation should be allowed to die rather than be kept alive by artificial means. Still, even if we accept the concept of a right to die, other questions arise. Who gives permission for the patient to be taken off life-support systems? Should active euthanasia be allowed (causing death with a deliberate overdose of painkillers, for example) or only passive (failing to take all measures possible to avoid death)?

Disagreements also occur over how ethical standards should be applied. For example, a person may argue that the biblical commandment "Thou shalt not kill" forbids abortion. But the same person may support the death penalty. What happens to "Thou shalt not kill" then? Similarly, a person who opposes the death penalty may believe that euthanasia is sometimes permissible. Yet it can be argued that this also involves taking a life.

Life-or-death questions are not the only ethical issues under consideration in our society. Many people think government needs to develop stricter ethical standards. We hear calls for more ethics in business, science, journalism, and other professions. But ultimate responsibility for ethics lies with individuals. Public behavior depends on private choices. The ethics of each of us helps form the ethics of all of us.

ANN E. WEISS
Author, *Bioethics: Dilemmas in Modern Medicine*

ETHIOPIA

Ethiopia, once called Abyssinia, is the oldest independent nation in Africa. It is also one of the oldest countries in the world; its emperors claimed descent from a son of the Queen of Sheba and King Solomon. Located in eastern Africa, Ethiopia is situated in the area known as the Horn of Africa.

Ethiopia's last emperor was Haile Selassie I, who was deposed in 1974 in a military coup led by Communist army officers. The following year the 83-year-old monarch was murdered on the orders of the new government. This regime ruled Ethiopia with an iron fist until 1991, when it was overthrown by rebel forces. Since then, Ethiopia's leaders have had to contend with a land devastated by famine, years of civil war, and the loss of its northernmost region, Eritrea, which provided Ethiopia with its only outlet to the sea.

▶ THE PEOPLE

Ethnic Groups, Language, Religion. Ethiopia's extremely rugged terrain has isolated many of its people, often preserving ways of life and languages as they were long ago.

The Ethiopian mother and child at right are Oromo, one of three major ethnic groups that are part of the country's varied population. Ethiopia's rugged terrain consists mainly of a high plateau, scored by numerous valleys and steep mountains. The Great Rift Valley of eastern Africa cuts Ethiopia nearly in two.

The various peoples include three main groups—the Oromos, Amharas, and Tigreans. The ancestors of the Amharas and Tigreans originated in southern Arabia. Generally dark-skinned and slender in appearance, they inhabit the northern part of the country. There are also a number of black Nilotic people and nomadic Somalis. The Somalis live mainly in the Ogaden region of southeastern Ethiopia.

For centuries the country's ruling families were Amharas, and until 1974, Amharic was the official language of Ethiopia. Today, the main languages, in addition to Amharic, are Tigrinya, Gallinya, and Arabic. Amharic comes from an ancient Semitic language called Ge'ez, which is used in the service of the Ethiopian Orthodox Church.

About 45 percent of the people are Christian, and about 45 percent Muslim. Most of the remainder follow age-old traditional African religious beliefs. There were a dwindling number of Ethiopian Jews (sometimes called Falashas) in the country until 1991, when the last 17,000 were airlifted to Israel.

Way of Life. Most Ethiopians live in rural (country) villages and earn their livelihood as peasant farmers or herders of livestock. A typical village home is made of mud, with a thatched roof and a floor of earth. Some houses may be made of stone, or of plaster over wood, with corrugated iron roofs.

Life is hard for most of the people. To earn even a bare subsistence from their small plots of land, farmers must work from early morning until darkness falls, seven days a week. Few can afford to own oxen or other work animals, and so must pull the plow themselves, usually helped by sons. At home, the women feed their families, care for the small children, provide all the needs of the household, and wait on the men and boys.

Food and Dress. The staple food is *injera*, a large pancake-like bread, which is usually eaten with chicken or goat stew and a very spicy sauce. *Talla*, a beer made from barley, and *tejj*, a wine made from fermented honey, are served with meals.

The traditional Ethiopian garment is the *shamma*, a large white shawl, sometimes decorated with embroidery and worn draped over the shoulders and arms. Underneath a *shamma*, men may wear shorts or tight white trousers and a white shirt, while women usually wear a long, loose white dress. In the cities, men often wear European-style clothing, but most women prefer the *shamma*.

▶ **THE LAND**

A Varied Landscape. Ethiopia has a varied landscape, which rises from below sea level to a height of more than 15,000 feet (4,600 meters) above it. About two thirds of the land consists of a high plateau slashed and scored by valleys and steep-sided mountains. The Great Rift Valley, a deep depression that runs through eastern Africa, splits Ethiopia almost

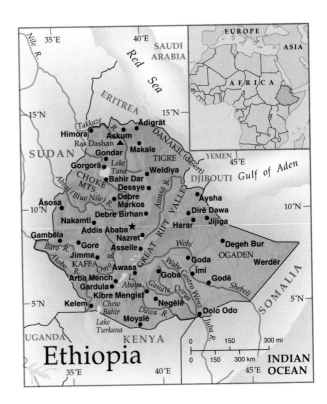

Ethiopia

in two. Swamps and jungles in the southwest contrast with the deserts of the north and southeast.

Lake Tana in northwestern Ethiopia is the country's largest lake. A chain of smaller lakes stretch from Addis Ababa, the capital, southwest into neighboring Kenya. The Blue Nile, known in Ethiopia as the Abbai, rises in the northwestern highlands and flows into Lake Tana. The river spills over the Blue Nile Falls, creating one of the country's most majestic sights. The falls are also called Tisisat, or "smoke of fire," because of the rising mist, which has the appearance of smoke. See the article on the Nile River in Volume N.

Climate and Natural Resources. Climate varies with elevation. The lowlands are very hot, with temperatures of 120°F (50°C) not uncommon along the Red Sea coast. The central plateau, however, has a moderate climate. Most rain falls between June and September, but rainfall has been erratic in recent years and in 1992–93 the country suffered through the worst drought of the century.

Few mineral resources have been discovered in any quantity, although Ethiopia is believed to have as yet untapped deposits of minerals. There are small deposits of platinum and potash (used in making fertilizer), and some gold is mined. Forests, which once covered more than one quarter of the land, have been greatly reduced. The loss of forested areas, along with the present-day practice of cutting down trees for fuel, has led to widespread erosion of the soil.

▶THE ECONOMY

Agriculture. Agriculture has long been the basis of Ethiopia's economy. The most important commercial crop is coffee, which accounts for 60 percent of its export income. The word "coffee," in fact, is thought to be derived from Kaffa, the region in southwestern Ethiopia where most of the country's cof-

fee is produced. The chief food crops include teff, barley, corn, sorghum, chick peas, beans, lentils, and oil seeds. Teff is the cereal grain from which *injera* is made. Sugarcane and tropical fruits are grown in the lowlands.

Years of drought and civil war combined to destroy much of the country's agriculture, including its great herds of cattle, once the largest in Africa. The resulting famine caused the deaths of millions of Ethiopians. Millions more fled to refugee camps, where international organizations have provided emergency food and medical aid.

Industry and Transportation. The processing of agricultural products is Ethiopia's chief industry. Livestock yield canned meat, leather, hides and skins, and footwear. Other manufactured products include textiles, cement, wood pulp, and glassware.

Most people live far from any roads and usually travel on foot. In rural areas, mules are an important means of transportation. Ethiopia has two major railroads. Ethiopian Airlines flies to neighboring countries as well as to Europe and Asia.

▶CITIES

Addis Ababa (meaning "new flower") is Ethiopia's capital, commercial center, and largest city, with a population of close to 2 million. Founded in 1887, it is the country's most modern city, but it was constructed haphazardly and is a mixture of modern buildings and small wooden structures. Refugees from the rural areas have swelled its population.

Most Ethiopians are peasant farmers who eke out a bare subsistence from their plots of land. The farmer shown above is relatively fortunate in having oxen to help him plow. Years of drought and civil war have devastated the country's agriculture. Addis Ababa is Ethiopia's capital, largest city, and commercial center. It was founded in 1887 by the future emperor Menelik II as part of his drive to modernize the country. Like most of Ethiopia's major cities, Addis Ababa lies in the high central plateau, where the climate is temperate.

ETHIOPIA is the official name of the country.

LOCATION: Eastern Africa.

AREA: 426,372 sq mi (1,104,303 km²).

POPULATION: 55,000,000 (estimate).

CAPITAL AND LARGEST CITY: Addis Ababa.

MAJOR LANGUAGES: Amharic, Gallinya, Tigrinya, Arabic.

MAJOR RELIGIOUS GROUPS: Muslim, Christian.

GOVERNMENT: Republic. **Head of state**—president. **Head of government**—prime minister. **Legislature**—National Assembly.

CHIEF PRODUCTS: Agricultural—coffee, teff, barley, corn, sorghum, chick peas, beans, lentils, oil seeds, sugarcane. **Manufactured**—processed agricultural products, textiles, cement, wood pulp, glassware. **Mineral**—salt, potash.

MONETARY UNIT: Birr (1 birr = 100 cents).

One of the city's most impressive buildings is Africa Hall, which houses the United Nations Economic Commission for Africa. It also has been the site of conferences and meetings of the Organization of African Unity, which was established in Addis Ababa. Other places of interest include the Jubilee Palace, once the residence of Ethiopia's emperors; the Cathedral of St. George; the Great Mosque; and Addis Ababa University.

Aksum is a small city in the northern part of the country whose history dates back more than two thousand years. Legend has it that the Queen of Sheba lived here and that her son Menelik was born here. Gondar was Ethiopia's capital from the 1600's to the 1800's.

▶GOVERNMENT

Until 1974, Ethiopia was a constitutional monarchy. Real political power, however, rested with the emperor, who ruled with nearly absolute authority. Following the revolution that overthrew the monarchy, a new constitution, adopted in 1987, officially established a Communist form of government, with a single political party, the Workers' Party of Ethiopia. The Communist government itself was overthrown in 1991.

A transitional (temporary) government was formed by the Ethiopian People's Revolutionary Democratic Front (EPRDF), an alliance of many political groups but dominated by the Tigre People's Liberation Front (TPLF). The transitional government was made up of the Council of Representatives, whose 87 members represented many different ethnic and political groups. The council selected the president, who in turn appointed the prime minister.

In 1994, elections were held for a constituent assembly, with the EPRDF winning the great majority of the seats, but not all opposition parties participated. The assembly approved a new constitution, which provided for a federal type government and the division of the country into nine states. Under the constitution, the states have local self-rule and the right to secede from Ethiopia, if they wish. The first elections for the new legislature, the National Assembly, were held in 1995.

▶HISTORY

Early History. According to Ethiopian tradition, the country's emperors were descended from Menelik I, son of the Queen of Sheba and King Solomon. The Ethiopian empire grew out of the early kingdom of Aksum. Christianity was introduced by missionaries in the A.D. 300's. When Muslims swept across North Africa in the 600's, they brought the religion of Islam to the region. Although Ethiopia was able to preserve its Christian faith, it was surrounded by hostile Muslim states. Isolated from its trade and cultural contact with Asia, it declined in importance. In the centuries that followed, various kingdoms rose and fell in Ethiopia.

Modern Ethiopia. The founder of modern Ethiopia was Emperor Menelik II, who ruled from 1889 to 1913. During his reign, Ethiopia's territory expanded, the country was modernized, and Addis Ababa was made the national capital. Haile Selassie I became emperor in 1930. He abolished slavery, set up a modern educational system, and established friendly relations with the European powers. When Italy invaded Ethiopia in 1935, Haile Selassie appealed to the League of Nations for support. But the Italian government ignored the league. Italian forces occupied Ethiopia until 1941, when they were driven out by the British during World War II.

Below: Emperor Haile Selassie I appealed to the League of Nations (forerunner of the United Nations) for help in 1936, after Italy's invasion of Ethiopia. The Italians were driven out in 1941, during World War II. Ethiopia's last emperor, he was overthrown in 1974 and murdered the following year. *Right:* In recent decades, drought and civil war caused the deaths of millions of Ethiopia's people and forced countless others to become refugees in their own land.

Communist Rule. Years of civil war, famine, and authoritarian rule had eventually cost Haile Selassie much of his support, and in 1974 the emperor was overthrown by the military. He was murdered the following year. (For more information, see the biography of Haile Selassie I in Volume H.)

The military government expanded education and health services and announced a program of land reform. In 1977, Lieutenant Colonel Mengistu Haile Mariam, one of the leaders of the coup, took complete power by murdering his opponents. In 1987, Mengistu proclaimed Ethiopia a Communist state.

Civil War and Loss of Eritrea. For nearly thirty years, rebel groups waged guerrilla war against the government. The Eritrean People's Liberation Front (EPLF) began fighting for the independence of the Eritrea region in 1970. The Tigre People's Liberation Front (TPLF) began a struggle for independence in 1974. The government also fought a war (1977–78) with Somalia, which claimed the Ogaden region.

A major campaign against the Communists began in 1991. Mengistu fled the country and a rebel coalition installed a new government. Interim president Meles Zenawi agreed that Eritrea would be granted independence if its people voted for it. A referendum, held in 1993, was passed overwhelmingly.

Recent Events. In 1995, under a new constitution, the Ethiopian People's Revolutionary Democratic Front (EPRDF) won the country's first multiparty elections, and Meles became prime minister. The EPRDF was returned to power in 2000. The following year, Parliament elected Girma Woldegiorgis to the largely ceremonial post of president.

In 2000, after two years of border disputes, Ethiopia launched a major military offensive against Eritrea. A peace accord was finally signed that year, but Ethiopia did not accept the ruling of the United Nations Boundary Commission until 2004. Meantime, famine had returned, threatening people mainly in the south. In 2003, archaeologists announced the discovery in Ethiopia of the oldest known fossils of modern humans—three human skulls dating back 160,000 years.

Elections in 2005 returned Meles and the EPRDF to power. But protesters accused the ruling party of electoral fraud.

PETER SCHWAB
Author, *Ethiopia*

See also ERITREA.

ETHNIC GROUPS

An ethnic group is a group of people who feel close to each other because they share the same culture and because their ancestors came from the same country or area. The members of a particular ethnic group often enjoy the same kind of music or art or food their parents and grandparents enjoyed. Common interests bind them together and sometimes influence their actions. "Ethnic," the adjective used to describe these groups, comes from the Greek word *ethnos*, meaning "people" or "nation."

Perhaps the easiest way to understand what an ethnic group is, is to point out what it is not. All the citizens of a country do not necessarily belong to one ethnic group. The citizens of the United States, for example, all may carry a United States passport and all may qualify to vote, but they belong to many different groups. Most citizens of Canada belong to one of the two large ethnic groups (French-speaking descendants of French settlers, and English-speaking descendants of English settlers) or to one of the smaller ethnic groups whose members are, or are descended from, immigrants from other European countries. But whatever their ethnic backgrounds, all these people are Canadian citizens.

A family is not an ethnic group. Members of a family have the same ancestors and often share a common "culture"—perhaps certain jokes and words that other families do not know. But the family is too small a unit to be called an ethnic group.

▶ HOW ETHNIC GROUPS ARE FORMED

In many countries there are groups of people who feel closely linked because of their origin and culture: the Indians and Pakistanis in England, the North Africans in France, the Irish in England, the Italian-Americans in the United States. All these groups are made up of immigrants and their descendants.

Immigration is not the only way an ethnic group is formed. Ethnic groups are also formed when a country expands to include people of different cultures and origins. When the United States expanded in the early years of its history, Spanish-speaking groups and Indians were included within its borders. Russia expanded to include many ethnic groups besides Russians.

Sometimes an ethnic group is given a legal definition. For example, until the 1960's many states of the United States defined blacks by law and restricted their activities.

Jews were legally defined in Nazi Germany, where they suffered severe persecution and finally genocide (the killing of a people). Jews are, of course, members of a religious group, but they are also an ethnic group. Many Jews who are not religious think of themselves as part of the Jewish ethnic group.

Ethnic groups are sometimes legally defined not for the purpose of discriminating or taking action against them, but for just the opposite reason. For example, there is a law in the United States requiring large American employers to report the numbers of their employees who are black, American Indian, or Spanish-speaking (or descendants of Spanish-speaking ancestors). The purpose of this law is to make sure that employers do not refuse to hire members of these ethnic groups.

▶ NEW IDEAS ABOUT ETHNIC GROUPS

For a long time most multi-ethnic nations (nations made up of many ethnic groups) believed in the idea of assimilation, or the blending of all groups into one large group. These nations felt that they could be strong only if individual ethnic groups forgot their origins and allowed their languages and cultures to disappear. Assimilation was the goal of Czarist Russia. In the early 20th century the United States followed a policy of "Americanization" of all immigrants.

Although many countries still cling to the idea of assimilation, some multi-ethnic nations, such as the United States and Canada, are changing. The old ideal of assimilation is being replaced by a new ideal called "cultural pluralism." Cultural pluralism means that each ethnic group continues to enjoy and keep alive its special culture in whatever way it chooses.

▶ ETHNIC GROUPS IN THE UNITED STATES

In the United States the processes of assimilation and acculturation (taking on a new culture) have gone very far. Except for the newest Spanish-speaking groups (Mexican-American and Puerto Rican), almost all

FACES OF AMERICA

American ethnic groups have given up their distinctive languages. Their cultures—family life, education, occupations, and beliefs—have all become quite similar.

Intermarriage is one factor that has contributed to the blending of ethnic groups. As marriages between Italian-Americans and Puerto Ricans or between Irish-Americans and German-Americans have increased, growing numbers of Americans come from many different ethnic backgrounds. Some people of mixed backgrounds choose to be part of one particular group. Others feel there is no need to be anything but "American."

In the United States, as in many other countries, people may think of themselves as members of different "ethnic groups" at different times and under different circumstances. For instance, German-Americans from Texas might think of themselves as Texans when they are in one of the northern states or as Americans when they are in Europe. In fact, Americans of any ethnic group who travel abroad often begin to think of themselves simply as Americans because their culture is so different from that of the countries they are visiting.

Because there has been so much merging among ethnic groups in the United States, it is sometimes difficult to distinguish them clearly. Yet many people still feel strong ties to their past. In recent years there has been a revival of interest in individual cultures.

Today many people believe that society is enriched by the contributions of a variety of ethnic groups. People have begun to show great interest in their roots and in the culture of their ancestors—their history, values, art, dress, and food. Along with this interest has come a new feeling of pride in one's own ethnic background.

Nathan Glazer
Harvard University
Co-author, *Beyond the Melting Pot*

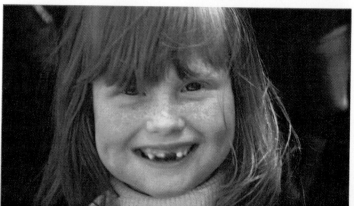

Even at a very young age, children begin to learn the rules of etiquette. These rules, which may vary from country to country, are based on consideration for others.

ETIQUETTE

Have you ever stopped to consider why you share your belongings with others? Or why you say "please" when you ask for something and "thank you" when someone does something for you? These behaviors are designed to help people get along with one another.

Etiquette is the set of rules that guide how people behave toward one another. Actually, people follow not one but several codes of etiquette. Most people are concerned with a social code of behavior—that is, how people treat one another in daily life. There is also military etiquette, the special set of rules that people in the military follow. Protocol is yet another kind of etiquette. It is used by government officials and diplomats.

Etiquette also varies from culture to culture. In some countries, people greet each other by shaking hands. In other countries they bow in greeting. In many countries a host goes through doors after a guest as a sign of courtesy. But in some parts of the world, the host goes ahead of guests as a sort of honorary form of protection for them.

▶ THE HISTORY OF ETIQUETTE

The first etiquette rules probably came about when people began to band together to hunt and to protect one another. If nothing else, these prehistoric people needed rules about sharing the food they had gathered. As people began to live together in larger, more complex groups, they created more rules to help them get along with one another. Eventually, etiquette became a strict set of rules about social behavior.

People have learned about etiquette from their families and also by reading etiquette books. Such books have been written at least since the days of the Roman Empire, and children have often been their target.

From the 1500's through the early 1900's, children also learned etiquette in school. Most reading primers consisted of verses and advice on correct behavior. Children were advised on such points as the proper way of kneeling before their teachers, the value of remaining silent until spoken to, and the folly of using a dinner knife as a toothpick.

Over the years, people were expected to follow an increasingly complicated set of rules. Many of the rules seem silly today. For example, in Western countries in the 1800's, a young man could not speak to a young woman he knew until she had first acknowledged him. Little girls curtsied and little boys bowed when introduced to someone. Not long ago, when a man and woman went out on a date, she was expected to sit in the car while he walked around it to open her door and help her out.

▶ ETIQUETTE TODAY

Since the 1960's, manners have become much more relaxed. Etiquette today is based on treating everyone with the same degree of kindness and consideration, and it consists mostly of common sense. It is helpful, though, to know some rules about how to behave in certain situations.

Greetings and Introductions. When you meet someone you have not seen for a while, it is polite to say hello. Young people often greet each other casually and always use first names with one another. Greetings to adults are more formal. As a sign of respect, stand up when you greet someone older and call the person by name. Young people do not usually call adults by their first names until the adults have asked them to do so.

This diagram of an informal table setting shows the correct placement of the following items: (1) salad fork; (2) dinner fork; (3) plate; (4) knife; (5) dessert spoon; (6) soup spoon; (7) bread plate and butter knife; (8) water glass; (9) teacup, saucer, and spoon.

It is easy to make an introduction if you remember that it is merely a polite way of making two people known to each other. Young people are usually introduced to older people rather than the other way around. If you are at a party and have not been introduced to everyone, it is quite proper for you to introduce yourself to someone else. When you meet someone for the first time, it is polite to shake hands with them.

Table Manners. Probably more has been written about table manners than any other area of etiquette. Almost all the rules are designed to make eating pleasant. There are far more rules than can be listed here, but the basics of good table manners are easy to learn.

To begin with, meals are a special time to sit down and talk with family and friends. Because of this, the dinner hour is not the time to act rowdy, talk loudly, or argue with anyone. The days are long past when children did not speak at the dinner table except when spoken to. But certain topics of conversation are still ruled out. In general, do not discuss anything that will ruin anyone's appetite, such as what you dissected in science class and any descriptions of serious injury or illness.

There are lots of rules about how to eat specific foods. But you need only a few guidelines to get along well. Learn to hold and use a knife, fork, and spoon correctly. Never use your fingers to push food onto your fork or spoon. Eat quietly and always keep your mouth closed when chewing food. Sit up straight at the table. It is polite to wait for your host or hostess to begin before you start to eat.

At a restaurant or at someone's home, you may be served a food you have never seen before. If you do not know how to eat it, you can say, "I've never eaten this. Can you tell me about it?" Or you can wait and watch your hosts eat the food and do what they do.

A formal table setting may have more knives, forks, and spoons than you are used to seeing. If you do not know which one to use for which course, follow this rule: Start from the outside and work in. A salad fork, for example, is placed outside the dinner fork, when salad is served before the main course.

If you must leave the table for any reason during a meal, ask to be excused. Finally, do not forget to compliment the cook. Especially at home, people too often take meals for granted.

Telephone Manners. Good telephone manners also help life run smoothly. Remember that the only impression callers have of you is made by your voice. Try to speak in a normal, pleasant tone.

If the caller asks to speak to someone who is home, say, "Just a minute, please, I'll call her to the phone." If the person is not home, offer to take a message. Make sure you write down a correctly spelled name and a number. Do not forget to give the message to the person who got the call.

Be thoughtful about when and how long you use the phone. Do not let friends call late at night or during dinner. Do not tie up the phone for hours, especially if someone is waiting for a call or planning to use the phone.

Visiting. When you visit someone, you are a guest. This means that you are extended various small courtesies, but it also means that you have some responsibilities.

When you arrive at someone's house, greet other family members. Elderly people especially appreciate a few minutes' attention. Ask them how they are feeling or comment on something they are doing.

As a guest your role is to be more a follower than a leader. Your host will suggest activities, and unless you hate the suggestion, you should try to go along with it. Wait until food and drinks are offered to you.

Finally, do not outstay your welcome. If you have been invited for an afternoon swim, do not stay until someone has to invite you to dinner. Your friend may have other plans, so leave shortly after the swim. This way you will be a welcome guest the next time you visit. Always thank your host for the visit.

Making Guests Comfortable. "The shoe is on the other foot" when a friend visits as your guest. Then you must do everything possible to make your guest feel comfortable. The key to this is to anticipate your guest's needs.

If someone is visiting overnight or for several days, explain the routine of the household. Your guest will then feel comfortable and will know what is expected. Make a special effort to take all of your guest's needs into account.

Take special care to share things with your guest and to give him or her special treatment—the best seat for watching television, for instance. Try to suggest activities that you know your guest will enjoy. Finally, when your guest is leaving and thanks you for the visit, thank her or him for coming.

Parties. Party manners are not very different from the manners you use when you visit someone's home, but they are sometimes a bit more formal. Since you are not the only guest at a party, it is important to go along with the crowd. Act enthusiastic about whatever activities have been planned.

When you arrive, greet your host and anyone who is there to help with the party. When you leave, say good-bye to these same people and thank them for giving the party or for helping. Offer to help the host—or just lend a hand if you see that something needs doing. A particular kindness at a party is to talk to someone who is shy or a stranger.

Thank-You Notes. When someone gives you a gift, you should send a handwritten note of thanks. A thank-you note need not be long, but it should be sincere and specific. Mention the gift by name. You might describe something you particularly like about it—its color or its shape—or how you will use it. On the other hand, if you really do not like the gift and probably will not use it, a more general note may help hide this fact.

Manners at Home and in Public. If you remember to be thoughtful and considerate toward other people, you will behave properly wherever you are—at school, in restaurants, on buses, and in theaters, as well as at home.

At a theater you should walk quietly to your seat. If you have to pass in front of people, excuse yourself and be careful not to step on their toes. Avoid talking, rattling candy pa-

RULES for BEHAVIOUR, 1787

CHILDREN'S BEHAVIOUR at the TABLE

COME NOT to the Table without having your Hands and Face washed, and your Head combed.

Ask not for any Thing, but tarry until it be offered thee.

Find no fault with any Thing that is given thee.

If thou wantest any Thing from the Servants, call to them softly.

Make not a Noise with thy Tongue, Mouth, Lips or Breath, in eating or drinking.

Take not Salt with a greasy Knife.

Spit not, cough not, nor blow thy Nose at the Table, if it may be avoided; but if there be necessity, do it aside, and without much Noise.

Stuff not thy Mouth so as to fill thy Cheeks, be content with smaller Mouthfuls.

Blow not thy Meat, but with Patience wait until it be cool.

Smell not of thy Meat, nor put it to thy Nose; turn it not the other Side upward to view it upon thy Plate.

Throw not any Thing under the Table.

Spit not forth any Thing that is not convenient to be swallowed, as the Stones of Plumbs, Cherries, or such like; but with thy left Hand, neatly move them to the Side of thy Plate.

Foul not the Napkin all over, but at one Corner only.

Stare not in the Face of any one, especially thy Superiours, at the Table.

Pick not thy Teeth at the Table, unless holding up thy Napkin before thy Mouth with thine other Hand.

Drink not nor speak with any Thing in thy Mouth.

When thou risest from the Table, having made a Bow at the Side of the Table where thou sattest, withdraw.

From *A Little Pretty Pocket-Book* first printed by John Newbery, London, 1774; first American edition issued by Isaiah Thomas, Worcester, Mass., 1789. Reprinted at the press of The *Virginia Gazette*, Williamsburg, copyright D. Adair, 1949.

According to these "rules for behaviour" from the 1700's, children should not ask for anything at the table or complain about the food.

pers, pushing on the seat in front of you, or bobbing your head from side to side. These things spoil the show for other people.

At a fast-food restaurant, you should eat as politely as you would at any restaurant or at someone's house. In many of these restaurants, you are expected to clear your table when you have finished eating.

As you can see, there are many kinds of situations where knowing how to act is helpful. Most situations, though, can be handled by following one simple guideline: Treat others as you would like to be treated. That as well as "please" and "thank you" will get you through almost any awkward moment.

MARJABELLE YOUNG STEWART
Author, *White Gloves and Party Manners*

ETYMOLOGY. See WORD ORIGINS.

EUGENE. See OREGON (Cities).

EULER, LEONHARD. See MATHEMATICS, HISTORY OF (Profiles).

EUROPE

On a world map or globe most of the continents can be seen plainly as masses of land set in the vast expanse of the oceans. Australia, Antarctica, and Africa are well defined, although Africa is attached to Asia by the Isthmus of Suez. North and South America, although joined at the Isthmus of Panama, also stand out as large individual landmasses. Europe, however, seems to be an extension of Asia. In fact, geographically, Europe and Asia are sometimes regarded as a single great continent called Eurasia, with Europe as an enormous peninsula. But because Europe has a distinctive history and culture, it is usually considered a separate continent.

The idea that Europe is a separate continent is a very old one. It is believed by some

authorities that many centuries before the birth of Christ, the people of the Middle East divided the world they knew into three parts: One part was their own familiar region. They called the land to the east Asu—the Land of the Rising Sun. They named the land to the west Ereb—the Land of the Setting Sun. It may be from these ancient names that we get the modern names Asia and Europe.

Geographers do not always agree on the boundary between Europe and Asia. But most consider it to run from the Atlantic Ocean westward to the Ural Mountains and the north shore of the Caspian Sea, then along the

Caucasus Mountains to the Black Sea, and southward through the Bosporus and Dardanelles straits. The Urals also divide the giant nation of Russia into European and Asian areas.

Europe, with just 8 percent of the world's land area, ranks as the second smallest continent after Australia. But its placement at the crossroads of the trade routes between Asia, Africa, and the Americas—and its impact on world history—has given the continent a global importance far greater than its small size would suggest.

Europe was the birthplace of ideas that helped shape the modern world. From ancient Greece came the idea of democracy and the spirit of scientific inquiry. From Rome came the idea of just laws and the first attempts to unite Europe. In the northern European lowlands people learned to rotate the crops they planted from year to year. This helped keep the soil fertile and made it possible to establish permanent settlements. Europeans were also the first to make use of machines to replace human labor on a large scale. The Industrial Revolution in the 1700's and early 1800's made Europe the world's workshop. From the late 1400's, European ships roamed the seas, dominating world trade and exploration for the next four centuries. Enormous colonial empires were carved out in North America, South America, Africa, Asia, and Australia. European settlers carried their traditions and languages to all parts of the globe.

Clockwise from opposite page, top left: The Eiffel Tower in Paris, France, Europe's largest city; a Latvian girl wearing a traditional bow; Polish farmers driving a horse-drawn hay wagon; cyclists competing in the annual Tour de France bicycle race; green pastures along the Atlantic coast in Galway, Ireland; the Parthenon in Athens, Greece; a chamois standing before Mont Blanc, the highest peak in the Alps.

THE NATIONS OF EUROPE

Country	Capital
Albania	Tiranë
Andorra	Andorra la Vella
Austria	Vienna
Belarus	Minsk
Belgium	Brussels
Bosnia and Herzegovina	Sarajevo
Bulgaria	Sofia
Croatia	Zagreb
Cyprus[1]	Nicosia
Czech Republic	Prague
Denmark	Copenhagen
Estonia	Tallinn
Finland	Helsinki
France	Paris
Germany	Berlin
Greece	Athens
Hungary	Budapest
Iceland	Reykjavík
Ireland	Dublin
Italy	Rome
Latvia	Riga
Liechtenstein	Vaduz
Lithuania	Vilnius
Luxembourg	Luxembourg
Macedonia	Skopje
Malta	Valletta
Moldova	Chişinău
Monaco	Monaco-Ville
Netherlands	Amsterdam
Norway	Oslo
Poland	Warsaw
Portugal	Lisbon
Romania	Bucharest
Russia[2]	Moscow
San Marino	San Marino
Serbia and Montenegro	Belgrade
Slovakia	Bratislava
Slovenia	Ljubljana
Spain	Madrid
Sweden	Stockholm
Switzerland	Bern
Ukraine	Kiev
United Kingdom	London
Vatican City	Vatican City

[1] Cyprus is geographically part of Asia, but it belongs to the European Union.
[2] Russia includes land in Europe and Asia. Small areas of Turkey, Azerbaijan, Georgia, and Kazakhstan also lie in Europe.

FACTS and figures

LOCATION AND SIZE: Europe extends from: **Latitude**—71° 10′ N to 36° 10′ N. **Longitude**—66° E to 9° 30′ W. **Area**—(including Russia in Europe and adjacent islands)—approximately 4,000,000 sq mi (10,360,000 km²). **Highest Point**—Mt. Elbrus, 18,510 ft (5,642 m). **Lowest Point**—Caspian Sea, 92 ft (28 m) below sea level.

POPULATION: 729,000,000 (estimate includes Asian Russia but none of Turkey).

PRINCIPAL LAKES: Caspian Sea (between Europe and Asia), Ladoga, Onega, Vänern, Vättern, Saimaa, Balaton, Constance.

PRINCIPAL RIVERS: Volga, Danube, Dnieper, Don, Pechora, Dniester, Rhine, Elbe, Vistula, Loire, Tagus, Neman, Ebro, Oder, Rhône.

PRINCIPAL MOUNTAIN RANGES: Caucasus—Mt. Elbrus, Dykh Tau, Mt. Kazbek; **Alps**—Mont Blanc, Dufourspitze, Monte Leone, Barre des Écrins, Matterhorn; **Pyrenees**—Pico de Aneto; **Sierra Nevada**—Mulhacén.

following World War II, Europe was roughly divided into two political camps. Most of the Eastern European nations became satellites of the Soviet Union, the world's first Communist state. Much of Western Europe allied itself with the democratic United States. This division of the continent came to an end between 1989 and 1991, when the Eastern European Communist countries replaced their governments with democratically elected ones, and the Soviet Union itself collapsed.

By the turn of the century, the 15 member nations of the European Union (EU) had made great strides toward forming an economic bloc large enough to rival that of the United States. Unity was also furthered by expanding European Union membership to include several nations that had formerly belonged to the Soviet Union.

▶ THE NATIONS OF EUROPE

Europe is made up of all or part of 48 countries. The nations of northern Europe include Norway, Sweden, Denmark (known as the Scandinavian countries), Finland, and the distant island of Iceland. The United Kingdom and Ireland are a part of western Europe. (The United Kingdom includes the island of Great Britain and a small area in northern Ireland.)

France, the largest nation in western Europe, is ringed on three sides by eight other

But in the 1900's, two world wars (1914–18 and 1939–45) almost destroyed Europe and its rich heritage. Many cities were completely devastated. Out of the ashes and rubble, Europeans had to rebuild their nations. In the years

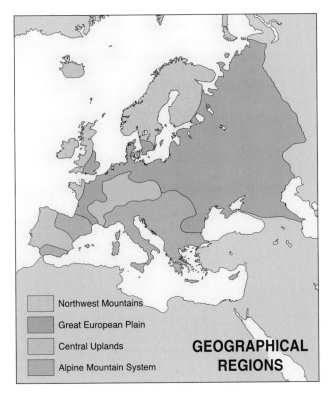

At the end of the last Ice Age, melting glaciers carved narrow channels called fjords through the towering cliffs of the Northwest Mountains region in Norway.

nations. On the low-lying plains of northwestern Europe lie Belgium, the Netherlands, and Luxembourg. Spain and Portugal both occupy the Iberian Peninsula of southwestern Europe, with Portugal being the most westerly country on the European mainland. Italy lies in southern Europe. Switzerland, Germany, and Austria are situated roughly in central Europe, while Poland, Hungary, the Czech Republic, and Slovakia lie in east central Europe. Serbia and Montenegro, Croatia, Slovenia, Bosnia and Herzegovina, Macedonia, Romania, Bulgaria, Greece, and Albania occupy the Balkan Peninsula in southeastern Europe. The Baltic States—Latvia, Lithuania, and Estonia—are so called because of their location on the Baltic Sea in northeastern Europe. Moldova, Ukraine, and Belarus lie at the eastern edge of the continent.

Europe also has several tiny countries: Andorra, nestled in the Pyrenees mountains; Liechtenstein, between Switzerland and Austria; Monaco, an enclave on the southern coast of France; the island of Malta in the Mediterranean Sea; mountainous San Marino in Italy; and Vatican City, realm of the pope, situated within the city of Rome.

Several countries lie in both Europe and Asia. They include Russia (Europe's largest country) and small parts of Azerbaijan, Georgia, Kazakhstan, and Turkey. Geographically, the island nation of Cyprus in the eastern Mediterranean Sea belongs to Asia, but it is linked politically and economically to Europe.

▶ LAND

Europe stretches from the Atlantic Ocean in the west to the Ural Mountains in the east. The northernmost point on the European mainland is Cape Nordkyn in Norway. The most southerly point on the mainland of Europe is Point Tarifa in Spain.

Land Regions

There are four major geographical regions of Europe: the Northwest Mountains, the Great European Plain, the Central Uplands, and the Alpine Mountain System.

The Northwest Mountains, made up of high plateaus, rugged mountains, and deep valleys,

GEOGRAPHICAL REGIONS

Northwest Mountains

Great European Plain

Central Uplands

Alpine Mountain System

The Great European Plain extends from the Atlantic Ocean to the Ural Mountains. Poppies bloom on the plain in the Burgundy region of northern France.

extend from western France through parts of the United Kingdom and the Scandinavian Peninsula, then sweep to the northeast along the Arctic coast all the way to Russia. In Scandinavia the land rises steeply along the Atlantic coast but slopes rather gently down to the Gulf of Bothnia and the Baltic Sea. During the Ice Age, glaciers deepened the short valleys near the coast. After the ice retreated, the ocean water flowed in. These narrow arms of the sea are called fjords. Although the Northwest Mountains receive ample precipitation, the rugged terrain makes farming difficult.

The Great European Plain, the largest of the European land regions, is the most densely settled part of the continent. Its fine harbors, vast network of railroads, and many rivers and canal systems have made it a leading center of transportation and industry.

The Great European Plain is shaped like a funnel. The narrow end lies at the foot of the Pyrenees in southwestern France and grows wider as it extends northeast. It includes a large part of western and northern France, most of Belgium, the Netherlands, northern Germany, Denmark, and nearly all of Poland and Russia. The plain is widest in western Russia, where it stretches from the Arctic Ocean to the Black Sea. Its eastern boundary is formed by the Ural Mountains.

The Central Uplands lie between the Great European Plain and the Alpine mountains to the south. They reach from the Atlantic coast of Spain through France and Germany to central Europe. As in the Northwest Mountains, farming in this region is limited due to the rugged landscape. Major sections of the highlands include the Massif Central, the Vosges mountains, and the Ardennes.

The Alpine Mountain System stretches from the Franco-Italian border through central Europe and the Balkan Peninsula. The

Wheat, corn, and other grains thrive in the vast grasslands of Ukraine. This part of the Great European Plain has been called the Breadbasket of Europe.

Sierra Nevada range in Spain parallels the Mediterranean coast. The Pyrenees form the border between Spain and France. Many of the islands in the western Mediterranean, such as Corsica, Sardinia, and the Balearics, are also mountainous. The backbone of the Italian peninsula is formed by the mountains of the Apennines.

The mountains north of the Po River are called the Alps. The Alps form a mountain barrier between southern Europe and western and central Europe. However, there are natural passes through the Alps. It is through these passes that Roman legions marched northward in their conquest of Europe. Later it was through the same passes that the conquerors of the Roman Empire entered the Italian peninsula.

One branch of the Alps, called the Jura Mountains, borders the Swiss plateau on which most of the Swiss cities are built. Two branches of the Alps circle the Great Danube Plain and part of the Balkan Peninsula. The Carpathian Mountains form the northern branch of the Alps. The southern branch is known as the Dinaric Alps.

The towering Caucasus Mountains, between the Black and Caspian seas, are often considered part of the Alpine Mountain System. The Caucasus form a high wall that shuts Europe off from the Middle East. Both the highest and the lowest points in Europe are in the Caucasus. They are Mt. Elbrus, which is 18,510 feet (5,642 meters) above sea level; and the Caspian Sea, part of which lies about 92 feet (28 meters) below sea level.

Rivers, Lakes, and Coastal Waters

Several arms of the Atlantic Ocean penetrate deeply into the continent. No point in the western part of Europe is more than 500 miles (800 kilometers) from a seacoast. Only the plains of the eastern European steppe are far from the sea.

The deepest penetration by the Atlantic Ocean is the Mediterranean Sea in the south. The peninsulas of Italy and the Balkans divide the Mediterranean into separate parts, such as the Ligurian, Tyrrhenian, Adriatic, Ionian, and Aegean seas.

The Mediterranean Sea extends to the east to form the Black Sea and the Sea of Azov. The seas form part of Europe's southern border. They provide a link between the land-locked heart of Eurasia and the ancient trade routes of the Mediterranean. The Caspian Sea is all that remains of an arm of the Mediterranean that once stretched east to the Aral Sea.

The Caucasus Mountains mark Europe's southeastern boundary. Mount Elbrus, Europe's tallest mountain, is located there.

The northern branch of the Atlantic is the Baltic Sea. It may be entered from the North Sea by way of the Danish straits. For more information, see the articles ATLANTIC OCEAN, MEDITERRANEAN SEA, and OCEANS AND SEAS OF THE WORLD in the appropriate volumes.

For centuries transportation in Europe has moved along a network of rivers and canals. The Volga, Europe's longest river, rises in the hills near Moscow, capital of Russia, and flows through the Russian heartland, before emptying into the Caspian Sea. Two other rivers—the Dnieper, which flows through Russia and

Ukraine, and the Dniester, forming part of the border of Moldova—empty into the Black Sea. The Don, another important Russian river, flows into the Sea of Azov. The famed Danube, Europe's second longest river, is the major waterway of central Europe.

Several broad rivers wind across northern and western Europe and end in the North Sea or the Baltic. They include the Rhine, the Weser, the Elbe, and the Vistula. These rivers are navigable (deep enough and wide enough for ships) for most of their length and carry traffic from the coast to the interior. Six major rivers flow to the Atlantic—three Spanish (the Tagus, Douro, and Guadalquivir) and three French (the Seine, Loire, and Garonne). The Ebro in Spain and the Rhône in France empty into the Mediterranean. The most important river in northern Italy, the Po, flows into the Adriatic Sea. For more information on Europe's rivers, see the article RIVERS in Volume QR.

The Caspian Sea, which is actually a lake, lies on the border between Europe and Asia. It is the world's largest inland body of water. The largest lake entirely within Europe is Ladoga, in Russia. Three other large European lakes are in Scandinavia: Saimaa in Finland

INDEX TO EUROPE PHYSICAL MAP

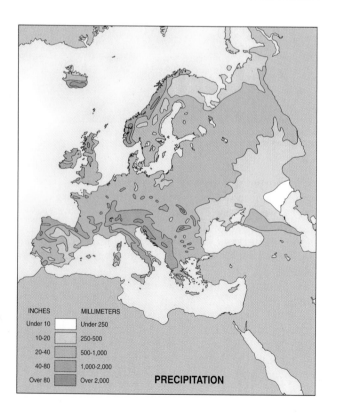

INCHES	MILLIMETERS
Under 10	Under 250
10-20	250-500
20-40	500-1,000
40-80	1,000-2,000
Over 80	Over 2,000

PRECIPITATION

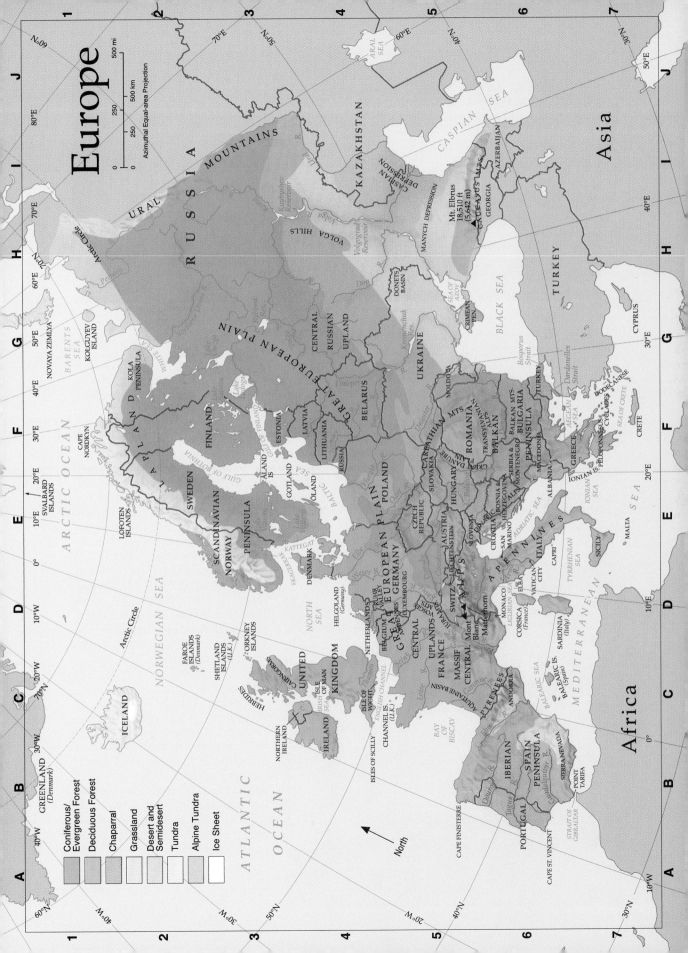

Europe

Azimuthal Equal-area Projection

500 mi
0   250   500 km
0   250

Legend (vegetation):
- Coniferous/Evergreen Forest
- Deciduous Forest
- Chaparral
- Grassland
- Desert and Semidesert
- Tundra
- Alpine Tundra
- Ice Sheet

North

The Danube, Europe's second longest river, rises in the Black Forest region of Germany and flows 1,771 miles (2,850 kilometers) through central Europe to the Black Sea.

and Vättern and Vänern in Sweden. Lake Balaton in Hungary is that country's most popular vacation spot. Lake Constance on the border of Switzerland, Austria, and Germany is another famous tourist attraction, as are the lakes in northern Italy—Como and Garda. Italy and Switzerland share lakes Lugano and Maggiore. Important Swiss cities are built on the banks of lakes Zürich, Geneva, and Lucerne. For more information on Europe's lakes, see the article LAKES (Europe and Asia) in Volume L.

The gleaming domes of a Greek Orthodox church decorate the landscape of Thíra (also known as Santorini), one of the many islands in the Cyclades chain in the south Aegean Sea.

Islands

Europe encompasses thousands of islands. Five of them—Iceland, the United Kingdom, Ireland, Malta, and Cyprus—are nations unto themselves.

Among the most important island groups are the Faeroe Islands (Denmark); the Lofoten and Svalbard (Norway); the Åland (Finland); the Hebrides, Orkneys, Shetland, Isles of Scilly, and Channel Islands (United Kingdom); the Azores (Portugal); the Balearic and Canary Islands (Spain); and the Cyclades, Dodecanese, and Ionian Islands (Greece). Notable individual islands include Capri, Elba, Sardinia, and Sicily (Italy); Corsica (France); Crete (Greece); Greenland (Denmark); Helgoland (Germany); Madeira (Portugal); and the Isle of Man and Isle of Wight (United Kingdom).

Climate

Western Europe's climate is influenced by the North Atlantic Drift, an ocean current that brings mild sea air from the west and accounts for the generally moderate temperatures, both in winter and summer. Precipitation (including rain and snow) is heaviest in mountainous areas, such as the west coast of Norway and in many parts of the Alps.

Southern Europe has a Mediterranean climate, with mild, wet winters and warm, dry summers. Because of the warming influence of the Mediterranean Sea, winter temperatures rarely fall below 48°F (9°C). Storms are infrequent and days are usually sunny.

The greatest extremes of climate, with the coldest winters and hottest summers, are found in the inland regions of the continent. The lowest winter temperatures occur in northern Russia and in interior areas of the Scandinavian Peninsula.

Although most of Europe receives enough rainfall for crops to grow, some regions receive very little rain. The land in the southern part of Russia and the interior plateau of Spain is too dry for farming and is used for grazing livestock. In other areas, crops can be grown only with irrigation.

Plant Life

The most northerly zone of vegetation in Europe is the tundra. In the tundra zone of Lapland and northern Russia, reindeer graze on mosses, lichens, and low scrub growth during the summer. But animals must move south in search of food during the winter months. Below the tundra is a vast area known as the boreal forest, or taiga. It forms a wide belt all around the world and includes parts of Sweden, Finland, and Russia. The taiga is Europe's chief source of softwoods, such as pine, spruce, hemlock, and fir.

South of the taiga, running through much of central Europe, are temperate deciduous forests of larch, ash, beech, birch, elm, maple, and oak. Grasslands cover much of Ukraine and southwest Russia. Chaparral covers the dry, southernmost regions of Europe. In the Mediterranean region laurel, cypress, cedar, evergreen oak, cork oak, and olive trees are common. A typical form of Mediterranean

Windmill on the River Zaan, the Netherlands

WONDER QUESTION

Where and what are the Low Countries?

The Low Countries are a region in northwestern Europe lying between France and Germany. Historically, they include the modern nations of Belgium, the Netherlands, and Luxembourg—sometimes called the Benelux countries. Geographically, the region takes its name from the low-lying plains of the Netherlands and northern Belgium along the North Sea coast. At one time the entire region was known as the Netherlands (meaning "low countries"), but that name now applies just to the one country. The Netherlands are sometimes mistakenly called Holland. Holland is actually the largest province of the Netherlands.

Combined, the Low Countries are smaller in area than the state of South Carolina. But their importance is far greater than their small size would suggest. They form one of the most densely populated regions of Europe and one of its major manufacturing centers.

The Low Countries were united by the dukes of Burgundy in the late 1300's and 1400's. By marriage, they passed to the Habsburg rulers of Austria and Spain. The great wealth of the region was then based in large part on cloth weaving. The Netherlands was the first to win full independence, from Spain in the 1600's. In 1815, the Netherlands and Belgium were united in a single kingdom. The Belgians, unhappy with the union, declared their independence after a revolt in 1830. The tiny Grand Duchy of Luxembourg dates its modern era of independence from 1839.

Left: The cork oak, a tree native to the Mediterranean region, is cultivated in Spain and Portugal. Its bark tissue is used in many products, from bottle stoppers to baseballs. *Below:* Tulips and other flowers are commercially grown in Holland, a province of the Netherlands.

vegetation is the maquis—a mixture of scrub plants that look lifeless in the summer but blossom during the rainy season.

Wildflowers are a part of the landscape everywhere in Europe. They are most beautiful in the mountains, especially in the Alpine pastures. Even the semi-arid steppes of southern Russia have a carpeting of colorful wildflowers in the early spring.

Animal Life

Many animals that once roamed throughout Europe are now found only in zoos. Some, however, are still found in fairly large numbers in the wild. Rabbits and hares are caught everywhere. Deer are hunted during the hunting season. Mink, ermine, sable, and some varieties of fox are trapped in the forests of northern Russia for their fur. Fox hunting with dogs, once a popular sport in Britain, has been outlawed.

Birds have survived better, although game birds, such as grouse, partridge, and wild duck, are diminishing in number. Among the more familiar European birds are skylarks, nightingales, finches, and starlings. Storks, which used to be numerous, are now rare.

Fish have suffered from the pollution of many lakes and rivers, although fishing is still popular. Probably the best-known freshwater fish is the trout. The sturgeon of the Caspian Sea is caught for its roe (eggs), known as caviar.

Natural Resources

Forests. Northern Europe and other mountainous regions of the continent are densely forested. Southern Europe once had many forests, but long ago the land was cleared to provide lumber for building and other wood products. These old forests were replaced with cultivated fields and grasslands. Today, however, due to strict conservation measures, Europe's forests are expanding by more than 1.25 million acres (500,000 hectares) every year. Many forestlands are further protected to minimize the destruction caused by pollution and other environmental hazards.

Soils. Only parts of eastern, central, and southern Europe have fertile soils. But European agriculture has a high level of productivity because fertilizers are used to enrich the soil where it is poor.

Minerals. Russia and Ukraine have deposits of many of the most important minerals needed in industry. Outside of these countries, however, Europe is not rich in minerals, aside from coal. Iron ore is produced mainly in Sweden and France. There are also relatively small deposits of copper, lead, zinc, bauxite (aluminum ore), silver, and chrome in various parts of Europe. Nearly all European countries must import the minerals they need for their economies.

Environmental Issues. As a heavily populated continent with generally high living standards and limited natural resources, Europe is especially concerned about environmental problems. Europe's vulnerability was demonstrated in 1986 when a nuclear accident at Chernobyl in Ukraine (then part of the Soviet Union) spread nuclear contamination for thousands of miles around. In addition, acid rain, one of the many results of industrial pollution, has affected the forests and lakes of Scandinavia and Germany. In Germany a small but active environmental and political group, the "Greens," has members elected to the legislature. Efforts are being made to clean up the Mediterranean Sea, which suffers not only from industrial pollution, but also from recreational pollution caused by the many tourists who come to the region each year.

▶**PEOPLE**

Although it is the second smallest continent in area, Europe (including European Russia) is the third largest in population, after Asia and Africa. Europe is the most densely popu-

Europe is filled with many interesting birds and mammals. *Left:* Colonies of storks build large nests out of sticks on rooftops and other ledges. *Below:* A dense coat of sharp spines protects the European hedgehog from most predators. *Bottom:* Herds of reindeer are raised in Lapland and elsewhere within the Arctic Circle.

lated of the continents. Its people make up more than 12 percent of the world's total population. The population in most European countries has remained stable, with little or no increase in the rate of growth. However, immigration is swelling the population figures in western Europe.

Europe's population density varies greatly from region to region. Few people live in the northern part of Scandinavia and in some of Europe's more mountainous regions. Industrial areas, however, are heavily populated. There are also dense populations in some rural areas where farming depends on a great deal of human labor, as in parts of the Mediterranean region. A zone of high density runs from the United Kingdom and northern France well into the interior of Europe. A second area of high population density is found in the Po River basin and Arno River valley in northern Italy.

Ethnic Groups

For such a relatively small region, Europe has many different ethnic groups. Ethnic divisions exist even within a single country. Some examples include the English, Welsh, Scots, and Irish in the United Kingdom; the German-, French-, Italian-, and Romansch-speaking peoples of Switzerland; the Flemings and Walloons in Belgium; the Bretons in France; and the Basques in Spain. The arrival of peoples from former European colonies has added to Europe's cultural mix. These include Indonesians in the Netherlands; Algerians in France; and Jamaicans, Pakistanis, and Indians in the United Kingdom.

Many ethnic groups have lived together in peace for centuries, as in Switzerland. But ethnic identity has sometimes led to violence, as in the case of the Basques in Spain who demand their own homeland. Religion has sometimes contributed to ethnic unrest, as in Northern Ireland, where Protestants and Roman Catholics have clashed.

Languages

Europe has three major

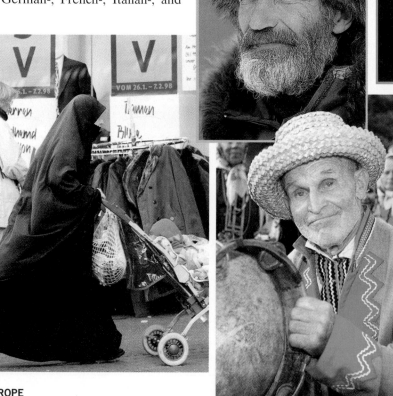

language groups, all branches of the Indo-European language family—Germanic, Romance, and Slavic. Each group consists of a number of different but related languages.

The Germanic languages are German, English, Dutch, Danish, Swedish, Norwegian, and Icelandic. The Romance languages, which are derived from Latin, are Italian, French, Spanish, Portuguese, Romanian, Catalan (spoken in the Spanish province of Catalonia), and the Romansch of Switzerland. Slavic languages are Russian, Ukrainian, Belarusian, Polish, Serbo-Croatian, Czech, Slovak, Bulgarian, Slovene, and Macedonian. The languages of Latvia and Lithuania are considered part of a larger Balto-Slavic group.

Separate European language groups include Greek and Albanian. Celtic languages, once spoken widely in Europe, are now used by a relatively few people in Ireland, Wales, and Scotland and by the Bretons in the French province of Brittany.

Several languages of Europe do not belong to the Indo-European family. They include Finnish and Estonian, which are closely related; Hungarian (Magyar), which is more distantly related to Finnish and Estonian; and Basque, which is spoken in the Pyrenees mountain region of Spain and France.

European languages contributed to the spread of European customs, manners, and values to much of the world. English, French, Spanish, and Portuguese are today spoken by millions of non-European people, and English has become the preferred second language in many countries.

Faces of Europe (*clockwise from opposite page, far left*): A Muslim woman and her baby in Germany; a dogsled musher in Finland; a palace guard in Sweden; a woman in Greece in traditional dress; a fisherman in Portugal; a Basque man and his cow in Spain; a "bobby" (policeman) in the United Kingdom; a farm woman in Sweden; a Ukrainian at a midsummer celebration.

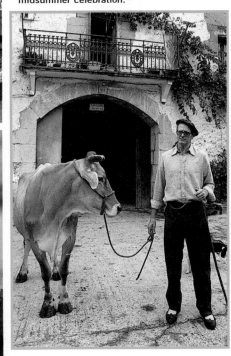

INDEX TO
EUROPE POLITICAL MAP

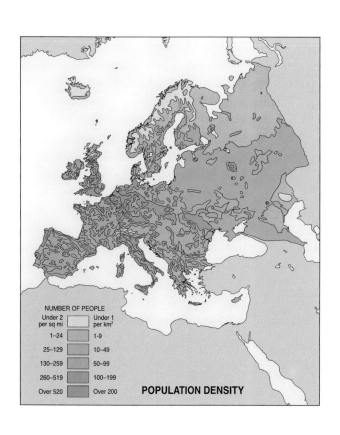

NUMBER OF PEOPLE

Under 2 per sq mi	Under 1 per km²
1–24	1–9
25–129	10–49
130–259	50–99
260–519	100–199
Over 520	Over 200

POPULATION DENSITY

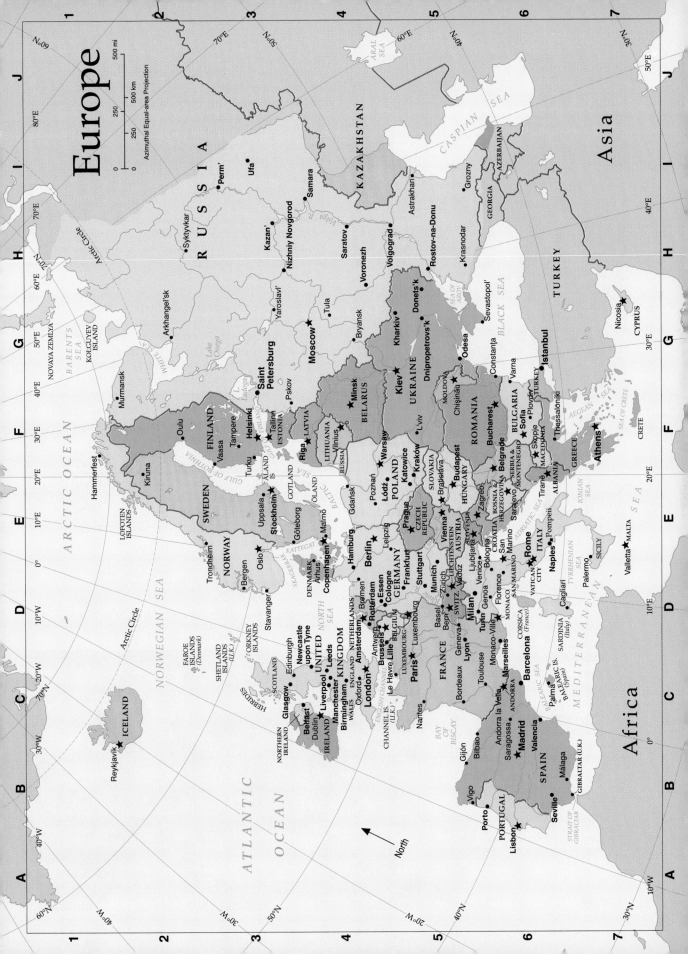

Europe

Crowds gather in St. Peter's Square in Vatican City to worship in the presence of the pope, the supreme head of the Roman Catholic Church.

Religion

Most Europeans are Christians. There are three chief religious groups—Roman Catholic, Eastern Orthodox, and Protestant. The break between the Roman Catholic and Orthodox churches came about as a result of the rivalry between Rome and Constantinople, after the fall of the Roman Empire in the A.D. 400's. The Protestant Church emerged during the religious Reformation of the 1500's, when many Christians split from the Roman Catholic Church.

Ireland, France, Belgium, Italy, Spain, Portugal, Austria, the Czech Republic, Slovakia, Poland, Croatia, Slovenia, and southern Germany are chiefly Roman Catholic. The Scandinavian countries, Finland, the

Public school attendance is required in Belarus and elsewhere throughout Europe. Most European countries have an extremely high literacy rate.

United Kingdom, Iceland, northern Germany, Estonia, and Latvia are largely Protestant. Switzerland and the Netherlands are about equally divided between Roman Catholics and Protestants, and many other countries also have mixed religious populations. The Eastern Orthodox faith is found chiefly in eastern and southeastern European countries—Russia, Ukraine, Belarus, Bulgaria, Romania, Greece, and Serbia and Montenegro. Albania is unique in being the only nation in Europe with a Muslim majority. Bosnia and Herzegovina also has a considerable Muslim population.

Education

Almost all Europeans are literate (able to read and write). Only a few countries have a literacy rate below 97 percent.

In most countries, children attend school from the age of 5 or 6. At about 11, they take tests that determine further schooling. Most qualify to study at a comprehensive or technical school. Those with highest marks attend an academic secondary school that prepares them for study at a university.

Some European universities are very old and have distinguished histories. Among the oldest are the University of Bologna (founded in 1088) in Italy, the University of Oxford (1249) in England, and the Sorbonne (1253) in France. They set standards of excellence that made them models for later universities everywhere.

Family Life

In the rich fabric of European traditions there are some common threads of behavior.

A favorite pastime of many Europeans is to relax at an outdoor café and have a drink or a meal while watching other people stroll by.

Skiing is a popular sport as well as a regular form of transportation for Europeans living in small villages in mountainous regions.

The family is the basic social unit, and many activities revolve around the home and family events. In many parts of Europe, especially in the southern and eastern regions, it is still the custom for several generations of a family to live together. Children are trained to be polite and quiet in the presence of adults, but their upbringing is not as strict as it was before World War II. The father of a family has traditionally been the main wage earner, but more and more European women are seeking jobs outside the home.

Living standards vary throughout Europe. They are highest in western and northern European countries, both in the cities and in rural (country) areas. In eastern and southern Europe, city dwellers are more likely to have modern conveniences than country dwellers.

Food and Drink

Although the French style of cooking is the best known, each nation of Europe has its own food specialties. These include the roast beef and Yorkshire pudding of England, the *smörgåsbord* (buffet of cold and hot appetizers) of Sweden, the numerous varieties of pasta of Italy, the goulash (paprika-flavored beef stew) of Hungary, and the *mousáká* (ground lamb and eggplant) of Greece, to name just a few. Wines from France, Germany, Italy, and Hungary; cheeses from the Netherlands, France, and Switzerland; chocolates from Belgium and Switzerland; and caviar from Russia are world famous.

Dress

While each European nation or region has its own distinctive dress, such traditional clothes are usually worn only on special occasions, and most Europeans wear modern dress. European teenagers, like those the world over, are fond of blue jeans.

Sports and Recreation

Soccer is the most popular sport throughout Europe, although basketball has grown in popularity in recent years. Cricket is played in the United Kingdom. Skiing is a traditional sport in Norway and in the Alpine regions of Switzerland, France, and Austria. Bicycling is both a popular sport and a common form of transportation.

Vacationers come from all over the world to enjoy the Riviera and other sparkling beachfronts along the Mediterranean coast. Tourism is one of Europe's most profitable industries.

▶ECONOMY

Europe's economy suffered tremendously after World War II, but it recovered with the help of the Marshall Plan, an economic aid package offered by the United States. The creation of the European Economic Community (EEC, or Common Market) in 1957 further strengthened economic conditions.

Services

In recent years, heavy industry has declined, while such service industries as government and banking have gained strength. Shopping has increasingly become a leisure activity, and many stores have begun lengthening their hours of operation to attract buyers. Also of growing importance are the so-called knowledge industries, involving research and the use of advanced computers and other modern technologies.

Tourism is one of Europe's largest and most varied service industries. Most non-Europeans who vacation there come from the United States and

The manufacture of automobiles and other motor vehicles and transportation equipment is an important industry throughout Europe.

Japan. Mountainous regions, particularly the Alps, the Pyrenees, and the Cairngorms in Scotland, attract skiers. The beaches of the Mediterranean draw sun-seekers, with the Riviera being a particularly fashionable destination. Dozens of cities such as London, Paris, Rome, and Vienna, are magnets for those interested in the arts.

Manufacturing

The chief manufacturing regions of Europe lie in a belt extending from the United Kingdom through northern France, Belgium, and the Netherlands into Germany, Poland, the Czech Republic, the Donets Basin area in Ukraine, and the Urals region of Russia. Concentrations of heavy industry are also found in Italy's Po Valley, parts of Switzerland, and central Sweden.

Europe's manufactured products include steel, textiles, machinery, and processed foods; motor vehicles and transportation equipment; and petrochemicals. Western Europe has long been

Wine grapes are grown in most southern European countries. *Above:* The vineyards of the Bordeaux region of France produce some of the world's finest wines.

industrialized, but industry developed in eastern Europe only after World War II.

Agriculture and Fishing

Although Europe is a small continent, it is one of the most important agricultural areas of the world. It produces substantial amounts of the world's wheat, oats, rye, potatoes, dairy products, and meat. The land is intensively farmed and yields are generally high.

In western Europe, farms are usually small and under private ownership. In some countries, such as France, the government has encouraged farmers to combine their lands into larger plots so that they can be more productive. The cooperative movement, where farmers share in the cultivation and sale of crops, is strong in Scandinavia.

Land use varies, depending on the characteristics of a particular region—its type of land and climate. The region just south of the taiga consists largely of pastureland, where dairy cattle and other livestock are raised. Here the main crops grown are fodder (food) for livestock. Milk, butter, and cheese are the main products, but chickens are also raised for their meat and eggs. The Netherlands and Denmark are among Europe's leading producers of dairy products. Some kinds of vegetables can also be grown here. In addition, greenhouses are used to grow crops such as tomatoes and grapes, which otherwise would not ripen.

Farther south is a region where grains, especially wheat and rye, are the most important crops. Sugar beets and potatoes are also of great economic importance in this region. Some cattle are raised as well. Grapes are grown in vineyards, and apples, pears, and cherries are cultivated in orchards. One of Europe's largest grain-growing regions is Ukraine, a land of vast plains and rich black soils.

In the southern part of this region, where summers are warmer, corn competes with wheat for importance. Europe's corn-growing area extends from northern Portugal through southern France and northern Italy into the Danube River basin and then eastward to the borders of the Caspian Sea. Vegetables and fruits are grown in truck gardens near the large cities and are sold in local markets. In the mild climate of the Black Sea region, citrus fruits, tea, and grapes can be grown.

Land use changes dramatically in the Mediterranean region. Much of the land here is too rugged to be productive, and summers are too dry for summer crops to be grown without irrigation. If water is available for irrigation, fruits and vegetables grow abundantly. Many areas are famous for their wine grapes. Oranges are a typical crop, and large yields of rice can be obtained. Olives and figs grow well on the hilly slopes. Sheep and goats are more plentiful than dairy cattle.

Since the days of the Vikings the people of the region have turned to the sea for a living. The North Atlantic is one of the world's leading fishing grounds. The shallow seas bordering northwestern Europe have long provided substantial harvests of cod and herring. Commercial fishing traditionally was an important part of the economies of coastal areas of the United Kingdom, Norway, Denmark, France, the Netherlands, Germany, and

Vast petroleum and natural gas deposits were discovered beneath the North Sea in 1959. The North Sea has since become a major source of oil and gas production.

Portugal. Iceland depends on fishing for most of its income. The Mediterranean Sea, historically, has also been a major fishing region. Although fishing is still carried out in both regions, it is now of less importance.

Energy

Petroleum has surpassed coal as the leading source of energy in Europe, but coal remains important. Western Europe's chief coal mining area extends from Britain into northern France and through Belgium into Germany. The major concentrations of bituminous (soft) coal are in Britain and Germany's Ruhr Valley. Eastern Germany has large deposits of lignite (brown coal).

Some of Europe's largest coal deposits are found in the Donets Basin in Ukraine. Poland is also one of the chief coal-producing countries in eastern Europe. Russia has large deposits of coal and oil. Romania produces oil both from its Ploesti fields and from offshore deposits in the Black Sea.

The chief petroleum and natural gas fields in western Europe are located in the North Sea. These especially benefit the United Kingdom and Norway, and to a lesser extent Denmark, the Netherlands, and Germany. Much of western Europe's oil, however, must still be imported.

Sweden, Switzerland, Austria, and France have abundant sources of hydroelectric power (energy produced from rushing or falling water), which partly offsets their lack of coal and oil. Russia also produces enormous amounts of hydroelectric power, with two of the world's largest hydroelectric power stations located on the Volga River.

Nuclear power is especially important in western Europe because of its limited deposits of petroleum. France, Germany, the United Kingdom, and Sweden are among the chief producers of nuclear energy. However, several western European nations, including Sweden and Germany, are reconsidering their nuclear power programs because of the safety factor. Sweden and the United Kingdom are expected to phase out their nuclear power plants.

Trade

Trade is essential to Europe's prosperity. In spite of extensive agriculture, most western European nations cannot grow enough food to feed their relatively large populations. Because of their limited natural resources, most countries must also import raw materials for their industries. The United Kingdom, for

Left: Eurostar trains provide passenger service between Britain and France by way of the Chunnel, an underwater tunnel in the English Channel. *Above:* Rotterdam-Europoort, the world's busiest port, provides a gateway to the industrial centers of northern Europe.

example, must import about half its food and industrial raw materials.

Today's European Union (EU), an extension of the Common Market, was founded to remove trade restrictions among the member countries. It is now the largest single trading bloc in the world. For more information see the article EUROPEAN UNION following this article.

Transportation

Railways. Europe has more railroads per square mile than anywhere else in the world. Much freight is still carried by trains that link key industrial regions. Modern passenger trains moving at high speeds are a comfortable way to travel. In 1994, for the first time in history, Britain and the European mainland were connected by rail with the opening of the underwater Channel Tunnel (popularly known as the Chunnel).

Roadways. The number of private automobiles has increased tremendously as the people of western Europe have improved their standard of living. There are far fewer cars in eastern Europe. European roads vary in quality. Although there are modern highways, such as the Autobahn in Germany and the Autostrada in Italy, many of the smaller, narrower roads cannot handle the growing traffic.

Airways. All of Europe's major cities have international airports. Air France, British Airways, Aer Lingus (Ireland), Alitalia (Italy), Lufthansa (Germany), and KLM (the Netherlands) are just a few of the continent's major airlines.

Ports and Waterways. Europoort, which serves Rotterdam and the interior of the Netherlands, is Europe's largest port. Other leading European ports include Le Havre and Marseilles in France; Antwerp in Belgium; the British port of London; Hamburg and Bremen in northern Germany; Naples in Italy; and Odesa on the Black Sea in Ukraine.

Canals were being built in Europe long before there were railroads. They connect the navigable rivers and are used to transport freight.

Among the many navigable rivers in Europe, the most important are the Rhine, the Danube, and the Volga. The Rhine is one of the world's most traveled rivers. It is usable by ships from its outlet, the city of Rotterdam in the Netherlands, to the town of Basel in Switzerland. The Rhine is connected by canal with the Danube. The Volga and its many tributaries are Russia's most important waterways. A system of canals links different regions to the Volga.

▶ MAJOR CITIES

Europe has more than 30 urban centers with populations of more than 1 million people. The two largest, with more than 9 million each, are **Paris**, the capital of France, and **Moscow**, the capital of Russia. **Istanbul**, a city that lies in both Europe and Asia, also has more than 9 million residents. Europe's next largest city, with more than 7 million people, is **London**, the capital of the United Kingdom.

Other interesting capital cities in western Europe are **Amsterdam** (the Netherlands), **Copenhagen** (Denmark), **Stockholm** (Sweden), **Oslo** (Norway), **Rome** (Italy), **Madrid** (Spain), **Lisbon** (Portugal), and **Vienna** (Austria). The largest capitals in central, eastern, and south-eastern Europe include **Prague** (Czech Republic), **Belgrade** (Serbia and Montenegro), **Budapest** (Hungary), **Bucharest** (Romania), **Warsaw** (Poland), and **Athens** (Greece).

For more information on each of these cities, see the separate articles in the appropriate volumes. Articles on the Spanish city of **Barcelona**; the Italian cities of **Florence**, **Genoa**, and **Venice**; the Swiss cities of **Geneva** and **Zürich**; and the Russian cities of **Kiev** and **Saint Petersburg** also appear in the appropriate volumes.

▶ CULTURAL HERITAGE

Among the most striking reminders of the long European artistic tradition are the ruins of ancient temples in Greece, where Western civilization began more than 2,500 years ago. Later the Romans, who studied the ancient Greeks, represented European culture. For more information, see the articles GREECE, ART AND ARCHITECTURE OF; POMPEII; and ROME, ART AND ARCHITECTURE OF in the appropriate volumes.

Most of Europe's capitals and other major cities have an Old World charm dating back at least one thousand years. *Clockwise from right:* Trolley cars pass through the main square of Zagreb, the capital of Croatia; gondolas ply the Grand Canal in Venice, Italy; pedestrians rest beside shaded tree-lined boulevards in Madrid, the capital of Spain.

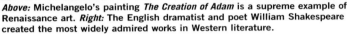
Above: Michelangelo's painting *The Creation of Adam* is a supreme example of Renaissance art. *Right:* The English dramatist and poet William Shakespeare created the most widely admired works in Western literature.

During the Middle Ages, Christianity was the most influential force in European art and architecture. In the West, its greatest examples are still found in the religious paintings and soaring Gothic churches of the period. In the East, in the Byzantine Empire centered in Constantinople, a distinctive form of art developed that still remains a part of the Eastern Orthodox church. For more information, see the articles BYZANTINE ART AND ARCHITECTURE, CATHEDRALS, GOTHIC ART AND ARCHITECTURE, and ROMANESQUE ART AND ARCHITECTURE in the appropriate volumes.

The classical tradition of ancient Greece was given new life during the Renaissance, which began in Italy in the 1300's and later spread to the rest of western Europe. The works of the great European painters of this and later periods can be seen in museums throughout the world. For more information, see the articles BAROQUE ART AND ARCHITECTURE, RENAISSANCE ART AND ARCHITECTURE, and MODERN ART. Also see the art and architecture articles associated with individual countries in the appropriate volumes.

Western music began in Europe centuries ago. The opera, symphony, concerto, ballet, and other familiar musical forms are all European in origin. For more information, see the articles BALLET; BAROQUE MUSIC; CHAMBER MUSIC; CLASSICAL AGE IN MUSIC; HYMNS; MIDDLE AGES, MUSIC OF THE; MODERN MUSIC; OPERA; and the music articles associated with individual countries in the appropriate volumes.

As in music, many forms of literature were perfected in Europe, including the novel, essay, and such types of poetry as the ode, epic, and sonnet. Western science, art, and philosophy originated in Greece and, literally, had a "rebirth" in Italy during the period known as the Renaissance. A list of the great thinkers and scientific discoverers would include names from many European countries. Later, new European ideas about science, society, government, and economics began to influence other parts of the world. For more information, see the articles ENLIGHTENMENT, AGE OF; HUMANISM; RENAISSANCE; and ROMANTICISM in the appropriate volumes.

▶HISTORY

Prehistoric Times. Modern humans were already living in Europe during the last Ice Age. After the ice retreated and the climate warmed, about 15,000 years ago, populations began to move. The early Europeans lived by hunting and fishing and only slowly became animal herders and farmers. Stone was first used for tools and weapons, followed by copper and bronze and later iron. Europe was very backward in comparison with the highly developed civilizations of Egypt and Babylon. But those ancient Europeans had an artistic sense, as indicated by the wall paintings that can still be seen in caves in southern France and Spain.

IMPORTANT DATES

1600?–1400? B.C.	Period of Minoan civilization.
753 B.C.	Traditional date of the founding of Rome.
500? B.C.	Beginning of the Golden Age of Greece; Athens became the center of Greek civilization.
431–404 B.C.	Peloponnesian War between Athens and Sparta led to the decline of Athens.
218–201 B.C.	Second Punic War; Roman armies defeated Hannibal and Carthaginian army; marked rise of Roman power.
31 B.C.	Roman Empire established.
A.D. 324	Emperor Constantine, first Christian Roman emperor, made Constantinople his capital.
395	Roman Empire divided into eastern and western halves.
476	Traditional date for fall of Western Roman Empire.
711	Muslims invaded Spain.
800	Charlemagne crowned "emperor of the Romans."
800?–1000	Period of greatest Viking power; about 1000, Vikings reached North America.
1054	Eastern Orthodox Church cut ties with Rome.
1066	Normans invaded England.
1096	First Crusade to Holy Land began.
1215	King John signed Magna Carta, cornerstone of English liberties.
1270	Last Crusade to Holy Land began.
1300?	Renaissance began in Italy.
1387?	Chaucer began writing *The Canterbury Tales*.
1453	Constantinople (now Istanbul) fell to the Ottoman Turks, ending the Byzantine Empire.
1453?–55?	Johann Gutenberg issued first Bible printed in movable type.
1492	Christopher Columbus made his first voyage to the Americas.
1497–98	Vasco da Gama found sea route to India.
1513	Vasco Núñez de Balboa became first European to see Pacific Ocean.
1517	Martin Luther posted 95 theses on church door in Wittenberg, beginning Protestant Reformation.
1519	Ferdinand Magellan began first round-the-world voyage.
1536	John Calvin published *Institutes of the Christian Religion*.
1543	Nicolaus Copernicus published *On the Revolutions of the Heavenly Bodies*, a description of solar system.
1545	Council of Trent opened, with aim of reforming Roman Catholic Church.
1571	Turks defeated at Battle of Lepanto; Turkish naval power declines in the Mediterranean.
1588	English fleet crushed the Spanish Armada; beginning of England's importance as a world power.
1601?	William Shakespeare's *Hamlet* first produced.
1607	First English colony in America founded at Jamestown (Virginia).
1609	Johannes Kepler published his *New Astronomy*, describing laws of planetary movement.
1618–48	Thirty Years' War involved most of Europe.
1620	Pilgrims landed at Plymouth Rock.
1687	Sir Isaac Newton published his *Mathematical Principles of Natural Philosophy* (*Principia*), describing laws of motion and gravitation.
1689	Parliamentary government established in England; Bill of Rights proclaimed.
Mid-1700's	Industrial Revolution began in Britain.
1775	Britain's American colonies started the War for Independence.
1789	French Revolution began.
1804	Napoleon became emperor of the French.
1815	Napoleon I defeated at the Battle of Waterloo.
1859	*On the Origin of Species by Means of Natural Selection* published by Charles Darwin.
1861	Victor Emmanuel II became first king of Italy.
1867	Karl Marx finished the first volume of *Das Kapital*, his revolutionary work on Communist theory.
1870–71	France defeated in Franco-Prussian War.
1871	German Empire founded.
1914–18	World War I.
1917	Revolution in Russia overthrew the czar.
1922	Union of Soviet Socialist Republics established.
1933	Adolf Hitler became chancellor of Germany.
1939–45	World War II.
1945	United Nations founded.
1949	North Atlantic Treaty Organization (NATO) formed.
1956	Hungarian rebellion against Communist rule suppressed.
1958	European Economic Community (Common Market) founded.
1961	Soviet Union's *Vostok 1* became first manned space capsule to orbit the Earth.
1962	Twenty-first Ecumenical Council opened.
1968	Czechoslovakia's attempt to liberalize Communist rule ended by Soviet troops.
1973	United Kingdom, Ireland, and Denmark were formally admitted to the European Economic Community (EEC).
1974	Government coup in Portugal led to independence for Portuguese territories in Africa.
1981	Greece was formally admitted to the European Economic Community.
1986	Spain and Portugal officially became members of the European Economic Community.
1989	Soviet Union began political and economic reforms; popular governments elected in former Communist nations of eastern Europe.
1990	Germany was reunited as a single nation.
1991	Soviet Union recognized the independence of Latvia, Lithuania, and Estonia; Russia, Ukraine, Belarus, and Moldova became independent nations.
1991–92	Slovenia, Croatia, Macedonia, and Bosnia and Herzegovina declared their independence from Yugoslavia, leaving a smaller Yugoslav state made up of Serbia and Montenegro. Civil war erupted, mainly in Bosnia.
1993	Czechoslovakia split into two separate nations: the Czech Republic and Slovakia.
2002	The euro replaced the national currencies in 12 of the 15 member nations of the European Union; major flooding along the Danube and other rivers in Central Europe caused billions of dollars in damages.
2003	The two remaining republics of Yugoslavia renamed the country Serbia and Montenegro.

Ancient Greece and Rome. Civilization came to Europe by way of the eastern Mediterranean. The island of Crete was known for its great culture as early as 2000 B.C. Somewhat later the Greek city-states developed. The most important of these was Athens. Greek art, science, poetry, drama, and philosophy formed the cornerstone of European civilization. It was also in Greece that the idea of democracy was born. Greek merchants as well as those from Phoenicia (in what is now Lebanon) established colonies along the European coasts of the Mediterranean. For more information on

Europe was the birthplace of Western civilization. *Above:* Cave paintings discovered in southwestern France date back 17,000 years. *Left:* In Roman times, the forum was the center of business and government administration.

pean continent and made it part of the civilized world. The Latin language and the Christian religion, which spread through western Europe in the later centuries of the Roman Empire, helped unite Europe.

The Roman Empire in the West gradually weakened under attacks from Germanic

ancient Greece, see the article GREECE, ANCIENT in Volume G.

During the last centuries before Christ, Rome gradually extended its power from its central location on the Italian peninsula. At its height, during the first centuries A.D., the Roman Empire ruled most of the island of Great Britain, western and southern Europe, and nearby regions of Africa and Asia. On the continent the Roman boundary roughly followed the Danube River. Beyond that lay a Europe inhabited largely by Germanic peoples but influenced by Roman ideas. Roman roads and settlements had opened the Euro-

tribes on its borders and eventually fell to them in the A.D. 400's. However, the eastern half of the Roman Empire, located at Constantinople (modern Istanbul) and known as Byzantium or the Byzantine Empire, flourished for a thousand years more. See the articles ROME, ANCIENT in Volume QR and BYZANTINE EMPIRE in Volume B.

The Middle Ages and the Renaissance. The period following the end of the Western Roman Empire is known as the Middle Ages. Familiar to us as a time of warring nobles, knights in armor, and fortified castles, it was also a period in which western Europe was split into many small kingdoms and principalities. Western Europe was briefly united, from 800 to 814, under Charlemagne. A little more than a century later, Otto I, in imitation of the Roman Empire, established the Holy Roman Empire in what is now Germany and parts of Italy and eastern Europe. Although it lasted in name until the early 1800's, the Holy Roman Empire became little more than a federation of many small states.

Beginning in the 1300's, Europe underwent a rebirth of interest in ancient Greek and Roman art and literature. This rebirth of classical learning, called the Renaissance, led to one of the greatest periods of artistic creativity in European history. It originated in Italy and, over the next 300 years, spread through western and northern Europe.

For more information on these periods, see the articles CHARLEMAGNE, HOLY ROMAN EMPIRE, MIDDLE AGES, and RENAISSANCE in the appropriate volumes.

Empire Building and the Reformation. In 1453, Constantinople, the capital of the Byzantine Empire, fell to the Ottoman Turks, who began their long rule of southeastern and parts of central Europe. Christopher Columbus' first voyage of discovery to the Caribbean Sea in 1492 began the great age of exploration and settlement of the Americas, as Spain, Portugal, England, France, and the Netherlands established colonies in the New World. See the articles COLUMBUS, CHRISTOPHER and EXPLORATION AND DISCOVERY in the appropriate volumes.

The religious disputes between Catholics and Protestants that had begun with the Reformation reached a head in the Thirty Years' War (1618–48). Starting as a religious war, it eventually became a political one.

France emerged from the war as a leading power in Europe, a role it kept for nearly 300 years. England and the Netherlands built empires based on sea power and trade. Spain's great wealth was drawn from the gold and silver of its colonies in America. Habsburg emperors ruled Austria, parts of Italy, and the states of the Holy Roman Empire.

See the articles REFORMATION and THIRTY YEARS' WAR in the appropriate volumes.

Two Revolutions. The Industrial Revolution began in Britain in the mid-1700's and transformed Europe. Goods once made by hand were now made by machines. The steam engine was the first of many inventions that would forever change methods of transportation. Cities expanded as people moved from the countryside to work in the growing factories. Britain's head start in becoming an industrialized nation helped make it a world power. See the article INDUSTRIAL REVOLUTION in Volume I.

The French Revolution (1789–99), which overthrew the French king, stressed liberty and equality, radical ideas in Europe at the time. But France had a republican government only briefly. In 1804, Napoleon, whose armies had conquered much of western Europe, made himself emperor of the French. Napoleon was finally defeated by an alliance of European nations led by Britain in 1814 and again in 1815, and the French monarch was restored to the throne. See the articles FRENCH REVOLUTION and NAPOLEON I in the appropriate volumes.

Nationalism and Imperialism. The 1800's was a period of growing nationalism. European peoples still under foreign domination struggled to win independence, while others sought unification as nations. Belgium gained independence

In the early 1800's, the French emperor Napoleon I nearly succeeded in conquering all of Europe. He was defeated in 1815 by an alliance of nations led by Britain.

Vladimir Ilich Lenin, a Communist revolutionary and founder of the Soviet Union, was among the most influential leaders of the 1900's.

from the Netherlands in 1830. Greece freed itself from Ottoman Turkish rule that year, and other south-eastern European countries were eventually to do the same. Although Hungary failed in its attempt to win independence from Austria in 1848, it became a partner in the Austro-Hungarian Empire. Italy was united as an independent nation in the second half of the 1800's, and Germany was created out of the states of the former Holy Roman Empire in 1871.

During the middle and late 1800's, European powers carved out new colonial empires in Africa and Asia. Britain—whose empire included Canada, India, and Australia and rivaled that of ancient Rome—and France were the chief imperial powers. But Belgium and Germany also joined the race to acquire African colonies. See the article IMPERIALISM in Volume I.

Two World Wars. The map of Europe took most of its present shape as a result of World War I (1914–18). The new countries of Austria, Hungary, Czechoslovakia, and Yugoslavia emerged from the ruins of the Austro-Hungarian Empire. Poland, which for more than a century had been partitioned among its neighbors, was again made an independent nation. In Russia, revolutions in 1917 overthrew the czar and led to the creation of the Soviet Union, the world's first Communist state. Finland won independence, along with Latvia, Lithuania, and Estonia, but the latter three were later absorbed into the Soviet Union.

World War II (1939–45) was equally far-reaching in its political impact. It left Britain

EUROPE BEFORE WORLD WAR I

EUROPE AFTER WORLD WAR I

The European Parliament is an elected body of the European Union (EU), an organization that promotes political and economic unity among its member nations.

and France weaker than they once were. The Soviet Union came to dominate eastern Europe, whose countries were under the rule of Communist governments. For more information, see the articles COMMUNISM, WORLD WAR I, and WORLD WAR II in the appropriate volumes.

Modern Europe. Western Europe recovered rapidly from the war's destruction, with economic aid from the United States through the Marshall Plan. In eastern Europe, recovery was much slower, as countries that were once mainly agricultural sought to industrialize quickly. The years following World War II were also marked by the gradual independence of former European colonies, mostly throughout Africa and Asia.

Between 1989 and 1992, democratic movements spread rapidly across eastern Europe.

Germany was reunited in 1990. In 1991, Yugoslavia broke into various independent republics, which resulted in numerous civil wars throughout the Balkans. The Soviet Union also broke apart at the end of 1991, and from it emerged seven independent nations—Russia, Ukraine, Belarus, Moldova, Latvia, Lithuania, and Estonia. In 1993, Czechoslovakia peacefully split into two separate nations, the Czech Republic and Slovakia. And in 2003, Yugoslavia was renamed Serbia and Montenegro.

In 2003, several European nations, including Britain, sided with the United States in the Iraq War, while others—notably France and Germany—objected to the campaign. Further divisions were indicated in 2005 when the EU nations split on accepting Europe's first unified constitution.

DALE R. LOTT
SAMUEL VAN VALKENBURG
Author, *Elements of Political Geography*

Reviewed by JEREMY BLACK
University of Exeter

See also BALKANS; EUROPEAN UNION; LAPLAND; SCANDINAVIA; articles on individual European countries and cities.

EUROPEAN UNION

The European Union (EU) is an organization of 25 European nations. Originally planned as an economic union to promote growth and cooperation, the EU now seeks to establish a political union as well.

Taken together, the nations of the EU form an economic superpower. They have a combined population greater than that of the United States and represent the world's largest trading bloc. Their achievements have not been won without disputes, however, which arise most often when the interests of

individual nations come into conflict with the interests of the union as a whole.

Organization

The EU is administered by the Commission of the European Union, headquartered in Brussels, Belgium. It is made up of 25 members (one from each nation), appointed to 4-year terms. The commission is headed by a president, who serves a 6-month rotation.

Additional bodies include the Council of Ministers, the European Parliament, and the

European Court of Justice. The Council of Ministers is the chief decision-making body. The European Parliament (EP) is made up of 732 members who are elected by the citizens of the member countries to 5-year terms. The Court of Justice, located in Luxembourg, is made up of 25 judges who interpret laws and settle treaty disputes.

History

The dream of a united Europe is centuries old. After World War II (1939–45), European leaders sought unity as a way to restore Europe's prosperity and prevent future wars. They saw economic union as the first step. In 1951, France, West Germany, Italy, the Netherlands, Belgium, and Luxembourg signed a treaty, creating the European Coal and Steel Community (ECSC). It eliminated trade barriers for coal and steel among member nations and allowed industry workers to travel freely within the ECSC.

The success of the ECSC encouraged its members to broaden their area of cooperation. In 1957 they signed two new treaties in Rome. These established the European Economic Community (EEC) and the European Atomic Energy Community (Euratom). The EEC, better known as the Common Market, was far-reaching in scope. It sought to abolish remaining trade barriers among its members by forming a single economic union in which all of their goods, services, labor, and capital could move without restraint. Euratom was organized to promote research and development in the peaceful uses of atomic energy.

The early achievements of the EEC led to expansion in membership. In 1973, Denmark, Ireland, and the United Kingdom joined the union, followed by Greece in 1981; Portugal and Spain in 1986; and Austria, Finland, and Sweden in 1995. The community became known as the European Union in 1993.

The most far-reaching step toward integration was the Treaty on European Union, better known as the Maastricht Treaty. Ratified in 1993, it sought to create a monetary union among the member states. But to qualify, member nations first had to get their national budgets under control by reducing debts and inflation. In 2002, 12 of the then 15 member nations adopted a common currency known as the **euro**. (Great Britain, Denmark, and Sweden chose not to participate.)

In 2000, the EU established the European Security and Defense Policy (ESDP), with a rapid-reaction force to carry out peacemaking and humanitarian and rescue missions. In 2003, a European Constitution was drafted, the first step toward forming a European government.

In 2004, ten additional nations joined the EU—Cyprus, the Czech Republic, Estonia, Hungary, Latvia, Lithuania, Malta, Poland, Slovakia, and Slovenia.

The EU's first constitution was signed by the leaders of the 25 member nations in 2004 and was overwhelmingly approved by the European Parliament the following year. However, it still faced ratification by the individual member nations. By mid-2005, ten nations had ratified the document. But progress stopped abruptly when it was soundly defeated in referendums in France and the Netherlands.

Reviewed by DEREK PRAG
Former Director of Publications
European Community

EVANSVILLE. See INDIANA (Cities).

EVAPORATION. See HEAT.

MEMBERS OF THE EUROPEAN UNION

Member	Year Joined
Austria	1995
Belgium	1951
Cyprus (Greek)	2004
Czech Republic	2004
Denmark	1973
Estonia	2004
Finland	1995
France	1951
Germany*	1951
Greece	1981
Hungary	2004
Ireland	1973
Italy	1951
Latvia	2004
Lithuania	2004
Luxembourg	1951
Malta	2004
Netherlands	1951
Poland	2004
Portugal	1986
Slovakia	2004
Slovenia	2004
Spain	1986
Sweden	1995
United Kingdom	1973

*West Germany only until 1990.
Note: Additional members under consideration include Bulgaria, Croatia, Romania, and Turkey.

EVEREST, MOUNT

The summit (top) of Mount Everest is the highest spot in all the world. On a sunny day it can be seen from some points at least 160 kilometers (100 miles) away. When viewed from afar, the summit looks calm and beautiful. But it is a desolate wasteland of wind-blasted snow and rock. If the wind is blowing (and it usually is), a great plume of snow and ice particles stretches out downwind for a vast distance. For the top of Everest is so high that it reaches into the jet stream, where winds over 300 kilometers (200 miles) an hour are not uncommon.

The official height for Mount Everest is 8,850 meters (29,035 feet). The huge peak is located on the border between Nepal and Tibet, just north of India. It is part of the giant Himalayan mountain range. Seen from the Ganges Plain of India, Mount Everest lies far back among the other mountain peaks. Many of these peaks look higher because they are closer in view. But seen from Tibet, Mount Everest towers above all the others.

Mount Everest was first calculated to be the highest mountain in the world in 1852 during the Great Trigonometrical Survey of India. It was named for George Everest, the former surveyor-general of the survey. But it has another name, given long before by the people of Tibet. To these reverent and poetic people it was Chomolungma—Goddess Mother of the World.

In the last 100 years, mountains have increasingly challenged our spirit of adventure.

The higher or more difficult the mountain peak, the greater is the desire to climb it. Everest, being the highest of all, naturally stood as one of the supreme challenges for all mountaineers. But it was not until December 9, 1920, that permission was granted to approach the mountain on its north side, through Tibet.

Then nine attempts were made on that side without success. Climbers did reach over 8,500 meters (28,000 feet) without oxygen, and they learned that they could sleep, live, and work at almost that height, at least for a while. They also learned from hard experience quite a bit about the best food, fuel, clothing, and equipment to take. At these altitudes everything must be as light as possible, as efficient as possible, and as reliable as possible. People are living in a semi-vacuum with only a fraction of the oxygen they need. So they have no extra energy to deal with bulky or inefficient equipment.

Everest continued to resist all attacks. Climbers began to despair and to say that the task was beyond human endurance. But others refused to give up. Tibet was taken over by the Chinese in 1950, and the route on the North Face was closed. But a new route was pioneered on the southwest side through Nepal. The Swiss almost succeeded in 1952. Then in 1953 the British made an all-out attack. Under the leadership of Colonel John Hunt, ten climbers were selected. They and the tons of necessary equipment were transported to the mountain. Every detail was carefully planned. As far as possible, every prob-

Mount Everest, in the Himalayan mountain range on the border between China and Nepal, is the world's highest mountain.

lem was foreseen, for the British realized that this might be their last chance to be first to the top. They hoped to accomplish it in time for the coronation of Queen Elizabeth II.

Supplies and equipment were relayed up the mountain. Camps were set up about every 300 to 600 meters (1,000 to 2,000 feet). Then finally, on the morning of May 29, 1953, two climbers set out for the summit from their high camp at 8,500 meters (27,900 feet). They were Edmund P. Hillary and Tenzing Norgay. The latter was a Sherpa—a member of one of the hill tribes that live in the high valleys around Everest. On that historic morning the two climbers accomplished one of the great mountaineering feats of all time. They had climbed Everest.

As the news was flashed throughout the world, it was deemed appropriate that one person from the East and one from the West should have shared in the victory. The victory was also shared with all other members of their party and with all those who had gone before on Everest, without whom the final success could never have been achieved.

In 1956, following the same route as the British, the Swiss put four men on top. In 1960 and 1962 India tried but failed. On the old northern route in Tibet, the Chinese tried in 1960 and failed. In 1962 a four-member American expedition under the leadership of Woodrow Wilson Sayre also tried the north route. They used no oxygen, no porters, and no fixed camps, carrying everything they needed for 42 days on their own backs. The expedition carried to about 7,750 meters (25,400 feet) and then was forced to give up.

In 1963 another American expedition, under Norman G. Dyhrenfurth, succeeded in putting six men on the summit. Four climbed by the now traditional Nepalese route up the southwest ridge of the mountain. But William F. Unsoeld and Thomas F. Hornbein climbed an entirely new route, which they had pioneered, on the west ridge of Everest. They made the first traverse of a major Himalayan peak when they descended by the route that the others had come up the same day. In 1965 a second Indian expedition, led by Lieutenant Commander M. S. Kohli, succeeded in reaching the summit. Their Sherpa guide, Nawang Gombu, had been on the 1963 Dyhrenfurth expedition. He thus became the first person to climb Mount Everest twice.

In 1975, Junko Tabei of Japan became the first woman to climb to the summit of Mount Everest.

In 1975, Junko Tabei of Japan, part of an all-woman team, became the first woman to climb to the summit of Mount Everest. In 1988, two teams of climbers reached the top from opposite sides of the mountain, the first time two groups climbed at the same time.

The 50th anniversary of the first ascent was celebrated in 2003. Edmund Hillary was made an honorary citizen of Nepal, and special medals were awarded to others who had also reached the top of Mount Everest.

For years Everest has fired the imagination of people of spirit and courage. Although it has now been conquered, the mountain still stands as a symbol of challenge, of beauty, and of human aspiration.

WOODROW WILSON SAYRE
Author, *Four Against Everest*

EVERGREENS. See TREES.

EVERS, MEDGAR. See CIVIL RIGHTS MOVEMENT (Profiles).

EVERT, CHRIS. See FLORIDA (Famous People); TENNIS (Great Players).

EVOLUTION

Have you ever wondered why human beings look somewhat like chimpanzees and monkeys but quite different from bears? Or have you wondered how dolphins came to be such good swimmers? The science of evolution answers questions like these. Evolution means change in life through time.

Scientists think about evolution in two ways. First they think of all living things as being connected in a branch-like pattern, called the tree of life. Just as we can trace our own individual ancestry back through our parents, grandparents, and great-grandparents, we humans can trace our ancestry back to animals that were the ancestors of all primates (monkeys, apes, and humans), then to the ancestors of all mammals, to the ancestors of all animals, right back to the ancestors of all living things.

This branching pattern shows us how plants and animals are related to one another through their ancestors. It explains, for example, that gorillas are not our direct ancestors but that we share a common ancestor with them. More distantly, we also share common ancestors with dogs, frogs, jellyfish, and mushrooms.

The second way scientists look at evolution is through its usefulness in explaining why living things change over time. The most important reason is natural selection (explained later in this article). Natural selection helps scientists understand how and why living things evolve from one form to another.

▶ EVIDENCE OF EVOLUTION

Large changes in life-forms take place over thousands or millions of years. We cannot watch the

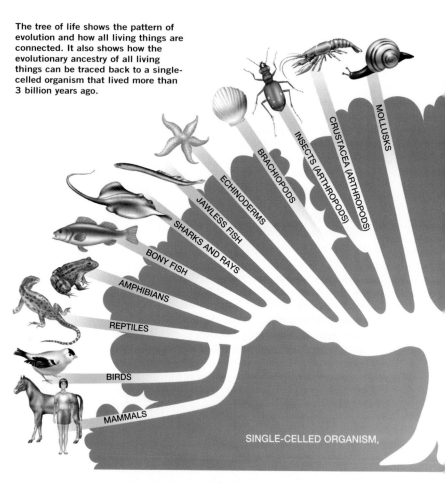

The tree of life shows the pattern of evolution and how all living things are connected. It also shows how the evolutionary ancestry of all living things can be traced back to a single-celled organism that lived more than 3 billion years ago.

MOLLUSKS

CRUSTACEA (ARTHROPODS)

INSECTS (ARTHROPODS)

BRACHIOPODS

ECHINODERMS

JAWLESS FISH

SHARKS AND RAYS

BONY FISH

AMPHIBIANS

REPTILES

BIRDS

MAMMALS

SINGLE-CELLED ORGANISM,

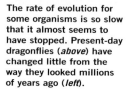

The rate of evolution for some organisms is so slow that it almost seems to have stopped. Present-day dragonflies (*above*) have changed little from the way they looked millions of years ago (*left*).

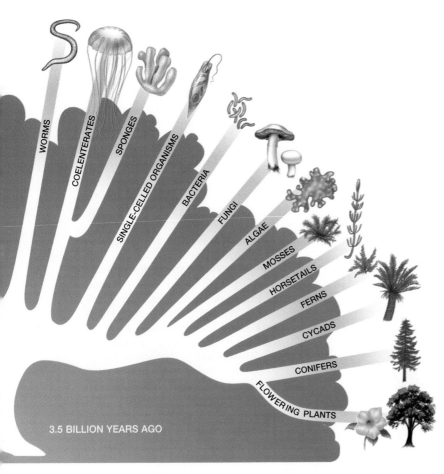

WORMS
COELENTERATES
SPONGES
SINGLE-CELLED ORGANISMS
BACTERIA
FUNGI
ALGAE
MOSSES
HORSETAILS
FERNS
CYCADS
CONIFERS
FLOWERING PLANTS

3.5 BILLION YEARS AGO

Many scientists believe that the *Archaeopteryx*, which showed features common to both birds and dinosaurs, supports the idea that birds evolved from dinosaurs.

changes take place and so cannot observe evolution directly. Instead, scientists look for various types of evidence that evolution has occurred.

The Fossil Record

Important evidence for evolution comes from fossils, which are the remains of ancient life. Fossils are often found in sedimentary rocks, which form when layers of loose material, such as sand or clay, are compressed over time. In all parts of the world, sedimentary rocks may contain the remains of plants or animals that lived when the rocks formed.

In the 1600's and 1700's, scientists began to realize that layers of sedimentary rock could be used as a kind of calendar for the Earth's history. Since the layers of rock built up over time, any lower layer must be older than those above it. Geologists were able to determine the ages of rock layers all over the world by comparing their positions in sequences of sedimentary rocks.

By about 1830, scientists had made an important observation: Different fossils are found in rocks of different ages. The oldest known rocks, which are about 3.8 billion years old, contain no fossils. Fossils of single-celled organisms, such as bacteria, are the only fossils found in rocks about 3.5 billion years old. Invertebrates with shells become common in rocks about 530 million years old. Eventually fish fossils appear, and in younger rocks are fossils of amphibians, then reptiles, and then mammals. Human fossils are found only in the youngest, and highest, rock layers. Thus the sequence of fossils shows that life on Earth has changed through time. It shows that evolution has taken place.

Fossils also show that certain groups of animals or plants have evolved from other groups. For example, fossils indicate that amphibians evolved from fish that were capable of breathing air and moving on land. The fossil *Ichthyostega* is a **transitional**, or intermediate, form that demonstrates this. It had legs that were developed enough to carry it on land, but it also had many features of its fish ancestors, such as scales, a tail fin, and the same kind of teeth.

Transitional forms in other fossils show that reptiles evolved from a group of amphibians, that mammals evolved from a group of reptiles known as therapsids, and that birds probably evolved from dinosaurs. The birdlike fossil *Archaeopteryx* is a transitional form supporting this last idea. Like a bird, it had feathers and a wishbone. But it also had teeth, clawed "fingers" on each wing, a long bony tail, and other skeletal features that were nearly identical to those of small meat-eating dinosaurs.

Evidence from Modern Species

Even without a fossil record, there is other evidence that evolution has taken place.

Descent with Modification. Different species often share similar features, which suggests that they inherited those features from a common ancestor. For example, the front limbs of all four-legged vertebrates have the same basic structure: one bone in the upper arm, two bones in the forearm, then the bones of the wrist and palm, then five fingers. This is as true for lizards, birds, bats, and whales as it is for human beings.

It is hard to imagine that this same bone arrangement is best for all the different actions of front limbs in these animals: running (lizards), supporting wings (birds and bats), swimming (whales), or grasping (humans). But it is easy to imagine that a common ancestor of these animals had this bone arrangement. The original structure of the front limbs was inherited with some changes by all the ancestor's descendants. English naturalist Charles Darwin (1809–82) called this **descent with modification**. It provides important evidence to scientists studying how animals may be related to one another.

Shared features between related animals sometimes appear only in the embryo form. For example, close study of human embryos shows that in early stages of development, human embryos have tails and gill arches, somewhat like those found in fish and chicken embryos. At birth, humans certainly do not have tails or gills. But the brief appearance of these structures during the embryo's development shows that they once existed in an ancient ancestor and were inherited by all its descendants.

Protein Studies. Studies of certain molecules essential for life also provide strong evidence for evolution. Cytochrome C is a protein that helps organisms produce energy. Biologists have been able to determine the sequence of building blocks—called amino acids—that make up this protein. When they compare the 104-amino-acid sequence in human Cytochrome C to that in other

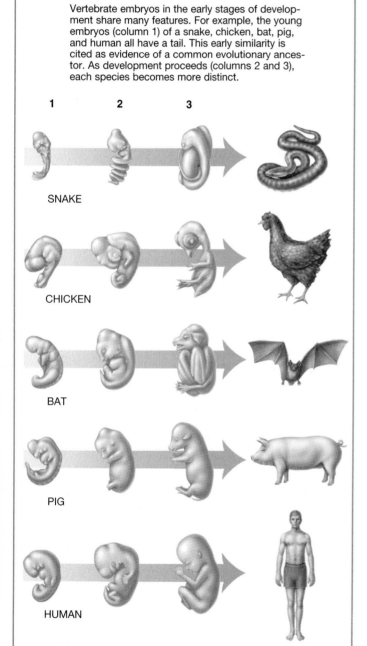

Vertebrate embryos in the early stages of development share many features. For example, the young embryos (column 1) of a snake, chicken, bat, pig, and human all have a tail. This early similarity is cited as evidence of a common evolutionary ancestor. As development proceeds (columns 2 and 3), each species becomes more distinct.

1   2   3

SNAKE

CHICKEN

BAT

PIG

HUMAN

PIECING TOGETHER THE THEORY OF EVOLUTION

Modern ideas of evolution were first developed by Charles Darwin. Darwin was born into a wealthy family in England in 1809. At age 23, he set off on a five-year voyage around the world in a naval ship, the H.M.S. *Beagle*.

During the voyage he saw many unfamiliar plants and animals. He found strange fossils, and he noticed how animals were beautifully adapted to their ways of life.

Darwin's visit to the Galápagos Islands, located in the Pacific Ocean, was perhaps his most significant. There he made observations and collections that would be instrumental in developing his ideas. He saw finches with beaks suited to various ways of life, mockingbirds that differed dramatically between islands, and giant tortoises. He was told that a knowledgeable person could tell which island a tortoise had come from by the shape of its shell. This led Darwin to speculate on how such differences arise. After years of study and thought, he suggested a process by which life had evolved. He called the process natural selection.

At nearly the same time, another English naturalist, Alfred Russel Wallace, came to the same conclusions based on his own travels. Although the two scientists had similar ideas about evolution, Darwin is more famous because of the carefully detailed arguments in his book *On the Origin of Species*, published in 1859.

When Darwin died in 1882, the theory of evolution was incomplete and still needed much work. In particular, Darwin had not understood why offspring resemble their parents. Austrian priest and botanist Gregor Mendel (1822–84) was the first to understand genetics, that is, how offspring inherit features from their parents. In the first half of the 1900's, Mendel's and Darwin's work were woven together to form the modern theory of evolution. The main scientists involved in this work were English geneticist J. B. S. Haldane (1892–1964), English biologist Ronald Fisher (1890–1962), American geneticist Sewall Wright (1889–1988), and American paleontologist and zoologist George Simpson (1902–84).

species, they find that it is identical to the sequence in chimpanzees, 1 amino acid different from rhesus monkeys, 10 amino acids different from whales, and 35 amino acids different from wheat.

Similarities and differences of other proteins—including DNA, the genetic material itself—show that organisms share recent ancestry with some species and distant ancestry with others. Protein studies also give scientists information about how long ago two different organisms branched off from a common ancestor. For example, these studies support fossil evidence showing that humans and chimpanzees are descended from a primate ancestor that lived about 5 million years ago.

Vestigial Structures. Some of the most unusual traits shared by different species are those called **vestigial structures**. These are the remains of structures that have been inherited from an ancestor but that have become useless. Vestigial structures can be understood in terms of descent with modification.

For example, pythons have the remains of hind leg bones, even though snakes do not have legs. However, the ancestor of snakes had legs. The python's useless hind leg bones are vestigial structures.

The human appendix is also a vestigial structure. Useful for digestion in animals that eat mostly plants, it was important to our distant ancestors. In modern humans, however, it is of no use.

Geographic Distribution. The way in which different species are distributed throughout the world provides additional evidence for evolution. For example, similar species are found together in certain areas. All types of kangaroos are found in Australia and nearby islands. This is because the ancestor of kangaroos lived in Australia, and it evolved there over time.

Also, specific plants and animals are not found in every place on Earth that could provide a suitable habitat. Tropical ocean islands are ideal habitats for frogs, but no frogs are found there. This is because the ancestor of frogs lived on the mainland, and no species were able to spread to distant ocean islands.

HOW EVOLUTION TAKES PLACE

The foundation of modern evolutionary theory was laid by Charles Darwin. To explain evolution, Darwin needed to discover a reason why organisms would change over time. His explanation, called natural selection, is the most important part of the theory of evolution. (To a scientist, the word "theory" means a statement of what are held to be the general laws, or causes, of something known or observed. Theories are well-studied explanations that fit the available evidence.)

Natural Selection

Natural selection is based on three basic facts about plants and animals in nature. The first is that individual organisms within a species vary slightly from one another and that these differences are inherited from parents to offspring. This is easy to see in human beings. We are all the same species, yet each person is unique. Children resemble their parents because they inherit traits from each parent.

The second fact is that in nature, plants and animals produce more offspring than can survive to adulthood. This causes a competition for limited resources such as food, which the organisms need to survive and reproduce.

Third, some individuals are better (or worse) competitors for these resources, based on their individual traits. Darwin concluded that organisms with traits that are helpful in a certain environment will, on average, survive and reproduce better than those with less favorable traits. The favorable traits, or variations, will be passed on to more offspring and will become more common in the overall population. This is natural selection.

A clear example of natural selection comes from a study of finches that live on the Galápagos Islands located in the Pacific Ocean—the same species seen by Darwin in the 1800's. (For more information on Darwin's travels and studies, see the feature in this article.) Medium ground finches eat the seeds of plants growing on these small islands. Biologists studying the birds measured their beaks and found that the beaks varied in size, and—as expected—the beak size of offspring resembled that of their parents.

In 1977, no rain fell during the typical wet season on the Galápagos Islands. Plants did not grow or produce seed. Food became so scarce that many birds died. On one island the number of medium ground finches decreased from 1,200 to 180 that year.

Biologists observed that finches with smaller beaks died in greater numbers than large-beaked finches. They discovered that birds with larger beaks survived because they were able to eat the largest, hardest seeds that birds with smaller beaks could not crack open. In the struggle for limited food during a drought, large-beaked finches suddenly had an important advantage.

After the drought ended, biologists observed that the beaks of the next generation of finches were larger, on average, than before the drought. Natural selection, over the course of a single generation, had caused an increase in beak size.

Genetics and Inheritance

When Darwin developed his ideas about natural selection, he knew that offspring resembled their parents, but he did not understand how inheritance works. Scientists today know that a molecule called DNA contains the information that directs how an organism will develop. The information in DNA exists in sections called **genes**, which are made up of four building blocks called **bases**. The arrangement of genes and the arrangement of bases within each gene are the **genetic code** that makes each individual unique.

Each cell in an organism's body contains two sets of the genetic code, but only one set is found in a sperm or an egg. When a male and female reproduce, a sperm and an egg fuse to produce a single cell with two complete genetic codes, one set from the mother and one set from the father. From this cell an offspring develops. This is how we inherit traits from both parents.

Sometimes part of the genetic code changes accidentally. It may be miscopied, part of it may be left out, or an extra piece may be added. These are called **mutations**. Most mutations in genes are harmful, but not all. Some mutations produce slight variations in organisms without causing them harm, and, rarely, some mutations are beneficial.

In the example of medium ground finches, small mutations in the genes that control

The process of inheritance makes each child unique, even though some traits are clearly passed down from parents to their offspring.

beak size produced, at some time in the past, some birds with slightly larger beaks. Larger beaks became an advantage during the drought, helping some birds survive.

In summary, mutations produce the variation on which evolution works. Without variation, there is no evolution, because there is no possibility of change.

Adaptation

Darwin was fascinated with the features of organisms that helped them fit so beautifully into their environment. Scientists call such features **adaptations**. For example, the long neck of the giraffe is an adaptation for eating leaves from the tops of trees. The bright color and fragrant scent of many flowers are adaptations for attracting insects that will pollinate the plant.

Adaptations result from the operation of natural selection. Ancestors of the giraffe did not have long necks. But those individuals that had slightly longer necks than others could find more food, simply because they could feed on leaves that others could not reach. Longer-necked giraffe ancestors therefore had more offspring than shorter-necked giraffes. The result, over many generations, is the giraffe we know today, the tallest land animal in the world.

Some fox species show clear adaptations to the special environments they inhabit. For example, the Arctic fox is superbly adapted to the tundra and polar ice of the far north. Its thick white winter coat provides warmth and protective camouflage. Its hairy footpads help it walk easily in the snow. And its short well-furred ears minimize heat loss.

Adaptation to a similar environment can cause organisms to appear similar, even if they are not at all closely related. The body shapes of sharks, dolphins, and the extinct ichthyosaurs (prehistoric marine reptiles) are very much alike, even though one is a fish, another a mammal, and the third a reptile.

We know from fossil evidence that these species did not inherit this body shape from a common ancestor. Instead, it arose independently in each group. How? Natural selection worked to produce the same solution to the

Adaptations make it possible for organisms to survive in their environments. A cactus' thick stems store water (*far left*); an Arctic fox's heavy coat and small ears conserve heat (*left*); and the bottom-dwelling flounder not only blends in with the seafloor, but both its eyes are on the same side of its head (*above*).

challenge of swimming fast in the sea. The shape is an adaptation to their underwater lifestyle. This is called **convergent evolution**. Each species converged, or moved together, toward a similar trait.

Speciation

Speciation is the name for the process by which one species branches into two or more new species. Speciation most commonly occurs when a single species is divided into groups that live in separate geographic areas. This can occur when some individuals migrate to a new area or when the population is divided by some natural event, such as flooding, an earthquake, or a volcanic eruption.

When a species is geographically divided, individuals in one area no longer have contact with individuals in the other area. In particular, the two groups no longer reproduce with each other.

How does this separation produce new species? Natural selection does the work. For example, the environment in the two areas is unlikely to be identical. One area might be hotter or drier than the other. It might have more predators or different food resources. As the organisms struggle to survive, natural selection will favor those that are best suited to each environment. Over time, the populations living in the two areas will become increasingly different from one another. Eventually the two types will change, or evolve, into distinct species.

Once this happens, the process of speciation cannot be reversed. Even if the two groups came to occupy the same area again, they could no longer interbreed. In fact, this is how species are identified: They cannot breed with individuals outside of their species and still produce fertile offspring.

The speciation process described here is called **allopatric speciation**. It occurs because populations of organisms are living in other (*allo-*) places (*-patric*).

Rates of Evolutionary Change

How fast does evolution take place? Sometimes it happens very quickly. In just a few decades, many species of insects have evolved the ability to survive insecticides, such as DDT. Viruses and bacteria also evolve quickly. Antibiotics, in general, are less effective today than when they were first widely used in the 1940's because some bacteria have evolved the ability to resist them. New virus species have recently evolved, including the AIDS virus and the virus that causes the canine disease called parvo.

The fossil record provides information about the rates of evolution throughout the Earth's history. It shows that in some kinds of organisms, small evolutionary changes occurred little by little over long periods of time, perhaps millions of years. This kind of slow change is called **gradualism**.

Other kinds of fossils show a different pattern of evolution. For example, clams and sea snails apparently evolved very little for a million years or more. Then, evolutionary change occurred quickly, perhaps during a few thousand years. This kind of evolution has been called **punctuated equilibrium**. Long periods of little change (equilibrium) are broken up, or punctuated, by shorter periods when new species form more rapidly. Scientists continue today to research which type of evolution is more common and in what kinds of fossils.

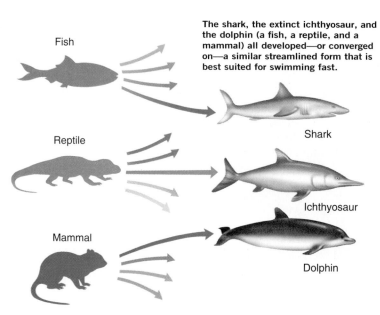

The shark, the extinct ichthyosaur, and the dolphin (a fish, a reptile, and a mammal) all developed—or converged on—a similar streamlined form that is best suited for swimming fast.

Fish

Shark

Reptile

Ichthyosaur

Mammal

Dolphin

What is artificial selection?

Along with nature, human beings can also influence how a species changes over time. Vastly different forms of a single species have been produced through careful breeding by humans. People—not nature—choose which organisms will reproduce. This is called artificial selection. Some of the forms produced in this way are so different that they resemble different species.

For example, all dogs belong to a single species, *Canis familiaris*. But because of selective breeding, modern dog breeds look very different from one another.

It is possible that the different forms created by artificial selection will someday become distinct

The Old English sheepdog (*left*) and the Chinese crested (*right*) belong to the same species. However, through selective breeding (artificial selection), they have been developed into very different looking dogs.

species—or they may not change for a thousand years. It all depends on the future course of evolution.

▶ HUMAN EVOLUTION

The fossil record includes a number of extinct species that belong to the same family as our species, *Homo sapiens*. The oldest members of the human family include several species of *Australopithecus*, a primate that lived in Africa between about 4 million and 1 million years ago. *Australopithecus* could walk upright, like a human; possessed a slightly larger brain than that of similarly sized apes; and showed several features that were intermediate between those of apes and modern humans. You can read more about our human ancestors in the article PREHISTORIC PEOPLE in Volume P.

▶ EVOLUTION AND RELIGIOUS BELIEFS

Some people do not accept evolution because it contradicts their religious beliefs. Most religions offer accounts of how God created the world and human beings. For example, Chapter 1 of the Book of Genesis in the Bible states that God created all living creatures in their present form during a six-day period. The view that this biblical account is literally true is called **creationism**. Creationists believe that life has not changed since God's creation of the world and that evolution's explanation of how life has changed through time must therefore be false.

In the early 1900's, creationists tried to keep ideas about evolution from being taught in public schools. Some states even passed laws making it illegal to teach evolution in public schools. In 1925, John T. Scopes, a Tennessee high school teacher, was convicted in a highly publicized trial of teaching evolution. The Scopes trial was often referred to as the monkey trial because, according to evolution, monkeys and humans share common ancestors. After this trial many years passed before schools began teaching evolution in science classes. Today creationists want their beliefs taught along with evolution.

Laws that would force creationism to be taught in public school science classes have been overthrown in United States courts. The courts ruled that creationism is a religious belief rather than a scientific theory. The United States Constitution does not allow the teaching of religion in public schools, in order to protect the religious freedom of all citizens.

However, many religious people accept evolution as the explanation for the history of life; some believe that God used evolution as a way of creating life.

COLIN HUGHES
University of North Dakota

PATRICIA H. KELLEY
University of North Carolina at Wilmington

See also CELLS; DARWIN, CHARLES ROBERT; EARTH, HISTORY OF; FOSSILS; GEOLOGY; LIFE (Adaptation); MENDEL, GREGOR JOHANN; PREHISTORIC ANIMALS; PREHISTORIC PEOPLE.

EXPERIMENTS AND OTHER SCIENCE ACTIVITIES

In school you learn many facts. For example, you learn that the Earth revolves around the sun, and that plants need carbon dioxide to grow. But do you ever find yourself wondering, "How do they know that?" Most likely, the answer is that someone did an experiment to find out. By performing experiments, we gain a better understanding of the world around us.

▶ **LEARNING BY EXPERIMENTING**

In ancient times, people believed that thinking and observation were all that were necessary to solve a problem. For example, Aristotle said that a basic quality of air was "lightness." This being so, a large quantity of air would weigh less than a small quantity. Aristotle never tested his idea, but people believed it because Aristotle was known to be a great thinker.

It was not until 1620—2000 years later—that Galileo tested and disproved Aristotle's ideas about air. Galileo took two identical containers. He pumped a large quantity of air into one and sealed it so that the air could not escape. Then he weighed both containers. The container with the pumped-in air weighed more. An experiment was needed for an old idea to be replaced with a new one.

What Is an Experiment?

An experiment is one method a scientist may use to solve a **problem**. A good experiment follows a step-by-step process known as the **scientific method**. First, the problem must be recognized and clearly stated. Next, the experimenter does research to learn about the problem and then makes an educated guess about a possible solution. This guess is called a

One of the best ways to learn about the world around you is to conduct experiments. These young investigators are studying paper towels to determine which brand is the most absorbent.

hypothesis. The experimenter tests the hypothesis by following a **procedure** that can show whether the hypothesis is true or false.

During the procedure, the experimenter makes **observations** and keeps careful records of the results that are observed. Then the experimenter draws a **conclusion** about whether the hypothesis is true or false.

Deciding on the Problem

A good deal of a scientist's time is actually spent thinking rather than handling equipment. Often the hardest task in carrying out an experiment is deciding exactly what the problem is—and wording the problem in the form of a question—so that it can be answered by carrying out an experimental procedure.

A good kind of problem question is one that can be answered by "yes" or "no." If the problem is such a question, it should be possible to design the procedure and carry out the rest of the experiment. A well-designed problem also involves a change in a single **experimental variable**. An experimental variable is the object or condition that is being tested. For example, let us take the problem "Will a plant exposed to sunlight grow to a greater height than a plant kept in a dark closet?" The experimental variable is sunlight, and the answer to

---

STEPS OF THE SCIENTIFIC METHOD

1. State the problem.
2. Gather information about the problem.
3. Form a hypothesis.
4. Perform experiments to test the hypothesis.
5. Make observations.
6. Record and analyze the data.
7. Draw a conclusion.

the question might be either "yes" or "no." By designing and performing the proper procedure, we can find out which answer is correct.

A different kind of problem question asks how one factor changes as the experimental variable changes. We can illustrate this kind of question with an experiment involving magnetism. The problem is this: How does the force of attraction between a magnet and a nail change as the distance between the magnet and the nail is increased? In this problem the distance between the magnet and the nail is the experimental variable. The magnetic force of attraction is the factor that changes because the experimental variable has been changed. Experiments show that the magnetic force decreases as the distance increases.

Here are some other problem questions that ask how a certain factor changes as the experimental variable is changed.

1. How does the pitch produced by a violin string change as the length of the string is changed?
2. How does the volume of a certain mass of water change as its temperature is increased from 32 to 68°F (0 to 20°C)?
3. Fruit flies can be raised in containers of different sizes. When this is done, how does the size of the containers affect the number of flies that can develop and survive?

When you are deciding on a problem for an experiment, you should make certain that the question is definite. For example, the following question is not suitable for use as the problem of an experiment because it is not definite enough: What are the effects of adding fertilizer to the soil in which plants are being grown?

First, the question should specify the kind of fertilizer to be used. But the main difficulty with the question is that the fertilizer may have many effects on plants. It may affect the plant's height, color, leaf size, and so on. An experiment should examine only one factor that changes. The original question should be replaced by a number of problem questions. Each one should be concerned with one kind of change. One suitable problem question might be this: How is the height of bean seedlings affected if a complete fertilizer is added to the soil in which they are grown? (A complete fertilizer is a fertilizer that contains three elements that plants must have to grow. They are nitrogen, phosphorus, and potassium.)

Controls in Experiments

Most experiments include **controls**. The controls in an experiment are treated exactly the same way as the test group, except for the experimental variable. In order to answer the question "How does complete fertilizer affect the height of bean seedlings?" you must have two groups of plants. One group, the experimental group, is grown in soil containing fertilizer. The second group, the control, is grown in soil without fertilizer. The effect of the fertilizer is discovered by comparing the heights of the plants in the two groups.

Before beginning an experiment, it is important and necessary to think about what all

CONTROLLED EXPERIMENT WITH PLANT FERTILIZER

Every experiment must have an experimental group and a control group. The three plants on the right are the experimental plants. They are planted in soil that contains complete fertilizer (fertilizer that contains nitrogen, phosphorus, and potassium). The plants on the left are the control plants. They are planted in soil that does not contain fertilizer. All plants from both groups get the same amount of water and sunlight. Compare the growth of the control plants with the growth of the plants that got the complete fertilizer.

REPORT OF AN EXPERIMENT

Problem: *How is the height of bean seedlings affected if complete fertilizer is added to the soil in which they are grown?*

Hypothesis: *Bean seedlings grown in soil containing complete fertilizer will be taller than bean seedlings grown in soil without added fertilizer.*

Materials: *Bean seeds, six small pots, a marker for labeling, potting soil, complete fertilizer, water, and a sunny window.*

Procedure:

1. *Label three pots "Contains Fertilizer" and three pots "No Fertilizer."*
2. *Fill the three pots labeled "No Fertilizer" with potting soil.*
3. *Mix more potting soil with fertilizer as instructed on the fertilizer package. Add the fertilizer-soil mixture to the three pots labeled "Contains Fertilizer."*
4. *Plant three bean seeds in each pot. Poke the seeds into the soil about 1/2 inch (1.3 centimeters) deep and cover them with soil.*
5. *Water the pots and place them on a table near a sunny window.*
6. *Every two days water beans by adding 2 tablespoons (30 milliliters) of water to each pot.*
7. *Measure the height of the seedlings once a week for four weeks.*

Average Height of Bean Seedlings Weeks One Through Four

	Contains Fertilizer	No Fertilizer
Week 1	0.5 inch	0.35 inch
Week 2	1.0 inch	0.8 inch
Week 3	3.6 inches	3.5 inches
Week 4	7.9 inches	7.6 inches

Conclusion: *The hypothesis was correct. Bean seedlings grown in soil containing fertilizer grew taller than bean seedlings grown in soil that did not contain fertilizer.*

of the possible experimental variables are. For example, if you are testing the effects of fertilizer on plant height, you want to be sure that the other factors that might affect plant growth, such as sunlight and water, are the same for both groups of plants.

Observation and Measurements

When we carry out experiments, we usually compare things. For example, in the previous experiment we would compare the height of bean plants grown with complete fertilizer to the height of bean plants grown without fertilizer. We do not simply place the plants side by side and look at them to see which plants are taller. Instead, we measure the height of each plant with a measuring device, such as a ruler. We record the measurements and then compare the measurements. What we actually do is compare the lengths of the plants with a standard length, which may be an inch (or a centimeter).

Scientists use different kinds of measuring instruments. Each measurement involves a comparison with a standard. Using a thermometer, for example, we compare the temperature of an object with a standard of temperature. This standard is the degree Fahrenheit (or Celsius).

Some scientific instruments aid our senses and make better observation and measurement possible. Telescopes and microscopes make objects look larger and closer. With these aids, we can clearly see objects that we could not see without them. Microphones and amplifiers allow us to hear sounds that we would otherwise be unable to hear.

Other instruments enable us to observe things that cannot directly stimulate our senses. For example, without instruments we cannot judge weight very accurately. When we use a spring balance, we measure how much the weight stretches the spring. In this way we make a fairly accurate measurement of the weight.

In some instruments, the factor we wish to measure produces an electric voltage that causes a needle on the dial of a meter to move. The photocell in a light meter produces a voltage that increases as the intensity of the light increases. In turn, the meter needle swings farther from zero as the light intensity increases.

The careful use of measuring instruments makes accurate measurement possible. The work of measurement is highly important in scientific activities because some problems can be solved only if all measurements are extremely accurate.

How to Write a Report

For every experiment that is performed, the experimenter writes a report. A report usually gives information about the problem, the hypothesis, and the materials used. It also explains the procedure that was followed, the observations made by the experimenter, and the conclusion that was reached. If a report is well written, a person who is unfamiliar with the experiment should be able to follow it and repeat the experiment in exactly the same way.

An experimenter should start writing the report even before beginning the experiment, and continue to write it as the experiment goes along. All observations and measurements should be added as they are made, and any mistakes should be written down. If a scientist waited until the experiment was finished to try to write the report, many important details might be forgotten. A sample report for the fertilizer experiment is shown on the opposite page.

Why Should an Experiment Be Repeated?

Three bean plants were grown in soil containing complete fertilizer. Three other plants were grown in soil without fertilizer. This experiment was designed to determine the effect of fertilizer on the growth of plants. There was a reason for having at least three. If only one plant had been grown in each case, we might not have been sure that the results were trustworthy. For example, one of the seeds might have been defective and might

---

Astronomy

See For Yourself

How the Length of a Shadow Changes with the Seasons

Problem:
Does the angle of the sun in the sky change during the year?

Background:
The Earth's axis is tilted at an angle of 23.5 degrees to the plane of its orbit around the sun. This causes the amount of heat and light the Earth receives from the sun to vary from place to place and to change throughout the year. This is the main cause for the seasons. This activity will help explain why it is hotter in the summertime than in the wintertime.

Materials:
An assistant, a yardstick, and a measuring tape.

Procedure:
The following procedure will need to be repeated once a week for several weeks or more. It is important to make your observation at the same time each day. If the day is overcast you may have to wait to make your observation until the next day.

1. Prepare a data sheet on which you can record the date, time, and length of the shadow of the yardstick.
2. Find a spot outside where the view of the sun is not blocked by buildings or trees.
3. Have an assistant hold the yardstick straight up on level ground.
4. Use the measuring tape to determine the length of the shadow cast on the ground by the yardstick, and record the information on your data sheet.

Graph your data on simple graphing paper or using a computer. You should expect to see a pattern by your third or fourth observation. But the changes will be more dramatic if you extend the course of your experiment. Be sure to notice what happens to the shadow as you approach spring, summer, autumn, and winter.

Going Further:
If you lived at the equator, do you think you would get the same results? What if you lived at the North or South Pole?

not have grown properly. If we had used more than three plants in each part of the experiment, our results would have been even more reliable.

A scientist may repeat one experiment a number of times before feeling confident that the results and conclusion are correct. After the scientist reports what has been discovered, other scientists may repeat the experiment several times to test the reliability of the experiment. Scientists insist that they should be able to obtain the same results as the original experimenter before they accept that person's results as correct. This is what scientists mean when they say that the experiment must be **reproducible** (able to be reproduced) to be acceptable.

Can an Experiment Fail?

Thomas Edison believed that no experiment could be a complete failure. When he was developing the incandescent light, he searched for a substance that could serve as a filament for the lightbulb. Edison tested thousands of different substances before he found one that he could use in a practical, long-lasting lightbulb. While Edison was still hunting unsuccessfully for a good filament, he was asked whether he considered the experiments to be failures. He answered that they were not failures

WORKING SAFELY

Safety is extremely important, regardless of the kind of science activity you undertake. You should know certain basic science-safety rules and should always observe them.

• Do not use 110-volt electricity in science activities unless you are working under the supervision of someone who is an expert in handling such electricity. Any voltage greater than 30 volts is considered dangerous.

• Do not heat anything to a high temperature—and do not boil or burn anything—unless someone who is experienced is present. Observe all the fire-safety rules. These rules are designed to help prevent damage to property and injury to yourself or others.

• Do not carry out chemical reactions unless you know what the results will be. You should never perform a chemical experiment to "see what will happen." The result might be a fire, an explosion, or the release of a poisonous gas. All work with chemicals should be done under the supervision of a capable, responsible person.

• Do not grow cultures of bacteria or molds except in a laboratory that is specially equipped for that purpose. There are definite safety procedures that must be followed to prevent infection and possibly serious harm from the bacteria or mold cultures. This work should be supervised by someone who knows how to handle bacteria and molds safely.

• A piece of broken glass is an extremely sharp object, which—as you know—can cause severe wounds and dangerous bleeding. Use precautions that will help keep glass from breaking. For example, do not heat or cool a piece of glassware very rapidly.

• Wear proper clothing while you are performing a science activity. Scientists wear laboratory coats to protect themselves. Ties or scarves should not be worn near any kind of tool or machine that has moving parts. Long hair should be pinned up securely or tucked under a cap.

• Wear safety goggles or glasses if there is danger of injury to your eyes from chemicals or from objects that may be thrown through the air.

• Never work on any science activity that can possibly be dangerous without supervision by an adult.

• Know first aid, and have simple first-aid equipment where you can easily get to it.

Remember that these are only some of the general science-safety rules. An expert who is capable of supervising your work will know many other detailed safety precautions.

See For Yourself

How to Observe the Greenhouse Effect

Problem:
What is the greenhouse effect and how can we demonstrate it?

Background:
According to some scientists, the temperature of our planet is slowly increasing. One possible reason for the warming is the increase of gases such as carbon dioxide in the atmosphere from the burning of fossil fuels. Carbon dioxide traps the heat from the sun in the lower atmosphere, and the Earth's temperature rises. This is similar to what happens in a greenhouse. Radiation from the sun can pass through the glass walls of the greenhouse, but it becomes trapped as heat and cannot leave. Therefore the plants stay nice and warm.

Materials:
Two shoe boxes, sand, two thermometers, tape, and a sheet of clear plastic, plastic wrap, or glass.

Procedure:
1. Half fill each shoebox with sand and place a thermometer in the sand of each box. Cover one box with the plastic or glass sheet. If you are using plastic wrap, cover the box and secure the ends tightly on each side with tape.

2. Place both boxes in a sunny spot.
3. Record the temperature in each box every 15 minutes for two hours.

Graph your results to compare the temperature of both boxes. Does the sand in one box heat faster than the sand in the other box? The temperature in the covered box should be warmer for most or all of the readings.

because, as a result of the experiments, he knew thousands of substances that could not serve as the filament of an incandescent bulb.

Edison was right. You can learn something from every experiment, including those that seem to fail.

▶ **OTHER TYPES OF SCIENCE ACTIVITIES**

Not all science activities are experiments. An experiment is designed to solve a problem by making changes in a variable and must have a control group. But much can be learned from any science activity. You can obtain valuable information by simply observing conditions as they are, without conducting experiments.

For instance, you might want to find out two things about robins: (1) When do they begin to raise families in the spring? (2) When do they begin to get ready to migrate in the autumn? First, you would observe the number of birds in each group of robins that you see in the spring. For a short time after robins have migrated from the south, they may be in fairly large flocks. Make a note of the date on which you begin to see no more than two robins together. That is when they have formed pairs to build nests, mate, and raise families of baby robins. Then, in the autumn, make a note of the date on which you first see flocks of robins. That is when they are about to migrate to the south.

Often it is valuable to make a map of a small area, such as a pond and its shores, and to record on the map the location of various kinds of plants and animals. Such information can help you learn more about the kinds of environments that different species prefer.

Making a scientific collection can be an interesting hobby, but it can also be much more than that. By studying a collection of insects, you can learn much about the characteristics of the insects and their relationships and classification. There is a good deal to be learned from each kind of collection you might make. (For more information about nature collections, see the article NATURE, STUDY OF in Volume N.)

How to Build an Electric Motor

Problem:

How is an electric motor constructed and how does it work?

Background:

Electric motors run on magnetic fields and electricity. In this activity you will build a simple electric motor. You might need help from an adult for this activity. Before you begin, you should learn about electric motors and how they work. See the article ELECTRIC MOTORS in this volume.

Materials:

A pen, a size D battery, a size D battery holder, a small magnet, 8 inches (20 centimeters) of 20-gauge enamel wire, two medium-size paper clips, and wire strippers.

Procedure:

Follow the diagrams to help you assemble your motor.

1. Wrap the wire around a small section of the pen about 20 times to make a coil. Leave about 1½ inches (4 centimeters) of free wire on each end.
2. Pull the coil from the pen and hold it gently so that it does not lose its circular shape.
3. Wrap each free end of the wire around the coil a few times to hold the loops of the coil together.
4. Hold the coil in a vertical position, and remove the top half of the insulation from the protruding free ends using a wire stripper. It is important that only half the insulation is removed.
5. Partially straighten out a paper clip, as shown in the diagram. Repeat this with a second paper clip.
6. Attach the ends of the paper clips securely to the battery holder. Rest the ends of the coil in the loops

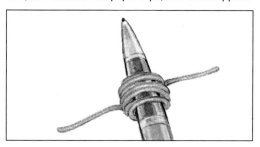

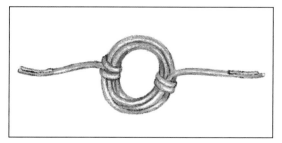

Many people are interested in illustrating scientific topics by taking photographs, making drawings, or constructing models. In doing so, they learn much about the topic.

Many "virtual" experiments are available to try on the World Wide Web. Using these experiments you can explore the human body, visit outer space, or perform other tasks that would be too expensive or difficult to try at home. Ask your science teacher to help you.

▶ SCIENCE FAIRS

Each year professional scientists meet at conventions, where they talk about the experiments and other science activities they have carried out. A science fair is a kind of science convention for students. Its main purpose is to give young scientists a chance to exchange information about their science activities.

Almost any kind of science activity may be suitable for presentation at a science fair. Collections, models, records of observations, illustrations, and experiments are all worthwhile. Regardless of the kind of activity you

choose to present, it should have the following characteristics:

1. It should be something you yourself have done, although you may have been supervised by someone else.
2. It should be an activity that you began quite a while before the science fair, rather than something you prepared specially for the fair.
3. It should concern a topic in which you are truly interested.
4. It should be an activity from which you gained new understanding of the topic.
5. It should not be a dangerous activity.

Before you begin to work on your exhibit, you should learn about the science fair, the types of exhibits it will include, and how much space is available. Your science fair exhibit should catch a visitor's attention. It should also explain itself. Your goal should be an exhibit that lets the visitor understand your project quickly. For information on of the paper clips. Bend the paper clips toward each other if necessary.

7. Insert the battery into the battery holder.

8. Place the magnet on top of the battery holder, just below the coil. Spin the coil. Be sure that the coil does not touch the magnet when it spins. You may need to adjust the coil and the paper clips so that the coil is balanced and remains centered as it spins.

9. Spin the coil to start your electric engine. If everything is set up correctly, the coil should continue to spin on its own.

Going Further:
Can you think of ways to build a bigger or more powerful engine? What happens if you add more magnets or use a more powerful battery?

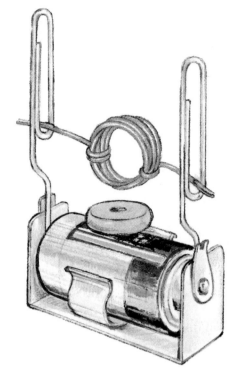

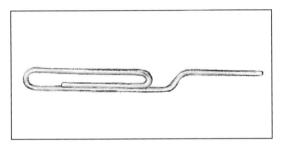

planning, conducting, and presenting a science fair project, see the article SCIENCE FAIRS in Volume S.

Who wins at a science fair? Everyone who enters. Of course, if there are official awards, only a few students can win them. But every student who presents a project at the fair gets other rewards. These include (1) the joy of discovering the answer to a problem all by yourself; (2) the feeling of satisfaction that comes from accomplishing something worthwhile; (3) the feeling of self-confidence you get from knowing that you can keep working on a big task until you finish it; and (4) possibly the beginning of a hobby that may give you pleasure and satisfaction for many years.

▶ IDEAS FOR EXPERIMENTS AND OTHER SCIENCE ACTIVITIES

Scientific exploration can be an exciting adventure. How do you begin to work on a science activity? The first step is to decide what area of science interests you and what questions you want to answer. Next, you should find out as much as you can about the topic you will be exploring. One of the best methods of doing background research is reading.

There are many articles in this encyclopedia that give information about different areas of science. The best way to find information about a scientific subject is to look up key words in the index pages of this encyclopedia. Such key words could be "ants," "constellations," "electricity," "plants," "rocks," and "weather." At first you may need help deciding which key words to use. You will find it helpful to study the section "How to Use the Index" at the beginning of the index pages in Volume A. Once you have decided on a subject, you might also want to do research looking for key words in the index pages of other books or using the search mode of a computer.

Among the ideas listed below, you might find some you would like to try. The activities in this section are grouped under the headings Astronomy, Earth Science (Including Pollution), Physics and Electricity, Chemistry,

Life Sciences (Biology), and Health and Fitness. As with all scientific investigations, the ideas presented here might lead you to research a topic further and create your own experiment or study.

Two kinds of activities are presented: detailed activities and ideas. Complete instructions are not provided for all of the suggested activities. It is up to you to find out which procedures work well and are best to follow. During the course of your research you may find a better way to conduct the experiment. This will depend on what materials you can obtain and the time and effort you put into your project.

Before you begin an activity, take time to review the scientific method. The most important step for a successful project is to have a well-defined problem. Before the experiment is actually performed you should make a list of materials you will need. Some of the materials you will find at home. Other materials may need to be purchased or obtained from your school science lab with your teacher's permission.

In some cases you might need the assistance of an adult when preparing or performing an experiment. Even the most experienced scientists work with lab assistants. Safety when performing lab experiments or any type of science activity must be the top priority. Be sure to read each activity completely before proceeding.

It is important to keep a complete and accurate record of your data. Even if you make a mistake you should write it down. Some of the most important discoveries in science—such as the discovery of penicillin—were made because of mistakes!

How to Make a Pinhole Camera

See For Yourself

Problem:
How does a pinhole camera work?

Background:
Light from a candle flame or other bright object travels out in all directions, but only the light falling directly on the hole of a pinhole camera can get into the camera and reach the screen. Since the object is larger than the hole, the light from the top of the object is directed down and falls off the bottom of the screen. Light from the bottom of the object is directed up and falls on the top of the screen. The image appears upside down. The pinhole camera you will make is for viewing an image with your eyes rather than for taking pictures.

Materials:
Waxed paper, a rubber band, and a cylindrical box, such as an oatmeal box.

Procedure:
1. Remove the lid from the box, and stretch the waxed paper across the open end of the box. Fasten the waxed paper in place with the rubber band, and pull the paper around the edges to smooth out wrinkles.
2. With a steel darning needle (or other round sharp object), punch a neat hole in the center of the end of the box opposite the end that is covered with waxed paper.
3. Point the hole toward any bright object, such as a lightbulb or a candle flame. The image of the object is focused upside down on the waxed paper

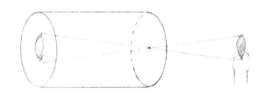

"screen." If you move the pinhole camera toward the object, the image remains upside down but becomes larger.

Going Further:
It is also possible to make a pinhole camera that you can use to take pictures on film. Do research and then try making your very own camera.

Research and experimentation are exciting ways to learn about the world around you. Many of the activities listed in this section can bring you hours or days of enjoyment and wonder. The thrill of discovering something new is a feeling you will want to share with your family, friends, and teachers. The love of discovery through experimentation may also be the stepping stone you need to focus on a career in science.

Astronomy

Astronomy is the study of the position, size, and other characteristics of the moon, sun, planets, galaxies, and other objects in space.

- Learn to identify the constellations using star charts. List the names of the constellations you find in the sky. What are the names of their brightest stars? Learn how the constellations and stars that belong to them got their names.
- Observe and plot the path and phase of the moon as it moves across the sky from night to night. How is the moon's motion different from the motion of the planets, sun, and stars? Keep an accurate record of the moonrise over a period of one month, and chart its position relative to the constellations using a star chart.
- A meteor is a streak of light in the sky caused by a particle of dust entering the Earth's atmosphere and burning up. Have you ever seen a meteor? Several times each year the Earth encounters swarms of dust from the tails of comets. We observe the dust as meteor showers that are seen in a particular area of the sky. Find out when and where in the sky the next meteor shower is going to occur, and try to observe it. Count how many meteors you see.
- Four of the planets are bright enough to see with the unaided eye. They are Jupiter, Saturn, Mars, and Venus. Learn to identify and locate one or more of these planets in the night sky, and follow their motion for several weeks as they change position in the sky. Use an astronomy book to find out when and where to locate the planet you want to watch. Why do the planets' positions change over periods of time? How does the motion of an inner planet, like Venus,

See For Yourself

How Fast Your Reaction Time Is

Problem:
Do different people have different reaction times in response to a change in their environment?

Background:
Reaction time is the amount of time it takes to respond to a change in the environment. It may be the time it takes to hit the brakes on your bike when an animal runs onto the sidewalk in front of you, or the time it takes to catch a ball. Professional baseball players must have excellent reaction times to be able to swing the bat and hit a fastball that is traveling at over 100 miles (160 kilometers) per hour.

Materials:
A yardstick and an assistant. The more people you can get involved, the more fun you will have with this activity.

Procedure:
1. Hold a yardstick vertically with the zero mark on the bottom. Have your assistant position one hand around the yardstick at the zero mark, without touching the stick.
2. Without warning, let go of the yardstick. Your assistant should try to catch it. Record the number mark at which it was caught.
3. Repeat several times and compare. Does reaction time get faster with practice? Switch positions.

Going Further:
Try distracting the person doing the catching by talking to them or changing the length of time before the yardstick is dropped. Compare the values of the distracted and undistracted times. Can you think of any situations where a distraction could increase reaction time and create a dangerous situation?

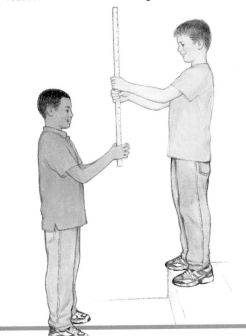

See For Yourself

How to Identify Acids and Bases

Problem:

What effects do acids and bases have on the color of a red cabbage indicator solution?

Background:

An **indicator** is a substance that changes color in the presence of an acid or a base. For example, red litmus paper will turn blue when placed into a liquid that is a base. Blue litmus paper will turn red when placed in a liquid that is an acid. In this activity you will make an indicator using items found at the grocery store. Vinegar will be your acid, baking soda your base, and water your neutral control.

Materials:

A red cabbage, water, vinegar, baking soda, and three glasses. You will also need an adult to help with the first part of the experiment.

Procedure:

1. Chop up the red cabbage and let it simmer in water on low heat until the solution is dark purple. Let the solution stand and cool, then drain the purple cooking liquid into a container and store it in the refrigerator until you need it.
2. Pour some water into a glass and some vinegar into another glass. Pour water into a third glass and dissolve a little bit of baking soda in it. Pour some of your cabbage solution indicator into each glass.
3. Record your results. What color does the indicator turn in an acid? In a base? In a neutral solution?

compare to the motion of an outer planet, like Saturn?

- Venus changes phases just as the moon does. Use a telescope to view Venus, and keep a record showing the changing phases of the planet. What is the relationship between the phase displayed by Venus and the planet's position in the sky? At some times of the year Venus is more easily seen in the morning sky rather than the evening sky.
- Observe the planet Jupiter using a telescope at no more than 50 power. You also can observe Jupiter using binoculars. Just be sure to rest the binoculars on something to hold them steady. Make drawings showing the positions of Jupiter's four largest moons: Io, Europa, Ganymede, and Callisto, as they revolve around the planet. The moons will look like bright, tiny stars in line with Jupiter's equator.

- Use a telescope to observe Saturn over a period of several months. Keep a record of how the angle of Saturn's rings changes in relation to the Earth.
- If you have access to a 35-millimeter camera (not automatic), a camera tripod, and a shutter cable release, you can demonstrate the rotation of the Earth by photographing the movement of the stars. Use black-and-white film with an ASA (American Standards Association) film speed of 400 or faster. Set up the camera on the tripod so it points toward Polaris, the North Star. You will need to use long exposures, from 5 to 30 minutes, in order to see the star trails.
- Following the procedure on star trail photography above, use color film (with

an ASA film speed of 400 or faster) to take 30-second time exposures of sections of the sky that contain bright stars. The resulting photographs will show the true colors of the stars, which cannot be seen by the unaided eye. Learn the names of these stars and compare their colors. The color of a star is directly related to its surface temperature. Cool stars are red, while very hot stars are blue. Is there a pattern to the distribution of cool, moderate, and hot stars in our section of the galaxy?

Earth Science (Including Pollution)

Earth science is the study of the Earth, its history, and the forces that change it. Earth science can be divided into a number of different areas, including geology, oceanography, hydrology, and meteorology.

- Air pollution can be studied using a microscope, a microscope slide, and petroleum jelly. Smear a thin layer of petroleum jelly on a microscope slide and let it sit outside in a clear spot overnight. Or prepare several slides and put them in different locations. Look at the slides under the microscope to see the solid particles that pollute the atmosphere in your area. Do research to find out what these particles are. Do some locations have more air pollution than others?
- Study water pollution by gathering water specimens from sources near your home. Use a microscope to examine a drop of water from each source. Make sketches of what you observe. Obtain test papers for pH (acid or base), lead, nitrates, and sulfides, and test the water samples. You can obtain most of these test papers from sci-

---

Chemistry

How to Make Polymer "Slime"

See For Yourself

Problem:
What is a polymer? How can you make a polymer in your kitchen?

Background:
A polymer is a chemical compound made up of repeating structural units. Many of the products we wear, work with, or play with are made of polymers such as plastic or nylon. In this activity you will make polymer "slime." Before you start, learn more about polymers and how they are produced in the article PLASTICS in Volume P.

Materials:
White glue, food coloring (optional), several plastic cups, paper towels, wooden spoons, borax (can be found in the detergent section of a grocery store), and water.

Procedure:
1. Combine equal amounts of glue and water in a container and mix well.
2. In another container make a saturated solution of borax by adding the borax slowly to warm water. After each addition, make sure that the borax

is dissolved before adding more. When no more borax will dissolve (you will see it settling on the bottom), the solution is saturated.
3. Add the food coloring to the borax until it is the color you would like your slime to be.
4. In the plastic cups, combine the glue mixture and the borax solution and stir. Allow it to sit for a couple of hours and your slime will begin to form. Experiment with different amounts of glue and borax to find a slime texture that you like. It can be watery or more like putty.

Going Further:
More complex polymers can be made with a combination of other substances. Research polymers and plastics to find other polymers you can make at home.

ence hobby stores or from your teacher. Water pollution can also be observed by placing a small amount of water in a pan and boiling it away to see what residue is left behind. Get an adult to help you use the stove.

• Study the salinity of the oceans. Do research to find out which ocean contains the highest percentage of salt and why. Can the salt be removed from ocean water? How would you do this?

• Show how streams and rivers are formed. Take a long board and cover it with dirt and sand. Use bricks to place the board at a slight angle. Set up a hose so that water runs gently down the board. Observe what happens as the water flows. What happens if you repeat the experiment with a faster flow of water? What happens to the sand that is washed off the board?

• Create your own weather station. It is easy to build a thermometer, a barometer, a rain gauge, and a wind speed indicator from materials you have at home. See the article WEATHER in Volume W if you need help.

• What is the shape of a tornado? A tornado is funnel-shaped, and its high winds create a vortex that lifts whatever is in its

Physics

See For Yourself

How to Create Layers of Liquids

Problem:
Which liquids are more dense and less dense than water?

Background:
Density can be defined as the amount of matter contained in a given volume. Scientists compare the density of all substances with the density of water, which is 1.00 at room temperature. A liquid that is less dense than water will float above water, while a liquid that is more dense than water will sink. In this experiment you will compare the densities of several household liquids with the density of water.

Materials:
A clear glass or jar, 4 cups, water, rubbing alcohol, salad oil, corn syrup, food coloring, and spoons.

Procedure:
1. Pour about $1/4$ cup (60 milliliters) of each liquid into separate cups.
2. Dye each liquid a different color using several drops of food coloring. Stir to make the colors uniform.
3. Pour the colored water into the clear glass. Then pour the colored corn syrup into the glass. Does it float above the water or sink below the water?
4. Gently pour the salad oil into the glass. Observe whether it is more or less dense than water.
5. Carefully add the rubbing alcohol to the glass. Is it more or less dense than water? Is it more or less dense than salad oil?
6. Record your observations. Which liquids are denser than water? Which liquids are less dense than water? Which liquid is the most dense? The least dense?

Going Further:
Solids have different densities just as liquids do. For example, a ping pong ball will float on the water in a swimming pool, but a baseball will sink. Experiment with the densities of small solid objects. Gently drop a small object such as a grape or a cork into the stack of liquids. Does it sink or float? Do some objects settle between layers of liquids?

path. Create your own tornado in a jar using water, glitter, soap, and food coloring. Shake the jar to suspend the glitter, then twist the jar. Observe the funnel shape that is formed by the swirling water. Do all tornadoes look the same?

- Collect and identify rocks and minerals. See the article MINERALS in Volume M to learn how to determine the hardness of your specimens.
- How many different temperatures can you find near your home? What is the temperature (1) on the pavement, (2) on a sunny sidewalk, (3) on the grass under a tree, (4) in a birdbath? Try many different places and make a chart of your discoveries. Repeat your observations on different days and at different times of year. Also find out how many different temperatures are inside your home.

Physics and Electricity

Physics is the study of energy and matter. Electricity is one form of energy.

- Build an electromagnet by wrapping insulated wire around a large nail and connecting the wire to a battery. How can an electromagnet be strengthened? Is it possible to increase the strength indefinitely?
- Study the effects of static electricity by rubbing a balloon with a silk scarf or on a carpet. Make a record of the things the balloon will and will not stick to.
- How much friction is there between an object and a surface? Place a block of wood near one end of a board. Keep a record of how high you raised the board before the block began to slide. Cover the bottom of the block with sandpaper (rough side out) and test its friction. Repeat the experiment with paper, cloth, and other materials covering the bottom of the block.
- How do gears work? Make a collection of different size gears and show what type of machine they are used in.
- Build a crystal radio using a plastic container, insulated wire, a germanium diode, and a telephone headset. Simple instructions can be found in an amateur electronics manual.

How to Use Chromatography to Separate the Components of a Dye

See For Yourself

Problem:
How many different colors make up the black ink in a felt-tip pen?

Background:
Scientists often use a method called paper chromatography to separate a mixture into the chemicals of which it is composed.

Materials:
A circle of filter paper about 4 inches (10 centimeters) in diameter (a piece of a coffee filter will work), a felt-tip pen with water-soluble ink, and a glass of water.

Procedure:
1. Make two parallel cuts from the edge to near the center of the paper filter. The result should be a strip about 1/2 inch (1 centimeter) wide and about 2 inches (5 centimeters) long.
2. Use a felt-tip pen to place a spot of ink on the strip about 3/4 inch (2 centimeters) from the edge.
3. Bend the strip at right angles to the rest of the filter paper. Support the filter paper on the rim of a glass tumbler that is filled with water to a height at which it barely touches the bottom of the filter paper strip. Make sure the ink spot is not underwater.
4. The water will begin to creep up the paper strip. Observe what happens to the ink spot. As the water reaches the ink, it should carry the ink along.
5. Record how many colors separate from the ink. They will appear as bands of color on the paper.

Going Further:
Repeat the experiment using other colors of ink. Are some colors used in more than one ink? Why is it important to use water-soluble ink for this experiment?

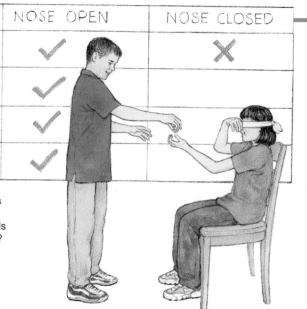

	NOSE OPEN	NOSE CLOSED
CHERRY	✓	✗
ORANGE	✓	
LEMON	✓	
LIME	✓	

How Your Sense of Smell Affects Your Sense of Taste

Problem:
Is your sense of taste affected when you cannot smell your food?

Background:
Many animals use their keen sense of smell rather than sight to identify foods. Have you noticed that a dog always smells its food before it eats it? Maybe you have noticed that food does not taste as good when you have a cold. Is this because your stuffy nose is not smelling as well?

Materials:
A friend or helper, a blindfold, and flavored candies.

Procedure:
1. Make a chart listing the flavor and color of the candies. For each candy have two columns labeled Nose Closed and Nose Open.
2. Blindfold your assistant. Have your assistant pinch his or her nostrils together. Have your assistant taste each candy and try to guess the flavor. Let them keep it in their mouth for only a short time. Keep track of how many flavors your assistant correctly identifies.
3. Repeat the experiment, this time with your assistant's nose unpinched. Again record how many

flavors are correctly identified. What do you conclude? Does the sense of smell affect the sense of taste? Try the experiment with more volunteers.

Going Further:
Do other senses affect your sense of taste? Have volunteers guess the flavor of fruit drinks that are sipped from glasses covered with paper so the color cannot be seen.

• Make a spectroscope, using a diffraction grating, a small box, and a mirror. (A diffraction grating is a plate of glass ruled with closely spaced, parallel grooves or slits. When the different colors making up white light are reflected from or passed through the grating, each color bends by a different amount and a spectrum is created. Diffraction gratings can be purchased at science hobby stores.) What kind of spectrum do you see when you look at (1) an incandescent lamp and (2) a fluorescent lamp? When do scientists use a spectroscope?

• How can you see magnetic fields if they are invisible? Magnetic fields can be observed using iron filings in a bottle of mineral oil or baby oil. Cut a piece of steel wool into tiny pieces and place them in a bottle of baby oil from which the label has been removed. Hold a magnet to the side of the bottle. What happens to the filings? They should align themselves with the magnetic field.

• Make a musical instrument using glasses of water filled to different heights. How can you change the pitch of the notes? Can you play a simple song? Dye the water in the glasses different colors using food coloring and write "music." See if a friend can play and guess the song.

• Experiment with aerodynamics. Make paper airplanes of different styles. See what qualities make them fly the farthest, the highest, and the straightest. Do several trials to make sure your results are reproducible, and record your results.

• Cohesion is the force of attraction between molecules of the same substance. It is responsible for the **surface tension** of water. Surface tension allows a water bug to hop across the water of a pond, or a stone to "skip" across a lake. To learn about surface tension, take a dish of water and sprinkle some pepper on top of the water. Add several drops of dishwashing soap to the center of the dish. What happens to the pepper? Why? What does this tell you about cohesion?

Chemistry

Chemistry is the science that deals with the composition and properties of matter and how matter interacts to produce new substances through chemical reactions.

- Study the properties of metals and their resistance to corrosion. Put different metals into containers filled with salt water and let them sit for three days. Examine each metal and record how it reacted to the saline (salt solution).
- Make a study of iron rust. What causes it? How can you prevent rust from forming on an iron nail? What happens chemically when rust occurs?
- Study the effects of sunlight on different materials. You might use rubber, plastic, paper, and cardboard. Place the materials in a sunny spot, such as on a windowsill, for one week. Make sure to have control items that are not placed in the sun. Compare the two sets of objects. How do the objects exposed to sunlight change?
- Turn water into an acid. Use pH paper to test the pH of a glass of water. The pH should be about 7. Then use a straw to blow carbon dioxide from your breath into a glass of water that is a third full. After several minutes test the pH of the water again. How long does it take to turn water with a pH of 7 into carbonic acid with a pH of 4?
- What chemical changes take place when sulfur is added to a metal? An egg contains sulfur. Break an egg into a small bowl and beat it until it is uniform. Polish a silver spoon, a copper penny, and an iron nail until they are clean and shiny. Place these items in the beaten egg and place the bowl in the refrigerator for 24 hours. Observe the changes that take place in the appearance of each item.
- What is starch? How can you test for the presence of starch in different foods and substances? Some substances to test are flour, sugar, a halved potato, paper, and white cloth.

- How does temperature affect the rate of a chemical reaction? Try dissolving effervescent antacid tablets in glasses of water at different temperatures. In which temperature does the tablet dissolve most quickly? Do you know why? What is the temperature in your stomach?
- Make raisins go scuba diving. Pour some unflavored seltzer water into a clear glass, then drop about ten raisins into the glass one at a time. Wait several minutes and then observe the raisins. Why do the raisins move up and down in the glass?

Life Sciences (Biology)

Biologists study the origin, classification, and life functions of plants and animals.

- Is light required for seed germination?
- Do magnets placed around a plant affect its growth?
- Compare the growth of plants grown in natural light versus artificial light.
- Can plants move? The responses of plants to stimuli such as light and gravity are called tropisms. Geotropism is the response of plant growth to the pull of gravity. Grow small plants in several pots. Lie one pot on its side, suspend one pot upside down (if you can keep the soil from falling out), and keep one plant upright. Does the direction of plant growth change? How long does it take to see a change?
- Grow seeds of one kind of plant in different kinds of soil. You might try sandy soil, enriched soil, and clay. In which kind of soil do the seeds sprout the fastest? Do the soils need to be watered at the same times? Are the results the same for other kinds of seeds?
- Collect cones from a variety of **conifers** (evergreen trees such as pines). Use a field guide to help you identify the trees that the cones came from. How are they the same? How are they different? Are all of the cones from the same tree identical? Explain your findings.
- How many different kinds of plants can you find in your neighborhood? Collect leaves and create rubbings using crayons or ink. Use a reference book to identify each kind of leaf. Before you begin, be sure you can identify poison ivy, poison

oak, and other leaves that contain irritants so you can avoid picking these!

- Can plants be grown without soil? Plant seeds in six small pots containing vermiculite, which can be purchased at lawn and garden stores. Moisten the vermiculite in three of the pots with water. To the other three pots add a chemical solution containing the essential nutrients required by the plant. This method of feeding plants is called **hydroponics**. Compare the growth of the plants in the two sets of pots.

- How does overcrowding affect plants? Sow some seeds thickly in a pot. In your control, sow the same kind of seeds thinly. Do not thin out the plants that sprout. Find out the percentage of seedlings in each group that die within a few weeks. Find out the average heights of the living plants. Compare the crowded plants with the plants that are well separated.

- How many different kinds of birds can you find in your neighborhood? Use a bird guide to identify each kind. Set up a feeding station. Keep a record of the kinds of birds that visit the feeder each day. Which of these birds do you see only in the winter? Which do you see for just a few days?

- Entomology is the study of insects. Bugs can be found in many places if you are looking for them. Watch a population of insects over a period of time. Do the insects perform different kinds of "jobs?" What kind of food do you see the insects collecting?

- Many scientists study genetics using fruit flies. You can do your own study of fruit flies. Put some fruit in a jar and place it outside on a day when the temperature is above 60°F (16°C). If you find fruit flies in the jar, cover the jar with a cloth held on with a rubber band. Study the reproduction of the fruit flies, the stages in the life cycle, and the way the number of the fruit flies in the jar changes. Try checking the flies' eye color using a magnifying glass. What is the ratio of flies with red eyes to flies with white eyes?

- Do you know what makes plants green? It is a pigment called chlorophyll. Remove the chlorophyll from a leaf by placing it in boiling water for two minutes (get an adult to help). Then put the leaf in a glass or jar containing rubbing alcohol and set the glass in a container of warm water. Check the glass after about an hour. The alcohol should be green. How does the leaf look now? What happens if you try this experiment in the autumn with a leaf that has changed color? Why do leaves change color in the autumn?

- The yeast used to make bread are living things, and like all living things, they must eat and give off waste products. Make an observation of yeast. Put a packet of dry yeast into warm water. Add a small amount of sugar and watch what happens over an hour. What happens if you change the temperature of the water? What happens if you add more sugar or no sugar? Use a microscope to observe the yeast cells more closely and make drawings of what you see.

Health and Fitness

- Your stomach produces hydrochloric acid, which helps digest food. Do this demonstration to see how acid helps the digestive process. Put vinegar in a jar and then place a chicken bone in the jar so it is totally submerged in the vinegar. Let the chicken bone sit in the jar for several days and then remove the bone and examine it. What changes have occurred? Repeat the experiment putting another chicken bone in a jar containing a cola soft drink. Does the cola contain an acid?

- Your eyes adjust to the amount of light available. This is called a simple reflex. To see this reflex, take a flashlight and shine it into a volunteer's eyes and observe what happens. Do the pupils get larger or smaller? Doctors use this simple eye test to see if the brain is functioning normally after a head injury.

- High blood pressure is a major health problem. Blood pressure is measured using a device called a sphygmomanometer, which can be purchased at any pharmacy. Learn to measure your blood pressure. Keep a record of your blood pressure and the blood pressures of your family members. Does blood pressure change during times of activity or stress?

How Cold Temperatures Affect Seed Germination

See For Yourself

Problem:
Do cold temperatures have an effect on seed germination?

Background:
A seed is a living thing, and under the right conditions it will begin to germinate, or sprout. In this experiment you will study the effects of cold on seed germination.

Materials:
Seeds (beans are a good choice), paper towels, three shallow bowls or petri dishes, and resealable plastic bags.

Procedure:
The time of this activity can vary from one to three months, depending on the time you have available.

1. Place about 100 seeds in each of three plastic bags and seal them. Place one bag in the refrigerator, one bag in the freezer, and one bag at room temperature.
2. At the end of one month, remove thirty seeds from each of the bags. Place the thirty seeds from one bag into a dish that contains moist paper towels. Be sure to label the dish. Repeat with the seeds from the other bags.
3. Keep the seeds at room temperature and check them every day to make sure the paper towels are moist but not soaking wet.
4. Monitor the seeds for a month (if necessary) and count the number of seeds that germinate in each group.
5. Record your findings. Did the seeds that were stored in the freezer germinate as well as the seeds that were stored at room temperature?

Going Further:
Repeat the experiments using another kind of seed. Are some kinds of seeds more sensitive to cold than others?

ROOM TEMP.

REFRIGERATOR

FREEZER

- What makes a person's pulse speed up? Take a friend's pulse several times under normal conditions. Have your friend exercise strenuously, and then take the pulse again. Does it quicken? Is there any way to slow down the pulse quickly? Can a person slow down the pulse by thinking relaxing thoughts? Try these tests on other friends. Show your findings on graphs or charts.
- Did you know that making a cake involves chemical reactions? What do the different ingredients in a cake made "from scratch" do? With the help of an adult, bake several small cakes, leaving out an ingredient (eggs, oil, or baking powder, for example) in each one. Visually examine and taste each cake and try to determine what each ingredient is needed for. Do not forget to bake a control cake with all of the ingredients.
- The body needs energy for all the activities it does in a day. The measure of how much energy a given food will provide when eaten is called a calorie. Most boys and girls need between 2,000 and 2,800 calories a day. Learn to read the nutrition labels on the foods you eat, and then keep track of the number of calories you eat and drink for one day.

PHILIP J. IMBROGNO
Science Department, Windward School
White Plains, New York

See also SCIENCE FAIRS.

EXPLORATION AND DISCOVERY

In the course of human history people have been driven to explore the unknown in order to discover more about the world in which they live. No one knows the names of the first explorers or what their discoveries were. Undoubtedly they were curious to know what was across the river or over the next hill. On occasion they must have had to search beyond their familiar territories to find more plentiful food supplies.

As civilizations advanced, the reasons adventurers set out to explore became more varied. Some sought shorter trade routes and valuable goods for commerce, such as gold, silver, precious gems, silks, and spices. Others sought glory for their nations or personal wealth and power. Some wished to teach their religion to other cultures. Still others wished to learn more about other lands and peoples, to find uncrowded living spaces, or to discover answers to scientific questions. Many were simply motivated by a desire to be the first to discover and explore unknown lands. Certainly most sought excitement and adventure. Today explorers continue to investigate new frontiers that include not only the earth but the universe beyond.

▶EXPLORATION BY ANCIENT CIVILIZATIONS

The earliest explorers were prehistoric people who sought fresh lands for hunting and living. Anthropologists believe that the human race first developed in East Africa. They think that hundreds of thousands of years ago people migrated from Africa through the Middle East and into Europe and Asia. Australia and the New World were only settled by humans much later—within the past 50,000 years.

The starting point for the history of exploration is the Old World. The ancient civilizations that developed on the shores of the Mediterranean Sea sent forth the earliest expeditions of which we have any record.

The Egyptians

As early as 2500 B.C., the Egyptians were sending their ships through the Red Sea to the mysterious land of Punt. Punt was a highly developed trading civilization that modern scholars believe was located along Africa's east coast, somewhere south of present-day Ethiopia. Little is known of the people of Punt, but they appear to have had ties with central Africa and Arabia.

Just as A.D. 1492 is a famous date in exploration, so too is 1492 B.C. In that year Egypt's Queen Hatshepsut dispatched an important expedition to Punt to resume the trade relationship that had fallen off. Her envoys (representatives) returned with gold, silver, ivory, and leopard skins, as well as wood and incense of the myrrh tree.

Portuguese explorer Ferdinand Magellan led the first successful expedition around the world. In 1520 he navigated his ships through the Strait of Magellan, a natural waterway connecting the Atlantic and Pacific oceans.

The Phoenicians

The Phoenicians were an ancient people who originally lived in cities along the coast of the eastern Mediterranean. Many historians think the Phoenicians were the first true explorers. They were fearless sailors fired with curiosity and the desire to expand their world.

By 1100 B.C., Phoenician ships were sailing all around the Mediterranean and Red seas, mostly to increase trade with other civilizations. Phoenician sailors ventured far north in Europe, visiting the British Isles, where they traded for tin from the mines of Cornwall. They also traded for amber from the shores of the Baltic Sea. Wherever they found a market for their goods, they established settlements. Phoenician colonies sprang up in Sicily and Sardinia as well as along the coast of Africa. Carthage, founded by the Phoenicians, became the most important city in northern Africa. They also settled in Cádiz, on the coast of Spain.

About 600 B.C., Phoenician ships may have sailed from the coast of the Red Sea all around Africa from east to west. Hanno (?–480 B.C.), a Phoenician navigator from Carthage, was probably the first person ever to sail out of the Mediterranean Sea through the Strait of Gibraltar into the Atlantic Ocean beyond. On the

This article describes selected discoveries of the earth's geographic regions over the course of human history. For more information on territorial exploration, consult individual articles on explorers (such as COLUMBUS, CHRISTOPHER); continents (such as AFRICA); and countries (such as PORTUGAL). For more information about exploring the world's oceans, consult the articles OCEANOGRAPHY and UNDERWATER EXPLORATION. For more information about exploring the universe, consult the article SPACE EXPLORATION AND TRAVEL.

Early seafarers, such as the Roman in this ancient mosaic, explored the Mediterranean Sea. Only the most daring ones ventured out into the Atlantic Ocean.

Atlantic coast of what is now Morocco, Hanno established seven Phoenician colonies. Many scholars believe that he also sailed along the Atlantic coast of Africa as far south as modern-day Sierra Leone. But the Phoenicians kept their discoveries a secret to prevent rivals and pirates from threatening their monopoly on trade with the new areas.

The Greeks

Like the Phoenicians with whom they competed for trade, the ancient Greeks were also great seafarers. With few exceptions, however, the Greeks were not as interested in discovering or exploring new lands.

Around 330 B.C., Pytheas (?–300 B.C.?), an explorer and geographer, became the first Greek to discover Britain. In an account of his voyages, he described the coasts of the British Isles as well as the Netherlands. Pytheas also discovered a land he called Ultima Thule, which was probably Iceland. He is credited with helping to prepare what were most likely the world's first accurate maps and navigational charts, which would allow other seafarers to repeat his voyages.

Two centuries later, around 100 B.C., a Greek mariner and merchant named Hippalus observed and described the pattern of monsoon winds in the Indian Ocean. Hippalus discovered that between May and October the winds blow steadily from the southwest and that between November and March they blow from the northeast. This information was of great importance to early mariners sailing the Indian Ocean between ports on the Red Sea and the Far East (Asia).

The Roman Empire

The Romans were far more practical-minded than the Greeks and the Phoenicians and did not really engage in exploration for its own sake. In building and maintaining their far-flung empire, however, some Romans did venture to the northernmost parts of Europe and into Asia as far as India. They maintained regular ties between the Mediterranean world and the British Isles, the farthest outpost of the Roman Empire.

▶THE VIKINGS AND THEIR VOYAGES

Around A.D. 800, several groups of Scandinavians (called Vikings, Northmen, or Norsemen) began a flurry of exploration, seeking both adventure and new homelands for their fast-growing population. They were expert seamen and set out in long, graceful, narrow, open boats called *knorrs* that could either be sailed or rowed.

The Vikings became great colonizers during the Middle Ages. They crossed the Baltic Sea into eastern Europe and founded colonies in what later became Russia. Crossing the North Sea, they settled in France in the province of Normandy and in the British Isles, where they were regarded as the Danish invaders. They even sailed into the Mediterranean and founded trading colonies in Sicily and Spain.

The Vikings then ventured farther out into the Atlantic than earlier sailors had dared to go. About 850 the Vikings colonized Iceland. A century later, around 982, Eric the Red (950?–1000?), a Viking leader exiled from Iceland, discovered Greenland and colonized its west coast. Using Greenland as a base, Viking mariners sailed farther west. Eric's son, Leif Ericson (975?–1020?), reached the shores of North America about the year 1000 and explored an area he called Vinland on the eastern coast of North America. There he founded a short-lived settlement.

No one knows just where the Viking settlement of Vinland was. Places ranging from Newfoundland to Virginia have all been suggested as possible locations. However, today it is generally thought that Vinland was somewhere along the coast of Newfoundland.

Old Norse sagas tell of the Vikings' bold adventures, and scientists and historians now recognize the achievements of Eric the Red, Leif Ericson, and their associates in exploring and colonizing the North Atlantic.

In the Middle Ages, many people undertook long, difficult journeys for religious reasons. Some of them wished to make pilgrimages to shrines in the Holy Land, in Rome, and elsewhere. Places associated with the apostles and saints were often focal points. Many of these early travelers were scholars who kept careful written records of their travels and provided lively, detailed accounts of their adventures and observations.

Still other religious travelers of the Middle Ages were monks and priests who sought to spread Christianity to new lands. A popular legend told of the voyage of St. Brendan (484–577), an Irish monk who sailed westward across the Atlantic and visited the coast of North America. In 1976–77, British adventurer and explorer Tim Severin built a replica of an ancient Irish craft and reproduced St. Brendan's voyage, proving that the old legends could, in fact, be true. Irish monks may have reached North America centuries before the Vikings did and almost a thousand years before Columbus.

The Crusades

At the Council of Clermont in 1095, Pope Urban II issued a dramatic call to Christians to take action against the Muslims in the Middle East, who were then in control of the Holy Land, where Jesus Christ had lived. Christian men, women, and children in Europe responded by launching the Crusades, a series of military campaigns and pilgrimages to win back the Holy Land from the Muslims. Many people participated and for many different reasons. Religious individuals went because they believed it was their duty as Christians to free the Holy Land from the Muslims. Ambitious nobles joined, hoping to win additional lands in the Middle East.

The Crusaders did not achieve most of their objectives. Eventually the Christian armies were forced out of the Middle East. Nevertheless, the Crusades affected the future development of exploration in several ways. The Crusades introduced or made popular in Europe many new ideas and goods, including pepper, lemons, muslin and damask cloth, glass mirrors, and even sherbet. In time the demands of Europeans for these and other useful goods from Eastern lands stimulated the search for sea routes to the East.

In 1275, Venetian merchants and explorers Niccolo, Maffeo, and Marco Polo visited the great Mongol emperor Kublai Khan at his court in the Chinese city of Cambuluc.

The Crusades reawakened European interest in all the lands that lay to the east. One of the earliest travelers to the Far East was Giovanni de Piano Carpini (1182?–1252?). In 1245, Pope Innocent IV dispatched Carpini, a Franciscan monk, as an emissary (agent) to the Mongols in Asia. Carpini started from Lyons in France and followed an overland route through Kiev in Russia. Passing north of the Caspian Sea he traveled across central Asia to the court of Genghis Khan at Karakorum in Mongolia. He covered the 3,000 miles (4,800 kilometers) on horseback in only 106 days. Carpini returned to Europe in 1247 with a lively account of his travels that aroused the interest of others, including the Venetian merchants Niccolo and Maffeo Polo, father and uncle of Marco Polo.

Marco Polo

Marco Polo (1254–1324) was a young Venetian who, with his father and uncle, spent more than twenty years in Asia. When they returned from their travels, they told such amazing tales that they were not believed.

Marco Polo's father and uncle first journeyed to the Far East in 1266. They were received in China by the Mongol chief, Kublai Khan, at his capital, Kaifeng. Three years later they returned to Venice with wonderful tales of Asian splendor. In 1271 they launched

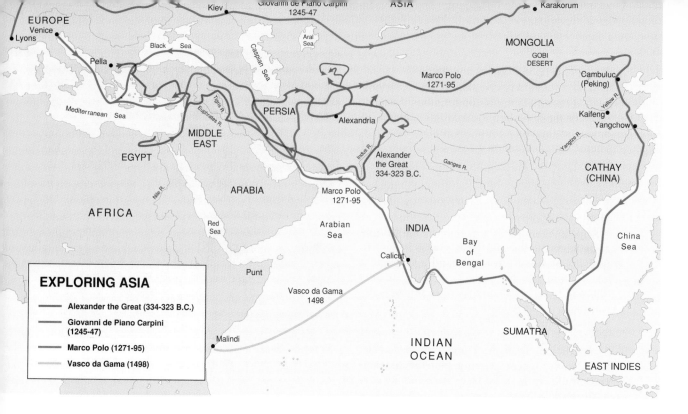

EXPLORING ASIA

—— Alexander the Great (334-323 B.C.)

—— Giovanni de Piano Carpini
(1245-47)

—— Marco Polo (1271-95)

—— Vasco da Gama (1498)

another expedition to the Khan's court, this time accompanied by the young Marco Polo and two Roman Catholic priests. At this time, the Khan's huge empire encompassed most of Asia, including both India and China.

In 1275 the Polos reached the Chinese city of Cambuluc, which is now Peking (Beijing). The Khan took a liking to young Marco and used him to conduct business in various parts of his empire. Marco was appointed ruler of the city of Yangchow for three years. After more than a 20-year absence, the Polos returned to Venice in 1295.

The next year, during a Venetian war against Genoa, Marco Polo was taken prisoner. He was held captive for two years, but he used this time to compose and dictate *Description of the World,* a book about his travels. The book described parts of the world virtually unknown in Europe at the time, including the Middle East, Persia (now Iran), Japan, Sumatra, and China. Polo had also traveled through many parts of eastern Africa and as far south as Zanzibar during his long absence from Venice. He vividly described the customs of the peoples he had observed and many products as yet unheard of in Europe, including gunpowder, coal, paper, paper money, and asbestos.

For almost six centuries, Marco Polo's book was Europe's main source of information about China and the Far East. Many parts of Asia visited by Marco Polo remained unexplored by other European travelers until the late 1800's.

Ibn Batuta

Europeans were not the only travelers and explorers of the late Middle Ages. Ibn Batuta (1304–77?), a Muslim, is thought to have covered more territory than any other traveler of his time. Many people consider him an Islamic equivalent of Marco Polo.

Beginning in his birthplace of Tangiers (in present-day Morocco), Batuta's travels took him across North Africa and through Syria to the Muslim pilgrimage capital of Mecca in Arabia. He explored much of the Middle East. He also traveled into the African interior as far as Timbuktu (in present-day Mali) on the Niger River. There he marveled at the order, wealth, and power of the Mali Empire and recorded all his observations in a lengthy account called the *Rihlah*. This narrative, discovered many years later by French explorers, contains remarkably accurate information on the geography and customs of the lands Batuta visited.

▶THE AGE OF EXPLORATION AND DISCOVERY

The Age of Exploration and Discovery, which began in the late 1400's and continued throughout the 1500's, was the greatest period of overseas exploration in the history of the world. This period occurred in the middle of the Renaissance, a period in European history when life took on fresh movement and vitality. The Renaissance spirit stirred people's curiosity about other lands and peoples and stimulated overseas exploration.

During this time, Portugal, Spain, England, and France emerged as proud national states. They began competing with each other for the rich resources and markets of foreign lands and began investing in overseas expeditions. However, the Turks, who conquered the important commercial city of Constantinople (present-day Istanbul) in 1453, stood between Europe and Asia. This fact encouraged Europeans to look for an all-water route to Asia. In addition, church leaders wanted to bring Christianity to peoples in foreign lands. Many explorers were more interested in converting people to Christianity than in finding gold, silver, and spices.

This 1543 map shows how much Europeans had learned about geography in the fifty years following Columbus' discovery of the New World. Two continents are missing —Australia and Antarctica, which had not been discovered. The mapmaker, Battista Agnese of Venice, shows Magellan's expedition around the world and the "Inca treasure route" across the Atlantic Ocean.

The Portuguese

The Portuguese court helped spark the Age of Discovery. Prince Henry the Navigator (1394–1460) was a great patron of exploration. In 1416 he established the Portuguese naval academies for the study of astronomy, geography, and navigation. He also encouraged Portuguese sailors to explore the west coast of Africa. Prince Henry himself was a stay-at-home adventurer. Still, he made major contributions to history by encouraging and financing voyages of exploration and developing the science of navigation. Unfortu-

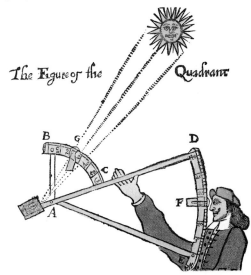

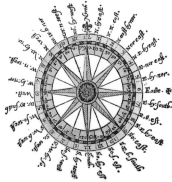

The quadrant (*top*) and compass card (*above*) were among the navigational instruments available to explorers during the Renaissance. Sailors used quadrants to determine their latitude, or distance from the equator. They used magnetic compasses to determine the direction in which they were traveling.

nately, Henry died before achieving his dream that someone would find a sea route to Asia by sailing around Africa.

King John II of Portugal hired Pedro de Covilhã (1450?–1526?) to explore various parts of the Middle East as well as Asia and Africa. Covilhã disguised himself as an Arab and acted as a secret agent in uncovering information about the rich spice trade in the East. His travels took him from Yemen to Calicut, India. He then investigated the city of Goa, which later became a Portuguese colony. He also spent time in Persia and Mozambique. He sent reports to the Portuguese monarch on the riches of the seaports he visited and on the navigational problems presented by the monsoon winds that blow across the Indian Ocean. But he never returned to Portugal. Covilhã's efforts helped Portugal extend its empire and to become a major sea power in the 1400's and 1500's.

In 1488, under the patronage of King John II of Portugal, Bartholomeu Dias (1450?–1500), a Portuguese navigator, became the first European to sail around the southern tip of Africa. He called it the *Cabo Tormentoso*, or Cape of Storms, but the king later renamed it the Cape of Good Hope. Dias' voyage opened up navigation to India by proving it was possible to sail around Africa.

Christopher Columbus Finds a New World

Christopher Columbus (1451?–1506), who was born Christoforo Columbo, was raised in the Italian port city of Genoa. He went to sea at an early age and made several lengthy voyages to Ireland, Iceland, the east coast of Africa, and various ports on the Mediterranean. He settled in Portugal after being shipwrecked there, became a mapmaker, and married a Portuguese woman.

Columbus believed the theory, then held by many scholars, that the earth was, indeed, round. Possibly encouraged by his reading of the Norse sagas and the writings of Marco Polo and others, Columbus became convinced that he could reach the Far East by sailing westward across the Atlantic.

Columbus spent seven years trying to get financial support for his venture. He appealed to the senate of his native city of Genoa, to the kings of Portugal and England, and to other wealthy people. Finally, on April 17, 1492, the king and queen of Spain, Ferdinand and Isabella, agreed to pay for the trip. They were eager to find a route to the Far East that was not already traveled by the Portuguese. A little more than three months later, on August 3, 1492, Columbus, a crew of about 120 men, and three small ships set sail from the Spanish port of Palos.

Columbus himself commanded the *Santa María*. The *Niña* was commanded by Vicente Yáñez Pinzón and the *Pinta* by Martín Alonso Pinzón. They stopped first in the Canary Islands. After a total of ten weeks at sea, the *Pinta*'s lookout, Rodrigo de Triana, sighted land at about 2 o'clock in the morning on October 12.

Columbus named this land—which is now believed to be Watlings Island in the Bahamas—San Salvador. Cuba was discovered on October 28, and the island of Hispaniola—now shared by the countries of Haiti and the Dominican Republic—was reached one month later. The *Santa María* was shipwrecked, but Columbus arrived back in Spain with the *Niña* and the *Pinta* on March 15, 1493, claiming, as he believed, that he had been to Asia.

When Columbus set out to find a westward route to the Indies, he had severely miscalculated the circumference of (distance around) the earth. Asia is twice as far away as he believed it was. Therefore, when land was sighted, he assumed he had reached his intended destination because he had sailed the expected distance.

Columbus made three additional voyages of discovery to the New World, reaching the islands of Puerto Rico, Dominica, Jamaica, and Trinidad as well as the coast of South America. During his last voyage, from 1502 to 1504, he explored portions of Central America and part of the Gulf of Mexico. His discoveries brought him fame and some wealth. However, Columbus never realized that he had found a new world. He died believing that he had merely discovered an unknown portion of Asia.

Today it is clear that Columbus was not the first European to cross the Atlantic and reach the Western Hemisphere. The Vikings and perhaps other mariners had preceded him. But in a very real sense, Columbus can be called the discoverer of the Americas, because his voyages were widely publicized and he was the first to open up the New World to further exploration, colonization, and development.

Spain and Portugal Divide the World Between Them

In 1493, Pope Alexander VI attempted to settle a territorial dispute between the kings of Spain and Portugal. On a map of the then-known world, he drew an imaginary line that ran from north to south through a point one hundred leagues (350 miles, or 560 kilometers) west of the Cape Verde Islands in the Atlantic Ocean. This line, known as the Papal Line of Demarcation, assigned each country a global region for Christian missionary work and played an important role in the future exploration of the Americas.

Christopher Columbus' four voyages to the New World (1492–1504) expanded people's knowledge of the earth's geography and opened up two new continents to European settlement.

The Papal Line of Demarcation barely touched on the east coast of South America. The Pope granted to Spain the right to claim any lands to the west of that line, which included almost all of the New World (although no one at the time yet realized this). Portugal was granted the right to claim all lands east of the line, including Africa, India, and the Far East.

The following year, in 1494, the Treaty of Tordesillas moved the Papal Line of Demarcation about another 1,000 miles (1,600 kilometers) to the west, which enabled Pedro Cabral to claim Brazil for Portugal when he discovered the territory six years later.

In 1529 the Treaty of Saragossa extended the Tordesillas treaty line around the globe. This line, which cut through Asia and Australia, clearly established the Spanish and Portuguese regions of influence in the Eastern Hemisphere. However, both treaty lines were largely ignored by explorers from other countries, such as Britain, Holland, and France.

Vasco da Gama Sails Around Africa to India

In 1497 the Portuguese navigator Vasco da Gama (1460?–1524) became the first European to reach India by sailing around the Cape of Good Hope at the southern tip of Africa.

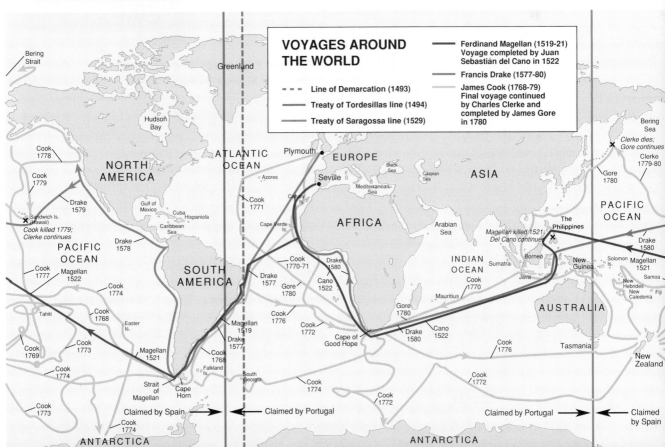

VOYAGES AROUND THE WORLD

- - - Line of Demarcation (1493)

— Treaty of Tordesillas line (1494)

— Treaty of Saragossa line (1529)

— Ferdinand Magellan (1519-21) Voyage completed by Juan Sebastián del Cano in 1522

— Francis Drake (1577-80)

— James Cook (1768-79) Final voyage continued by Charles Clerke and completed by James Gore in 1780

Manuel I of Portugal had commissioned the sea journey, which took more than two years to complete. Following Bartholomeu Dias' success in rounding the Cape of Good Hope and sailing part of the way up Africa's eastern coast, da Gama sailed from Portugal in 1497 with a fleet of four ships. He rounded the Cape of Good Hope and continued up the continent's eastern coast to Kenya. Da Gama then sailed eastward across the Indian Ocean to Calicut, a port city in India on the Arabian Sea. He returned to Portugal in 1499 with a rich cargo of pepper, ginger, cinnamon, cloves, and nutmeg, which were worth many times the cost of the journey. Unfortunately, many of his men died of scurvy (a disease caused by a lack of vitamin C) before reaching Lisbon.

Vasco da Gama's voyage had covered nearly 24,000 nautical miles (44,500 kilometers) and lasted two years. It was a remarkable feat of sailing. More important, it allowed the Portuguese and other Europeans to develop by sea the valuable trade in spices and other goods from India. In 1502, da Gama led a fleet of twenty ships on his second voyage to India and established Portuguese trading centers in India and along Africa's east coast. Portuguese merchants became rich dealing in spices and other luxuries as they sought to control navigation and trade on the Indian Ocean.

Ferdinand Magellan Sails Around the World

More remarkable than the expedition of Vasco da Gama was the voyage of Ferdinand Magellan's ships around the earth. Magellan (1480?–1521) was a Portuguese nobleman who made his great voyage for Charles I, the king of Spain. His goal was to discover a sea route to Asia and the Spice Islands by sailing southwestward across the Atlantic Ocean. In September 1519, he set out with five ships and a crew of 243 men.

Magellan relied on his compass, astrolabe, and navigational skill to guide his ships through the dangerous waters ahead. He crossed the Atlantic to Brazil, sailed down the east coast of South America and wintered at Port St. Julian. It was not always a quiet period. A mutiny had to be crushed, and one of the ships was wrecked in a storm. Finally, Magellan set forth again, searching for a strait, or passageway, through which his ships could pass around South America.

As he sailed farther south and moved farther away from the equator, storms, ice, and bitter-cold weather threatened the expedition. One of his ships deserted, but Magellan would not give up. At last he found a strait (now called the Strait of Magellan) and sailed through with his remaining three ships. It required 38 days to travel the roughly 350 miles (565 kilometers) from ocean to ocean.

The three remaining ships then sailed into the Pacific Ocean. The crew suffered many hardships. They drank bad water and ate wormy biscuits, rotting ox hides, and sawdust. Then scurvy attacked them. Joints swelled, and gums became spongy and bled so that eating any kind of food became torture. The sailors who died were buried at sea. At last, the survivors reached the islands known today as the Philippines.

There Magellan and a small group of his men became involved in a fight with the natives. Magellan was struck down and killed. His remaining men, led by Juan Sebastián del Cano continued the voyage home. Finally, in September 1522, almost three years after their departure, 18 men and one ship returned to Spain, having circumnavigated the earth.

Magellan's expedition remains one of the most remarkable feats of navigation of all time. As a result of this voyage, people at last had more accurate ideas about the earth's size and shape, the extent of the Pacific Ocean, and the placement of the continents.

The First Englishman to Sail Around the World: Sir Francis Drake

Sir Francis Drake (1540?–96) was the first Englishman to sail around the world. In 1577, more than 50 years after Magellan's voyage, Drake sailed from England leading a fleet of five vessels, including his flagship, the *Golden Hind*. He crossed the Atlantic to the coast of Brazil and then sailed southward, through the Strait of Magellan and up the west coast of South America, raiding Spanish settlements along the way. He continued on and sailed up the coast of North America, claiming the region of central California—which he named New Albion—for England. He then crossed the Pacific and Indian oceans and sailed up the west coast of Africa. He reached England in 1580, his ship laden with treasure. For his achievements, Queen Elizabeth I knighted him aboard the *Golden Hind*.

▶ EXPLORING NORTH AMERICA

After Columbus opened up the New World, many European explorers came to the Western Hemisphere to investigate the new lands. These expeditions can be classified in three broad categories: Spanish, British, and French. First came the Spanish expeditions, even though some of the explorers, including Columbus, were Italian-born.

The Spanish

Columbus, who had been sponsored by the king and queen of Spain, first sighted land in the New World in 1492. He later explored for Spain portions of the West Indies and Central America.

Numerous Spanish expeditions followed. In 1513, Juan Ponce de León (1460?–1521) discovered Florida and explored much of it, searching for the fabled Fountain of Youth. From 1520 to 1521, Hernando Cortés (1485–1547) conquered the Aztec Empire of Mexico and made the first thorough exploration of Mexico for Spain. About 1540, Francisco de Coronado (1510–54) also explored parts of Mexico and what is now the southwestern United States. During the same period, Hernando de Soto (1500?–42) explored much of what is now the southeastern United States

and became the first European to discover the Mississippi River.

The British

In 1497 a British expedition led by Italian John Cabot (1451?–98) explored eastern Canada. This was probably the first recorded European landing on the North American continent. More than a century later, Henry Hudson (?–1611) explored the Hudson River, now in New York state, and discovered Hudson Bay in northern Canada.

Much wilderness remained unexplored for the next 175 years. In the late 1700's, George Vancouver (1757–98) and Scottish explorer Alexander Mackenzie (1764–1820) explored large portions of northwestern North America.

The French

The French also sought to control territory in North America. One of the earliest French expeditions was led by the Italian mariner Giovanni da Verrazano (1485?–1528). In 1524 he sailed along North America's east coast between North Carolina and Nova Scotia.

Beginning in 1534, Jacques Cartier (1491–1557) made three voyages for France. In 1535 he explored the regions of Canada along the St. Lawrence River, later the center of the col-

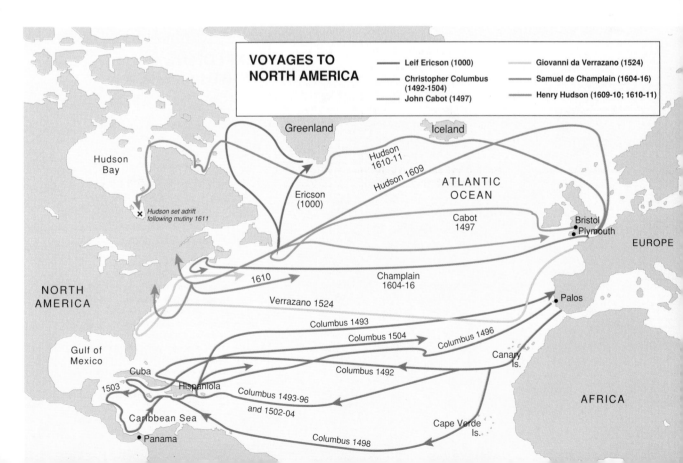

VOYAGES TO NORTH AMERICA

— Leif Ericson (1000)
— Christopher Columbus (1492-1504)
— John Cabot (1497)
— Giovanni da Verrazano (1524)
— Samuel de Champlain (1604-16)
— Henry Hudson (1609-10; 1610-11)

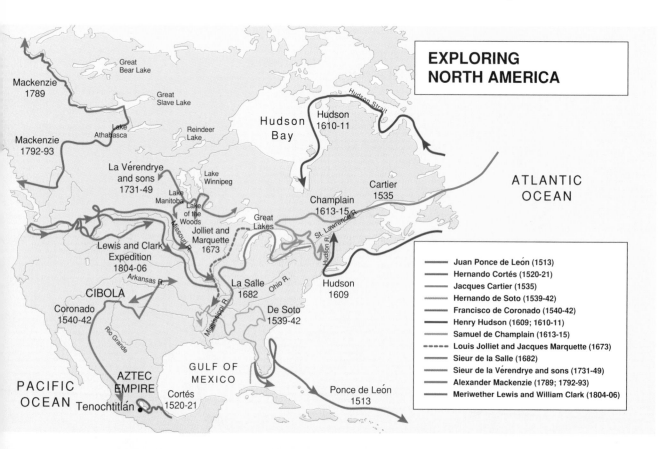

In 1673, French explorers Father Jacques Marquette and Louis Jolliet entered the Mississippi River from the Wisconsin River. They traveled as far south as the Arkansas River before being turned back by hostile Indians.

ony of New France. From 1605 to 1609, Samuel de Champlain (1567?–1635) explored much of the Atlantic coast of Canada. On later expeditions, Louis Jolliet (1645–1700), Father Jacques Marquette (1637–75), and Robert Cavelier, Sieur de la Salle (1643–87) explored the Mississippi River in what is today the midwestern United States. In the 1700's, Sieur de la Vérendrye (1685–1749) and his sons investigated central Canada.

In 1763, New France was taken over by the British following the French and Indian War, but the French influence remains strong in Canada to this day, particularly in the province of Quebec.

Americans Explore America

After the United States purchased the Louisiana Territory from France in 1803, Meriwether Lewis (1774–1809) and William Clark (1770–1838) led an expedition to explore it. From 1804 to 1806, under the guidance of Sacagawea (1787?–1812), an Indian woman, Lewis and Clark went up the Missouri River, over the rugged Rocky Mountains, and down the Columbia River to the Pacific Ocean. The Columbia River had been named by American explorer Robert Gray (1775–1806), who sailed into the mouth of the river in 1792 after completing a voyage around the world, the first under the American flag.

EXPLORING NORTH AMERICA

Mackenzie 1789
Great Bear Lake
Great Slave Lake
Hudson Strait
Hudson 1610-11
Hudson Bay
ATLANTIC OCEAN
Mackenzie 1792-93
Lake Athabasca
Reindeer Lake
La Vérendrye and sons 1731-49
Lake Winnipeg
Lake Manitoba
Lake of the Woods
Jolliet and Marquette 1673
Great Lakes
Champlain 1613-15
Cartier 1535
St. Lawrence R.
Missouri R.
Lewis and Clark Expedition 1804-06
Arkansas R.
La Salle 1682
Ohio R.
Hudson R.
Hudson 1609
CIBOLA
Coronado 1540-42
Mississippi R.
De Soto 1539-42
Rio Grande
PACIFIC OCEAN
AZTEC EMPIRE
Tenochtitlán
Cortés 1520-21
GULF OF MEXICO
Ponce de León 1513

- Juan Ponce de León (1513)
- Hernando Cortés (1520-21)
- Jacques Cartier (1535)
- Hernando de Soto (1539-42)
- Francisco de Coronado (1540-42)
- Henry Hudson (1609; 1610-11)
- Samuel de Champlain (1613-15)
- Louis Jolliet and Jacques Marquette (1673)
- Sieur de la Salle (1682)
- Sieur de la Vérendrye and sons (1731-49)
- Alexander Mackenzie (1789; 1792-93)
- Meriwether Lewis and William Clark (1804-06)

▶EXPLORING SOUTH AMERICA

It is not certain which European explorer reached South America first. Columbus explored portions of the northern coast on his third voyage to the New World. Amerigo Vespucci may have explored parts of the South American coast in 1499 and 1501. Pedro Álvares Cabral (1468?–1520) accidentally discovered Brazil in 1500 when he sailed off course on an eastward voyage to India. He claimed the territory for Portugal, according to the terms of the Treaty of Tordesillas (1494).

Early in 1516, Juan Díaz de Solís (1470?–1516) discovered the Río de la Plata, the great inlet between present-day Argentina and Uruguay. Another Spanish explorer, Francisco Pizarro (1470?–1541), explored the west coast of South America and conquered the Inca Empire of Peru between 1531 and 1533. Diego de Almagro (1475?–1538) led an expedition to conquer Chile in 1535. Pedro de Valdivia (1500?–1553) explored Chile from 1540 to 1547. In 1541, Francisco de Orellana (1500?–1549) reached the interior of South America. He investigated the length of the Amazon River and was the first explorer to cross South America from west to east.

For almost 200 years, little progress was made in exploring South America's interior. Major cities continued to develop along the coasts of the continent, but the dense forests and hostile Indian tribes of the interior regions discouraged investigation and settlement. The

WONDER QUESTION

Why was the New World named "America"?

The continents of the New World—North and South America—were named after Italian explorer Amerigo Vespucci. In 1507, German mapmaker Martin Waldseemüller mistakenly believed Vespucci had discovered the New World. Waldseemüller created a map and called the new lands ''America'' for Amerigo. Actually, Vespucci explored the coasts of South America for Spain (1499–1500) and Portugal (1501–04). He was the first person to recognize that South America was a continent, separate from Asia.

situation changed between 1800 and 1804, when Baron Alexander von Humboldt (1769–1859), the great German naturalist, investigated many areas of Central and South America. And from 1841 to 1843, British explorer Sir Robert Schomburgk (1804–65) surveyed Guyana and claimed it for Great Britain.

Aztec turquoise (*above*) and Inca gold (*right*) were among the Indian treasures plundered by Spanish invaders. By 1521, Cortés had conquered the Aztec Empire of Mexico, and by 1533 the Empire of the Inca of Peru had fallen to Pizarro and his forces.

EXPLORING SOUTH AMERICA

— Amerigo Vespucci (1499)

— Pedro Álvares Cabral (1500)

— Vasco Núñez de Balboa (1510-13)

— Juan Díaz de Solís (1516)

— Francisco Pizarro (1531-33)

— Pedro de Valdivia (1540-47)

— Francisco de Orellana (1541)

— Alexander von Humboldt (1800-04)

— Robert Schomburgk (1841-43)

On three separate voyages from 1768 to 1779, British captain James Cook explored the uncharted Pacific Ocean, where in 1778 he discovered the Hawaiian Islands. The following year, Cook (standing foreground) was killed there during a native uprising.

▶ EXPLORING THE PACIFIC OCEAN

The Pacific Ocean covers about 30 percent of the earth's surface. However, it was unknown to the European world until 1513 and was not fully explored for centuries. In 1513 the Spanish explorer Vasco Núñez de Balboa (1475–1519) discovered the Pacific when he and his followers marched the 40-odd miles (65 kilometers) across the Isthmus of Panama, a strip of land that separates the Atlantic and Pacific oceans.

Balboa had first come to the New World in 1501. He settled on the island of Hispaniola but fled to Panama in 1510 to escape creditors. Once in Panama, Balboa managed to seize control of the colonial government from his rival, Martini Fernandez de Encisco, whom he had beheaded.

Balboa managed to win the respect, support, and friendship of the native Panamanians. Many of them agreed to accompany his brigade on the difficult march across the narrow isthmus, tracing much the same route that builders of the Panama Canal would follow nearly four centuries later.

When Balboa and his men reached the shore of the ocean in 1513, he claimed the "Great South Sea" and all the lands washed by its waters for the king of Spain. In 1520, Magellan renamed the huge, unexplored body of water *Mar Pacifico* (Pacific Ocean), which means "peaceful ocean."

The Voyages of Captain Cook

Captain James Cook (1728–79) was perhaps the most distinguished explorer of the 1700's. More than 250 years after Balboa discovered the Pacific, Cook explored the ocean, where he sighted Antarctica, explored the coasts of New Zealand and eastern Australia, and discovered the Hawaiian Islands.

Cook joined the Royal Navy at the age of 27, after serving as a shipping apprentice in England. In 1759 he surveyed Canada's St. Lawrence River, and from 1763 to 1767 he was in a party that explored the coasts of Newfoundland and Labrador.

From 1768 to 1771, Cook made his first expedition to the Pacific Ocean in a research vessel called the *Endeavour*. His primary goal was to chart the path of the planet Venus in the night sky, but along the way he also explored the coasts of New Zealand and eastern Australia. After two years away, he returned to England by way of the Cape of Good Hope, having sailed around the world.

From 1772 to 1775, Captain Cook commanded the ships the *Resolution* and the *Adventure* on a voyage in the South Pacific. During this journey he explored the Antarctic Ocean and the New Hebrides Islands, and discovered New Caledonia.

In 1778, Cook discovered the Hawaiian Islands, which he named the Sandwich Islands after the Earl of Sandwich. Then, after searching unsuccessfully along North America's northwest coast for a route to the Atlantic Ocean, he returned to Hawaii where he was killed by natives during an uprising.

Cook was an organized adventurer. He kept detailed records of his observations in journals and took along artists to make paintings and drawings of the people, places, plants, and animals he encountered on his voyages. In addition, by enforcing strict dietary and sanitary codes, Cook kept his crew healthy and prevented them from developing scurvy, a constant threat on lengthy voyages when fresh fruits and vegetables were not available.

▶ **EXPLORING AUSTRALIA**

For centuries geographers and philosophers had thought that there was a great continent in the South Pacific. Sixteenth-century Portuguese and Spanish mariners in the Pacific actually claimed to have sighted a great southern continent, but the first reliable report of the sighting of Australia came from Willem Jansz (1570?–?) of Holland, who explored the northern coast of Australia in 1605 or 1606. Then in 1642, Abel Tasman (1603–59), also from Holland, discovered the island now known as Tasmania off the southern coast of Australia. He also explored part of Australia's coast, but the continent was left largely undisturbed for almost 100 years.

In 1699, William Dampier (1652–1715), an Englishman, explored Australia's northwestern coast, its waters, and nearby islands and declared the continent unfit for habitation. In 1770, Captain Cook explored the eastern coast and claimed it for England. In 1788, Captain Arthur Phillip was sent to Australia to establish a penal colony for convicts. The site he chose was called Port Jackson (present-day Sydney). In 1829, England claimed the entire continent and began establishing free colonies as well as additional penal colonies.

In the 1800's a number of adventurers from Great Britain explored various parts of the Australian continent for the first time. These included Robert O'Hara Burke (1820–61) and William John Wills (1834–61), who died of starvation in the attempt; Edward John Eyre (1815–1901); John McDouall Stuart (1815–66); and Charles Sturt (1795–1869). By crossing Australia from north to south and east to west, these explorers were able to map and describe the entire continent.

Breadfruit plants and kangaroos (*above* and *right*) were two of Captain Cook's discoveries on his first voyage to the South Pacific (1768–71). Artists on his ship, the *Endeavour*, made scientific drawings of the unusual plants, animals, places, and peoples they encountered.

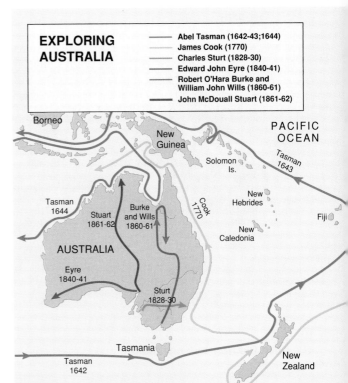

EXPLORING AUSTRALIA

—— Abel Tasman (1642-43;1644)
—— James Cook (1770)
—— Charles Sturt (1828-30)
—— Edward John Eyre (1840-41)
—— Robert O'Hara Burke and William John Wills (1860-61)
—— John McDouall Stuart (1861-62)

Borneo
New Guinea
PACIFIC OCEAN
Solomon Is.
Tasman 1643
New Hebrides
Fiji
New Caledonia
Tasman 1644
Stuart 1861-62
Burke and Wills 1860-61
Cook 1770
AUSTRALIA
Eyre 1840-41
Sturt 1828-30
Tasmania
New Zealand
Tasman 1642

►EXPLORING AFRICA

Because the Mediterranean Sea was not a barrier but a highway of trade and communication, the North African coast had been well known to the peoples of Europe since ancient times. It was the site of the highly advanced civilizations of Egypt, Carthage, and other early cultures. The ancient Romans may have penetrated the interior of Africa, but most of the continent south of the Sahara remained relatively unexplored by Europeans. Europeans called Africa the "Dark Continent" because they knew so little about it. Africa was considered a place of mystery, inhabited by exotic people and dangerous wild animals. Many parts of Africa were not explored by Europeans until the late 1800's, and some remote parts of the continent remain little known even today.

In 1364, French sailors are said to have founded colonies on the east coast of Africa and in the Canary Islands, off the northwest coast of Africa. Over the next four centuries, other African coastal settlements were established by explorers from Portugal, the Netherlands, and Great Britain.

In 1770, Scottish explorer James Bruce (1730–94) traveled to the source of the Blue Nile. Among the many 19th-century adventurers who explored and charted Africa's rivers, lakes, jungles, and mountains were Mungo Park (1771–1806) of Scotland, Richard Burton (1821–90) and John Speke (1827–64) of England, and Heinrich Barth (1821–65) of Germany.

Stanley and Livingstone

Perhaps the most famous of all the African explorers, however, were Scottish physician and missionary David Livingstone (1813–73) and American journalist Henry Morton Stanley (1841–1904). Between 1840 and 1873, Livingstone explored Africa, preached Christianity, and made several important discoveries. He crossed the Kalahari Desert and found Lake Ngami in 1849. He discovered the Zambezi River in 1851 and in 1853 traveled along it, crossing the African continent from east to west. Crossing back, he discovered Victoria Falls in 1855 and continued on to Mozambique on the east coast in 1856.

In 1859, Livingstone became the first British explorer to describe Lakes Chilwa and Nyasa in Malawi. On his final expedition, he returned to East Africa in 1866 to locate the source of the Nile. He explored Lake Tanganyika and was the first European to see Lakes Mweru and Bangweulu in the area that is now Zambia.

In 1869 the journalist Henry Morton Stanley was sent by an American newspaper, the New York *Herald,* to search for Livingstone after more than two years had passed with no news from him. In November, 1871, Stanley found Livingstone in a village near Lake Tanganyika and greeted him with the now-famous words, "Dr. Livingstone, I presume?" He and Livingstone explored Lake Tanganyika together until 1872, when Stanley returned to the United States. Livingstone died two years later in Zambia, and his body was shipped

Henry Morton Stanley, a newspaper reporter for the New York *Herald*, was sent to Africa in 1869 to look for Dr. David Livingstone. The British explorer had been "lost" for more than two years. In 1871, Stanley (center left) found Livingstone in Ujiji on Lake Tanganyika. His greeting was soon famous: "Dr. Livingstone, I presume?"

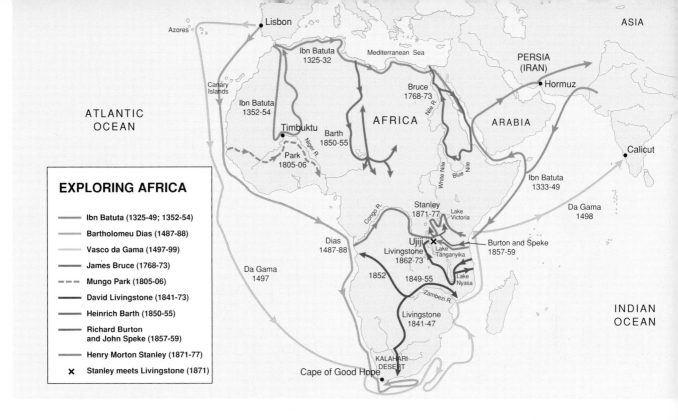

EXPLORING AFRICA

─── Ibn Batuta (1325–49; 1352–54)

········· Bartholomeu Dias (1487–88)

─── Vasco da Gama (1497–99)

─── James Bruce (1768–73)

- - - Mungo Park (1805–06)

─── David Livingstone (1841–73)

─── Heinrich Barth (1850–55)

─── Richard Burton
and John Speke (1857–59)

─── Henry Morton Stanley (1871–77)

✕ Stanley meets Livingstone (1871)

back to London for burial in Westminster Abbey.

Stanley returned to Africa in 1874, and in 1875 he explored Lake Victoria and Lake Tanganyika and then followed the course of the Lualaba and Congo rivers. In 1877 he became the first European to trace the Congo River to its mouth. He made two more expeditions to Africa, from 1879 to 1884 and again from 1887 to 1889. In 1889 he discovered the Ruwenzori range, called the "Mountains of the Moon," in east central Africa.

▶ **EXPLORING ASIA**

Since ancient times, European explorers were lured into exploring Asia by the promise of Asian luxuries—spices, silks, and precious stones. Under Alexander the Great (356–323 B.C.), the ancient Greeks had pressed as far east as Afghanistan and into India. More than a dozen centuries later, the Mongol king Genghis Khan conquered much of Asia and had even reached Europe. The peace and good will achieved between Europeans and Genghis Khan and his grandson, Kublai Khan, in the 1200's enabled the Venetian explorers Niccolo, Maffeo, and Marco Polo to journey through Asia in relative safety.

The discovery of new sea routes in the 1400's was made possible by advances in the science of navigation. By 1498, the Portuguese explorer Vasco da Gama had sailed to India; Russian cossacks penetrated northern Asia and Siberia and reached the Pacific Ocean by the mid-1600's; Portuguese, French, Dutch, and English groups founded the East India trading companies also in the 1600's and extended European influence in Asia. But many parts of the continent—especially the mountains and deserts of central Asia—remained unknown.

In the 1700's and 1800's, a reawakening of interest in science and exploration prompted Europeans to explore portions of Asia that were still virtually unknown, including the territories from Arabia to Siberia. Swiss explorer Johann Burckhardt (1784–1817) and Englishman Charles Doughty (1843–1926) explored the Middle East, including Arabia. A Russian, Nikolai Przhevalski (1839–88), explored central Asia continuously from 1867 to 1885, filling in many gaps in the world's knowledge of that territory. In the 1800's, French explorer Marie Joseph François Garnier (1839–73) explored China, as did German explorer Baron Ferdinand von Richthofen (1833–1905), whose travels led to the publication of the first accurate atlas of that country.

In 1906, Norwegian explorer Roald Amundsen completed the first successful voyage through the Northwest Passage, an Arctic water route connecting the Atlantic and Pacific oceans. In 1911 he again distinguished himself by leading the first expedition to reach the South Pole.

▶ **EXPLORING THE POLAR REGIONS**

Soon after European explorers first ventured into North America, they began exploring the Arctic regions, searching for speedier sea routes that would link East to West—connect the Atlantic and Pacific oceans.

The Northeast Passage

The Northeast Passage is a water route through the icy Arctic waters north of Europe and Asia. It extends from the North Sea in Europe along the Arctic coast of Europe and to the Bering Sea and the Pacific Ocean. The Northeast Passage was sought by many European explorers: by Englishman Sir Hugh Willoughby (1500–54) and Dutchman Willem Barents (1550–97) in the 1500's; Englishman Henry Hudson in the 1600's; and Danish explorer Vitus Bering (1680–1741) in the 1700's. All tried but failed to find the passage.

The first successful passage through the Northeast Passage was made by Baron Nils Adolf Erik Nordenskjöld (1832–1901) of Sweden in 1878–79. He sailed eastward along the northernmost coast of Russia and through the Bering Strait. Clogged with ice for most of the year, the passage is navigable only from June through September unless icebreaker ships are used. The Russians later mapped, explored, and made the Northeast Passage into a regular shipping route. Today the passage is still used by the shipping industry, but the development of air commerce has greatly diminished its importance.

The Northwest Passage

The Northwest Passage is a route through the Arctic waters north of the North American continent. European sailors hoped that such a passage would reduce the time and danger of sailing all the way around the southern tip of South America.

Many navigators searched for the Northwest Passage in the 1500's and 1600's, including Englishmen Sir Martin Frobisher (1535?–94), Henry Hudson, and Sir John Franklin (1786–1847). Franklin actually came within a few miles of discovering the passage on an expedition from 1845 to 1847. He is sometimes credited with being its discoverer, even though his expedition met with a tragic end when he and his entire crew disappeared. Remains of their campsites were found in 1930.

Finally, the Norwegian Roald Amundsen (1872–1928) became the first to successfully navigate the passage on a herring boat named the *Gjoa*. The voyage, which took three years (1903–06), ran through Lancaster Sound and then south and west to the Beaufort Sea and Bering Strait.

Reaching the North Pole

In addition to finding northern water routes, explorers sought to reach the northernmost point on earth—the North Pole. This feat was finally accomplished by American Commander Robert Edwin Peary (1856–1920) on April 6, 1909, after more than eleven years of attempting to cross the icy landscape. In 1926 the American pilot (later Admiral) Richard E. Byrd (1888–1957) claimed to have made the first flight over the North Pole. On March 17, 1959, the U.S. nuclear submarine *Skate* surfaced through the ice at the North Pole.

Antarctica and the South Pole

Antarctica, the body of land surrounding the South Pole, is the world's fifth largest continent. Captain Cook, who sailed within the Antarctic Circle, first sighted Antarctica during his second Pacific voyage from 1772 to 1775. From 1819 to 1821, Russian Admiral Fabian von Bellingshausen (1778–1852) commanded the first expedition to sail around Antarctica. In 1823, Englishman James Weddell

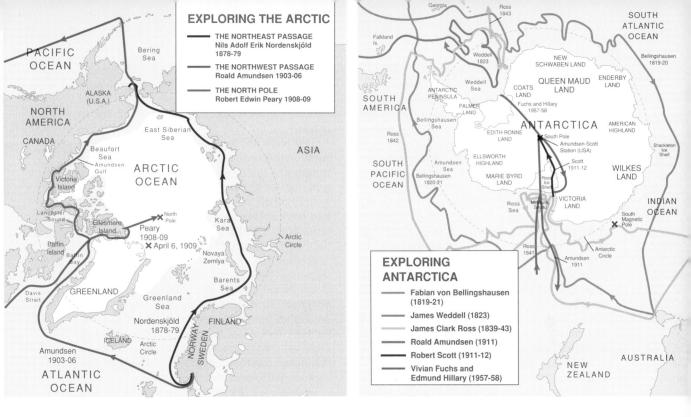

(1787–1834) sailed through the floating ice masses that border Antarctica and discovered the body of water that now bears his name, the Weddell Sea.

In 1839, Sir James Clark Ross (1800–62) led a British expedition to find the South Magnetic Pole. (He had discovered the North Magnetic Pole in 1831.) Ross stayed on to explore Antarctica until 1843.

In the early 1900's, Englishmen Robert Scott (1868–1912), Sir Ernest Shackleton (1874–1922), and Douglas Mawson (1882–1958) made epic journeys to Antarctica that greatly advanced our knowledge of the continent. On December 14, 1911, Roald Amundsen, the first person to sail the Northwest Passage, also became the first person to reach the South Pole. Traveling by dogsled and on skis, Amundsen won the race to the South Pole, reaching it just five weeks before Robert Scott reached it in January 1912. Tragically, Scott and his men perished in a storm on their return journey just a few miles short of their base camp.

After World War II (1939–45), scientific exploration of Antarctica began to accelerate. New Zealand explorer Sir Edmund Hillary (1919–) and Englishman Sir Vivian Fuchs (1908–99) in particular were active in Antarc-

tic exploration. Today scientific stations operated by many nations continue explorations in Antarctica, seeking information about weather and climate, plant and animal life, and the geology of the region.

▶ **EXPLORING THE OCEANS**

The surface of the world's oceans has been relatively well known for more than the past hundred years. But fully 70 percent of the earth's surface lies underwater, and until recently this vast undersea world has remained unexplored.

Underwater exploration began in ancient times. The Greek philosopher Aristotle (384–322 B.C.) wrote of divers who descended 100 feet (30 meters) to retrieve sponges. However, it was not until 1819 that the diving suit and helmet were invented, enabling divers equipped with air tubes to plunge to new depths. Underwater construction workers, salvagers, and pearl fishers welcomed these inventions. In fact, oceanography, the study of oceans and marine life, is now possible because of the development of specialized vessels and equipment.

The era of manned exploration of great ocean depths began in 1934 when Americans William Beebe (1877–1962), and Otis Barton descended to a record depth of 3,000 feet (915 meters) in a bathysphere designed by Barton. The bathysphere was a round, watertight observation chamber made of steel and equipped with windows. It could be lowered to the bottom of the sea, enabling divers to observe the plant and animal life there.

In the 1940's the Swiss scientist Auguste Piccard (1884–1962) developed the bathyscaphe. The bathyscaphe is a deep-sea diving apparatus equipped with a steel observation chamber that can descend without a cable to great depths. A lead-weighted balloonlike chamber that is filled with a fluid lighter than water (often gasoline) is used to raise and lower the bathyscaphe. In 1960 a bathyscaphe descended 35,800 feet (10,910 meters) to explore the Challenger Deep of the Mariana Trench in the western Pacific Ocean, the deepest known spot on earth.

After World War II, modern aqualungs, or scuba equipment, were developed by the great French environmentalist and oceanographic explorer Jacques-Yves Cousteau (1910–97). This greatly improved equipment enabled divers to descend safely to points on the ocean floor. Cousteau and his research ship *The Calypso* became legendary. For more information, see the biography of Jacques-Yves Cousteau in Volume C.

More recent underwater research vessels, called submersibles, are similar to small submarines. They can carry crews of two to six people, cameras, and scientific equipment to investigate the ocean floor at depths of up to 13,000 feet (3,950 meters). In February, 1986, submersibles were called in to search for the remains of the space shuttle Challenger. That same year a submersible investigated the wreckage of the luxury liner *Titanic*, which had been submerged for over 70 years under more than 2 miles (3 kilometers) of water in the North Atlantic Ocean.

Knowledge of the ocean is important to shipping, fishing, defense, and communications. Naval and commercial oceanographic programs drill cylindrical core samples from the ocean floor and analyze them for mineral content. Naval oceanographic research teams have also established temporary stations on the ocean bottom, to test the ability of humans to withstand underwater life.

Undersea exploration has enabled scientists to chart large areas of the ocean floor; they have prepared contour maps that show that it is even more varied than dry land. In addition, scientists have found there many strange and exotic forms of sea life as well as important deposits of oil, minerals, and other valuable resources.

French oceanographer Jacques Cousteau was a pioneer of underseas exploration. He helped develop scuba-diving equipment and built the first underwater diving station.

EXPLORING SPACE

The Space Age began on October 4, 1957, when the Soviet Union launched earth's first artificial satellite, *Sputnik I*. On January 31, 1958, the United States launched its first satellite, *Explorer I*. Until that time scientists had used telescopes to collect information about the stars, planets, moons, and other celestial bodies of the universe. Scientists today can explore space with much more sophisticated types of equipment, including artificial satellites, space probes, and spacecraft.

In recent years, space probes equipped with cameras and other instruments have landed on the moon, Venus, and Mars. *Voyager 2* had flyby encounters with Jupiter (1979), Saturn (1981), Uranus (1986), and Neptune (1989). The U.S. Mariner program made important studies of Venus and Mars in the 1960's. Exploration of Mars continued in the 1970's when the U.S. *Viking* unmanned spacecraft landed on the surface of the planet in 1974. In the early 1980's the Soviets successfully landed several *Venera* spacecraft on the surface of Venus. In 1989 the United States launched a planetary probe, the *Magellan*, also to explore Venus.

The era of manned space exploration began with the orbital flight of the Soviet cosmonaut Yuri Gagarin (1934–68) on board *Vostok 1* on April 12, 1961. The U.S. Mercury program began in 1960. On May 5, 1961, Alan Shepard (1923–98) became the first American astronaut in space on a Mercury *Freedom 7* flight that lasted only 15 minutes. On February 20, 1962, John Glenn (1921–) circled the earth three times in less than 5 hours on the *Friendship 7*. In 1965 the first missions involving more than one astronaut were attempted by both the American and Soviet space programs. The first active docking of two spacecraft in space was accomplished in 1966.

In 1961, President John F. Kennedy committed the United States to the goal of landing a person on the moon by the end of the decade. The *Apollo 11* spacecraft was launched on July 16, 1969, from the National Aeronautics and Space Administration (NASA) Center at Cape Kennedy (now Cape Canaveral) in Florida. Four days later on July 20, 1969, Neil Armstrong (1930–) and Edwin Aldrin (1930–) became the first astronauts to walk on the surface of the moon. The command module *Columbia*, manned by Michael Col-

The most exciting event in the history of space exploration was the landing of men on the moon. On July 20, 1969, American *Apollo 11* astronauts Neil Armstrong and E. "Buzz" Aldrin (shown here) collected data from the moon's surface. Astronaut Michael Collins remained in lunar orbit. The crew returned to earth on July 24th.

lins (1930–), remained in orbit around the moon. The *Apollo 11* mission and five later Apollo flights all returned safely to earth with samples of lunar rock and a large amount of scientific information.

From the start of the Space Age, the United States and the Soviet Union were the leaders of space exploration. In 1977, the United States launched the first space shuttle, designed to carry people and equipment into orbit and return to earth. With the breakup of the Soviet Union in 1991, the Russians scaled back their space efforts. Canada, Japan, and several European countries have set up their own space agencies, which have cooperated with Americans and Russians on several projects, including the International Space Station.

Space exploration is only in its infancy. The moon is the only place outside the earth that people have actually visited. But there is the whole solar system—with its planets, asteroids, and moons—not to mention the entire universe waiting to be explored.

A PARTIAL LIST OF SOME OF THE WORLD'S MOST FAMOUS EXPLORERS

Explorer's Name	Homeland	Date(s)	Major Accomplishments
Alexander the Great	Macedon	300's B.C.	Conquered much of the Middle East and Asia
Amundsen, Roald	Norway	1903–06; 1911	Discovered the Northwest Passage; first person to reach the South Pole
Armstrong, Neil	United States	1969	First person to walk on the Moon
Balboa, Vasco Núñez de	Spain	1513	Discovered the Pacific Ocean
Bering, Vitus	Denmark	1727–29	Explored Arctic region
Byrd, Admiral Richard E.	United States	1926; 1929	First to claim to fly over the North Pole; first to fly over the South Pole
Cabot, John	Genoa (Italy)	1497	Claimed North American territory for England
Cartier, Jacques	France	1535	Explored the St. Lawrence River in Canada
Champlain, Samuel de	France	1605–09; 1613–15	Explored the Atlantic coast of Canada; explored the Ottawa River and Lake Ontario
Clark, William	United States	1804–06	Explored American northwest with Lewis
Columbus, Christopher	Genoa (Italy)	1492–1504	First Age of Discovery explorer to discover the New World; explored islands off the east coast of North America
Cook, Captain James	England	1768–79	First to sight Antarctica and explore Pacific
Coronado, Francisco	Spain	1540's	Explored southwestern North America
Cortes, Hernando	Spain	1520–21	Conquered the Aztec Empire of Mexico
Da Gama, Vasco	Portugal	1497–99	First Age of Discovery explorer to sail around Africa to India and back
De Soto, Hernando	Spain	1539–42	Explored southeastern North America
Drake, Sir Francis	England	1577–80	First Englishman to circumnavigate the globe
Ericson, Leif	Greenland	1000	First European to land in North America
Eric the Red	Norway	982	Discovered and colonized Greenland
Gagarin, Yuri	Soviet Union	1961	First person to orbit the earth
Hudson, Henry	England	1609–11	Discovered the Hudson River and Hudson Bay
Jolliet, Louis	France	1673	Explored the Mississippi River with Marquette
La Salle, Sieur de	France	1669–71; 1682	Explored the Ohio Valley; explored the Mississippi River
Lewis, Meriwether	United States	1804–06	Explored American northwest with Clark
Livingstone, David	Scotland	1840–73	Explored much of the African interior
Mackenzie, Alexander	Scotland	1789–93	First European to cross Canada, east to west
Magellan, Ferdinand	Portugal	1519–22	Led first successful expedition to circumnavigate the globe
Marquette, Father Jacques	France	1673	Explored the Mississippi River with Jolliet
Nordenskjöld, Baron Nils	Sweden	1878–79	Discovered the Northeast Passage
Peary, Commander Robert E.	United States	1909	First person to reach the North Pole
Pizarro, Francisco	Spain	1531–33	Conquered the Empire of the Incas of Peru
Polo, Marco	Venice (Italy)	1271–95	Explored Asia and met Kublai Khan
Ponce de León, Juan	Spain	1513	Explored Florida, looking for Fountain of Youth
Ross, Sir James Clark	England	1831; 1839–43	Discovered the North Magnetic Pole; explored Antarctica
Stanley, Henry Morton	United States	1870's–1880's	Located Livingstone and explored Africa
Vancouver, George	England	1791–94	Explored northwestern Canada and Pacific coast
Vespucci, Amerigo	Florence (Italy)	1499–1504	Explored the coasts of South America

Consult the index for biographies of these and other explorers.

▶ TODAY'S FRONTIERS

Before the 1900's, explorers searched for new lands, but today it seems there are few places left to discover. However, there are many frontiers that we still know little about. We have much to learn about the world's mountains, caves, grasslands, deserts, rain forests, and polar regions. Exploration of the world beneath the ocean is still in its infancy. Space exploration has barely begun. There are many secrets of the universe that have yet to be discovered. And the human desire for adventure, knowledge, and even fame will continue to lure people to explore and discover more of the world around them.

CASS R. SANDAK
Author, *Explorers and Discovery*

See also NAVIGATION; SPACE EXPLORATION AND TRAVEL; UNDERWATER EXPLORATION; and articles on individual countries, continents, and explorers.

EXPLOSIVES

Explosives play a part in everyday life long after they have been used. For example, highways, railroads, and waterways carry food, materials, and manufactured products to distant parts of the country. All these—the highways, the railroads, the waterways, and many of the products they carry—were produced with the help of explosives.

Huge rocks are blasted to make way for highways and railroads. Underwater rocks are removed by explosives to make waterways safe for ships. Explosives are used to mine the many minerals we need. Trucks and trains carry food grown on land cleared with the help of explosives. The land is irrigated by dams that were built with the help of explosives. In the city, explosives are often used to dig foundations for buildings.

▶ WHAT IS AN EXPLOSIVE?

An explosive is a chemical or mixture of chemicals that, upon burning, produces a sudden, violent burst of gas that expands with great force. The heat of the explosion makes the gas expand to great size in less than a second. In an explosion, rapidly expanding material pushes aside and breaks anything in its way. The noise of an explosion is the result of the air being moved away.

Different kinds of explosives explode at different speeds and with different amounts of force. When the fuse of a firecracker is lit, it burns until the flame reaches the explosive powder inside. Then the firecracker explodes. But if the same amount of powder were heaped on the ground and lighted, it would simply burn with a flash. If the powder burns in the open, the gas that is formed escapes. In a firecracker, however, the gas is held in by the paper shell until enough gas is formed to burst it.

Most explosives burn and form gas so quickly that there is an explosion whether the gas is held in or not. However, they are usually sealed up anyway to make the explosive work better. Dynamite, for example, can burn ten times as fast as gunpowder. This extra-fast burning is so different from regular burning

A large building is quickly and safely demolished through use of carefully planned explosives. The building collapses inward, causing no damage to nearby property.

that scientists give it a special name: **detonation**. Fast-burning, detonating explosives, like dynamite, are called **high explosives**. The slower-burning ones, like gunpowder, are called **low explosives**. High explosives are much more powerful than low explosives.

▶HISTORY OF EXPLOSIVES

Black Powder. Many historians give the Chinese credit for inventing the first explosive —a kind of gunpowder—about A.D. 600. It is thought that gunpowder reached Europe in the 1200's from the Far East by way of the Middle East. One of the first Europeans to mention a kind of gunpowder known as black powder was the English scientist Roger Bacon (1214?–92?).

Although Europeans knew about black powder by the 1200's, it was a long time before anyone realized how useful it could be. Guns were being manufactured in the early 1300's. But it was not until the 1600's that people began using gunpowder for such purposes as mining. In 1627 black powder was used to blast rock in a mine in Schemnitz, Hungary (now Banská Štiavnica, Slovakia). Shortly after that it began to be used in tin mines in England.

Early settlers in America needed gunpowder in order to hunt food and to protect themselves on the frontier. Because they could not always be sure of getting powder from Europe when they needed it, they soon began making it themselves. The first black powder mill in America was built in 1675.

While gunpowder had been important for centuries, its use was limited to war, hunting, and mining until the early 1800's.

The Industrial Revolution brought a need for better transportation. Roads and railroads were built in many countries. In many places roadways had to be blasted out of solid rock. Canal building called for more blasting. The growing mining industry demanded a large supply of explosives. Gunpowder manufacturing became a big business.

Two discoveries in the 1800's made blasting even more popular. One was the invention of the "miner's safety fuse" in 1831 by William Bickford of England. A fuse was originally a length of slow-burning cord that led into a charge of black powder. When the flame reached the powder, it went off. But fuses of this type did not burn evenly. Users could

Never touch anything that looks like an explosive. If you find anything that looks like these explosives, report it immediately to the police or fire department.

never be sure how long a fuse they needed for safety. Mines were often too damp for a cord fuse to burn in, so miners would set off their charges by trails of gunpowder sprinkled on the ground or by straws or paper tubes filled with powder. These were even more uncertain than a cord fuse and caused frequent accidents, which resulted when the charge went off too soon. Bickford's fuse always burned at the same speed. Users could always be sure of how long a fuse to use in order to give them time to get away.

In 1857, the American inventor Lammot du Pont discovered that black powder could be made by using sodium nitrate instead of potassium nitrate. This formula became widely used because it delivered more energy at a lower cost.

Nitroglycerin. The history of modern high explosives began in the 1800's with the manufacture of cellulose nitrate, or guncotton (so named because it was made from cotton). Then, in 1846, Ascanio Sobrero, a chemistry professor at the University of Turin in Italy, discovered a chemical compound called nitroglycerin. Although nitroglycerin was a powerful explosive, it was almost useless because its strange behavior was not understood. It was very sensitive and often exploded accidentally. Yet it sometimes failed to explode when it was supposed to.

The Swedish inventor Alfred Nobel, donor of the Nobel Prizes, solved the problem. He discovered that nitroglycerin could always be made to explode if it were set off by a **detonator**. A detonator, or blasting cap, is a small metal tube about 1⅛ to 5 inches (3 to 13 centimeters) long. It contains explosives that are easily set off by the heat from a burning safety fuse, or from an electric current sent through special electrical wires. Blasting caps are dangerous to handle. They are powerful enough to blow off fingers. **If you find a blasting cap, do not touch it. Call a police officer, fire fighter, or sheriff.**

Dynamite. Even after Nobel discovered how to use nitroglycerin, many people did not use it because it was too dangerous. It could be set off by a slight jar. Because it was a liquid, it was difficult to ship. Many accidents occurred while it was being shipped.

Nobel solved this problem, too. In 1866 he discovered that nitroglycerin could be controlled by mixing it with a claylike material called kieselguhr. This mixture was a solid. It was easy to handle, and it was not so likely to explode accidentally when dropped or jarred. It was called dynamite.

The new explosive was a big success. Soon Nobel's factories were making thousands of tons of it a year.

▶ MAJOR TYPES OF EXPLOSIVES USED TODAY

Modern research has produced many different explosives. Some of these are used only for military purposes. Other kinds are used for blasting rock in mining and construction operations.

Low Explosives

Most explosives in use today are high explosives, but black powder, a low explosive, is still used. The use of black powder today is limited to the manufacture of safety fuses, fireworks, igniters for cannon powder, hand loads for rifles and shotguns, and similar specialty applications.

High Explosives

Nitroglycerin is hardly ever used by itself because it is difficult to handle. It is used to make various forms of dynamite. But explosives that do not contain nitroglycerin have replaced dynamite for many uses. Instead of nitroglycerin, most explosives used today contain large amounts of ammonium nitrate. Ammonium nitrate is the same material that farmers use to fertilize their crops. The ammonium nitrate is mixed with other chemicals to produce safe and low-cost explosives.

Blasting Agents. Ammonium nitrate is also the most important ingredient of blasting agents. Blasting agents cannot be exploded by means of sparks, a safety fuse, or even a blasting cap. They can be exploded by use of a high explosive charge, such as a stick of dynamite. This high explosive charge is called a **primer**. The primer, in turn, needs a detonator to set it off.

Water-Based Explosives. In recent times, a new family of explosive products has found a large and expanding market. Chemicals that burn and chemicals that supply oxygen are

Explosives come in many forms. *Top:* A worker loads sticks of dynamite into a mine wall. *Bottom:* This water gel explosive is poured from a truck into a hole drilled in the ground.

Large, powerful explosions are used in road building and surface mining. *Right:* Rock is blasted to clear a path for a new road. *Below:* At a surface mine, a worker fills holes in a layer of coal with an explosive. When the explosive is detonated, broken chunks of coal can then be loaded into trucks and hauled away.

dissolved or mixed in water to make explosives that are much safer to make and use than dynamite because they contain no nitroglycerin. These materials are called **slurries**. The two types of slurries, **water gels** and **emulsions**, are made by different manufacturing processes. Water-based explosives have taken over much of the market formerly served by dynamite.

Present-day Forms of Dynamite. The kieselguhr in Alfred Nobel's original dynamite was replaced long ago with more effective ingredients. These include small particles of materials that can burn (such as wood, starch, and nut shells) and chemicals that supply oxygen (usually ammonium nitrate and sodium nitrate). Nitroglycerin is added in an amount of 10 to 30 percent to obtain the desired explosive properties, density, and plasticity. Dynamite can vary from a loose powder to a gelatinous material that looks like bread dough.

Military Explosives. Explosive weapons are used extensively during war. Most military explosives are too expensive for commercial use. They must meet the special requirements of military service, for which commercial explosives do not qualify. For example, they must remain stable even when exposed to extreme temperature changes. And they must not explode when subjected to impacts such as those that occur when an artillery shell is fired from a gun.

Military explosives usually are known by initials—probably because their real names are long and complicated. Important military explosives include TNT (trinitrotoluene) and

RDX (cyclonite). Mixtures of these explosives are used to fill bombs, warheads, torpedoes, mines, and artillery shells. Some military explosives are combined with other explosives and waxes to produce what are popularly known as plastic explosives. "Plastic," as used here, means "easily molded or shaped." It does not mean that these explosives are made of plastic.

▶ USE OF EXPLOSIVES

Many industries use explosives in many different ways. Explosives are extremely efficient and helpful tools. For example, many of the minerals used in the construction of automobiles, homes, factories, and roads are mined with explosives.

Explosives in Mining

Today the mining industries use most of the explosives that are made. In fact, the coal industry alone is the largest user of explosives in the world.

In underground mining, explosives are used to break off large pieces of coal or ore. These pieces are then broken up into smaller pieces by machines.

Coal or ore is strip-mined when it is very close to the surface of the ground. Explosives are used to blast away the unwanted rock on the surface so that the coal or ore can be dug up easily.

Metals such as copper, iron, aluminum, gold, and silver could not be mined without explosives. Minerals used to make cement, concrete, glass, and gypsum board are also mined with explosives.

Explosives in Construction

Although most people do not realize it, large, growing cities use explosives almost every day. The only easy way to make large holes in solid rock is to use explosives. Foundations for tall buildings—and sometimes even small houses—are dug with the help of explosives.

Experts must use great care when using explosives near buildings and people. Many small explosions are used instead of a few big ones. Before the explosives are detonated, the ground is covered with large woven steel nets called **blasting mats** to protect people and buildings against flying rock.

Large buildings can be torn down with relatively small amounts of explosive carefully placed to destroy basement supports. Experts can collapse a building into its own basement without harming the neighboring buildings.

Many types of tunnels are built with the aid of explosives. New York City's subway trains travel through many miles of tunnels that were cut through solid rock. This was done mostly with explosives. It was done so carefully that people on the street did not even know that anything was going on underneath them. In areas where rock is near the ground surface, explosives are used to blast trenches for water and sewer lines.

Without explosives, road and highway systems could not be built in mountainous areas. When roads are being built in such areas, great masses of rock must often be cleared away to lessen the need for sharp curves and steep grades. Explosives again are employed to do the job.

Explosives on the Farm

Explosives are a very helpful tool to farmers. They can save farmers a great deal of work. For example, after cutting down trees on a piece of land that is to be farmed, the farmer must remove the tree stumps. It is much simpler to blast them than dig them out. Large rocks can be broken down in the same way. By setting off small explosions in a row, a farmer can dig a ditch with much less work than by other means.

Finding Oil with Explosives

One way of finding out what is under the ground is to drill a hole and study the material that the drill brings up. But this is very expensive. Scientists can obtain a great deal of information on the underlying rock structure and on the possible location of oil deposits by **seismic prospecting**. This kind of prospecting involves creating vibrations and then studying how the vibrations are bent and reflected by different layers of underground rock. The vibrations can be made by setting off an explosion. They are recorded by a machine called a **seismograph**.

FRANK A. LOVING
E.I. du Pont de Nemours and Company
Reviewed by CALVIN J. KONYA
Author, *Surface Blast Design*

See also FIRE; FIREWORKS; FUELS (Solid Rocket Fuels); NITROGEN; NOBEL, ALFRED.

EXPRESSIONISM

The art movement known as expressionism flourished in the early 1900's. Expressionist artists turned away from representing scenes and objects realistically. Instead, the artists tried to reveal their inner feelings through their art. The subjects they chose to paint were often unsettling, frightening, or even grotesque. Their painting techniques, too, were designed to arouse an emotional response in the viewer. Distorted shapes, vivid colors, and twisting or swirling lines were frequently used to show strong emotion.

Much art throughout history has had expressionist qualities. This is especially true of primitive and folk art, medieval religious art of Germany and other areas of northern Europe, and some romantic art of the early 1800's. However, modern expressionism did not begin until the 1880's. The Dutch artist Vincent van Gogh was among the first to state

The swirling lines, vivid colors, and disturbing subject of *The Scream* (1893), by Norwegian artist Edvard Munch, are characteristic of expressionist art.

expressionist goals. He said that he deliberately exaggerated nature to "express . . . man's terrible passions." In *The Starry Night* (1889) and other works, agitated brush strokes and looming shapes express Van Gogh's emotional suffering and inner turmoil. At about the same time, other artists, notably the Belgian James Ensor and the Norwegian Edvard Munch, used similar techniques to create works of great emotional intensity.

About 1905 the first modern expressionist groups began to form. In France, a group of artists led by Henri Matisse used bright, intense colors and bold but flat shapes in a way that was expressive rather than realistic. Their highly untraditional approach led critics to call them *les fauves* ("the wild beasts"), and their particular expressionist style became known as fauvism. In Germany, a similar group called *Die Brücke* ("The Bridge") was formed by Ernst Ludwig Kirchner and other artists.

A second group of German expressionists, *Der Blaue Reiter* ("The Blue Rider") was organized in 1911. It included Franz Marc and the Russian artist Wassily Kandinsky. Gradually, some of the Blaue Reiter artists moved from painting recognizable images to painting colors and shapes that suggested feelings and moods but did not represent any real object. This kind of painting is called **abstract expressionism**. Other notable expressionist artists were Georges Rouault of France, Paul Klee of Switzerland, Oskar Kokoschka of Austria, and Max Beckmann and Emile Nolde of Germany.

The expressionist movement also extended to literature and music. The plays of the Swedish dramatist August Strindberg, the fiction of the German-Czech writer Franz Kafka, and the music of the Austrian composer Alban Berg are all characterized by disturbing subject matter, intensity of emotion, and the expression of inner states of mind.

Expressionism faded as a unified movement after World War II. But its goals and techniques continued to have a strong influence on modern art. In the United States and much of Europe, abstract expressionism, in particular, became one of the most important art movements of the later 20th century.

Reviewed by HOWARD E. WOODEN
Director Emeritus
The Wichita Art Museum

See also GERMANY, ART AND ARCHITECTURE OF; MODERN ART.

EXTINCTION

Would you like to ride on a dinosaur's back, pet a woolly mammoth, or hold a saber-toothed kitten in your arms? Unfortunately, such things are possible only in the movies, because all of these animals are extinct. A species of plant or animal becomes extinct when its last living member dies. And once it has become extinct, that species will never be found alive on Earth again. Extinction lasts forever.

▶ WHAT CAUSES EXTINCTION?

Species of plants and animals may become extinct if changes occur in their environment, although change does not always cause a species to die out. If the environment changes slowly, the species may be able to adapt or to move away, allowing it to survive. For example, if the world's climate were to cool slowly, causing glaciers to spread out from the polar regions, plants and animals could migrate toward the equator, where the climate is warmer. Or individuals with warmer fur might be able to survive, and the species could then adapt to the cooler climate. However, if the environment changes too much or too quickly, the species may not be able to migrate or adapt. In that case, extinction may result.

▶ RATES OF EXTINCTION

Most species that have ever lived on Earth are now extinct. Extinction is thus very common, but it usually occurs at a very low rate. That is, only a small number of species become extinct at any one time.

However, there have been times during the history of the Earth when a large number of species have become extinct within a short period of time (a few million years at most, which is short in comparison to the age of the Earth). These episodes of rapid extinction of many species are known as mass extinctions. They are studied in detail by paleontologists, scientists who study the fossil remains of these species.

At five different times during the history of the Earth, episodes of mass extinction have killed off at least three-fourths of all species alive at that time. Paleontologists refer to these episodes with the names of the geological time periods in which they occurred. The five largest mass extinctions occurred at the ends of the periods known as Ordovician (440 million years ago), Devonian (365 million years ago), Permian (250 million years ago), Triassic (205 million years ago), and Cretaceous (65 million years ago).

The Ordovician and Devonian mass extinctions affected mostly marine invertebrates such as trilobites and corals. The mass extinction at the end of the Permian Period came very close to wiping out all life on

Scientists study fossil evidence to determine why mass extinctions occurred. Fossils of a trilobite (*above*), a marine animal, and a diplomystus (*right*), a relative of the modern herring, are remains of two species that died out millions of years ago.

Earth. Only about 4 percent of all plant and animal species, on land and in the sea, survived this extinction. The Triassic and Cretaceous extinctions also affected both sea and land animals, including the dinosaurs, which disappeared at the end of the Cretaceous.

▶ STUDYING EXTINCTION

Finding out what caused a particular extinction is like solving a murder mystery. Clues can be found by comparing the kinds of species that became extinct with those that survived. For example, if most of the species that became extinct lived in warm climates, this might suggest that cooling climates killed off these species. Scientists also look for clues in the rocks that formed during the time of the extinctions.

Cretaceous rocks, for instance, have provided clues that led some scientists to suggest that dinosaurs (and other animals and plants that became extinct at the same time) were wiped out by a giant meteorite impact. These rocks contain a layer of clay that is rich in the element iridium, which is common in meteorites. Some mineral grains in these rocks show that they were involved in a great explosion, such as would happen if a meteorite collided with the Earth. Evidence of a huge crater has even been found in the Yucatan Peninsula of Mexico.

If a huge meteorite did strike the Earth, it would have blasted dust (ground-up rock) into the atmosphere. The dust would have kept sunlight from reaching the Earth, so that plants could not grow. Animals that ate plants (and animals that ate those animals) would also be affected. Other effects of an impact include acid rain, wildfires, and climate change.

Not all scientists agree that a meteorite impact caused the Cretaceous extinctions. The Cretaceous was also a time of large volcanic eruptions, and volcanoes can cause some of the same effects as a meteorite impact. Scientists continue to study the Cretaceous mass extinction, as well as the other mass extinctions. Many possible causes of these extinctions have been suggested, among them a cooling climate for the Ordovician and Devonian extinctions and sea level and ocean chemistry changes for the Devonian, Permian, and Triassic. Evidence is still being collected to test these theories.

▶ THREATS OF EXTINCTION TODAY

It may seem surprising, but one of the greatest mass extinctions in the Earth's history is happening right now. Thousands of species are disappearing each year because of the activities of humans. Species that are in immediate danger of dying out are known as endangered species.

By converting forests to farms and building roads and houses, humans destroy the habitats of many plants and animals. This process, called deforestation, drives out native species. And if its habitat disappears completely, a species becomes extinct. Between 1973 and 1988, more than half a million square miles (about 1.5 million square kilometers) of land were deforested in developing countries around the world. This is roughly equal to the areas of Spain, France, and Germany.

Hunting also causes extinction. The dodo bird and passenger pigeon were both hunted to extinction. Some whale species came close to the same fate. Even today, animals such as the black rhinoceros, elephant, and some parrots are hunted or captured illegally, threatening their survival.

Extinctions may also occur when humans introduce new species to areas where they do not live naturally. Animals and plants brought to new areas can kill or drive out native species. For example, cats and rats introduced to islands have caused the extinction of many species of ground-nesting birds that had no defense against these predators. Sometimes the diseases or parasites brought by new species do just as much harm.

Pollution is another human-caused threat to the survival of some species. Oil spills and toxic chemicals harm waterways and coastal areas. Smokestack emissions and automobile exhausts add pollutants to the air, causing acid rain. Environmental damage caused by pollution can pose a serious threat to species that cannot move away or adapt.

It is estimated that between 18,000 and 55,000 species become extinct each year because of the factors described here. If these rates are accurate, we are currently experiencing a mass extinction comparable to the largest extinctions in Earth's history.

PATRICIA H. KELLEY
University of North Carolina at Wilmington

THOR A. HANSEN
Western Washington University

EXTRASENSORY PERCEPTION (ESP)

Ordinarily the information we get about the world around us comes to us through our five senses: sight, hearing, smell, taste, and touch. Most scientists feel that these are the only routes by which we can get information.

But what about the following case: A husband and wife were at the theater. Suddenly the woman told her husband that they must go home immediately, because their son had just hurt himself seriously. When they arrived home, they found that their son had indeed been hurt, but the family doctor had taken care of it. The baby-sitter had decided not to spoil the parents' evening by phoning the theater. Or, consider this case: A young man, Willis, was very close to his grandfather who lived in another state. One night Willis struggled awake, hearing his grandfather's voice calling his name. Opening his eyes in the strangely bright bedroom, he saw an image of his grandfather smiling at him. Startled, Willis put on the light. The clock showed 1:10 A.M. At 6 that morning Willis' brother phoned with the sad news: Grandpop had died during the night, just after 1 A.M.

Perhaps you have heard stories like these and have wondered how the woman could have known about her son, or how Willis could have seen his grandfather. It seems unlikely that they could have obtained that information through the regular senses.

Scientists, too, have wondered about these experiences. In the 1930's, J. B. Rhine, a psychologist at Duke University, invented the term extrasensory perception (ESP) to describe this unusual manner of obtaining information. "Perception" is the act of becoming aware of something, and "extrasensory" means "without or outside the senses." Thus ESP means obtaining information without using our normal senses.

Does ESP exist? If it exists, how does it work? These questions are the starting point for the science of **parapsychology**, a term meaning "beyond psychology." While psychology deals with the mind, parapsychology deals with the mind and with the more unusual occurrences it may experience, such as ESP. Initially, most parapsychologists started as psychologists, but today ESP research is done by physicists and engineers as well.

▶ESP IN HISTORY

Belief in ESP is as old as recorded history. Ancient Greeks consulted oracles—persons who were believed to be able to give information about future events or events in a distant land. In the Middle Ages, alchemists (early chemists) sought ways to use ESP. Francis Bacon (1561–1626), often called the father of the scientific method, devoted part of a book to ESP experiments. He felt that what many regarded as superstitious or magical would eventually be understood as something "clean and pure natural."

This feeling was shared by the scientists and scholars who, in 1880, founded the Society for Psychical Research in London. An American branch followed shortly, but it was not until the 1930's, when Rhine established the Parapsychology Laboratory at Duke University in North Carolina, that parapsychology became a legitimate topic for research and debate on the university campus. Today ESP research goes on at laboratories and universities around the world.

▶ESP IN THE LABORATORY

As you read the examples above, you probably realized that it would be difficult to build a science on such stories alone. Memory and ordinary perception are not that reliable. Perhaps the mother's hunch was just that—a hunch—but over the years she had forgotten the times she had run home on a hunch and found no problem. Maybe Willis' experience was just a vivid dream, and he was not really sure of the time, but his memory shaped the event into something that seemed more important to him as a way of helping him deal with his sadness. It is certainly possible that the events really did happen as reported, but scientists would never be able to tell without exhaustive investigations of each case.

Realizing this, Rhine developed laboratory experiments of ESP that could be repeated and used by other scientists. His technique was simple. He devised a set of special cards that were similar to ordinary playing cards except that each had one of five symbols on it: a cross, a square, wavy lines, a circle, or a star. There was nothing magical about the shapes; they were just easy to tell apart and easy to remember. A standard deck of "ESP cards" consisted of five of each symbol, for a total of 25 cards.

With the cards hidden from view, a person would try to guess the symbols. By just guessing, a person has a one-in-five chance of being correct on any card. Purely by chance a person should average five correct guesses per pack. But, when a person does considerably better than five correct guesses per pack and does this for hundreds of tests, Rhine reasoned that the person must somehow be getting information to help identify the hidden cards. This information, he thought, must come through ESP.

Not everyone was willing to accept Rhine's claim that his experiments had demonstrated ESP. Some scientists argued that perhaps the subjects were unconsciously getting clues to the card's identity through things like reflections on shiny surfaces or accidental whispers by the experimenter. But Rhine and his colleagues were able to show that these suggestions could not explain the results of many of his experiments, and Rhine's team went on to conduct successful experiments where the subject was separated from the cards by great distances.

The Duke researchers identified three types of ESP. When a subject seemed to be obtaining the information from another person's mind, it was called **telepathy**. Sometimes persons would guess cards that nobody was looking at, and this was called **clairvoyance**. Finally, in some cases a person could guess the order of cards in a deck that only later would be shuffled and assigned to that test. This last type of ESP—seeing into the future—was called **precognition**. In practice researchers have found that it is difficult to separate these categories, so today they often use the term GESP (for general ESP) to refer to any type of ESP.

In time, ESP research spread from Duke to many other laboratories. Researchers began to design experiments that were more like real-life ESP experiences. In the 1960's, researchers at Maimonides Medical Center in Brooklyn, New York, conducted a long series of experiments that demonstrated that ESP could influence the dreams of some individuals. While a subject slept and dreamed in an isolation room, an agent, elsewhere in the building, tried to communicate by ESP the contents of an emotionally and visually rich picture or slide set. Later analyses of the dreams revealed that often the subjects incorporated elements of the target picture into their dreams.

While similar work continues today, other scientists have added a new twist. In recent experiments specially ''gifted'' subjects try to view—by ESP—a distant location. An agent will visit one of a large number of possible target sites, while back at the laboratory the subject is asked to describe or sketch the scene that comes to mind. Some subjects have proved to be remarkably successful in these tests. Some of this research, known as remote viewing, has been funded by U.S. government agencies.

▶ **A CONTROVERSIAL SCIENCE**

Although microcomputers and other high-technology electronics have replaced cards in the laboratory, ESP research remains controversial. Hundreds of successful ESP experiments have been conducted, but still parapsychologists cannot design an experiment that will allow any scientist, even a skeptical one, to demonstrate ESP in his or her laboratory. For this reason, many scientists simply do not trust experiments conducted by parapsychologists—there are just too many ways that an experiment can go wrong and give misleading results. It may not seem fair to parapsychologists, but whenever one group of scientists makes an unusual claim—and ESP is a very unusual claim—other scientists will demand very strong evidence.

Another problem is that scientists have not yet developed a theory that would help us understand how ESP fits in with the findings of other branches of science. In science it is possible that a new finding will be accepted on the basis of a single experiment if there is a good theory to explain the results. But because there is no such theory of ESP, the experimental findings remain isolated from mainstream science.

Polls of scientists have shown that most are willing to keep an open mind about ESP, but only a much smaller number—about 20 percent—are willing to say that it is an established fact. For the present, ESP research must remain on the controversial frontier of scientific understanding.

RICHARD BROUGHTON
Director of Research
Institute for Parapsychology
Foundation for Research on the Nature of Man

EYE

Our eyes are perhaps our most important sensory organ. In a single glance, eyes provide us with countless pieces of information, such as the size and shape of objects, colors, distance, and movement. A person without sight cannot read a newspaper, drive a car, watch a movie, catch a ball, or do many other things that people with sight can easily do.

Although it takes no effort to open your eyes and look around you, ''seeing'' is actually a complex process.

▶WHAT IS SIGHT?

Eyes, nerve fibers, and the brain are the three components needed to produce sight. The eyes alone cannot see anything without a brain to interpret the images and without nerve fibers to relay the messages.

Sight begins when light enters the front of the eye by passing through the clear **cornea** and **lens**. These structures bend the rays of light to focus an upside-down image onto the **retina**, the lining at the back of the eyeball. The retina contains specialized cells that are sensitive to light. When light strikes these cells, they send a message along the **optic nerve** that leads from the eye to vision centers in the brain. In the brain the messages are interpreted, and we see.

Because our eyes point forward, a similar image of our surroundings is formed in each eye. These two images are combined in the brain, providing us with binocular vision. (Binocular means ''two eyes.'') Binocular vision gives us information about how far away objects are. This ability to sense distance is called **depth perception**.

Some animals, such as most birds, have eyes on the sides of their heads. Each eye sees different images. Such animals have good side vision and can see larger areas than we can, but they do not have good depth perception. (A person who loses sight in one eye does not have depth perception either.)

▶STRUCTURES SURROUNDING THE EYE

Our eyes are very delicate. For protection each is located in a deep cavity in the skull called the eye socket, or **orbit**. A pad of fat surrounds the eye and cushions it from direct contact with the socket. Connected to the back of the socket and to the surface of the eyeball

Eyes provide so much information that they may be our most important sensory organ. Eyeglasses, like those shown here, correct eye defects and improve sight.

are six eye muscles, called **extraocular muscles**. Their job is to keep the eyes working together by pointing them both toward the same object at the same time.

Also inside each eye socket is the **tear gland**. This gland produces tears, which keep the surface of the eye moist. When something irritates the eye or when we experience strong emotion, the gland produces extra tears, and we cry. Attached in front of the eye at the rim of the socket are the eyelids. When they blink, they sweep the surface of the corneas and keep them clean. Eyelashes, which grow from the eyelids, help keep dust out of the eyes.

▶PARTS OF THE EYE AND HOW THEY WORK

The eyeball is nearly round and about the size of the ball used for table tennis. Its outer surface is a tough protective layer made up of the **sclera** and the **cornea**. The sclera is white and forms most of the outer surface at the sides and back of the eye. Attached to the sclera at the front of the eye and bulging slightly is the clear cornea. The cornea's curved shape bends light rays and helps direct them toward the back of the eye.

Just inside the sclera lies the **choroid** layer.

The eye from the front

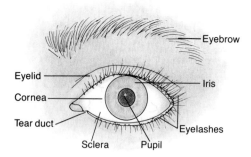

How the eye moves

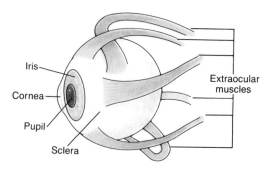

At the back of the eye, this layer contains many blood vessels that nourish some parts of the eye. Near the front of the eye, the choroid layer contains the ring-shaped **ciliary body** containing the **ciliary muscle**. This muscle automatically focuses the lens when looking at objects close up or far away.

Part of the choroid forms the colored **iris**, which is visible through the clear cornea. The amount of pigment in the iris gives eyes their color. The circular opening in the center of the iris is the **pupil**. All light passes through the pupil before going further into the eye.

The amount of light entering the eye can be controlled by changing the size of the pupil. This is done by two muscles in the iris. One muscle is made up of many spokes, extending outward away from the pupil. In dim light, this muscle automatically contracts, opening the pupil wider and letting in more light. The other muscle is close to the pupil and is shaped like a ring. In bright light, this muscle contracts to make the pupil smaller, thus reducing the amount of light entering the eye.

The lens is a clear, rubbery structure located behind the iris and pupil. It is held in place by thin fibers, called **zonules**, connected to the ciliary body. Changing tightness of the zonules alters the shape of the lens and causes it to focus on near or far objects. The process of focusing the lens in the eye is called **accommodation**. The lens is responsible for about one third of the focusing power of the eye. The remaining focusing occurs in the cornea.

The retina makes up the inside surface at the back of the eye. This layer contains two types of **photoreceptors**, or light-sensitive cells. These are the **rods** and **cones**.

Rods are slender, rod-shaped cells that work best in dim light. Cones are tapered and cone-shaped cells. They work best in bright light and allow us to see fine detail. The pres-

Inside the eye

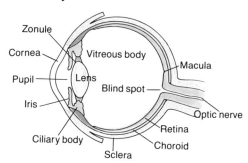

ence of three different types of cones, which are especially sensitive to red, green, or blue light, allows us to see color. A retina contains about 120 million rods and about 7 million cones.

When light reaches the rods and cones, it is absorbed by a light-sensitive chemical in the cells, called **visual pigment**. This triggers a message that passes through the back of the retina to a nerve cell called a **ganglion cell**. Each retina contains about one million ganglion cells. Each ganglion cell has a long nerve fiber that leaves the eye in the optic nerve. Through the optic nerve, the nerve impulses move out of the eye and into the visual centers of the brain. There the pattern of nerve signals from the eye is interpreted as sight.

The most important vision region of the retina is a small depression at the back of the eye called the **macula**. The macula contains about 50,000 cones and no rods. We use the macula for all detailed vision when we look directly at an object. You are using the macula now as you read these words.

In the back of the eye where the optic nerve is located, a small section of the retina is missing. Because this area contains no photorecep-

FOCUSING ON AN OBJECT

When a person with normal vision looks at an object, an upside-down image of the object falls directly on the retina. If the eyeball is too short or too long, a clear image falls behind or in front of the retina. When this happens the person is either farsighted or nearsighted. Eyeglasses or contact lenses cause the image to fall directly on the retina so the person sees clearly. The upside-down image is then interpreted by the brain and turned right side up.

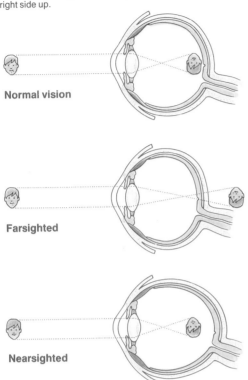

Normal vision

Farsighted

Nearsighted

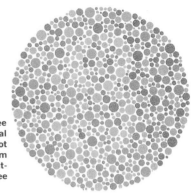

Some people do not see colors in the normal way. Often they cannot distinguish red from green. Look at this pattern of dots. Can you see a number?

tors, light striking this part of the retina cannot be seen. This area is called the **blind spot.**

A jellylike substance called the **vitreous body** fills the large cavity between the lens and the retina. Its job is to press the retina against the choroid.

The cavities at the front of the eye, on both sides of the iris, are filled with a watery fluid called the **aqueous humor.** This clear fluid is rich in nutrients and takes over the function of blood to nourish the lens and cornea.

▶ DISORDERS OF THE EYE

The most common disorders that affect our eyes are problems in the focusing power of the cornea and lens. These problems are often easily corrected with eyeglasses or contact lenses.

In a person with nearsightedness, also called myopia, the focal point of the eye is in front of the retina instead of directly on it. This results in the inability to focus clearly on distant objects, such as words on a blackboard or

traffic signs. In farsightedness, also called hyperopia, the image is focused behind the retina. This results in the inability to focus clearly on objects close up, such as words on a page.

As people get older, their lenses become less rubbery and cannot focus easily. This condition, called presbyopia, is one of the reasons why some people with good vision when young need glasses in middle or old age.

A person with astigmatism has an unevenness in the surface of the cornea. This causes a portion of an object to be in focus and the remainder of the object to be out of focus.

Infections sometimes develop in and near the eye. Conjunctivitis is an infection of the moist tissues surrounding the eye. A stye is a swelling in the eyelid caused by an infection of a small oil gland.

Cloudy areas in the lens, called cataracts, can develop in older individuals. The cloudy lens can be removed and replaced by a clear plastic lens.

Glaucoma is a disease caused by high pressure inside the eye. The pressure builds up because fluid drainage from the eye is blocked. Unless treated, continued pressure can damage the optic nerve, causing blindness.

Strabismus is a condition in which the eyes are crossed, or not directed toward the same object. It is caused by a defect in the extraocular muscles. It may be corrected by surgically shortening or lengthening one of the muscles early in life.

Night blindness is the loss of sight in dim light. It is usually caused by not eating enough foods containing vitamin A. Color blindness is an inherited disorder caused by the absence of one of the three cone cell types. People who are color-blind usually cannot distinguish between red and green, but some people see no color at all—only black, white, and shades of gray.

▶PROTECTING OUR EYES

Because eyes are delicate structures and can be injured easily, special care must be taken to protect them. Flying debris, such as wood chips from a saw, filings from a grinding wheel, or small sticks and stones thrown by a lawn mower, can severely damage the eyes. Always wear protective goggles whenever you are near these kinds of hazards.

Goggles also should be worn to protect the eyes when playing certain sports. In racquetball, for example, the ball is small enough to go under the eyebrow and hit the eye.

Intense light can severely damage the eyes. Never look directly at the sun. This can destroy the macula. Looking directly at black (ultraviolet) light may also damage the eye.

If dust or debris gets onto your cornea or inside your lid—and blinking will not remove it—do not rub your eye. Rubbing may cause the debris to scratch the cornea. Ask an adult for help. The debris should be removed gently with the edge of a soft tissue. *Never* use a sharp object for this purpose. Sharp objects should never be used near the eyes.

If you think you may not see as well as your friends, have your eyes checked. You may need glasses. An ophthalmologist or an optometrist can check your eyes. An ophthalmologist is a medical doctor (M.D.) who will test your eyes and can also treat all eye disorders, diseases, or injuries. An optometrist is trained to fit eyeglasses and contact lenses but is not a medical doctor. If you already have glasses, wear them and have them checked regularly.

JOE G. HOLLYFIELD
Author, *The Structure of the Eye*
See also BLINDNESS; LENSES.

EZRA

Ezra was a Jewish priest and scribe who lived in Persia (now Iran) in the 400's B.C. As a scribe, he studied the Torah (the first five books of the Bible's Old Testament) and explained its meaning to the Jewish people. But Ezra did much more than that. His story is told in the Bible in the books of Ezra and Nehemiah.

During Ezra's lifetime, the Jews were returning to Palestine, their homeland, after many years of exile. The Babylonians had captured the Jews and deported many of them to Babylonia. But when King Cyrus of Persia defeated the Babylonians in 539 B.C., he let the Jews return. Many of the Jews were delighted to return to Palestine, but they had problems in their homeland. One of the greatest was a lack of strong religious leaders.

Ezra learned of the problems the Jews were having in Palestine, and he decided to help them. Under the authority of the king of Persia, Ezra went to the Holy Land in 458 B.C. A large number of Jews went with him. Ezra also took a copy of the Torah with him.

In Palestine, Ezra found that some Jewish men had married non-Jewish women. This was against Jewish law and threatened to weaken the unity of the Jewish people. Without unity the Jews would not be able to defend themselves from their enemies. Ezra persuaded the men to marry only women of their own faith.

Ezra settled in the city of Jerusalem. One day he summoned the people to the public square, where a wooden platform had been set up. There he read the Torah to the people. He wanted them to hear the Bible stories that told what God had done for their ancestors. He also pointed out how often their ancestors had foolishly disobeyed God.

When the people heard Ezra, they wept and confessed they had not been paying much attention to their religion. Then Ezra made them promise that they would live by the laws and rules of the Torah. They vowed they would "walk in God's Law, which was given by Moses, the servant of God."

It is believed that Ezra spent the rest of his life in Jerusalem—teaching the Torah and strengthening the religious life of his people. He is greatly honored for his work and is sometimes called the father of Judaism.

LLOYD R. BAILEY
Duke University

Index

HOW TO USE THE DICTIONARY INDEX

See the beginning of the blue pages in Volume 1.

Ebola virus   **R:**100
Ebrāhīm, Mount (Iraq)   **I:**312
Ebro River (Spain)   **R:**241; **S:**372
EB virus *see* Epstein-Barr virus
Ecatepec (Mexico)   **M:**247
Eccentricity (of spacecraft orbit)   **S:**340d
Ecclesiastes (book of the Old Testament)   **B:**163
Ecclesiasticus (apocryphal book of the Bible)   **B:**164
Eccrine sweat glands   **G:**226
Ecevit, Bülent (prime minister of Turkey)   **T:**349
ECG *see* Electrocardiograph
Echeverría, Esteban (Argentine writer)   **L:**68
Echeverría Álvarez, Luis (Mexican president)   **M:**251
Echidnas *see* Spiny anteaters
Echinacea (plant used for medicinal purposes)   **H:**119, 120
   picture(s)   **H:**120
Echinoderms (spiny-skinned sea animals)   **S:**426–27
Echmiadzin (Armenia)   **A:**420
Echo   **E:**49
   behavior of sound   **S:**259
   echolocation of bats   **B:**103
   echo sounding   **O:**37–38
   radio echoes used in radar and sonar   **R:**38–41
Echo (in Greek mythology)   **G:**367
Echo 1 (communications satellite)   **S:**54
Echolocation (using echoes to locate things)   **E:**49
   bats   **B:**103
   dolphins   **D:**276, 277
   echo sounding in oceanography   **O:**37–38
   whales   **W:**149
Echoscopy (medical use of sonar) *see* Ultrasonography
Echo sounder (device using sonar to measure ocean bottom)
   O:37–38, 39
Eckert, John (American engineer)   **C:**490
Eclectic reading programs   **R:**110
Eclipses   **E:**50–52
   astronomy, history of   **A:**468
   lunar and solar eclipses   **M:**448–49
   Pluto and Charon   **P:**342
   picture(s)
      confirmation of general relativity theory   **R:**144
Ecliptic (of the sun)   **S:**110; **Z:**386
Eco, Umberto (Italian author)   **I:**409
Ecological processes (that provide renewable resources)
   C:523–24
Ecology (science that deals with how living things are related
      to one another and their environment)   **B:**199;
      E:53–55; **L:**201–6
   Arctic region   **A:**381
   biomes   **B:**206–12
   Carson, Rachel   **C:**121
   earth science   **E:**8
   ecosphere   **N:**63
   endangered species   **E:**208–11
   nature, study of   **N:**67–70
   sharks, overfishing of   **S:**145
Econometrics (application of mathematical techniques to
      economic theory)   **E:**63
Economic Advisers, Council of   **P:**451; **T:**326
Economic and Social Council, United Nations   **U:**65–66
Economic assistance *see* Foreign aid programs
Economic Development Administration (EDA)   **C:**455
Economic geography   **G:**103
Economics   **E:**56–63
   American Indians' contributions to world cultures   **I:**166
   banks and banking   **B:**52–59
   budgets, family   **B:**427–28
   business   **B:**470–73
   capitalism   **C:**103
   Communist system   **C:**472–74; **U:**37–39
   Consumer Price Index   **C:**533
   Depression, Great   **D:**119–20
   depressions and recessions   **D:**121–22
   energy supply   **E:**219

Enlightenment, Age of   **E:**298
food supply and   **F:**351
human rights   **H:**285
inflation and deflation   **I:**227–28
international trade   **I:**270–71
Marx, Karl   **M:**117
money   **M:**412–15
New Deal   **N:**138h
Nobel prizes   **N:**270–71
Organization for Economic Cooperation and Development
   O:220
poverty   **P:**418–20
socialism   **S:**224
social studies   **S:**227
Southeast Asian crisis   **S:**332, 336
stocks and bonds   **S:**454–59
tariff   **T:**23
taxation   **T:**25–26
trade and commerce   **T:**264–65
unemployment insurance helps control recessions   **U:**29
What is the amazing invisible hand?   **E:**60
Economic sanctions *see* Sanctions
Economics and Statistics Administration (ESA)   **C:**455
Ecosphere   **N:**63
Ecosystem (complex community of living organisms and the
      environment in which they live)   **B:**198; **E:**54
   coyotes and their environment   **C:**580
   forests and forestry   **F:**374–77
   national forest management   **N:**32–33, 34
Ecosystem functioning   **E:**54
Ecosystems ecology   **E:**54, 55
ECSC *see* European Coal and Steel Community
Ecstasy (MDMA) (drug)   **D:**331
ECT *see* Electroconvulsive therapy
Ector (foster father of King Arthur)   **A:**438a
Ectothermic animals *see* Cold-blooded animals
Ecuador   **E:**64–69; **L:**48, 49, 55
   holidays   **H:**160
   Latin-American architecture   **L:**61
   Organization of Petroleum Exporting Countries   **O:**222
   What were the enchanted islands?   **E:**66
   map(s)   **E:**65
   picture(s)
      banana crop   **E:**68
      Cotopaxi volcano   **A:**250
      flag   **F:**230
      Otavalo market   **S:**288
      people   **E:**64
      petroleum industry   **E:**68
      plateau in Andes   **S:**276
      Quito   **E:**65, 67; **L:**56
      volunteer working on irrigation project   **V:**390
Ecumenical councils (of Roman Catholic Church)   **R:**286–87,
      291, 294
   early Christian Church   **E:**45
   Nicaea, Council of (A.D. 325)   **R:**286
   Pope John XXIII   **J:**113
   Trent, Council of (1545–1563)   **G:**377; **R:**291
   Vatican Council II   **R:**294
Ecumenical (Unity) movement (among churches)   **C:**294;
      P:494
Eczema (skin condition) *see* Dermatitis
Edam cheese   **D:**10
Edberg, Stefan (Swedish tennis player)   **T:**96 *profile*
   picture(s)   **T:**96
Eddas (early Scandinavian poetry)   **N:**277; **S:**58h
Eddington, Sir Arthur Stanley (British astronomer)   **A:**474
      profile
   picture(s)   **A:**474
Eddy, Mary Baker (American founder of Church of Christ,
      Scientist)   **M:**148 *profile;* **P:**494
Eddy, William A. (American meteorologist)   **K:**266b
Eddystone Light (Plymouth, England)   **L:**227
Edelman, Marian Wright (American advocate for the
      disadvantaged)   **W:**35 *profile*

Edema (fluid accumulation in the body)   L:270, 350
Edentata (order of mammals)
     anteaters   A:296
     picture(s)
          three-toed sloth as example   M:76
Ederle, Gertrude (American swimmer)   S:536
     picture(s)   S:536
Edessa, County of (Crusader state)   C:599
Edgerton, Harold (American inventor)   I:282 *profile*; P:215
     picture(s)   I:282
Edge tools   L:342; T:227–28
Edgeworth, Maria (Irish writer)   I:326
Edict (decree or order) *see* individual edicts by name, as Milan,
     Edict of
Edinburgh (capital of Scotland)   S:87; U:50, 59, 236
     picture(s)   S:88
Edinburgh, Duke of *see* Philip (prince of the United Kingdom)
Edinburgh Castle (Scotland)   U:54, 59
     picture(s)   U:58
Edinburgh Festival (Scotland)   M:555
Edison, Thomas Alva (American inventor)   E:70–73
     birthplace in Ohio   O:70
     communication, history of   C:466, 467
     experiments cannot be complete failures   E:384–85
     incandescent lamp   E:145, 150; I:284; L:234–35
     motion pictures, history of   M:487
     patents held by   P:99
     phonograph   P:194–95; R:122
     quoted on genius   Q:22
     telegraph   T:51
     picture(s)   W:271
Edison National Historic Site (West Orange, New Jersey)
     N:172
Edith Cavell, Mount (Alberta)   J:54
Edith Macy Conference Center (Briarcliff Manor, New York)
     G:217
Edition (in engraving and etching)   E:294, 326
Editor, letters to the   L:160a
Editorials (essays giving opinions of editors or publishers)
     N:198
     cartoons   C:127
Editors and editing
     book publishing   B:325–26
     computer-based editing   V:332f, 332g, 332h–332i
     encyclopedias   E:206–7
     magazines   M:16, 17
     media's rights and responsibilities   C:471
     motion pictures   M:485
     newspapers   N:199–201
     writing process   W:331
Edmond (Oklahoma)   O:91
Edmonds, Sarah Emma Evelyn (American woman who fought in
     the Civil War)   C:344 *profile*
     picture(s)   C:344
Edmonton (capital of Alberta)   A:170; E:73
     picture(s)   A:170
Edmontonia (dinosaur)   D:176
Edmonton Oilers (ice hockey team)   I:31
Edo (Japan) *see* Tokyo
Edom (Biblical character) *see* Esau
Edo period (in Japanese art)   J:49
Education   E:74–88 *see also* the articles on professions; the
     education section of continent, country, province, and
     state articles; the names of curriculum subjects
     adult *see* Adult education
     African American history   A:79f, 79g–79h, 79p–80
     agricultural education   A:96–97
     Australia's School of the Air   A:500
     Bethune, Mary McLeod   B:154
     blind children   B:258
     child development   C:223–26
     colonial America   C:412, 418
     computer graphics, uses of   C:484
     deaf, education of the   D:50–51

debates and discussions   D:52
Dewey, John   D:144
disabilities, rehabilitation of people with   D:179, 180
driver education   D:326–27
Education, United States Department of   E:89
etiquette, history of   E:337
foundations   F:391
French system   F:404–5
Gates, Henry Louis, Jr.   W:138
guidance counseling   G:401–2
Hispanic Americans   H:149
homeschooling   H:196
humanism   H:284
industrial arts   I:213
Internet   C:488
job retraining   P:419
journalism, careers in   J:139
kindergarten   K:246–50
knighthood, education for   K:276
Land Ordinance of 1785 began system of giving land
     grants for schools   O:67; P:517
language arts   L:36
learning   L:98–106
learning disorders   L:107–8
legal education   L:90–91
libraries   L:171–86
Mann, Horace, was father of American free public school
     M:87
mental retardation, children with   R:191
Middle Ages   M:295
Morrill Act of 1862 for land-grant colleges   P:517
museums' educational programs   M:522
National Geographic Society   N:41
National Honor Society   N:42
nursery schools   K:246–50
parent-teacher associations   P:66–67
Peace Corps   P:104
physical education   P:222–23
pioneer life and education   P:257–58
poverty, weapon against   P:419, 420
preparatory schools   P:443–44
preschool education   K:246–50
programmed instruction   P:483
psychology   P:499–511
reading   R:108–11
Rousseau, Jean Jacques   R:339
schools   S:60–61
science education   S:75
science fairs   S:76–78
Should students attend year-round school?   E:85
social studies   S:227–28
Soviet school system   U:35
space museums' programs   P:274
statistics, uses of   S:439
storytelling   S:463–65
study, how to   S:470–72
teachers   T:37–38
tests and test taking   T:118–23
toys for young children   T:249
uniforms in public schools   E:88
universities and colleges   U:219–26
vocations and education   V:376
What makes students interested in schoolwork?   P:510
picture(s)
     Australia's School of the Air   A:499
     rural Mauritanian women learning to read   M:179
     schoolchildren in Belarus   E:356
     teacher using the Internet   C:462
     Ugandan schoolchildren   U:5
Education, United States Department of   E:89; P:447
Educational television *see* Public broadcasting
Educational tests *see* Tests and test taking
Educational video games   V:332c
Education for All Handicapped Children Act (United States,
     1975)   R:191

Education Index   I:115

Education of Henry Adams, The (book by Henry Adams)   A:11, 214

Education Sciences, Institute of (United States)   E:89

EDVAC (first computer)   O:55

Edward (prince of England)   E:192

Edward, Lake (Uganda–Democratic Republic of Congo)   L:26; U:5

Edward I (king of England)   E:**90**, 239–40; S:88; W:4

Edward II (king of England)   E:**90–91**

Edward III (king of England)   E:**91**, 241
  Hundred Years' War   H:292
  knight's code of honor   K:275
  picture(s)   E:240

Edward IV (king of England)   E:**91**, 241; H:110

Edward V (king of England)   E:**92**, 241–42
  What happened to the princes in the Tower?   E:241

Edward VI (king of England)   E:**92**, 191, 242, 243; R:132
  Reformation   C:292
  picture(s)   E:92

Edward VII (king of Great Britain)   E:**92**, 252, 253
  picture(s)   E:92

Edward VIII (king of Great Britain)   E:**92**, 192, 254
  picture(s)   E:92

Edward II (play by Christopher Marlowe)   M:104

Edwardes, George (English theatrical producer)   M:553

Edwards, Jonathan (American preacher and writer)   A:202
  picture(s)   A:202

Edwards, Jonathan (British athlete)   T:263

Edwards Bello, Joaquín (Chilean writer)   C:254

Edwards Plateau (Texas)   P:427

Edward the Black Prince (prince of Wales)   E:**91**; K:276

Edward the Confessor (king of England)   E:90
  London   L:292–93
  William the Conqueror and Edward   E:238; W:174

Edward the Elder (king of England)   E:90

Edward the Martyr (king of England)   E:90

EEC *see* European Economic Community

EEG *see* Electroencephalograph

Eels   E:**93–94**
  benthic ocean life   O:26
  changes in the marketplace   F:221
  migration   F:183, 201
  picture(s)
    how fish swim   F:198

Effigy mounds (of North American Indians)   I:298

Effigy Mounds National Monument (Iowa)   I:298

Effort arms (of levers)   W:249

EFNEP *see* Expanded Food and Nutrition Education Program

Eforie (Romania)   R:298

EFT (banking system) *see* Electronic funds transfer

Egede, Hans (Norwegian missionary and founder of Nuuk, Greenland)   G:374, 374a

Eggbeater-gear drill (tool)   T:229
  picture(s)   T:229

Egg cell *see* Ovum

Eggleston, Edward (American writer)   A:212

Eggplant   V:290, 291

Eggs   E:**95–98**
  amniote eggs   P:433
  bees   B:119–20
  beetles   B:125
  birds   B:224, 230
  centipedes and millipedes   C:169
  crocodilian   C:593
  crustaceans   C:602
  dinosaurs   D:176
  Easter symbol   E:44
  egg farming and poultry raising   P:415–16
  fish   F:195–98
  flightless birds   O:243, 245
  frogs and toads   F:477–78
  insects   I:232
  metamorphosis   M:237, 238

  reproduction   R:176–79
  shrimps   S:168
  snakes   S:214
  sulfur-containing proteins   S:486
  turtles   T:357–58
  picture(s)
    insects   I:233

Eggs (used as food)
  altitude affects cooking   H:91
  baked goods, ingredient in   B:387–88
  cooking   C:543
  egg farming and poultry raising   P:415–16
  food shopping   F:349
  important agricultural products   A:90, 95
  livestock   L:272

Egg tempera (artist's paint)   P:30

Egley, William (English artist)   C:298

Egmont, Mount (New Zealand)   N:237

Egrets (wading birds)   H:**124**
  picture(s)   B:226, 236

Egypt (Arab Republic of Egypt)   E:**99–105** *see also* Egypt, ancient
  Arabic literature   A:342
  Aswan High Dam   L:32
  Cairo   C:7–8
  Israel, relations with   I:376
  Napoleon's invasion   N:10
  Nasser, Gamal Abdel   N:17
  Nile River   N:260–61
  Sadat, Anwar el-   S:2
  Suez Canal   S:480–81
  World War II   W:299, 307
  map(s)   E:101
  picture(s)
    agriculture in Nile Valley   M:301
    Cairo   A:47, 343; C:7, 8; E:101
    costume, traditional   C:373
    cotton crop   E:102
    desert   D:129
    feluccas on Nile River   N:260
    flag   F:230
    Great Pyramid of Cheops   B:394
    Great Sphinx and Pyramid of Chephren   W:258
    irrigation   E:100; F:257
    Nile River   E:99; R:236–37
    people   A:345
    petroleum industry   E:102
    pyramids   A:47; E:106; P:556, 557
    satellite photograph   E:21
    schoolchildren   M:298
    women carrying water   W:73

Egypt, ancient   A:234–35; E:103–4, **106–9**
  air conditioning by evaporation   A:101
  alchemy   C:207
  Alexander the Great conquered   A:178
  antibiotics, discovery of   A:310
  archaeological specialties   A:350
  architecture *see* Egyptian architecture
  art *see* Egyptian art
  ball games as religious ceremonies   B:23
  beekeeping   H:212
  bottles, history of   B:346
  bread making   C:540
  calendar   C:14
  canal system   C:89
  candles, use of   C:96
  cat was sacred animal of   C:137
  Cleopatra   C:355
  clocks   C:371
  clothing, history of   C:374
  dance accompanies rites of worship   D:22–23
  development of cities   U:235
  education   E:77
  engineering projects   E:227

Electron gun (in television cameras)   T:62, 63
Electronic books   B:322
Electronic calendar systems   O:56
Electronic clocks   C:370–71
Electronic communication see Telecommunications
Electronic computers see Computers
Electronic eavesdropping see Bugging
Electronic funds transfer (EFT) (banking system that moves
        money electronically)   B:58; M:415
    picture(s)   M:415
Electronic games   G:19
Electronic instruments (in music)   M:546
Electronic locks   L:284
Electronic mail see E-mail
Electronic music   E:155–57; M:398–99, 544
    digital keyboards   P:242
    electronic carillon bells   B:142
    guitar   G:412
    rock music   R:264
Electronic Numerical Integrator and Calculator see ENIAC
Electronic organ   K:239; O:218, 219
Electronic photography   P:216, 218 see also Digital cameras
Electronics (science dealing with flow of electrons)   E:158–62
    airport security checks   A:127
    artificial ear implants   E:6
    automation, applications in   A:530
    color separations in printing   P:473
    computers   C:480–94
    crystals, properties of   S:250
    electron microscopes   E:163–64; M:285
    Finland, economy of   F:136–37
    fishing industry, use in   F:218
    gravure printing   P:479
    high-fidelity systems   H:131–33
    ions and ionization   I:287–89
    lasers   L:46a–46d
    lasers, uses of   L:46c
    liquid crystal display   C:604
    locks   L:284
    microscope   M:285
    music   E:155–57
    navigation, electronic   N:76–77
    photoelectricity   P:196–97
    radar and sonar   R:38–41
    radio   R:50–61
    radio astronomy   R:66–73
    robots   R:252–56
    television   T:61–67
    toys   T:251
    transistors, diodes, and integrated circuits   T:274–78
    video games   V:332b–332c
    video recording   V:332d–332i
    What is nanotechnology?   E:162
    picture(s)
        electronic devices   T:39
        Oklahoma industry   O:89
        Southeast Asian industry   S:332
Electronics engineering
    picture(s)   E:224
Electronic synthesizers (used in the production of music)
        E:156, 157
    disco music   R:264
    keyboard instruments   K:239
    modern music   M:544
Electronic total station (for surveying)   S:520
    picture(s)   S:519
Electronic typewriters   O:57; T:373
Electronic Viewfinder (EVF) (type of digital camera)   P:203
Electronic watches   W:45, 46
Electron jump   R:43, 44
    diagram(s)   R:43
Electron microscopes   E:163–64; M:285
    bacteria, study of   B:10
    microbes, study of   M:278

viruses, study of   D:188
    picture(s)   M:285
Electrons (atomic particles)   A:485, 487, 488, 489; C:202,
        204
    bonding   M:151–52
    chemical structure   C:201
    cosmic rays   C:563
    electric current production   T:274–75
    electronics, science of   E:158–62
    elements   E:166
    how X-rays are made   X:349
    ions and ionization   I:287–89
    lasers   L:46a
    magnetism, causes of   M:31
    Millikan's oil-drop experiment   M:310
    negative charges of electricity   E:135–36
    nuclear energy   N:366
    oxidation and reduction   O:287
    photoelectricity   P:196–97
    radiation   R:43
    radioactive elements   R:64
    semiconductors   M:153
    shells   C:202–3
    static electricity   T:185
Electron tubes see Vacuum tubes
Electrophoresis (in biochemistry)   B:189
Electroplating   E:165
    gold in electronic devices   G:248
    ions and ionization   I:289
    knives, forks, and spoons   K:285
    silver   S:178
    tin-plated steel   I:337
Electro-pneumatic brakes (of railroad trains)   R:84
Electropolishing (electroplating in reverse)   E:165
Electroreceptors (of sharks)   S:143
Electrorefining (of metals)   M:234
Electroweak force (in physics)   S:69
Electrum (alloy of gold and silver)   M:413
Elegiac lyrics (in poetry)   G:355
Elegy (poem written in memory of the dead)   P:352–53
"Elegy Written in a Country Churchyard" (poem by Thomas Gray)
        P:352
Elementary and Secondary Education, Office of (United States)
        E:89
Elementary particles see Subatomic particles
Elementary schools   E:76, 81, 84, 85; S:60–61
    colonial America   E:82
    guidance counseling   G:401
    language arts   L:36
    physical education   P:222
    reading   R:108–11
    picture(s)   E:74
Elements, chemical   E:166–78 see also Periodic table
    alphabetical table of elements with their symbols,
        numbers, weights, discoverers, and year discovered
        E:170–78
    alphabetical table of symbols for the elements   C:200
    aluminum   A:194f–195
    atomic theory   C:209
    atoms   A:483, 485
    chemical structures   C:198
    chemistry, history of   C:206–7, 209, 210, 211
    Curies' discoveries   C:614
    defined by Boyle   C:208
    definition   C:204; L:198
    fertilizer elements   F:96
    gold   G:247–49
    helium   H:106
    hydrogen   H:316
    iodine   I:287
    ions and ionization   I:287–89
    iron   I:329
    magnesium   M:27
    matter   M:176

Elements, chemical (cont.)
    metals M:233
    nitrogen N:262
    nuclear energy N:366–67
    oxygen O:288–89
    periodic table C:202, 209–10; E:168–69
    radioactive elements R:64–65
    silver S:177–78
    spectroscopic analysis O:184
    stars S:430, 431
    sulfur S:485–86
    tungsten T:332
    uranium U:229–30
    What is the island of stability? E:167
    zinc Z:385
Elephanta Island (Bombay, India) B:310b
Elephant bird
    picture(s) O:244
Elephantfish F:192
Elephant Rocks (Missouri)
    picture(s) M:370
Elephants E:179–84
    Africa A:53
    circus acts C:307
    defense M:74
    endangered species E:209; M:76
    ivory I:415–16
    Ivory Coast, symbol of I:417
    Jumbo C:310
    largest land animals A:271
    life span A:83
    Nast cartoons C:127; N:17
    reproduction M:67
    picture(s) A:265; E:179
        African elephant E:180; M:69
        ancestors E:183
        circus performers C:307
        costumed elephant carrying passengers E:184
        eating plants M:72
        Hannibal used elephants H:26
        hauling teak log M:559
        Indian elephant A:443; E:180
        mud baths E:182
        Serengeti Plain T:17
        trunk, uses of E:181
"Elephant's Child, The" (story by Kipling) K:261–64
Elephant seals (Sea elephants) (animals) H:199; S:107, 108
    picture(s) C:21; O:25; S:108
"Eletelephony" (poem by Laura E. Richards) N:275
Eleuthera Island (Bahamas) B:17
Eleutherius, Saint (pope) R:292
Elevated railways T:288
    picture(s)
        New York City U:189
Elevation (on maps) M:96
    continents' elevations compared C:538
    photogrammetry in mapmaking O:184
Elevator (control surface of an airplane) A:113–14
Elevators E:185–87
    do not use when escaping from fire F:150
    How fast can the fastest elevators climb? E:187
    diagram(s) E:186
    picture(s)
        glass-enclosed E:186
Elevators, grain see Grain elevators
Eleventh Amendment (to the United States Constitution)
    U:156
Elf owls O:285
Elfreth's Alley (Philadelphia, Pennsylvania) P:180
    picture(s) P:181
Elgar, Sir Edward (English composer) E:188, 293
Elgin, Lord (Thomas Bruce) (British diplomat) G:350
Elgin Marbles (sculpture from Greek temples) G:350; M:525
    picture(s) G:350; L:295
El Greco (Spanish painter) see Greco, El

El Guerrouj, Hicham (Moroccan athlete) O:120; T:263
Elhuyar, Juan J. and Fausto d' (Spanish chemists) T:332
Eli (Biblical character) B:159
Elia (pen name of Charles Lamb, for *Essays of Elia*) E:321;
    L:34
Eliezer, Israel ben (Jewish teacher) J:145
Elijah (prophet) E:189; P:96
Elijah Muhammad (leader of the Nation of Islam) *see*
    Muhammad, Elijah
Elion, Gertrude (American scientist) I:282 *profile;* M:208h;
    O:227
    picture(s) I:282
Eliot, George (pseudonym of Marian (Mary Ann) Evans, English
    novelist) E:189–90, 286; I:222; N:359; R:114
Eliot, John (American missionary) M:148
Eliot, T. S. (Thomas Stearns Eliot) (American-born English poet,
    playwright, and critic) E:190
    American literature A:214a–214b
    drama, history of D:305
    English literature E:287–88, 290
    essays E:321–22
Elisha (Biblical character) E:189
Elixir of Love, The (opera by Gaetano Donizetti) D:285
Elizabeth (English queen; consort of George VI) E:192
Elizabeth (New Jersey) N:175
Elizabeth, Saint (mother of John the Baptist) B:159; J:125;
    S:18d *profile*
Elizabeth I (queen of England) E:191, 242, 243–44
    colony of Virginia named for T:165
    Drake, Sir Francis D:296
    English music E:291
    Mary, Queen of Scots M:118
    Puritans' opinion of P:550
    Raleigh, Sir Walter R:101
    Reformation C:293; R:132
    Spanish Armada S:393
    picture(s)
        Armada Portrait W:265
Elizabeth II (queen of the United Kingdom of Great Britain and
    Northern Ireland) E:192, 254; U:60
    Canada, Queen of C:74
    Commonwealth of Nations head C:461
    picture(s) C:74; E:192, 254; G:274; P:84; S:88; U:60
        Canada's dollar coin D:263
        in House of Lords U:61
Elizabeth I (empress of Russia) I:414; R:376
Elizabethan Age (England) E:243–44
    art and architecture E:258
    drama D:300–301; L:259
    English literature E:271–73
    music E:291–92
Elk (hoofed mammals) D:80; E:193; H:218
    locomotion of animals A:278
    migration M:75
    National Elk Refuge W:337
    picture(s) C:434; E:193; M:76; N:290
        American elk B:208
        National Elk Refuge W:338
Elk Island National Park (Alberta) A:167
Elk's horn ferns see Staghorn ferns
Ellesmere Island (northwest of Greenland) C:56; I:365;
    N:410
Ellesmere Island National Park (Canada) N:412
Ellice Islands see Tuvalu
Ellicott, Andrew (American surveyor) W:36
Ellington, Edward Kennedy "Duke" (jazz pianist, composer, and
    orchestra leader) J:61 *profile*
    picture(s) J:60
Elliot, James (American astronomer) U:232
Elliott, Robert (American politician)
    picture(s) U:143
Ellipse (in geometry) G:123 see also Conic sections
    Mars and Moon, orbits of M:446
    shape of a satellite's orbit S:53
Elliptical galaxies U:214

Ellis, Joel (American doll maker)   **D:**266
El Lisht (Egypt)   **E:**113
Ellis Island (immigration station, New York City)   **I:**90; **L:**169
  picture(s)   **I:**87
      immigrants' Christmas dinner in 1910   **I:**89
Ellison, Ralph Waldo (American novelist)   **A:**79L, 219; **N:**363;
  O:94 *profile*
  picture(s)   **O:**94
Ellora (India)   **I:**139
Ells (measures of length)   **W:**109
Elmer Gantry (novel by Sinclair Lewis)   **L:**162
Elmira system (of reforming criminals)   **P:**482
El Morro (fortress in Puerto Rico)
  picture(s)   **P:**526
Elm trees
  Dutch elm disease   **E:**209; **P:**287, 289
  leaves and flowers   **T:**309
  picture(s)   **M:**137; **N:**323; **T:**302
      uses of the wood and its grain   **W:**223
El Niño (Pacific Ocean current)   **O:**18; **W:**83, 94
  computers used to predict arrival   **C:**486
  coral reefs, impact on   **C:**556
  fish migration   **F:**201
  oceans and climate   **O:**36
El Obeid (Sudan)   **S:**479
Elobey Islands (Equatorial Guinea)   **E:**309
Eloquence (speaking well)   **H:**284
El Paso (Texas)   **E:**194; **T:**134
  picture(s)   **E:**194
El Salvador   **E:**195–99
  Central America   **C:**172, 173, 174, 175
  Honduras, dispute with   **H:**209
  Latin America   **L:**49
  map(s)   **E:**196
  picture(s)
      earthquake-caused landslide   **E:**199
      flag   **F:**230
      girl picking coffee beans   **E:**195
      Izalco   **C:**173
      Izalco volcano   **E:**195
      San Salvador   **E:**197
Elssler, Fanny (Austrian ballerina)   **D:**25
Elster, Julius (German physicist)   **P:**196
Eluard, Paul (French poet)   **F:**442
Elvers (Glass eels) (young eels)   **E:**94; **F:**201
Elves (in Norse mythology)   **F:**10–11, 12; **N:**280
Ely Cathedral (England)
  picture(s)   **G:**268
Elytis, Odysseus (Greek poet)   **G:**359
Elytra (wings of beetles)   **B:**123; **I:**240
E-mail (Electronic mail)   **C:**470, 488, 491; **O:**56
  computer bulletin boards   **L:**160b
  deaf people, use for communication by   **D:**50
  electronic postmarks   **P:**402
  electronics in business   **E:**162
  inventions   **I:**286
  telecommunications   **T:**50
  television   **T:**71
Emajõgi (river, Estonia)   **E:**324
Emancipation (Manumission) (of slaves)   **A:**79b; **S:**192, 197
Emancipation Proclamation   **A:**6b; **E:**200–201
  African American history   **A:**79g
  Civil War, United States   **C:**340, 497
  Lincoln, Abraham   **L:**246
  slavery   **S:**197
Embabeh, Battle of (1798)   **N:**10
Embalming (preservation of the dead)   **F:**493
Embankment dams (made of earth and rock)   **D:**18, 20
  picture(s)   **D:**17; **D:**19
Embargo Act (United States, 1807)   **J:**71; **M:**12; **U:**179; **W:**9
Embarkation for Cythera (painting by Watteau)
  picture(s)   **P:**25
Embassies (headquarters of diplomatic service)   **F:**371
  United States territory   **S:**434
Embden, Gustav (German biochemist)   **B:**186

Emberley, Ed (American author and illustrator)
  picture(s)
      illustration from *Drummer Hoff*   **C:**236
Embla (first woman in Norse mythology)   **N:**279
Embolism, air (danger to divers)   **S:**188
Embroidery (needlecraft)   **N:**97–100
  picture(s)
      Inuit parka   **I:**191
      stitches   **N:**99
Embryos (first stages of development in plants or animals)
      E:95, 97–98 *see also* Cells; Eggs
  baby   **B:**2; **R:**179
  baby kangaroos   **K:**175
  brain development   **B:**368
  chromosomes   **G:**78
  descent with modification   **E:**374
  livestock research   **L:**273
  mammal reproduction   **M:**68
  plant reproduction   **P:**294, 307, 312
  seeds, structure of   **F:**286; **N:**431
  stem cell research   **B:**214
  picture(s)
      chicken embryo   **K:**254
      human embryo at six weeks   **B:**368
      vertebrates   **E:**374
Embryo transfer (method of breeding cattle)   **D:**11
E=mc² (Einstein's equation for light and matter)   **R:**47
Emerald Isle (name for Ireland)   **I:**317
Emeralds (gems)   **G:**69, 71, 73, 74
  amulets   **G:**72
  Colombia   **B:**303; **C:**405; **S:**284
  picture(s)   **G:**74
      necklace   **G:**69
Emerald tree boa (snake)
  picture(s)   **A:**280
Emergency medical services (EMS)   **A:**199; **F:**157
Emergency medical technicians (EMT's)   **A:**199; **F:**162; **M:**205
  picture(s)   **M:**514
Emergency rooms (in hospitals)   **H:**248
Emergents (plants rooted in shallow water)   **W:**147–48
Emergents (tallest trees in a rain forest)   **R:**99
Emerson, Ralph Waldo (American writer and teacher)   **E:**202
  American literature   **A:**209
  "Concord Hymn" (poem)   **E:**202
  quotations   **Q:**21, 22
  Thoreau, Henry David   **T:**181
  Transcendentalism   **A:**210
  picture(s)   **A:**205; **E:**202
Emery (form of corundum)   **G:**391
Emigrants (people who leave their homes to live and work
      elsewhere)   **I:**87 *see also* Immigration
Emigré writers (in Arabic literature)   **A:**342
Émile (book by Rousseau)   **E:**82; **R:**339
Eminent domain (government's right to take land from its owner)
      R:112d
Emission-control devices (of automobiles)   **A:**547
Emission nebulas (in astronomy)   **N:**96
Emission standards (for diesel engines)   **D:**162
Emmer wheat   **W:**158
Emmett, Dan (American composer)   **N:**22
Emotions (feelings)   **E:**203–4
  adolescence   **A:**24–26
  asthma attacks can be brought on by   **A:**463
  connotations of words   **S:**116
  diseases, emotional   **D:**187
  divorce, attitudes toward   **D:**230–31
  emotional deprivation is a type of child abuse   **C:**222
  emotional disabilities, people with   **D:**178, 179
  grief   **G:**380
  holistic medicine   **H:**171
  lie detection   **L:**193
  mood disorders   **M:**221
Empedocles (Greek philosopher)   **C:**206; **G:**107
Empennage *see* Tail assembly
Emperor goose (bird)   **D:**347

Emperor penguins B:244; P:120b, 122–24
  picture(s) B:236
"Emperor's New Clothes, The" (story by Hans Christian
    Andersen) A:247–49
Emphysema (lung disease) D:192; L:345; S:207
  acid rain's effects A:10
  smoking is the main cause of H:75
  picture(s) D:192
Empire Day (Great Britain) H:167
Empires (in political science) *see* Imperialism
Empire State (nickname for New York) N:210
Empire State Building (New York City)
  picture(s) N:210, 226, 299
Empire State of the South (nickname for Georgia) G:132, 133
Empire State Plaza (Albany, New York) *see* Nelson A.
    Rockefeller Empire State Plaza
Empire style (in furniture design) F:513
Empire waistline F:65
Empiricism (philosophical theory of John Locke) L:281
  Hume, David H:288
Employee Benefits Security Administration (EBSA) L:2
Employee Retirement Income Security Act (ERISA) (United
    States, 1974) L:6
Employer's liability *see* Workers' compensation
Employment *see* Labor; Vocations; Work, world of
Employment and Training Administration (ETA) L:2
Employment Standards Administration (ESA) L:2
Empty Quarter *see* Rub' al Khali
Empty sets (in mathematics) S:128
Ems telegram (in European history) F:452
Emulsion (mixture of one liquid with tiny droplets of another
    liquid)
  explosive slurries E:422
  photographic film P:204, 214
Emus (Australian birds) A:506; O:245
  picture(s) O:244
Enamel (of teeth) T:43
Enameling E:205
  decorative arts D:74
  jewelry J:96
  pottery P:408
Enamels (paints) P:33
Encaustic (method of painting) P:17, 30
  Johns, Jasper J:114
Enceladus (moon of Saturn) S:58
Encephalitis (disease) D:201; R:191
  vectors of disease V:282, 283, 284, 285
"Enchanted Princess" (old German fairy tale) F:23–25
Encina, Juan del (Spanish dramatist) S:387, 392a
Enciso, Martín Fernández de (Spanish colonizer) B:20
Enclave (territory of one country within the boundaries of
    another country)
  Angola's Cabinda A:259
  Belgium's Baarle-Hertog B:131
  Gambia, The G:8
  Lesotho L:156
  San Marino S:35–36
  Spanish cities in Morocco S:375
Enclosure system (for English land holdings) I:217
Encoding (of sound sent over the Internet) R:61
Encounter (sculpture by Richard Lippold)
  picture(s) D:135
Encyclicals (papal letters) R:294
Encyclopaedia Britannica E:207
Encyclopedia Americana E:207
Encyclopedias E:206–7; R:129
  Diderot, Denis F:439
  subscription book publishing P:524
Encyclopédie (work containing many important ideas of the
    Enlightenment) E:297
Endangered species (of animals and plants) E:208–11
  Africa A:53
  antelopes A:298
  ants of endangered ecosystems A:324

apes and their environment A:327
bears B:107
biogeography G:101
birds B:248
California condors V:394
cats, wild C:150
cloning L:210
conservation C:525
crocodilians C:594
deer D:82
doves and pigeons, species of D:290
elephants, threats to E:184; I:416
fishing industry problems F:219
Florida F:264–65
flowers F:287
Hawaiian goose D:348
herons, bitterns, and egrets, former status of H:124
hoofed mammals H:220
laws prohibiting hunting of H:301
lizards L:277
mammals M:75–76
manatees M:77
marsupials M:115
modern zoos help save Z:389, 393
National Forest System protects N:33
oxen, wild O:286
pandas C:263; O:148
parrots P:86
primates P:457
rabbits and hares, distinctive species of R:26
sharks and rays S:145
snakes S:218
spotted owls O:285
tigers T:198
whales W:151, 153, 155
zebras H:243; Z:379
Endangered Species Act (United States, 1973) E:210–11;
    F:502
Endara, Guillermo (president of Panama) P:49
Endeavour (Captain Cook's ship) C:539
Endeavour (United States space shuttle) S:340j, 348, 355,
    364
  International Space Station S:349, 363
  space stations S:366
  picture(s) S:365
    cockpit mock-up S:338
    and Hubble Space Telescope S:367
    and *International Space Station* S:349
    Mae Jemison demonstrating weightlessness G:324
Endecott, John (Puritan colonist) T:173
End-effectors (of robot arms) R:253, 255
Endgame (play by Beckett) I:328
Endive (vegetable) V:290
Endocarditis (heart disease) H:84
Endocardium (inner layer of the wall of the heart) H:80
Endocrine system (of body's ductless glands) B:287,
    291–92; G:227–28
  adolescence A:24
  hormonal diseases D:194–95
  hormones H:227
Endocrinology (study of hormones) B:187–88
Endodontist (in dentistry) D:115
Endometrium (lining of the uterus) M:219
Endoplasmic reticulum (of the cell) C:160
Endoscope (instrument for examining the inside of the body)
    F:106; L:237
Endosperm (food-storing tissue of seeds) F:286; P:307
  corn endosperm, use of G:282
  seeds, structure of N:431
  wheat B:385; F:276
  picture(s)
    wheat kernel W:157
Endothermic animals *see* Warm-blooded animals
Endowments *see* Foundations
"Endymion" (poem by John Keats) E:282

Enemy aliens *see* Aliens

Energy **E:**212–17, 219–23 *see also* Energy supply; Fuels
  body cells' use of **B:**297
  body's energy cycle **B:**298
  chemical changes of matter **M:**178
  chemical energy needed for life **L:**195
  conservation of *see* Conservation of energy
  ecosphere's energy cycle **N:**63
  Einstein's formula: $E = mc^2$ **R:**142
  engines **E:**229–31
  food energy is measured in kilocalories **N:**423
  heat **H:**86–94
  hydrogen is an important source **G:**60; **H:**316
  law of conservation **M:**174–75
  light **L:**212
  nutrition **N:**425
  organisms need energy **B:**195–96
  photosynthesis and the energy of sunlight **P:**219–21
  physics, history of **P:**234–35
  physics is the study of **P:**228, 229
  quantum theory **L:**222–24
  radiation **R:**42–47
  recycling saves energy **R:**125
  relativity **P:**231
  transfer through food chain **L:**205
  volcanic energy **V:**384
  work, power, and machines **W:**246–47
  X-rays **X:**349–51

Energy, United States Department of **E:**217–18; **P:**447
  Human Genome Project **G:**86

Energy Efficiency and Renewable Energy, Office of (United States) **E:**217–18

Energy Information Administration **E:**218

Energy supply **E:**219–23
  air conditioning and energy conservation **A:**103
  biotechnology and the environment **B:**214
  Energy, United States Department of **E:**217–18
  fuel coal **C:**390–91
  garbage power **E:**222
  geothermal energy **E:**221–22
  Is there a new source of energy in the oceans? **O:**42
  North America **N:**293–94
  nuclear energy **E:**221, 222; **N:**366–73
  ocean, uses of the **O:**28
  Ocean Thermal Energy Conversion **E:**223
  power plants **P:**421–23
  rubber tires as source of **R:**348a
  solar energy **E:**222; **S:**239–40
  tidal energy **E:**222
  United States **U:**94
  waterpower **E:**221; **W:**69–70
  wind energy **E:**222

Energy therapies (category of alternative therapy) **A:**194e

Enewetak (Pacific atoll) **M:**113

Engagement rings
  picture(s) **J:**95

Engelbart, Douglas (American inventor) **I:**282 *profile*

Engelberger, Joseph (American inventor) **R:**253

Engels, Friedrich (German Socialist leader) **C:**473
  Marx and Engels **M:**117
  picture(s) **C:**472

Engel* v. *Vitale (1962) **S:**509

Engineering **E:**224–28
  automated drawing software **A:**533
  automobiles **A:**539–56
  aviation **A:**559–72
  blueprint **B:**263
  bridge construction **B:**395–401
  building construction **B:**436, 438–39, 440
  Corps of Engineers **U:**102, 106
  lasers, uses of **L:**46c
  materials engineering **M:**151
  mechanical drawing **M:**200
  modern architecture **A:**373–74

oceanography, careers in **O:**42
  railroad construction **R:**79
  Stonehenge **S:**462
  surgery helped by advances in engineering **S:**513
  surveying **S:**519
  tunnel building **T:**337–38
  work, power, and machines, principles of **W:**243–52

Engineering plastics **P:**328

Engineers (of railroads) **R:**86

Engineers, Corps of, United States **O:**78; **T:**290; **U:**102, 106

Engine rooms (of ships) **O:**32

Engines **E:**229–31 *see also* Fuels
  airplane **A:**115–17
  airplane models **A:**105
  automobiles **A:**540, 546–47
  diesel engines **D:**160–62
  energy **E:**216
  internal-combustion engines **I:**262–65
  jet propulsion **J:**90–92
  missiles **M:**344–45
  rockets **R:**257–62
  steam engines **S:**443–45
  turbines **T:**341–43
  Watt, James **W:**77
  diagram(s)
    jet engines **J:**91
  picture(s)
    automobile designing and testing **A:**553

England **E:**232–34 *see also* United Kingdom
  architecture *see* English architecture
  art *see* English art
  Christmas customs **C:**301
  cotton industry, history of **C:**570
  education **E:**74, 81, 83
  Enlightenment, Age of **E:**298
  fairs and expositions **F:**16, 18
  folk dance **F:**300, 302–3
  food **F:**331
  history *see* England, history of
  horse racing **H:**236
  land features **U:**52
  leather through the ages **L:**111
  literature *see* English literature
  London **L:**291–98
  music *see* English music
  New Year customs **N:**208–9
  parks **P:**76
  railroads, history of **R:**86–87
  Stonehenge **S:**462
  textiles, history of **T:**144, 145
  theater **T:**160
  picture(s)
    businessman reading newspaper **U:**57
    fields and hills **U:**52
    London *see* London (capital of the United Kingdom)—
      picture(s)
    Oxford University **E:**80
    punting on the Cam River **U:**49
    Sissinghurst Gardens **P:**76
    Stonehenge **A:**468

England, Church of **C:**292–93; **P:**491, 493; **U:**47–48
  British monarch is head of **U:**60
  Henry VIII and Elizabeth I establish Protestantism **E:**242–43
  Henry VIII was head of **H:**114
  hymns **H:**324
  Parliament, representation in **U:**61
  Pilgrims wanted to separate from **T:**170
  Puritans wanted to simplify the church service **P:**550; **T:**172
  Reformation **R:**132

England, history of **E:**235–55 *see also* Commonwealth of Nations; United Kingdom
  Albert, Prince **A:**163

Epstein-Barr virus   **B:**262; **D:**195
Equal Employment Opportunity Commission (EEOC)   **C:**326; **L:**8, 87; **W:**213
Equalitarian family   **F:**42
Equality
   Communism, beliefs of   **C:**472–73
   Quakers, beliefs of   **Q:**4b
Equality League of Self-Supporting Women   **W:**212b
Equality State (nickname for Wyoming)   **W:**334, 335
Equal Pay Act (United States, 1963)   **W:**212b
Equal Rights Amendment (ERA)   **C:**327; **U:**202; **W:**212b, 213
   National Organization for Women (NOW)   **N:**43
   Paul, Alice   **P:**101
   text   **W:**213
Equal Rights Party (in United States history)   **P:**372
Equal sets (in mathematics)   **S:**128
Equations
   algebra   **A:**182–84; **M:**157
   chemical   **C:**199–200, 204
   number puzzles and games   **N:**393, 395
   proportion   **R:**107
Equator   **E:**9, 10, **308**; **M:**96
   climate   **C:**361
   latitude zero degrees   **L:**77, 78
   low air pressure zone   **W:**82
   rainfall   **R:**97
   seasons   **S:**109–10
Equatorial Guinea   **E:309–10**
   picture(s)   **E:**309
      flag   **F:**230
Equestrian sports *see* Horseback riding
Equestrian statues (monuments)
   picture(s)
      Bernini's statue of Louis XIV   **B:**152
Equiano, Olaudah (American writer and seafarer) *see* Vassa, Gustavus
Equidae (horse family)   **H:**235
Equilateral triangles   **G:**121
   diagram(s)   **G:**121
Equinoxes ("equal nights") (position of the sun)   **S:**110–11
Equity (of a business)   **B:**311
Equivalence, principle of (relativity)   **G:**325
Equivalent fractions   **F:**398
Equivalents (in topology)   **T:**236
Equivalent sets (in mathematics)   **S:**128
Equus caballus (horse species)   **H:**235
E.R. (television program)
   picture(s)   **T:**71
ERA *see* Earned run average; Equal Rights Amendment
Era of Good Feelings (Monroe's administration)   **M:**423, 425–26
Erard, Sébastien (French harp maker)   **H:**36
Eras (geologic time)   **F:**383; **G:**110
   ice eras   **I:**10
   prehistoric animals   **P:**432–34
Eraser, kneaded (used in charcoal drawing)   **D:**311
Erasmus (Dutch scholar)   **E:310**; **N:**120c
   Christianity and the Renaissance   **C:**291
   German literature   **G:**177
   Holbein portraits of   **H:**159d
   humanism   **H:**284
   Renaissance humanist   **R:**159, 160
   picture(s)   **N:**120d
Eratosthenes (Greek geographer and astronomer)   **G:**105
   astronomers of ancient Greece   **A:**468
   geology, history of   **G:**107
   Sieve of Eratosthenes finds prime numbers   **N:**385
Erbakan, Necmettin (prime minister of Turkey)   **T:**349
Erbium (element)   **E:**172; **F:**107
Ercilla y Zúñiga, Alonso de (Spanish soldier-poet)   **S:**389
Erdogan, Recep Tayyip (prime minister of Turkey)   **T:**349
Erebus (in Greek mythology)   **G:**362
Erebus, Mount (volcano, Ross Sea)   **O:**46
Erech (Sumerian city)   **A:**230

Erechtheum (temple on the Athens Acropolis)   **A:**238; **G:**348
   picture(s)   **G:**349
Erevan (Armenia) *see* Yerevan
Erewhon (book by Butler)   **E:**286
Ergonomics   **I:**215
Ergot (rye fungus)   **R:**390
Ergs (giant sand dunes)   **A:**186; **S:**6
Erhard, Ludwig (German economist and political leader)   **G:**165
Erickson, Milton (American doctor)   **H:**329
Ericson, Leif (Norse sailor and explorer)   **E:311–12, 400**
   Canada, history of   **C:**79
   Eric the Red   **E:**312
   Vikings   **V:**342–43
Eric the Red (Viking chieftain)   **E:312, 400**
   discovery and exploration of Greenland   **G:**374a
   Leif the Lucky and Greenland   **E:**311
   Vikings   **V:**342
Eridanus (constellation)
   picture(s)
      barred spiral galaxy   **U:**215
Erie (Indians of North America)   **I:**175
Erie (Pennsylvania)   **P:**133, 135
Erie, Lake (one of the Great Lakes)   **G:**328, 329
   Ohio   **C:**356; **O:**64, 65, 69
   picture(s)
      barges   **O:**71
Erie, Lake, Battle of (1813)   **O:**75; **P:**153; **W:**9
   picture(s)   **O:**75; **W:**8
Erie Canal   **C:**90; **E:313–15**; **N:**224
Erie-Ontario Lowland (United States) *see* Great Lakes Plain
Eritrea   **E:316–17, 330, 334**
   map(s)   **E:**316
   picture(s)
      flag   **F:**231
      plateau   **E:**316
Eritrean People's Liberation Front   **E:**334
Ermines (weasels)   **F:**504; **O:**254, 255
   picture(s)   **O:**255
Ernst, Max (German painter)   **M:**394
   picture(s)
      The Little Tear Gland That Says Tic-Tac   **M:**395
Eros (Cupid) (Greek god)   **G:**363; **V:**266
Erosion   **E:318–19**
   caves and caverns formed by   **C:**155
   conservation   **C:**524
   Dust Bowl   **D:**355–56
   ever-changing earth   **E:**16; **G:**115–16
   forests help prevent erosion   **F:**376
   grasses and soil   **G:**319
   ice ages   **I:**8
   Kansas   **K:**180, 189
   landforms   **G:**99
   land management in agriculture   **A:**95–96; **F:**62
   landslides   **A:**558
   mountain formation   **M:**502–3, 504, 505
   mountains damaged by human activities   **M:**507
   ocean movements, effects of   **O:**19–20
   rivers, work of   **R:**236
   Saskatchewan crop practices   **S:**44
   soils formed by   **S:**234
   water shapes the land   **W:**51
   wetlands help prevent erosion   **W:**148
   picture(s)   **G:**116
      Guilin Hills (China)   **E:**11
"Eros Turannos" (poem by Edwin Arlington Robinson)   **A:**214b
Erratics (Wanderers) (rocks transported by ice)   **I:**8
Error (in baseball)   **B:**83
Error correction (in telecommunications)   **T:**49
Ersary (tribe of Turkmenistan)   **T:**351
Ershad, General Hussain Mohammed (president of Bangladesh)   **B:**51
Ervin, Sam, Jr. (American political figure)   **W:**60
Erving, Julius (American basketball player)   **B:**95i–95j *profile*
   picture(s)   **B:**95i

Erymanthian boar (in Greek mythology) G:366
Erythrocytes *see* Red blood cells
Erythromycin (antibiotic) D:209
Erythropoietin (hormone) B:261; K:244
Esau (Edom) (Biblical character) B:159; I:345
Escalante, Silvestre Vélez de (Spanish explorer) C:442; U:254
Escalators E:187–88
   diagram(s) E:187
   picture(s) E:187
Escape lever (in watches) W:45
Escapements (devices in timepieces) C:369–70, 372; W:45, 46
Escape velocity (of a spacecraft) S:340c, 340d
   rockets R:258
   satellites, artificial S:53
Escape wheel (in watches) W:45
Escarpment (rock formation)
   Allegheny Front O:269
   Brazil S:276
   Niagara Escarpment O:124
Escheat (reversion of property to the state) W:177
Escher, M. C. (Dutch artist) E:320
   tessellations G:126
   picture(s)
      Day and Night (woodcut) E:320
      tessellation with butterfly shapes G:126
      woodcut with optical illusions O:177
Escherichia coli (bacterium)
   picture(s) A:311; V:361, 365
Esch-sur-Alzette (Luxembourg) L:347
Escobar, Marisol (American artist) *see* Marisol
Escorial (palace, near Madrid, Spain) S:383
   picture(s) S:382
Escrow (a legal agreement, real estate term) R:113
Esdraelon, Plain of (Israel) I:371
Esdras I and II (apocryphal books of the Bible) B:163
Esenin, Sergei (Russian poet) R:383–84
Eskimos (a people of North America) *see also* Inuit
   Alaska A:144, 150
   picture(s)
      Alaska A:150
Esmeraldas (Ecuador) E:67, 68
Esmeraldas River (Ecuador) E:66
Esophagus (Gullet) (food passage tube) B:280
   birds B:222
   digestive system D:163
   peptic ulcer D:198
ESP *see* Extrasensory perception
Esparto wax W:78
Esperanto (universal language) L:40
Espinel, Luisa (American performer) A:405 *profile*
Espionage *see* Spies
ESPN (sports television channel) C:516
Espoo (Finland) F:137, 138
Esposito, Phil (Canadian hockey player) I:30 *profile*
Espresso coffee C:397
Espronceda, José de (Spanish poet) S:389
Esquire (form of address) A:21
Essays E:321–22; L:258
   compositions C:477–78
   English literature E:274, 278
   magazines M:19
Essen (Germany) W:307
Essenes (ascetic Jewish sect) D:47
Essential amino acids N:423
Essential oils O:79
   herbs and spices H:119
   perfumes P:150
   tea T:34
Essex (aircraft carrier) W:315
Essex Junction (Vermont) V:312, 319
Estate (property that a person owns) L:88; W:177
Estates-General (French legislative body) F:415, 467, 468
Estefan, Gloria (Cuban American musician)
   picture(s) H:146

Esterhazy, Ferdinand (French army officer) D:325
Esterházy, Miklós, Prince (Hungarian nobleman) H:67
Esters (chemicals used as lubricants) L:335
Estevanico (Estéban) (Moorish explorer) A:79d
Esther (book of the Old Testament) B:160, 163
   Purim P:549
Esther, Feast of *see* Purim
Estimation (in arithmetic) A:391
Estivation (Summer sleep) (resting state of animals) H:128
   crocodilians C:594
Estonia E:323–25
   disintegration of Soviet Union C:460
   independence U:44
   lakes L:33
   non-Slavic peoples in former Soviet Union U:34
   World War I W:290
   World War II W:296, 312
   picture(s)
      choral singing E:324
      flag F:231
      Tallinn E:325
      windmills and sheep E:323
Estrada, Joseph (Philippine president) P:188
Estrela, Serra da (mountain range, Portugal) P:392
Estrogens (hormones) G:228; H:227, 228
Estuaries (of rivers) R:237
E.T.: The Extra-Terrestrial (motion picture, 1982) M:497
   picture(s) M:496
Etching E:326–27 *see also* Engraving
   glass G:234
   illustration of books I:80
   Rembrandt's work D:365
   techniques of the graphic arts G:303, 305, 307
   Whistler, James Abbott McNeill W:162
Eternal City (Rome, Italy) R:305
Ethan Allen Homestead (Vermont) V:314
Ethane (gas) F:488
Ethanol (Ethyl alcohol) A:172; C:201; D:11; F:489; P:315
Ethelred II (king of England) E:238; V:343
Ether (general anesthetic) A:254–55, 256
   medicine, history of M:208a, 208c
   picture(s)
      early use S:512
Ether, luminiferous (early theory of light) R:140
Etherege, Sir George (English dramatist) E:277
Ethical, legal, and social implications program (of the Human Genome Project) G:90
Ethics (branch of philosophy) E:328–29; P:192
   animal rights A:261
   biotechnology, issues in I:286
   cloning L:210
   criminal behavior, definition of C:584
   fundamentalism F:492
   genetics G:89, 90
   Hindu moral and religious laws of conduct H:140
   lawyers L:91
   medical ethics D:237; M:208h–209
   religious moral codes R:145
   science, modern S:75
   Ten Commandments T:72–73
   U.S. citizenship applicants must have good moral character N:61
   vegetarian diet for ethical reasons V:293
Ethiopia E:330–34
   Cuban military intervention C:610
   Eritrea is former province E:316–17
   geomythology G:107
   Haile Selassie I H:4
   lakes L:33
   literature A:76b, 76c
   Mussolini attacks (1935) W:295
   painting A:75
   sculpture A:73
   Somalia and the Ogaden region S:255

European Coal and Steel Community (ECSC) E:369
European Command, U.S. U:108
European Commission on Human Rights H:287
European Community see European Union
European Constitution E:369
European corn borers see Corn borers, European
European Economic Community (Common Market) (now European
    Union) E:369 see also European Union
    Germany G:165
European Great Horses see Great Horses
European Organization for Nuclear Research (CERN) C:493
European Parliament E:369
    picture(s) E:368
European plan (of hotel rates) H:256
European rabbits R:25, 26
European Recovery Program see Marshall Plan
European Security and Defense Policy (ESDP) E:369
European Southern Observatory (Chile) T:60
European Space Agency S:339, 359, 365, 368
European Union (formerly European Community) B:135; E:342,
    361, 368–69; I:271
    Austria, sanctions against A:525
    Brussels headquarters B:134
    French farmers' protests F:409
    United Kingdom U:54, 62
    picture(s)
        Brussels headquarters B:134
European Union, Treaty on (1991) see Maastricht Treaty
European War (1914–1918) see World War I
Europium (element) E:172
Europoort (Rotterdam, Netherlands) E:361; N:120c
    picture(s) E:361; N:120b
Eurostar trains
    picture(s) E:361; L:288
Eurydice (in Greek mythology) G:367
Eurypterids (Sea scorpions) (early invertebrates) F:386, 387
Eurystheus, King (in Greek mythology) G:365, 367
Eusebius, Saint (pope) R:292
Euskera see Basque language
Eustachian tube (of the ear) E:4
    picture(s) E:5
Eutelsat (satellite network) S:339
Euthanasia (mercy-killing) D:237; E:329
Euthelopus (dinosaur) D:173
Eutrophication (in bodies of water) D:141; W:63, 65, 66
Eutychian, Saint (pope) R:292
Evaluation (of students by teachers) T:37
Evangelical movements (in religion)
    Costa Rica C:565
    Russia R:358
    picture(s)
        Brazilian Protestants B:373
"Evangeline" (poem by Longfellow) N:356
Evangelists, The (authors of the Gospels) B:165–66
Evans, Sir Arthur (English archaeologist) A:358
Evans, Edmund (English printer) C:233
Evans, Janet (American swimmer) S:537 profile
    picture(s) S:537
Evans, John (American governor) C:442 profile
Evans, Marian (Mary Ann Evans) (English novelist) see Eliot,
    George
Evans, Mount (Colorado) C:438
Evans, Oliver (American inventor) D:100 profile
    automobiles, first experiments with A:539
    first automated flour mill F:277
    steam engines S:445
    steam-powered bucket dredge D:322
Evansville (Indiana) I:153
Evaporated milk D:9; F:342
Evaporation H:92
    air conditioning A:101
    effect on amount of salt in lakes L:24
    fog resulting from F:290
    hydrologic (water) cycle W:49

irrigation water loss I:340
liquid gases L:253
rain R:93–94
refrigeration process R:133
water, forms of W:48
water desalting W:56
water supply, effects on the W:55
weather, creation of W:82
Evaporators (in cooling systems) A:102; R:133
Evaristus, Saint (pope) R:292
Eve see Adam and Eve
Evelyn, John (English diarist) E:276
Evening Star (name for Mercury or Venus) P:278; V:303
Event horizon (in physics) S:433
Even-toed hoofed mammals F:81–82; H:216, 218–20
Even Up (card game) C:109
Everest, George (English military surveyor) E:370
Everest, Mount E:370–71; H:137; M:505
    China C:261
    Hillary, Sir Edmund H:136
    mountain climbing M:499
    picture(s) A:438g; E:370; M:501
    table(s)
        first ascent M:500
Everett (Washington) S:112
Everglades (swamp in Florida) F:262, 263, 265
    Douglas, Marjory Stoneman F:274
    wetlands W:145, 146
    picture(s) F:262
        satellite picture S:53
Everglades National Park (Florida) F:270
Evergreens T:308
    Christmas customs C:297
Evergreen State (nickname for Washington) W:14, 15
Evers, Charles (American political figure) M:363
Evers, James Charles (American civil rights leader) C:329
    profile
Evers, Medgar (American civil rights leader) C:329 profile;
    M:363
    picture(s) C:329; N:25
        memorial (Jackson, Mississippi) M:351
Everson v. Board of Education (1947) F:163
Evers Williams, Myrlie (American civil rights leader) see
    Williams, Myrlie Evers
Evert, Chris (American tennis player) F:274 profile; T:96
    profile
    picture(s) T:90, 96
Everyman (15th-century morality play) E:271; G:181
"Everyone Sang" (poem by Siegfried Sassoon) F:124
Evesham, Battle of (1265) E:239; H:109
Evidence (in law courts) C:575; J:163
    forensic science F:372–73
Evil (moral concept) K:292
Evolution E:372–79
    biological anthropology A:301
    biology B:197, 199, 200
    birds B:247
    Darwin, Charles Robert D:40–41; G:110–11; S:67
    Earth, history of E:24–29
    fish F:184
    flightless birds O:242
    fossils give evidence of F:382, 383, 385, 386–87
    fundamentalists' opposition to theory F:492
    genetics and heredity G:81–82
    genocide, justification of G:96
    horses H:243
    Huxley, Julian Sorell H:309
    Huxley, Thomas Henry H:310
    Leakey family L:96–97
    living things' adaptation to change L:197–98
    mammals M:75
    marsupials M:113
    niche specialization P:434
    plants, history of P:299–301

Protestant sects' differing beliefs   P:491
Roman Catholic Church, challenges to   R:293
science, milestones in   S:72
Scopes trial   B:416; D:36; S:84; T:87
theory (in biology)   B:203
What is artificial selection?   E:379
Evren, Kenan (Turkish general and political leader)   T:349
Ewe (a people of Africa)   G:194; T:216, 217
music   A:79
Togo-Ghana border cuts through their homeland   A:61
Ewe (language)   T:216
Ewes (female sheep)   S:147
Ewing, Patrick (American basketball player)
picture(s)   B:95c
Examinations see also Tests and test taking
civil service   C:331
Examinations, physical see Physical examinations
Examining rooms (in hospitals)   H:248
Excalibur (sword of King Arthur)   A:438b
Excavation (in engineering)
building construction   B:433
dredges used in   D:321–22
earth-moving machinery   E:30–32
mining   M:321–22
Excavations (archaeological)   A:353–55
picture(s)   A:350
Excellency (form of address)   A:21
Excepted service (in civil service)   C:331
Exchange (trade and commerce)   T:264–65
money   M:412–15
Excise taxes   T:25
Excitability (of neurons)   B:363
Excited state (of electrons)   L:46a
Exclamation points (punctuation)   P:542
Excommunication (from the Roman Catholic Church)
Luther, Martin   C:292; R:130
Patriarch of Constantinople (1054)   R:289
Execution see Capital punishment
Executive agreements (in international relations)   P:452
Executive branch (of the United States government)   U:164, 169–70
Executive Office of the President (United States)   P:446, 451
Executive orders (of United States presidents)   P:450
prohibited discrimination against African Americans   A:79L, 79n
Executive power (of United States presidents)   P:449–50; W:43–44
Executor (feminine: executrix) (of a will)   W:177
Exemptions (from income tax)   I:111
Exercise (for physical fitness)   P:224–27 see also Sports
astronauts during weightlessness   S:342
bones, effects on   S:184a
diabetes, prevention of   D:145
dogs, care of   D:259–60
health   H:75
heartbeat   H:81–82
heart disease, helps prevent   H:84
jogging and running   J:111
karate   K:194
lungs   L:344
obesity, treatment of   O:6
occupational therapy   O:15
physical education   P:222–23
picture(s)
astronauts during weightlessness   S:344
Exeter (New Hampshire)   N:160
Exhaust gas (from engines)
air pollution   A:123, 125
air pollution controls in automobiles   I:265
carbon monoxide poisoning   P:355
rocket propulsion   R:257, 258, 260
Exhaust manifold (of an automobile)   A:547
Exhaust systems (of engines)   A:546, 547; I:265
Exhibits (for science fairs)   S:78
Exhibits (in law courts)   C:575

Existentialism (in philosophy)   F:443
drama   D:305
French novels   N:362–63
Exobiology (study of life in outer space)   A:476b
Exocrine glands   B:291; G:226–27
Exodus (book of the Old Testament)   B:159
Exodus (delivery of the Hebrews from Egypt)   B:159; P:95
Exoskeleton (outside skeleton)   A:265, 267; C:601
ants   A:318
arachnids   A:348
crabs   C:581
lobsters   L:279
shrimps   S:167, 168
Exosphere (layer of Earth's atmosphere)   A:482; E:21
Exothermic reactions (in chemistry)   F:140
Expanded Food and Nutrition Education Program (of the 4-H)   F:396
Expanding universe theory see Inflation theory
Expansion (in physics)
heat   H:92–93
ice, action of   W:48, 51
Expansion valve (in a refrigeration system)   R:133
Expatriation (giving up citizenship)   C:324
Experience Music Project (museum, Seattle, Washington)   M:528
Experiment (in research) see Research, scientific
Experimental Aircraft Association   A:572
Experimental poetry   A:217–18
Experimental science   S:67, 71–72
Experimental variables see Variables (in scientific experiments)
Experiments and other science activities   E:380–97
abacus, how to use an   A:2–3
acids and bases, how to identify   E:390
air, expansion of   B:36
air pressure   G:57
air resistance   F:34
Archimedes' principle   F:251
barometer, how to make a   W:89
biologists: how they explore nature   B:204
bread mold   A:307
buoyancy   F:252–53
camera, pinhole, how to make a   E:388
chemical reactions   C:199
color wheel, how to make a   C:427
composting with worms   W:320
constellations, imaginary creation of   C:532
dew point apparatus, how to make   W:84
electricity   E:136–37, 393
electric motor, how to build an   E:386–87
electromagnet, how to make an   M:30
electromagnetism   F:366b
friction, reduction of   W:244
garden to observe animal pollinators of flowers   F:286
gases, properties of   G:57–58, 59
gravity, effect of   W:245
greenhouse effect, how to observe the   E:385
gyroscope, properties of   G:436
ideas for experiments and other science activities   E:387–97
leaves, sunlight requirements of   L:116
light, principles of   L:215, 217
liquids, how to create layers of   E:392
liquids, properties of   L:254, 255
magnets and magnetism   M:28–29, 30
map making   M:98
matter, properties of   M:172–77
microscope, how to build Van Leeuwenhoek's   M:286
microscopes, some things to see with   M:283
minerals, how to identify   M:315
mushrooms, spore prints of   F:498
musical glasses   S:264
musical sounds, how to show the principles of   M:546, 549
nature, study of   N:68

PHOTO CREDITS

E

Cover © Pierre Tremblay—Masterfile
2 Leonard Lee Rue III—The Image Bank
3 The Metropolitan Museum of Art, Purchase, Alfred N. Punnett Endowment Fund and George D. Pratt Gift, 1934
7 The Granger Collection
8 © Satellite Composite View of Earth by Tom Van Sant and the Geosphere Project, Santa Monica, California. With assistance from NOAA Photo Library, NASA, Eyes on Earth, technical direction Lloyd Van Warren. Source data derived from NOAA—TIROS-N Series Satellites; © Satellite Composite View of Earth by Tom Van Sant and the Geosphere Project, Santa Monica, California. With assistance from NOAA, NASA, Eyes on Earth, technical direction Lloyd Van Warren. Source data derived from NOAA—TIROS-N Series Satellites.
11 © Hiroji Kubota—Magnum Photos
12 © David Paterson
13 © Stephen J. Krasemann—Peter Arnold, Inc.
14 © James Balog—Black Star
15 NASA; © E. R. Degginger; © Frank Rossotto—Stocktrek.
16 © Peter French—Bruce Coleman Inc.
17 © Bruce C. Heesen and Marie Tharp, Date (1977), reproduced by permission of Marie Tharp
18 © Steve Wilkings—The Stock Market; © E. R. Degginger.
19 © Peter Ryan/Scripps/Science Photo Library—Photo Researchers
21 NASA/Science Photo Library—Photo Researchers
22 © William K. Hartmann (all photos on page).
23 © William K. Hartmann (all photos on page).
26 © Tony Brain—Science Source—Photo Researchers; © Fred Bavendam—Peter Arnold, Inc.; © Michael Furman—The Stock Market.
28 © Ferrero/Jacana—Photo Researchers
30 Courtesy of Caterpillar Inc.
31 © Phil Mougamer—Third Coast Stock Source
32 © Kelly Culpepper—Transparencies; Courtesy of Caterpillar Inc.
33 © Herman Kokojan—Black Star
34 © James Balog—Black Star
36 © Lawrence S. Burr
38 © Earthquakes and Geological Discovery by Professor Bruce A. Bolt, W. H. Freeman and Company, New York
40 UPI/Bettmann Newsphotos
41 © Ken Cobean—Black Star
43 Art Reference Bureau
44 © Margaret Mead—The Image Bank
46 © Alain Keler—Corbis-Sygma; © Steve Vidler—Leo de Wys.
48 International Museum of Photography at the George Eastman House
50 © Roger Ressmeyer—Starlight
51 © Dennis di Cicco—Peter Arnold, Inc.; © Roger Ressmeyer—Starlight.
52 © Dennis di Cicco; © Pekka Parviainen/Science Photo Library—Photo Researchers.
53 © Michael Busselle—Stone
54 © Brad Markel—Liaison Agency
55 © Alan Briere—Liaison Agency
56 © Allen Russell—ProFiles West/Index Stock
57 © B. Thomas—H. Armstrong Roberts
58 © Carl Frank—Photo Researchers
59 © Allen Russell—ProFiles West/Index Stock; © David R. Frazier—Photo Researchers.
61 © Z.E.F.A.,U.K.—H. Armstrong Roberts
62 The Granger Collection; The Granger Collection; © Alon Reininger—Contact Stock Images.

63 © Bernard Gotfryd—Woodfin Camp & Associates; © George Rose—Liaison Agency; © Theo Westenberger—Corbis-Sygma.
64 © Stephanie Dinkins—Photo Researchers
65 © François Gohier—Photo Researchers
66 © François Gohier—Photo Researchers
67 © Joachim Messerschmidt—Bruce Coleman Inc.
68 © James D. Nations—DDB Stock Photo; © Gianni Tortoli—Photo Researchers.
70 The Granger Collection
71 The Granger Collection (all photos on page).
72 The Granger Collection; North Wind Picture Archives.
74 © Mary Kate Denny—PhotoEdit; © Lee Day—Stockphoto.com.
75 © Bill Weems—Woodfin Camp & Associates
76 © Jim Harrison—Stock, Boston/PictureQuest
77 Scala/Art Resource, NY
78 The Granger Collection
79 © Giraudon/Art Resource, NY
80 The Granger Collection; Fine Art Photographic Library, London/Art Resource, NY.
81 The Granger Collection
82 The Granger Collection (all photos on page).
83 The Granger Collection; Stockphoto.com.
84 © Damian Dovarganes—AP/Wide World Photos
85 © Michael Newman—PhotoEdit
86 © Rusty Kennedy—AP/Wide World Photos; © Sam Pellissier—© SuperStock.
87 © Tony Freeman—PhotoEdit
88 © A. Ramey—Woodfin Camp & Associates
90 UPI/Bettmann Newsphotos
91 The Bettmann Archive
92 The Bettmann Archive; UPI/Bettmann Newsphotos; The Metropolitan Museum of Art, The Jules Bache Collection, 1949.
93 © Tom McHugh—Photo Researchers; © Mike Neumann—Photo Researchers.
94 © Jane Burton—Bruce Coleman Inc.
95 © Jane Burton—Bruce Coleman Inc.
96 © Jane Burton—Bruce Coleman Inc. (all photos on page).
97 © Zig Leszczynski—Animals Animals; © Jane Burton—Bruce Coleman Inc.
98 © Kim Taylor—Bruce Coleman Inc. (all photos on page).
99 © Lee Boltin; © Fred Salaff—FPG International.
100 © Kurt Scholz—SuperStock
101 © James R. Pearson—FPG International; © Jim Pickerell.
102 © SuperStock; © Jim Pickerell.
103 Giraudon/Art Resource
104 The New York Public Library, Astor, Lenox and Tilden Foundations
106 © SuperStock; © Scala/Art Resource, NY.
107 © E. Strouhal—Werner Forman Archive/Art Resource, NY
108 © SuperStock; © Carl Purcell—Photo Researchers.
109 © Egyptian National Museum, Cairo, Egypt/Index, Barcelona/The Bridgeman Art Library
110 Giraudon/Art Resource
111 © Norman Owen Tomalin—Bruce Coleman Inc.
112 The Louvre, Paris; Giraudon/Art Resource.
113 Giraudon/Art Resource; The Metropolitan Museum of Art, New York, Gift of Edward S. Harkness, 1926.
114 © Farrell Grehan—FPG International
115 © Ray Manley—SuperStock; © Lee Boltin.
116 Art Resource (all photos on page).
117 © Geoffrey Clifford—Wheeler Pictures
118 The Bettmann Archive
119 UPI/Bettmann
120 The Bettmann Archive
121 The White House Collection, © copyright White House Historical Association
122 United Press International; U.S. Army.
123 AP/Wide World Photos
124 UPI; The New York Times.
126 The Bridgeman Art Library
127 © Charles Neibergall—AP/Wide World Photos
128 © Mario Tama—Getty Images
129 AP/Wide World Photos
130 © Ouahab—AP/Wide World Photos
135 © F. Stuart Westmorland—Tom Stack & Associates
137 © Gary Milburn—Tom Stack & Associates; Culver Pictures.
138 The Granger Collection; Historical Pictures Service, Chicago.
141 National Portrait Gallery, London
142 © Tom Stack—Tom Stack & Associates
143 © Dan Budnik—Woodfin Camp & Associ-

ates; © Tony Freeman—PhotoEdit.
144 © Ken Ross—The Viesti Collection, Inc.
145 © Ken Ross—The Viesti Collection, Inc.
148 © Tony Freeman—PhotoEdit; © The Stock Solution; © Margot Granitsas—The Image Works.
151 © Mike Powell—Woodfin Camp & Associates; © Alex Webb—Magnum Photos; © Pat Lanza Field—Bruce Coleman Inc.
153 © Robert Harding Picture Library; © Patrick Piel—Liaison Agency.
155 © Ted Thai—Corbis-Sygma
157 © Mike Kidulich—Journalism Services; © De Wildenberg—Corbis-Sygma.
158 © Ellie Bernager—Liaison Agency; © Leonard Lessin—Peter Arnold, Inc.
159 © Jose L. Pelaez—The Stock Market; © Larry Mulvehill—Photo Researchers; © Peter Cade—Stone; © Paul S. Conrath—Stone.
160 © Nelson Morris—Photo Researchers; © World Perspectives—Stone; Liaison Agency.
161 © Bruce Lee Smith—Liaison Agency; Courtesy, Sony Corporation; © Michael Gaffney—Liaison Agency; © Adam Hart-Davis—Science Photo Library—Photo Researchers.
162 Department of Defense/Liaison Agency
163 © David Scharf
164 © David Scharf
179 © Sven-Olof Lindblad—Photo Researchers
181 © Zig Leszczynski—Animals Animals; © Klaus D. Franke—Peter Arnold, Inc.; © Zoological Society of San Diego.
182 © Clem Haagner—Ardea London Ltd.
183 © Wildlife Education
184 © Georg Gerster—Comstock, Inc.
186 © Cameramann International Ltd.; Courtesy of Otis Elevator Corp.
187 © Cameramann International Ltd.
189 The Granger Collection
190 UPI/Bettmann Newsphotos
191 The National Portrait Gallery, London
192 © Karsh of Ottawa—Photo Trends
193 © Ken N. Johns—Photo Researchers
194 © Keith Bernstein—Woodfin Camp & Associates
195 © Douglas Engle—AP/Wide World Photos; © SuperStock.
197 ©Luis Romero—AP/Wide World Photos
198 © Alison M. Jones/Danita Delimont, Agent
199 © La Prensa Grafica/AP/Wide World Photos
200 The Granger Collection (all photos on page).
202 The Granger Collection
203 © Jose Luis Pelaez—The Stock Market; © Michael Grecco—Stock, Boston.
205 Scala/Art Resource; The Granger Collection.
206 H. Roger-Viollet—Liaison Agency
207 © Grolier, Inc.
208 © J. Lotter—Tom Stack & Associates
209 © D. Clendemen—U.S. Fish and Wildlife Service
210 © Tom & Pat Leeson—Photo Researchers; © Kerry T. Givens—Tom Stack & Associates; © François Gohier—Photo Researchers; © Frans Lanting—Photo Researchers.
211 © Anup Manoj Shah—Animals Animals; © Jany Sauvanet—Photo Researchers; © Brian Parker—Tom Stack & Associates; © John Cancalosi—Tom Stack & Associates.
212 © Comstock, Inc.
213 © Dan Budnik—Woodfin Camp & Associates
217 U.S. Department of Energy (all photos on page).
219 © Robert J. Langlotz—Black Star
220 © Kenneth Garrett—Woodfin Camp & Associates
221 © Jeff Perkell—The Stock Market
222 © Gazuit—Photo Researchers
223 Infraspection Institute (all photos on page).
224 © Rob Outlaw
225 © David Brenizer—Transparencies
226 © Rob Outlaw; © Charles West—The Stock Market.
228 © Dallas & John Heaton—Miller Comstock, Inc.
232 © Leo de Wys; © Patrick Ward—Stock, Boston.
233 © Adam Woolfitt—Woodfin Camp & Associates
234 © Adam Woolfitt—Woodfin Camp & Associates; © Topham—The Image Works.
235 Reproduced with the permission of the Controller of Her Majesty's Stationery Office
236 © Topham—The Image Works; © Larry Mulvehill—Photo Researchers.
237 The British Library; The Bettmann Archive. Art Resource
238 Art Resource
239 The British Library; The British Museum.

240 Weidenfeld & Nicholson; The National Portrait Gallery, London.
241 The National Portrait Gallery, London
242 Art Resource
243 The National Portrait Gallery, London
245 The British Museum
247 The British Museum
249 The National Portrait Gallery, London; The Tate Gallery, London.
250 The National Trust—Photographic Library; Barnardo's.
251 The Mansell Collection; Royal Archives—Windsor Castle.
253 Topham—The Image Works
254 Alpha/Globe Photos
255 © Morvan—Sipa Press; © David Caulkin—AP/Wide World Photos; © David Baruchli—AP/Wide World Photos.
256 The Granger Collection; © Anthony Howarth—Woodfin Camp & Associates.
257 The Granger Collection
258 © Rita Bailey—Leo de Wys; The Granger Collection.
259 Art Resource; The Granger Collection.
260 The Granger Collection
261 The National Portrait Gallery, London; Art Resource.
262 The Granger Collection
263 The Granger Collection
264 © David Hockney; Hirshhorn Museum and Sculpture Garden, Smithsonian Institution, gift of Joseph H. Hirshhorn Foundation, 1966; Hirshhorn Museum and Sculpture Garden, Smithsonian Institution, gift of Joseph H. Hirshhorn, 1966.
268 The Granger Collection
270 The Huntington Library
273 The National Portrait Gallery, London (all photos on page).
274 The Granger Collection
275 The National Portrait Gallery, London
277 The Granger Collection
278 Lessing J. Rosenwald Collection, Library of Congress, Washington, D.C.
279 The Granger Collection
280 North Wind Picture Archives; Grolier Archives; The Granger Collection; The Granger Collection; North Wind Picture Archives; The Granger Collection.
281 North Wind Picture Archives; The Granger Collection; The Granger Collection; The Granger Collection; The Granger Collection.
282 The Granger Collection; The New York Public Library, Astor, Lenox and Tilden Foundation; The Bettmann Archive; The Bettmann Archive; The Granger Collection; North Wind Picture Archives.
283 The Bettmann Archive; The Granger Collection; The Granger Collection; Hulton/Bettmann; © Courtesy, Harcourt Brace Jovanovich, Inc.; Courtesy of The New American Library, Inc.
285 The Granger Collection
286 The Granger Collection
287 *The Strand* magazine—Courtesy, Gaslight Publications
288 © David A. Hardy, from the private collection of Bob Monkhouse
289 The National Portrait Gallery, London; The Granger Collection; The National Portrait Gallery, London.
290 The Granger Collection; © Miriam Berkley—Alfred A. Knopf Inc.; © Larry Silbert.
291 National Portrait Gallery, London—Art Reference Bureau
294 Courtesy of Mrs. John Buckland-Wright—Illustration Research; Art Reference Bureau.
295 Giraudon/Art Resource, NY
296 The Granger Collection; Giraudon/Art Resource, NY; © Erich Lessing—Art Resource, NY; Erich Lessing—Art Resource, NY.
297 The Granger Collection (all photos on page).
299 Cameramann International Ltd.; © Melinda Berge—Bruce Coleman Inc.; Cameramann International Ltd.
300 © Ken Straiton—The Stock Market
301 © Grant Heilman Photography
302 © Bastide—Liaison Agency; AP/Wide World Photos.
303 © Grant Heilman Photography
304 © Hans Reinhard—Bruce Coleman Inc.
305 © Rick Windsor—Woodfin Camp & Associates
306 © Steve Elmore—The Stock Market
309 © Sean Sprague—Panos Pictures
310 © Christine Nesbitt—AP/Wide World Photos
311 The Granger Collection